WOMEN, GENDER, AND THE WEST

ALSO IN THIS SERIES:

What Is Gone
by Amy Knox Brown

Their Lives, Their Wills:
Women in the Borderlands, 1750–1846
by Amy M. Porter

Divinely Guided:
The California Work of the Women's National Indian Association
by Valerie Sherer Mathes

Divinely Guided Revisited

THE WOMEN'S
NATIONAL INDIAN
ASSOCIATION
BEYOND
CALIFORNIA

Valerie Sherer Mathes

TEXAS TECH UNIVERSITY PRESS

Copyright © 2025 by Valerie Sherer Mathes

All rights reserved. No portion of this book may be reproduced in any form or by any means, including electronic storage and retrieval systems, except by explicit prior written permission of the publisher. Brief passages excerpted for review and critical purposes are excepted.

This book is typeset in EB Garamond. The paper used in this book meets the minimum requirements of ANSI/NISO Z39.48-1992 (R1997). ♾

Designed by Hannah Gaskamp
Cover design by Hannah Gaskamp
Cover photograph courtesy of Department of Special Collections, Princeton University Library [Navajo Mission Collection, circa 1895–1908 (WC116)]

Library of Congress Cataloging-in-Publication Data

Names: Mathes, Valerie Sherer, 1941– author Title: Divinely Guided Revisited: The Women's National Indian Association beyond California / Valerie Sherer Mathes. Description: Lubbock, Texas: Texas Tech University Press, 2025. | Series: Women, Gender, and the West | Includes bibliographical references and index. | Summary: "A history of the Women's National Indian Association (WNIA), a volunteer organization promoting the US government's assimilationist Indian policy and performing broad philanthropic and humanitarian non-Indian work"—Provided by publisher.
Identifiers: LCCN 2025008444 (print) | LCCN 2025008445 (ebook) |
ISBN 978-1-68283-258-5 paperback | ISBN 978-1-68283-259-2 ebook
Subjects: LCSH: Women's National Indian Association (U.S.)—History | Indians of North America—Cultural assimilation—History | Indian women—Political activity—United States—History | Women political activists—United States—History | Women social reformers—United States—Women social reformers—United States
Classification: LCC E98.C89 M383 2025 (print) | LCC E98.C89 (ebook) |
DDC 305.48/897—dc23/eng/20230314
LC record available at https://lccn.loc.gov/2025008444
LC ebook record available at https://lccn.loc.gov/2025008445

Texas Tech University Press
Box 41037
Lubbock, Texas 79409-1037 USA
800.832.4042
ttup@ttu.edu
www.ttupress.org

Contents

Abbreviations / vii
Illustrations / ix
Preface / xi

Introduction / 3
The Dawn of an Indian Reform Movement

Chapter 1: The Founding of the WNIA / 11

Chapter 2: The Washington, DC, Auxiliary as a Case Study / 29

Chapter 3: Constance Goddard DuBois / 65
Mission Indians, Basketmaking, and the Indian Industries League

Chapter 4: New York Reformers and the Montana Piegan Station / 97

Chapter 5: The WNIA and Indian Health Care / 127

Chapter 6: Mary Louise Eldridge / 157
Missionary and Field Matron among the Navajo

Chapter 7: William Henry Weinland / 179
Supervisor of the Ramona Mission

Chapter 8: Cornelia and Anna Taber and C. E. Kelsey of the NCIA / 205

Chapter 9: Dorcas J. Spencer / 237
The Hupa Indians and the WCTU

Conclusion / 253

Appendix / 257
Notes / 271
Bibliography / 343
Index / 361

Abbreviations

ABHMS: American Baptist Home Mission Society
ARCIA: Annual Report of the Commissioner of Indian Affairs to the Secretary of the Interior
ASQ: Amelia Stone Quinton
BIC: Board of Indian Commissioners
CFL: Charles Fletcher Lummis
CGD: Constance Goddard DuBois
CHS: California Historical Society
CIA: Cambridge Indian Association
GPO: Government Printing Office
IBC: Indian Board of Co-Operation
IRA: Indian Rights Association
ITKA: Indian Treaty-Keeping Association
ITKPA: Indian Treaty-Keeping and Protective Association
LB: Letter Book
LMC: Lake Mohonk Conference of the Friends of the Indian
LR: Letters Received
LS: Letters Sent
M. E.: Methodist Episcopal (Church)
MLE: Mary Louise Eldridge
NARA: National Archives and Records Administration
NIA: National Indian Association
NIDA: National Indian Defense Association
NCIA: Northern California Indian Association

ABBREVIATIONS

OIA: Office of Indian Affairs
RG: Record Group
SC: Special Case
SI: Secretary of the Interior
WBHMS: Women's Baptist Home Mission Society
WCTU: Woman's Christian Temperance Union
WHW: William Henry Weinland
WNIA: Women's National Indian Association

Illustrations

18	Fig. 1: Amelia Stone Quinton
39	Fig. 2: Sara Thomson Kinney
42	Fig. 3: Harriet Ward Foote Hawley
43	Fig. 4: Katherine Elizabeth Foote Coe
61	Fig. 5: Alice Cunningham Fletcher
68	Fig. 6: Constance Goddard DuBois
74	Fig. 7: Frances Campbell Sparhawk
86	Fig. 8: Lake Mohonk Conference, 1899
111	Fig. 9: Dutcher family picnic
120	Fig. 10: Arthur Dutcher cutting oats
123	Fig. 11: Arthur Dutcher and friends
128	Fig. 12: Susan La Flesche Picotte
143	Fig. 13: Navajo family, Navajo Methodist Mission, Jewett, New Mexico, c. 1902
160	Fig. 14: Mary A Tripp and student picnic
166	Fig. 15: Henrietta G. Cole and pupil
169	Fig. 16: Mary Louise Eldridge on horseback
175	Fig. 17: Eldridge and Navajo family
181	Fig. 18: Moravian Mission House, Bethel, Alaska
185	Fig. 19: Sarah Morris and students
200	Fig. 20: Reverend and Mrs. William Henry Weinland
218	Fig. 21: Anna Haviland Ferris Taber
229	Fig. 22: Fourth Zayante Indian Conference, 1909
234	Fig. 23: Annie E. K. Bidwell and Zayante Conference attendees
246	Fig. 24: Dorcas J. Spencer and friends
250	Fig. 25: Indian women at a WCTU Meeting

Preface

The Women's National Indian Association (WNIA), a volunteer group of middle- and upper-class white women, grew out of the Baptist Home Missionary Society organized on May 17, 1877, in the First Baptist Church of Philadelphia. The association, which existed until 1951, initially engaged in reforming the government's Indian policy through petitioning but later focused on changing Indian behavior and beliefs through missionary work. In 1895 Amelia Stone Quinton, the first general secretary and later longtime president, described the WNIA as a Christian organization, born from a missionary spirit with a lengthy history of missionary activity. To implement their work, the association founded more than sixty missionary stations from Florida to California, some two-thirds of which were created during Quinton's tenure. She also organized the majority of the more than one hundred auxiliaries located in almost every US state and territory.

To understand the role that the WNIA played within the late nineteenth century Indian reform movement, this book begins with a history of the association, its placement within the movement, and a brief study of its larger, more active state branches in Connecticut, Massachusetts, and New York. Since missionary work was most often funded by individual auxiliaries, the history of two very diverse ones is included. The Washington, DC, auxiliary, one of the smallest and therefore less financially able to fund extensive missionary work, was, by far, the most politically active because its membership included wives of sitting congressmen. In sharp contrast, the slightly larger Northern California Indian Association financed a number of mission stations and engaged in innovative approaches to achieve its reforms, including the founding of an annual conference where Indians actually dictated the agenda.

PREFACE

To better illustrate the complicated process of founding and operating a mission station, the Epworth Piegan Indian Mission in Montana is included because of its interesting backstory. Unlike the typical station, organized and run by the national association's Missionary Committee, this mission was founded and solely run by an auxiliary. Moreover, because Indian health care was part of the work carried out within a missionary station, chapter 5 deals with the role of WNIA medical missionaries, the building of several full-scale Indian hospitals on the Navajo Reservation, and the Connecticut auxiliary's unique program to fund the complete medical education of Susan La Flesche Picotte, the first Indigenous woman to became a physician. However, missionary work was actually accomplished on the ground, in a one-to-one contact situation, involving extensive travel and primitive living conditions on the part of the missionary. As examples, chapters 6 and 7 are devoted to the missionary efforts of Mary Louise Eldridge in New Mexico and Rev. William Henry Weinland in California, detailing their longtime work and their role as supervisors of WNIA stations.

Although the WNIA membership primarily focused on Indian reform and missionary work, many also engaged in philanthropic and humanitarian efforts in other reform arenas. For example, the association formed a close partnership with the Woman's Christian Temperance Union (WCTU). Chapter 9 is devoted to the history of a WNIA member, Dorcas J. Spencer, who was also a lifelong member of the California branch of the WCTU. Also, to emphasize the wide range of reform interests of WNIA members and to broaden the understanding of their role within the larger reform arena of the day, their non-Indian reform work is emphasized when available. The diversity reflected merits that the association's role as a reform association be viewed as historically important as that of the WCTU, the National Woman Suffrage Association, the American Woman Suffrage Association, and the General Federation of Women's Clubs.

I have written this book from the perspective of WNIA reformers, letting them tell the story through their own words. Because they used the term "Indian" in their writings, I do so as well, inserting tribal names for clarity. A direct and strong "Indian voice" seldom appears in WNIA literature, as Indigenous peoples were not consulted and therefore their letters, speeches, and praises were not recorded. I have included all the examples that I have found during four decades of research. It is also possible, however, to attribute the presence of such a voice by inference. If Native parents continually sent their children to WNIA boarding schools, sought aid from WNIA medical missionaries or in association hospitals, and regularly participated in church services and other activities within a mission station, it can be assumed that they found some value in what was being offered, even though they did not publicly express it.

Like their fellow reformers, members of the WNIA promoted the government's policy of assimilation—an approach viewed today as harmful. Not all reform work, however, should be painted with the same negative brush. As in other social movements, there was good along with the bad. I have made a point to include all the many examples I have found of positive philanthropic and benevolent social reform work carried out by these dedicated WNIA members.

Although I owe a large debt to many librarians and archivists who have helped me over the years, for this specific book, I am indebted to the following: the Mudd Library at Princeton; the Autry Museum of the American West; the Harriet Beecher Stowe Center; the Smithsonian Museum; California State Polytechnic University, Humboldt; the Huntington Library; Archives of the Episcopal Church; Mohonk Mountain House Archives; Archives of the Presbyterian Historical Society; the Farmington Museum; and the Litchfield Historical Society. I am also indebted to the scholars who have graciously read all or parts of this book and have provided invaluable insight and suggestions. They are: Patricia "Patty" Tharp, former president of the San Juan County Historical Society; Lynn Downey, archivist, writer, and historian; Larisa K. Miller, archivist; Donald L. Fixico, Regents and Distinguished Foundation Professor of History at Arizona State University; and Helen M. Bannan, professor emerita, University of Wisconsin–Oshkosh. Helen, who wrote her dissertation on the WNIA and contemporary reformers, has been especially generous with her time. I also owe special thanks to Travis Snyder, editor in chief of Texas Tech University Press, who has worked closely with me during the writing of this book.

VALERIE SHERER MATHES
SONOMA, CALIFORNIA, 2025

Divinely Guided Revisited

Introduction

The Dawn of an Indian Reform Movement

During the last quarter of the nineteenth century, four evangelically driven Indian reform associations were founded with the intent of "civilizing" and Christianizing the American Indian, breaking up communally held reservations and allotting lands individually. Historian Francis Paul Prucha, S.J., identifies these "friends of the Indian" as the Women's National Indian Association (WNIA), the Boston Indian Citizenship Society, the Indian Rights Association (IRA), and the Lake Mohonk Conference of the Friends of the Indian.[1] He writes that the seeds for this movement were planted with the arrival of the first Western European settlers to the shores of America. Two cultures, with radically different world outlooks, collided, resulting in military encounters and "fraud and deception and injustice of men toward other men," creating an "Indian problem" that no one could ignore and that provided "fertile ground for seeds of reform, which sprouted again and again."[2]

English professor Russel Blaine Nye in *Society and Culture in America* notes that "evangelical religion made social reform a moral imperative." He explains that "if social evil were the result of individual sin and selfishness, then progress came from reforming individuals by religious conversion." Thus it was the reformers' duty to "convert the nation, rather than to try to argue it into virtue or legislate it into benevolence." One instrument to achieve this outcome was the voluntary missionary society, which was composed of clerics and laymen who published journals, organized speakers' bureaus, held conventions, and lobbied in state capitals and before Congress. Of the four reform associations, the WNIA, an outgrowth of a woman's missionary society, engaged in all of the activities outlined by Nye, although he was writing of an earlier movement and of different associations. Members of Nye's voluntary missionary societies were all clerics. WNIA members were not, although their all-male advisory board did include prominent ministers, and association meetings were often held in local churches. Nye also writes that women were prominent figures within many of the reform societies, later becoming "a powerful force in the feminist struggle for equal rights."[3]

The reform movement of the 1840s dealt primarily with women's rights, treatment of the insane, and peace crusades. Its adoption of public education, however, tangentially touched Indians, as education was viewed as a potential way of bringing about Indigenous transformation. William Medill, Commissioner of Indian Affairs from 1845 to 1849, viewed the opening of manual labor schools for Indians as the beginning of "a new era in the progress of Indian civilization." He proposed such in his 1848 report. Prucha concludes that these schools "were the first of a long succession of panaceas that were to erase the past and create a bright new future for the Indians."[4] Medill, like most humanitarians of the day, believed that the ultimate solution to the "Indian problem" was assimilation, and one road toward that end was to impose a manual labor school education upon the children "until they became civilized enough to be adopted into the mainstream of American life." To reduce the government's obligation and expenses, Medill also recommended that missionary societies participate in this endeavor.[5] Decades later, the WNIA was positioned to do just that.

Reformers traditionally referred to Indians as children or childlike, and a government policy of paternalism slowly emerged, eventually growing to restrict their freedom of action, including even dictating treaty terms "to chiefs unable or afraid to reject them, and set[ting] about to change the fundamental cultural patterns of the Indians in a self-righteous paternal manner."[6] In 1871 congressional legislation ended Indian participation in treaty making altogether, declaring that Indian nations and tribes were no longer recognized as independent. Fifteen years later, in *United States v. Kagama*, Indians were declared to be wards of the nation, communities dependent upon the US for their political rights.[7] These changes prompted Prucha to conclude that "the Indian Office assumed the paternalistic mantle that theoretically belonged to the Great Father, the president."[8]

Amelia Stone Quinton, a co-founder of the WNIA, challenged this paternalistic approach in an 1886 pamphlet, writing that "though savages, they [Indians] are not children, and less than children can they thrive and develop nobly under the rod." Describing this approach as archaic, she inquired of her readers if it was not time for a Christian nation to adopt an intelligent policy toward its so-called wards, viewing them instead as "men and women, with all the natural rights of maturing which we ourselves possess?"[9] Under Quinton's tenure, first as general secretary and later as president, the WNIA gradually adopted a maternalistic agenda as it carried out women's work for Indian women.[10]

The "Indian problem" worsened during the Civil War years as settlers pushed westward, forcing Plains tribes to defend their lands. In 1869, the Ulysses S. Grant administration responded with the peace policy, a multifaceted approach, including treaty making with warring tribes, the establishment of reservations, and the assignment of Indian agencies largely to Protestant denominations, giving missionary boards the power to nominate agents and other personnel in an effort to improve the quality of Indian agents.[11] Such a political move was possible, notes Prucha, because the United States was openly a Christian nation, and its citizens and their government were "dominated by a religious sentiment that affected all aspects of national life—including Indian policy."[12]

Another component of the peace policy was the Board of Indian Commissioners (BIC), composed of unpaid philanthropists, humanitarians, and prominent Protestant laymen, who exercised joint control with the Interior Department in the purchase and inspection of goods and disbursement of funds. To make well-informed decisions, commissioners also undertook investigative reservation tours.[13] Every winter the BIC met in Washington with representatives of various Protestant missionary groups to learn of their year's work and to discuss Indian matters. According to Prucha, these meetings served as a "useful platform from which to preach the reforms devised" because it brought evangelical churches into a semiofficial association with the very men who made government policy.[14]

Post–Civil War America continued to be dominated by this reformism, which, fed by reports of new injustices towards the Indians, resulted in an increased "intensity with which evangelical Christians moved into Indian affairs." These well-intentioned but seriously misguided eastern humanitarians "mounted an aggressive campaign to revolutionize the relations of the Indians to American society."[15] United and well organized, they were convinced they finally had the answer to the "Indian problem." Sharing a common philanthropic and humanitarian outlook and drawing upon local church support, they worked harmoniously between and within their respective groups to promote the government's policy of assimilation without consulting with or getting any input from Indians. Utilizing various forms of propaganda to "awaken and inform the national conscience and thereby bending Congress and federal officials to their will," these reformers effectively shaped government policy, giving "new drive and a new orientation to Indian-white relations in the United States."[16]

Historian William G. McLoughlin writes that evangelicalism had "made Americans the most religious people in the world."[17] Therefore, these "friends of the Indian" were not a small peripheral group of men and women who unjustly pushed a reform program upon Congress. Instead, they represented a large and powerful segment of Protestant church membership. When they spoke, they were "expressing views that were widely held, consciously or unconsciously," making them "the chief channel through which this Americanism came to bear upon the Indians." According to Prucha, if the reformers erred, it was because "the America they represented was so satisfied with its vision of the world that everyone was expected to accept and conform." Therefore, he concludes, it was the Indians' fate that the solution for this problem which "had troubled the national conscience throughout the nineteenth century should have been formulated when such a reform group was in command."[18]

Thus, with good intentions, these reformers, accustomed to living in a society defined by rugged individualism, set out to end the Indians' communal way of life and to dissolve tribal relations with the government. "Indianism" had to be stamped out and replaced by a uniform Americanism—continuing the government's paternalistic approach to Indian affairs. Reformers achieved their goal in 1887 with the passage of the General Allotment or Dawes Act which divided up tribally held reservation lands, allotting the land individually as private property and opening up unallotted lands to homesteading, transferring some ninety million acres from Indigenous to white ownership.[19]

Not all reformers pushed assimilation, however. Based on his Midwestern upbringing espousing working-class and agrarian causes, Thomas A. Bland held different beliefs from those of elite eastern philanthropists. In late 1885 he founded the National Indian Defense Association (NIDA), which rejected forced assimilation. He appealed to Indians to actively participate in reform, encouraging them to speak at NIDA meetings and in the *Council Fire*, a periodical he edited. Bland focused "upon using the federal government to provide resources and opportunities for Indigenous nations while simultaneously protecting the integrity of communally held land." He and the NIDA tried to "create a permanent alternative to the assimilation process by providing incentives to Indian communities and allowing Native people to embrace mainstream culture and societal values only if they chose to do so." The NIDA's main argument against allotment was that it provided no self-determination, leaving the Indian without a future voice.[20]

To better understand the amicable relationship among the three male-dominated associations and the WNIA, a brief history follows. (A detailed discussion of the origins of the WNIA is the subject of the next chapter.) The Boston Indian Citizenship Committee was founded two years after the WNIA in the summer of 1879 by a small group of well-educated, politically connected philanthropists, businessmen, ministers, lawyers, and legislators. It was inspired by Thomas Henry Tibbles's initial fund-raising tour on behalf of the small Ponca tribe, which had been removed by force from their Nebraska homeland to the Indian Territory.[21] Chief Standing Bear, with his wife, a small party of followers, and the body of his son, had returned to their tribal homelands to bury the boy and were arrested by federal troops commanded by General George Crook. Tibbles, an assistant editor of the *Omaha Daily Herald*, hired two lawyers to defend Standing Bear before the US District Court of Nebraska in *Standing Bear v. Crook*. This case was decided in favor of the defendant. Supported by the Boston Committee, Tibbles returned to Boston with Standing Bear and his interpreter Susette La Flesche and her brother Francis, children of Joseph La Flesche, the last recognized chief of the Omaha tribe, on a lecture tour of the eastern United States to heighten awareness of the plight of the Poncas and to raise money.[22]

Helen Hunt Jackson, poet and novelist, attended one of the lectures and in articles and a chapter in *A Century of Dishonor* alerted the reading public to this egregious injustice.[23] Her writings and the efforts of the Boston Committee resulted in investigative hearings before the U.S. Senate, a presidential commission, and congressional compensation for the Poncas. Once their goals were achieved, a prominent Committee member inquired of Albert K. Smiley, founder of the Lake Mohonk Conference, if they should "dissolve as no longer needed." Smiley responded that it would be "wise" to continue, for an occasion might arise where it would be an "advantage to have an organization ready to take up some unexpected phase of the subject."[24]

Following Smiley's advice, the Boston Committee continued to function until the second decade of the twentieth century, with some members regularly attending the annual Lake Mohonk Conference, joining a branch of the IRA, or working closely with WNIA auxiliary members in the Boston and Cambridge areas. The Boston Committee did not go national, establish auxiliaries, maintain a lobbyist in Washington, DC, or hold annual conventions. They were, however, along with the WNIA, the earliest organization to promote the recognition of treaty obligations, Indian citizenship, and allotment. Although it was initially an all-male association, some women did join early on. In most cases they were wives of existing members. Once the WNIA established their auxiliaries in Boston and Cambridge, many women, now no longer dependent upon their husbands' connections, joined the WNIA. The early female membership in the Boston Committee may well be a reason for the close working relationship between male and female Indian reformers in the Boston and Cambridge area.[25]

During the summer of 1882, political reformer Herbert Welsh and his friend Henry Pancoast made an investigative tour of the Great Sioux Reservation.[26] That December, forty prominent Philadelphia philanthropists, mostly Episcopalians and Quakers, gathered in John Welsh's home and founded the IRA. John Welsh, a former ambassador to England, had been a successful merchant, enabling his son, Herbert, to dabble in philanthropy and Indian reform. The younger Welsh's interest in Indian reform may also have been influenced by his uncle, William Welsh, a wealthy merchant and a lay Episcopalian philanthropist, who had served for a short time as the first chairman of the Board of Indian Commissioners.[27] After resigning from the BIC, Welsh continued as a private citizen to devote his time to Indian reform, acting as a semiofficial government inspector and publishing reports at his own expense, thus throwing "a glare of light upon fraudulent transactions relating to government contracts."[28] He and his wife, Mary Ross Welsh, also founded the Indian's Hope Association, a branch of the Episcopal Church's Women's Auxiliary to the Board of Missions in 1868, running it out of their Philadelphia Spruce Street mansion.[29]

The IRA, founded a decade and a half after William Welsh's Indian's Hope Association, was a nonpartisan, nonsectarian organization intent on securing civil rights, impartial justice, education, and individual title to land for Indigenous people.[30] Rev. George Dana Boardman, pastor of the First Baptist Church, also attended the founding meeting. By this time, two of his own parishioners, Mary Lucinda Bonney and Amelia Stone Quinton, co-founders of the WNIA, had already been engaged in Indian reform for five years. A close working relationship developed between these two Philadelphia-based associations.

Welsh had hoped to emulate Quinton's WNIA structure with branches diffusing knowledge of Indian reform through public meetings and publications. However, unlike WNIA auxiliaries which governed their own activities, those established by the IRA were used "to raise funds, distribute literature, and inspire letters and petitions in behalf of causes identified by the Philadelphia leadership." In 1888, the IRA had twenty-eight branches, over half of which were moribund, while in 1885 the WNIA already had fifty-six auxiliaries operating in twenty-seven states.[31] Two IRA exceptions were the Boston branch, which drew members from the Boston Committee, and the Cambridge branch, organized by Welsh in March 1885 with Reverend Samuel Longfellow, the younger brother of Henry Wadsworth Longfellow, as president. The latter branch also welcomed women members.[32] Welsh's willingness to run a central office staff in Philadelphia distinguished the IRA from the Boston Committee. When he was absent on one of his numerous western reservation tours, his clerk, Mathew K. Sniffen, handled affairs.[33] Much of the association's political effectiveness was due to the employment of Charles C. Painter, the Washington, DC, agent, who represented IRA policies before Congress.[34] Welsh, following Quinton's lead, addressed public meetings, organized branches, toured western reservations, and worked to raise funds to keep his association solvent.

The Lake Mohonk Conference of Friends of the Indian was an annual forum founded in 1883 by Quaker schoolteacher Alfred K. Smiley, who as a BIC member was displeased with the limited time the Board had to deal with issues brought before it by representatives of missionary societies and Indian associations during their annual winter Washington, DC, meeting. He included an extra BIC meeting during the regular fall Mohonk Conference. Attendees, personally invited by Smiley, included congressmen, Indian commissioners, interior secretaries, representatives from various religious societies, clergy from Protestant denominations, members of congressional Indian committees, Army officers, heads of Indian schools, presidents of universities and colleges, members of national Indian reform associations, and editors of secular and religious newspapers.[35] They conferred and recommended policies to be considered by officials of the Indian Office. An inner circle, or Business Committee, determined topics, selected speakers, and made recommendations to include in the yearly platform. Quinton often served as a member. The conferences succeeded because Smiley emphasized "the Quaker tradition of seeking agreement through unity" and the adoption of the Quaker belief of female equality, a principle that enabled reform-minded women to participate on an equal footing with the men.[36] In 1884 four women attended; in 1885 there were twenty-six, a dozen of whom were WNIA members, including Quinton.[37] Beginning that year the conference also offered a session titled "Woman's Work for the Indian."[38] In 1890 there were seventy-two women, only fifteen of whom were WNIA members, reflecting an increasing interest in Indian reform among other home missionary societies and female educators.[39]

Although the history and role of the WNIA is recognized by scholars of Indian history, it is often overlooked by those writing about women's volunteer associations. Anne Firor Scott in *Making the Invisible Woman Visible* describes the role of such groups as filling societal needs at a time when no government took the responsibility for basic human services. She writes that a social history of nineteenth-century America that fails to analyze "the effect of women's voluntary associations is somewhat akin to discussing plant growth without mentioning photosynthesis." Scott lists four categories: church-related groups, a direct descendant of prewar missionary and benevolent societies; the Woman's Christian Temperance Union; women's clubs; and two national suffrage associations, the National Woman Suffrage Association and the American Woman Suffrage Association. The WNIA, which patently fits within the first category, is neither discussed in the text nor listed in the index.[40] Scott can be excused for this oversight because at the time she wrote her book, the only histories of the WNIA were unpublished dissertations.[41]

Like the three relevant male-dominated associations, the WNIA initially had been interested in reforming the government's Indian policy; however, when the IRA took over much of its political work, the women returned to their missionary roots, operating much like a home missionary society, establishing more than sixty mission stations across the country. The following chapter is a short history of the association's founding.

CHAPTER 1

The Founding of the WNIA

On May 5, 1880, Mary Lucinda Bonney,[1] president of the Women's Home Missionary Society of Philadelphia's First Baptist Church and founder in 1850 of the Chestnut Street Female Seminary,[2] suggested to three members of her missionary society that they join her to become a Committee of Ways & Means and aid in the distribution of petitions and leaflets on behalf of their Indian work.[3] This was not the first women-driven petition movement in support of Indians. In 1829, Catharine Beecher, daughter of Presbyterian minister Lyman Beecher and sister to Harriet Beecher Stowe, had written a petition protesting the removal of the Cherokee from their southeastern homelands.[4] Bonney's action moved her missionary society further along the road to becoming the Women's National Indian Association, an association of middle- and upper-class white women, initially engaged in reforming the government's Indian policy, later turning almost exclusively to missionary work until they disbanded in 1951.

The most active of Bonney's three society members was Mrs. Amelia Stone Quinton, a former organizer for the Brooklyn branch of the Woman's Christian Temperance Union (WCTU), who had only recently moved to Philadelphia.[5]

The two other particularly dedicated society members were Mrs. Mariné Chase, a member of the American Association for the Advancement of Science,[6] and Mrs. George Dana Boardman (née Ella Covell), wife of the pastor at First Baptist Church and the founder of the home missionary society of which Bonney was president.[7] That autumn the women voted to invite members from other religious denominations to join them, becoming an "independent undenominational Committee," calling themselves the Central Indian Committee.[8]

The two most influential committee members were Bonney and Quinton. The date of their first meeting is unknown. Quinton was rumored to have taught at the Chestnut Street Seminary; however, there is no evidence that she did. The two most likely met when Quinton moved to Philadelphia following her lengthy stay in England. It is not clear if she had gone abroad to rest from her extensive reform work on behalf of the WCTU or to seek out distant new fields to spread her temperance message. However, on the voyage over to England Amelia Stone met Richard Linton Quinton, a professor and lecturer of historical and astronomical topics. They married in 1878 in All Saints Church in Highgate, London.[9] While in England, Quinton gave temperance lectures in private homes and churches. Following the couple's move to Philadelphia, it was logical for Mrs. Quinton, raised in the Baptist faith, to join the First Baptist Church and the home missionary society, giving, as Bonney described, "her entire time to the movement and to mission work in connection with it."[10]

Bonney, older by almost twenty years, was financially comfortable because of her profitable female seminary. She funded their Indian work while Quinton served as the primary organizer. Their successful partnership was based on a shared background and beliefs. They were born in the "burned-over district" of Upstate New York—known for its evangelical revivals and dedication to social reform—and were raised in Baptist homes, marrying Baptist clergymen.[11] They both taught in the South and brought extensive humanitarian and philanthropic experience to their reform work.[12] They were well educated for their time, although Bonney had the advantage of attending Emma Willard's Troy Female Seminary for two years, a prep school that provided its female students with a curriculum similar to that found in colleges educating young men.[13] According to Anne Firor Scott, Troy's graduates became "agents of cultural diffusion, spreading Willard's ideas about women's capacities,"[14] a task that Bonney readily accepted.

Bonney's petition efforts on behalf of the Indians were not the first in which members of Philadelphia's First Baptist Church had taken up such an interest.

More than half a century earlier, on January 20, 1819, the 1,500-member congregation had supported a memorial petition to Congress decrying the activities of white Indian traders, who continually defrauded the Indians of their property, corrupted their morals, and led "them to the most contemptible ideas of civilization and religion." The memorialists petitioned Congress to pass legislation not only to regulate Indian trade but to instruct the Indians in living a "civilized" life.[15] Although trade regulation had begun in 1790 with the passage of the first Indian Trade and Intercourse Act, enforcement was spotty, and traders had continued to engage in fraudulent practices. This First Baptist Church petition, along with those of other churches and missionary societies, resulted in the March 3, 1819, passage of the Civilization Fund, establishing an annual $10,000 fund [$251,810 in 2025 dollars] to support the education of Indians in missionary schools. Congressional monies were later augmented by treaty provisions.[16] Now, more than sixty years later a missionary society founded within the same church would grow into the WNIA and establish its own private Indian boarding schools.

This 1819 petition had been sent under the signature of its pastor, Henry Holcombe. Born in Prince Edward County, Virginia, Holcombe served in Pipe Creek, South Carolina, and Savannah, Georgia, before being unanimously elected by the First Baptist Church in late September 1811. He began his pastorate in January 1812, serving until his death in 1824 in what was described at the time as the richest and most prestigious Baptist church in the country. Holcombe was well known for his previous benevolent work, including the founding of an asylum for homeless girls and promoting the growth of African American churches. Once in Philadelphia, he and his wife, the former Frances Tanner, quickly became involved in the city's Female Hospitable Society for the Relief and Employment of the Poor, founded two decades earlier by a Quaker woman. This 1819 petition on behalf of the Indians was a natural progression of his humanitarian interests on behalf of his community and parishioners.[17]

Decades later, on May 17, 1877, Ella Covell Boardman founded the Women's Home Missionary Society within the same First Baptist Church to engage in missionary work for the Indians. Her husband, who had been appointed in 1863 and served for the next three decades, was the son of Baptist missionaries serving in Burma (now Myanmar). Reverend Boardman and his wife strongly believed that church members should engage in missionary work. Therefore, Ella Boardman had organized her home missionary society with the goal of promoting the "Christianization of homes by means of mission schools, etc. with special reference to the freedmen, Indians, and immigrant heathen populations of our country," tying together the various groups that Holcombe and his wife Frances had worked among decades earlier.[18]

Boardman had organized her society only two weeks after attending a May 1, 1877, illustrated lecture at her husband's church by George Washington Ingalls, the General Missionary to the Indians for the American Baptist Home Mission Society (ABHMS). A former agent at the Nevada Paiute Agency and the Union Agency in Indian Territory (present-day Oklahoma), Ingalls lectured that day on "Missionary Work Among Indians" as part of a national campaign to encourage the formation of local affiliates of the Women's Baptist Home Mission Society (WBHMS), only recently formed.[19]

The previous August, Ingalls's efforts on behalf of the Indians had also inspired Mrs. Emily Lucas Blackall, author, philanthropist, and a founder and treasurer of the Woman's Baptist Foreign Missionary Society of the West, and her husband Rev. C. R. Blackall, of the Chicago-based Baptist Publication Society, to attend the annual meeting of the Choctaw-Chickasaw Baptist Association, established in 1872 by Rev. Joseph Samuel Murrow. Mrs. Blackall, with the aid of Mrs. Czarina Bond, a Choctaw woman, met with other Indigenous women, who upon learning that some missionary societies were sending missionaries to foreign destinations, requested that several be sent to them. On August 15, 1876, the Choctaw and Chickasaw Woman's Home Mission Society was formed with forty-six Indian members. Describing this society as "the first Baptist women's home mission society with a national scope," historian John M. Rhea concludes that it was not white women who initiated reform among Indian women but "Choctaw and Chickasaw Indian women who rattled the consciences of these Northern Baptist women, sparking them to engage in Indian activism."[20]

Sometime after returning from the Indian Territory, Emily Blackall participated in the founding on February 1, 1877, of the Women's Baptist Home Mission Society at the Michigan Avenue Baptist Church in Chicago. Ella Boardman's missionary society of Philadelphia women was only one of many such groups organized in answer to Ingalls's call. During their first general meeting, the WBHMS passed a resolution describing their group as carrying "forward the work of Christian women for the evangelization of the heathen and semi-heathen people and homes in our country."[21]

Until May 1880, Boardman's First Baptist auxiliary continued as a WBHMS affiliate, collecting money and goods on behalf of Indian women in the Indian

Territory.²² That month, at Bonney's suggestion, she and three society members formed the Committee of Ways & Means, separating from the WBHMS to raise money for their own Indian work. According to Rhea, one possible reason for this separation was the founding in the spring of 1879 of the Women's American Baptist Home Mission Society, a rival women's missionary group in Boston, which conspired with the all-male American Baptist Home Mission Society to dissolve the WBHMS board and use their funds. Ultimately, the Chicago and Boston societies came to a mutually beneficial agreement, with each remaining independent, meeting once a year in a joint session. Quinton and Bonney continued to remain active in the WBHMS even after their Philadelphia-based home missionary society had become independent.²³

Only recently has the traditional origin story of the WNIA come into question. Although the role of Boardman's society has always been known, official WNIA literature never once mentioned the Women's Baptist Home Mission Society or George Washington Ingalls. In a 2020 article reexamining the association's early history, historian John Rhea concludes that "for 120 years, historical accounts have faithfully repeated Bonney and Quinton's WNIA history without questioning its claim of spontaneous origin or its factual accuracy."²⁴ Bonney, in her 1881 historical sketch, claimed to have alerted home missionary society members to the pressures brought by various groups to open Indian-held lands in the Indian Territory for white settlement. Characterizing this invasion as "a vast moral evil to our own nation," she believed it hindered the process of Christianizing the Indians and encouraged society members to initiate a petition drive protesting such action.²⁵ Again, essentially taking credit for the association's founding, Bonney repeated a similar version in a September 1894 autobiographical sketch written at Quinton's request, explaining she had learned from newspapers that Missouri Senator George Vest "had been pressing Congress for 13 years to open the Oklahoma lands to settlement by whites." Amazed that a senator would encourage such "injustice," and describing it as morally wrong, she expressed her feelings to Quinton, whose "heart and conscience were stirred," and the two women pledged to do what they "could to awaken the conscience of Congress and of the people." Bonney had clearly written that "this was in 1879," and "thus was begun what finally issued as the Women's National Indian Association."²⁶ However, based on Rhea's recent research, it might be more accurate for current scholars to consider 1877, the year Boardman established her society, as the WNIA's founding date.²⁷

In describing their use of a selective chronology, Rhea asserts that Bonney and Quinton chose to omit their relationship with the WBHMS to cover up their association with Ingalls, a disgraced Indian agent,[28] and their "participation in a pitched interdenominational battle with Northern Baptist men over control of women's Indian missionary work" to "hide embarrassing, potentially damning facts about the complex evolution of their Indian social activism and the WNIA's subsequent formation." He suggests this mutually sanitized narrative was presented to protect the women's "political status as Indian reformers and national ambassadors of Christian motherhood." By "reconnecting the WNIA with the historical forces that gave birth to its Indian activism, it becomes clear that Bonney and Quinton played key roles in the development of post-bellum maternalism," Rhea writes, concluding that "the development of the WNIA was an important contribution to the lateral spread of women's rights." In their struggle with the ABHMS for control of their home missionary societies, Bonney, Quinton, and other evangelical women had "contended with a politically seasoned group of white protestant men—and won." Therefore, Rhea concludes, the WNIA "merits a place in women's rights history as much as the activities of East Coast suffragists and the overtly political endeavors of women's rights activists."[29]

Like earlier women reformers, Bonney and her little group turned to petitioning, considered a feminine tactic that did not require "women to step out of the normal circle of their private lives."[30] Their first petition completed, Bonney invited Boardman and Chase to accompany her to Washington, DC, to present it to President Rutherford B. Hayes at the White House. On February 14, 1880, Boardman personally handed the 300-foot-long petition signed by 13,000 citizens from fifteen states to the president, who according to Bonney "expressed his sense of the timeliness of the memorial."[31] The petitioners requested government officials take steps to prevent encroachment upon the Indian Territory and guard Indian rights guaranteed by the "faith of the nation."[32]

Chase, on the recommendation of her friend, Henry B. Whipple, Episcopal Bishop of Minnesota, had written ahead to President Hayes and his wife requesting an interview. Bonney later explained that the presidential couple had received them "most courteously and cordially" that day.[33] Hayes was quite familiar with the work of missionary-minded women because his wife, Lucy Ware Webb Hayes, was the first president of the Woman's Home Missionary Society of the Methodist Episcopal Church, founded in Cincinnati in 1880. Mrs. Hayes and her fellow members organized schools and sent female missionaries to work among poor whites,

Blacks, Indians, and Chinese.[34] Three years later, Lucy Hayes's personal missionary efforts and those of several WNIA members would interconnect with the founding in Philadelphia of an auxiliary of the American McAll Society.[35] Hayes served as president of the McAll auxiliary, Chase as executive secretary, later as president, and Frances Lea,[36] a new member of the Central Indian Committee member, as treasurer.

On December 11, 1880, Lea attended her first formal meeting of the Central Indian Committee, with Chase sitting as chairman. The group had already grown to eight members, representing five different Protestant denominations.[37] During their second meeting on December 31, 1880, Quinton suggested they rename themselves the Indian Treaty-Keeping Association (ITKA), which she described as "simple, descriptive & unostentatious." They also listened to the reading of Whipple's recent letter to Chase in which he had included a list of senators who "would best aid in presenting" their next petition. The name change was adopted.[38] During the fourth meeting, on March 17, 1881, members accepted Chase's resignation, selecting Bonney to succeed her. At the June 3, 1881, meeting with eight committee members and six visitors present, Bonney presided over the adoption of a new constitution. Calling themselves the Indian Treaty-Keeping and Protective Association (ITKPA), members chose Bonney as president, Quinton as general secretary, and Boardman as treasurer.[39] They declared their object as awakening "a Christian public sentiment which shall move our Government to just dealing with the Indian tribes among us."[40]

The November 30, 1881, minutes reflected the extensive organizational work already accomplished by Quinton, including addresses given since the last meeting, circulars and appeals written, and the founding of branches outside Philadelphia based on a decision made during the November 3 meeting. Quinton had already organized in Amsterdam and Gloversville, New York, and would soon add Newark, New Jersey; Brooklyn, New York; Hartford, Connecticut; Providence, Rhode Island; and Boston, Massachusetts, to the list.[41] The membership decided to keep Philadelphia as their headquarters. In the spring of 1904 it was moved to New York City, operating out of a rented room in the Presbyterian Building on Fifth Avenue.[42]

Chase's resignation in 1881 and Boardman's fragile health shifted the workload to the capable shoulders of Bonney and Quinton. By April 1881, this small group of determined women had distributed hundreds of thousands of pages of information, numerous press articles and petitions, prompting Bonney to declare that all material "coming to the eye, conscience, and heart of Christians, pastors,

CHAPTER I

Figure 1. Amelia Stone Quinton, co-founder of the WNIA, longtime president, and chair of the Missionary Committee, sent this studio photograph taken by G. J. Pruden, a Homer, New York, photographer, to Reverend and Mrs. William Henry Weinland on September 16, 1898. (The Huntington Library, San Marino California, William H. Weinland Collection, [photCL 39 (202)].)

editors and other thought makers could not fail to bring forth fruit from seed thus sown on good ground."⁴³

Quinton and Chase carried their second petition, signed by 50,000 people from all thirty-eight states and several territories, to Washington, DC, in late January 1881. The petitioners requested honorable governmental dealings with all Indians, the prevention of white encroachment upon reservations, and the recognition of Indian treaties unless changed by consent of both parties.⁴⁴ In the meantime, members continued gathering signatures for their third petition, preparing additional information to present to the public, dealing with the various organizational issues and name changes, and rewriting their constitution to reflect new goals. Massachusetts Senator Henry Laurens Dawes, who presented their second petition before the Senate, introduced their third on February 21, 1882, with 100,000 signatures. Years later, Quinton wrote that Dawes had closed the Senate debate with "a brilliant speech of thrilling eloquence, giving telling facts of outrages upon Indians by the Government and white settlers, and the speech was received with prolonged applause."⁴⁵ As chairman of committee resolutions for the WBHMS, Quinton reported that while they were continuing their own work "for the Christianization of the Indian homes," society membership cordially endorsed "the efforts of the Indian Treaty Keeping and Protective Association to secure for all Indian tribes the same governmental justice and protection that are enjoyed by the other races within our national limits."⁴⁶

During their October 3, 1882, meeting, members of the ITKPA executive board voted to introduce educational and missionary work. To incorporate these new objectives, that same day the membership adopted a new constitution, describing themselves as Christian women "deeply deploring the long catalogue of unjust dealings of our government with Indians . . . and conscious of personal responsibility for efforts to secure the adoption of a just, protective and fostering Indian policy." To that end, they defined two goals. The first was to strengthen public sentiment to encourage the government to adopt a policy including a common-school education and citizenship. In the second, they declared that by adding their own educational or missionary work on behalf of the Indians, they hoped "to hasten as much as is in our power their civilization, christianization and enfranchisement." To reflect their nondenominational approach, the new executive committee would include two or more members from each religion denomination determined by their officers. And finally, they changed their name to the National Indian Association.⁴⁷ Two months later, when the Indian Rights

Association was founded, they became known as the Women's National Indian Association.

Of the three male-dominated Indian associations, the IRA had the most profound impact upon WNIA work. Its founding enabled the women to shift their priorities from Indian policy reform and protecting Indian rights to missionary work, returning to their missionary roots.[48] In their 1883 annual report, the association announced that the IRA would be taking over much of their efforts to "secure civil and political protection for the Indian," freeing their membership to devote a portion of their work "to uplifting Indian homes; to aiding the vastly needed work within Indian hearts, minds and souls, while not intermitting the effort to secure to the race civil rights."[49] Although they would still continue traditional petition drives, the WNIA now claimed fieldwork as their province, devoting their time, energy, and money to the founding of missionary stations across the country. Within these stations, which provided a physical infrastructure of chapels, missionary cottages, educational facilities, and in some cases hospitals, WNIA members and support staff followed the government's assimilation program—a policy they had helped create.

The WNIA's move to assume school and missionary work caused Francis Paul Prucha to describe the association as taking "on many of the characteristics of a home missionary society."[50] Such an idea was not foreign to Rev. Joseph Flavius Cook, who in his March 2, 1885, remarks delivered at Boston's Tremont Temple had recommended that Indian associations "lock hands with the home Missionary Societies [and] assist in sending to the front those who are willing to devote their lives to the teaching of a pure Gospel among the dusky tribes." Cook, warning reformers not to depend upon politicians or on government schools to reform the Indians, concluded that "the longest root of hope for the Indian is to be found in the self-sacrifice of the Christian Church." The WNIA not only followed his advice but printed some of his remarks on the front cover of their 1885 missionary report.[51]

The WNIA further clarified their new missionary endeavor before a mass meeting at St. George's Hall, Philadelphia, in 1884, announcing that "while the men of the last few generations were oppressing the aborigines, or suffering them to be oppressed, the women were forgiving (as not knowing what they did) and pitying them for their ignorance, sins and sufferings." And the "daughters of those women have developed compassion into action, forbearance in justice, sympathy into public sentiment, and have fairly and fully organized a great reform."[52] These daughters, much like the women in the home missionary societies, soon assumed leadership roles that heretofore had been nonexistent.

The WNIA's shift from their initial work of promoting Indian rights to working among Indian women, uplifting their homes, prompted Margaret Jacobs in *White Mother to a Dark Race* to declare that when the WNIA turned to these "gender-appropriate maternal reforms," they had finally become a "full-fledged maternalist organization," as they "concentrated on reaching Indian women and children, first through sending women missionaries and field matrons to remote Indian communities." Jacobs described maternalists as using traditional women's associations "with motherhood to justify their participation in reform politics, a male-dominated realm, by arguing that they were merely extending their natural role as potential mothers who had values and skills that were necessary to solve the major problems of the day."[53] In an 1886 pamphlet, Quinton addressed the issue of Indian homes when she wrote that it was incumbent upon the "good women of the white race" to begin to create a safe happy home for Indian women—"a home from whose sacred precincts her sons shall go forth strong men, gentle and well taught, men of integrity, law abiding citizens and Christian patriots."[54]

In her article on American missionary women, Dana L. Robert describes the formation of various missionary societies as "the first organized woman's movement in the history of American churches." However, she also relates that conservation men gradually began to oppose the recognition of such societies.[55] WNIA literature does not reflect any such opposition. Instead, reformers of both genders appeared to work harmoniously. The association's monthly periodical, *The Indian's Friend*, notes that WNIA members hailed "with joy the advent of the Indian Rights Association," recognizing their respective work as aligned with one another. Each association agreed to appoint a member of their own executive board to attend the other's board meetings and "to secure practically the united influence and co-operation of both for the work of each." They continued in "fellowship, not always holding identical views on the smaller issues, but ever in substantial unity and in hearty accord to the great aims of their work."[56]

Mrs. J. B. Dickinson (née Mary Caroline Lowe) in her November 1885 presidential address described the relationship between the WNIA and the IRA as cordial, much like an elder sister contemplating "the strength and prowess of a younger brother with grateful emotions," a sibling able to mass his "forces against the legal and political barriers in the way of Indian elevation."[57] Unitarian minister Edward E. Hale, editor of *Lend a Hand*, a journal he founded to support organized charity, confirmed this relationship, describing the two associations as "having the same end in view," working "together in perfect harmony, although, from the necessities of the case, along somewhat different lines."[58]

The correspondence between Quinton and Herbert Welsh also reflected cordial personal relations between their respective Philadelphia headquarters, calling upon one another for support when needed. Individual members, including Constance Goddard DuBois and Mary Louise Eldridge, whose histories appear later in this book, felt comfortable writing directly to IRA officials. A personal request from a member of a Northern California Indian auxiliary resulted in the raising of $312 by the IRA to enable the purchase of a small tract of land for a homeless band.[59]

A particularly cordial working relationship developed within the Boston/Cambridge area, where the Massachusetts Indian Association (MIA) and its branch, the Cambridge Indian Association (CIA), both WNIA auxiliaries, worked closely with the Boston Indian Citizenship Committee and the Cambridge branch of the IRA.[60] Joint public meetings were common, and male reformers often addressed the women's associations.[61] Ellen A. Goodwin, president of the CIA, wrote of her association's joint efforts with the Cambridge IRA in sending petitions to Congress, emphasizing friendly terms between members. "Most of our public work has been done with them," she wrote, and "almost all the public meetings that have been held in Cambridge have been under the auspices of the two Associations combined."[62]

The secretary of the Cambridge IRA, William Lawrence, was in agreement, writing: "the Massachusetts Indian Association, which has been organized since our last Annual Meeting, has worked in harmony with us."[63] In 1886, for example, the CIA not only sponsored a public address by Boston Committee member James Bradley Thayer, a Harvard law professor, but funded the printing and distribution of 2,000 copies of his speech.[64] This sentiment of cooperation, multiplied numerous times over by WNIA members, and the effective cross-gender interaction they had with the mostly male-dominated reform associations, explains their ultimate success in the reform arena.

Mary Dickinson, a prominent educator, accomplished poet, member of the New York City Indian Association (NYCIA), and president of the national association in 1885 and 1886 before Quinton assumed that position in 1887, understood the role played by women in reform movements.[65] Like many WNIA members, she was active in a number of organizations. She was superintendent of education for the WCTU; secretary of the Women's Bible Society of New York; president of the Women's National Council;[66] general secretary from its inception of the International Order of the King's Daughters and Sons, an international, interdenominational Christian philanthropic organization;[67] and on the advisory committee of the League for Social Services, a "clearing house of practical philanthropy."[68] Dickinson was a fervent believer in the power possessed by Christian women working within an organization to do good for society. In a 1901 article, she had explained that "it would be foolish to deny that extreme phases of religious teaching have always found more devoted followers among women. In every abnormal movement," she continued, women not only outnumber men, "but outrank them in advocacy and outdo them in sacrifices for whatever cause has won their allegiance." She concluded that "woman's greater devotion is not necessarily an admission of her greater weakness and credulity."[69] It did not matter what kind of work women engaged in, Dickinson believed. Whether it was "social, scientific, legal, educational, philanthropic, secular, or religious—the light by which we have seen the world's need, and the power by which we adapt woman's work to the need, both radiate, directly or indirectly, from the cross."[70]

Welcoming the attendees to the annual WNIA meeting in November 1885, Dickinson reminded them that before they began their discussions on current progress and "a consideration of practical plans for its prosecution," they needed to remember that their missionary work was "divinely given and divinely guided." They had started as pioneers "when the field of opinion was at best almost a wilderness," and it had not been "a light task to cut down old obstructing theories and dead tangles of incoherent sentiment existing in the minds of women with regard to the Indians' true status and claims." She assured them that their labor had not been in vain. Eighteen new auxiliaries had been gained during the year, with a total of fifty-six scattered across twenty-seven states. Members had "thrust under the public eye, over twenty thousand leaflets and pamphlets," and their voices had been heard in more than four hundred meetings. Their work was "increasing by every means the intensity of public sentiment till it shall move at last with resistless might against the great wrongs to this Indian race, [and] is to say the least, with God's blessing, well begun."[71]

Although it is impossible to ascertain the number of women who joined the WNIA, based on a small sampling of one hundred reformers who joined the movement in the 1880s, Helen M. Bannan provides interesting details about the reformers' backgrounds. She chose individuals who had either attended at least two reform conferences or had achieved some prominence in the movement. Only twenty, however, were women. Ninety percent of the total sampling were between the ages of forty and eighty, with 72 percent living in either an urban or suburban area. Eighty percent had either a college or a female seminary degree, and one-third were involved in church organizations. Twenty-three percent were either Congregational or Presbyterian, with Quakers being the next largest group at 17 percent. Forty-two percent were from the Mid-Atlantic, with 24 percent from the Washington, DC, area, explaining why that small auxiliary was so successful. Even though women represented slightly less than one-quarter of the sampling, a rough profile emerges of a mature, older, well-educated woman, more than likely living in an urban area, and involved in a church organization.[72] Based on their husbands' or parents' professions, it also becomes quite evident that many of these women were financially secure.

WNIA members were further burdened by the nineteenth-century expectation that women live up to the ideals of "true womanhood"—purity, submissiveness, piety, and domesticity—with their home being viewed as their "proper sphere." This belief credited women "with a moral authority which implicitly empowered them to extend their moral influence outside the home," although work within a church community was still viewed as an extension of their "proper sphere."[73] The writings of numerous clerics reinforced this role. For example, Rev. J. F. Stearns in 1837 had declared that women were not only the mainspring of society but were "fitted by nature" to the cause of Christian benevolence.[74] Such declarations prompted Bannan to conclude that as "real women responded to the 'true woman' model," they got down off of their pedestal, left the home, and, because they were viewed "as moral guardians of society," they joined various reform movements and engaged in charity and missionary work.[75] By doing so, these female reformers expanded their "proper sphere" to include distant Indian reservations, passing on these beliefs to Indian women.

"True womanhood," however, went against the cultural practices of many Indian tribes. In her article on Southern tribes, Theda Perdue argues that the "economically productive, politically powerful, and socially significant" role of some Indigenous women was "sacrificed to the cult of true womanhood." Using Cherokee women as an example, Perdue explains that they were the original agriculturalists, farming land inherited through their female line, while Cherokee men lived "in the household of his wife's lineage, and buildings, garden plots, and sections of the villages' common field belonged to her lineage." Prosperous

Cherokee towns had emerged, composed of numerous matrilineal households of several generations. Cherokee society slowly changed due to pressure from resident missionaries, the emergence of mission schools teaching domestic arts to young girls, intermarriage with whites, and the rise of a Cherokee elite emulating white society and expecting their wives to conform to the ideals of "true womanhood." The most prominent change was a redefining of gender roles in farming, which had now become the domain of men. Thus, Indigenous women lost control of their land rights.[76]

In less than a decade of its founding, the WNIA had become a formidable force. A brief summary of the work of just one branch in Cambridge reveals the breadth of their influence. Cambridge reformers funded the salary of a teacher at Round Valley Reservation in Northern California; supported the Boston Committee in their efforts to provide legal work for the Mission Indians of California; funded work in Alaska; provided money for home loans to Indians through the Connecticut branch; aided Apache prisoners in the Mount Vernon Barracks in Alabama; donated money to introduce a herd of reindeer into Alaska; and raised funds for a school among the Hualapai in Arizona.[77] Their major effort, however, would be on behalf of the Navajos, the subject of chapter 6.

As the years passed and new opportunities for women opened up in other fields, WNIA membership declined. In late 1901 the association rewrote its constitution, becoming the National Indian Association to enable men to join. A noted author and member of the Massachusetts Indian Association, Frances Campbell Sparhawk, long in favor of such a move, commented that "when men work together they make a camp; when women work together they make a nunnery; when men and women work together they make the home."[78] In her dissertation, Helen M. Wanken asserts, however, that men "did not flock to the Association." The transformation was only nominal and superficial, for by that time the "most striking characteristic of the organization" was "its static nature," with each year bearing "an uncanny resemblance to the last."[79]

Wanken writes that the WNIA had never intended to last as long as it did; therefore, it "never rethought its approach." World War I took a toll from which the association never really recovered. Furthermore, Quinton's death in 1926 removed the association's most prominent symbol. Then the Depression brought its own difficulties. Money had always been tight, but now even more so. Recruiting methods remained old-fashioned, with too much dependence upon church contacts. By the 1930s, upper- and middle-class women had been voting for a decade, although the association itself had remained essentially apolitical. Cultural pluralism had gradually become part of the government's Indian policy, but members had remained largely assimilationist in their beliefs, questioning this new philosophy which intended to destroy much of the work they had accomplished since their founding. The extensive network of auxiliaries and branches that Quinton had so carefully crafted began to decline as the membership aged. The confederated nature of the association left the national headquarters powerless to stop the erosion. By the end of 1941, only four auxiliaries were left, three in New York (New York City, Brooklyn, and the Madeline C. Haynes branch at Binghampton) and the Massachusetts Indian Association. To save money, the NIA cut back on its publications, leaving only *The Indian's Friend*, which became bimonthly in 1915. In 1932 it went from eight published pages to half that number, becoming a simple newsletter instead of a periodical devoted to Indian issues that had once included national political news on Indian affairs. In 1940 it went from being professionally printed to poorly mimeographed.[80] As members aged, they had difficulties attending meetings. Funding became scarce, and in 1949 the New York City auxiliary and the national association, now headquartered in New York City, merged.[81]

At an April 18, 1951, meeting at the Allerton Hotel in New York City, attended by only twenty-three delegates, the association disbanded. When the books were closed on May 31, 1951, all remaining monies were turned over to the Charles H. Cook Christian Training School in Phoenix, Arizona.[82] The June 1951 issue of *The Indian's Friend* reported final monies received from six auxiliaries and branches, several of which had already disbanded.[83] In four instances, monies turned over were the principal and interest on various funds, including $3,657 from the Cornelia Taber Fund of the Northern California Indian Association[84] and $4,143.33 ($50,963 in 2025 dollars) from sales of shares of Continental Baking, Canada Dry Ginger Ale, and dividends from the two stocks on behalf of the Bryn Mawr Indian Association.[85] At one point in time there had been over one hundred auxiliaries.

Wanken writes that the association was not missed. Not only had its goals been injurious to the very people they set out to help, but it had outlived its time. However, she writes, there is a temptation to dismiss their work as much too practical to solve "the Indian problem." It is easy to "snicker at the sewing classes, the mission boxes, and the model Christian homes which these women held in such high esteem." Wanken tempered her criticism when she reminded her readers that these WNIA members lived in the era of the "Cult of True Womanhood," where "domesticity was raised to the status of a religion." Homemaking was the one skill they had as women to transfer to the cause of Indian reform. During "the nineteenth century, they can be forgiven for their lack of foresight."[86] Although "today we are critical of these reformers' ethnocentricity, their biases, their prejudices," their story still needs to be heard, she concludes.[87]

The main strength of the WNIA was always centered in its branches and auxiliaries, not in its headquarters. And Quinton had organized almost all of the auxiliaries, initially starting close to Philadelphia, gradually venturing further afield, making several transcontinental organizing trips, her first in 1891, which lasted seven and a half months.[88] The following chapter begins with a brief overview of Quinton's early organizing efforts, concluding with a case study of the Washington, DC, auxiliary, a history heretofore unexplored. With no branches, this auxiliary seldom ever comprised more than fifty members. Nevertheless, it succeeded because of a strong foundation established by its first two presidents, Harriet and Kate Foote, each remarkable women in their own right.

CHAPTER 2

The Washington, DC, Auxiliary as a Case Study

Amelia Stone Quinton was the driving force behind the Women's National Indian Association, writing leaflets and pamphlets and speaking before women's groups, ministers' conferences, educational assemblies, and missionary meetings. During 1880 alone, she addressed 150 different groups and sought out influential individuals to help promote her association's work, making more than a hundred visits in one week in and around Philadelphia. Throughout her decades of organizing, she continually called upon prominent local leaders, especially mayors, governors, and government officials, for introductions to influential women in every location she was about to visit. She also turned to local pastors for permission to host meetings in their churches.[1]

With Philadelphia as the permanent headquarters, in November 1881 Quinton began organizing associate committees in Gloversville, Syracuse, Auburn, Clifton, Rochester, and Buffalo, New York, shortly thereafter moving into New Jersey, Connecticut, and Massachusetts. By the October 27, 1883, annual meeting in St.

George's Hall Parlors in Philadelphia, the WNIA had grown to twenty-six auxiliaries, with branches in eleven states and the District of Columbia.[2] On that day president Mary Lucinda Bonney welcomed delegates from Boston, Cambridge, Albany, New York City, Brooklyn, New Jersey, and Delaware. Between 1879 and this meeting, the membership had already raised $5,678.60 for their Indian work.[3]

In 1884 during a five-month period, Quinton traveled some ten thousand miles, establishing state branches in Michigan, Illinois, Indiana, Wisconsin, Minnesota, Dakota Territory, Iowa, Nebraska, and Kansas, bringing the total number of auxiliaries to thirty-eight.[4] While in Dakota Territory in July, she visited Mary C. Collins, a Congregational missionary working at the Oahe Mission on the Great Sioux Reservation. During this visit, Quinton gave a Bible reading to the Indian women (translated by Collins), attended an Indian prayer meeting, visited several Indian villages, made house calls, slept one night wrapped up in buffalo robes beneath a wagon, and spent a second night in a new Indian-built lodge.[5]

Four years later Quinton met up with Collins, not in a remote setting on a distant reservation but at Albert K. Smiley's annual conference at his Mohonk Mountain House, a castle-like Victorian resort hotel in the Shawangunk Mountains near New Paltz, New York. Quinton, who had attended her first meeting in 1885, joined some fifty reformers at what she described as the "magnificent mountain estate of 3,000 acres," which was "affluent in picturesqueness and variety of scenery."[6] At this 1888 autumn meeting, Quinton and Collins addressed the conference, their comments published in the proceedings. In heartfelt remarks, Collins described how strange it was to "stand before so many white people and feel that they are all interested in this great cause," reminding some of them that they had been a guest at her mission. Quinton followed, explaining that because she had not been "long among Indians," visiting only half a dozen tribes during her last organizational tour, she appreciated the importance of testimonies from missionaries like Collins, able to describe conditions firsthand.[7]

Following her July 1884 reservation visit, Quinton had returned to Pierre, South Dakota, organizing the Dakota Women's Indian Association on the fourteenth. She enthusiastically ended that year's report relevant to these new auxiliaries with: "do not its records prove that this work had a Divine origin and has had Divine guidance and blessing?" She also informed members that plans were being made for St. Louis and Cincinnati and doors were standing wide open in the South, "bidding us to enter, and it is hoped that an organizing tour may be taken there before another spring shall come."[8]

Helen M. Wanken credits Quinton for her 1884 tour. Although recognizing the support she received by local citizens and ministers, who had opened their churches to her, Quinton's accomplishments were "... phenomenal. Good genes and a burning zeal allowed her to adhere to a brutal schedule."[9] Also, Quinton was willing to put aside her own comfort, enduring more than sleeping beneath buffalo robes in later years when visiting distant missionary stations. Her hard work enabled the WNIA in 1885 to report fifty-six branches in twenty-seven states and territories.[10]

To promote Quinton's organizing efforts, the WNIA published a pamphlet in 1882 with tips on how to organize properly for those willing to undertake the task on their own. It included a brief historical sketch, a copy of the current constitution and bylaws, and the petition for 1883. In a section on suggestions, members were encouraged to distribute association leaflets and pamphlets, secure signatures on the year's petition, and hold union meetings at some church to be addressed by a pastor or "by some speaker specially familiar with, and on the right side of, the Indian question." The last three pages were devoted to facts about the current condition of the Indians to be used as suggested talking points during a meeting. Although members were encouraged to organize in their own hometowns, association bylaws clearly gave Quinton, as the general secretary, the authority to organize and transact all business, and she undertook this task with élan, founding the majority of all auxiliaries.[11]

Four years later Quinton wrote her own pamphlet recommending that any "lady who is beloved and 'well reported of for good works' invite two or three or more" of her friends "or leading spirits, from each religious denomination"[12] to her home or church parlor and explain the "objects, scope and methods of work" of the WNIA. Once gathered, they could then organize into a branch of a state association or of the national association, adopt a constitution, elect officers, and hold public meetings. Quinton even provided the order for business meetings, listed required committees, explained duties, and suggested model resolutions to be sent to state legislatures. She recommended that monthly meetings be held in a church parlor or vestry with a member reading an original paper on any Indian topic, a copy later sent to other branches. Each auxiliary was urged to set up a library to include government reports, Indian school newspapers, and specific books. Those who did not feel called to create a full-fledged branch were encouraged to form an Indian committee, which had no constitution and held no regular meetings. To support members interested in organizing on their own, three years later the association published another pamphlet with additional details. Dues were set at $1 a year, $10 for a life membership, or $50 for an honorary member, with a quarter of the money going to headquarters in Philadelphia.[13]

By the November 1886 annual meeting, the association had grown to eighty-three branches in twenty-eight states and territories, with "the greatest activity and the greatest financial success" from its New England branches. Collectively WNIA auxiliaries held some four hundred or more meetings, a number of which had been addressed by prominent judges, senators, bishops, and Army officers. In addition, the association issued forty-nine thousand copies of pamphlets and leaflets, including five written by Quinton. Some auxiliaries, such as that in New Haven, Connecticut, which had organized on November 20, 1885, published their own circulars and leaflets, seventeen in 1886 alone. Association members sent memorials to the Interior Department on behalf of retaining competent Indian Office officials and sixty-five petitions on various Indian-related subjects to Congress, all reprinted in the *Congressional Record*. The increased secretarial work to support such effort had required Quinton to stay close to headquarters when she much preferred to be out organizing. To deal with over eighty auxiliaries and various government officials, she and her assistant wrote thousands of letters, "more than seven hundred a month at a time," sending out "more than eighteen thousand parcels of literature" as they pushed their goals of influencing the public and the government, and aiding the Indian "in civilization, industrial training, self-support, education, citizenship, and Christianization."[14]

During 1887, the WNIA experienced another growth spurt due to Quinton's long-planned trip to the South. By year's end, she had given fifty-eight public addresses before church meetings and auxiliaries and at Sunday schools and had taken over as the national president in October. There was even talk of publishing a monthly periodical.[15] In April, armed with letters of introduction from Interior Department officials, Southern congressmen, and personal friends, Quinton arrived in Richmond, Virginia, on the 27th to meet with Governor Fitzhugh Lee, a nephew of Robert E. Lee. The large gathering of influential women responded warmly to her plea. After founding an auxiliary in Richmond, Quinton traveled on to Raleigh, North Carolina; Columbia, South Carolina; Atlanta and Rome, Georgia; Nashville, Tennessee; Louisville, Kentucky; and Wheeling, West Virginia, establishing an Indian association in each city. The total number of branches had now reached 104.[16]

With the exception of the West Virginia and Kentucky associations and the one in Washington, DC, little information on Southern auxiliaries appeared regularly in the *Annual Report*, and when it did, according to historian Rose Stremlau, it was seldom a robust agenda. Southern members tended to be less active; attended fewer annual conventions, probably because their branches were short-lived; and were "less connected into established reform networks than their northern counterparts." Stremlau blames this lack of success on the national leadership's failure to make new efforts to organize in the South. However, she also attributes this inactivity to Southern women's aversion to the image of the "crusading woman," viewing such public work as dishonorable for Southern wives and daughters. For the same reasons, the WCTU was also not as successful in the South. Furthermore, by advocating for the assimilation or integration of Indians into American society, the WNIA "inadvertently endorsed the dismantling of a particularly volatile boundary in southern society, i.e., intermarriage and interracial sexual activity."[17] Only one Southern auxiliary was long-lived—the one founded in the nation's capital.

In 1891, Quinton founded additional auxiliaries as a result of her more than seven-and-a half-month-long cross-country organizational tour. She not only visited existing missionary stations and inspected new potential fields but gave numerous public addresses, "awakening interest in sections of the country hitherto unacquainted" with the WNIA. Leaving Philadelphia in late February, she spent March visiting the Seminoles in Florida before touring through Georgia, Alabama, and New Orleans, organizing committees and Indian associations in Georgia and Louisiana, and then traveled into New Mexico and Arizona in May and June to organize an Indian association in Albuquerque and an Indian Committee in Fort Defiance, Arizona. She spent July, August, and part of September in California, where she established seventeen branches, before heading for Oregon, Washington, and Colorado. During this tour she organized a total of thirty-four new auxiliaries.[18] Organizational growth for the next few years was uneven. In 1894 there were eight auxiliaries added, but the following year it dropped to six, and to five in 1896.[19]

Wanken describes the WNIA as a loosely knit federation, where in "one sense the composite of the auxiliaries might be considered to equal the Association." Although auxiliaries contributed to association funding, their success depended upon the "levels of interest and presence of an aggressive local leader." Some auxiliaries worked on behalf of tribes within their own state or opened their own missionary stations, schools, and hospitals, further reducing their support of mission stations directed by the national Missionary Committee. Most often, auxiliaries simply paid their dues, held occasional meetings, and/or sent a box or two of used clothing and other items to a mission station of their choice. The real power of the WNIA was in those auxiliaries with multiple branches and large memberships such as Massachusetts, Connecticut, and New York, with the two New England states competing for the position of the association's "banner society."[20]

Quinton had organized the Massachusetts Indian Association (MIA) in late January 1883. By the end of the first year it already had a membership of 356. The WNIA annual report of 1888 reported there were sixteen branches with a combined membership of thirteen hundred.[21] One of the most recognizable members was Alice Mary Longfellow, eldest daughter of Henry Wadsworth Longfellow, who served as president from 1901 to 1906.[22] Massachusetts women funded various projects over the years, beginning in 1884 with the salary of Mrs. H. O. McGlashan, WNIA missionary to the Otoe Indians of the Indian Territory. Two years later they provided the salaries of Claudia White of Rockville, Maryland, and Anna Boorman of Jersey City, New Jersey, WNIA missionaries at the Round Valley Reservation in Northern California,[23] and in 1887 supported the work of Dr. and Mrs. L. M. Hensel, medical missionaries to the Nebraska Omahas. The auxiliary also underwrote educational work among the Chiricahua Apache prisoners at Mount Vernon Barracks in Alabama; missionary work on the Navajo Reservation; educational work among the Hualapai of Arizona; and the building of a new wing of the school dormitory at the association's Greenville Indian Industrial School in Northern California.[24]

Wanken describes the early years of the MIA as "filled with an enthusiasm characteristic of youth," and for a short period the association experienced phenomenal growth. However, within three years of their founding, the number of pamphlets they distributed dropped, prompting Wanken to suspect it was because they changed from arousing the "public conscience to one of practical self-help programs for the Indians themselves." But when attendance also dropped precipitously, she concluded that many members "had enrolled in name only."[25] Adequate funding was a constant issue; dues were low, and donations never assured. When branch numbers in 1890 declined, Mary Dewey, the association's corresponding secretary, exclaimed that many of the ones "we counted so proudly three years ago, have withered and become little better than dead wood."

Although Wanken writes that there were "symptoms of degeneration, within both the Massachusetts society and the parent association," the MIA was one of the six to continue until the national association dissolved in 1951.[26]

With the exception of the Cambridge Indian Association (CIA), which was singular in its Indian work, almost nothing has been written on individual MIA branches. A small collection of records relative to their Stockbridge auxiliary, however, provides the opportunity for a brief look at their work, which, unlike that of the Cambridge Branch, was not particularly inspiring but was probably more traditional of the average auxiliary. Had there been more extensive records and detailed histories of the work of its officers, the picture might have been different. Many members of the Stockbridge auxiliary, founded in 1886, were wives and daughters of prominent religious leaders and statesmen, a theme common for most New England branches but not expanded upon in available association records.[27] By January 1887, they had sixty members and had hosted two of the more prominent Indian reformers as speakers. One was General Samuel C. Armstrong, founder in 1868 of Hampton Normal and Agricultural Institute in Hampton, Virginia, which originally educated African Americans, a decade later admitting Indian students.[28] The second speaker was Armstrong's close personal friend, Charles C. Painter, the IRA's agent in Washington, DC. In addition to listening to such compelling speakers, Stockbridge members in 1887 donated $350 ($11,782 in 2025 dollars) for an unidentified Indian cottage.[29] The following year, they numbered fifty-five members and contributed $200 toward missionary work and an unidentified teacher's salary.[30] The membership and contributions fluctuated; some years they donated only an occasional box of items for Indian schools. In 1894, they had a spurt and added a few more members, raising $152. Nine years later they raised a similar amount, but membership had dropped to thirty. In 1905 they raised almost $100.[31] Then, two years later, with no explanation, the branch disappeared from the annual report. By 1908 the MIA had only four branches remaining.[32]

Because so little research has been done on the majority of WNIA branches, it is difficult to know if the experience of the Stockbridge auxiliary was typical. However, one small auxiliary with a remarkable legacy, and of which little has been written, was the Washington Women's Indian Association in Washington, DC. It was not only one of the smallest, holding fewer meetings than any other auxiliary, its membership was so closely connected to Congress that it spent much of the time watching legislation, sometimes adjourning when Congress did.[33]

A number of the members were wives of sitting congressmen and senators and of other prominent politicians. Because these women also held membership in their home state auxiliary, often as officers, they tended to be quite influential. Furthermore, the auxiliary's location in the United States capital provided it with a continual large pool of influential speakers, including but not limited to Indian reformers, government officials, visiting Indian dignitaries, and various Indian delegations, all eagerly seeking to address the auxiliary's well-informed and well-connected audience. The primary reason this auxiliary was so successful was that its first two presidents, Harriet Ward Foote Hawley and her sister, Kate Foote Coe, prominent members of the Connecticut Indian Association, were perfect examples of what Helen Wanken describes as "aggressive local leaders."[34]

The eldest of ten children, Harriet Ward Foote was born in Guilford, Connecticut, on June 25, 1831, to Elizabeth (Eliza) and George Augustus Foote. Her father's older sister Roxana was married to the prominent theologian Lyman Beecher, making Harriet Beecher Stowe and her famous brother, Rev. Henry Ward Beecher, Harriet's cousins. Harriet Foote not only had the advantage of receiving a better than average education (along with her brothers), she also formed a keen interest in public affairs primarily because her father had served in the state legislature for five terms. One source described her as a "radical abolitionist."[35] In December 1855, Harriet married Joseph Roswell Hawley, who after he had been admitted to the Connecticut bar five years earlier had entered a law partnership with John Hooker, husband of Harriet Beecher Stowe's sister Isabella. At the beginning of the Civil War the Hawleys were living in Nook Farm on the western edge of Hartford, where Joseph, who had left his law practice, was now editing the *Hartford Evening Press*, of which he was also part owner. Mark Twain was their friend and neighbor.[36] When the Civil War broke out, Joseph Hawley organized a company of volunteers and participated in more than a dozen engagements, eventually rising to the rank of major general in command of the 7th Regiment.

Harriet Hawley, plagued throughout her life with unidentified health issues, was not able to join her husband in the Carolina Sea Islands until November 1862. For the next two years, she followed him from camp to camp briefly pursuing a journalist career, writing seven newspaper articles, four from Florida, describing her personal experiences as she covered war conditions in the South, "evoking in detail the exotic and sensory delights of Florida." Although many women recorded their Civil War experiences, few did so for newspapers, prompting the authors of an article on Hawley to write that "for a woman to have done this in the period was extraordinary." Harriet Beecher Stowe, after reading her cousin's articles in the *Hartford Evening Press*, published her own observations in the *New York Independent*, a Congregational journal, which her brother, Henry Ward Beecher, edited. "Rather than a cousin copying the celebrated author, the reverse was true; Stowe, in fact, would eventually emulate her cousin."[37]

In a January 2, 1863, letter signed H.W.F.H. and as a correspondence of the *Press*, Hawley described New Year's Day at Beaufort, South Carolina, with the 1st South Carolina Volunteers, an African American Regiment, and the warm greeting the 7th Regiment had received from Col. Thomas Wentworth Higginson.[38] This letter appeared on January 14 in the family's newspaper.[39] Hawley also shared her experiences with her Hartford readers while at Fernandina, Florida, noting especially their medical facilities. She also wrote from St. Augustine. Her final letter was on February 7, 1864.

Shortly thereafter, Hawley returned north, actively engaged in nursing. *The Nation* recorded that she "spent three years during the war in the military hospitals, nursing the patients and teaching the art of nursing to others."[40] By April 1864 she was working in the Armory Square Hospital in Washington where she had started a new ward, described by Mrs. Annie W. Halstead, who had arrived at the hospital only days after the Battle of the Wilderness in early May, "as twice as large as any other, and of a complex nature as to its diseases and wounds." In a memorial letter written after Hawley's death, Halstead described her friend as carrying "in her heart an intense devotion to her country, and her soldier husband, which was the unfailing spring of her work for the soldiers then, and for the Indians and all down-trodden, sorrowing humanity to the end of her life."[41]

General Hawley mustered out of the military in 1866. He was subsequently elected governor of Connecticut, returning to his editorial duties when he lost the next election. When he was appointed in 1872 to fill a vacancy in the House of Representatives, Harriet accompanied him to Washington, DC. He was reelected in 1879 and then elected to the Senate in 1881, serving until his death in 1905. While living in Washington, Harriet engaged in philanthropic work, serving as a member of the board of directors of the Garfield Hospital, which had been opened in May 1884 in honor of President James A. Garfield, who had been assassinated in 1881. She later became "interested in the welfare of a House of Refuge for fallen women."[42]

Most of Hawley's attention was occupied with running the Washington, DC, auxiliary, which according to Laura Sunderland, the auxiliary's first secretary, had been organized on March 3, 1882, following an address by Quinton in Harriet's own parlors with the purpose of lifting up "a voice of protest against all existing wrong and oppression to the Indian, and to secure, if possible, wiser legislation in the future." Hawley was chosen as the first president of the new Washington group, while Electa Allen Sanderson Dawes, wife of Massachusetts Senator Henry Laurens Dawes, became one of almost a dozen vice presidents.[43] Less than a month earlier, on February 22, 1882, Hawley had joined Quinton and Eliza Stout Keifer in presenting the WNIA's third petition to President Chester A. Arthur at the White House.[44]

Although Electa Dawes had first met Hawley during the founding of the Washington auxiliary, Quinton had been introduced to her months earlier while securing the names of prominent Hartford women from Rev. Heman Lincoln Wayland, editor of the *National Baptist*, and husband to Elizabeth Arms Wayland, a member of Philadelphia's First Baptist Church. Through Hawley, Quinton had been introduced to Mrs. Sidney Joseph Cowen (née Sarah Sophia Tyler), who had agreed to organize a group of women from various Protestant churches to listen to Quinton describe the work of the WNIA. In mid-November 1881, they formed an Indian Committee, later becoming the Connecticut Indian Association.[45]

There had been an earlier, lesser-known meeting in October 1880, described in a historical sketch of the Connecticut Indian Association as "undoubted an earlier impulse" for this Indian work. This meeting, held in Cowen's rooms in the City Hotel in Hartford, included Mrs. John Coddington Kinney (née Sara Thomson), Miss Louise Riley, Mrs. M. B. Riddle, and Harriet Hawley. The five women pledged "to further the speedy organization of definite work" for the Indian cause. Thus, "in the semi-consecration of that day was formed the germ that later developed into active life,"[46] reflecting that Hawley's interest in Indian reform had predated the formation of the Washington, DC, auxiliary and her presidency.

By 1884, the Washington auxiliary had grown to thirty-six members, with meetings continuing to be held in the Hawley home.[47] On January 22, 1884, Hawley attended her first Board of Indian Commissioners (BIC) meeting in the parlor of the Riggs House in Washington, DC, accompanied by Mrs. Eliphalet Whittlesey (née Ann Augusta Patten), whose husband was the BIC secretary and a member of the WNIA advisory board.[48] Once a year the BIC met in Washington, DC, to confer with various Indian reform associations and

MRS. SARA T. KINNEY
STATE REGENT CONNECTICUT DAUGHTERS OF THE AMERICAN REVOLUTION

Figure 2. Sara Thomson Kinney, longtime president of the Connecticut Indian Association, is photographed wearing her Daughters of the American Revolution medals. She was also a member of the Connecticut Societies of the Colonial Dames of America. (CT Daughters of the American Revolution, Inc., CTRDAR Archival Library.)

representatives of missionary societies engaged in Indian work. Hawley, representing the Washington auxiliary, was invited by current chairman Clinton B. Fisk to address the conference.[49] An unidentified observer described her as "slight and delicate, and leaning on crutches, with a look of great sweetness in her face." Although he could not recall what Hawley had said, the observer was struck "by the whole effect of what she said."[50] During the following year she and her association continued to hold influential mass meetings with addresses by Senators George G. Vest of Missouri and Zebulon B. Vance of North Carolina, as well as Senators Hawley and Dawes, and General Armstrong.⁵¹

Beginning in 1885, the Washington auxiliary, like the Connecticut Indian Association, began to raise money in support of an Indian home-building program.⁵² The idea had been initially suggested to the Washington membership by ethnologist Alice Cunningham Fletcher in February of that year "to aid a young Omaha couple in Hampton to build and furnish a cottage and start life on the reservation, the money to be loaned them and paid back when they were able." During that meeting, $135 was collected. By the following year Washington members had raised $369.50 towards the program. In 1889 they contributed $60 towards a home for Edward Bearskin, a Winnebago Indian.⁵³

Fletcher had initially presented the idea of an Indian home loan program before the September 1884 Lake Mohonk Conference, explaining that it would enable students returning from eastern boarding schools "to make civilized homes to be the centres of civilization among the tribes." Such an experiment was already being tried at Hampton, she explained.⁵⁴ Her idea found support among WNIA members, especially with the Connecticut Indian Association's president, Sara T. Kinney. On November 13, 1884, her association selected Philip and Minnie Stabler, Omaha Indians and graduates of Hampton, as candidates for the first WNIA-built home. A week later, General Armstrong "made a strong and earnest plea in support," and at the annual meeting in January 1885, Kinney announced a new department "establishing among the Indians of small centers of civilization which should be the property of the individual, not through charity, but as the prize of his own self-respecting industry."⁵⁵ In her secretary's report for the 1885 annual meeting of the WNIA, Quinton announced this new Indian Home-Building Department, inaugurated by the Connecticut and Washington auxiliaries. Unanimously approved during the October 23, 1885, meeting of the WNIA Executive Board, Quinton later described it as "Miss Alice C. Fletcher's admirable plan for helping young Indian pairs, who at some Government or other school have had a term of instruction in civilized home life as well as in books."⁵⁶ Later, in a testimonial for Hampton Institute's tenth anniversary in 1888, Fletcher touted the program's success, describing the story of Hampton students who, after receiving "a few years of training in school and cottage life," had success on their home reservation, with acreage under cultivation and well-cared-for stock and tidy homes.⁵⁷

That same year, in her presidential address Quinton declared that "the Christian women of the nation [are] perfect[ly] able to supply what is needed and to do this mother-work for the Indian race." She thanked her membership for adding the home loan department to their work, announcing that twenty homes had been built in three years. "Let us women then give to the destitute tribes Christian homes and missions, for without these no race can rise."[58] Historian Lori Jacobson writes that "because the new department focused on Indian home life, it represented a 'feminine' field of reform that aligned with the WNIA's growing missionary endeavors and satisfied the group's need for distinction from the IRA." By reshaping its reform work, the WNIA "more closely align[ed] with the Protestant domesticity that characterized much of American women's culture in the late nineteenth century."[59] The Washington auxiliary had in their small way made this program successful, supporting it from the beginning.

Harriet Ward Foote Hawley died on March 3, 1886. Her death shook the membership. In its annual report, the national association, mourning the loss of one of its vice presidents, described her as "a Christian woman of sincere faith, of noble devotion to our righteous cause," one "widely known in high social and official positions and one always admired and beloved."[60] However, because the Washington auxiliary had lost its president, on March 11 they held a special meeting in the home of Electa Dawes at which time the attendees passed a resolution declaring they had just "suffered an overwhelming and irreparable loss." In a letter to Dawes, Laura Sunderland, the auxiliary's former secretary, had written that "not only the *head* but the *heart* of our Association is gone from us. We shall miss her unspeakably." Electa's daughter, Anna Laurens Dawes, described Hawley as a remarkable woman with "unbounded enthusiasm and a great patience," whose name was on the lists of numerous charities. She was, to Dawes, "a New England woman of the best type." Although often ill and always delicate, she attended to many duties, freely giving her help and influence. Because of her sacrifice for country and its soldiers, Anna explained, her coffin had been "draped in the colors she had loved and served, and her own State honored the memory of what she had done with half-masted flags, as for a public bereavement." Later that day, soldiers of the 7th Regiment placed a memorial tablet on the walls of the Congregational Church on Asylum Avenue.[61]

Alice Cunningham Fletcher, long associated with Hawley in non-Indian charity work, emotionally explained how difficult it was to speak of "one who was so closely linked to parts of [her] life." She described her friend's interests "as varied as the needs of our struggling humanity" and wondered how "one so frail could

Figure 3. Harriet Ward Foote Hawley, c. 1878–1880, poses in this Cabinet card photograph (a print mounted on cardstock). While she accompanied her husband, Joseph Roswell Hawley, as he led Union troops through the South, she recorded her experiences for the *Hartford Evening Press*. A member of the Connecticut Indian Association, she was also the first president of the Washington, DC, auxiliary of the WNIA. (Harriet Beecher Stowe Center.)

accomplish as much as she did." Fletcher concluded that "the value of such a life can only be read from the other side, where the ephemeral is not and where the eternal reigns." Ann Whittlesey, in her memorial letter, wrote that without

Figure 4. During the Civil War, Katherine Elizabeth Foote accompanied her sister Harriet. She is pictured in this circa 1863 daguerreotype with two of the many freedmen students she taught while employed by the New England Freedmen's Aid Society. Following her sister's death, she became president of the Washington auxiliary. (Harriet Beecher Stowe Center.)

Hawley's "patient, unwearied, watchfulness," the Washington auxiliary "would have made little progress during the past four years." She had given herself to the auxiliary "with a heartiness which insured its success, and but for her enthusiasm it would have been only a name."⁶² In her honor, the Washington auxiliary set up the "Hawley Memorial Fund" to build an Indian cottage. Contributions for 1890 had been $394.50. The following year the fund was completed.⁶³

Hawley's younger sister, Kate Foote, who had served as auxiliary vice president, assumed the presidency in 1886, traveling "extensively over sections of the country inhabited by the Indians," establishing schools and hospitals for them. She also represented and presided over Senator Hawley's household until he remarried the following year.⁶⁴ Katherine Elizabeth Foote was born on May 31, 1840, in Guilford, Connecticut. After graduating from Miss Dutton's Private School in New Haven and the Guilford Institute and High School, she taught school, initially in Guilford and later at the Hartford Female Seminary, founded in 1823 by her cousin, Catharine Beecher, who believed girls were capable of learning philosophical and scientific subjects.⁶⁵ During the Civil War, Kate had joined her sister in Beaufort where she taught former slaves as part of the New England Freedmen's Aid Society.⁶⁶ She followed Harriet into Florida where they both taught in St. Augustine, Fernandina, and Jacksonville. The *Hartford Courant* described Kate's teaching stint for two years as "not free from danger by any means, for there were alarms by day and night and fighting was going on, she saw a great deal of the life the soldiers led."⁶⁷

The war over, Foote turned to a literary career, writing fiction, contributing to *Century Magazine* and *St. Nicholas* magazine and serving for fifteen years as the Washington, DC, correspondent for the *New York Independent*.⁶⁸ Socially active in the national Daughters of the American Revolution (DAR), she was a charter member of the Mary Washington chapter in Washington and later a regent of the Susan Carrington Clarke chapter in Meriden, Connecticut. Foote also enjoyed travel, spending 1872 in Europe. Therefore, when she was invited by her friend, Alice Fletcher, to accompany her on a three-month tour of Alaska, she readily accepted.⁶⁹ The two women had forged a friendship initially as members of the Sorosis Club, a professional association for women founded in New York City by two prominent female journalists. Fletcher had been elected the association's recording secretary in 1872.⁷⁰

Fletcher, who had been mentored by Frederic Ward Putnam, director of Harvard's Peabody Museum of American Archaeology and Ethnology, had lived for four months among the Omaha Indians of Nebraska in 1881.⁷¹ Shortly thereafter, at the behest of fifty-three tribal members, fearing they might face the same fate as their Ponca kinsmen, she drafted a petition calling for the allotment of their reservation. With Henry Laurens Dawes's support, her petition was introduced before the Senate in December 1881, and the following August the Omaha Allotment Act became law. Months earlier, Fletcher had thanked Dawes in a February 1882 letter, explaining that her study of the Omahas had taken her into their homes, where she had become a familiar friend. With their daily life "fully open[ed]" to her, she had been able "to note their attainments and to discern much of the struggle by which it has been gained."[72] Based on her ethnological study of the Omaha Indians, the Indian Office appointed Fletcher in 1883 to serve as their allotment agent. Years later, in 1897, she returned to the reservation shocked to find "a demoralized people who were left to cope with every temptation that local whites could offer, especially alcohol and credit, and the Indians had little will to resist." She found that they were not even farming their own allotments but leasing them out and living on the rent. Although never admitting it publicly, according to her biographer, Fletcher recognized that "her radical and comprehensive program for Indian 'civilization' was a failure and had been a mistake."[73]

Worn out from her allotment duties and at loose ends, Fletcher had finally accepted an invitation issued three years earlier by Sheldon Jackson to visit Alaska.[74] Foote accompanied her. Jackson, a Presbyterian minister and newly appointed as Alaska's General Agent for Education, was aware of Fletcher's role as a powerful Washington, DC, insider and had been trying to get her support to establish a school system. During their trip, Fletcher and Foote took the opportunity to visit the Aleutian Islands, the Alaska Peninsula, and the Shumagin Islands. They also spent time among the Kwakiutl Indians, visiting several of their homes, and conferred with the missionary and his wife. During their travels, Foote had purchased at least two Chilkat blankets which she later donated to Yale's Peabody Museum.[75]

The Alaskan venture over, Foote returned to her presidential duties, officiating at auxiliary meetings and representing her members at various Lake Mohonk meetings and BIC conferences in Washington, DC. Unlike Quinton, whose comments on the work of the WNIA and its auxiliaries regularly appeared in the proceedings of both organizations, Foote's voice was silent. During the January 1888 BIC conference attended by both women, it was Quinton who during her address at a WNIA-sponsored evening meeting at the Unitarian Church singled out Foote and her Washington auxiliary to praise for their participation in the WNIA Indian home-building program. Six cottages were already occupied by Indian families, Quinton reported. She also explained that the WNIA was currently working on a plan to sponsor Christian "farmers to reside among the Indians who are taking their lands in severalty."[76]

The Washington auxiliary thrived under Kate Foote's leadership as her own obligations to the national association increased. In 1888, she became chairman of a new Committee on Indian Legislation, with the main purpose of keeping WNIA branches "informed of special legislation needed." She had been chosen because she was "politically astute, had a much broader understanding of legislative affairs than most in her organization, and consequently was able to apprise her sister reformers of which legislation suited their philosophy," writes Helen Wanken.[77] The editor of *The Indian Bulletin*, published by the Connecticut Indian Association, described Foote's long residency in Washington as affording her "somewhat exceptional opportunities for studying national questions," giving "weight to her communications from the Capital, and her comments on Indian matters are of special value to the associations throughout the country that are working for the advancement of this cause."[78]

Foote did not choose the bills that the WNIA supported or opposed. Suggestions were more than likely made by Herbert Welsh of the Indian Rights Association and Lake Mohonk members. She did, however, write a comment column which appeared in *The Indian's Friend* between 1888 and 1892, at times monthly, and several WNIA pamphlets detailing what she considered as vital legislation. In an 1889 pamphlet she explained that the business of the WNIA was "to educate the sentiment of the people until we make Congress see what we want." She concluded: "We must remember and look to it that our Congressmen are as good as their constituents, and if we ask attention in these matters it will be granted."[79] Occasionally Foote would read her report before the annual meeting. During a November 1889 meeting, emphasizing the influence of the WNIA, she proudly announced that "more consideration had been given the [Indian] question by Congress and the methods of agents had received closer investigation than hitherto," concluding that "the cause of civilization among the Indians has been helped in every way."[80] For a private citizen, Foote had unusual access to government documents, highlighting in one column her visit to the Indian Committee Room of the House to consult a file of bills brought before Congress.[81]

During her 1890 annual report at Lake Mohonk on WNIA missionary work, Quinton described Foote as "doing excellent service," calling attention to essential Indian-related legislation.[82] Others praised her political acumen. An observant reporter for the *Pittsburg Dispatch* described Foote as far more than a pretty face. Although "soft in repose," it held "a deal of power hidden in it, and only called into action when she converses." She was witty and "sarcastic without being ill natured, and original without spoiling her spontaneity," he noted, "nurtured in politics, and is a Republican by birth and principle."[83]

In addition to her written and oral political reports, Foote corresponded regularly with officials in the Indian Office on matters personally vital to her and her association. On November 15, 1887, she wrote to Commissioner John D. C. Atkins[84] on behalf of the Turtle Mountain Band of Chippewa in Dakota Territory, requesting he write the incoming chairman of the House Committee on Indian Affairs a "letter which can be used in getting an appropriation through at once" for them. Explaining that Chippewa lands had been opened to settlement without their permission and that they had not received any annuity payments, she feared they would suffer during the coming winter months. Foote had concluded that private assistance was insufficient.[85] According to the *Duluth Journal*, one hundred fifty-one tribal members died in the winter of 1887 to 1888.[86]

Months later, Foote wrote Atkins that the WNIA was interested in supporting the government Indian School at Keams Canyon, Arizona. Although the school's educational department appeared to be well attended, the industrial department did not include certain industries she felt useful to young Indian men. She suggested they add practical farming, the blacksmith trade, wagon making, and harness and shoe making, describing the industrial department of an Indian school as "of the greatest importance—almost more than reading & writing." She was not so worried about teaching Indian women because housework was "always on hand in any boarding school." She did, however, request three or four washing machines for the laundry and offered her association's help in getting her recommendations attended to.[87]

At times Foote's political articles included interesting background material. In a February 1889 column she described the most pleasant thing in the list as a petition written by Thomas L. Sloan and one hundred ten other Hampton students complaining about the present ration system employed by the Indian Office for reservation Indians. The students had described the items provided as encouraging both idleness and dependence, recommending instead that farming equipment and livestock be substituted. Senator Dawes, who presented the petition before the Senate, was so impressed by their wise ideas and the fact that all but three of the students had signed in their own handwriting that he spent time reading most of it out loud.[88]

Foote's influence and access to prominent reformers and public figures was apparent in a March 1889 column, in which she described meeting with Dawes, Herbert Welsh and Charles C. Painter of the IRA, Quinton, and Alice Fletcher in the office of General Eliphalet Whittlesey, secretary of the BIC, to write resolutions requesting certain policies they wanted the recently elected administration to adopt. They all carried the resolutions to the White House, presenting them to incoming President Benjamin Harrison and to Interior Secretary John W. Noble. Foote described their interviews as satisfactory, and that they had all come away "much pleased with the President and with General Noble."[89]

Often critical of Congress's failure to pass certain legislation, Foote was particularly displeased with the fate of a bill for the relief of the Mission Indians that had initially been submitted by the Indian Office in January 1884. It had passed the Senate but failed in the House and was thereafter annually resubmitted until its passage in 1891. The bill had been accompanied by a July 1883 report written by Helen Hunt Jackson and Abbot Kinney, special agents for the Interior Department, relative to the conditions and needs of California's Mission Indians.[90] In her 1888 pamphlet, Foote explained that the purpose of the Mission Indian Bill was to secure land for "those unhappy Mission Indians of California, in whom Mrs. Helen Hunt Jackson was so much interested." She had described it as "a just bill" which would "rescue them [the Indians] from a position in which they are between wind and water and not befriended by either." Two years later, in a September 1890 column, she again referenced the Mission Indian Bill, describing it as still "sleeping in the Committee rooms, while helpless, peaceful Indians are plundered and left defenceless," concluding, "it does seem as if justice were not only blind, but deaf and paralyzed."[91]

Foote was not the only WNIA member whose curiosity and empathy had been aroused by Jackson's various writings on the Mission Indians. On August 9, 1885, Mrs. Osia Jane Joslyn Hiles of Milwaukee, Wisconsin, had written a letter to the editor of the *Milwaukee Sentinel*, a copy of which she forwarded in her letter to President Grover Cleveland. Hiles had described Jackson's protest novel, *Ramona*, as "an impassioned prayer to the American people, imploring that the Indians shall not be disturbed in the possession of lands upon which they are settled." As a private citizen, Hiles made two investigative tours of Mission Indian villages in 1886 and 1888, spending three months visiting fourteen reservations and Mexican grants and five out of the six government schools on her second visit. Following her first of three presentations before Lake Mohonk, attending members established a Committee on Legal Defense of the Mission Indians to fund lawsuits on their behalf. Hiles eventually joined the Wisconsin branch of the WNIA, was appointed chairman of their Committee on Mission Indians, and wrote numerous articles for *The Indian's Friend*.[92]

During the summer and fall of 1890, Foote, following in the footsteps of Jackson and Hiles, toured a number of the same Indian villages that they had, as a special agent for the government's eleventh federal census, responsible for counting residents of the nineteen Mission Indian reservations in San Diego and Los Angeles Counties.[93] She was already familiar with their conditions, having read the Mission Indian bill and its accompanying Jackson/Kinney report. In one of her columns, she had recently described the bill as still "sleeping in the Committee room." Now, guided by Mission Agent Horatio Nelson Rust, Foote was about to see for herself the isolated Indian villages that Jackson had written about in her articles for the *New York Independent*, *The Century Magazine*, her 1883 government report, and *Ramona*.[94] In an extract from a letter, reprinted in the November issue of *The Indian's Friend*, she reported having arrived at the Mission Indian Agency at Colton, California, on August 18, 1890, explaining she had recently returned from "a seventeen days trip on a buckboard among the Mission Indians in the mountains of San Diego." It had been "a hard trip but very interesting," she recalled. Although not identifying the agent by name, Foote had described him as "a very good one," having "more success than I supposed possible among the better class of them."[95]

In a December 20, 1890, letter reprinted in *The Cambridge Tribune*, Caroline H. Dall, a literary scholar and a WNIA member, informed her readers that although Foote had been sent by the government to collect information for the census, she "did not forget her more sacred charge as she pursued her work." Foote, Dall explained, had undertaken this assignment so "that she might have government authority and aid in ascertaining what our association wanted to know." Dall assumed, based on the information Foote was gathering, that the WNIA would soon be raising money for a hospital at the Cupeño Mission Indian village of Agua Caliente located on the Warner Ranch in San Diego County.[96] Dall concluded that the association would be corresponding with the agency physician, and "when Mrs. Quinton is ready to work our association will be called up to help."[97]

Foote provided more details in a lengthy letter read by Albert K. Smiley before the October 8, 1890, Lake Mohonk Conference. Describing her travels through

San Diego and San Bernardino Counties, she explained how appalled she was to learn that Jackson's writings, which had "stirred up so much feeling among us all," had accomplished so little. Although Foote clarified that the Soboba Reservation[98] had been saved by the efforts of the IRA and that good reservation land had been set aside at Mesa Grande, she explained that "the bane of the work everywhere is the absence of the surveyor's work for want of that Mission Indian bill which hangs fires so in the House of Representatives."[99]

The lack of proper surveying had become apparent to Foote as she and Rust traveled through the Cahuilla Valley. She had explained in her Lake Mohonk letter that she had witnessed "the agent's face grow dark the day we drove away from the Conuila [sic] Valley reservation, as we stopped at a house belonging to a white man, a house just built near the reservation,—the fence was put so as to include a fine spring of water." Once they had passed the house, she wrote that Rust had given her "an angry, helpless glance," stating "the fence is on the wrong side of that spring, I am morally certain, but I cannot prove it for want of the linesman's work." As they moved further up the valley, Foote inquired about the absence of cultivated fields, prompting Rust to respond that he could not "reproach them for not planting and for not setting out trees, when they can turn to me and say, 'we do not know who shall gather what we plant.'" Finally at San Ysidro, Foote noticed one Indian with a small package, which he treated as a holy relic. Asking to see it, she discovered the paper had been signed by Abbot Kinney and Helen Jackson requesting that "all white people who should come in contact with these Indians to be considerate and kind in their treatment of them."[100]

Foote's census report was lengthy, detailed, and complex. She estimated unallotted Mission Indian reservation lands at 182,315 acres or 285 square miles and only partially surveyed, with a resident population in 1890 of 2,645. She had also included dates when reservations were established, altered, or changed by executive order.[101] Foote also provided a history of the Mission Indians, describing their culture, foods, ceremonies, marriage customs, and games. She explained that the US Court of New Mexico Territory had decided that "by virtue of the provision of the eighth article of the treaty of Guadalupe Hidalgo (1848) the Indians within its territory were citizens of the United States, and that they could not therefore be treated as the government had been used to treating the wild tribes." Thus, because government treaties were not negotiated, it was not necessary to "buy their lands of them," she explained.[102] Therefore, Foote asserted, local whites, who did not recognize Indians' right to public lands, simply filed on any parcel they wanted "no matter whether Indians were upon it or not." She provided several well-known historical examples and, to be thorough, enumerated specific "groups and clusters of Indians living off the reservation," listing size and locations. She then devoted an entire page to current conditions, sometimes using descriptions echoing ethnocentric views held by many whites, among them that the Indian presented a "serene, contented air, if he only has bread enough for the day." Foote viewed their poor little graveyards as "desolate looking places, because grass does not grow as in the east, and these homes of the dead have a bare, unblanketed look, without the friendly green turf to cover their repose."[103]

It is unclear how long Foote remained in California. However, when she returned home, the plight of the Mission Indians remained on her mind. In her January legislative column, she described their history as easily explained by four words: "conversion, civilization, neglect, outrage." The first two were the work of the Franciscan friars, while neglect and outrage "have been mainly our own," she concluded. "Justice and humanity alike demand the immediate action of Government to preserve for their occupation, the fragments of land not already taken from them." Not until her February 1891 column was she able to report the successful passage of the Mission Indian bill.[104]

This bill was one of the main topics discussed during the 1891 Lake Mohonk Conference, primarily because its host, Albert K. Smiley, was chairman of the three-man commission authorized by the bill to select reservations for each of the Southern California Mission bands. During his discussion, Smiley referenced Jackson's exhaustive report, prompting Senator Dawes to confirm that she had in fact drawn up the original draft of the bill. Smiley then explained that the commission's goal had been "to secure a home for all, trying not to pauperize them, but giving them a chance to go to work and earn their living under the protection of law." When invited to speak, Foote explained that "the white man has got to learn that he must respect the rights of the Indians," and that unfortunately many Californians referred to reformers, who were insisting that Indians had rights, derogatively, as "Eastern sentimentalists."[105]

Completing her census obligations, Foote returned to the helm of the Washington auxiliary. The list of speakers she welcomed in 1892 was impressive. At the First Baptist Church on February 19, her friend Alice Fletcher spoke on the early days of the auxiliary. Fletcher was followed by Indian Commissioner Thomas Jefferson Morgan,[106] an educator, who addressed the issues of Indian schools and the hospital he had proposed that the WNIA establish at Agua

Caliente, the same one alluded to by Caroline Dall.[107] Morgan concluded his remarks with strong praise for "the good influences and results from such societies" like the WNIA. At their March 18 meeting, members listened to William A. Kelly, the superintendent for seven years at the Indian Industrial and Training School in Sitka, Alaska. He regaled the audience with his stories of Indian customs, a history of the school, and the resources of the country. Charles C. Painter spoke on April 22. As the IRA's agent in Washington and its liaison to Congress, he had worked to secure the passage of the Mission Indian Bill and had been appointed to serve with Smiley on the California Mission Indian Commission to prepare their lands for allotment.[108] Briefly commenting on his role, Painter spent most of his time discussing the hospital at Agua Caliente, urging its construction. By June the Washington auxiliary had raised the $100 pledged for a cottage for the physician.[109]

Also in attendance that day was Annie E. K. Bidwell, WNIA's western vice president, who also enthusiastically urged the building of the hospital. Since her 1868 marriage to John Bidwell, she had been engaged in efforts to assimilate the small band of Mechoopda Indians living and working on her husband's Chico, California, estate. Bidwell, who had been raised in Washington, DC, where her father J. C. G. Kennedy had served as superintendent of the Census Bureau, returned often to visit her family and to give addresses on her California Indian work before the Washington, DC, auxiliary.[110] Her younger sister, Sarah Jane, who in 1888 had married Thomson H. Alexander, a prominent DC attorney, served for a time as corresponding secretary of the auxiliary.[111]

During the auxiliary's May 21 meeting, Quinton delivered "a stirring account of her journey of eight months through the Southern and Western states." She was followed by Dr. Susan La Flesche, whose education at the Woman's Medical College of Pennsylvania had been paid for by the Connecticut Indian Association. Before an audience, including a number of Woman's Christian Temperance Union members, La Flesche spoke of the increased intemperance among her people, the Omahas, after the Nebraska State legislature's passage of legislation permitting liquor sales to Indians. Following years of drinking, the doctor's own husband died in 1905.[112] Quinton, in Washington, DC, to confer with the Indian commissioner, addressed the auxiliary in mid-January 1893 in the parlors of the First Congregational Church at their first meeting of the year. By now the auxiliary had forty-seven members.[113]

That same mid-January day in 1893 Kate Foote had "described in her own graphic way her allotting of lands among the Mission Indians."[114] On July

28, 1892, of the previous year, the Wilmington, Delaware *Evening Journal* had announced Foote's presidential appointment as "a special agent to make allotment of lands in severalty to the Indians."[115] Immediately upon receiving President Harrison's telegram, Foote had written Commissioner Morgan asking if she should come to Washington first, and how soon did he want her to go to California? She explained she could not simply "plunge into the depths of Southern California at a moment's notice."[116] A bit of mystery surrounds this appointment, as does her role on the census. It is unclear if she requested these government assignments, if her politically powerful brother-in-law, Senator Hawley, had suggested her, or if her reputation as a politically astute reformer was already known to the Indian Office, and the appointment had originated from within that office.

Morgan informed Foote on August 5 that she would receive $8 a day ($281 in 2025 dollars) compensation and "actual and necessary traveling expenses, exclusive of subsistence." In order for funds to be credited to her, Interior Secretary Noble had designated her as "a Special Disbursing Agent," required to "file an official bond in the penal sum of $2,000" ($70,285 in 2025 dollars). She was to provide at least "two sureties to the bond," totaling "twice the penal sum" or $4,000, half of "which must be in *real estate*."[117] Two weeks later, Morgan informed Foote that her bond had been received and approved, and her commission would be forwarded separately. He passed on advice from her brother-in-law, Senator Hawley, that due to the hot weather in Southern California, she should delay her departure for a short time. In the meantime, Morgan requested that she come to his office for instructions.[118]

Charles C. Painter was particularly disturbed to learn that Foote had been selected, writing to Herbert Welsh that her appointment was an "infernal shame and outrage." Calling her a sentimental appointment, Painter was fearful that "what had been so hopefully begun out there will be suffered to peter out in utter failure."[119] However, Foote's attention to detail proved Painter's concern unwarranted. When the surveyor assigned to her, Edward L. Dorn, was unable to do his work at Rincon, La Jolla, and several other reservations without the original 1891 Mission Commission's field notes, Foote wrote Morgan on October 22, 1892, requesting copies from his office or the authority to have copies made in either the Los Angeles or San Francisco land office. "It is an absolute necessity for the surveyor," she wrote, noting that the copy costs for two reservations would only be $8.25.[120] On November 3, enclosing a copy of Foote's letter, Morgan informed Cyrus Bussey, acting interior secretary, that because the Indian Office had never been furnished the field notes in question and thus could not copy them for her, it would be easier if she could have copies made in the land office or the surveyor general's office in California. He therefore authorized that she be allowed to spend no more than $100 in photocopy costs.[121]

Two days later Bussey informed Morgan that according to Foote "the existing roughness of the lands in the Rincon reservation" made it "absolutely impossible to subdivide the same into regular shapes for allotment and do justice to the Indians." Therefore, he suggested that to ensure the "Indians may receive the arable lands with the best water privileges," she be instructed to have Deputy Surveyor Dorn "subdivide the lands into such irregular lots as may be necessary."[122] On November 18, Acting Commissioner Robert V. Belt notified Foote that she had been granted authority to spend up to $100 for copies of the "field notes of the surveys" of any reservations she needed in order to make the allotments.[123]

On November 24, Foote telegraphed Morgan, requesting he order her to report to him in Washington by December 5. "The work here is done so far as it can be at present," she had written.[124] On December 17, Foote tendered her resignation. A week later, Interior Secretary Noble responded that he had accepted it.[125] John F. Carrere of Spokane was appointed as her replacement. On January 9, 1893, Painter informed Morgan that he was displeased with Carrere's appointment; he had hoped that Edward L. Dorn would be chosen. As a member of the original 1891 Commission, Painter had spent eleven months in the various Mission villages working with two surveyors, one of whom had been Dorn. Initially, Painter had "grave apprehensions" learning of Foote's initial appointment, describing her as "a lady from the east, entirely unacquainted with such work as this." He had only been mollified upon learning that she had employed Dorn as her surveyor.[126] Therefore, it was important to Painter that Dorn continue the project.

Dorn, Painter explained, was a university graduate, a man of high character, and a longtime resident of the state, who was a "practical land and water surveyor." Employed by the 1891 Commission to lay "out the several reservations set apart for the Mission Indians," Dorn was "thoroughly acquainted with the situation." Both Painter and Smiley had hoped that he would be appointed. When that did not happen, Painter urged Morgan to make sure that Carrere was informed that Dorn was still in camp on the reservation of Palm Springs[127] "where he was left by Miss Foote, awaiting her return." Painter almost pleaded that Carrere "be authorized, if not directed," to employ Dorn as surveyor. His appointment was essential because the work done at Rincon "requires further attention from him for its completion," warned Painter, who feared "great injury to the Indians" if an allotting agent "ignorant of the situation, brings with him a surveyor also ignorant." Painter, as a member of the Mission Indian Commission, had "given a great deal of attention to the interests of the Mission Indians," and he did not want his many years of labor on their behalf to have been "fruitless." Therefore, he forcefully urged that Dorn be appointed.[128] At least until early 1894, Dorn was still employed as allotment surveyor.

On February 17, Foote responded to Mr. J. H. Bradford, a financial official of the Interior Department, that the bill he was referring to was for "copies of the field notes of Rincon necessary in the surveying there," and that it had been made out to Dorn instead of to her. She had been authorized to spend such money, explaining that the surveyor general of San Francisco had not only continually delayed appointing Dorn as Deputy Surveyor but had refused to send the field notes for the survey at Agua Caliente No. 2 "without which the work of survey could not go on."[129] Dorn had been forced to travel to San Francisco to sort the situation out, learning among other things that his appointment had been held up because of "the irregularity of the allotments at Rincon" which, Foote explained to Bradford, she had been authorized to make.[130]

When he arrived in San Francisco, Dorn discovered that the surveyor general was temporarily out of the office, his daughter having been left in charge. Although she claimed there were no field notes, Dorn succeeded in locating them as he hunted "over their shelves & notes" and through "the disordered mess," thus enabling the continuation of his surveying work at Agua Caliente. This entire oversight had forced Foote to explain to Bradford that Dorn's experience showed "*us* the animus of the office in the shape of active opposition." When she returned to Washington, Foote enlisted the help of the interior secretary, and orders were sent to "the Surveyor General's Office to appoint Mr. Dorn as Deputy Surveyor & to approve his plats when sent to that office." In defense of the bill in question, Foote informed Bradford that Dorn's journey and the expense "were worth the trouble." They had not only acquired the necessary notes to continue the survey but had learned "the exact knowledge of the reason for delay." Therefore, the expense should be considered legitimate. Foote had concluded that the final "result is as important to my surveyor as myself."[131]

Foote's prestigious appointment as allotting agent was not well known by the WNIA membership, considering that the association had backed the 1887 Dawes legislation which had formalized the process. Only a small notice was printed in the November 1892 issue of *The Indian's Friend* reporting that she had begun allotting land on the Rincon Reservation early the previous month, meeting frequently with the Indians. In a short extract of one of her letters, Foote explained that she had been going "out every day to see the surveyor's work and to talk with each allottee about his land, and I am to be on horseback every day soon."[132] At Rincon she had distributed twenty acres to heads of households for farming or one hundred sixty acres of grazing land. To single non-heads of households she had given ten acres apiece, secured for twenty-five years, distributing in total some 2,000 acres of Mission Indian lands. She also assured members of her auxiliary in another letter that she had felt safe living in her adobe home on the Rincon Reservation, never even locking her doors or trunks.[133]

Once home, Foote entertained members of the New Haven branch with an address on her experiences as an allotting agent in May 1893. Like Quinton, she endured primitive experiences in the field, both in transportation and housing, conditions she would never have encountered in either sophisticated Washington, DC, or in Connecticut. The New Haven *Morning Journal* reporter described her as the "brilliant Washington correspondent of 'The Independent,'" who had recently "finished the work she was sent out by the government to do" among the same Indians that Helen Hunt Jackson wrote about in her novel *Ramona*. He concluded that Foote's "account of her experiences among them will undoubtedly prove most interesting."[134] Shortly thereafter, Foote addressed the New York City Indian Association, a talk described as "very interesting, sometimes amusing, and at every point instructive," deepening the interest of this New York association in "the Ramona Mission for those dusky brothers and sisters."[135] And in distant California, Agent Francisco Estudillo in his August 1893 report of the Mission Tule River Consolidated Agency declared that Foote had made fifty-one allotments in severalty at Rincon. At first he explained that the Indians had been reluctant to have their lands allotted, but he convinced them "it would be a benefit to them in many ways."[136]

In September, Foote, who had taken an interest in Mission Indian day schools during her visit, wrote Daniel M. Browning, Morgan's successor as Indian commissioner, about the possibility of establishing a government school at Los Torres and Martínez.[137] One November day, while at Palm Springs, she had set out to explore the land and the residents around Indio, discovering two small Mission villages, with some one hundred fifty residents, and between thirty and forty children. "Isolated as these people have been from their desert surroundings," she described them as "less contaminated by contact with the outer edge of white civilization than almost any of the Indian reservations in this country." The children were "bright & healthy looking & their parents want a school there." She was very interested in their well-being and spoke of "their need & desire of a school to Commissioner Morgan." Although promoting education in general, Morgan for an undisclosed reason did not heed her suggestion. Therefore, Foote waited patiently until his successor, Browning, took office, writing him on September 4, 1893, making the same request.[138] Browning, like Morgan, chose not to build the school.

As late as February 1894, Foote was still hearing pleasant things about her role as an allotting agent. Miss Ora M. Salmons, the Rincon schoolteacher, informed *The Indian's Friend* that the residents of her village were doing well now that their lands had been allotted. "They have felt the impetus of owning their own land as was hoped; have fenced it, raised corn, and planted fruit trees as never before." Salmons explained that her own students had helped plant trees and flowers around their new government school, built on a hill which their parents had graded to make more accessible.[139]

Her census and allotment duties completed, Foote oversaw the appearance of a number of prominent speakers before the Washington auxiliary during the remainder of 1893. One of the more interesting was Grace Howard, who was engaged in missionary work among the Sioux at Crow Creek. The sickly eldest daughter of Joseph Howard Jr., a prominent New York City war correspondent, Grace had been sent to live in the milder climate of Hampton, Virginia, in 1885, where she became interested in the Indian work at Hampton Institute. Concerned about "the helpless condition of the Indian students upon their return to their Indian homes," she decided to establish a mission. With the consent of War Department officials, she toured several Sioux agencies, choosing a site for her project twelve miles from the agency on the Crow Creek Reservation. With a strong belief that Christian women should aid Indian girls returning from Hampton, she conferred with Rev. Henry Ward Beecher on her plan and, with his approval, an endorsement from her father, and a subscription book, privately circulated among her father's prominent friends, she funded the Grace Mission, "in which the Indian girls may be qualified to act as instructors for their less favored sisters."[140] Praised for her "interest and zeal in the Indian cause," Howard was described as leaving "home, friends, the comforts of civilized life and all the gayeties [sic] and pleasures of our great metropolis to spend her life" among the Sioux people.[141]

Howard, in a lengthy article in the February 1890 issue of *The Indian's Friend*, explained that for the last two years her work had been more of a missionary effort than industrial. At times she had several married couples from Hampton living with her in the mission, the men doing work around the mission facility and the wives engaged in housework. Howard took in girls as young as five from the agency school at the camps. They mostly engaged in housework for her. Although her nearest neighbor was a quarter of a mile away, Howard, who sincerely believed that her Grace Mission was influential, testified to numerous daily visitors, including old people who stopped by for a cup of tea, or young women who used her sewing machine. She described her "large sitting room into which [her] front door opens, [as] an attractive picture to me in the evening, when my own girls and the young boys about gather around the big table to enjoy the games and books." During haying season, she set up five tents behind the stable, explaining that when a tribal member came to work for her, he brought his entire family, referring to them as "part of mine until the work is done."[142]

Two other interesting speakers were Alice M. Robertson, a teacher among the Creeks living in the Indian Territory, and Rev. Hollis Burke Frissell, chaplain and vice principal at Hampton Institute, who brought a delegation of students, two of whom addressed the auxiliary, while others presented a musical selection. Robertson, known affectionately as "Miss Alice," was the daughter of missionaries to the Creek Indians and the granddaughter of Reverend Samuel A. Worcester, missionary to the Cherokees during removal. As supervisor of the Creek Indian schools, Robertson founded a boarding school for Indian girls, which eventually became the University of Tulsa. She boasted a number of firsts during her career: the first female clerk in the Indian Office, the first female postmaster at Muskogee, and the first woman elected to Congress from Oklahoma.[143] Reverend Frissell also had a distinguished career, becoming the second principal of Hampton Institute following the death of General Armstrong in 1893 and serving on the board or as a trustee of numerous African American associations.[144]

The highlight of that year for the Washington auxiliary was to host, at Foote's invitation, the annual WNIA meeting. The association's *Annual Report* described the "brightness which broke through the heavy snow-clouds on the afternoon of December 5th, 1893," as the membership was welcomed "to the national city, gleaming from White House to Capitol in the first snowy ermine of the season, and glorious under a brilliant sunset." One hundred fifty guests attended a reception at the Corcoran Art Gallery to meet with the more than eighty delegates from thirteen states and the District of Columbia.[145]

The following year, in addition to her usual duties as auxiliary president, Foote was invited by the Business Committee of the 1894 Lake Mohonk Conference to write the resolution for the twelfth conference to express the feelings of the three hundred guests who had been welcomed by Smiley to his resort hotel that year. Advised to make it "hard and soft, long and short," Foote described the conference as "golden, glowing, glorious in the matter of weather, of open fires, and the hospitality of our hosts, Mr. and Mrs. Smiley." Her only regret was that Smiley had limited his meeting to three days instead of giving it the week he had originally desired.[146]

In February 1895 the Washington auxiliary reluctantly accepted Foote's resignation. On January 8, 1895, she married Judge A. J. Coe, the first judge of the Meriden Municipal Court, and moved to Meriden, Connecticut.[147] Wishing her "the best of all earth's blessings and the great happiness she so richly merits," the editor of *The Indian's Friend* had begun the column with the thought that Foote, "who had given lands and homes in severalty to various Indians, would never desire either for herself, but be ours 'to have and to hold' for Indian works, till every Indian had his own." That was not to be the case, and the auxiliary welcomed Mrs. A. G. Wilkinson, formerly their first vice president, as their new president.[148]

A month after her marriage, Foote responded to William N. Hailmann, Superintendent of Indian Schools, who had written her about the need for a school for certain San Diego County Indians.[149] She explained that his letter had come just as she was getting married, and then her husband had become sick. Briefly noting she was sending him information on a potential location for the school, she devoted one full page to Charles C. Painter's recent death, having learned of it from Hailmann's letter. Sincerely sorry to learn of his passing, she responded that Painter "will be a great loss because he knew so much about the Indians from a practical point of view."[150]

Kate Foote Coe's move to Meriden did not end her association with the WNIA. On April 2, 1895, she gave an address before the Meriden Indian Association in the First Congregational Church on the work of government

Indian schools such as Hampton, Carlisle, and the day schools among the Mission Indians. She also spoke about mourning ceremonies among the Mission Indians based on information gathered during her time as allotting agent. Some time that year she also became president of the Meriden branch of the WNIA.[151]

Under Wilkinson's presidency, the Washington auxiliary prospered, and interesting speakers continued to address their public meetings. The April 1895 issue of *The Indian's Friend* described the March 15 meeting in the red parlor of the historic Ebbitt House and the reading of three letters. Members were especially pleased to hear from Dr. Rebecca Cooper Hallowell, the medical missionary funded by the New York City Indian Association at Agua Caliente on the Warner Ranch in Southern California.[152] Of particular interest was a letter from Fletcher, read before the meeting by Jane Gay, who had accompanied Fletcher between 1889 and 1892 to photograph her allotment activities among the Nez Perce.[153] Fletcher's letter called the auxiliary's attention to Nettie (Henrietta) Fremont, a young Omaha woman, who wanted a college education. The auxiliary immediately set up the Nettie Fremont Educational Fund. The third letter was from Bidwell, describing stories of the lives of several of the Mechoopda Indians in the Chico Rancheria. The keynote speaker at that meeting was General John Eaton, former superintendent of Tennessee schools and U.S. Commissioner of Education from 1870 to 1886, who addressed the issue of Indian education, providing some interesting facts about the Carlisle Indian Industrial School, founded in 1879 by Richard Henry Pratt, an Army officer with a strong belief in Indian assimilation. Pratt served as school superintendent from 1879 to 1904.[154]

Fletcher personally addressed the reformers at the April 19 meeting, reminding them of the seriousness of their work, and that "public sentiment must be enlightened and enthused; this was hard work, but a necessity," she assured them. "The longer I live and observe the surer I am that the right step was taken when land in severalty was secured for the Indians." She then spoke of the value of education, believing the best opportunities were offered at eastern government boarding schools. Praising the WNIA work as remarkable and enlightening and stirring up public opinion, she encouraged the membership to "take courage; hold on; you are needed to-day, you will be still needed in the future." At the end of the meeting it was announced that enough money had been raised for Nettie Fremont's first two years of college. The July issue reported that the young Indian woman would be attending Swarthmore College in Pennsylvania.[155]

Figure 5. Alice Cunningham Fletcher, pictured here, was privately tutored by Frederic W. Putnam, director of Harvard's Peabody Museum. She lectured widely on the new discipline of anthropology, authored books, engaged in field work among various tribes, and served as allotment agent for the Omaha, Winnebago, and Nez Perce Indians. (National Anthropological Archives, Smithsonian Institution [No. 4510].)

During 1896, the auxiliary held five meetings. Quinton gave a "delightful and encouraging address at the January meeting, reporting gratifying evidences of progress seen everywhere on her extended trip through the West." During another meeting, the auxiliary hosted Francis E. Leupp, a member of the BIC and the IRA, and later Commissioner of Indian Affairs, who explained the workings of the Teller Bill, having made a similar presentation before the twenty-fifth annual January BIC conference in Washington.[156] Presented to Congress by Colorado Senator Henry M. Teller, the legislation was an attempt to remove Indian affairs from partisan politics by replacing the Indian commissioner with a three-man commissioner—two civilians, one from each political party, and an officer of the regular Army. However, it offered little continuity as all three officials were replaced every four years, just as was the commissioner after each presidential election.[157]

By 1900, the Washington auxiliary was almost twenty years old, had doubled its membership, and had raised enough money to purchase a steel loom for the New Jersey Association's work among the Hopi tribe at Keams Canyon, Arizona. In the WNIA missionary report, the New Jersey–sponsored missionary wrote that "the Indians are very much interested in it," later reporting the weaving of the first blanket.[158] Two years later Washington members again hosted the national meeting in the capital. President, Mrs. Mary E. C. Wilbur, welcomed delegates, reminding them it had been nine years since they last met there. Attendees were toured from the Senate Reading Room "through the various electrically illuminated apartments and galleries adorned with pictures and statues in view of the wealth of volumes, periodicals, manuscripts and maps of that magnificent building." Months later the auxiliary reported that after going through financial difficulties with deaths and "changed localities of members," it was finally strong enough to have shared "its hospitality last December." Now at full strength, "who can predict what a life of achievement lies before it!" The auxiliary had also just published its first history, written by Wilbur.[159]

The Washington auxiliary continued with successful public meetings and speakers during the remainder of the decade, reporting in 1906 the addition of fourteen new members, six regular meetings and five public meetings, and that they "go into the new year with everything paid." Eager to get ideas before the public, they provided as usual a venue for reformers and Indians alike. Two in the latter category were attorneys William Wirt Hastings[160] and Robert Latham Owen,[161] mixed-blood members of the Cherokee Nation, representing the Cherokee in negotiations with the government. Although WNIA literature made no reference to their addresses, topics discussed most likely included the fate of the Cherokee and the other four of the Five Civilized Tribes (Muscogees [formerly Creek], Choctaw, Chickasaw, and Seminoles) as their homelands in the Indian Territory[162] were advancing toward statehood. Hearings had begun in 1904 on the "Twin Territories" (Oklahoma Territory and a formalized Indian Territory, reorganized in 1890). Although both were eligible for individual statehood, the territories were combined in 1907 to form the state of Oklahoma.[163] The fate of the five tribes was again on the minds of Washington auxiliary members as they listened to George W. Woodruff, assistant attorney general assigned to the Department of the Interior, address the same subject on December 27, 1907, in the home of Sarah Jane Alexander, Bidwell's sister.[164]

Washington members reported taking "up its work for 1907-08 with hope and faith that much good will be accomplished through its efforts, with God's help."[165] They exceeded their goal, with a total of ten new members and seven executive and four parlor meetings, with topics discussed ranging from the legal status of the Five Civilized Tribes to "professions for which the Indian is Adapted."[166] In 1910 they elected a new president, Mrs. William H. Chany (née Jane Douglas Butler),[167] who was active in in the Daughters of the American Revolution, the Mayflower Society, the Twentieth Century Club, and the Association for the Blind. The following year the auxiliary invited Dr. F. A. McKenzie, an Ohio State sociologist, to describe the recent October conference in Columbus, Ohio, attended by fifty, mostly middle-class professional Indian men and women, who addressed major issues facing the country's Indian population. McKenzie had played a role in the formation of this organization, the Society of American Indians, by holding the conference planning meeting on his campus in April 1911. Members of the Washington auxiliary were most eager to learn about this first pan-Indian reform organization founded during the Progressive Era. For those unable to attend, *The Indian's Friend* included a brief article on the new organization.[168]

By the second decade of the twentieth century, fewer reports on any auxiliaries appeared in the association monthly. Issues of *The Indian's Friend* were cut back, first to ten a year in 1912 and then in January 1915 to six. Auxiliaries with their own periodical, such as the Connecticut Indian Association, or others like the Massachusetts, New York, and Northern California Indian Associations which published their own annual reports, were less impacted by these cutbacks. The Washington auxiliary, however, was dependent upon the occasional article in the monthly periodical and the short statement about their work in the *Annual Reports*. The little news that was printed reflected continued growth, albeit at times small, and the appearance of prominent speakers, and the auxiliary's ongoing support of missionary stations funded by the national association. On November 19, 1913, Washington women held a bazaar at the Willard Hotel to raise funds to benefit the national association's Good Samaritan Hospital at Indian Wells, Arizona, on the Navajo Reservation. Similar events on behalf of the hospital were held annually by the auxiliary until late 1919, when it was turned over to the permanent care of the Woman's Board of Home Missions of the Presbyterian Church.[169] On December 10, the membership attended a gathering at the home of General Richard L. Hoxie and his wife Lavinia "Vinnie" Ream Hoxie, a prominent sculptor. She was best known for her statue of Abraham Lincoln, which stands in the rotunda of the US Capitol Building. She had been awarded the commission for it in 1866, at age eighteen. During the social hour, Vinnie entertained auxiliary members in her studio, describing the statue of Sequoyah she was making for the state of Oklahoma to be placed in the Capitol.[170]

For the remainder of the decade, the auxiliary continued their handful of meetings; even the war years did not seem to deter their efforts. When the Navajo hospital at Indian Wells was turned over, auxiliary members immediately adopted the Rocky Boy Mission, founded that year in Montana among the Rocky Boy Band of Chippewa and Cree.[171] In 1933, "owing to changes in membership" and the death of Mrs. A. G. Wilkinson, the former president, described as their "prime mover for many years," the Washington auxiliary disbanded, turning over all monies to the national association.[172] Only a handful of the more than one hundred original WNIA auxiliaries were still functioning.

It is remarkable that this single auxiliary, with a membership that rarely exceeded more than fifty members at any one time, remained viable for so long. Although its initial success was due to the extraordinary leadership of the Foote sisters, succeeding presidents also proved to be capable. The auxiliary remained successful because it served as a magnet, drawing influential speakers, many of whom were Indigenous, enabling members and visitors, unable to visit the West, to have firsthand contact with the people they had vowed to help. A major downside was that their small membership made funding their own missionary station impossible. Despite that shortcoming, their philanthropic work was still impressive, including funding the medical efforts at the Agua Caliente village on Warner Ranch; work among the Yuma; work with the Klamath, at the Yainax Mission; and support for the Navajo hospital at Indian Wells, to name a few.

Unlike the Washington auxiliary which had no branches, the Connecticut Indian Association, to which both Foote sisters belonged, did, even in small towns liked Waterbury. And strength was in numbers. Beginning in 1897 and for the next decade, Constance Goddard DuBois, a member and officer of that branch, played a prominent role in alerting government officials and reformers of the plight of the residents of several small Mission Indian villages in and around Chula Vista, south of San Diego. She toured their villages during the summer to gather information for articles and lectures written and delivered during the winter months in Waterbury. Although she arrived relatively late to the reform movement, her influence was considerable. She collaborated with the IRA's Herbert Welsh and other reformers, engaged in cultural preservation by recording Indigenous myths and music, encouraged traditional Native basketmaking, and worked toward the purchase of additional lands near existing reservations to promote subsistence agriculture. Constance Goddard DuBois is the subject of the next chapter.

CHAPTER 3

Constance Goddard DuBois

Mission Indians, Basketmaking, and the Indian Industries League

In addition to serving as presidents of the Washington, DC, auxiliary, Harriet Ward Foote Hawley and Kate Foote Coe had been members in good standing of the Connecticut Indian Association. And Harriet's husband, Senator Hawley, even after his wife's death continued to serve on the association's advisory committee.[1] Connecticut women had initially organized on November 15, 1881, as a committee of the Indian Treaty-Keeping and Protective Association in Hartford, Connecticut, with 61-year-old Sarah Sophia Tyler Cowen as their first president. During the Civil War, Cowen had been a member of the Hartford Soldiers' Aid Society, working on behalf of Connecticut soldiers on the battlefield and in hospitals. After the war, she shifted her philanthropic efforts to Indian reform.[2]

For the next two years, Cowen's committee primarily devoted themselves to "arousing the public's ire against United States Indian policy."[3] Then in 1883 members reorganized as the Connecticut Indian Association and elected Sara Thomson Kinney, a resident of Hartford, as president, a position she held for the next three decades. Interested in genealogical research, Kinney was a member of the Society of Mayflower Descendants, the DAR, and the United Daughters of 1812.[4] Then, four years later, twenty-six Connecticut women, serving as "a body politic," were granted a charter, the said object of which was "to protect the rights and promote the education and civilization of the Indians . . . with reference to their full admission into full citizenship." Along with Cowen and Kinney, this group of women also included Harriet Beecher Stowe, author of *Uncle Tom's Cabin*, who was listed as an honorary vice president in the *Annual Report* of that year. Her brother, Henry Ward Beecher, was a strong supporter of the association, and his granddaughter, Annie Beecher Scoville, who lived in Stamford, Connecticut, served as chairman of the WNIA Home Building and Loan Department for almost two decades, beginning in 1898.[5] With hard-driving Quinton at the helm of the national association, all auxiliaries thrived. By 1888, the Connecticut association had eleven branches, with one in Waterbury, which Kinney had personally organized on June 15, 1888.[6] One of the more prominent members of this branch was novelist Constance Goddard DuBois, later elected its president.[7]

DuBois was born in Zanesville, Ohio, in the late 1850s to John Delafield DuBois and Alice Goddard DuBois and attended the Female Seminary in nearby Putnam. The 1870 census placed the family living in Charleston, West Virginia. DuBois, who never married, also lived for a time in Watertown, New York, before moving to Waterbury, Connecticut, about 1889 to share a home with Dr. Caroline Root Conkey, a graduate of the Woman's Medical College of the New York Infirmary for Women and Children, who had opened up a practice there. Sometime after moving to Waterbury, DuBois joined the WNIA affiliate there, as did Conkey.[8]

DuBois was atypical of the average WNIA member, who most often simply attended meetings, paid dues, and participated in petition drives. Beginning in 1897 and for the next decade, she traveled almost every summer to visit family members who had moved to Chula Vista, south of San Diego.[9] Once there, she spent weeks on investigative field trips, visiting isolated Mission Indian villages, taking photographs,[10] gathering information for her articles and lectures, and writing letters on behalf of the Indians to reformers and officials. Late to the movement, by the time of her first visit to Southern California, most WNIA work at the Ramona Mission among the Mission Indians, begun in June 1889 under Rev. William Henry Weinland, was winding down, and missionary efforts had been transferred either to the Moravian Board or to Southern California auxiliaries, headquartered in Redlands. This lack of institutional support did not deter her. From her first visit in 1897, DuBois, carrying a copy of Helen Hunt Jackson's official 1883 report to the Interior Department, toured remote Mission reservations, quoting from the report in her letters written from the field and in articles from home.

Then, during the long Waterbury winters, DuBois lectured before women's clubs, church groups, and Indian associations, describing the fragile condition of the Mission villagers, displaying their baskets, hoping, as political scientist Erik Krenzen Trump writes, that these "reform-minded white women would make ideal consumers." His analysis of her few available lectures reveals "insights into how an image of Indian artistry was constructed for a female, reform-minded audience." As an amateur ethnologist, DuBois not only brought "a unique kind of authority to the lecture," but as an expert on basketry, she also verified the quality and discussed designs while displaying and equating them with fine china or silver.[11] Moved by the extreme starvation she personally witnessed among the Indians, DuBois spent her own money and encouraged basketmaking and the development of a Native lace industry for sale in eastern markets to earn extra monies to feed hungry villagers.[12]

Like Jackson and several other WNIA members, DuBois used her literary skills to benefit the Mission Indians. She wrote for two different audiences. Her articles, written in her role as an activist Indian reformer and appearing in *The Indian's Friend*, *The Land of Sunshine*, and *The Southern Workman*, printed at Hampton Institute, exposed the extreme poverty faced by them and generated a correspondence with officials in the Indian Office and prominent reformers including Herbert Welsh; Charles Fletcher Lummis, Indian advocate and later founder of the Southwest Museum and of the Sequoya League, a West Coast–based reform organization;[13] and C. E. Kelsey, the general secretary of the Northern California Indian Association (NCIA).[14] DuBois's letters and articles resulted in several investigative tours by prominent officials and clergymen and monetary support for starving Indians. As an amateur ethnographer, writing primarily on Kumeyaay (Diegueño) and Luiseño mythology and religious ceremonies in an effort to preserve their traditions, DuBois corresponded with noted anthropologists and ethnologists Alfred L. Kroeber, Clark Wissler, Franz Boas, and Frederick W. Hodge, and engaged in fieldwork for the American Museum of Natural History and the Department of Anthropology of the University of California, with articles published in major anthropological journals. She also

Figure 6. Constance Goddard DuBois, pictured here circa 1900, was an editor, author, and amateur ethnologist, preserving the mythology and religious ceremonies of the Diegueño and Luiseño, and was president of the Waterbury, Connecticut, auxiliary of the WNIA. (Autry Museum of the American West [P. 32203].)

made sound recordings of Indigenous music, and with the aid of interpreters, recorded their myths.[15]

Described as "a historical novelist turned ethnographer,"[16] DuBois had published her first article in 1884, her last in 1909, writings novels in between.

From 1893 to 1897 she also served as the general secretary of the Gray Memorial Botanical Association and the first editor of the *Asa Gray Bulletin*, at times writing an occasional short article. When the publisher's office moved from Waterbury in 1897, she resigned to devote more time to her own writing.[17] Beginning with *A Soul in Bronze: A Novel of Southern California* (1898), her fifth novel, DuBois wrote exclusively on California's Mission Indians.[18]

Like Quinton, Hiles, and other WNIA members, DuBois had been influenced by Helen Hunt Jackson's novel, *Ramona*, dedicating her own California novel to Jackson, "whose warm heart and enlightened sympathy [had] made her the Friend of the Indian."[19] Lummis serialized DuBois's novel in *The Land of Sunshine*, which he also edited. Initially describing it as "somewhat suggesting *Ramona* in its zeal and fire and in its scope . . . daring in its conception, and fuller of exciting incident," he later called the novel "the peer of *Ramona*."[20] In the May 1899 issue, which included the final installment, Lummis wrote that DuBois's novel "unquestionably takes its place in the small class which is next after *Ramona*," describing the story as "of singular truth to one side of California life—and to a very large side of creation—a story of deep interest and of noble love."[21] Months later, Welsh, publisher and editor of a Philadelphia weekly called *City and State*, reviewed the H. S. Stone & Company edition of DuBois's book in his December 1900 issue, describing it as having "a skillfully developed plot, which insures the interest of the casual reader, and the local color and atmosphere of southern California are presented in a marvelous way."[22] The previous month he had published her article, "Our American 'Reconcentrado,'"[23] an exposé of the destitute condition of the Mission Indians in the San Diego area.

Welsh's father had been a successful Philadelphia merchant and philanthropist who had served as the US minister to the Court of Saint James. The younger Welsh, with inherited wealth and motivation from "his concept of Christian responsibility," engaged in full-time reform activities. He was most noted as a founder of the powerful and influential Philadelphia-based Indian Rights Association, serving as its longtime executive secretary. In May 1895, he had founded *City and State* in an "unremitting effort to arouse reform sentiments in Philadelphia," envisioning it as providing continuous education to various reform elements.[24] Welsh's publication of DuBois's article in his periodical had far-reaching consequences for both her and the Mission Indians.

DuBois's portrayal of their dire situation was clearly a cry for reformers to act. She described how white settlers had "crowded in and stolen their land, driving them further and further back, until now they are beyond the limit where human beings can live, and starvation is their only future." She wished her readers could envision the desert-like land where these Indians were expected to "make a living and rise toward the refinements of civilization." The residents of La Posta and Manzanita, located near the Mexican border, were facing slow starvation; those at La Posta lived on "a heap of rocks where a goat could hardly find a footing"; and the villagers at Inyaha, Laguna, and Los Conejos were subsisting only on green corn and manzanita berries. Everywhere she saw "a terrible poverty caused not by any fault of their own, but by the desperate conditions to which they are condemned by our fault as a nation." She called these destitute reservations "our American 'reconcentrados,'" likening the Indians' situation as hardly less cruel than that faced by the rural Cubans reconcentrated into camps under orders of Valeriano Weyler y Nicoul during the Spanish-American War. If the government could not place these Indians "in conditions where they can help themselves, we must not hold ourselves absolved from Spain's guilt in the treatment of the Cubans," she concluded.[25]

DuBois also described the residents of the Diegueño village of Santa Ysabel as "driven up upon the savage and inaccessible heights of Vulcan Mountain—ninety-seven human beings left face to face with starvation on land where only goats could find a living."[26] She had first visited the village on St. John's Day in late June 1897. By the time of her arrival, the local priest and people had already left the annual morning service. All that remained was the ruins of the 1818 *asistencia* or sub-mission of Mission San Diego de Alcalá, "leveled by time and washed by winter rains," its walls "sunk into indistinguishable heaps of earth." The ceremony had been performed in an old brush church with walls of fresh-woven green boughs, and the mission bells still hung on its rude framework of logs instead of in the belfry. When DuBois returned in the summer of 1900, "the mission bells hung silent and deserted. The last Indian was gone."[27] She later eulogized Santa Ysabel in "The Song of the Death," describing the mission as "now but a name. Its adobe walls, washed by a century's rainstorms, have crumbled into ruin. Its silver bells are voiceless, but eloquent in silence as reminders of the past."[28]

That summer of 1897, DuBois had also visited Mesa Grande, a Kumeyaay village eleven miles from Santa Ysabel, to watch the feather dance. What she most noticed was the reservation's "rugged, barren hillsides where it is impossible to gain a living from the soil."[29] Her descriptions of inhospitable sites to which the Indians were forced to live became a common thread throughout many of her articles and the primary reason why she suggested the purchase of tillable lands either by the government or private interests to augment Indian landholdings. It was more than likely during this visit to Mesa Grande that she first met Mary Watkins, appointed to a government teaching position on September 1, 1896. Watkins became a confidante, accompanying DuBois on her investigative tours, helping to distribute food and clothing, recording stories and songs, and collecting baskets to be sold in eastern markets.[30]

DuBois had combined her 1897 and 1900 observations into the November *City and State* article that she assumed would be read primarily by local Philadelphian reformers. However, Rev. H. B. Restarick of St. Paul's Episcopal Cathedral in San Diego also read it and wrote to her. She sent him additional information on basketry, explaining that "years ago the Indian women made baskets to hold household stores of every kind, . . . now old tin cans serve the purpose which the baskets did." She also explained that the practice of sending the girls off to boarding schools at the very time they should be honing their basketmaking skills had limited those learning the craft. Restarick, inspired by her article, wrote the *San Diego Union and Daily Bee* of his intention to visit these reservations to see to both "their needs and the judicious distribution of relief," explaining that "when Mrs. Watkins and Miss Dubois write of Indians 99 years old lying on the ground, dying, covered only by a few rags, this is not pleasant to think of as happening in our country."[31] Restarick was joined by the Right Rev. Joseph Horsfall Johnson, Bishop of the Los Angeles Diocese of the Episcopal Church, on a ten-day, three hundred-mile-long tour of nine reservations. They set out on December 5, 1900. Newspapers were soon printing descriptions of starving Mission Indians.[32] While Restarick and Johnson were touring Mission reservations, DuBois was attending her first WNIA annual meeting in Philadelphia, at which she encouraged Indian lacemaking by reading a letter from the president of the Pasadena branch, who had enclosed a sample of lace work by a ninety-year-old Mesa Grande Indian woman.[33]

DuBois's Indian writings and Watkins's efforts on their behalf began to gain more exposure in the press. A mid-December 1900 news item in the *Los Angeles Herald* revealed that "it was through the efforts of Miss Constance Goddard DuBois, author of 'A Soul in Bronze,' and Mrs. Watkins, a government teacher, that the existing conditions among the Indians was brought before the public."[34] Watkins, earlier mistakenly identified as a Mrs. Walker, had appealed in a letter to the people of San Diego not to forget the children. "Little babies are rolled up in an old apron," she wrote, "no wonder that there are rows of tiny graves; that the death and birth rate are about even."[35] Several weeks later Bishop Johnson traveled to Washington, DC, to confer with Thomas R. Bard, a California member of the Senate Indian Committee, who introduced him to Indian Commissioner William A. Jones.[36] The Bishop made "an earnest plea for the relief of the Indians," describing them as starving. Shortly thereafter a San Diego newspaper reported that funds had been secured for Mission Indian relief.[37] At year's end, Johnson and Restarick joined Lummis and former Mission Agent Horatio Nelson Rust and others in signing a lengthy memorandum and memorial to Commissioner Jones, detailing the threat to Mission Indian lands and announcing a permanent association of citizens (the Sequoya League) being formed "for the sole purpose of remedying—and keeping remedied—as many as possible of these abuses" against Mission Indians.[38]

DuBois's writings soon led to a renewed interest in the Mission Indians on the part of the WNIA. A January 1901 issue of their periodical, *The Indian's Friend*, quoted extensively from Bishop Johnson, who in his recent tour with Restarick explained he had traveled "through an almost completely barren country, made still more barren by three years of drought, witnessing scenes that made his heart ache." Johnson had found misery and destitution in all but one reservation. DuBois later quoted him as stating that "if the policy of the Government is to exterminate its unfortunate wards, it has made a good start in that direction."[39] In the February issue, Johnson described Indians nearly everywhere he had traveled as "destitute, discontented and unhappy." Their white neighbors, however, described them as "industrious when given a chance to work."[40]

Bishop Johnson offered such an opportunity in the summer of 1901 when he appointed Mrs. Sophie R. Miller,[41] an Episcopal missionary, to the Mesa Grande Reservation to conduct Sunday school classes and to teach lacemaking and basket-weaving in an effort to create a small cottage industry for Indian women. DuBois visited her that summer, describing Miller as "eminently fitted for the place" and willing to "look after the drawnwork, which was an industry the women already possessed and one that could be done at their homes more conveniently in some cases than the lace work." Desirous that men have a similar opportunity, DuBois persuaded Miller to begin teaching wood carving and to learn leather carving.[42]

In mid-October 1901, a San Diego newspaper reported that Miller had gone to Los Angeles to study lacemaking with Sybil Carter.[43] Carter, a deaconess of the Episcopal Church, a member of its home missionary society, and later WNIA president in 1906, had begun to teach lacemaking to the Anishinaabe (Ojibwa) women on the White Earth Reservation around 1889, at the invitation of Episcopal Bishop Henry Whipple of Minnesota.[44] By 1906 the Sybil Carter Lace Industry Association, founded to market Indian-made lace to eastern consumers, listed ten schools teaching lacemaking, two in California—at Mesa Grande and La Jolla.[45] Historian Jane Simonsen writes that since the production of lace required clean hands and a clean house, Carter had "reported that making snow-white lace promoted cleanliness and good hygiene." Although Simonsen concludes that "once again, labor is subsumed under the rhetoric of civilization that linked whiteness with progress," she also explains that many Indian women "embraced the opportunity to earn wages."[46] It was often the government-appointed field matron[47] who managed the labor of Indian women, with her missionary cottage divided between living quarters and a working space for an Indian cottage industry. Mamie Robinson, the field matron at Campo, a Kumeyaay reservation near the Mexican border, worked closely with DuBois, especially in the buying and selling of Indian-made baskets.

Two months after Miller had begun her studies with Carter, DuBois praised the Episcopal missionary's work during the 1901 WNIA annual meeting.[48] DuBois described her as bringing "the basket work back to the perfection of that early time when no one made haste for gain," explaining that "the art instinct is the primitive woman's birthright." DuBois also credited Bishop Johnson for proposing to have an industrial building constructed at Mesa Grande to enable Miller to expand her work and to include neighboring reservations. With elderly women like those at Manzanita still engaged in basketmaking, DuBois believed a market could be created with Campo storekeeper, H. M. Johnson, serving as agent as well as encouraging new basket makers. The final products could be shipped to New York City for sale at Wanamaker's and the Hyde stores.[49] DuBois remained adamant that the sale of Indian crafts be "kept out of the hands of the dealers," with the money forming a perpetual fund to continue the purchase of new baskets.[50] As Erik Trump writes, this "vision of an arts-based economic self-sufficiency may have been unrealistic," but it "reflected a desire to find creative, female-based solutions to the Indian 'problem.'"[51] Unfortunately, by 1905 Lummis, who described DuBois as "a practical philanthropist," had pressured her to let the Sequoya League take over some of the marketing, although the Indian Industries League continued their role, opening a salesroom in Boston.[52]

Figure 7. Frances Campbell Sparhawk, philanthropist and author of numerous books, was also chair of the WNIA's Indian Industries League, which at her suggestion invited male members. (Image from *A Woman of the Century*, ed. Frances E. Willard and Mary A. Livermore (Chicago: Charles Wells Moulton, 1893), 682, https://www.alamy.com.)

Under the umbrella of the WNIA executive board, the Indian Industries League had begun as an effort to establish a division of Indian industries, replacing the association's earlier Department of Indian Civilization, created to teach industries to students returning from government boarding schools.[53] This new work was combined into the Committee on Indian Libraries and Industries in 1891 with Frances Campbell Sparhawk, a resident of Newton Center, Massachusetts, in charge.[54] A gifted writer, Sparhawk saw her short fiction and essays appear in prominent eastern magazines shortly after her graduation from the Young Ladies' Academy in Ipswich. Her first book was published in 1881, and by 1890 she was incorporating into her novels the various challenges facing educated Indian youths upon returning to their reservation. A strong supporter of the educational policies of Richard Henry Pratt, founder of the Carlisle Indian School, Sparhawk, a former teacher and editor of their school paper, *The Red Man*, attributed the difficulties facing returned students upon "an unhealthy environment," in no way based on "any inherent weakness peculiar to the red race." According to Helen Wanken, Sparhawk's upper-class-background "colored her opinion on exactly what possibilities were open to whites, but it did not make her aspirations for Indians any less admirable." Sparhawk viewed her organization as opening opportunities for individual Indians and in turn encouraging the rise of self-supporting industries in Indian communities.[55]

In 1894, a separate Indian Industries League was formed "to establish self-supporting industries in Indian communities," with Sparhawk as secretary and general manager. In October of that year, the League applied to become an auxiliary at large of the WNIA, with Sparhawk advocating for male membership. Welsh, Smiley, and several members of the Boston Indian Citizenship Committee and of the Board of Indian Commissioners joined Amelia Stone Quinton, Sybil Carter, Mrs. Lyman Abbott (née Abby Frances Hamlin), wife of the editor of *Christian Union*, and many of the presidents of state auxiliaries in this new endeavor. Within two years the League was solely responsible for Indian industries.[56] It seemed "incongruous for an organization, which for decades preached 'rooting out Indianness,' to care whether traditional Indian basketry, beadwork, pottery, and weaving were preserved," while at the same time remaining true to their original goals of Americanizing and civilizing them, writes historian Helen Wanken. According to the latter, it was their flexibility in accepting this dichotomy that enabled the WNIA, an assimilationist organization, to accomplish as much good as they did.[57]

Erik Trump expands on the reasoning behind the encouragement, revival, and sale of Indian arts by the League, attributing it to "a combination of broader societal shifts in attitudes toward Indian culture," including the "growing respect for Indians among fieldworkers, the influence of several key League members, and simple pragmatism." It was easier and cheaper to develop Native industries that already existed, Trump concluded.[58] For example, Mary Louise Eldridge, the subject of chapters 5 and 6, promoted Navajo weaving during her tenure as government field matron and as supervisor of WNIA efforts on their reservation, working closely with the Indian Industries League.

In 1901, the WNIA established a Department of Indian Industries with Nellie Blanchan De Graff Doubleday, wife of New York publisher Frank Nelson Doubleday, as chair.[59] One of the key League members identified by Trump,

Doubleday, an assimilationist, nevertheless promoted Indian arts, arguing that total assimilation was misguided "because it falsely posited Anglo culture as superior to Indian and because it robbed Indians and white Americans of important cultural resources." Trump attributed Doubleday with laying "out a defense of why reformers should redirect their energies toward native arts." According to her, "most of the cultural history of Indian tribes" resided in the art of Indian women, and, therefore, its preservation ensured that "a great store of knowledge that would otherwise vanish" was preserved.[60] Two years later DuBois, serving on the League's executive committee, convinced Doubleday to cooperate with her in the selling of Mission Indian–made baskets. According to Trump, both reformers went beyond philanthropy, defending "Indian culture from charges that it was 'savage,' and in their advocacy of Indian arts they openly challenged certain assimilationist goals."[61]

DuBois's exposé in *City and State* had led to the investigative tours of Restarick and Johnson, had increased publicity in Southern California newspapers, had served as a possible nudge toward the founding of the Sequoya League, and had engaged DuBois in an extensive correspondence with reformers and government officials. One of the more influential was Herbert Welsh, a relationship that provided DuBois with access to the powerful IRA, which early in 1901 published her second article as an association pamphlet. Her letters in turn provided Welsh with valuable firsthand information about local conditions without his leaving his Philadelphia home. Although he was known for extensive tours of Indian country, there is no evidence that he ever visited Southern California. Instead, that responsibility was assigned to the association's Washington, DC, agent, Samuel Brosius, who made at least one tour of Mission villages with DuBois and Watkins.[62]

During the summer of 1900, several months before the publication of her article in *City and State*, DuBois had written Welsh, apologizing that her Waterbury auxiliary was unable to fund a small project requested by Brosius. All auxiliary funds were pledged to the WNIA national office in Philadelphia, she explained, and since "literature is not lucrative," she had no spare money of her own. She was personally trying to raise funds for starving Indians, many of whom were living on "Manzanita berries, [as] their only food." However, since Welsh and the IRA were providing legal support to the Warner Ranch Indians, currently facing eviction, she would be pleased to share any information gleaned from her August visit to Mesa Grande, Santa Ysabel, and Warner Ranch that would support his association's efforts.[63]

The Warner Ranch case was already a cause célèbre, one that DuBois later described as widely noticed with "the public heart and conscience" stirred.[64] The 44,000-acre ranch, which included five Indian villages, covered most of the San Jose Valley in northern San Diego County. It had been named after Jonathan Trumbull Warner, who after becoming a Mexican citizen had received a land grant in 1844. Helen Hunt Jackson, in her government report, had described the Cupeño village of Agua Caliente, one of the five on the ranch, as "most flourishing and influential," with hot springs bubbling "up in a succession of curious stone basins in the heart of the village," enabling residents to earn money renting their little adobe homes to sufferers of rheumatism.[65] The New York City association of the WNIA was currently sponsoring Dr. Rebecca C. Hallowell as a medical missionary. At the time of Jackson's visit, the ranch was owned by former California governor John G. Downey, who initially had been considerate of its residents; by 1890 he had begun threatening to evict them.

DuBois also explained in her July letter to Welsh that she had recently returned from the Santa Ysabel Ranch, which Jackson, in her government report, had recommended the government purchase as a reservation for all the Indians. The current residents of Santa Ysabel had been driven to "an inaccessible barren mountain, an extinct volcano, where nothing will grow," DuBois related to Welsh. She would send him "fuller reports later on, hoping that in some way help may be given." She concluded her letter, expressing the great faith she had in Welsh's knowledge of the methods of the government and in his power "to aid these needy people."[66]

From Mesa Grande a month later, DuBois wrote Mathew Sniffen, IRA clerk and business manager for *City and State*, of the possibility of his association's sponsoring a congressional bill to purchase a new reservation for the Warner Ranch Indians and other villagers facing eviction. Describing the potential Warner eviction as "too cruel for words," DuBois attested that many other Mission Indians were forced to live on rats and acorns.[67] Her solution for all evicted Indians was the purchase of the 18,000-acre Santa Ysabel Ranch. It was large enough for the building of a boarding and day school, with space for basket-making and drawn work (embroidery) for the women and dairying and farming for the men. Off on a four-day trip to "distant reservations where starvation reigns," she asked Sniffen to have Brosius confer with Watkins at Mesa Grande, describing the schoolteacher as "a trustworthy Christian woman whose heart and soul are in her work." In conclusion, DuBois characterized the IRA as "the one tower of strength, hope, and comfort in all this sad business." Three weeks later, she wrote Sniffen from Chula Vista that she had just returned from a trip to the destitute reservations of Volcan, La Posta, and Manzanita.[68]

In early December, writing from home, DuBois informed Sniffen that she would be in Philadelphia to attend the annual IRA meeting on the eleventh. He extended an invitation for her to speak before attendees on the topic of the Mission Indians. Welsh later complimented DuBois on her address, impressed not only by her great enthusiasm and energy but with her "broad view of things and practical common sense. These are certainly most necessary if one wants to do good in the world," he had concluded.[69] The previous month he had published her article in *City and State*.

In mid-February, DuBois informed Lummis she was writing a descriptive book on the Mission Indians, calling it *An Indian Summer in Southern California*. She already had written three chapters, "each one a sort of sketch in itself." She would send them for his magazine if he paid her "not less than ten dollars a number" and allowed her to correct the final proof, describing her style as "a poor thing but mine own."[70] The following month, on the seventh, she lectured on the topic of the Indian in North America at Friend League Hall in Waterbury, with an admission fee of 10 cents for non-league members. Five days earlier, the *Waterbury Democrat* had alerted the public to her upcoming address, describing DuBois's study of the Mission Indians as exhaustive, enabling her to speak on a subject "which has such fascination for all lovers of 'Ramona.'" Afterwards, the *Democrat* reported that she had painted "the pathetic picture of their [the Indians'] present condition, driven from their homes by the Americans into the desert, where a bare existence only is possible." Her visits to their homes and her attendance at their "simple church services" had enabled her to present "a striking contrast to the ordinary conception of the Indian character."[71]

In April, DuBois's article on the Connecticut Indian Association's efforts on behalf of the Mission Indians was published in their periodical, *The Indian Bulletin*. She stated that "it should be the object of our Association to urge upon the Government the duty of restoring to these Indians enough good land with water upon it to suffice for their self-support." In the meantime, the membership should "aid each community with such tools or means of industry as may prove to be of most urgent necessity." As an example, she pointed out that her Waterbury branch had purchased a ninety-dollar wood-wagon for Mesa Grande, enabling the Indians to cut and haul their own wood. She suggested that other branches could send plows, or road-building tools, or seeds, or assist the women in "the encouragement of the native basketmaking, and the drawn-work [lacemaking] taught them by the Spanish." DuBois described the field as "made ready to our hand; a people already well started towards civilization," concluding, "what more important work can we find than to aid them to such means of self-support as still exist for them in the pitiful conditions where the white man's greed has forced them."[72] Her plan was sound and plausible, building upon a foundation that already existed.

Early in 1901, the IRA printed DuBois's article, "The Condition of the Mission Indians of Southern California," as one of their many pamphlets. She had begun her sixteen-page-long article describing the history of the Mission Indians as unique, having learned numerous trades taught by the Franciscan missionaries that "were practically applied in the daily life of the Mission community." And because these seeds, planted by the early friars, were still bearing fruit, as evidenced by their "tiny patches of level land" laboriously cultivated, she declared it was "not laziness which has brought them to want and despair." Instead, living on their heaps of rocks, the Indians had been expected "without tools, without water, and with miserable soil, to support a family and rise to the refinements of civilization." It was "the extremest cruelty, a pitiless irony, to require of the Indian that which would be an impossible task for a white man with all his superior advantages," she wrote. To provide readers with an accurate description of the true nature of their lands, she had included a list of the thirty reservations prepared for her by Mission Indian Agent Lucius A. Wright, with populations, distance from the agency, and land conditions. In almost one-third of the reservations, she noted there was "no water." She had omitted Manzanita from the list (population, fifty-seven) because the land was worthless, and Los Conejos, where the "people there said to be in very bad condition from poverty of land." She recommended the immediate allotment of the few good reservations.[73]

The IRA's Samuel Brosius was unimpressed with DuBois's article, explaining to Rev. William Henry Weinland, WNIA supervisor at the Ramona Mission in Southern California, that although he had "misgivings" about it, he was "not conversant sufficiently with the facts to take any part in the matter even by suggestion." Brosius had also been struck by DuBois's "advocacy of the continuation of the Mission Agency," explaining that "some time ago [he was] convinced that the agency should be abolished. If you cannot control a thing, *kill it*," he had concluded.[74] Brosius then wrote Welsh, explaining that although DuBois had "not radically erred" in her article, the effect of her writings was "overwrought, since one not very conversant with the situation would only apply her statements to the whole Mission Ind. Field." He described her view of the Indians' needs as too extreme and much too sympathetic, pointing out that Charles L. Partridge, an Indian advocate from Redlands, California, in a *Los Angeles Express* article, had criticized "such giving and refers to the Indian as being in a position of self-support." Brosius concluded that "it was most unfortunate that the friends of the Indian should waste their efforts in criticism when their united effort was so badly needed in the work of securing aid from Congress."[75]

Brosius proved to be quite disingenuous. Although critical of DuBois's pamphlet, in 1906 when trying to secure a $100,000 congressional appropriation to purchase land for some Northern California groups, he had copies made, presenting one to each senator.[76] One wonders whether, had the author of the pamphlet been a male, would Brosius's reaction have been the same, or was he simply reacting to a strong-opinioned woman whose writings had finally made the public take notice of the poor condition of the Mission Indians.[77]

Brosius was correct in that there was considerable disagreement among reformers. DuBois, Johnson, and Restarick viewed the condition of the Mission Indians as dire, while Charles L. Partridge, and his sister, Henrietta, secretary of the Redlands Indian Association, presented a more hopeful view. Accompanied by Reverend Weinland, superintendent of the Ramona Mission, and Mrs. Charles Meigs, a member of the Redlands association, the Partridges toured ten of the thirty-three Mission reservations for five days in mid-April 1901, representing a population of 1,000, or some two hundred families. They had found only three families whom they defined as destitute. As Brosius had pointed out, Partridge was critical of the indiscriminate distribution of supplies to any one village, viewing it as tending "to pauperize rather than to help the recipients." Balancing his report was another less graphic essay by DuBois explaining that the differing opinions among the friends of the Mission Indians was due to the number and "varying circumstances of the Indians included under this name."[78]

This disparity between reformers became even more complicated when Louise Hoppock, president of the Southern California Association, presented an uplifting view of the condition of the Mission Indians during an informal talk before the New York City Indian Association in May. She explained that "the majority of the Indians were found to be indignant over the reports of their starving condition." Quinton, serving as editor of *The Indian's Friend* at the time, fearful that such disagreement would hamper reform efforts, wrote in her editorial that the "harrowing statements 'of papers and travelers' and also those of Mr. Partridge could both be true though seemingly contradictory." She explained there was both deep poverty and real suffering at the same time as the more progressive Indians were getting "outside work and maintaining their families."[79] Later that summer, Quinton informed Weinland that DuBois had been greatly disturbed by Hoppock's address, fearing that such testimony would ruin the plans that she and her friends had made to purchase land for evicted Mission Indians. Quinton's greatest hope was that "all the friends of the Mission Indians of all types should *agree* upon *some* plan, and then push it. It needs *all* the forces for success," she had concluded.[80] DuBois eventually came to the same conclusion, writing in one of her articles that "contradictory accounts of their condition have been given by reliable people because it is impossible to summarize in a word the varying conditions in which they are found."[81]

DuBois expanded her correspondence to include Indian Commissioner William A. Jones, writing to him on January 15, 1901, concerned about a reclamation project to irrigate desert lands. She believed that improving the land would only bring an influx of white settlers. Jones assured her that Indian lands were safe, that "reservation trust patents in common" had been issued for many Mission reservations, and that land allotments in severalty had already been accomplished on several reservations. Furthermore, patented reservations were "absolutely secured to the Indians." Those not patented had been withdrawn from "entry and settlement and set apart" as executive order reservations.[82] Therefore, Jones explained, there was no way "by which such settlers can obtain title to land in said reservations under the public land laws."[83] Kate Foote's work at Rincon and that of other allotting agents was protecting Indian lands.

Seeking additional assurance, in early June DuBois wrote to Welsh that ever since she had written the pamphlet for his association, she had been urging Brosius and others to encourage the government to set aside "all the desert land now occupied by Indians, withdrawing it from [white] settlement." Only on the desert had the Indians been left alone, primarily because no one desired that land. However, the current movement to irrigate desert lands would result in the Indians' being driven off. Because Brosius had been successful in getting government instructions sent to the Los Angeles Land District office ordering that Indian rights be respected, she inquired if Welsh could have this order expanded to cover Indian-held lands in San Diego, Riverside, and San Bernardino Counties.

"Prevention is better than cure," she concluded, "it would be very little trouble for the Government to make all the Mission Indians secure in such lands as they now have, poor enough at the best."[84]

From Waterbury the previous month, DuBois informed Welsh that she had indirectly learned that the Warner Ranch Indians had lost their legal case—a loss she described as "nothing less than a crime." It made her "heart bleed to think what this enforced exile will mean to those people." She also provided Welsh with a bare outline of a plan with Nellie Doubleday to organize a corporation in California and the East to raise money to purchase the Santa Ysabel Ranch, which adjoined the reservations of Mesa Grande and Volcan. The price was "said to be $150,000.00, no small sum," but Doubleday had "influence with certain millionaires and does not despair of raising the money provided the scheme in all its details is so consistent as to present no difficulties in theory." Desirous of Brosius's assistance in developing the plan, she asked Welsh to forward her letter, and to provide his own opinion.[85]

Quinton was familiar with DuBois's plan to purchase the Santa Ysabel Ranch, turning one of the buildings into a school for Mission Indian teachers, and that she also wanted a mission station at Mesa Grande. In an August 1901 letter to Weinland, the former had written that it was unfortunate that the WNIA currently had no funds available to support DuBois. She had already explained to an unidentified DuBois supporter that her association had turned over all of their missionary work to the Moravian Board. However, eventually the WNIA might be able to "start a mission down there somewhere."[86] Unfortunately, the opportunity never presented itself.

In early July 1901, DuBois again returned to Southern California, and later in the month joined Brosius on a trip to "the poorer bands of the Indians, going by way of San Diego, to Mesa Grande, etc."[87] Brosius, in a letter to Reverend Weinland, explained that both DuBois and Mary Watkins, the government teacher at Mesa Grande, had accompanied him on a five-day trip to Mesa Grande, La Posta, and Manzanita. He described La Posta and Manzanita "in a sad plight—not over eight or ten acres available for farming for either band, the latter numbering about sixty souls." To emphasize his point, he asked: "Who of us would be willing to undertake to make a living upon such lands? Eight acres for 60 people at Manzanita!" He had, however, found some suitable land for pasture at Mesa Grande. Brosius was especially critical of Watkins, describing her as "too easily hoodwinked by the Indians, and in the habit of giving promiscuously when they importuned." While traveling to Manzanita, he had tried to impress upon both women "that true charity consisted not in giving, and thus weakening the manhood of a people, but to encourage them to self support, in all ways that would not have such a tendency." Based on what he had learned during the tour, Brosius felt he now had the "strength to fight for what is best much more intelligently than heretofore." He hoped that a three-man government committee would be sent to investigate the condition of the Indians and locate new lands for their use.[88] Unfortunately, he said nothing about either DuBois or Watkins influencing his thinking in any way.

On the same July day that Brosius wrote to Welsh, DuBois had sent a letter to attorney William Collier seeking his legal advice. Collier, serving his third year as the Special Attorney for the Mission Indians, responded four days later, pleased that she was willing to sacrifice herself by visiting remote villages, witnessing "some of the most pronounced horrors of the Indian service," which even some special agents "rarely see or know anything about." Her inquiry was correct: "no filings of any kind are permitted or accepted upon land known to be occupied by the Indians." He would be spending the next month looking over possible lands for government purchase for the Warner Ranch Indians and other groups for which eviction suits were pending. Although it was a sentimental suggestion, he was not convinced that trying to buy portions of Warner Ranch was the practicable way to proceed, as the hot springs at the village of Agua Caliente could not accommodate residents of the other four villages. Furthermore, the benefits at the springs were poorly distributed among current residents. Collier affirmed that he would be driving over to Mesa Grande to call on Watkins and that he hoped to meet up with DuBois during her summer visit.[89]

In October 1901, DuBois's articles on the Warner Ranch eviction appeared in *The Indian's Friend* and *The Land of Sunshine*. In the former, she had written that "humanity, justice, and a wise economy" urged immediate land purchase by Congress—sufficient land not only for those evicted but "overflow from the more destitute reservations." Initially championing allotment in severalty for the Mission Tule Agency, she had decided against it when she learned that "conditions in this field [were] peculiar and require separate treatment," realizing that the Indians first must be educated about their legal responsibilities; otherwise, through ignorance, they could lose what they had. In his October 1901 report, William Collier expressed similar misgivings.[90] It is unknown whether DuBois had conferred with him before writing her article. She was particularly concerned that the industrious and agricultural Mission Indians not be degraded by being accorded rations, "except as a temporary expedient for exiles." They only asked for tools and land. She concluded that "to starve on barren rocks would be a kindlier fate than to sink into the ranks of paupers."[91]

In a *Land of Sunshine* article, DuBois informed readers of the Warner Ranch Indians' loss in the Supreme Court. "Now they are waiting on sufferance of the owners until Congress meets this winter, when it is hoped that something will be done to provide a home for them." She urged readers to bring pressure to bear upon legislators to "realize that a question of humanity apart from politics is still of importance enough in this country to demand immediate solution." The old and the sick needed to be cared for "and in this rich and generous State it should be possible for the Government's wards to have the conditions of self-support bestowed upon them," she concluded.[92]

The history of the legal battle of the Warner Ranch Indians was long and complicated. The initial suit, *John G. Downey v. Alejandro Barker*, called for the eviction of the residents of Agua Caliente and the nearby Luiseño village of Puerta la Cruz. It was filed in July 1892 in the Superior Court of San Diego. A second suit, *John G. Downey v. Jesus Quevas, et al*, covering La Puerta, a Luiseño village, and San Jose and Mataguay, two small Kumeyaay villages, followed. The cases were eventually combined. The trial began in June 1893. Downey's death and the substitution of his nephew as plaintiff slowed the process. In December 1896 the court ruled against the Indians, and their lawyers, supported by the IRA, appealed to the California Supreme Court, which in October 1899 again ruled against the Indians. The case went to the federal Supreme Court; arguments were held in March 1901. On May 13, the Court upheld the lower court's decision. Despite the combined efforts of the IRA, which had funded the lawyers and provided the bond; the WNIA, which had established a medical missionary station at the village of Agua Caliente, with the hope of building a hospital; and the Sequoya League in their first reform effort, the Warner Ranch Indians, after decades of threats, lawsuits, and intimidation, were facing eviction.[93]

Reformers were surprised. They had expected the same outcome as in 1888 when the IRA had successfully defended the Mission village of Soboba.[94] But times had changed. A new home for the Warner Ranch Indians was selected in December 1901 during a week-long meeting between a special agent of the Interior Department and Agent Lucius A. Wright. The Indians, however, rejected it. Charles Fletcher Lummis then entered the picture. Having attended Harvard at the same time as Theodore Roosevelt, he went to Washington, DC, and personally lobbied the president for the creation of an advisory commission to select a new home. The Warner Ranch Indian Commission was created on May 28, 1902, with Lummis, Charles Partridge, and Russell C. Allen of the Sweetwater Fruit Company as members. Attorney William Collier, who served as their advisor on water rights, accompanied them on their investigative tours. DuBois had learned personally from Partridge in an August 12, 1902, letter that he had been selected to serve, explaining that the commission did not have sufficient money to buy even part of the Warner Ranch.[95] Following a month spent inspecting various Southern California sites for purchase, in October 1902 the commission selected the Pala Reservation as the Indians' permanent home.[96]

The much-publicized removal of the Warner Ranch Indians took place in May 1903.[97] Later that September they were joined at Pala by the San Felipe Indians, whose plight had been overshadowed by publicity devoted to the Warner Ranch villagers. DuBois was intimately familiar with San Felipe, having during her 1901 visit personally witnessed their intense attachment to their homes, describing in the *Southern Workman* that a "hut of adobe thatched with tule is dear to him than many a more lordly mansion ever is to its owner." During her overnight stay, she had slept in a new adobe home with glass windows and a shingle roof. The following day, the Indians expressed great sorrow at their having to move, explaining that their neat adobe chapel, just recently built, and this new home would have to be left behind.[98]

DuBois's articles on the Warner Ranch Indians appeared in *The Indian's Friend* and *The Land of Sunshine* the same month as her attendance at the annual Lake Mohonk Conference. During her allotted time, she described her previous summer's camping trip to several Mission villages, explaining she had traveled for several hundred miles in a wagon to visit "Indians living in the remote reservations far beyond the tourists' line of travel." Extreme desert conditions had forced her and her traveling companion, presumably Watkins, to continually inquire in advance about the availability of water for them and their horses. She saw "old Indians lying dying on the ground, with their head on a stone, ragged, absolutely without provision." Few current Mission Indian reservations, she explained, could adequately support their residents. Instead, the Indians were forced to "eke out their scanty harvests with Manzanita berries and acorns, boiled grass, or anything that can fill the stomach." Later that month, DuBois gave an address on the same trip before the annual meeting of the Waterbury auxiliary, after which

Figure 8. Attendees of the Lake Mohonk Conference of Friends of the Indians are photographed on the east porch of Mohonk Mountain House in 1899. Although no women reformers attended the first conference in 1883, this photograph reflects their large attendance a decade and a half later. (Mohonk Mountain House Archives.)

the membership elected her their first vice president. Early the following month, she spoke before a group at the Christ Church Parish house, displaying Indian baskets, pottery, bead work, and other crafts and at month's end attended the twentieth annual meeting of the Connecticut Indian Association in Hartford.[99]

During the first week of December 1901, DuBois traveled to Boston to attend her second WNIA annual meeting. There she discussed the Connecticut association's missionary work for the year, reporting their support of hospital work among the Wisconsin Oneidas and the Navajos, and their aid to Mission Indians, especially along industrial lines, with a pledge of $100 toward buying Indian baskets and drawn work. She also reported on Sophie Miller's lacemaking efforts at Mesa Grande, the prospect of teaching the men to carve, and her visits to remote Mission villages during the past six summers.[100] DuBois would attend only one more meeting of the national association in 1903, at which time she gave the Connecticut association's missionary report and explained that her branch, with its seventy-five members, was supporting destitute elderly Indians at Mesa Grande.[101]

That same December, DuBois had another article printed in *The Southern Workman* in which she suggested that the "friends of the Indians" organize and form a corporation to purchase land near each of what she described as desperately needy reservations and hire a farm superintendent to oversee the Indians as day farm laborers. In this same industrial center, a teacher could be hired to supervise the women in basketmaking and drawn work, such as had already been introduced successfully at Mesa Grande. She reminded her readers that in the past the Franciscan fathers had supervised Indians in such practical tasks as carving wood and horn, embossing leather, working in silver, iron, and copper, and binding books, concluding that "the occasion is ripe for some such scheme of extended industrial opportunity in private dealing with the nation's wards." She added that "the vexed Indian problem may find its ultimate solution in the assistance lent by non-political initiative to governmental methods, both tending to one end."[102]

Home in Waterbury in mid-February 1902, DuBois thanked Lummis for sending three issues of his magazine, which had been renamed *Out West* the previous month. She indicated that in the coming summer she intended to again look for land to purchase in the vicinity of Campo, a piece large enough for space for an industrial teacher and her work. It is unknown what happened to her plans to purchase the Santa Ysabel Ranch. In the winter of 1902, DuBois's newest concern was the need for a resident missionary for the Indians. She relayed to Lummis that the previous summer she had intended to walk over the mountains to visit an elderly blind woman, who lived a mile from Manzanita. She had never found the time, but she explained a missionary would have done so. However, she emphasized that the missionary should not be one who simply tried to convert the Indians "when they are already good Catholics." She lamented that the poor Indians had nothing; not even the local priest visited them. Needing assistance, DuBois expressed a willingness to work with Lummis and his Sequoya League, although she much preferred to pursue an independent course, helping out where she could, especially around the Campo region which laid heaviest on her heart. She explained she was currently sending money to a local Campo storekeeper to purchase provisions for the old and sick.[103]

Although Campo was not assigned a missionary, it did receive a government field matron, an appointment that DuBois credited to the efforts of her Waterbury branch but for which Charles E. Shell, Superintendent and Special Disbursing

Agent at Pala, personally took credit. Sometime in 1904, Mamie Robinson was appointed as a field matron to the San Diego County Kumeyaay reservations of Campo, La Posta, Manzanita, Laguna, and Cuyapipa (Cuyapaipe), commonly referred to as the Five Campo Reservations, supervised by Shell and located in the Sierra Madre Mountains near the Mexican border.[104] DuBois described these small reservations as having little tillable land and a combined population of only one hundred forty individuals, largely old and infirm, with a few children, all in dire need of aid.[105] Robinson, who remained until 1909, was assisted by two young Mesa Grande Indians, Frances Lachappa and Rosalia Nejo, whom Lummis described as "educated, refined, of high character, and of clear intelligence." Under Robinson's supervision, the two young Indian women started a school and taught Indian women to sew, remake clothing, cook, and weave baskets. Nejo was employed by the Sequoya League, which provided money for local supplies and school lunches. Agent Shell, pleased with their work, provided them with a wagon and team to better visit local families.[106]

Edward H. Davis, a confidant of DuBois, described Lachappa and Nejo as doing great work at Campo, sending their photographs to her. In 1885, Davis, an artist, artifact collector, and photographer, had moved to San Diego for his health, eventually settling in Mesa Grande.[107] He informed DuBois that the two young Indian women could "reach the people so much better than a white matron." The villagers, he explained, had become dependent upon them, for they served as "a constant object lesson & inspiration to those poor creatures, showing the possibilities that may be latent in themselves." Although they were working under difficult circumstances, Davis noted that the Sequoya League had recently donated a bit of money for them. Months later he described their work at Campo as an unqualified success: the school already had fourteen pupils, and "whole families have moved to Campo so as to have their children receive the benefit of the school." Sympathizing with DuBois's continual struggle to secure funds for her Indian work, he wrote that he wished he had money to help her.[108]

In October 1903, DuBois hosted the annual meeting of the Waterbury auxiliary in her home, delivering "an interesting talk on her recent trip to California." During that meeting she was elected association president.[109] Two months later, curious about the current condition of the Warner Ranch Indians, who had been removed to Pala in May of that year, she wrote to Agent Shell on December 19. He responded late in the month that both they and the former residents of San Felipe were getting along nicely. He had not been forced to issue rations yet. Portable houses had been erected and able-bodied men were hard at work farming, some on the ten acres each head of a household had been given. Shell had, however, found some elderly individuals who were destitute in several nearby reservations and had issued rations.[110]

The following October, DuBois wrote Lummis that she was sorry she had not been able to visit him before she left California, explaining that she had spent ten days at Campo during the summer becoming acquainted with Mamie Robinson. "You may trust her to do anything in her power for the Indians," DuBois had written from the Lake Mohonk Conference, which she described as very crowded but at the same time very interesting, explaining she had managed "some private conversations which will be useful." Like fellow reformers, she believed the solution for the Mission Indians was for the government to purchase additional lands near current reservations, retaining both old and new. "I do not think they would consent to a distant removal, nor is it necessary," she concluded.[111]

In November, DuBois informed Lummis that she was pleased he was going to visit the five Campo reservations to see the conditions under which they were living and make a record and a report. She explained to Lummis that Collier, both in his last letter and his last visit, had heartily agreed with the idea of purchasing small farming tracts near present settlements, enabling the Indians to "go back and forth to work their crops as a white man does on his farm." To her dismay, she had just learned from him that Agent Shell was currently proposing to move the Indians to the desert, digging wells for them, and that the government favored his plans. Convinced Shell was mistaken in this approach, she had earlier conferred at Lake Mohonk with Indian Commissioner Jones, who had "heartily agreed that these Indians should not be moved from their present homes." Shell, DuBois explained, was new to the job and "does not realize how hopeless has been the condition of the desert Indians." Not only did it take years for wells to be dug, they often failed, reminding Lummis of the futile attempt at Martínez where "the contractor was dishonest, machinery broke, supply was a failure, [and] the Indians [left] in despair." And according to Collier, it had cost the government $10,000 to get a decent water supply at Torres. Furthermore, if the Indians were moved, the industrial school she was planning could not be built, and the basket work would cease. Fearing that the entire desert would eventually be irrigated by white homesteaders, DuBois concluded that it was far better to keep the Indians in their homes, to create industrial opportunities for the women and a school for the children, and to provide small plots of land nearby for the men to farm.

That way the men could "stay at home and not have to travel as they do now so far from work that home life is practically broken up."[112]

In mid-November, Lummis suggested to DuBois that she no longer send money to H. M. Johnson, who was currently distributing her funds to the indigent. Instead, he recommended E. H. Weeger as "that rare bird, a trader who really thinks more of the Indians than of himself"—a "most painfully honest trader." And in reference to her basket project, Lummis suggested that she deal directly with him, assuring her that his wife and daughter could easily sell many.[113]

Late in the month, Lummis informed DuBois that joined by Agent Shell and Wayland H. Smith, secretary of the Sequoya League, he had traveled by wagon to the five Campo reservations on November 7 and had taken forty-four photographs to be used for a future public presentation and to illustrate an article in his magazine.[114] Unable to locate any land adjacent to the reservations fit to recommend for government purchase, Lummis incorrectly presumed that since the Indians had only lived in their present homes for a generation, they might consent to move. He had made the same assumption about the Warner Ranch Indians, who had fought long and hard to remain in their homes. In the summer of 1903, Mary Watkins had informed DuBois that the residents of Agua Caliente were so determined to stay that "they tried to kill Mr. Lummis for he talked too much, not understanding their condition of mind."[115] Lummis also explained that Shell no longer favored sending Campo Reservation residents to the desert, unless they wished to go. "And doubtless they would not wish" to do so, he concluded. Lummis had also secured $200 worth of seed grain from residents of San Diego and raised over $130 for the old and sick for the upcoming winter.[116]

In March 1905, Edward Davis informed DuBois that he had sent Commissioner Francis E. Leupp some photos of old, blind, half-starved Indians at Mesa Grande to make him aware of their current condition. "It [had] reached the right spot," he happily concluded. In mid-May, Davis offered DuBois accommodations in one of the floored tents he was constructing as well as the use of a horse part time during her usual summer visit.[117] She, however, had a far better offer. On June 23, Clark Wissler, the acting curator of the American Museum of Natural History in New York City, provided her with a railway ticket and $130 to purchase specimens for the museum, $50 of which she could use for recording songs and myths. Additional funding was possible if she could find interesting materials. According to Erik Trump, DuBois's anthropological work was important in that it "held the power to combat negative stereotypes about

Indians," for it gave her the opportunity in her historical articles to revise the opinion that Indians were "a naturally indolent race, disinclined to work of itself" by documenting their actual struggle to eke out a living in the most inhospitable environments.[118]

DuBois ended that summer of 1905 presenting a paper on religious ceremonies and myths of the Mission Indians at the American Anthropological Association meeting in San Francisco in late August. On August 18, Alfred L. Kroeber, of the Department of Anthropology at the University of California in San Francisco, wrote to her at Chula Vista, apologizing for being unable to meet her in person. He enclosed a program, noting that her paper would probably be presented on the afternoon of the first day and that he had arranged for both a Columbia and an Edison phonograph to play her recordings.[119] An article in the *Riverside Enterprise* reported that she had accompanied her paper with "phonograph records of weird songs of the Indians."[120] In early September, Kroeber wrote to her in Waterbury, explaining that because she had left so quickly, he had not had the opportunity to mention that papers presented during the meeting were to be published in the *American Anthropologist*. He hoped she would agree to have it included.[121]

A month earlier, Agent Shell had written to DuBois complaining that he was having difficulty securing sufficient money to purchase food and clothing for the elderly and dependent Indians under his charge. He suggested that she write to Lummis on their behalf, cautioning her to keep his name out of it, otherwise "if known [it] might result in much mischief."[122] Instead, from Chula Vista DuBois wrote directly to Indian Commissioner Leupp, who informed her he had recommended that the Interior Department allow Shell to spend $500 from time to time as needed, assuring her that his office was "alive to the situation" and would do "whatever the conditions will justify and its means will allow."[123] In response to another letter, proposing he send $500 every two months to Shell, Commissioner Leupp explained that his total appropriation for the Mission Indians was only $5,000 plus "a small unexpended balance of an old appropriation for the 'Relief of Destitute Indians' which has to be held subject to drafts of driblet sums to meet practically mortal emergencies."[124] DuBois again wrote the commissioner in late October concerned about who the department would be sending to purchase the land for the Indians. She had suggested either William Collier or Charles L. Partridge, both familiar with the California terrain. Leupp assured her that she "need not be at all worried about [his] sending an Eastern person there, for nothing was further from [his] thought."[125]

CHAPTER 3

While DuBois was busy touring and corresponding on behalf of the beleaguered Mission Indians in the southern part of the state, the Northern California Indian Association, the NIA San Jose affiliate, was already hard at work on their solution for the homeless Indians of their part of the state. To address their plight, during the summer of 1903, C. E. Kelsey, the auxiliary's general secretary, had presented a memorial letter to President Theodore Roosevelt during his June trip to Northern California. The following January, a formal petition, supported by the WNIA, the IRA, Lake Mohonk, and Lummis and the Sequoya League, was presented before Congress by Senator Bard. The legislature appropriated $10,000 for a census and a formal investigation of the condition of these Northern California tribes. Appointed to conduct the census, Kelsey traveled thousands of miles. In June 1906, Congress authorized $100,000 ($3,553,322 in 2025 dollars) for land purchases. To aid the bill's passage, Brosius had handed copies of DuBois's pamphlet to the senators. However, he made sure to clarify that the real service had been done by Kelsey's personal report.[126] Two years later Congress made a second appropriation of $50,000.[127]

Upon learning that Kelsey might be visiting Southern California, in late October 1905 DuBois wrote recommending he consult Robinson at Campo and include Collier in his tour group, explaining that there was a great need around Campo to find suitable land to purchase. Kelsey thanked her for her "information and especially for the practical suggestions as to remedial measures," promising her he would visit Campo as soon as he was able to.[128] A month later, DuBois learned from Kroeber that if she returned to Southern California the following summer he hoped "to be able to arrange to have [her] do some work" for his Anthropology Department, enabling her to collect all myths and ceremonials possible.[129] In May, Kroeber declared he had received permission for her work, recommending $300 for two months—$5 a day to be used to gather "myths and ceremonies in notes and on the phonograph, but not including archeological work or collecting." He added that a small separate amount might be found for the collection of specimens.[130]

DuBois responded that the New York Museum had already secured a railroad pass and reduced transportation for her, prompting Kroeber to immediately correspond with Wissler about her obligation to his museum. Once assured that there was none, Kroeber informed DuBois on June 20 that $300 would be available from the National Bank of Commerce of San Diego, with a smaller amount made available for her to collect anthropological specimens.[131] Months later, he congratulated her on her successful fieldwork, especially having secured "a few pieces of old feather work." He would be pleased if she could find some old used baskets because the anthropology museum had only a few unused specimens of Luiseño or Diegueño basketry.[132] In a short statement in a September issue, the *Pittsburg Press* reported that DuBois had completed "an important investigation of the ceremonies, myths and religion of the Louisene [*sic*] or Mission Indians" for the University of California.[133]

That September, while still at Mesa Grande, DuBois wrote to Kelsey, who responded that after making a fairly exhaustive examination of the Campo reservation months earlier, he had found "no place in that whole country that fulfills the requirements." He described the situation as simply "a choice between the less and the less fit." One problem at Campo was the presence of a very large strip of alkali land as well as the potential of a large supply of liquor readily available from neighboring white settlers. Kelsey was beginning to doubt the wisdom of buying separate tracts adjoining each of the little reservations as DuBois and others had suggested.[134] In early November, Kelsey informed DuBois that he planned to return to Campo mid-month. His preference was to purchase "one of the many farms to the north and move the Indians there, but that may be among the impossibilities" if owners refused to sell.[135]

In mid-November, with winter approaching, DuBois, concerned especially about the elderly, wrote Commissioner Leupp to ensure that money was readily available to feed them. He responded that government authority had been granted to the superintendents of the San Jacinto, Pala, and Mesa Grande schools to expend monies for the purchase of subsistent supplies for the old and infirm Indians under their charge.[136] In the meantime, she was being continually updated on the current conditions at the Five Campo Reservations by Robinson and Watkins. Setting aside her correspondence, in mid-December DuBois attended the twenty-fifth annual meeting of the Connecticut Indian Association, one of thirty women at the business meeting. She presented her report on the work of the committee on Indian industrial arts, noting there was only $1.58 remaining of the $200 they had raised.[137]

In January 1907, Robinson thanked DuBois for her ten-dollar check, expressing concern about a comment she had made about feeling unwell. Fortunately, the Indians were doing unusually well despite recent snows and extreme cold. The reason, no doubt, was her continued issuance of rations. In the meantime, Robinson and her assistants were making cotton flannel underwear for the

CHAPTER 3

Indians. She informed DuBois that Kelsey had visited in December, taking bids on various properties, and that by March it would be known what lands would be purchased. Robinson also noted that the women were making fewer baskets that winter because their husbands had had a good crop of beans and potatoes. In a February letter, she wrote that she would be getting two more baskets in the mail and that the work on the flannel underwear continued. Robinson concluded that she was sorry to learn that DuBois was not so well. The latter had begun to complain of nerve strain as early as 1905, prompting Erik Trump to remark that if physical pain and mental illness had not cut short her career, DuBois "would likely have become a prominent member of the intellectual elite that 'discovered' the American Indian in the 1910s and 20s,"[138] an era dominated by an assault on assimilation led by such prominent figures as John Collier and Mable Dodge Luhan.[139]

Several days later Watkins also wrote to DuBois, again concerned about her health issues, wishing her absolute winter rest like that of bears and squirrels. She reminded her friend that a mere seven years before even the agent "did not know that Campo's poor people existed." He only paid them a visit after Watkins had written to him. Now with DuBois's help, wonderful "changes are coming," the schoolteacher concluded, asking DuBois if she could "have accomplished as much in any other work?"[140] Lummis also praised her efforts on the Indians' behalf, explaining that the Los Angeles Public Library, the fourteenth largest in the country, was creating a special "Autograph Archive of People who Count." He sent her a special page to sign and requested she return it in the enclosed mailing tube.[141]

DuBois's undisclosed illness, however, did not prevent her from continuing her correspondence with government officials. In early May she learned from Acting Commissioner Charles F. Larrabee that with Kelsey's recommendation, the Department of the Interior had been authorized on February 23, 1907, to purchase certain tracts of land for the Campo Indians for $14,560 (worth $495,348 in 2025 dollars)—a parcel with an abundance of running water. At the present time the department was not contemplating any removals, allowing the Indians to retain both tracts of land. The May 10 issue of the *San Diego Union and Daily Bee* quoted Kelsey as declaring that now every tribe and band in Southern California had been provided with a parcel of good land.[142]

DuBois was reelected as president of the Waterbury Indian Association on January 27, 1908, and during the annual meeting of the Connecticut association in early December reelected to the Committee on Indian Industrial Art. However, at year's end, she sent out an open letter to the Waterbury Indian Association explaining that although she was not well enough for active work, she could not forget the old pensioners in the mountains of San Diego County. With cold weather approaching and the association's Indian fund low, she was making her annual appeal for the old, blind, infirm, and helpless. The $536 she spent the previous year had been divided between four different villages, leaving about ten cents a day for each. Because she knew every person receiving aid, she could vouch "for the great necessity of continuing this work." With government resources limited, there was no use looking to them for support. She had included an undated letter from Edward Davis, who had enclosed a list of each individual Indian receiving assistance, describing them as "desperately poor, lacking nearly everything to make them comfortable," concluding that if donors "could see these old people in their homes they would never grudge the money."[143]

A November 1910 issue of the *Bridgeport Times* reported that Mrs. Mary Watkins, a friend of DuBois, was the principal speaker at the annual meeting of the Connecticut association. Watkins described the wonderful work that DuBois had accomplished, asserting that ever since her first visit to California in 1897 DuBois had given herself to bettering the condition of the Indians. Watkins related her travels with the reformer from "reservation to reservation distributing flour and other foodstuffs among the suffering Indians," noting that of the two hundred six people living on the reservation when DuBois first arrived, only seventy remained. Watkins concluded, they "are dying out in this proportion all over the West."[144]

By 1909, DuBois had disappeared from the public record. The 1930 federal census placed her in the Hartford Retreat Insane Asylum. Her death certificate recorded she had suffered from senility for twenty years, cerebral arteriosclerosis for fifteen years, and chronic myocarditis for eighteen years. The day before her death, on August 18, 1934, she suffered a cerebral hemorrhage.[145] Constance Goddard DuBois was buried in Riverside Cemetery in Waterbury, Connecticut.

During one short decade of work DuBois almost singlehandedly had kept the plight of the Mission Indians before the American reading public. She had written to and worked with some of the most prominent Indian reformers of her day, reflecting a strong sense of collaboration on the part of various reform groups and other philanthropists interested in the Indians' welfare. She helped bring about a resurgence of Native basketmaking and preserved traditions that might otherwise have been lost as she recorded their songs, stories, and myths. Although supported by her Waterbury auxiliary and the larger national association, DuBois had carried out most of her work alone, spending long hours touring remote villages, taking photographs, collecting museum specimens, and later writing her articles and addressing public meetings in Connecticut and elsewhere. She had made a difference for those living at Mesa Grande and Campo, feeding the hungry and encouraging the women to engage in their traditional crafts to augment family incomes. Her work on their behalf is a perfect example of how the WNIA, even as it promoted the government's policy of assimilation, continued to improve the daily lives of many Indians.

While supporting her Native basketmaking program, DuBois had worked closely with Nellie Doubleday, who like many WNIA members also wore numerous hats. Under her pen name, Neltje Blanchan, Doubleday wrote a number of nature books on such varied subjects as gardening, wildflowers, and birds. She also was a member of the WNIA's Department of Indian Industries and treasurer of the Bay Ridge Branch of the Brooklyn Indian Association, a WNIA affiliate. To support her association's Epworth Piegan Indian Mission in Montana, Doubleday had written a pamphlet in 1892 titled *The Piegan Indians*. The missionary work of this Brooklyn-funded Indian mission is the subject of the next chapter.

CHAPTER 4

New York Reformers and the Montana Piegan Station

New York women, like their Connecticut counterparts, played a prominent role in the work of the Women's National Indian Association.[1] The first three WNIA presidents, Mary Lucinda Bonney, Mary Lowe Dickinson, and Amelia Stone Quinton, were from the state of New York, and the first two branches organized outside of Philadelphia were in Amsterdam and Gloversville, New York, where in June 1881 Quinton met with and organized local women. Speaking before Chautauqua-like public meetings, women's groups, and in personal meetings with the wives of leading clergymen, Quinton began to spread word of her association's work. One such meeting of clerics' wives in Syracuse consented to be the first WNIA state committee.[2] In August 1881 Quinton held meetings in Western New York, returning in September to

Clifton Springs Sanitarium to address "persons of best influence" who "took impressions home with them to various sections of the country, feeling the need of earnest action against our national wrongs to Indians."[3] Between October 7 and the 24, 1881, Quinton organized Indian committees in Rochester, Syracuse, Auburn, and Buffalo, and added another on November 10 in Brooklyn, followed by an address in a New York City church.[4]

A committee, the least complicated of all the different forms of WNIA organizations, generally required Quinton to return and reorganize. She did so on December 4, 1882, where during a ladies' union meeting in a Brooklyn church, she organized the Brooklyn Indian Association. The following day, with fifteen women present, Quinton organized the New York City Indian Association (NYCIA) in the Madison Avenue home of Mrs. William E. Dodge (née Melissa Phelps).[5] The decision to meet in her home was strategic on Quinton's part, for Melissa Dodge's husband, a philanthropist long interested in various reforms, had been appointed to the first Board of Indian Commissioners in 1869. Devoted Presbyterians, the couple were also members of the National Temperance Society, Mr. Dodge having served as its first president.[6]

The first president of the newly organized NYCIA was Angeline Ensign Newman, daughter of Rev. Datus Ensign, an early Methodist minister in northern New York State, and the wife of Bishop John Philip Newman, a prominent Methodist Episcopal cleric. While living in Washington, DC, Reverend Newman had served three terms as Chaplain of the Senate and was pastor to President Ulysses S. Grant and family. Angeline Newman's interest in Indian reform could well have dated from her husband's work with Grant, whose "peace policy" had included the assignment of Indian agencies to various Protestant denominations. Her husband's association with Grant continued between 1879 and 1882 when he served as pastor of the Central Church in New York City, where Grant was a trustee.[7] As an astute organizer, Quinton, who had wisely chosen Angeline Newman, often sought out prominent clerics and their wives to support her crusade, always considering the possibility of holding her educational meetings in their churches.

Within two years of its founding, the NYCIA had grown to eighty members, raised $600, printed and distributed more than one thousand pages of information, influenced publication in the city's daily press of numerous articles on Indian issues, and sent petitions to Congress for suggested legislation. Newman resigned in 1884 and was succeeded by Mrs. D. P. Kidder (née Harriette Smith), who before she became the second wife of prominent Methodist Episcopal minister Daniel Parish Kidder in 1842,[8] had graduated from the Amenia Seminary in New York, the first woman ever enrolled; taught in Methodist women's schools in three states; and served as principal of the Worthington Seminary in Ohio. After marriage and before she became president of the NYCIA, she had founded the Orphan's Asylum in Newark, New Jersey, and the Mother's Association in Evanston, Illinois. These and other accomplishments prompted *The Christian Advocate* in her obituary to describe Harriette Kidder as engaging in "nearly a century of distinguished social and humanitarian service."[9] According to *The Indian's Friend*, the NYCIA thrived under her faithful and able care, with the membership contributing $500 to the national association's Indian Home Building Fund for the construction of several cottages for young Indian couples in Sitka, Alaska. Kidder served until 1887, replaced by Mrs. Theodore Irving, described in *The Indian's Friend* as a writer, with the power to "interest and charm as a speaker," and a firm believer that knowledge of "the past and present status of the Indian was all that was necessary to interest intelligent, right-minded men and women in his behalf."[10]

In 1890 the NYCIA raised $1,000 for teachers' salaries and the building of a chapel at the Mission Indian village of Soboba, part of the Ramona Mission complex. Five years later the association had raised a total of $8,800 ($335,028 in 2025 dollars), monies going to hospital work, the Home Building Fund, and the Home for Aged Indian Women at Porcupine Creek, on the Pine Ridge Agency in South Dakota.[11] Branch membership had grown to include auxiliaries in Harlem, organized November 1887; the Yonkers-on-Hudson Branch, founded in 1890, which supported the Maternity Hospital in Sitka and the Home for the Aged Indian Women; the Poughkeepsie Branch founded in February 1891;[12] the Kingston Branch organized in 1893; the Hopewell Junction branch formed in 1895; and one in New Rochelle.[13]

A year after founding the NYCIA, on March 22, 1883, Quinton organized the Women's Eastern New York Indian Association in Albany.[14] Two years later, during a visit to one of their meetings, Quinton suggested they form branch associations in Poughkeepsie, Hudson, Troy, Utica, and Syracuse. The membership agreed, and Mrs. William Winslow Crannell (née Elizabeth Keller Shaule), the association's general secretary, organized in Poughkeepsie on June 2, 1885, and at Troy, May 18, 1885.[15] Crannell, in her 1887 report, noted their new branch at Syracuse, which Quinton had organized on February 1, 1886, already had fifty-one members. Her own branch in Albany had held eight regular meetings with prominent speakers including General Samuel C. Armstrong and the Rev. R. B. Frissell of Hampton Institute. Crannell reported that their goal for the coming year was to raise $500 to support a missionary among one of the more than eighty tribes and parts thereof with no resident missionary. She explained that the "government opens all reservations to us, and gives us free rent for the work," to teach children to read and write English, young parents "to make comfortable and attractive homes out of scanty materials," and women "how to cook the foods of civilization," but "*most surely, teaching all within reach, in the simplest ways, redeeming Christian truths.*" Crannell reminded her fellow members that the annual dues of $1 constituted only about two cents a week.[16]

On September 29, 1884, the Western New York Indian Association was organized in Rochester with two hundred women attending,[17] and on March 2, 1885, Quinton organized an Indian committee in Buffalo, with a Brewster, New York, auxiliary also announced.[18] During 1889 the Saratoga Indian Association was organized on February 7, as well as one in Hamilton on February 4, its president informing *The Indian's Friend* that they had grown to fifty members and that WNIA co-founder, Mary Lucinda Bonney Rambaut, had returned home to Hamilton and "is our constant aid and inspirer."[19] At a January 23, 1896, meeting of the Thursday Morning Club, Quinton organized an Indian committee in New Rochelle and on September 14, 1897, an Indian committee in Binghamton.[20] Thus in less than two decades New York was crisscrossed with WNIA auxiliaries with a membership large enough to support the national association's missionary stations as well as fund their own auxiliary missionary work.

Once the WNIA determined to undertake the founding of missionary stations in 1883, Quinton, as head of the national Missionary Committee, was poised to direct the process. From the beginning she wrote the lengthy annual missionary reports, selected missionary sites, visited completed missions, and wrote to Indian Office officials for lands grants, field matrons, or whatever she felt essential to promote their work. She often traveled to Washington to personally confer with Indian commissioners and interior secretaries on urgent issues. Although she visited the Indian Territory in 1884 on her first missionary-associated trip, in her other role as the WNIA's secretary, she had been on the road for more than a year organizing new affiliates. In that year alone, Quinton covered more than 10,000 miles throughout Pennsylvania and neighboring states, founding new auxiliaries and addressing public meetings, urging the women in her audiences to join.[21] She carefully stressed the missionary role of the WNIA, explaining that even though for "the first years wholly devoted to gaining political rights for the Indians," the association had emerged "from the missionary spirit as was afterward the planting [of] missions in the tribes."²² She was the embodiment of the perfect leader for the WNIA missionary effort.

In one of her many addresses, Quinton described "the Indian problem" as largely in the hands of Christian women; their "work and heart are needed, and *because* these are *needed, God* has already employed both." Although the initial impulse of the WNIA was to engage in missionary work on behalf of Indian women and children, she explained they first had to "create a strong, *united Christian sentiment*" within the country in order to "achieve just Congressional action on behalf of Indians."²³ The IRA's founding and its assumption of most of the WNIA's political efforts had freed the membership to begin missionary work among Indian women, to minister to "their great sufferings from barbarism," to enlighten "their physical, mental and spiritual ignorance," and to teach them "of a Savior longing to help them."²⁴

Quinton had proposed the initial guidelines for this new missionary undertaking in a February 13, 1883, resolution, which had passed without debate.²⁵ That year's *Annual Report* recorded that work would begin among women and children. Following white cultural assumptions about what was thought best for Indigenous people, maternalistic WNIA missionaries were to teach Indian children to speak, read, and write English and their mothers "how to cook the foods of civilization and how to care for their children." Jane Simonsen noted that by adopting this specialization, "the WNIA carved out a niche for itself by stressing the need to address Indian women in particular."²⁶ Quinton and her Missionary Committee selected sites for their stations from a listing of over sixty tribes without a resident missionary, provided by Indian Commissioner Hiram Price in his 1882 annual report. The WNIA later published the list in an association pamphlet.²⁷ Over the years, Quinton refined her original goals, recommending a first-class mission to include a night school for adults; domestic art and industrial training; medical and hospital support; and instruction in gardening, farming, and mechanic arts, along with Christian teaching on weekends and Sunday.²⁸

By 1893, Quinton settled on a simple statement of "pioneer missionary work in tribes unprovided with religious teaching and domestic instruction."²⁹ After retiring as president in 1905, she remained chairman of the Missionary Department, now called the Department of Missions, describing their work two years later as twenty-three years old and unique. Their original plans had been to go to tribes without missionaries, secure "wherever practicable land among them, with their consent and that of Government," build a cottage home for the missionaries, and a chapel if possible, and then hand the mission over, free of charge, with all of its properties, to "whichever of the great Home Mission Societies should adopt the station for permanent work." They then started anew with the next project. She explained their work had already expanded into almost twenty states—"all with the object of "saving and [the] elevation of our native pagan tribes."[30] Ultimately the WNIA established over sixty missionary stations during more than seventy years of activity, more than half under Quinton's watch.[31]

WNIA missionary effort was a continuation of that undertaken by earlier individuals and missionary societies as part of the settler-colonial process. In his book on Protestant missions, Robert E. Berkhofer described the "conversion to Christ and civilization" as an instructional issue, viewing mission stations as "educational establishments in the broadest sense." If persuaded by the right reasoning, the Indian would adopt the ways of the dominant society, learning how to farm, pray, and behave. Berkhofer concluded that the functions of "piety, learning and industry" were to be taught in all stations whether "large model communities in the form of manual labor boarding schools or small model families as represented by a missionary couple."[32] Although Berkhofer was describing missionary work undertaken a century earlier, he could easily have been describing the work of the WNIA, which founded both types of stations. The Epworth Piegan Indian Mission in Montana, whose history appears in this chapter, serves as an example of Berkhofer's small model families and the most common type employed by the WNIA. The national association did fund several large model communities, such as the Greenville Boarding School and two hospitals on the Navajo Reservation. The histories of these hospitals appear in following chapters.

With assimilation as an ultimate goal, Berkhofer wrote that "missionaries and their supporters believed both Indian institutions and Indian 'character' had to be transformed."[33] Quinton "took it on faith that assimilation was the most logical path . . . to overcome hatred of Indians and inspire a sense of moral culpability in powerful white Americans to transform native people."[34] She believed in the power of Christianity to transform American Indians into "civilized" citizens. Thus, WNIA-sponsored missionaries conducted regular church services while their wives taught Indian women white housekeeping skills using their association-funded missionary cottage as a laboratory.³⁵ In so doing, the WNIA not only implemented the government's Indian policy but helped shape it.

In 1884, association president, Mary Lucinda Bonney, informed her membership that following recommendations from Interior Secretary Henry Teller and Commissioner Price, the national association had selected the Ponca Agency in the Indian Territory to be their first mission station project. In May 1884, a Miss Howard and a Mrs. McGlashan arrived. Because the agency served three tribes—the Ponca, Pawnee, and Otoe—Agent John W. Scott suggested that two separate stations be set up. After weeks of observation, Howard chose the Poncas, and McGlashan the Otoes. The Pawnee were assigned to the Woman's Home Missionary Society of the Methodist Episcopal Church, which had applied earlier for a station. In reporting the arrival of the two WNIA missionaries to "labor among the women of these tribes in teaching them the arts and economies of domestic life," Agent Scott described their effort as "highly important and praiseworthy" since "the education of the Indian woman has been heretofore entirely neglected."³⁶

The Brooklyn Indian Association had been the first New York auxiliary to support the national association's missionary work, assuming funding of the Ponca and Otoe Indian mission stations in the summer of 1884. The following year they began the process of transferring the missionary work to the care of the Brooklyn Women's Congregational Committee, composed largely of members of the Brooklyn auxiliary. To raise money, these women, with the consent of their pastors, asked each of their Congregational churches to contribute $100.³⁷ In support, Henry Ward Beecher, pastor of the Plymouth Congregational Church in Brooklyn Heights, invited Quinton on December 18, 1885, to address his congregation. Beecher, a leader of the Second Great Awakening and a former abolitionist who also supported the moral power of women, was a charismatic spokesman for evangelical Christianity. One of six sons of clergyman Lyman Beecher, he had two activist sisters, Catharine Beecher, founder of the Hartford Female Seminary, author of *A Treatise on Domestic Economy* (1841), and leader of the first women-driven petition on behalf of the Indians; and Harriet Beecher Stowe, author of *Uncle Tom's Cabin* and a member of the Connecticut Indian Association. A half-sister, Isabella Beecher Hooker, had founded the Connecticut Woman Suffrage Association, and a granddaughter, Annie Beecher Scoville, later served as chairman of the WNIA's Home Building and Loan Department.

In a letter published in the March 31, 1887, issue of *The National Baptist*, Quinton described having approached Reverend Beecher's invitation with trepidation. She had begged "to be excused from mounting the high platform," but his "gentle, reassuring humor broke the spell of fright," putting her at ease long enough to ask the congregation to share in the cost of a missionary's salary and his cottage. Reverend Beecher then mounted the platform, spoke of "his father's deep interest in Indians" and of his own concern, concluding it would be a great gratification to him if his congregation took up the project, paying "a share of what we owe to the Indians." Five hundred dollars was raised, enabling Quinton to transfer the Ponca and Otoe missionary stations to the Brooklyn Congregational Committee in February 1886.[38] In June of the following year, this same work was transferred to permanent control of the Woman's Home Missionary Society of the Methodist Episcopal Church, which had initially assumed missionary work among the Pawnee, thus consolidating all Methodist Episcopal Indian work within the Indian Territory.[39]

Brooklyn members did not wait long to begin their next work. In 1889 they raised $500 for three months' salary, traveling expenses, and a missionary cottage in the Indian Territory for Reverend Joshua H. Given, a Kiowa native, who was also a Presbyterian minister. A graduate of Carlisle Indian Industrial School and of Lincoln University and its Theological Seminary, Given was already known to Brooklyn Indian Association members, having addressed one of their meetings in January 1884.[40] Instead of turning over initial funds collected by Brooklyn members to the WNIA, monies were passed directly to the Presbyterian Board of Home Missions, which from the beginning had agreed to take over the station once it was up and running.[41]

In January 1889, Joshua Given addressed Brooklyn members at Association Hall. A *Brooklyn Eagle* reporter described him as a student missionary, a "tall, athletic man of about 30," who spoke "in a slow and deliberate manner that was decidedly impressive." He explained that before visiting the Comanche and Kiowa reservation several months earlier, where he hoped to engage in missionary work, he had celebrated "the national holiday, the Fourth of July, with the good people of Philadelphia." Although not a citizen, he gloried in the country's institutions. Understanding from white friends that although he was American born, he was ineligible for citizenship, Reverend Given informed his audience that "no one has a right to deny me that which a foreigner may attain." His nine years of residency in Pennsylvania had entitled him to citizenship, he explained, "and I am bound to have it."[42]

During his most recent visit to the Kiowa Reservation, Given recounted, Chief Lone Wolf had accompanied him on the seventy-mile-long trip from the

Kiowa agency to his camp, declaring, "I had nothing with me but a sachel [*sic*] containing a change of clothing and a Bible." As they traveled on horseback, the young minister explained biblical teachings to the chief, who "saw the light from it and is now a firm believer in its teachings." Lone Wolf would later join the Baptist Church. At his camp, the chief proudly showed off "his waving fields of corn" and his almost seven hundred head of cattle. Given had been equally successful with the chief medicine man, who later not only became "a believer in the only true God" but sent his two daughters to the agency school. Based on his success with Lone Wolf and the medicine man, Given concluded that all the Indians really wanted was "good teachers and good Christians for the advancement of this work."[43]

In a September 30, 1889, letter in *The Indian's Friend*, Given described the warm welcome he had received by his people. He not only attended a council of the Kiowa, Comanche, and Wichita, who shared the reservation, but was welcomed by Lone Wolf into the society of chiefs. As he traveled around the reservation holding religious meetings, Given could see that some of his people were, like their chief, engaged in farming and stock raising.[44] Sometime during 1890, John Charlton, a member of the Board of Indian Commissioners, tasked to visit and report on Indian boarding schools, wrote that Given had "returned to labor among his people, with whom, it is expected, he will have a great influence."[45] With Joshua Given well situated, in late 1889 the WNIA Missionary Committee reported that the Brooklyn Auxiliary was contemplating the establishment of a mission among the Montana Piegans,[46] one of the tribes on Price's list as having neither church or missionary, "making it certain that thousands must live and die without Christian instruction unless new instrumentalities are raised up to evangelize them." Brooklyn women intended to be that instrument.[47]

The Algonquian-speaking Piegans were part of the Blackfeet Confederacy which included the Kainai (Blood) and the Siksika (Northern Blackfeet), whose range in the early eighteenth century covered the northern Great Plains, the upper reaches of the Missouri River in Montana, and the high plains in Saskatchewan and Alberta.[48] Formerly a dominant force on the northern plains, by the 1850s and 1860s the Blackfeet, after negotiating federal treaties, had been forced to settled down on a reservation. Under the Grant-era "peace policy," the Methodist Episcopal Church had been assigned control of the Blackfeet Agency which included 7,500 Northern Blackfeet, Blood, and Piegan. The Methodist Mission Board had recommended John Young, a member of the Pacific Street Methodist

Episcopal Church in Brooklyn, as their agent. Although not an ordained minister, he did organize a Sabbath school at his agency in December 1876.[49] The following year he lamented that "his duties are such that beyond Sabbath service, my opportunities are few," and that his church had not yet provided a minister.[50] Young reemphasized the need for a missionary in his 1881 report.[51]

George Bird Grinnell, ethnologist, conservationist, naturalist, ornithologist, avid sportsman, and editor in chief of *Forest and Stream*, was well acquainted with the Piegans, visiting them for the first time in the fall of 1885. He made subsequent treks to the Northern Plains, revisiting them and the Cheyenne and writing a number of classic ethnographic books on them and other Plains tribes. In a letter to the editor of the *New York Times*, reprinted in an April 1889 issue of *The Indian's Friend*, Grinnell clearly stated he was not an eastern sentimentalist but had for nearly twenty years "seen a great deal of Indians: have lived with them, have met them on the warpath, on the hunt, and in the village." He described their treatment as one "that ought to make every American ashamed of his government and of himself." He singled out the Piegans, describing the "disgraceful state of things now existing at the Blackfeet Agency." Once numerous, they had been reduced to fifteen hundred because of disease, war, and famine—the most serious loss of life, some six hundred, could be blamed on "the failure of the supply of buffalo and the dishonesty of their agent" four years earlier. The survivors were, Grinnell wrote, "discontented, discouraged, and hopeless, because, instead of being helped on in their struggle toward civilization, obstacles [were] constantly put in the way of their advancement." During a visit the previous autumn, he learned from his Indian informants that Agent Marcus Baldwin was enriching himself at their expense, listing seven specific charges against Baldwin in his public letter.[52]

The precarious situation facing the Piegans to which Grinnell had referred should have been obvious to government officials. As early as 1875, Blackfeet Agent John S. Wood reported that each year "the vast herds that once swept the prairie like a tempest become less," the continental railroad having broken up the path of their annual migration.[53] Food insecurity increased every year. A severe early frost destroyed the grain crop in 1881; the next year a disease killed off half the Piegans' horse herd. In 1883, Agent John Young reported that "now that all game is gone from their reservation, no support can be derived from hunting." Until they could properly be instructed in farming, he concluded, "humanity requires that they and their children should not be allowed to suffer hunger."[54]

Young's replacement, R. A. Allen, who took over on April 1, 1884, presented a similarly dismal picture.[55]

In late June 1884, the *Times* ran the headline "Indians Dying from Starvation." Similar headlines followed.[56] From her Colorado Springs home, poet, author, and Indian reformer Helen Hunt Jackson read one newspaper with an article describing there was "too much wheat on hand this fall" and an account of starving Piegans on another page. Inspired by this juxtaposition, she wrote a poem entitled "Too Much Wheat," which was published on the front page of the November 6, 1884, issue of the *New York Independent*. She had written: "Hundreds of men lie dying, dead, / Brothers of ours, though their skins are red; / Men we promised to teach and feed. / They starve like beasts in pens and fold, / While we hoard wheat to sell for gold."[57]

Newspaper headlines and Jackson's poem drew reformers to the cause. In October 1884, the IRA sent their Washington, DC, agent, Charles C. Painter, to tour several Indian agencies in Montana.[58] In this, his first investigation, Painter presented compelling reports, which, accompanied by continued news accounts and IRA pamphlets, put the plight of the Piegan squarely in the public spotlight. Painter blamed the Indian Office and Congress for a situation that should have been anticipated. Responding in his October report, Commissioner Price defended his office, putting the blame directly and entirely on Congress, for it had appropriated the money three months late and far less than his office had requested, driving the Blackfeet, Blood, and Piegan Indians "to great straits to sustain life during the winter and spring of 1883 and 1884."[59]

WNIA members joined with the IRA to secure congressional funding. During her November 1884 presidential address, Mary Lucinda Bonney argued that if it had been the Irish who were starving, "Congress and the people would be alive to the exigency," and ships loaded with provisions would be ploughing their way across the Atlantic. "And yet 'the wards of the nation' send forth their cries with little response." She called upon her membership to act, to protest and pass resolutions "to express the depth of [their] convictions that these dying Indians should be speedily relieved." Members unanimously adopted resolutions to be sent to President Chester A. Arthur, and the WNIA Executive Board directed Quinton, the association's general secretary at the time, to Washington to confer with leading officials. Quinton concluded: "Could a clearer illustration be given of the value of organized effort for ensuring justice to the oppressed?" During a mass meeting held that evening at Association Hall in Philadelphia, Herbert

Welsh addressed the crowd. In his customarily forceful and earnest manner, he described the condition of the Piegans and other starving Montana Indians, and his association's efforts on their behalf. Public pressure, directed by the IRA and supported by the WNIA, forced Congress in January 1885 to appropriate $50,000 ($1,648,448 in 2025 dollars) to feed the starving Indians.[60]

Brooklyn reformers had not been the first to consider missionary work among the Piegans. In June 1886, Sarah J. Williams, MD, a graduate of Mount Holyoke Seminary and of a four-year medical course in Philadelphia, with fifteen years of experience and a postgraduate course in diseases of the eyes, had offered her services to the WNIA Missionary Committee as the Piegan medical missionary. However, the New Haven Women's Indian Association, a branch of the Connecticut Indian Association, had already applied for a mission station. After meeting with Williams, New Haven reformers elected to support her. In July, the Indian Office approved, and Indian Agent Marcus D. Baldwin cordially granted his permission. The WNIA Missionary Committee announced that Williams had arrived in Montana,[61] but no further mention was found in any WNIA literature until the 1888 publication of Ellen Terry Johnson's historical sketch of the Connecticut Indian Association.[62] In her sketch, Johnson, the wife of Professor Charles F. Johnson of Trinity College, finally confirmed that "the Blackfeet Agency, where the first missionary post was established, proved too extensive a field for this especial enterprise." In the WNIA's 1894 missionary report, it was confirmed that unidentified obstacles had emerged "and the maintenance of the mission proved impracticable at that time."[63] In the meantime, Connecticut women had shifted their missionary efforts to the 1,500 Shoshone and Bannock Indians at Fort Hall Idaho. Agent Baldwin, more than any single individual, regretted this failed medical station. In his August 1887 report to the commissioner, he wrote of the death of his eleven-year-old daughter on December 20, 1886, due to insufficient medical care at the agency.[64]

Half a decade had passed since the famine, and the Brooklyn branch was poised to invest in the Piegans' future. From the very beginning of its founding, this branch had been successful. Well-attended meetings and prominent speakers were reported by the *Brooklyn Eagle* and other newspapers.[65] In a February 1888 article, highlighting their city's benevolent women, the *Brooklyn Eagle* singled out Mrs. George Stannard (née Cornelia W.), current president of the Brooklyn Indian Association, describing her as "tall and stately, with a sweet, dignified bearing," a "woman of rare executive ability." The *Eagle* claimed that "probably no other woman has given as much of her time and attention to benevolent undertakings," listing philanthropic work that included the presidency of the Working Girls' Home, Indian Association Maternity, Homeopathic Central Dispensary, Hospital for Mental and Nervous Diseases, Diet Dispensary, and Women's Union Missionary Society for Heathen Lands. She was also the first vice president of the Home for Consumptives.[66] Although Stannard did not have the opportunity to oversee a mission in Montana, her predecessor, Mrs. J. B. Plummer, did. In a December 1893 issue the *Eagle*, reporting on a fair held by the Brooklyn Association at Henry Ward Beecher's Plymouth Church, noted that Plummer had "succeeded very well and will now be able to go ahead with the work of their missionary headquarters among the Piegan tribe in Montana."[67]

In addition, Brooklyn reformers raised sufficient monies to pay for an investigative visit by Rev. Dr. Daniel Dorchester, Superintendent of Indian Schools, to the Blackfeet Agency on their behalf. Unfortunately, he was unable to do so until the fall of 1892, when, with the support of the agent, he selected a mission site and secured, with Blackfeet permission, the removal of those tribal members who lived on the land in question. It was reported that with government consent, one hundred sixty acres "of the best land on the reservation, well situated and well watered, and within a mile of the present new agency buildings," was turned over to the Brooklyn auxiliary.[68]

With a firm commitment from Brooklyn reformers, Quinton, again serving as editor of *The Indian's Friend*, reprinted two articles, alerting her membership to Piegan needs and creating an association-wide interest in support of the new project. In the April 1889 issue, she reprinted George Bird Grinnell's *New York Times* letter. Having recently toured the reservation government school, he described the Piegan children as "bright and intelligent and extremely interested in their work." But he had also learned from their current agent, R. A. Allen, that the Indians had not yet rebounded from the terrible famine they had endured between 1883 and 1885, which had taken the lives of a quarter of their population.[69] In the August issue, Quinton reprinted Agent Marcus Baldwin's 1886 report to Commissioner John D. C. Atkins. The agent portrayed reservation residents as showing "a disposition to work, and a desire to merit approval," explaining that "kindness, patience, and perseverance will eventually place them upon the same plane as the white man." He decried his inability to stop intoxicating drink from entering the reservation, concluding the "Indian ought not to be subject to these temptations: he needs protection as well as assistance." In her editorial, Quinton called attention to the inconsistencies between Baldwin's report and Grinnell's letter, hoping earnestly that "the hour has already struck when succor and instruction shall display tyranny and darkness among the Piegans."[70]

To promote the need for such missionary work, in 1892 Nellie Blanchan De Graff Doubleday, treasurer of the Brooklyn Indian Association's Bay Ridge branch, wrote a leaflet titled *The Piegan Indians*.[71] *The Indian's Friend* reported in their August issue that she had recently read from it before a fall branch meeting.[72] In it she described the dreadful accounts of starving Piegans, remarking afterwards that based on the current Indian commissioner's report, the government's policy was obviously failing them. Clearly the Indians were having a difficult climb to civilization, and the Brooklyn Women's Indian Association was prepared to "establish earnest missionaries among them, and in a building large enough to conduct their work on a liberal basis." Her Bay Ridge Association would supply "this home with comforts, so that the Indians on that desolate reservation may have at least one sufficient object lesson before them—that of a civilized Christian Home." By this time, the WNIA had created innovative approaches to encourage a "civilized" Indian home, in keeping with nineteenth-century America's view that a woman's place was the home.[73]

Rev. Eugene S. Dutcher, a member of the Methodist Episcopal Board, was a potential candidate as missionary. Although it is unclear who initially suggested him, Quinton had at least met him at Fort Defiance, Arizona, during her extensive 1891 cross-country organizational tour. When learning that he and his wife, Mary Bishop Dutcher, were currently unengaged, Quinton wrote to them on September 28, 1892, inquiring if they would be interested in serving as WNIA missionaries at the rate of $500 per missionary or $1,000 for a couple. "We expect to build a cottage in the spring, & a *chapel*, we *hope* later," she explained and that for WNIA workers "the house [was] rent free. May I hear from you soon, after which I can write more fully."[74] Dutcher accepted, and the Epworth Piegan Indian Mission became a state mission, funded by the Brooklyn auxiliary and its Bay Ridge branch. With his arrival in 1893, the Piegans would finally get their first Methodist Episcopal missionary, one promised two decades earlier during the "peace policy" era.

As chairman of the WNIA Missionary Committee, Quinton tried to visit each station at least once. On July 1, 1893, she descended from her Great Northern Railroad car at the small station at Kipp in Montana's Teton County at the end of a 1,600-mile-long trip begun in Chicago on June 28. She had come to

Figure 9. On their way to a missionary conference, the Eugene S. Dutcher family sets up camp for the evening at the edge of a Montana lake in this undated photograph. (National Anthropological Archives, Smithsonian Institution, Eugene S. Dutcher Photographs [92-9].)

Northwestern Montana at the invitation of Dutcher and his wife to visit the government Indian school exhibition at the Blackfeet Agency and to attend their July 4th celebration. The invitation offered her an opportunity to visit a large number of Piegans in one location "without delay or prolonged travel." With her July duties in hand and describing his invitation as "a call to see work which had long held the heart," she set out with only a few hours of notice, arriving ahead of her telegram. Therefore, no one was waiting at the station to escort her the eight miles to the Brooklyn-funded mission or the mile beyond to the government school. The small community of Kipp offered "only the little station, some railroad shops, a store containing the post office, with a little café near, and a few other roofs beyond," she informed readers of *The Indian's Friend*. After talking to the telegrapher, the storekeeper, and the postmaster, who although kind and interested had neither horses nor wagons available, she finally located a customs collector willing to drive her to the mission and school.[75]

Quinton's visit to observe Dutcher's success in Christianizing and educating the Piegans was her way of fulfilling, on her association's behalf, what she perceived to be a moral debt owed the Indigenous populations by the United States, "a Christian nation occupying their [Indian] former heritage." In an early editorial, she had described this debt as "greater than that touching any of the new-comers upon our soil." Until the gospel was spread across the continent, the WNIA would toil on to awaken attention, move hearts, and gather "means for supplying the many-sided work needed on the reservations," where "men still stand in enforced idleness, . . . women suffer and perish from the many cruelties and bereavements of savagery and a vicious white vicinage, . . . [and] their children, if spared, grow up in squalid want and barbarism." Quinton truly believed that independence, education, and the Christian faith could "give to [Indian] life here either happiness or value."[76] A woman of her time and of some social standing, she embodied the philanthropic impulses of evangelical Christianity with the prejudice and racism inherent in the late nineteenth-century federal government's assimilationist policy.

Eugene and Mary Dutcher, accompanied by their two small children, had arrived on April 1, 1893, temporarily residing in the government schoolhouse until, with the assistance of the Indians and funds from Brooklyn, Dutcher had enlarged the existing small log cabin. Blackfeet Agent, George Steell, welcomed them, reporting that "the field for missionary labor here is large," concluding that when fully operational, this mission "will help materially toward the advancement of these Indians."[77] In an 1899 article, George Bird Grinnell described Dutcher's efforts as "a practical form of missionary work, seldom seen, which cannot be too highly applauded." After preaching on Sunday in the little church built with his own hands, Dutcher took his carpenter's tools on weekdays and helped hang doors, set window frames in Indian houses, and set fence posts or string wire on the reservation. While thus engaged, Mary taught the women to bake bread and sew. Grinnell concluded that "missionary work such as this, where practical religion is made a part of the daily life, and soul and mind and body are cared for at once, accomplishes lasting results."[78]

Arriving at the Epworth Mission, Quinton was greeted with "a warm hand-grasp and luminous-eyed greeting" by the six-foot-two pastor and his "happy faced young wife," while their one-year-old and three-year-old children looked on. She described Dutcher as "busy on the walls of our Piegan Jerusalem," which then was only a foundation of what would eventually become a three-room cottage, with the existing cabin as the kitchen. Quinton pronounced the family "in perfect health and blithe of heart, though only the cabin, two horses and grass and sky, save on one side, could be seen." In the distance was "the glorious, snow-capped Rocky Mountains stretch[ing] along the western limited of the reservation."[79] Buoyed up by her usual optimism, only Quinton could envision this stark mission in such grand terms.

Following this greeting, Quinton was driven to the Willow Creek Boarding School, a mile away, where at teatime she was cordially welcomed by Superintendent W. H. Matson and the teachers and students. She described the Piegans as "bright, alert, cheerful-looking" and their children as "healthy, happy, and to be doing capitally well especially in English speaking." Initially Agent Steell had been forced to order parents to send their children to school, reinforcing his command with the use of tribal police. Now, however, Quinton wrote, the Indian parents were "well pleased to have them there."[80] It was not uncommon for parents to resist sending children to school, which in many cases often meant distant off-reservation boarding school. Even reservation boarding schools, like Willow Creek, required time away from home. It is unknown if Piegan parents were more inclined to send their children once the school was removed from its original unfavorable site inside the agency stockade, "subjected to the disturbing, distracting, and generally demoralizing influences incident to frontier post life" to the more judicially selected site at Willow Creek. But even this new location had its downside. It was "wholly without shelter, fully exposed to the heavy winds," and in the winter the snow drifted in huge heaps around the building. This school, like all government boarding facilities, was expected to be agriculturally self-sustaining, difficult in Montana's extreme winters. Although it had a successful dairy, raising chickens had proven difficult what with the large number of camp dogs.[81]

Steell's arrival at the school afforded Quinton an opportunity to confer with him on agency affairs. Unfortunately, her reports did not include details of their discussion. Based on her one visit and comments "learned from various persons beside [Steell's] friends and employees," she formed an opinion of the agent far different from that expressed by Grinnell, who had personal dealings based on numerous visits. Quinton described the agent, who had taken charge of the agency in October 1890, as doing more "for the civilization of these Indians than all his predecessors in office," having "abolished the lounging about the agency" and inducing "the Indians to go out and take individual holdings of land." Grinnell, on the other hand, described him "as a man merely more bearable than his drunken, thieving predecessors."[82] Quinton saw what she wanted and what the WNIA was promoting—Piegans mostly living in "civilized" log houses, with livestock and wagons—improvements which could have been made under previous agents. Thus, based on an assumption that he had been responsible for these changes, she became outraged upon learning he was to be replaced because new regulations required the appointment of Army officers as agents to remove the appointment from the political process.[83] Asking her readers that if the goal of the government was to "civilize and elevate Indians," and the agent was accomplishing that goal, why remove him, she had concluded, "if not for Indian benefit then we have the open confession that the Indian Department is controlled for the white man's benefit."[84]

During the morning of July 4, Quinton attended Sunday school, reporting, "we have never seen any children more obedient to orders or more prompt in marking time." She began to notice more and more tents being set up on the prairie, as the Indians began to gather for the upcoming celebration.[85] In her rosy prose, she described the twenty or thirty colorful tents with bright streamers and shouting children on agile ponies "careening over the undulating grass stretches" as proud parents watched in blessed content. The day ended in a grand sunset and its "glorious but gentle radiance, ever like the hushing from a sacred psalm." The only shadow on this bucolic scene was a broken arm, sustained by the daughter of the chief when she tumbled off her pony. Because the agency doctor was twenty-two miles away, it took a full day before her arm was cast. On July 4th the children's presentations, mostly patriotic in nature, presented by "wee ones of seven to those of seventeen," were followed by short speeches from Quinton, Dutcher, and Steell, and ended with a visit to the tents for a holiday dinner provided by the government. Fireworks at the school concluded festivities, with Quinton wondering how "these scenes must appear to our new fellow-citizens who now saw such for the first time."[86]

Departing the Willow Creek Boarding School on July 5, Quinton paid a short visit to the Dutchers' "cheery" log cabin with its homemade furniture. From there, the agency interpreter drove her the fourteen miles to the agency headquarters, covering only part of Dutcher's pastorate, which stretched out twenty-five miles. They had passed the "long lines of prairie graves, more of them on the sod or even with it than under it, sleep the six hundred who starved to death not ten winters ago," Quinton reported. She was unimpressed with the existing agency, describing it as a series of dilapidated log buildings around a "quadrangle inside the old stockade which was decorated with ghastly buffalo skulls."[87]

The next day Quinton traveled four miles onto the reservation to visit Piegan homes, a practice she followed on all tours. She found most settled on "holdings of their own in log houses, with gardens, and other lands under tillage, and stock about them." She described one home in which five Piegan women lived, with earthen floors and a rough bench as the only furniture. She envisioned how "easy it would be to win them to a healthful bath, to clean simple garments instead of tattered blankets and a rugged skin, and to teach them to neatly comb their long raven or gray locks." Viewing them critically through her ethnocentric prejudice, Quinton only saw a meager lifestyle, compared to what she envisioned as a fully civilized community. However, she felt she was witnessing the beginnings of meaningful work, expressing pleasure in having seen "the image of God in these men and women, [and] of having felt their capabilities as well as their needs." She had expected to see only sadness during this visit but instead saw smiling faces and a "cheerful energy of some and the apparent jollity of a few."[88] Unfortunately, her report, which appeared in *The Indian's Friend*, provided no details on the missionary efforts of the Dutcher family since their April arrival.

Quinton spent the remainder of July and all of August and September 1893 in Chicago focusing on the WNIA's participation in the World's Congress of Representative Women. She had already given seven addresses during the Congress in May before heading to the Blackfeet Agency and would give several more each in August and September.[89] The *Times* described it as "a wonderful gathering of brainy women and a most impressive one, as showing their progress in the latter half of this century." Quinton was listed among the attendees.[90] When available, she or her temporary private secretary, Miss Clarabel Gilman, secretary of the Jamaica Plain auxiliary of the Massachusetts Indian Association, sat at Desk 39 of the Woman's Building handing out WNIA pamphlets and other literature.[91]

During the second week of October, Quinton set out for the Hudson Valley of New York to attend the October 11, 1893, opening session of the annual Lake Mohonk Conference. During her allotted time, she spoke about her Montana visit, describing the "Christly principles" that had taken hold among the Piegans. She had found expressive faces and genuine feeling among these people, who had "already made remarkable progress, and [were] eager to go forward." The school was a capital one; the July celebration was "an inspiration and a joy," and Agent Steell was an "honest, sensible, and practical man," who "has made marked success with them." She explained to Lake Mohonk attendees that she had learned that after three years of service he was to be replaced by an Army officer, a result of a recent reform to improve the quality of agents. Although pleased with any reform that improved the Indian service, she strongly believed that competent agents like Steell should be retained, informing the conference that the Piegans were so anxious about his removal that they had petitioned the Indian Office on his behalf.[92]

Quinton would spend the next several years trying to secure Steell's rehiring, protesting his removal before every conference and association meeting she attended. Although she had only met him during her one visit to the reservation, she viewed him as a good agent, overcoming the Indians' fears and prejudices, winning their confidence and abolishing alcohol. It was not that she was displeased with his replacement, for L. W. Cooke, Captain, 3rd Infantry, was also well spoken of. Quinton simply believed that good agents should be retained, even after a presidential election in which a new party assumed office.[93]

According to Francis Paul Prucha, between 1884 and 1896 the change in political parties in the executive branch had "brought the spoils system into new prominence," and incompetent political hacks were often appointed as agents. Like many reformers, Quinton favored merit appointments. Although the 1883 passage of the Pendleton Act provided the use of competitive exams in the selection of some government employees, agents were not yet covered under the legislation.[94] Quinton was supported in her efforts by Herbert Welsh, who spent more than a decade demanding that civil service rules be applied to the Indian service.[95] He saw the "key to the proper solution of the Indian problem" as the Indian agent. If good men were appointed and retained, "so long as they faithfully perform their duties," Welsh believed, the IRA "would never have been organized" as much of their work was to counter "the disastrous results too often caused by placing the unworthy, if not dishonest, men in charge of Indian agencies."[96]

Quinton had voiced her opinion on this issue of retaining competent agents as early as the January 6, 1887, BIC annual conference with missionary boards and Indian rights associations. Following her discussion of the missionary work of the more than eighty WNIA auxiliaries, she explained to the Board that her association desired "that civil service reform rules should be applied to the Indian service," and because the IRA was also very much interested, this "will be one of the lines that we shall especially work on this year."[97] A year later, during her November 7, 1888, annual WNIA address in Philadelphia's Methodist Episcopal Church, Quinton reported that although the association's first duty was to secure legal justice for the Indian with male reformers leading the work and women doing their utmost to help, equally as important was *"that the Indian be taken out of politics"* by "putting into offices, both great and small for management of Indian affairs, only those who are proved fit for such service."⁹⁸ Three weeks later, the *New York Times* reported that she hoped that women's influence "should be brought upon President Harrison to induce him to apply civil service reform rules to Indian affairs."⁹⁹

Invited to speak during the October 1891 Lake Mohonk Conference following Welsh's lengthy address on civil service reform, Quinton stated that everywhere during her more than seven-month-long cross-country organizational tour she had found "a great desire among Indians for some settled officials, for something permanent, and a feeling that there ought not to be this constant change." Aggrieved by "the great evils from this want of power and permanence," she lamented that just when an Indian commissioner finally learned his role, a new administration was elected, and reformers had to reeducate the new appointee.¹⁰⁰ Two years later, at Lake Mohonk, she again called for the application of civil service reform.¹⁰¹ Steell's removal had been the final straw. Following Quinton's address on that October day in 1893, Welsh had stood up to address the conference, declaring that George Bird Grinnell had given him "the same characterization" of Steell that Quinton had just presented. After receiving Grinnell's letter, Welsh immediately wrote to Commissioner Daniel M. Browning to see if Steell might be retained "on the simple ground that his work was of utmost value." Browning responded that even though no charge had been brought against him, the president "deemed it almost mandatory under the [new] law to appoint army officers as Indian agents."¹⁰²

At the end of October, Quinton informed Welsh that she had written to President Grover Cleveland and two acquaintances from Georgia, intimate friends of Interior Secretary Hoke Smith, who had previously practiced law in Atlanta, in hopes of finding some support for Steell. The latter's case was a perfect example of how poorly the present system worked. He was not only an exemplary agent, but Indians and the local white population alike wanted him retained. If a suitable man was appointed and kept in office, the whole issue of the so-called Indian problem would be settled. "We women are very much interested in it," and "we think both administrations are just as naughty as they can be," Quinton concluded.¹⁰³

When Quinton joined other reformers on December 15, 1893, at the annual Board of Indian Commissioners' meeting in Washington, DC, Agent George

Steell's removal was still very much on her mind. During her allotted time, she addressed the WNIA's current work, describing their recently adopted resolutions, one of which recommended extending civil service classification to include agents, special agents, and inspectors.[104] This topic was in keeping with the afternoon session at which Theodore Roosevelt addressed the case for a merit system during this, his third time before the BIC. He had been appointed by President Harrison in 1889 as a U.S. Civil Service Commissioner, a position he held until May 1895.[105] Not until the Roosevelt presidency would the position of Indian agent finally become subject to civil service rules.[106]

At meeting's end, the BIC proposed a resolution to include the extension of civil service rules to agency clerks, assistant teachers, carpenters, engineers, and government farmers. Another resolution urged the president to adopt a fitness and merit test for Indian agents and the passage of legislation "removing their appointment entirely from the arena of politics." Quinton, in perfect agreement, demanded: "Let us make it our business to see that the Congressmen are awakened." Declaring that "God is alive and on the throne," she concluded: "I do bespeak for all friends of the Indian [that] the most earnest work in carrying out that part of the resolution especially [is] asking Congress to take the matter out of politics."[107]

Shortly thereafter, Quinton informed Rev. William Henry Weinland, the WNIA's missionary among Southern California's Missions Indians, that she had again been appointed to the BIC's business committee. They would soon be asking for congressional legislation ordering that agents be appointed for their "*fitness & kept* in, till *unfit*, & I believe we shall get that," she confided to Weinland. It was now the time "for radical work & I'm doing all I can for it & driving work day & night."[108] In mid-January she informed Welsh that she had heard from General Eliphalet Whittlesey, secretary of the BIC, that Roosevelt and other reformers might not be able to get a law putting agents under civil service reform. "If not, we must bring such pressure to bear upon Mr. Cleveland that he will be glad to say 'I will appoint no agents who have not the endorsement of the civil service committee.'" Ever optimistic, she believed the president "can be made to say that cordially."[109]

As a member of the BIC business and resolutions committee, Quinton carried the conference resolutions to President Cleveland at the end of their mid-January 1895 meeting. Although many of their resolutions dealt with Indian education, the BIC had heartily pledged to support Interior Secretary Hoke Smith "to develop a competent, permanent, non-partisan Indian service."[110] Philip C. Garrett, a Philadelphia lawyer, executive board member of the IRA, and a member of the BIC, reported that their committee was kindly received by the president and Smith, and as evidence of their accepting of conference demands, the Interior Department had submitted the names of all agents to reformers for their consideration.[111] As late as 1899, Quinton, still concerned about retaining good agents, noted in her address before a special meeting of the Cambridge Indian Association that it took new appointees at least two years to learn their duties, and then they were replaced with "men wholly inexperienced, with everything to learn all over—describing it as a "waste of time and money." It was even worse for the Indians, who had learned "to love a good agent devotedly and mourn deeply at losing their friend."[112]

Steell's replacement occurred at the same time as Eugene and Mary Dutcher's arrival on the reservation. Their work continued seamlessly through the change of personnel, and beginning in 1893, *The Indian's Friend* began publishing extracts from their letters. In November 1893, Dutcher described his family as "snugly settled in the new cottage and are blessed with good health," explaining that the new agency buildings were progressing rapidly with the school building nearly finished.[113] The January 1894 issue included a chatty letter from Mary Dutcher, explaining to Quinton that the number of tents constructed between the mission and the agency had doubled since her visit. She also expressed surprise with the Piegans' good behavior and work ethic. When passing a group of fifty tribal members gathered for a horse race, she confided to Quinton that they had been "perfectly civil and courteous." Mary was most impressed with those hired by Agent Cooke to work on the new three-mile-long irrigation project near the Willow Creek school. Facing bitter cold and fierce winds, they worked willingly. She described their attitude as vastly to their credit.[114] Unfortunately, these letters provided no information on any actual missionary work, although they did reveal Mary Dutcher's ethnocentric preconceptions.

The February issue of the periodical described Christmas activities, providing more details. Gifts from various auxiliaries were distributed and several small trees decorated. More than two hundred Indians had attended the festivities, arriving on foot, horseback, or in wagons. "We thought this a fine festival for our first year," wrote Reverend Dutcher, thanking WNIA members for their support.[115] A March letter referred to the mission's afternoon Sunday school of fifteen to twenty Willow Creek school students, viewed as "very teachable and

Figure 10. Arthur Dutcher, Reverend Dutcher's brother, is photographed mowing oats with the mission's horse team. The Epworth Piegan Mission chapel can be seen in the background, upper right. (National Anthropological Archives, Smithsonian Institution, Eugene S. Dutcher Photographs [92-9].)

attentive." The May issue described an Easter service with one hundred Piegans in attendance and the baptism of fourteen children, with a comment that everyone was "prospering and the future looks bright. We praise the Lord for the many evidences we have that this work has the divine approval," Dutcher concluded. In a letter in the September issue, he reported on the partly laid twenty-six-foot by forty-foot chapel foundation. When completed it would include a vestibule and a bell tower. Although the Brooklyn auxiliary and its Bay Ridge branch had raised most of the money, reservation residents also contributed, with the Piegans, even "out of their deep poverty," giving "a large proportion of the money." Describing their missionary work as exceptionally difficult, Dutcher concluded that "the success of this mission is one to inspire work on the hardest field."[116]

Mary Dutcher's lengthy August letter described recent improvements accomplished by working with leading tribal members, assisted by some white men living on the reservation. The Piegans had hauled most of the lumber for the new chapel, and afterwards Mary and her husband fed them "a nice dinner of vegetables, butter, milk, etc.," all produce grown at the mission "to which they did ample justice, and they were as good natured and jolly as anybody you ever saw." The mission garden was producing plenty of potatoes and turnips and some cabbage and beets, and the hay crop was enough to feed their horses. The Dutchers had traveled some 1,863 miles visiting homes and received eight hundred sixty-three Indian visits to the station. And, before the Willow Creek school closed for the summer, Mrs. Dutcher explained that they had held Sunday school at their cottage for four months for the boys, the weather being too inclement for the girls to attend. Unfortunately, their cottage-home was much too small to accommodate all the children. The couple were both looking forward to opening the chapel, hopefully in the coming week, to accommodate a larger Sunday school and regular attendance by adults. And they intended to hire an interpreter to aid in their ministry.[117]

A year and a half into his missionary work, Reverend Dutcher wrote an article for *The Gospel in All Lands*, explaining that Agent Steell had initially invited Piegan leaders to a council meeting to discuss the need for the mission, and the Indians had willing given written consent. Dutcher then described the purpose of the mission as providing the Piegans with religious and industrial training. To achieve the first goal, he held regular religious services in the missionary cottage, the Indian camps, and later in the chapel, and for the second goal, he and Mary used their "mission home and farm [as] an object lesson to the Indians." While she reinforced the lessons with additional instruction to the Indian women in their cabins or tents in the interests of maintaining a home and habits of cleanliness, the reverend instructed the Indian men in the care of their cattle and in useful farming techniques.[118]

In his article, Dutcher listed reasons why he believed he had achieved his goals among the Piegans: 1) he had gained their confidence; 2) more were attending services than the facilities could accommodate; 3) they were contributing to the chapel fund; and 4) more sick children and elderly were coming in for medicine and advice. Dutcher was so pleased with his achievements that he was considering the building of a small industrial training school.[119] The Brooklyn auxiliary obviously agreed with his assessment for on August 1, 1894, it turned the station over to the Missionary Board of the Methodist Episcopal Church, free of charge. The *Brooklyn Eagle* described the parcel as 160 acres of well-watered property with a chapel and cottage.[120] Brooklyn women had spent close to $4,000 renovating the cabin, constructing stables and a chapel, fencing in a hundred acres, digging

CHAPTER 4

a well, and purchasing farm equipment, furniture, horses, a farm wagon and a buggy, and paying the missionaries' salaries.[121] The Dutchers remained on site after the transfer.

The July 1894 issue of *The Indian's Friend* included a rare glimpse into the missionary work at Epworth through the letter of a Piegan leader. As is so common, the Indian voice is often silent, for they were seldom consulted. One summer Sunday, Wolf Tail (described in the article as "a leading Indian") visited the Dutchers asking them to write a letter to Quinton. He had expressed a hope to the WNIA president that she would return to the reservation so he could visit with her again. He described his wife and family as well, explaining that "all the Indians [were] working hard." He liked the "missionaries here very well," much preferring Epworth Mission to St. Ignacius, the Holy Family Mission of Fort Shaw, because it had "a good Sunday School to teach the children" and the missionaries gave out many presents that made the Indians happy and kept them warm. Every Sunday Wolf Tail proudly wore the clothing given to him by the Dutchers. He also related to Quinton that he had been encouraging his people and other chiefs around the agency to help the missionaries build "a big church here so that all the people that come can get in, and so that more can come as they will be glad to." He suggested one way the Dutchers could get more Indians to attend services was to provide dinner for all. Wolf Tail also praised Agent Steell's "good rules," especially for ending the whiskey business on the reservation. "Whiskey is a very bad thing for the Indians," he wrote. Wolf Tail also liked the agent's rule that they "live on their own place," and not in a bunch anymore. Complaining that the trains were not running, he asked Quinton to either bring or send him some peacock feathers. He signed his letter, "your good friend, Wolf Tail."[122]

Although no longer a WNIA station, news of activities at Epworth occasionally appeared in *The Indian's Friend*. The February 1895 issue included accounts of Christmas activities, with the Dutchers writing that one hundred twenty-five Piegans slept in their tents in the mission's dooryard. Although the chapel was not finished, two hundred Indians had crowded inside for the Christmas service. In total, the missionaries reported that over three days, some seven hundred fifty Indians had attended the services.[123] The Dutchers were still at their post in late 1897, the November issue of *The Indian's Friend* reprinting excerpts from his letter. Noting there were some nineteen hundred Piegan residents, Dutcher explained he was continuing to hold regular services and Sunday schools, as well as meetings "at various places in the homes of the people, as our several years'

Figure 11. Arthur Dutcher, top right, is pictured with three Indian friends at the Epworth Mission. His sister-in-law, Mary Bishop Dutcher, is in the middle of the first row. Note that the young Indians pictured are dressed in "civilized clothing." (National Anthropological Archives, Smithsonian Institution, Eugene S. Dutcher Photographs [92-9].)

experience has taught us is best." He and his wife continued to make improvements, repainting the chapel, improving the parsonage, and fencing most of the mission lands, even hoping to establish a school "where Indian boys and girls who wish may get a more complete education than is furnished by the ordinary school."[124]

In early 1895, a year after the WNIA had transferred the Epworth Piegan Indian Mission, Interior Secretary Hoke Smith reappointed Steell. *The Indian's Friend* described this move as admirable, an illustration of permitting "no political considerations to prevent putting the right man in the right place over Indians."[125] Quinton made no personal comment on the appointment, but since she served as editor periodically, the comment may well have been hers. It is unknown whether her efforts on Steell's behalf had led to his reappointment.

Steell took charge on March 8, 1895, finding the new agency buildings on Willow Creek, some three miles from Durham Station, on the Great Northern Railroad line, almost completed. He was displeased with its location. The soft ground had already resulted in foundations settling, and the structures, built too far apart, made it inconvenient to move around. He did, however, speak positively about the Piegan Mission, describing the continued "hard work and kind words" of Dutcher and his wife.[126] His final report of August 15, 1896, was positive, portraying a people "quick to realize the value of an education," building "their own houses, and very neatly, too," and fencing in fine hay land, watered by irrigation ditches they had dug themselves.[127] The agent resigned sometime later, according to Grinnell, "shamed and stained by his lenience toward miners and white ranchers and by the suspicious increase of his own cattle herd." Although Grinnell had wavered in his characterization of Steell, in the end he complained to Herbert Welsh, "there seems to be something about the business of Indian agent which saps the morals of every man who takes the position."[128]

The Epworth Mission, one of more than sixty founded by the WNIA, represents what Robert W. Berkhofer describes as a small mission model headed by a missionary couple. It was chosen as a case study because of a more complicated backstory, illustrating the process of founding a mission. It also represented an example of an auxiliary-funded station as opposed to one initiated and controlled by the WNIA's Missionary Committee. Furthermore, in a small way, the Indians had consented, even contributing their own money towards a chapel. And if Wolf Tail's sentiment was even partially true, some Piegans willingly engaged in those aspects of the assimilation process that met their personal needs.

Although as early as February 1883 Quinton had established some guidelines, there was no standard blueprint; each tribe presented a unique situation. However, there were some commonalities. Each station began with an initial grant of government land upon which the WNIA built a missionary cottage, outbuildings, fencing, often a chapel, and provided necessary agricultural tools. Some sites included a boarding school, hospital, or both. The missionary work inside was similar. Male missionaries instructed the men to become better farmers and stockmen, while their wives or female missionaries promoted homemaking and domesticity, all work dutifully accompanied by heavy doses of Christianizing and "civilizing," with regular preaching and weekly Sunday schools.

The missionary was the key to the success of each station. Some were obviously better than others. All, however, were expected to make regular reports to the Missionary Committee, parts of which were extracted and printed in association publications to not only acquaint the far-reaching WNIA membership of their work but to provide the missionary with an opportunity to request needed supplies. Some sent long, informative letters, like Mary Louise Eldridge from her post in New Mexico, the subject of chapter 6; others, like Rev. William Henry Weinland, from his Ramona Mission in Southern California, the subject of chapter 7, had to be badgered to even report. Reverend Dutcher and his wife were somewhere in the middle to lower end of the spectrum.

One major issue confronted by all missionaries was dealing with Indian health matters, from a simple broken bone to a major epidemic of smallpox. Improper food storage, unsanitary cooking facilities, and contaminated water supplies were present on all reservations. Government hospitals were not established until the 1890s, and distant Indian agencies generally had only one doctor on staff, forcing the patient to either seek out a local medicine man or turn to their missionary. Although in their letters the Dutchers make no mention of engaging in any health work, a number of WNIA stations went to great lengths to provide proper care, employing medical missionaries, nurses, physicians, and building hospitals. To supplement their effort, the WNIA relied heavily on a government program that provided field matrons, white women employed to educate Indigenous women in proper household duties and care of their children, and to "incite among Indians generally aspirations for improvement in their life—morally, intellectually, socially, and religiously."[129] Lisa Emmerich explains that some reform-mind women were drawn to this novel program because it had "a romantic, exotic aura" and because by "emphasizing the reception of a down-trodden people through education and christianity," it resonated with those "who perceived themselves as teachers and nurturers."[130] She also writes that "health care was one area where field matrons developed new roles that brought them in closer contact with native culture and traditions."[131]

The following chapter explores the WNIA's efforts to provide health care to Indians within their stations, their participation in the field matron program, and the funding of a medical education for a young Omaha Indian woman.[132]

CHAPTER 5

The WNIA and Indian Health Care

In February 1885, the Committee on Indian Education of the Connecticut Indian Association unanimously voted to "take under its especial charge and guidance a young Indian girl, guaranteeing her support and education until she should graduate from a medical college." Mrs. Frances C. Palmer, chairman of the committee, announced for this plan the selection of Susan La Flesche, a member of Nebraska's Omaha tribe and salutatorian of her class at Hampton Institute. From the beginning, this young Omaha woman had made a strong impression upon reformers. Hampton founder General Samuel C. Armstrong described her "as about the finest, strongest Indian character we have had at this school. She is a level-headed, earnest, capable Christian woman, quite equal, I think, to medical studies," while Alice Cunningham Fletcher, bedridden in 1883 with an attack of inflammatory rheumatism, was impressed by the medical knowledge she demonstrated even before receiving formal training. Most important, Sara Thomson Kinney, association president, convinced

Figure 12. Studio portrait of Dr. Susan La Flesche Picotte, circa 1905. She was born on the Omaha Indian Reservation in Nebraska; her medical education was paid for by the Connecticut Indian Association. The first Indigenous woman physician, she was appointed by the WNIA as their medical missionary to the Omahas. (Nebraska State Historical Society Photograph Collections, [RG2026].)

both government officials and fellow reformers to fund La Flesche's medical education.[1] Connecticut Indian reformers came to view La Flesche much like a daughter. In 1894 she married Henry Picotte, a Sioux from the Yankton Agency and brother of her sister Marguerite's late husband Charles Diddock. When a son was born to the couple in December 1895, an article titled "A New Role" was printed on the front page of the February 1896 issue of *The Indian Bulletin*. The first line read: "The Connecticut Indian Association is a grandmother."[2]

Palmer reported that on March 14, 1889, Susan La Flesche had become "the first Indian woman ever regularly matriculated as a student in a medical college in our country, and year by year her progress and success has been watched with deepest interest by members of our Association." She explained that the young Omaha woman had graduated from the Woman's Medical College of Pennsylvania, with all expenses paid for by the Connecticut Indian Association. Soon after, La Flesche was awarded the coveted position of resident physician in Philadelphia's Woman's Hospital. That July, the US government appointed her as the official physician to the Omaha Tribe, arranging that she would live in the school building and take "care of all the children under government supervision among the tribe."[3]

After her graduation from medical college, La Flesche wrote Amelia Stone Quinton a letter to be read before the 1889 annual convention. She explained that she wished "that every Indian tribe had a National Indian Association working in its very midst"—a strong sentiment and a rare positive Indian voice for a reform association often criticized. After describing nonmedical activities at the school and at church, where she interpreted on Sundays and during evening prayer meetings, La Flesche expressed gratitude that already some nonprogressive tribal members were seeking her medical advice. "I feel so happy in my work to think that I can devote myself to my own people," she informed Quinton, describing her help "not only medically but in so many other ways."[4]

In the winter of 1890, the WNIA Missionary Committee named her their medical missionary among the Omahas; soon her letters and reports of success among her own people began to appear in *The Indian's Friend* and *The Indian Bulletin*, presenting another positive Indian acceptance of the WNIA, albeit of an Indigenous physician. In one quarterly report, La Flesche asserted she had seen some seventy cases in November alone, most patients coming to her office, although she had made twenty-four home visits. The most common ailments she treated were rheumatism, eye diseases, and other "light maladies." In December 1891 she reported that the "dreaded *Grippe* made its appearance and raged with more violence than during the two preceding years," with some families "rendered helpless by it, sometimes all the family but one or two being down."[5] The previous month, numerous Omahas had been to her office for nonmedical reasons, mostly for translating, letter writing, and help with basic daily business affairs.[6] After her marriage, she moved with her husband to Bancroft, Nebraska, some twenty-two miles from the Omaha Agency, where she practiced among more "Swedes, Irish, Danes, [and] Dutch" than Indians.[7]

La Flesche's success prompted Connecticut women to fund the medical education of Lewis Johnson, a young Tuscarora Indian from Western New York. When he failed to meet their standards, they withdrew their support and turned instead to educating Indian nurses at the Hartford Training Hospital. The first to graduate was Nancy Cornelius, born on the Oneida Reservation in Wisconsin. After attending Carlisle Indian School from 1885 to 1891, she entered the hospital's nursing program. When her medical studies were completed, she practiced in local private homes until 1899 when she went to work at the Oneida Mission Hospital, serving as its superintendent until 1905. Several other young Indigenous women were supported by the WNIA auxiliary, but none achieved Cornelius's prominence.[8]

While these exceptional Indians made important contributions to their communities, there never were enough Indian candidates for health-care programs to train and staff reservations or WNIA mission stations. To expand medical facilities within the Ramona Mission complex, originally founded in 1889 among the Mission Indians of Southern California, Quinton chose two white female physicians for new sub-mission sites selected during her 1891 organizational tour. Like La Flesche, they were both graduates of the Woman's Medical College of Pennsylvania. Dr. Anna Hayward Johnson, a government field matron, was assigned to provide medical care at Cahuilla, while Dr. Rebecca C. Hallowell, a physician who recently set up a medical practice in San Francisco, went to the Cupeño village of Agua Caliente on Warner Ranch.[9]

Born in New York City in 1855, Johnson graduated from Vassar in 1877 and from the Woman's Medical College of Pennsylvania in 1882, opening a medical practice in Orange, New Jersey, before accepting a position as resident physician at Hampton Institute.[10] A decade after receiving her medical degree, now newly employed as a government field matron, Johnson headed for Southern California. On November 1, 1892, Quinton informed Commissioner Thomas Jefferson Morgan that Johnson's "recommendations from Chaplain [Hollis Burke] Frissell & the other Hampton teachers are first class ones," and as a physician to the Cahuillas, she would "elevate the whole tribe & move them in many ways."

Quinton had requested that Morgan appoint Johnson as a field matron, to replace Miss C. M. Fleming, with the agreement that the WNIA would support her as they had Fleming.[11] Although Johnson was an official government employee, Quinton and her Missionary Committee assured Morgan they would view her "*in spirit* our helper too, & we as an Ass'n will aid her work for the Indians."[12] Johnson arrived on January 20, 1893, immediately assuming duties as a field matron and a WNIA medical missionary. Once settled in her WNIA-sponsored cottage, she began receiving medical supplies and other items from auxiliaries across the county.[13]

Five weeks into her work, Johnson informed Quinton that she had made three hundred twenty-two medical calls, and that Dr. C. C. Wainwright, the agency physician, had sent her what medicines he could spare. Others she had purchased with monies from the Newark branch. One day she rode thirteen miles to call on eight patients, gave medicine to twelve more, and provided meals for three very old Indians and another five who were quite ill. She described the fieldwork as hard, but no more difficult than expected, although it required all of her "strength of body, nerve and mind, and not only strength, but an everlasting calmness to attain which snatches of momentary solitude are necessary." Johnson soon fell in love with the Cahuilla valley, writing, "The rocks, the hills and mountains are dear to me already, and the meadow lark fills me with joy and thanksgiving."[14] In another letter she described the Cahuilla Indians as "so brave and steadfast in doing their part in the work, in lending me a hand, in giving me their confidence, that all helpers outside the field may rest assured that their aid, so generously given, is received with gratitude, no less deep because in Indian fashion not always spoken of."[15]

Johnson's one-room cottage served as "dining, reception, sewing, reading, bath and bed room, and also an office, drug store and church." Within this cramped facility she taught Indian women to sew on a sewing machine sent by the Pittsburgh, Pennsylvania, association and handed out Wainwright's medicines to three hundred fifty-eight individuals. The Riverside, California, auxiliary sent her books, carpenter tools, a cot, a mattress, bedding, and a pony-carriage, while Albert K. Smiley, from his winter home in nearby Riverside, sent her twenty dollars' worth of seed potatoes. In her spare time, Johnson taught Sunday school, with sixteen attendees the first Sunday and twenty-seven on the second. She already had received praise from two village leaders, who in letters to the WNIA Missionary Committee expressed their gratitude. Former village captain Gabriel Costa described Johnson as "the good and true friend of us Indians; everybody likes her and I do too." After she visited the sick, they got better, he explained. The current captain, Leonicio Lugo, wrote that his people were "very proud of our Dr. Anna Johnson. She is doing very nicely among us and all the people are very thankful." While the leadership expressed their gratitude in letters, local Indigenous residents expressed their thanks by supplying Johnson with "quail, duck, veal, beef, and eggs."[16]

One troubling issue faced by Johnson and all other reservation workers was the constant presence of alcohol. In an October 11, 1894, letter reprinted in the *Riverside Enterprise*, she railed against the hellish Indian fiestas, especially those held on saint days; they were only growing worse. She described the festivities at Soboba and Temecula as especially bad, with white, Indian, and Mexican men and women drunk from morning to night. Gambling went on twenty-four hours a day. She concluded with the comment that although "the men have passed a prohibition law, it is the women who must see that it is not a farce, a farce so rich in tragedy that our hearts cry out in agony."[17] Forced to resign in late 1894 because of her mother's poor health, Johnson eventually moved to Redlands, California, where she opened a private medical practice. She died on March 15, 1929, in Los Angeles County.[18]

Johnson's counterpart at Agua Caliente was Dr. Rebecca C. Hallowell. Two decades older, she had been born around 1833 in Pennsylvania and graduated from the Woman's Medical College in March 1878. Initially employed as a clinical physician at the Woman's Hospital of Philadelphia, she opened her own practice in Atlantic City, New Jersey, in 1884. By 1890 she was living and practicing medicine in San Francisco. The following year she served as a member of the Hospital Committee of the Northern California Women's Indian Association, an auxiliary Quinton had founded on August 10, 1891 during her first organizational tour to California.[19] A month later, after visiting the sulfur hot springs at Agua Caliente, one of five Mission Indian villages on the Warner Ranch, Quinton informed Commissioner Morgan that the small village would be of "inestimable value" as a site for "a small & inexpensive hospital" built by her association. More important, she knew of two women, perfect for the task, one a lady physician recently settled in San Francisco, whom the WNIA would willingly employ in medical and hospital work if Morgan would appoint her friend, Julia M. French, as a government field matron. Quinton described French as "a most excellent Christian woman & one in every way competent to instruct Indian women & girls in domestic arts & in morals, & in general elevation."[20]

The choice of Agua Caliente as a location for a WNIA-sponsored hospital resulted in a contentious atmosphere between Quinton and Mission Agent Horatio Nelson Rust. As early as October 1889, he had suggested to Commissioner Morgan that the village, with its hot and cold springs, would be a favorable place for a hospital, with the Mission agency physician as resident doctor.[21] After completing his tour with Quinton, Rust again reminded Morgan that the hospital was a longtime scheme of his, noting the centrality of the village as a positive factor, concluding that "with such a hospital and a kind physician the educational influence should be equal to any school we have." Although hoping that a hospital would be established "in part at least" by Quinton, he ultimately favored complete government control, suggesting that a new schoolhouse be constructed at Agua Caliente with the old one used temporarily as a hospital.[22] In a 1902 *Los Angeles Times* article, he expressed extreme displeasure with any WNIA participation, misrepresenting the situation and putting obstacles in the path of association work at both Agua Caliente and Cahuilla.[23] The 1903 removal of all Warner Ranch residents after an unsuccessful court case ended the prospect of a WNIA hospital.

Once receiving permission from Morgan to proceed with her plans, Quinton instructed Rev. William Henry Weinland, WNIA supervisor of Mission Indian work, to ensure that the hospital structure "*touch[ed]* the Hot Springs so as to have a free supply of the hot water." Believing that Rust "did *not* want the Indians to have *any* hold on the Springs," she informed Weinland to "look over *all* the pros and cons, guard the Indians and their hold on the Springs, and do what is *best* in way of selecting the site." A week later she cautioned Weinland to not "be taken in, or influenced by Maj. Rust, for all his arguments are specious & fallacious."[24] From the beginning, Rust was contemptuous toward Quinton, describing her in a later news account as his "old arch enemy." The agent, encouraged by Commissioner Morgan to establish a hospital at Warner ranch, disapproved of Quinton and her association's involvement in the entire process. Although correctly noting that one of the association workers was a doctor, he stated he soon "learned that they were there to do missionary work, and were poorly equipped even for that." Because of the WNIA's role in what he perceived as his hospital, Rust had written: "my plans were all frustrated, [and] my promise to the Indians broken." Complaining that Dr. Hallowell and field matron French simply drew their salaries and made missionary reports, he mistakenly concluded that they had never made "friends with the Indians."[25] Letters and reports printed in *The Indian's Friend* tell a different story.

Weinland, burdened with his own missionary work, was also given the responsibility of helping to settle Hallowell and French at Agua Caliente and Johnson at Cahuilla, serving at times as escort, driver, and carpenter, remodeling old buildings or constructing new ones. Spending hours in the saddle during August and September 1891, he traveled the eighty-six miles to Cahuilla to ready the cottage originally built for Fleming, now serving as Johnson's home. He had gotten lost on the first trip; undisturbed, he simply bedded down beneath a large tree, with his saddle for a pillow, declaring afterward he had "slept the sleep of Jacob in the wilderness." On April 20 he made a one hundred-fifty-mile-long buggy ride to Agua Caliente to consult with the Indians regarding the WNIA's hospital plans and to supervise repairs on a house rented for Hallowell and French.[26] Then, in early January 1893, at Quinton's request he met them at the train station nearest to Agua Caliente; Hallowell and French had met in Riverside, where French's brother lived, and then taken the train. Quinton had viewed this as a perfect opportunity for Weinland not only to become acquainted with the two women but to introduce them properly to the Indians. Hallowell was most impressed with the cleric, describing him as "pure gold," eager to see that they were comfortable.[27]

In turn, Weinland was equally pleased with the three new female appointees to his Ramona Mission, announcing their arrival in his January 14, 1893, report in *The Moravian*, the official organ of the Northern Province of the Moravian Church of America. He was particularly pleased with Dr. Anna Johnson because her appointment saved the villagers a seventy-five-mile trek to seek medical treatment from the agency physician. Convinced "that the constitution of the Indians and the peculiar line of diseases to which they are subject, call for special study and investigation," he believed that medicines had a different effect upon them. Possibly he hoped that Johnson would prove his theory correct.[28]

Weinland had informed the readers of *The Moravian* that Hallowell and French were at Agua Caliente to establish a hospital, a project long in the planning stage. "We need just such a place to which we can send chronic cases," he wrote. "It is our earnest prayer that as time passes, this small hospital may grow and develop into a very useful institution." The only obstacle was a lawsuit brought against the Indians by John G. Downey, an ex-California governor, who claimed the village springs were part of his property, when in fact the Cupeños had "lived there in undisputed possession for a century or more," building neat bathhouses and renting their adobe homes to summer visitors suffering with rheumatism.

Although Downey had hired some of the best lawyers, Weinland hoped that "God [would] overrule for justice and truth" and help in the Indians' defense.[29]

For the next six years the New York City Indian Association (NYCIA) and its branches at Harlem, Yonkers, Poughkeepsie, Kingston, and Hopewell Junction funded Hallowell's medical work. This support was in part possible because they had recently suspended their work at Soboba, transferring the monies to Hallowell.[30] In her first letter to her sponsors, Hallowell stated "that it has been supposed that we would turn one of our two rooms into a hospital at once." She wondered "how such patients can be nursed, cooked for, fed, bathed, etc. etc. and we live and cook and sleep in the other room I cannot quite see."[31] After reading that letter, Quinton immediately wrote to Weinland that she was personally "aghast!" When Dr. Wainwright sought approval for Hallowell to take in one or two of his surgical cases, Quinton had explained that this was their home, not a hospital. The WNIA did not object to Hallowell's tending to some patients but, she explained to Weinland, it would be unwise for her "to take one whom you expect to die, *at first* for fear the Indians might be afraid of her in case of death." In the meantime, since the Cupeños had not yet agreed to grant land for the hospital, Quinton informed Weinland that the plan was for Hallowell to tend to the Indians in their homes, win them over, and then build a hospital. In the interim, if Hallowell was willing to care for the sick, Quinton would authorize her to "get cots & beds etc. as needed." A tent, sent by an unidentified donor, could easily serve as a temporary hospital. However, Quinton made clear that any patients would be Hallowell's; Wainwright was to serve only as a consultant.[32] A cordial relationship soon developed between the two doctors, with Hallowell writing that during one of Wainwright's visits to a former patient, a heavy drinker, he had praised her for keeping the man alive so long.[33]

New York reformers, pleased with Hallowell's work, contributed $500 in 1894, prompting Quinton and the Missionary Committee to write, "We cannot but expect large and blessed results from its adoption by that able and deeply interested society." Hallowell and French were soon encouraging the Indians to install wooden floors and windows on the south side of each house to ventilate windowless adobe homes that had only a roof opening to allow smoke to escape. During an August 1896 address before a San Francisco audience, French explained that "one of the earliest steps toward civilization will be the admitting of light into the homes." Only then could the inhabitants see the wretchedness in which they had been living. With windows in and walls whitened, "the floor will soon be cleared of its loathsome rubbish," she concluded.³⁴ Hallowell's New York supporters described her work as often "done under the most discouraging circumstances, but nevertheless bright, cheerful letters were received" in which she listed illnesses tended to, including colds and rheumatism, and the treatment of one young boy who had severely injured his eye. She had performed reconstructive surgery to "prevent scarring and contraction," reporting he had been patient and trusting throughout the procedure.³⁵

During the early December 1896 WNIA annual meeting, the NYCIA described their work at Agua Caliente as "constant, efficient and of usual success." The missionary cottage was tastefully furnished, and the little front garden was "inspirational and a model for imitation, and there the industrial and medical work of the mission goes forward."³⁶ The WNIA missionary report for the following year, however, projected a difficult time ahead. On December 29, 1896, the California Superior Court had ruled against the Warner Ranch Indians in their eviction suit.³⁷ Nevertheless, two years later Hallowell traveled to New York City to appear before the NYCIA annual meeting, prompting corresponding secretary Aurora T. Green to describe her as possessing good sense and a "kindly, dignified presence" that "clearly indicated how she had come to win [the Indians'] love and confidence." The association pledged $800 towards her medical efforts for that year. During an earlier February meeting, Quinton had addressed the work accomplished by both Hallowell and French, describing their efforts to make the adobe missionary cottage attractive. It soon "became a striking contrast to the floorless, windowless, miserable hovels" around it and served as "an object lesson which in time produced the desired result." Quinton asserted that Hallowell had also won Indian mothers over by the expert care and healing of their sick babies.³⁸

The January 1899 issue of *The Indian's Friend* included a report presented during the WNIA's annual December meeting. Hallowell's efforts were described as varied and influential, as she combined her healing ministrations with religious instruction. Despite the drawbacks of the court case hanging over the work, it was reported that "there had been on the field real fruitage, social, moral and spiritual."³⁹ Then, at the first meeting in 1900, the NYCIA transferred its Agua Caliente station to Weinland and the Moravian Board, applying the unused portion of one of its memorial funds to the construction of the Rebecca Collins Hospital on the Navajo Reservation.⁴⁰ It was WNIA practice, once a station was fully operational, to turn it over, free of charge, to a local missionary society and open a new one. Hallowell subsequently moved to Los Angeles, where she opened a medical office. She died on October 13, 1901, at age 77, in Haddonfield, New Jersey.⁴¹

Johnson and Hallowell were not the only physicians employed in WNIA missionary stations. The association hired Dr. L. M. Hensel and his wife to serve as medical missionaries among the Omaha tribe in Nebraska. The couple had been described as "a Christian gentleman and able physician" and "an able teacher and missionary."⁴² Various Massachusetts branches paid his $1,000 salary, while the new Kentucky auxiliary paid her missionary salary of $500. Quinton was especially pleased that the WNIA was finally engaged in missionary work among the 1,200 members of the tribe, whose reservation lands had recently been allotted.⁴³

The Hensels arrived in November 1887 and were temporarily housed in cramped quarters in only one room in the old agency headquarters. In a January 2, 1888, letter, writing of conditions reminiscent of those later endured by Drs. Johnson and Hallowell, Hensel described life in their one room: "We cooked, toiled, rested, slept, entertained, examined the sick, and dispensed medicines; yet it was the very best that could be done under the circumstances." In addition, his wife had opened up a night school and a sewing class. Hensel expressed extreme displeasure with the practices of the local medicine men, describing them as "intolerably ignorant and cruel," especially pointing to their "barbarous manipulation with a flat-iron to cure nausea [which] often results in peritonitis." Eventually, WNIA auxiliaries in Maine, New Jersey, and Washington, DC, pledged funds to expand the original building and to add a hospital wing. When the entire home was finally opened for their use, Mrs. Hensel expressed great relief, explaining that the Indians "seemed as anxious as we felt for that time to come." In a January 14 letter, she wrote they were now using the large front room as the school.⁴⁴

The mission station was enlarged in the spring of 1889 when Benny Atkin, an Omaha Indian, and his mother, for an unspecified reason, gave the WNIA twelve acres at Omaha Creek, some nine miles from the agency.⁴⁵ Initial missionary efforts at this new Omaha Creek site were at first minimal: a Sunday school with two meetings weekly, and house-to-house calls until the Morristown branch of the New Jersey Indian Association funded a missionary cottage and the Bethlehem, Pennsylvania, auxiliary provided monies for a chapel, where Mrs. Hensel taught school that first summer. The combined cost of both structures was $1,212.⁴⁶

The WNIA Missionary Committee had initially decided to occupy the government-provided quarters only until they could move permanently to

Omaha Creek, where they believed the need was greater. However, once missionary work at the old agency began to grow, the Presbyterian missionaries, who worked nearby, and Alice Cunningham Fletcher, who had directed allotment of Omaha lands, as well as tribal leaders, advised against such a move. However, in order for work at the old agency site to expand, a formal grant of land directly from the Indians was needed as their reservation had been allotted, and the government could not gift it to the WNIA. Quinton turned to longtime supporter Senator Henry Laurens Dawes and to Indian Commissioner John H. Oberly. With their support, Congress on March 15, 1888, passed "An Act for the Relief of the Omaha Tribe," which included a provision authorizing Interior Secretary William F. Vilas, with the consent of the Omahas, to set aside land, not to exceed five acres, to the WNIA for missionary and educational purposes. The association and its successor were entitled to the land for as long as it was used for such purposes. On February 15, 1889, Oberly informed Quinton of the legislation, enclosing a copy of his instructions to the Indian agent to set aside the land. She responded three days later.[47] Commissioner Morgan, newly appointed, instructed Special Agent George W. Gordon to call an Indian Council on August 22, 1889, to explain to the Omahas the Interior Department's wish to set aside land to the WNIA and to implement the transfer.[48]

To prepare for his expanded mission, Hensel busied himself in the months before the council, traveling and hauling supplies almost daily between his two sites, supervising the new building at Omaha Creek and extensive repairs and improvement at the old site. He spent twelve weeks at Omaha Creek, leveling land, fencing five and a half acres, planting four thousand trees, and building a well and cistern with Indian labor. His daily travels between sites interrupted his missionary efforts, forcing him to acknowledge that this work had "been done in weakness and with imperfect hands," but he hoped what had been accomplished would speak for itself. Solely responsible for overseeing the construction at the sites, he excused the unavoidable reduction of the medical care he provided, explaining that he had not yet discovered or invented "any way to be in three places at once." He had still been able to make one hundred eighty medical calls, treat twelve patients in his makeshift hospital, and visit fifty Indian homes in September and October. He also praised the efforts of the Presbyterian Board for building the tasteful reservation church where Indians and whites alike worshiped on Wednesday evening, explaining that with Quinton coming, he had hired an interpreter, believing it "absolutely impossible to avoid mistakes and misunderstandings without" one.[49]

To make sure she would arrive at the council in time, Quinton had left Philadelphia on August 13, stopping along the way in Rochester, New York; Toledo, Ohio; and Chicago, Illinois, to make plans for meetings she intended to hold on her return. From Chicago she traveled directly to Bancroft, Nebraska, disembarking for the twenty-mile drive to the Omaha Agency.[50] The council grounds were on a large and pretty knoll where many Indian men and women were gathered, with one great circle of Indian men "in picturesque attitudes, with touches of bright color on some shoulders in the way of scarfs or shawls, the peace-pipe circulating among them." Their low conversations stopped when Agent Jesse F. Warner rose to open the proceedings, assisted by Hiram Chase, the first Omaha Indian to become a lawyer, as interpreter.[51] Gordon was introduced, and after reading the official document and explaining that a majority vote of adult males was required for acceptance, he recommended they approve, explaining that the land being set aside was for their sole benefit.[52]

Quinton was then invited to speak, reminding her Omaha audience of her 1884 visit during which she had agreed to carry their petition back to Washington. The Indians had requested the removal of white agency employees, with monies saved to be used for their benefit. Their petition had been granted, and she could now see "the great progress they had made since that date." Recognizing and acknowledging those who had been present during her earlier visit, she described the current missionary work of her association and of the "importance for their sakes of the grant of the five acres."[53]

The voting took longer than a week, with opposition from nonprogressive members. Wahonega, a representative of this group, explained to Quinton that his followers refused to sign because they felt that what the WNIA was proposing was "for the other party and that *our* people will not therefore be benefited by what you propose to do." He was referring to the application process needed to get a WNIA home building loan. Because fewer nonprogressives applied, most loans went to the more progressive tribal members. Quinton assured him that there was no favoritism. The WNIA "was the friend of *all*, and desired to help *all*." Finally, with Gordon's persistence and persuasion from Quinton, the document was formally signed on September 2.[54]

Unfortunately, Quinton's report provided few details of her activities during her two-week reservation stay. Nothing was mentioned about Hensel's improvements or his missionary and medical work. She did visit homes built with loans from the WNIA's Home Building Department, finding them neatly kept and "surrounded with evidences of industry, thrift, and a growing civilizing." She met with one homeowner, Noah La Flesche, a relative of Dr. Susan La Flesche. A recipient of a loan secured during the first year the department was under WNIA management, he proudly showed off his granary with five hundred bushels of wheat he had harvested.[55] On Sunday, August 25, Quinton also joined the Hensels in dedication ceremonies for the WNIA-funded chapel at Omaha Creek, "naming it Bethlehem Chapel with the grateful concurrence of the Indians."[56]

Several months after the Omaha council, Quinton attended the seventh Lake Mohonk Conference. During her appointed presentation time, she discussed her association's Home Building Department, explaining that returns from home loans that year had exceeded $500 ($17,380 in 2025 dollars). She related the accomplishments of Noah La Flesche, whose harvest of 2,000 bushels of corn meant he would be able to pay $200 toward his loan. She was most impressed with the many young Omaha men who had attended Carlisle and Hampton boarding schools and whose influence she believed would prove helpful to their people. She singled out Hiram Chase, who had recently been admitted to the bar, and his friend Thomas L. Sloan, a recent Hampton graduate.[57] As an interesting aside, she noted that Sloan had started a baseball club, believing that it would help his people learn "to think quickly, [and] to make decisions promptly." In the medical field, hospital work had been undertaken, and the association hoped to build a twelve-bed hospital with a large assembly room to be used as a classroom for social lectures, and a place where the young men could learn about their legal and political duties.[58]

The following May, the WNIA handed over their two Omaha stations, gratis, to the Presbyterian Board. This transfer included the five acres acquired during the 1889 council, a five-room cottage, barn and outbuildings, and the twelve acres gifted by Benny Atkin and his mother, with a new cottage and chapel. The Missionary Committee, however, retained "a share in the medical services of Dr. Susan La Flesche, the physician and a teacher in the Government school," supplementing her government salary by an annual payment of $250 to care for the Omahas in their own homes.[59]

The following year, a WNIA missionary report described La Flesche Picotte's well-furnished office as arranged like a drugstore but with plenty of games available to put Indian children at ease during their treatments. That July she had seen thirty-seven patients, one hundred eleven in August, and one hundred thirty the following month—both acute and chronic cases. Explaining that she truly enjoyed her work and was feeling "more interest in, and more attached to [her] people than ever before," she thanked the WNIA for all they had done for her and her people.[60] Two decades later, in January 1913, widowed and living in Walthill, Nebraska, Dr. Picotte succeeded in having a twelve-bed hospital built, with a grant from the Home Mission Board of the Presbyterian Church. It was never clear why the WNIA did not fund her hospital.[61]

The failure to build a hospital at Agua Caliente was not the only such aborted attempt. In 1891, the WNIA founded a short-lived Hospital Department under the chairmanship of Laura Elise Bates Tileston, who expressed an interest in Indian reform long before her WNIA membership. Following the 1877 death of her father, she and her mother and two sisters had moved to Hampton, Virginia, where she was hired along with her older sister, Etta, to teach at Hampton Institute.[62] In late autumn 1886, Tileston accompanied fellow teacher, Elaine Goodale,[63] an advocate for reservation day schools, to what is now South Dakota to open the White River Camp School, their model day school among the Lower Brule in an abandoned schoolhouse that Goodale had discovered during a visit the previous year. The two women introduced industrial training, with girls learning to sew and cook and boys tending gardens and learning carpentry. However, they also spent much of their time handing out medicines and preparing suitable food for those who were sick. Goodale later described Tileston, who had volunteered to join her, as possessed of an "unfailing flow of spirits under trying conditions" which was viewed as "a valuable asset." Dubbed "Miss Owl" by the Indians, Tileston was "as sensible as she was merry," winning instant popularity. She was also clever. When the Indian Office had refused to fund two positions for the White River Camp, she went directly to Bishop William Hare, Episcopal missionary working among the Sioux, and requested a commission as one of his missionaries.[64]

Two years later, Tileston returned to Dakota Territory. After a short time there, she wrote to Quinton that she had found a great need for an Indian hospital. It saddened her to visit the sick, finding no one near to make their pain easier "by the skillful touch or refreshing drink." She explained that for the past four years she had been corresponding with the government physician at the Lower Brule at Crow Creek Agency, who in turn had repeatedly written the Indian Office requesting medical assistance for them. Tileston was fully convinced that a hospital at each agency could be "made an important factor in furthering the work of civilization among Indians." She proposed putting up a "building for a really first-class hospital" at the agency, explaining that Miss Ada J. Porter, head nurse at Hampton for five years, was ready to take charge. Tileston believed that once the structure was built, she could get government support for furnishings and "a proper share of 'sick rations' issued annually."[65]

In an 1891 WNIA-published pamphlet, Tileston described hospital work as "one of the greatest present needs among the Indians." She soon was pleading for funds to build a hospital as well as a training school for nurses on the Crow Creek Reserve. When the government decided the following year to build their own hospital, she chose to use her current funding, $150 from the Jamaica Plain auxiliary and $390 from Hampton, to support a temporary hospital in a renovated four-room cottage until the proposed governmental facility was operational. To facilitate this effort, Commissioner Morgan appointed Ada Porter as a government field matron to care for the sick, teach hygiene in the schools, and visit Indian homes to show "the women better ways of living." Porter began work on June 18, 1891.[66] As late as 1893 she was still working in the newly built government hospital.[67]

Once Tileston was confident that the Crow Creek hospital was secure, she resigned as head of the WNIA Hospital Department, explaining that when she had agreed to assume the chairmanship, she "did not fully realize [that her] responsibility to the Association as well as to the work for Indians" would interfere with her duties as committee head.[68] No doubt part of her reason for stepping down was her responsibility to Tileston Hall, a day boarding school and a college preparatory school founded by her and her sister, Etta, in 1888. Located in Old Point Comfort, Virginia, overlooking Chesapeake Bay, the school specialized in languages, art, and music for students aged six to eighteen.[69]

It would take the WNIA almost a decade after Tileston's failed attempt to succeed in building their first full-service hospital on an Indian reservation. In 1899, the Rebecca Collins Memorial Hospital opened in the San Juan Valley, at Jewett, New Mexico, in the northeastern corner of the Navajo Reservation. The process had been complicated, requiring extensive monetary support from numerous WNIA branches and the multitasking skills of Mary Louise Eldridge, missionary, government field matron, and head of Navajo missionary work for the WNIA.[70] She not only hired the builder but supervised the construction on a thirty-five acre site at Jewett that she had donated for $1 from her one hundred sixty–acre homestead adjoining the reservation.[71]

Eldridge, a nurse in her forties, and her younger companion, Mary E. Raymond, had traveled from Lawrence, Kansas, under the auspices of the Woman's Home

Figure 13. A Navajo family arrives in front of the Navajo Methodist Mission at Jewett, New Mexico, circa 1902, to drop their child off at school. The small detached white building to the right of the school is Mary Tripp's cabin. (Department of Special Collections, Princeton University Library [Navajo Mission Collection, circa 1895–1908 (WC116)].)

Missionary Society (WHMS) of the Methodist Episcopal Church to establish a mission and school among the Navajos living along the San Juan River. They had arrived at Jewett in October 1891,[72] founding the Navajo Methodist Mission, which later moved closer to Farmington.[73] Embracing the government's new field matron program, the WHMS had applied for a position for Raymond before the two women had even left for New Mexico. A month after she and Eldridge had arrived, Raymond learned from Commissioner Morgan of her appointment.[74] Her early death prompted the local Indian agent to request that Eldridge be appointed in her place.

Less than a decade after the two missionaries had begun their Navajo work, the New York Indian City Association, long interested in opening a hospital among a tribe they viewed as unusually promising, turned their missionary work at Agua Caliente over to the Moravians. They dedicated the remainder of a memorial fund named after Rebecca Collins, a prominent Quaker philanthropist and association member, towards construction of a church near the Navajo Methodist Mission at Jewett.[75] Once this decision was made, New York City members put out an appeal for additional funding.[76]

Like all WNIA missionary stations, the hospital was a joint effort of numerous auxiliaries. The NYCIA provided $1,300 for construction costs and pledged $400 toward a physician's salary, with an additional $200 added by the Cambridge Indian Association (CIA), a branch of the Massachusetts Indian Association and a major sponsor of Eldridge's missionary work. New York and Brooklyn auxiliaries built the stable, while the Cambridge reformers also raised $305 by private subscription for furnishings. The NYCIA and Connecticut auxiliaries each pledged $500 toward the annual expenses of $1,500, while the Boston, Cambridge, and Jamaica Plain associations pledged the salary of a kindergarten teacher. In September 1899, Eldridge and an unidentified housekeeper, whose salary was paid by Cambridge reformers, moved in.[77] The *San Juan County Index* described the hospital as located "snugly up against the east side of the Hogback,"[78] with the nearest post office in Jewett. The eighty-five-foot-long structure, designed and built by W. R. Shawver, was "of goodly size and plain, neat architecture," a handsome building with a two-story-high central structure. A few yards' distance were the separate industrial building, a barn, and supply rooms.[79]

Earlier in July and August, Eldridge had informed her Cambridge sponsors of the frustrations she was having with supervising the construction work. She had, however, taken great pleasure in the Indian Industries League's stand-alone industrial building and its Indian room, for which she had also donated five acres from her homestead for $1.[80] In a July 20 letter, she wrote that the walls of the League building, constructed of adobe bricks, had been built in a mere four and a half days. It had been erected first to store doors, windows, and hardware for the much larger main hospital building, which took longer to build as it was constructed of the "finest lumber ever brought into this valley" and eighteen-inch-thick brick walls. While engaged in supervisorial tasks, Eldridge had also been dealing with a smallpox outbreak, traveling to distant camps to vaccinate more than eighty Navajos.[81]

In an August 28 letter, Eldridge described considerable sickness among the Indians, although there was no mention of smallpox. Sick herself, she was forced to hand out medicine to walk-ins while her assistant, Edith M. Dabb, visited the camps in her place.[82] On the positive side, Eldridge explained, Navajo crops were better than expected, and the hospital building, described as thoroughly well built, would be completed in a few days. It had been expensive, because all construction materials had to be hauled eighty-five miles over barely existing roads. For her own personal living space, Eldridge had decided to use the League's Indian Room, describing it as light and pleasant with its two handsome Singer sewing machines, knitting machines, and a cooking range to teach bread-making.[83] The League hoped that by the use of such new labor-saving devices, Navajo women could be trained in "regularity of occupation." Dabb, placed in charge of the industrial room, described the sewing machines as the most attractive part of the facility, and that the Navajo women were "pleased that the house [was] for them," concluding that the room was greatly helping to uplift the women.[84]

As superintendent of WNIA Navajo work, Eldridge regularly traveled the seventy miles of desert terrain between the association's hospital and its missionary station at Two Grey Hills. At times she was forced to camp at night alone because the entire trip was absent of Navajo homes. In one letter to her Cambridge sponsors, after noting the recent cold-blooded murder of three men, she wrote that when she stopped "for dinner and to rest my horses, I always have my revolver within reach, not for the Navajos but for tramps and desperadoes who are 'hiding.'"[85] On April 1, 1900, Mrs. Mary Pradt Harper, MD, former physician at the government hospital at Fort Defiance agency, joined Eldridge and Dabb.[86] During her first two months, Harper treated one hundred twelve cases and participated in a census that June, explaining that her numerous reservation trips to count residents had provided her with "a large volume of experience," enabling her to better understand the Navajo daily life.[87] Unfortunately, in August Harper suffered a debilitating stroke; the position she vacated was never filled.[88]

In August 1901, Eldridge toured Mary G. Burdette, corresponding secretary of the Women's Baptist Home Mission Society, and Rev. George H. Brewer, secretary of the New Mexico and Arizona Baptist Conventions, around the hospital environs. Burdette expressed her appreciation of Eldridge's kindness in acquainting them with the "the needs and the possibilities of the Navajos." Heavy rains and overflowing streams detained the two officials at Jewett long enough for them to visit a nearby Navajo settlement and view cultivated fields watered by the San Juan River through the Cambridge Ditch, funded by the CIA and built under Eldridge's direction. Typical of the ethnocentric view of the day, Burdette was "better pleased with the appearance of the cornfields than with the very primitive hogan which forms the home of the Navajo family." Eldridge also drove them to Two Grey Hills—a trip fraught with lengthy detours due to flooding and washed-out roads but enabling Brewer an opportunity to visit a group of Navajo farms at Toadlena, some eight miles northwest of the mission and a second encampment where the visitors lingered at a hogan to watch Navajo women at their looms. "We marvel that the women keep the blankets as clean as they do, as their rude looms are set up on one side of the hogan, and the wool lies on the floor," Burdette noted.[89] Brewer, impressed with the station, recommended to the Baptist Convention that they apply to the WNIA to take it over.

The November issue of *The Indian's Friend* reported the transfer of land and structures to the Baptists.[90]

Later that summer, a Mrs. Mary A. Vreeland described to Mrs. Hamilton S. Gordon, president of the NYCIA, her recent visit to the hospital. After traveling through a desolate terrain for miles, Vreeland had come upon "an oasis in the desert, twenty miles of cultivated fields, where not one existed" before. This oasis, she explained, had been created by ditches dug from the San Juan River by Navajo men under Eldridge's supervision, enabling river water to flood their fields of corn, wheat, melons, squashes, and beans. Vreeland described hospital work carried out in "a carefully constructed and well-equipped building with separate wards for men and women" furnished with comfortable beds, bathrooms, linen closets, and a well-stocked dispensary.[91] Observing that during a light month, some two hundred forty-one patients were treated, Vreeland described the affectionate reverence the Navajos showed toward Eldridge. Dabb had described to her the numerous times during the winter that Eldridge "crept on hands and knees around the dangerous curves, on her errands of mercy," as she climbed over the steep Hogback Mountains. "It is not to be wondered at when we consider her remarkable personality and loving devotion to their interests," Vreeland concluded. She was also impressed by the progress made by the children in the little boarding school.[92]

Around the same time as Vreeland's visit, F. L. Chase, a local rancher, who contracted with Agent G. W. Hayzlett for Navajo workers, reported to the *Durango Semi-Weekly Herald* that the hospital was "nicely situated and equipped," and that its quarters were "splendid, many white people not having as good accommodations." Eldridge, he noted, had an excellent knowledge of medicine and was "thoroughly acquainted with her work and never at a loss what to do." However, he found it odd that Eldridge and Henrietta G. Cole, both missionaries and women of culture, "should voluntarily bury themselves in the sand, as it were."[93]

In a February 1, 1902, letter, Eldridge provided a glimpse into her extensive time- consuming medical camp work, explaining that this was the only way she could reach "the greatest number of people." Loading her wagon with food, bedding, medicines, and a supply of cloth, she headed out to distant camps to "doctor the sick, make or have them make clothes for the very old, for the little children and the sick—plan for them about their farms, and ditches, and houses." Then, during the evening, men, women, and children gathered around her to discuss religion. Eldridge's long visits were possible only because of the complete confidence she had in her new assistant, Miss Mary E. Gaines, a nurse, to run the hospital while she was away. Once Eldridge returned home, the Navajos would come to her small personal living quarters, with its bed, a writing table, and a typewriter, located at one end of the Indian room, to talk business, to simply visit, run the sewing machine, or use the shoe making tools. "I am sure I do not know how I would get along without this room, as it keeps the noise and dust, etc., out of the hospital," Eldridge explained. If her Navajo visitors needed medicine, they went directly to the hospital.[94]

Years later, in 1911, Eldridge revealed more information about the Rebecca Collins Hospital to a member of the Presbyterian Board of Home Missions. She had personally contributed $300 toward the hospital, which she estimated costing about $2,300, with the Indian Industries League providing $350 toward their industrial building. Hospital furnishings had been about $500, exclusive of the almost $100 worth of bathtubs and heaters she had installed with the help of a friend. During the final year of operation, nearly six thousand medical prescriptions had been issued, and the wards were nearly always full of patients. Despite this apparent success, an earlier transfer had been necessary partly because of funding difficulties due to the death of a number of wealthier association member donors.[95] Once fully functioning, all association stations were handed over to a local missionary society to operate. However, the fact that Eldridge actually lived at the hospital meant that its 1902 transfer to the Board of Home Missions of the Presbyterian Church forced her to move down river some eighteen miles and open up a new missionary station, work again supported by Cambridge and Connecticut reformers.[96] By this time the WNIA had changed its name to the National Indian Association (NIA), enabling men to become members.

A decade after the transfer of the Rebecca Collins Hospital, the NYCIA funded a second Navajo hospital, the Good Samaritan Hospital at Indian Wells, on the Arizona part of the Navajo Reservation. The long, complicated process had begun under Quinton's watch as chair of the Missionary Committee, continued under her successor, John W. Clark, and involved considerable efforts on the part of Rev. William Riley Johnston and his wife Margaret Wray Johnston, a nurse, who supervised the running of the hospital. Although not a physician, she had honed her medical skills working alongside her missionary husband for some sixteen years. He had started work among the Navajos in 1896 at the Gospel Mission Union in Tuba City, Arizona. Dissatisfied with that organization's leadership, Johnston built an independent mission and school at Tolchaco on the Little

Colorado River near Leupp, Arizona, about 1900.[97] Later working with Quinton, he supervised the founding of an association station at Tuba City, funded by the NYCIA and the Brooklyn Association. Missionary work began in April 1903, and two years later the station was transferred to the Presbyterian Board.[98] Then, in 1910, with John W. Clark, Quinton's successor, Johnston opened another station initially at Castle Butte, northeast of Winslow. Because of an inadequate water supply, the work was moved to Indian Wells, where Clark reported that the New York City auxiliary "with its usual liberality and progressive spirit, proposes to begin hospital work" during the coming year.[99] The auxiliary donated $1,100 for the construction of a missionary cottage and a hospital which, according to *The Indian's Friend*, was to be called the Good Samaritan Hospital ("Kin-bi-jo-ba-i" or "the house in which they are kind") to "convey to the Indians the idea of the place that we wish them to have."[100] It was officially opened on April 1, 1913.

Construction costs and equipment exceeded $5,000, with estimated annual expenses of about $1,600. Built of adobe, mostly by Navajo workers earning market-based wages, the facility, far more extensive than the one at Jewett, consisted of a central building with a reception room; nurse's room; dispensary; two wards, one for women and a second for men with bathrooms and a sleeping porch for each; a kitchen and dining room; and closets for medical supplies, all on the ground floor. The cellar held the steam heating plant. The men's ward was named in honor of Hamilton F. Downing, the late husband of the president of the NYCIA, while the women's ward was named for Lucy Jane Wood, an active member of the Jamaica Plain, Massachusetts, auxiliary. The second floor served as living quarters for the Johnston family[101] and Margaret's assistant Viena Nevongoimsie Jenkins, a young Hopi girl who had been with her for six years. Mrs. Johnston, facility superintendent, was described in association literature as possessing "a large knowledge of medicine," with the ability to accurately diagnose diseases.[102] By the time the family moved into the hospital, Reverend Johnston had turned his Tolchaco mission over to the Presbyterian Board, although he continued working on their behalf. While not an official NIA worker, he and his interpreter often accompanied NIA workers to remote Navajo camps.[103]

Margaret Johnston began treating patients in mid-September 1912. From that time to the formal opening of the hospital, she cared for some one hundred ninety-six sick Navajos living in different remote camps. Between April 1, 1913, and the following October, leaving her Hopi assistant Viena to handle hospital patients, Johnston treated an additional three hundred seventy-seven Indians in various camps, and another sixty-six patients in the wards upon her return. To win over as many women and children as possible, she requested toys, books, and candies from her NIA sponsors. She noted in one report that she was not including the names of her patients because she still was a stranger to them, and it was "not considered polite to ask a Navajo his name."[104]

In early letters, Johnston lamented that "pioneer medical work among the Navajo Indians has its discouragements," largely because for generations "they have been under the influence of their medicine men." As time passed, however, she began to notice that "some of the most superstitious are coming to us for medical care." In a May 1913 letter, she recounted that she had treated an old medicine man who had been kicked by a horse. When he finally went home, she reported, he was "well and happy, praising our 'medicine.'"[105] Although forced to retire following several bouts of ill health and surgery in a Los Angeles hospital, she returned temporarily to resume her supervisory tasks.

Her first replacement was Dr. C. J. K. Moore,[106] who with his wife and children arrived on November 4, 1914, after a harrowing trip during which the wagon carrying part of their household goods turned over in Cottonwood Wash, immersing bedding, books, clothing, and groceries in three to four feet of muddy water, rendering them "utterly impossible to recognize." In his first letter, he concluded that this "is the greatest field for medical mission work on the Navajo reservation." During the next year, he visited Navajo camps and treated hospital patients. In 1915, 1,283 Navajos came to the dispensary for treatment; one hundred thirty-six were treated in their camps, with a total number of treatments estimated at two thousand forty, prompting *The Indian's Friend* to report that this was "conclusive evidence of the need for, and the value of, this work."[107] The NIA struggled with finances as World War I raged in Europe. Although wards were closed, the dispensary remained open, with medical work in the camps continuing, and the Binghamton, New York, branch, in honor of their late founder, Mrs. L. M. S. Haynes, equipping an emergency room to care for patients needing minor surgery. When Moore resigned to take another position, Margaret Johnston returned to work during July and August 1916.[108]

Margaret's replacement was to have been Dr. R. E. Gunn, a graduate of Iowa Medical College, but when he took seriously ill, Dr. Gwendolyn D. Thomas was hired, arriving on May 16, 1917. The one consistent presence was Reverend Johnston, who remained behind to assist his wife's various replacements. On June 12, after four weeks in the field, Dr. Thomas wrote, "How impossible it is for a city-raised person to comprehend the awful darkness in which people like these Navajos, live year in and year out!" She described a visit to a Navajo hogan to treat a sick child. Accompanied by Reverend Johnston, she arrived on a windy cold day only to find the sick child had been moved a mile away, placed on a sheepskin and covered by a dirty blanket.[109] The girl's two brothers and the medicine man were beside her. The latter had his medicines spread out around him—"sticks, some with feathers on them, others with rattlers from snakes, and these he would beat together all night long, singing in the minor key, trying to drive the evil spirits out of the child." It was too late for Thomas to give the child any of the medicines she had brought. All she could do was "to wash the dirt out of her eyes and mouth" and leave.[110]

Thomas reported treating trachoma, tuberculosis, rheumatism, dysentery, and heart trouble. A smallpox epidemic broke out in the fall of 1917, resulting in a hospital quarantine. On November 15, 1917, Thomas resigned, and Margaret Johnston returned again, this time supported by Dr. James D. Kennedy from Ganado, who made regular visits to the hospital and dispensary.[111] Johnston's reports were thorough, often lengthy, noting at year's end that smallpox cases had lessened but whooping cough and mumps were on the increase.[112] January 1918 was exceptionally busy, with one hundred thirty-three patients among the hospital, the dispensary, and the camps. Camp work had required fifteen trips, with a total of one hundred fifty-seven miles traveled. During May and June, she treated six hundred ninety-three patients and made twenty-one camp visits, traveling some four hundred fifty-nine miles.[113] At year's end there was a serious influenza epidemic, and both Mrs. Johnston and one of her daughters were infected. In its usual end of the year plea for funding, *The Indian's Friend* reminded the membership that it took $5,000 to support the hospital and dispensary.[114] Johnston continued at the Good Samaritan Hospital until December 1, 1919, when it was transferred to the care of the Woman's Board of Home Missions of the Presbyterian Church. During its seven years of operation, a total of 13,010 treatments had been given. John Clark reported that in addition to the demonstrated efficacy of mission- or government-provided health care, the perception of the powers of the Navajo medicine men had diminished, and there was a "growing feeling among the Indians in favor of scientific medical treatment."[115]

The NIA, which never had a truly solid financial foundation, could not build a hospital for every reservation. Therefore, to provide medical care at a nominal cost within many of their larger stations, the association actively participated in the government's field matron program. The roles of Ada J. Porter, Dr. Anna Hayward Johnson, Julia French, and Mary Louise Eldridge have already been detailed.[116] From its inception, the WNIA had focused on Indigenous women and children, while the government initially ignored tribal women, assuming they would benefit through their children's education in government-sponsored schools. Lisa Emmerich explains that because many Indian women "exerted a conservative force" within their tribe, the government had founded the field matron program to aid in their assimilation and to enable "American women who were looking for new outlets for their energies the opportunity to redeem the Indian women," in "the belief that the power of domesticity could bring Native Americans closer to the goal of assimilation."[117] Although mostly white women, at least a dozen field matrons were Indian, including Marguerite La Flesche Diddock, Dr. Susan La Flesche's sister.[118]

The program, initially begun in 1890 and funded the following year by a government appropriation act, was strongly supported by Quaker reformers, long noted for their missionary work among the Indians.[119] They had recognized the pivotal role of Indian women early on, as had some government officials, including Indian Commissioner Thomas Jefferson Morgan, who supported the idea of working with Indian women, aware of their role "as family moral and spiritual anchors." To test out the validity of such a program, Morgan, long acquainted with Quinton, had appointed her temporarily as a field matron to observe women and girls in their home environment as she crossed the country on her 1891 transcontinental organizational tour. She thoroughly approved of an approach focusing on Indian women, writing: "I find that in the tribes among which I have been the way is open, that women & girls can be easily taught & influenced, that they can be made ambitious to improve themselves & their Homes, & this seems *just* the *time* for this domestic & moral instruction to be given."[120] Aware of its compatibility with the goals of her association, Quinton embraced the program, regularly applying for field matrons for the cash-strapped WNIA.

Another strong advocate was Merial A. Dorchester, wife of Dr. Daniel Dorchester, Superintendent of Indian Schools, who had worked on behalf of the Brooklyn Association to acquire land for their Piegan mission. Mrs. Dorchester, appointed by Morgan as a Special Agent in the Indian School Service, was soon "channeling requests for appointments."[121] In a May 11, 1890, report to Morgan, she described the qualifications of a field matron as "middle aged women, of common sense and physical vigor; should be able to ride horse back, and endure hardships uncomplainingly; should have nerves so strong, that the filth and odors of a wickiup will have no terrors; and should have motherly hearts so warm and big that every red sister who wished or ought to wish, for a better life, would find in them the needed helper." They should also speak correct English, have some medical knowledge, and "possess all house-wifely wisdom with tact and patience to teach the same."[122]

To highlight the program, the Indian Office informed Indian agents that the field matron position had been created so "Indian women may be influenced in their home life and duties, and may have done for them in their sphere what farmers and mechanics are supposed to do for Indian men in their sphere." Initially, typical wifely duties, such as care of the home, meal preparation, sewing, and laundry were listed, but soon additional responsibilities such as ensuring "cleanliness and hygienic conditions generally, including disposition of all refuse" and care of the sick were added. Morgan, aware that women in both white and Indian households were the primary caretakers, directed field matrons "to teach some basic nursing skills" to break Indian women's reliance on shamans and folk remedies. With tuberculosis and infant death as serious concerns, field matrons were also encouraged to treat contagious diseases and to see to prenatal care.[123]

WNIA members who weighed in on the new program in *The Indian's Friend* included Annie Beecher Scoville, a graduate of Wellesley College, a teacher at Hampton Institute, and a member of the Connecticut Indian Association.[124] She gained firsthand knowledge of duties required during a summer vacation in 1896 living in the village of Running Antelope. A Hunkpapa leader at the Standing Rock Agency, the latter lived a mere ten miles from Sitting Bull's deserted camp.[125] From experience, Scoville described field matrons as missionaries of civilization, with the "final success of all Indian education, [and] the establishing of self-supporting homes . . . largely in her hands." A local Indian agent once described a matron's role as "doctor, nurse, cook, farmer, teacher, seamstress, and general counselor for the camp," prompting Beecher to conclude that "the days of barbarism and reservation life will be numbered" once the positions of matron and farmer were filled with experts, "carrying on the training of a people as intelligently as a mission or a college settlement is run."[126]

Another strong advocate of the program was Mary E. Dewey, corresponding secretary of the Massachusetts Indian Association. She saw the field matron's role in broader terms, describing them as friends, helpers, and guides to Indian women.[127] On the flip side, under its corresponding secretary, Cornelia Taber, the

Northern California Indian Association (NCIA) in San Jose, California, came to view its association as friend, helper, and guide to the field matrons. By 1910, the NCIA was supporting more of them than any other WNIA auxiliary, almost a dozen, working among 3,800 Indians. The membership provided financial support and their general secretary, C. E. Kelsey, described field matron work as crucial, especially in California where the Indian population was largely scattered, making it "impossible for the government to reach all the little bands." Kelsey's four-page pamphlet read much like an advertisement encouraging women to contact him for information to sign up for the program.[128]

NCIA matrons worked in remote areas, facing isolation and at times resistance from local white residents. In an undated manuscript, possibly written as a speech, Taber identified eleven field matrons "going in and out of Indian cabins from Del Norte to San Diego, preaching a gospel of work and salvation, stimulating the men, encouraging and comforting the mothers, teaching the little children."[129] Taber provided their sole connection to the outside world, sending their letters to *The Indian's Friend* to be published, encouraging association members to support them, giving them advice, making suggestions, and alerting the reform community to their crucial work. Her sympathetic approach made it easy for the field matrons to confide in her through their letters, which reflected activities that went far beyond the role envisioned by the Indian Office. Taber described them as nurses, fundraisers, policy advocates, cottage industry entrepreneurs, marketers of Indian baskets, mediators, and agricultural instructors, teaching farming techniques to the men. Because such activities were often accomplished under the guise of religion, they were not seen as stepping outside their womanly sphere.

Two NCIA field matrons, Mary Ellicott Arnold and Mabel Reed, published their experiences in *In the Land of the Grasshopper Song* in 1957.[130] Arnold, a graduate of Cornell and Annie Bidwell's niece, and her friend, Mabel Reed, went to live among a small band of some 700 Karok (Karuk) Indians in the Klamath and Salmon River country of Siskiyou County in Northern California in January 1908. Taber described them as former New York settlement house workers with "special training in agriculture and carpentry" who embodied "the best of our American culture in character and attainments." The two women immediately began teaching Indian children, organizing sewing classes, and starting a Sunday school in their own living room.[131] One day they treated a seriously ill Indian woman with lotion from an unmarked bottle, believing it to be medicine. Their patient got better, even though they later learned the miracle drug was hair tonic.¹³² After two years, expressing great sadness in leaving behind Karuk families they had grown to love, they returned east to engage in other reforms.¹³³ Lisa Emmerich explains that, like other field matrons, Arnold and Reed had experienced transculturation—the "reversal of the 'civilization' process," as defined by anthropologist A. Irving Hallowell. While immersed within an Indian culture, they had felt "the pull of tribal culture strongly enough to leave their own behind," making them candidates "for the Anglo-American parallel of an Indian assimilation experience."¹³⁴

Although Taber did not emphasize the NCIA field matron's role in providing medical care, her inclusion of their stories and letters in her *California and Her Indian Children* provided a strong insight into why this auxiliary was so successful, and why the field matron program was so vital to the WNIA's work in general. Taber writes of Mary Johnson, who in 1906 served in Requa, in Del Norte County on the north bank of the Klamath River, establishing Sunday schools for whites and Indians and encouraging Indian parents to send their children to public school. She attended Indian dances, confiscated whiskey, and helped "women to get their drunken husbands home safe."¹³⁵

Harriet M. Gilchrist, field matron in Coarse Gold, Madera County, corresponded with Taber between 1910 and 1914. A Canadian by birth, she could not be appointed as a full-time matron, thus her part-time salary was supplemented by a member of the NYCIA. The first summer of her tenure she wrote of a measles outbreak and of a sixteen-year old girl whom she had nursed back to health after a serious bout of pneumonia.¹³⁶ On December 15, 1910, she informed Taber of plans to begin church services again on New Year's Day and of having the children come to her home twice a week for singing, reading, writing, and sewing lessons. She complained that the government had cut appropriations, forcing matrons to buy medicines and sewing supplies with their own money.¹³⁷ In another letter, she wrote of receiving warm clothing for newborns from friends in Fresno and a fine supply of medicines from others, explaining that two local hospitals were now providing their medical care.¹³⁸

Minnie C. Randolph, a former teacher in Bishop, Inyo County, began her field matron duties by teaching sewing classes and visiting the sick. In a mid-February 1907 letter, she noted that her greatest need was for missionary support, expressing a willingness to work with a minister of whatever denomination the NCIA provided. The following spring, the NCIA and the American Sunday School Union of the Pacific Coast sent a young missionary student named Faucette to

Bishop.[139] Mrs. C. A. Johnson of Middletown, Lake County, wrote to Taber on May 10, 1910, that she was much encouraged "with some of the improvements [she] saw in [the Indians'] homes," especially in the dirtiest one she had previously visited, where she had discovered a family of mice living in the lower part of their stove. On a return visit, Johnson discovered the stove had been polished, the floors scrubbed, and clean bedding placed on the bed.[140]

These hard-working field matrons made it possible for the NCIA to reach Indian people in remote areas of Northern California, providing them when necessary with vital medical care. One field matron with advanced medical training who went far beyond her job description was Mary Louise Eldridge, a former Methodist Episcopal missionary, nurse, and superintendent of the WNIA's work on the Navajo Reservation, responsible for overseeing the construction of the Rebecca Collins Hospital. She spent years on the reservation pursuing a more practical approach to reservation conditions—encouraging the men to irrigate their crops and setting up industrial rooms so the women could more easily make their unique rugs to sell. More interested in furthering basic daily pursuits, she often neglected the Christianizing component of the field matron and WNIA program.

CHAPTER 6

Mary Louise Eldridge

Missionary and Field Matron among the Navajo

Mary Louise Eldridge and Mary E. Raymond first met on the Pine Ridge Reservation in South Dakota in 1890. Raymond, in her early thirties, had taught for several years in her native Iowa before moving with her father to Western Nebraska, where she continued her teaching career. As a member of the Woman's Christian Temperance Union, she wrote a column devoted to the temperance movement in her county newspaper—a stance that, although supported by her students, resulted in her dismissal. She accepted a position as the principal teacher in the government Indian school at the Pine Ridge Agency in 1888.[1] Her companion, Eldridge, thirteen years older, was a widow living with her daughter and elderly parents in Lawrence, Kansas. She was employed as a matron and head nurse in a girls' dormitory at Haskell Institute.[2] Following their appointment by the Woman's Home Missionary Society (WHMS) of the Methodist Episcopal (M.E.) Church as missionaries to the Navajos, the two women boarded a train in October 1891 at Lawrence, Kansas. Arriving in Durango, Colorado, they transferred to a stagecoach for the sixty-five-mile trip to Jewett, New Mexico, arriving on October 21.[3]

Shortly after they descended from the coach, a wagon, loaded with a tent and a few household items, arrived. Two men got out, erected the tent, set up a stove, and departed, leaving the women alone, "while two Indians wrapped in blankets sat at a distance and watched proceedings." Pinning a cloth over the tent opening, Eldridge and Raymond committed themselves to their missionary efforts,[4] and the Navajo Methodist Mission was born. For six weeks they lived in the tent before moving into a small newly built one-room house of rough boards on the north side of the river. To assure Navajo parents that their children would not be taken and placed in a boarding school, Eldridge deliberately had the house made so small that it could not include a school. Before long, the Navajos, curious about the women's activities, soon filled the little building to overflowing.[5] Less than a year later, a second structure was added, with mention of a school to open in the fall.[6] The WHMS reported that their missionaries had immediately begun to visit the sick and hand out medicine. However, "rather than launching a full-scale program of evangelism, [they] focused on practical social service," teaching the women to keep house, to cook, to spin using donated spinning wheels sent from the east, and supporting them in weaving and selling their Native blankets.[7]

In search of a worthy association project, in 1893, Ellen Susan Bulfinch, corresponding secretary of the Cambridge Indian Association (CIA), wrote letters to a number of newly appointed government field matrons, including Raymond, inquiring what supplies they most needed. The latter responded that because the reservation was mostly parched desert, the Navajos, who owned sheep, had to move frequently to ensure pasture and water for their flocks. As a result, "they have no good houses, only rude hogans, and, where they stop only a week or two, often only a rude stone pen with a wall about three feet high, even in cold weather." This situation, Raymond explained, made it difficult for a field matron to teach the women to properly keep house. What she wanted most for them was a home surrounded by irrigated land, stating that she and Eldridge preferred to help the Indians "do for themselves [rather] than to give to them." Therefore, Raymond requested money to buy a plough, a scraper, and three or four shovels to enable the men to break up the land and to build irrigation ditches to water their fields from the nearby San Juan River. In addition, she hoped to hire "a white man who understands irrigation thoroughly, to come for a day, and run the line for a good ditch." Impressed by Raymond's commonsense forthrightness, Bulfinch immediately authorized her association to send a $75 check.[8]

Thus began a decades-long partnership between Cambridge reformers and the Navajos and the funding and building of the Cambridge Ditch, which irrigated numerous farms, producing the oasis that Mrs. Mary A. Vreeland had witnessed when she first visited the Rebecca Collins Hospital at Jewett. An April 1894 issue of the *Cambridge Chronicle* confirmed that ditch work had begun with funding from Cambridge women, thus lending its name.[9] A year later, in a May 1895 letter, Eldridge expressed a wish that Cambridge members could walk with her along the length of the ditch "and see the Navajos all working in their fields, some planting, some irrigating, some grubbing and some plowing—and the ditch full of water." In November 1895, the CIA reported that the ditch, discussed during a meeting the previous year, was now completed.[10]

Eldridge's sponsors were not the only observers who saw value in her efforts on the Navajos' behalf. Their agent, E. H. Plummer, a first lieutenant in the 10th Infantry, also recognized her work and that of Raymond. In his August 1893 report, he described their efforts as accomplishing "more by deeds than by theories and is appreciable by the subjects through material benefit and assistance derived therefrom." He singled Eldridge out for providing "much valuable assistance to the Indians in that vicinity." Her August missionary report reflected his approval. She described receiving small items such as thread, needles, yarn, thimbles, combs, and even toilet soap as well as numerous small packages of bandages and flannels that she and Raymond either distributed or used in their work among the sick. WNIA auxiliaries across the country also donated carpenter tools, a sewing machine, two spinning wheels, and a large tent, along with a camp stove and an iron bedstead and mattress sent from Florence, Colorado, to be used as hospital facilities. The Pittsfield, Massachusetts, auxiliary had donated two large seed packages, and the WHMS had sent "a great deal of money" for medicines. Eldridge had also distributed five barrels of clothing and another barrel of oatmeal and wheat germ to the sick.[11] The following August, she reported receiving five more barrels and four boxes of clothing, two boxes of drugs from the Navajo agency, 149 packages of assorted seeds, and $375 from the Cambridge branch "to aid in taking out a ditch for the colony settled below the Hog Back." Eldridge concluded, however, that their greatest need was for a Christian Navajo to serve as interpreter.[12]

The missionary and field matron work among the Navajos along the San Juan River changed with Raymond's death on July 28, 1894. She had married Thomas

Figure 14. Mary A. Tripp of Round Lake, New York, seen here on a camping trip with her students, was employed by the WHMS as a missionary and teacher at the Navajo Methodist Mission at Jewett. When they sold their mission, Tripp purchased a small farm near Farmington as a replacement site. (Department of Special Collections, Princeton University Library [Navajo Mission Collection, circa 1895–1908 (WC116)].)

M. F. Whyte, owner of a trading post and ranch near the Hogback, early the previous year. In an August 17, 1894, issue, the *San Juan Times* described the marriage as "uncongenial and ill advised." Weeks before her death, Mary's brother had taken her home to El Dorado, Kansas, where, three days after the death of her infant son, Mary Raymond Whyte died.[13] A late July issue of the *Times* announced Eldridge's appointment as a field matron, describing her as "the right person in the right place, as regards Indian labor," concluding that with "governmental control or backing her scope of usefulness will be greatly enlarged."[14] That October the WHMS appointed Miss Mary A. Tripp of Round Lake, New York, to fill Eldridge's missionary role and to serve as a teacher. Eldridge, happiest in the field visiting the sick and needy, was, no doubt, pleased with the arrangement. To accommodate both women, a three-room adobe house was constructed directly south of the original structure, which was repurposed as a hospital.[15]

Historian Robert A. Trennert asserts that Eldridge, who understood some Navajo and had medical training, proved to be an effective field matron.[16] The month after her appointment, Agent Plummer praised her for caring for the sick and "assisting the Indians in every possible way," even saving a Navajo woman whom the medicine men had given up on. Under her guidance, some desperate tribal members had become steady, hard-working men. Plummer also announced that Eldridge intended to continue her work along the San Juan River. Bulfinch, the corresponding secretary of the CIA, also praised the field matron, portraying her as traveling up and down the river, "supervising the putting in of crops and the building of sorghum mills, [and] securing from the government a chain ferry boat on [the] river." Driving her great double wagon loaded with water for the Navajo men and their horses or traveling by horseback, her saddle bags filled with medicine, Eldridge visited remote camps, often alone, nursing the sick, consoling the bereaved, and everywhere teaching the "right ways of living." Bulfinch concluded that Eldridge was winning "the people's love by her sympathy."[17]

Captain Constant Williams, Plummer's replacement, also spoke highly of Eldridge's field matron work, describing it as "highly commended" as she lived a life of "hardship and devotion, and [that] whatever she undertakes she does well."[18] Eldridge's first report, a lengthy one, reflected a growing hardship among the Navajos. For the last seven years those living on the north side of the reservation had gradually grown poorer and poorer until the previous autumn when she described their condition as "pitiable." Their flocks had declined dramatically. During the two preceding winters, they had begun to eat their goats and sheep, with the poorer ones consuming their entire flocks so that by November 1894 they were eating their burros and horses, with many ending up with "stomach and bowel troubles and blood poisoning." Soon, Eldridge and Tripp were feeding many starving Navajos at the mission station, prompting her to write, "I do not see how many of them could have lived through the winter without the food given them."[19]

On the positive side with the generous support of Cambridge reformers, the Cambridge Ditch was now irrigating six hundred acres, "and the families under it had corn enough to last them through the winter." Eldridge believed that if the ditch were extended, it could easily cover several hundred more acres. On one raw December day during a visit to an isolated Navajo camp, she discovered eighteen small children with no moccasins, pants, or skirts and seventeen at the next camp "with practically no clothing at all." That spring she issued seeds and tools, and after the digging of little ditches, many Navajos were now cutting alfalfa and wheat with prospects of a fair crop of corn, melons, and squashes. Then, during May she reported to the *San Juan Times* that "two fine irrigating ditches have been completed near the Hogback," enabling the planting of corn, wheat, potatoes, and vegetables. The *Times* also described the M. E. mission as engaged in excellent work, teaching the Navajos "the wholesome independence which accrues from the cultivation of the soil."[20] The dire condition of the Navajos had kept both Eldridge and Tripp extremely busy, with Eldridge declaring that her field matron report covered only part of their exhausting year.[21]

Eldridge had incurred heavy expenses providing food and medicine to starving and sick Navajos, and in June 1895, she turned to Herbert Welsh for a $150 loan to purchase a team and a harness, requesting a year to repay it. While preparing for an upcoming month-long trip to a remote part of the reservation, she had discovered that one of her horses was unfit to drive. She needed a strong team to pull her wagon loaded with supplies, food, and bedding for herself and her assistant and grain for the horses. And since Rev. Howard R. Antes and his wife were currently staying at her mission, she could not leave them without a saddle horse.[22] Short of funds himself, Welsh sent the letter on to the Cambridge association, which promptly provided $50, the rest raised through private subscriptions, with Welsh contributing. When Eldridge later turned to him for money to build a ferry system across the San Juan River, the IRA contributed $150, with Commissioner Daniel M. Browning's office adding another $115. She purchased a flat-bottom boat and a cable.[23]

As WNIA missionary work increased among the Navajos, *The Indian's Friend* began printing more articles on crop failures, depleted flocks, and starving Indians. Members were encouraged to write their congressional representative and the Indian commissioner to demand that aid be sent them.[24] Welsh, long interested in their well-being, had toured the Navajo Reservation in the spring of 1884,[25] returning again in 1888 and in 1890, establishing good relations with their agents. In 1895, he sent Alfred Hardy of Farmington, Connecticut, a former industrial teacher at Fort Defiance School, to conduct a thorough IRA investigation. In the meantime, IRA membership, encouraged by Welsh, raised $1,300 for medical and agricultural supplies, part of which was sent directly to Agent Williams. During his early January to July visit, Hardy traveled over 1,800 miles on the reservation, gathering firsthand knowledge and spending five weeks at Jewett to personally observe Eldridge.[26] Later, during an early October address to the Lake Mohonk Conference, he described his time spent with her, concluding that the field matron's service was "second only to that of the agent in importance."[27]

Although the May 1895 issue of *The Indian's Friend* related that Navajos were still on the verge of starvation, by the following summer Agent Williams reported that harvests of the past year had been good, with better pastures for the sheep, and that field matrons Eldridge and Miss Laura E. Smiley "have performed their duties uncomplainingly and with great fidelity," despite riding "long distances in inclement weather."[28] Earlier, Mrs. E. W. Simpson of the WHMS had suggested to Commissioner Browning that he appoint a second field matron to work with Tripp at Jewett so that Eldridge would have opportunity to visit the more distant camps. At times, Smiley worked directly with Eldridge.[29]

Continually in the saddle or maneuvering a fully loaded wagon around the reservation had, by mid-year, worn Eldridge down, and she requested a month's leave to rest and to visit her elderly father and her daughter in Kansas, her mother having died earlier. With her request approved in August 1896 and with all expenses paid by Welsh and her Cambridge sponsors, she headed for Kansas. From there she traveled on to New York State to address the annual Lake Mohonk Conference in mid-October.[30] During her allotted time, Eldridge declared that she and Raymond had not been welcomed by either Agent David Shipley or the Navajos. The agent, not wanting missionary women reporting on him, had directed them to the very northern part of the reservation, where they were given only three-quarters of an acre, surrounded by two mountains on one side and a river and open plains on the other two sides. The Navajos, fearful the women would take their children, warned them that the "quicker [they] got off the better it would please them." However, undisclosed illnesses and economic hard times with no money to hire traditional medicine men to perform healing ceremonies had forced the Navajos to eventually welcome the women's medical advice. Before long, using proper tools purchased with a $75 check from the CIA, the men began digging ditches from the San Juan River to irrigate their crops. By the second year there was a good crop of corn and wheat.[31]

Eldridge also described the unique method Navajo women used to weave their blankets, stretching their primitive looms between two trees. After displaying one that would sell for $100, she explained that the price included shearing the sheep, washing the wool, spinning and weaving—a task taking some two hundred twenty days to complete. At best the weaver might get twenty-five cents a day for her labor. Eldridge maintained that the Navajos were not looking for handouts. Instead, they wanted tools and schools with industrial training.[32] Two months after her presentation, the WNIA-affiliated Indian Industries League, encouraged by her promotion of Navajo weaving, took Eldridge's "proposition to establish a simple industry among the Navajos" under consideration.[33]

During a second address, Eldridge described both a visit to a large peach orchard and her first Christian burial at the request of the eldest son of the deceased. She and Raymond had paid white neighbors to dig the grave; picked up the body, which had been removed through a hole in the hogan's west side, explaining that "it would not be right to take the body through the door" which faced east to greet the sun; and drove their wagon the two miles to the grave. The younger son had prepared a bed of blankets and skins with a saddle for a pillow, and the elderly gentleman was then covered with more blankets and his silver jewelry. "I think I never saw a more reverent company than was gathered for the first Christian burial among them," she declared.[34]

Eldridge's Lake Mohonk address on Navajo weaving had encouraged the Indian Industries League to support her work, especially now that she had convinced them that the Indians would "work when they have an incentive." In 1897, the League sent her a Lamb Knitting Machine and some medicines. After learning that she was overburdened with work, they paid for a housekeeper, freeing Eldridge to tend to the sick and supervise more weaving and farming. As a result of this additional support, the following May Eldridge informed Welsh that the WNIA mission station at Two Grey Hills was flourishing, and that the Navajos had received her kindly. There was even enough money to build a hospital room if they could get a deed to a little land.[35]

The station at Two Grey Hills, which had opened in March 1898, was the WNIA's newest reservation mission. Only weeks earlier, Eldridge had traveled from the Rebecca Collins Hospital, where she was living, to the new missionary cottage at Two Grey Hills, named in honor of J. Lewis Crozer,[36] to do some painting and to whiten the walls. During her visit, the sandstorms had become so fierce that she was unable to complete her task. However, the inclement weather had not deterred the Navajos from coming for medicines, some traveling sixty to seventy miles. A notice in the May issue of *The Indian's Friend* reported that

Eldridge had "oversight of the work" and would be in residence at the cottage for the present.[37] Several months later, in his August report to the Indian commissioner, Agent Williams complimented the field matron for continuing her "useful work among the Navajoes with the same energy which has heretofore characterized her," noting that Eldridge had recently "opened up a new field in the vicinity of the Two Grey Hills, where she is doing good work."[38]

In May 1898, Henrietta G. Cole, a WNIA-sponsored missionary, arrived at the new station, easing Eldridge's burden. Cole, a nurse formerly in charge of the infirmary at Williams College in Massachusetts, immediately began dispensing medicines, dressing wounds, and visiting sick Navajo women. During one eight-day period she tended to over three hundred twenty Navajos, who sought her out for "medical, industrial, and other help and instruction."[39] Eldridge was pleased with her new helpmate, describing Cole as sympathetic, with good common sense, and working well with the Indians, concluding she would soon became a tower of strength to their missionary effort.[40]

Shortly thereafter, Amelia Stone Quinton, fulfilling her role as chairman of the WNIA Missionary Committee, paid an official visit to the new mission located south of the association's Rebecca Collins Memorial Hospital. Quinton and Eldridge had met two years earlier at a Lake Mohonk Conference. During this September visit, Eldridge toured Quinton around two small neighboring groups of Navajo farms. At one site, some six miles to the northwest of Two Grey Hills, Quinton was able to see for herself how effective Eldridge's missionary efforts were on behalf of her association. She viewed stockades, log houses with fencing, and an irrigation system built by the 300 resident Navajos under Eldridge's close supervision. Quinton also observed how small the missionary cottage was now that there would be two women living there and recommended to her committee that it be enlarged to include a hospital ward and separate living quarters.[41] After her inspection tour, Quinton returned home by way of the Lake Mohonk Conference, where during her allotted time she described Eldridge's work as admirable, asserting that the latter had captured the "hearts of some of the leaders" and many of the Indian people, because she was willing to engage in tasks "not considered a part of woman's work." Quinton's visit to the nearby camp also enabled her to describe to the reformers gathered at the conference how the Navajos were learning "civilized ways."[42]

Under Eldridge's supervision, the WNIA station at Two Grey Hills continued to expand, with the appointment of a teacher by year's end. In a February 14,

Figure 15. Henrietta G. Cole, a nurse, formerly in charge of the infirmary at Williams College, is pictured here with Keno Woodie. Cole was employed by the WNIA to help Eldridge out at the Two Grey Hills Mission. (Department of Special Collections, Princeton University Library [Navajo Mission Collection, circa 1895–1908 (WC116)].)

1899, letter, Cole announced that Miss Sara Munger had arrived three weeks earlier and was "pleased with the Navajos." She had brought her own rocking chair and writing desk as well as pillows, bedding, and school supplies, and would be teaching kindergarten students in the Crozer cottage until the schoolhouse, funded by the Brooklyn auxiliary was opened at the end of the year.[43] Several months later, in a letter to Quinton, Eldridge described the Crozer cottage as "full of Navajos most of the time, coming and going," and that during her latest visit, she had taken Cole and Munger to visit some new Indian farms nearby. The three missionaries then revisited the two groups of farms that Quinton had toured the previous September. Eldridge reported their wheat, corn, and bean crops as better than she had seen anywhere that year with at least six new houses, all trim and neat. Cole was busy treating the sick, giving medicines out daily and sewing clothing for those who needed it. Cole had already become the "backbone of the work here, and the Navajos all love her," Eldridge had written. When the new schoolroom was completed, she would take over the present Indian room as a sickroom, and the room where Quinton had slept would become her living quarters, where the Navajos could come for their errands and for her instructions.[44]

Months later, in a letter to her Cambridge sponsors, Eldridge commented on how tired Cole had appeared during the June 1899 house-to-house visit. Even the Indians had remarked on it. They had grown so fond of Cole that Eldridge was concerned for them if the former had to leave because of health reasons. The positive news was that work had finally begun on the Two Grey Hills schoolhouse. Unfortunately, Cole was forced to return home to Williamstown for a well-deserved rest, with Edith M. Dabb, Eldridge's assistant, filling in temporarily. Once rested, Cole returned, much to everyone's relief, sending out a request for supplies for her Sunday school. The schoolhouse was finally finished, the day school opened, and all remodeling completed on the house and cottage.[45]

In 1902, Eldridge's field matron duties and the missionary efforts at the Navajo Methodist Mission changed drastically with the sale of the WNIA's Rebecca Collins Hospital to the Board of Home Missions of the Presbyterian Church. This circumstance also meant that Eldridge had lost her home at the hospital and that the WHMS had to make a decision about their own mission, located nearby. Ultimately, the Methodists determined it was unwise "for two denominations to carry on similar work in such close proximity" and also sold to the Presbyterians.[46] On Mary Tripp's advice, the WHMS purchased a forty-acre farm on the eastern edge of the Navajo reservation, four miles west of Farmington, on bottom land on the western bank of the San Juan some two miles below its confluence with the Animas River where a large concentration of Navajos lived. The land was fertile, with plenty of water, and peaches, grapes, and apples already growing in abundance.⁴⁷ The location would prove unfortunate, for nine years later, on October 6, the entire school washed down the San Juan River in a great flood.⁴⁸

Although the sale of the Rebecca Collins Hospital had left Eldridge homeless, WNIA auxiliaries immediately stepped into the void with the Massachusetts Indian Association's Cambridge auxiliary announcing that she had begun work for them "farther away on the river," among Navajos who were "suffering from lack of water, from disease and from dire poverty."⁴⁹ Initially, WNIA literature provided no specific location for this new station. Mrs. H. N. Wheeler, president of the CIA, merely reported that the hospital transfer had enabled Eldridge to undertake new work "among the less civilized Navajos" with the continued assistance of her auxiliary. She did report, however, that those Navajos who lived along the Cambridge Ditch were displeased with Eldridge's move, although Eldridge had assured them that she would visit often to make sure "that every one did his full share of work on the ditch, and if they allowed drinking or gambling they would surely hear from [her]."⁵⁰

Not until the summer of 1903 did the CIA identify Eldridge's new station as at Closiah, New Mexico, somewhere on the San Juan River. Later documentation revealed that it was about a mile from the training school at the Shiprock Agency.⁵¹ In the MIA annual report of that year, its Cambridge branch reported they had spent $590 towards a school building at Closiah and half of Gaines's salary as well as paying for a fanning mill and a well, and sending medicines, seeds, and six barrels of clothing. The Connecticut Indian Association, having recently turned over their state mission station at Fort Hall, Idaho, among the Bannocks and Shoshones to the Episcopal Board of Missions, paid the other half of Gaines's salary. Connecticut women also contributed towards a living space, a schoolroom, and an industrial room for Eldridge, who in an August 1, 1903, letter, described her new home, funded by both Connecticut and Cambridge members, as "exactly like the Indian home at Jewett, excepting a double window at the north end." Connecticut reformers also provided money for digging a well. Initially intended to be used primarily for the construction of adobe bricks, the well was soon providing water for over 100 Navajos.⁵² Writing from her new home in a February 27, 1903, letter, Eldridge described how exceedingly cold it was and reported that many elderly Navajos were dying. However, heavy snows meant plenty of water later for irrigating. The Cambridge Ditch Navajos were faring the best, she explained, for they had maintained their horses and had been able to engage in freighting all winter.⁵³

Figure 16. Mary Louise Eldridge, Methodist Episcopal missionary, government field matron, and WNIA supervisor, used various forms of transportation to move between remote Navajo camps. She is pictured here on horseback. (Department of Special Collections, Princeton University Library [Navajo Mission Collection, circa 1895–1908 (WC116)].)

Responding on July 3, 1904, to a June 11 letter from an unidentified IRA official, Eldridge noted that her mission was "on the north side of the Navajo Reservation on what is called the San Juan Dist.," and that she could only speak about that part of the reservation. There were no Native missionaries on the reservation and all religious services were delivered through an interpreter. Therefore, one of the greatest needs was for more Christian interpreters. She described the Navajos as childlike, needing much teaching and leading, although they were most anxious to be taught. She had found that the best way to reach them was to visit different camps and spend the night allowing them to gather and to ask her questions. They were particularly curious about the crucifixion and "how could God see his own son put to such an awful death." She explained the best way to reach them would be to send two Christian women to different camps—women "who expect to make this a life work, and they should also be able to care for the sick and advise in all kinds of work and home making, teaching the children and leading the older people to believe in the Great Spirit." The Indians' hearts "are reaching out for religious truth," Eldridge concluded. Reporting that the Navajos were currently building ditches and making homes, she included a partial list of many small ditches they had dug without any outside help.[54] During that summer Cole visited Eldridge at Closiah and, in a letter reprinted in *The Indian's Friend*, declared she doubted if she would return. The mission station, which she described as near the San Juan River in a beautiful grove of cottonwoods, had been extremely difficult to reach.[55]

Eldridge's work during the summer of 1905 unexpectedly changed when she was forced to resign her field matron position following an April investigation by Frank Mead, the General Supervisor of Indian Reservations.[56] Two years earlier, in September, newly appointed Navajo Indian Agent William T. Shelton had arrived on the reservation to establish the San Juan School and Agency, later renamed the Shiprock Agency.[57] Shelton proved to be a particularly tough taskmaster. David M. Brugge describes his incumbency as "marked by bitter controversies," while Robert S. McPherson writes that his iron fist directly impacted "all of the people in the Chuska Valley."[58] Prior to his arrival, Eldridge had pretty much dominated the San Juan area since 1891; confrontation between the two was inevitable. She had tried unsuccessfully to convince officials he was unfit and soon found it intolerable to work under such an unprincipled agent. Complaining about him to John S. Lockwood, president of the League, she had described her resignation as involuntary. Lockwood later confided some of what Eldridge had written to Constance Goddard DuBois, president of the WNIA's Waterbury, Connecticut, auxiliary.[59]

Following Eldridge's resignation, the Cambridge branch and the Connecticut Indian Associations immediately funded an independent mission for her, two miles from Farmington, near the recently resettled Navajo Methodist Mission School now headed by Tripp. So quick was the move that even Quinton, chair of the Missionary Committee, was unaware of the location. Announcing this new work among the Navajos, the *Cambridge Tribune* in an October 1905 article appealed for warm clothing, shoes, soap, combs, and sewing material to be sent to her. The mission, the Mary G. Fisk Home, was named in honor of the late secretary of the Cambridge branch and a frequent correspondent of Eldridge. In a multiroom house that had cost $700 to build, Eldridge cared for the sick, dressed wounds, dispersed medicines, and supervised sewing in an industrial room. During a two-month period, she saw four hundred thirty visitors and gave one hundred sixty sewing lessons, making garments and quilts.[60] But Eldridge's days at this comfortable new home were numbered. She would soon be living off the reservation in Waro's remote camp in the shadow of Mount Huerfano, some forty-five miles southeast of Farmington.[61]

Like many Navajos, Waro had returned in 1868 from the tribe's internment at Bosque Redondo to a newly created reservation that included only part of their original tribal homelands.[62] Therefore, his former home was now outside the current reservation boundaries. Although permitted to hunt on adjoining lands, tribal members had been cautioned not to "make any permanent settlements elsewhere."[63] Between 1878 and 1906, the original reservation was enlarged by ten presidential executive-order reservations,[64] which, unlike the original, were subjected to allotment following provisions of the 1887 Dawes Act.[65] Some of these new executive-order reservations were later withdrawn, removing protection from those Navajos already settled. Land ownership in the eastern part of the reservation was further complicated by the federal government's granting of alternate sections of land to the Atlantic and Pacific Railroad along a proposed route to California, with later transfers to affiliated rail lines. A complex checkerboard pattern emerged with tribal, federal, state, or county legal jurisdiction, and lands owned by individual non-Navajo landowners, Navajos with allotments, and Navajos occupying public lands.

At the time of Eldridge's first visit to Waro, he and his followers had been living on public lands at Huerfano for almost two decades, building homes, developing water sources, and farming. They asked her "to use her influence to protect them against the inroads of the Mexicans and white men who were taking their sheep and appropriating their lands."[66] After her mid-May 1906 visit, she alerted the IRA's Mathew K. Sniffen that she was writing to the association's Washington agent, Samuel M. Brosius, requesting that he pay a visit to Waro's isolated camp. All the Navajos were asking was to have the reservation line extended to protect their current land rights.[67]

In a May 21, 1906, letter to her Cambridge sponsors, Eldridge described in detail her tour of the remote camp at Mount Huerfano, one of six sacred mountains in Navajo cosmology. She had been accompanied by her interpreter, Frank Damon, and Dobe, a relative of Waro. They had spent their first night in a comfortable lodging house attached to a trading post, arriving the afternoon of the second day to find the Navajo men in the camp busy loading large sacks of wool to take to the nearby trading post. While awaiting their return and for others to come in from their distant fields for a formal meeting, Eldridge had visited Mount Huerfano, which she described as a "mountain of stone, standing all by itself," learning from one of the Navajos, through Frank, that his people visited the mountain "to sing and pray just the same as white people went to their churches."[68]

The Navajos, familiar with her work on their behalf, were pleased that Eldridge had come to explain how they could save the lands upon which they had built twenty homes and were now raising corn, beans, melons, squash, and some oats. Waro's followers had lived on this same land before their interment, forced at times to flee from raiding Mexicans, Apaches, or Utes. They explained that now they were free, no longer forced "to cover up their foot-prints" or walk backwards "to fool their enemies." Aware that outsiders could not file on lands upon which Navajos had made a home and developed a water source, they asked her to write a strong letter to the Indian Office requesting that the reservation line be extended to include their cultivated fields.[69]

In an incompletely dated letter to Brosius, written from the Mary G. Fisk Home, Eldridge described the camp as "rather pretty, being rolling land with a good stand of native grasses, and quite a good deal of cedar." The resident Indians had created watering holes for their livestock and built dams across the washes, enabling them to raise fields of corn, beans, melons, and squashes. She saw good wagons, harnesses, and saddles and described a "quiet and peaceable" people who were well clothed and appeared to be "in a very prosperous condition." She urged Brosius to tour the camp as soon as possible.[70]

Sometime during the summer of 1906 Brosius did visit Waro. During his fifty-mile drive there, he noted that the land was extremely arid, recalling not "having seen even a rivulet," although Waro and his followers had sufficient water to irrigate small fields and raise sheep. The IRA agent described the meeting as "altogether satisfactory," explaining through an interpreter that he had come "to devise means" for them to "secure title to their homes." Brosius filed a full statement with Commissioner Francis E. Leupp, who recommended that the allotment process commence.[71] Strong opposition from local whites, unwilling for the Navajos to have any land, forced Brosius to request that Eldridge return to the reservation in an official capacity to assist.

At the same time, having worked for sixteen years on behalf of the Navajos with little time off, Eldridge had grown weary and requested a leave, turning her duties at the Mary G. Fisk Home over to Mary Gaines and a Mrs. Ebbs.[72] In

October 1906, the CIA granted Eldridge a year leave. However, after only a few weeks of rest she agreed to accept Brosius's new "proposition to open up the work at Waro's Camp," some fifty miles southeast of Farmington, and devote her vacation time to "pioneer work, which has always been intensely interesting to her."[73] Unfortunately Brosius had been unable to secure a full-time field matron salary, raising only $300 in government funding. He turned to the Cambridge branch, which, with their funding tied up in the Fisk Home, was unable to contribute. Fortunately, an executive committee member stepped forward and offered $260, and the MIA contributed $420. With her leave extended to January 1908, Eldridge set off for El Huerfano. Her urgent appeals for medical supplies soon resulted in generous donations from Baltimore and various Massachusetts associations.[74] It is interesting to note that Brosius's relationship with Eldridge differed considerably from that with Constance Goddard DuBois. One must wonder if it was because Eldridge was older and therefore more "motherly" as opposed to a younger, brasher DuBois.

Life in Waro's camp was markedly different from that in the Mary G. Fisk Home. Instead of a new home specifically built for her needs, Eldridge lived in a twelve-foot by sixteen-foot tent, with a cot, writing table, some dishes and groceries, and a little camp stove, made of sheet iron, for warmth. She baked her bread in a Dutch oven and cooked her meals over the fireplace, eating them in the twelve-foot by fourteen-foot storeroom, which she had hired from Waro and where she kept her medicines and sewing machine. Altogether she described it as "a very primitive way of life. Once we went six weeks without seeing a white face." Although she never mentioned any companion, her use of the plural in her letters indicated she was not totally alone with the Navajos, possibly having been accompanied by an interpreter.[75]

On April 13, 1907, Eldridge informed Mrs. James B. Ames, honorary MIA president, that there was a great deal of illness at the camp. She quickly had everything under control, finding that her own health improved markedly in the higher altitude among the cedars, where it was far drier. She explained to Ames that with allotment underway, the Indians were well satisfied. They had even recently asked for two schools, a request that pleased her. She knew of no better influence "in the home than to have the children attend day school." Eldridge queried whether Ames was aware of the longtime contribution of the MIA's Cambridge branch toward her Navajo work. They had sent money during the starving times, and after the great drought, as well as to the Rebecca Collins

Hospital and its industrial room, and annually for medicines and supplies. They also funded a ferry boat in 1896, the digging of the Cambridge Ditch, the Indian room at Closiah, and the Mary G. Fisk Home. "Each helps and relieves and teaches hundreds of people every year, and helps in many other ways," she concluded. Eldridge also acknowledged Cambridge help for her current work, especially the medicines and part of her salary. She only wished she could make it clear to Ames "what good people these are out here at the Huerfano. I never have been treated with so much consideration," describing the Navajo men as possessing "good judgment and reasoning powers, far above the average."[76]

In an April 29, 1907, letter to Ellen Bulfinch, Eldridge explained that Waro's camp had been in the same place for between twenty-five and thirty-five years. She marveled how during those years camp residents had endured long-term mistreatment at the hands of the cowboys and Mexican sheep herders, who drove their herds and flocks onto the Natives' lands and appropriated their water holes, laboriously dug by hand. In one instance, she worked successfully with a local lawyer from Aztec to protect the land rights of at least one Navajo, and she was experimenting with forty pounds of seeds sent by the Agricultural Department to identify a grass that required less water. Her efforts had prompted Waro's followers to request she remain permanently. "They were afraid, if I went away, there would be no one to fight for them—what a reputation I am getting," she noted. Her intention was to remain only until the land was allotted and new workers came in to help them, and then return to the Fisk Home. Her visit stretched out for months, with the positive result that her health improved in the higher altitude. She confessed to Bulfinch that she was sorry she had not carried out her original plan to spend the winter "in the middle west and the summer in the Berkshire Hills at Williamstown," where she had lived for thirty years. She concluded that she did not "intend to do any more pioneer work, but I am glad to be able to help this camp."[77]

It is unclear when Eldridge moved from Waro's camp to the MIA's new mission site at Saahtoye.[78] In their November 1908 report, the association announced that "through the interest of the Cambridge Association," Eldridge had accepted their offer, and, with her interpreter, had set out for Saahtoye, twenty miles further from civilization, in Blanco Canyon where a spring of water had been fenced in for their benefit.[79] When she first accepted the offer, Eldridge had written, "I like it there,--I like the rustling, hustling Indians there." She may also have been persuaded because of the housing arrangements. Instead of Eldridge's having

Figure 17. In this undated photograph, Mary Louise Eldridge sits next to members of the Hosteen Teel family outside their traditional hogan, accompanied by a small lamb. (Department of Special Collections, Princeton University Library [Navajo Mission Collection, circa 1895–1908 (WC116)].)

to live in a tent, the MIA executive board used funds left by a board member, Miss M. M. Topliff, to build her a small house. Well settled in her new residence, during January 1909, Eldridge received three hundred twenty-eight Indian callers, seeking advice, medicine, or use of her sewing machine. Others simply came because they wanted to talk to a woman they had come to respect. The following month she saw two hundred fifty-six visitors. Those who traveled a long distance were offered the shelter of a tent. The government set aside forty acres at Blanco Canyon for this work along with the use of a nearby spring.[80]

Sometime in 1910 a health issue, requiring a move to a lower altitude, forced Eldridge to leave the Topliff Mission and returned to the Fisk Home. She was now sixty-one years old and had spent two decades serving the Navajos.[81] Although she had been able to endure the extreme isolation of Topliff, others could not, and the MIA was forced to employ two missionaries for companionship. They selected Mary L. Gaines, who had been filling in at the Fisk house for Eldridge, and her sister, Mrs. Wallace, at double the expense. A late November 1911 issue of the *Boston Daily Globe* described them as "willing to live on the edge of civilization for the purpose of giving help and education to the Indians of that locality."[82] In the meantime, Eldridge kept busy directing activities at the Fisk Home. She was in residence during the drenching October 1911 rainstorms that pounded Northern New Mexico and Western Colorado, causing the Animas River above Durango to flood downstream to the confluence of the San Juan and beyond, devastating one hundred fifty miles of river bottom and destroying five bridges on the San Juan. The Shiprock Indian School was covered with five feet of water, and the M. E. School, a mile below Farmington, was totally destroyed.[83] Frank Damon rescued the children, taking them to the Fisk Home. Unable to get a telegram through to her benefactors, Eldridge sent a letter via Gallup by employees to report that she was alive and their mission station safe. She described the scene around her as one of "ruin and desolation," with the country "all cut to pieces." She explained in her letter that the Navajo women had come "expecting their children were all drowned, but found them safe here."[84]

The *Boston Daily Globe* described the Fisk Home as "a refuge for the tribes for many miles around," where the sick and wounded could stay a night or longer "if need be, to be cured of their various ills." Its Cambridge sponsors kept Eldridge well supplied with the necessities. And its doors were always open to the unfortunate: students returning from eastern boarding schools with a problem for Eldridge to solve; the elderly who needed medicines and warm clothing; or the badly treated wife who simply sought a protector. The *Cambridge Tribune* described Eldridge as having served among the Navajos for so long that she had thoroughly gained their love and confidence. They came to her "for every conceivable kind of help—clothing, food, medicine, nursing, advice and instruction." She settled their disputes, taught the women to sew and cook, and fought "their battles against the injustice of some of their white neighbors." The hospital tent, funded with the $800 left to Eldridge by Jane L. Gray, was in constant use as Eldridge and her interpreter, Annie Mae Youree, cared for the sick.[85]

In a March 10, 1913, letter to her Cambridge sponsors, Eldridge wrote that although she had suffered only one case of grippe, the Indians had been very ill, requiring her to hand out much medicine. Housebound, she had not been to town since November—the river ice so bad, the boat so small, "and if one drove one never knew whether one was to make it all right or would get into the quick sand."[86] During 1913, the Cambridge branch reported spending $1,000 to maintain the Fisk Home where Eldridge was described as continuing her good work. There had been so much sickness during the year that she had been forced to put up a "shade of cottonwood boughs" for the overflow. At one point two girls and a man, too ill with typhoid to be turned away, were set up on the porches, and through it all, Eldridge remained in good health, putting up cherries, pears, and peaches.[87]

In 1914, the MIA, after seven years of helping the Navajos, closed its Topliff Mission at Blanco Canyon. This location had proven to be much too isolated, even for the current missionary sisters, with small surrounding Navajo settlements and a local superintendent who proved to be hostile. Eldridge herself remained so busy at the CIA's Fisk Home that she had no time for a vacation.[88] However, in 1915, with no explanation provided, Eldridge resigned from her post and the mission was closed. The following year at her urging, it was handed over to the Episcopal Church of New Mexico to be used as a hospital. The MIA also dismissed their workers and sold their mission house at Blanco Canyon, making enough money to pay off the Indian who owned the land upon which the Topliff missionary cottage stood. The war raging in Europe brought an end to any new projects.[89] With Eldridge no longer sending lengthy letters to her sponsors in Cambridge, news of her activities gradually disappeared. Occasionally she was reported to have traveled out onto the reservation. At the time of the 1920 census, she was living in Pagosa Springs, Colorado, with her son Silas; a decade later she was in Farmington with her daughter Ruth and son-in-law Harry Baldwin, where at age eighty-three, on March 28, 1933, she died. She was buried in Greenlawn Cemetery, Farmington.[90]

As a field matron, Eldridge had been expected to promote the transfer of white cultural ways to Indian women, but "even people of good will, church missionaries and federal matrons struggled with convincing people of another culture to accept their values," writes Robert A. Trennert.[91] The fact that many field matrons strived in vain to accomplish this goal may have been a good thing. Martha Knack writes that the program was "intended to introduce a series of skills that were both labor intensive and noticeably unrelated to subsistence production," confining women largely to indoor household work, limiting "their public movement as inappropriate," and severely restricting their "ability to participate in the political life of the society." Knack determined that had the program succeeded, "cross-cultural evidence suggests that the results might very well have been the very opposite of those intended—a lowered social status for Indian women."[92]

Eldridge may not have assimilated large numbers of Navajos or brought the gospel to others, but many hundreds of tribal people directly benefited from her medical skills and her agricultural expertise. She also eased their hunger, often using her own money to buy food. She provided two different ferry systems that made it safe to cross the treacherous San Juan River, and she supervised the education of numerous Navajo children. She also made it possible for their fathers to irrigate their fields through the Cambridge Ditch, the building of which she supervised, and to eat fruit off of trees she had provided.[93] The Navajo repaid her over and over with their devotion. There were plenty of Indian voices, especially within Waro's camp and among those who lived along the Cambridge Ditch, who could testify to her good works on their behalf. She endured primitive living conditions and traveled thousands of miles on horseback or in her wagons to remote camps to provide medical treatment. When necessary, she buried and consoled the bereaved. She went far beyond the Indian Office's vision of a field matron, "taking on the roles of nurse, farmer, civil engineer for irrigation projects, trader, hospital administrator, fund raiser, policy advocate, cottage industry entrepreneur and adoptive mother to Navajo children."[94]

Mary Eldridge did not focus primarily on converting the Navajo, being more intent upon meeting their basic daily needs. In counterpoint, Moravian minister Reverend William Henry Weinland spent much of his time preaching in his small WNIA-built chapel in the Southern California Mission Indian village of Potrero. Their methods differed considerably, but Eldridge and Weinland both served the WNIA and Indians faithfully.

CHAPTER 7

William Henry Weinland

Supervisor of the Ramona Mission

Reverend William Henry Weinland, a Moravian minister,[1] was the superintendent of the Women's National Indian Association's sprawling Ramona Mission in Southern California. His reports to Amelia Stone Quinton, chair of the Missionary Committee, turned into a decades-long correspondence and a lasting friendship. After Quinton purchased properties in Banning, California, and near Perris, she and Weinland became agricultural partners, growing seedless sultana grapes for raisins, as well as potatoes, beans, and fruit trees.[2] Their friendship continued even after he was no longer employed by the WNIA. His role, vital to the success of the association's work among the Mission Indians of Southern California, has never been narrated in its entirety.

Weinland ministered to the Mission Indians for four decades before he died on March 7, 1930, at age sixty-nine and was buried in San Gorgonio Memorial Park in Banning, California. The *Indian Truth*, published by the Philadelphia-based Indian Rights Association, described him as possessing "a sympathetic understanding of the Indians," with a judgment concerning their problems "that could be relied upon."[3] Weinland was a founder of the first Moravian Mission in Alaska; missionary and later superintendent of the Moravian Church's Southern

California Mission; a missionary for and later the superintendent of the WNIA's work; and pastor to countless Indians and whites at the Indian village of Potrero and at Banning. He was so well respected by WNIA-sponsored workers, government teachers, and field matrons that when he applied for the position of Mission Indian agent, they eagerly wrote lengthy letters on his behalf to the Indian Office. He was also, like some of his contemporaries, anti-Catholic,[4] not uncommon in this Protestant-driven reform movement. Even the prestigious Board of Indian Commissioners did not initially include a representative from the Catholic Church. At times Weinland struggled to teach his Protestant beliefs to Indians, who preferred the Catholic teachings of their ancestors learned from Franciscan friars in missions stretching from San Diego to Sonoma.

Weinland was born on January 23, 1861, in Bethlehem, Northampton County, Pennsylvania, to Henry Eugene Weinland and Sarah Ann Jones Weinland. He attended local Moravian schools, the Moravian College, and the Theological Seminary in Bethlehem, Pennsylvania. In 1884 he volunteered with Reverend J. A. H. Hartmann, of the Moravian Delaware Indian Mission at New Fairfield, Canada, for an exploratory expedition to Southwest Alaska. Sheldon Jackson, a Presbyterian minister, newly appointed as the General Agent for Education in Alaska, had, following the congressional passage of the 1884 Organic Act which created the district of Alaska and established a District Court there, invited the Moravian Church to build a mission and school. In May, Weinland and Hartmann embarked on a multi-month-long exploratory trip, sailing up the Kuskokwim River in Native skin canoes, identifying a site one hundred fifty miles upriver near a small Yup'ik Eskimo village (Mumtrekhlagamute) where they founded Bethel.[5]

On March 10, 1885, Weinland married Caroline Yost in Manhattan, New York, and two months later the newlyweds joined Reverend J. Henry Kilbuck and his wife, and Hans Torgersen, a lay missionary and carpenter, and sailed for Bethel with provisions and building supplies. While transferring lumber to their vessel, Torgersen slipped and fell into the water and drowned. Although untrained as carpenters, Weinland and Kilbuck, following Torgersen's plans, constructed the First Mission House in late summer and fall, 1885, the first in a series of churches, orphanages, and schools founded in Alaska by the Moravian Church.[6] According to Shelton Jackson's February 1, 1886, report, Weinland, who had initially been appointed as teacher of the government school at Bethel, was also commissioned to "establish and maintain a Signal Service station at that point."[7]

Figure 18. This c. 1884 photograph of a small wooden structure in Bethel, Alaska, is described as "possibly the First Moravian Mission House in Alaska." William H. Weinland, a missionary in Alaska at the time, was involved in its construction. (The Huntington Library, San Marino, California, William H. Weinland Collection, [photCL 39 (059)].)

Reverend Weinland and his family moved from Alaska in 1887 to Grace Hill, Iowa, after both Caroline and one daughter developed severe health problems. Shortly thereafter, the WNIA's Bethlehem, Pennsylvania, auxiliary expressed an interest in supporting a missionary station among the Cahuilla Indians in Southern California, and a meeting was arranged between Quinton and Bishop H. T. Bachman of the Provincial Elders' Conference of the Moravian Church in Bethlehem. The Conference recommended Weinland for the missionary post. In his history of the Moravian Mission in Southern California, Bishop Edmund de Schweinitz Brunner recorded that Quinton was already "well acquainted with the Moravian Church and believed that our liturgical forms fitted us in a peculiar manner for work among these Indians who had never known anything except the elaborate ritual of the Roman [Catholic] Church." It was clearly understood that the Moravian Church was only supplying the missionary; all founding expenses were to be borne by the WNIA.[8] On May 14, 1889, Weinland traveled from Iowa to meet with the Conference, and after agreeing to accept the position, returned home by way of Philadelphia where he conferred with Quinton. On June 19, the

Weinland family arrived in San Jacinto, present-day Riverside County, California, becoming the first Moravian missionary family sent to Southern California.[9]

Preparations for this station, designated the Ramona Mission in honor of Helen Hunt Jackson's 1884 novel, *Ramona*,[10] were underway even before Weinland's appointment. In the fall of 1888 members of the newly formed Atlantic City, New Jersey, auxiliary expressed interest in work among Southern California's Cahuilla Indians, raising $200 towards a missionary cottage and school. The October issue of *The Indian's Friend* described these Indians as "religious, industrious, and anxious to go forward in all the right ways."[11] In mid-February, Quinton wrote to Indian Commissioner John H. Oberly that the WNIA wanted to begin work in the Cahuilla Valley, requesting that the Interior Department provide the use of a school building as headquarters for this new missionary and educational work. When the latter responded that it was not "good policy to give missionary associations the use of government buildings," Quinton instead requested a five-acre parcel, wisely recommending that Mission Indian Agent Col. Joseph W. Preston and the agency physician make the selection. The following month she thanked Oberly for the grant.[12]

On May 31, 1889, Weinland wrote to Quinton for the first time. The following month, she thanked him for his letter, explaining that the government had agreed to the land grant, and that he was to join Agent Preston for the selection. She encouraged him to do as best he could with the $500 the WNIA had appropriated for his missionary cottage. She later recommended that he not build "so small & poorly as to have no comfort"; having already raised $700 for other purposes, she felt sure that "God will 'supply.'"[13] Weinland accompanied Preston to a scheduled meeting at the Cahuilla government schoolhouse on June 22, later writing that the Indian village leader, known as the captain, initially had been in favor of the mission "but evidently someone had in the meantime been trying to prejudice his people against us." In a second report, Weinland noted that a "Mrs. Ticknor had been called to her eternal reward, her place being taken by a Catholic lady, and through underhanded work, the Indians had been so prejudiced against" him as a Protestant missionary that they refused to receive him or grant the land.[14] Quinton concluded that "Catholic influence is behind their opposition," but "we will say nothing about that as we can prove nothing at present."[15]

Undeterred, a day after the Cahuillas refused permission, Weinland preached in San Jacinto's Methodist Episcopal Church, rented a house there on June 24, and requested that Quinton have the "land grant transferred to Saboba [*sic*] reservation."[16] Soboba, a small Serrano village in the San Jacinto Valley at the foot of the San Jacinto Mountains, some two miles from San Jacinto and some thirty miles south of Cahuilla, had recently been saved from eviction by a successful lawsuit funded by the Indian Rights Association. Weinland agreed with Quinton that he and his family should live in rented quarters in nearby San Jacinto, waiting to win the people's hearts. Meanwhile, she applied to newly appointed Commissioner Thomas Jefferson Morgan for a grant of land at Soboba.[17]

On June 28, aware of the role played by local government schoolteachers, Weinland visited Sarah Elizabeth Morris at Potrero, an Indian village at the mouth of a canyon in the San Gorgonio Pass, two miles from Banning on the Morongo Reservation between San Bernardino and the San Jacinto Mountains.[18] In addition to her regular schedule, Morris taught a Sunday school. Two days after that visit, the Weinlands traveled to Soboba to establish a foothold, organizing a Sunday school outdoors under the shade trees because the schoolhouse was too small to accommodate the assembly. In less than two weeks, Weinland had committed himself to a Sunday school and preaching at Soboba, a Friday sewing school overseen by his wife, Caroline,[19] and a Sunday service at Potrero, taking over Morris's Sunday school schedule in early July when she went on vacation. Riding his iron-gray horse or driving the family jump-seat surrey, on Sundays Weinland left San Jacinto for Soboba where he taught Sunday school from 10 a.m. to 12 p.m., followed by a sermon, and then traveled the twenty-three miles to Potrero, where he preached at 4 p.m., with the Indians sitting on benches he had built. On July 14 he had ministered to fifty-two Indians at Soboba and forty at Potrero. Amid his preaching schedule, he made house visits to the sick and, if needed, rode the long distance to agency headquarters in Colton.[20]

In a July 8 report to Quinton, Weinland described his June 28 visit to Morris, his first Sabbath meeting at Soboba, his building of the benches, and Soboba schoolteacher Mary L. Noble's reading of the Scripture in Spanish for the benefit of the adults. Describing his work as opening auspiciously, he explained that he was already planning regular weekly visits to other villages. Quinton, pleased with his report, described his letter as "full of encouragement and a spirit of rejoicing in the work."[21] In addition to ministerial obligations, Weinland began a systematic survey of the more than thirty Mission Indian reservations and their 3,000 inhabitants in San Diego and San Bernardino Counties. He rode "hither and thither through the two counties, preaching when possible, reading and praying with individual Indians, showing magic lantern pictures here and there—once displaying Pilgrim's Progress in a Roman Catholic chapel—and in every way seeking what openings for work might be found." If caught miles from home, he simply bedded down in a nearby government schoolhouse.[22]

Weinland's diligence impressed Mission Agent Horatio Nelson Rust, who described the Moravian cleric as cordially welcomed by the Indians. After attending one of his "simple, instructive services" and seeing "the interest manifested," Rust reported to Commissioner Morgan that he wished "that Christianity would put such a man in every Indian village on this coast."[23] Rust believed that the Catholic Church's neglect of the Mission Indians was a sure sign that they "had forfeited all rights to this mission field"; therefore he strongly supported Weinland's preaching in Catholic Mission villages. The cleric felt justified in doing so after both Hattie E. Alexander, government teacher at Rincon, and Ora Salmons, who taught at La Jolla, informed him that the Indians they taught were rarely visited by a priest. Initially, Weinland wisely limited his work, viewing an expansion over a territory as great as the Mission Indian Agency as accomplishing "very little at any one place," preferring "to do good work in a small field, at least at the beginning, and then to branch out as the Lord leads."[24] Commissioner Morgan was also impressed. Upon completing an extensive tour of Mission Indian reservations and schools, he informed Robert V. Belt, assistant commissioner, that Weinland was "greatly interested in the success of the [government] school and was anxious to cooperate with Miss [Sarah] Morris in every practicable way." Morgan assured Belt that the minister "and his wife ought to be a power for great good."[25]

In late July 1889, Weinland learned that Quinton had received "the *formal* 'permit' from the Indian Bureau" to build at Soboba with Indian consent. Because the village had only two hundred acres, she wisely requested only an acre, enough for a garden, house, lot, and pasture for a horse and cow.[26] However, after a priest held a service in the village, forbidding the Indians from attending those offered by Weinland, WNIA officials moved their missionary headquarters to Potrero. Unlike Soboba and neighboring Pechanga, Rincon, and La Jolla, which were predominantly Catholic, Potrero had fewer Catholics. The lines there had "been drawn pretty sharply," Weinland noted, "those who were Catholics still remain so, those who were not, stand with us."[27]

In a December 11, 1889, letter, Rust informed Weinland that he now had the authority "to select and set apart with the consent of the Potrero Indians a tract of land not exceeding five acres," requesting the best time for a meeting.

Figure 19. Sarah Morris, with her back to the camera, spent seventeen years living and working among the Indians. She is photographed here with an adult Indian woman and several students on the steps of the government schoolhouse on the Morongo Reservation. A visitor once commented on the age disparity of her students. This photograph is evidence of such an observation. (The Huntington Library, San Marino California, William H. Weinland Collection, [photCL 39(059)].)

The following month, *The Indian's Friend* confirmed the grant; land had been selected and lumber bought for the house and stable.[28] Although Potrero would become his official residence, Weinland continued his missionary work at Soboba.

The Ramona Mission had substations at La Jolla, Temecula, Pechanga, Potrero, and Agua Caliente and preaching stations at Soboba, Rincon, and Cahuilla. To promote the station, the WNIA published a pamphlet, describing the information in Jackson's *Ramona* as truthful. The unidentified author of the pamphlet, most likely Mrs. Osia Jane Joslyn Hiles, detailed the present conditions and hardships of the Mission Indians, followed with a brief history and current needs, concluding that facts presented "make their own silent appeal for whatever can now be done for the remnants of these tribes." The WNIA intended to provide "Christian instruction, Sunday schools, sewing schools; temperance, industrial, domestic and sanitary teaching; house-to-house visitation; a hospital department, and indeed whatever help and light are needed for Indian elevation, Christianization, and general well-being, and these will be provided as far and as fast as the means furnished will permit."[29] Weinland easily accomplished such goals at Soboba and Potrero.

In mid-January 1890, Weinland received permission from Quinton to spend all $500 on his cottage, "to make it proper & adequate." She also had inquired if he thought the Moravian Church would be willing to take the station over. The following month she authorized him to use $250 toward a chapel, then doubled the amount, explaining, "we certainly want a comfortable and nice looking little chapel where your home is and the headquarters are."[30] On February 12, the Weinlands moved into the Allegheny Cottage, a twenty feet by thirty feet two-story redwood structure, on a wire-enclosed five-acre parcel of land, half cleared and under cultivation, complete with a horse stable and buggy shed. The house was a $553 gift from the Western Pennsylvania Indian Association at Pittsburgh and Allegheny. Weinland informed WNIA members that his family was more comfortable there than at any time during the winter, and Caroline happily declared she could see Banning from their west window, describing the Indians as "very much pleased at our coming." The women and girls especially had received them kindly. Although "civilized," the Indians still "must be won [over] very much as are poor white people, and our work is very much like that of a city missionary," Caroline Weinland concluded. On April 20, 1890, Weinland presided over the dedication of the Potrero chapel, a gift of the Bethlehem, Pennsylvania, branch, and baptized his interpreter Captain John Morongo. Morongo, a Serrano leader, had, along with a few families of Cahuilla and Serrano people, been a longtime resident of Potrero. He had begun serving as agency interpreter with the tenure of the first Mission Indian agent, Samuel S. Lawson, and from the beginning had encouraged Weinland to makes his missionary headquarters in his village.[31]

On May 15, 1890, the WNIA Missionary Committee voted unanimously to transfer the Potrero station to the Missionary Board of the Moravian Church.[32] Quinton assured the Weinlands that their station was still much loved; it was "a grief to our hearts to part with you and them *officially*. You know that we do *not* part *otherwise*." To ensure Weinland's continued work for her association, she wrote to Bishop Bachman requesting that Weinland be appointed as WNIA counselor and advisor to take on the oversight of all the association's "new stations and work among the Mission Indians."[33] The Missionary Committee also engaged him to preach "at stated intervals for several [Mission] villages," confident that Weinland would provide "earnest and affectionate Christian instruction," an arrangement necessary because the WNIA could not afford to provide a church and regular Sunday preaching for each village.[34] Beginning on September 1, 1891, Quinton also employed Weinland as WNIA Traveling Missionary for one year at $400/year, later raised to $500.[35]

On September 27, 1890, Riverside resident Ida Goepp visited the Potrero mission, providing a glimpse into its activities. Weinland met her at the Southern Pacific Railroad station in Banning and drove her to the family's "perfectly plain two-story wooden structure made of California red wood" with a front yard boasting roses, chrysanthemums, and geraniums. Bessie, the Weinlands' four-year-old daughter, had stayed up to visit, chatting sociably during dinner. Once severely disabled, limited to the movement of only one finger on her right hand while living in Alaska, the child was now as active as her sister, Carrie, who had also been born in Alaska. Goepp remarked that all three children, including young Henry, were among the "healthiest, chubbiest little children" she had seen yet in California. The following morning Weinland brought out a large packing crate full of his Alaskan treasures, including maps, pictures and Native art to show her. He then escorted her on a tour to the Indian-built government school to observe Sarah Morris and her seventeen students in class and around the reservation to meet local residents. After dinner they stopped by the home of his parishioner, Captain John Morongo.[36] Goepp noted that the Indians enjoyed her visit, giving the guests "peaches and grapes." During the evening, Weinland officiated over a service in his "neat little wooden church, with its pretty little bell tower." Duly impressed, Goepp commented that visitors continually stopped by to spend time with Mrs. Weinland, and that the family's children had plenty of young Indian playmates, a sign of acceptance on behalf of both parties.[37]

Additional responsibilities prompted Weinland, on June 6, 1890, to turn over most of his duties at Soboba to Mary Sheriff, whose work was supported by the New York City Indian Association. She immediately established a Sunday school and sewing classes, made house calls, cared for the infirm, and held meetings, encouraging Indigenous women to engage in various domestic industries. Sheriff was well acquainted with Soboba, since she had been employed there in 1880 as the first government teacher among the Mission Indians. Initially, boarding in

San Jacinto, the valley's only town, she had ridden on horseback the two miles a day to teach in the small Indian-built adobe schoolhouse.[38] Two years later, Helen Hunt Jackson arrived, assigned by the *Century Magazine* to write articles on the Mission Indians and other California topics. "As we went from house to house," Sheriff later wrote, "I told her of the impending misfortune" of the threatened eviction of the village "and we discussed various ways of trying to help them keep their homes."[39] Jackson's writings had led to IRA involvement, a court decision, and a village saved. Sheriff remained at her post until 1885 when she married, William P. Fowler, a local ranch, misinformed that only single women could teach. Mary L. Noble replaced her.

Months after Sheriff took over, the Catholic Church delivered lumber for a new chapel. Not until August 2 did Reverend P. J. Stockman of San Bernardino apply to Morgan for permission to build. On September 5, 1890, Quinton inquired of Weinland if he thought it best to "*leave* Saboba [*sic*] & go where the Catholics will *not* hinder us. *We* are called to *peace* & there *are* places where we can work without war," she asserted. Eleven days later she wrote in despair: "How sad I am that the Catholics are rampant." On December 9, she declared, "I shall perhaps soon go to Washington and *if* so I shall do *all I can* about this Catholic matter you may be assured. Till then I know not what else to say."[40] The WNIA suspended work in 1891 when the Catholic church building was completed and transferred the money to needier missions. Sheriff, who lived in nearby San Jacinto, continued her Sunday work.[41] Persistent as ever, Weinland increased his activities, visiting Soboba five times during that winter and the following spring. Although attendance was sometimes good, he found a disturbing level of drinking and gambling. On an 1892 visit he found "the women too much engrossed in a game of chance and the men too drunk to attend service."[42]

A May 1891 visit to Potrero by Bishop Bachman provided more details of Weinland's ministry. Bachman described a pleasant hour spent with Weinland at Morris's school and a brief visit to Captain Morongo's nearby home. Although the captain was at the time in Los Angeles "where his presence [was] often required as an interpreter in the courts," the two clerics had a pleasant visit with Morongo's wife. In the afternoon, Weinland and Bachman visited a number of homes, "praying with and instructing the people." Bachman reported they were kindly received even by those who were nominally Roman Catholic, prompting him to conclude that the Indians were "an accessible and receptive people," and that the Weinlands enjoyed "the confidence and love of most of them."[43]

The following month Quinton arrived in California for the first time as part of a lengthy cross-country organizational tour. Escorted by Mission Agent Horatio Nelson Rust, from June 27 to July 24 she visited numerous Mission Indian villages, deciding upon Cahuilla and Agua Caliente as sites for new missionary work, and then organized auxiliaries up and down the state. She made no mention of Weinland in her report, although the planned new stations added considerable responsibilities to his supervisory work as he served as escort, driver, or carpenter, repairing existing buildings to be used as homes by the new WNIA workers—harkening back to his early days in Alaska.

In his January 14, 1893, report to *The Moravian*, the official organ of the Northern Province of the Moravian Church of America, Weinland announced the arrival of three new coworkers to the Ramona Mission—Dr. Rebecca C. Hallowell, Julia M. French, and Dr. Anna Hayward Johnson, the latter the new field matron at Cahuilla. He reported that Hallowell and French were at Agua Caliente to establish a hospital, a project long in the planning stage.[44] He had no idea that he would end up spending considerable time defusing a contentious situation between Quinton and Rust over the hospital. Rust, convinced the idea had been his, assumed he should control the situation. Weinland also would have his own personal issue with Rust over the placement of Johnson's cottage at Cahuilla. Rust, who at the time was ill and unable to visit the village for the selection process, later claimed to Commissioner Morgan that the cottage had been built without his consent or knowledge. When Quinton learned of Rust's objection, she informed Morgan that Weinland not only supervised its placement but had deferred to the village captain, who had indicated the only proper location. Both N. J. Salsberry, the government teacher, and C. M. Fleming, Johnson's predecessor as field matron, also had agreed. When Weinland and Rust finally met in Banning on September 3, 1892, the agent, informed of the location, made "not one word of protest." On a different occasion, when the brother of the carpenter who had built the cottage asked Rust about his initial objection, the agent replied he had "no fault to find with it whatever." Quinton, in assuring Morgan that Weinland, as the WNIA missionary superintendent, made all such decisions, concluded that Rust was displeased "because he thought our Association ought to have put the whole affair into his hands."[45]

The election in 1892 of a Democratic administration prompted Rust, a Republican, to resign his post. On March 15, 1893, Weinland wrote to Interior Secretary Hoke Smith, recently appointed by incoming president Grover

Cleveland, respectfully requesting "to be appointed to fill the vacancy thus created." He described his last four years living and working among the Indians as giving him "a thorough knowledge of the Indians themselves and an acquaintance with the best way of working with them," experiences he viewed as valuable for an agent. His graduation from the Moravian College also gave him the necessary educational qualifications, and his "successful management of two expeditions to North Western Alaska" provided him with both executive and business qualifications. He called Smith's attention to the personal letters of teachers and "other workers amongst the Indians, testifying to [his] fitness for the position."[46]

Weinland likely had been encouraged to apply by government teachers and WNIA workers eager to have a replacement they knew and trusted. Rust's confrontational personality had been objectionable to Indian leaders and whites alike. In contrast, in her letter, Rebecca C. Hallowell, medical missionary at Agua Caliente, described Weinland as faithful and devoted to the Indians—"a gentleman of unimpeachable integrity," who had "won the esteem and confidence of many of this section who are engaged in Indian work," while Julia M. French, field matron at Agua Caliente, described him as a "man of sterling integrity, singleness of purpose—and in every way above reproach."[47] Government teachers supporting him included Cahuilla teacher N. J. Salsberry, who deemed him eminently fit for the position of agent, possessing a "calm, patient and frank way of dealing" with the Indians, while Ora M. Salmons, who had taught at the Rincon Reservation since 1886, reckoned him a friend of the Indian "and in every way" fitted for the role. Mary Sheriff Fowler averred that the practical and morally strong Moravian minister was the best man to head the agency and that he had "the full *confidence* of the *people* of the various villages," as well as the "Americans of his acquaintance."[48] Dr. Anna Hayward Johnson, government field matron and medical missionary at Cahuilla, described "his absolute integrity, undoubted executive ability, education and experience with Indian nature [which] fit him to an unusual degree for the position." And Isabella M. Cadwallader, a teacher at Fall River Mills in Shasta County, in the north central part of the state, explained to President Cleveland that those supporting Weinland had "no ends to serve but the good of the Indians."[49]

Weinland informed Quinton on March 31 that he had applied for the position of Mission agent. Just home from a four-week business trip, she had corresponding secretary Mary L. Gibson respond. Gibson explained that since no appointment had been made yet, Quinton hoped "to secure Southern influence with Sec'y Hoke Smith and will press your application as soon as she thinks favorable & safe."⁵⁰ At the end of March, Quinton wrote to Smith, congratulating him on his appointment, enclosing letters earlier written on Weinland's behalf by French, Hallowell, and Fowler and a petition signed by a number of local Mission Indians. She also enclosed her association's endorsement, describing him as "a man of very quiet demeanor," with executive ability, integrity, and a devotion to the Indians. Since WNIA work was "domestic, industrial, medical, moral and religious," Quinton believed Weinland's appointment "would be the best possible aid" to the WNIA.⁵¹

As agent, Weinland no doubt would have well served the Indians, but the political spoils system was in play, and Francisco Estudillo, a member of a prominent Californio family and a Democrat, was nominated for the position on April 12. The youngest son in the family, he had been born in San Diego in 1844 and had served as a San Diego County supervisor, San Jacinto's first postmaster, and its second mayor. As a Spanish-speaking Catholic, Estudillo was welcomed by a large number of Mission Indians, some four hundred of whom gathered to greet him during a June 1893 fiesta at Morongo.⁵²

Quinton continued to encourage Weinland, working hard to overturn Estudillo's appointment.⁵³ She interviewed Smith and several senators in Washington, DC, trying to prevent confirmation. "Shall remit no exertion, & have many helpers in Wash'n," she confided to Weinland. Two days later she wrote that she had heard from Senator James K. Jones, a Democrat from Arkansas and current chairman of the Senate Indian Committee. If they could provide proof that Estudillo was "an intemperate man, or otherwise unfitted," his committee would not confirm. Quinton had already requested they delay until such testimony could be found. She encouraged Weinland to "do all you can, please, & so will I to prevent this confirmation."⁵⁴

Although Quinton failed to secure Weinland's appointment, she did succeed in ensuring that his children remained in the Potrero government Indian day school. In late April 1893, he complained about a new policy prohibiting white children living at Potrero from attending the school. Quinton immediately wrote to Commissioner Daniel M. Browning, Morgan's successor, explaining that Weinland was the pastor at the little Potrero church and was "a benediction and civilizer among the Indians." She viewed the attendance of "these well brought up little white children" as a "positive advantage to the little Indians." Because Browning was new and unfamiliar with WNIA work, Quinton explained her association's past relations with the government's educational work, describing it as most cordial, and trusting "that these mutually helpful relations may continue without interruption." A month later, Weinland learned that his children could continue to attend the school with the understanding that white students would "not occupy the time & attention of the teacher to the disadvantage of the Indian pupils."[55]

The July 1893 issue of *The Indian's Friend* announced a severing of the five-year-long association between the WNIA and Weinland, claiming his personal ministry at Potrero required "all his time and strength." His duties were taken over by his former assistant, Edward Helmich. The true reason for the change, however, was the perennial lack of WNIA resources.[56] Quinton always struggled to finance her stations. Before she could rehire Weinland, she had to negotiate with the Moravian Board and wait until the WNIA Seminole Mission station was transferred and for Helmich to leave his post. He did so in October, moving to Pennsylvania.[57]

During the summer of 1894, Quinton wrote that from her end "all seems to be peaceful & progress certainly has been made" at both Cahuilla and Agua Caliente.[58] Part of this tranquility was due to Rust's departure and to Weinland's return as superintendent. His new report in the February 1894 issue of *The Indian's Friend* reflected monthly visits to both Cahuilla and Agua Caliente as well as several visits to Soboba, and conferences with WNIA-sponsored workers. He had also attended several temperance lectures and had been invited to preach at Palm Springs, where there was a church and an adjoining Indian village. In the March issue of the periodical, Weinland reported conducting his usual morning service at Potrero, traveling on to Palm Springs to preach in the afternoon and evening, and afterwards visiting nearby Indian homes. His December report reflected visits to various villages and an improvement in attendance.[59]

In the spring of 1895, Weinland hosted another one of Quinton's California visits. Driven by a sense of obligation to carry on Jackson's legacy among the Mission Indians, she had come again to establish another WNIA station with Weinland's able assistance.[60] Quinton had grown quite fond of the Weinland family and was always eager to visit her summer home near Perris. The visit began with a two-week carriage trip through Mission villages, joined by Louise Hoppock, president of the Redlands Indian Association, and Albert K. Smiley, Lake Mohonk Conference founder, now a permanent resident of Redlands. The small party of reformers was welcomed to Rincon by Salmons and hosted at Agua

Caliente by Hallowell and French, as well as Josephine Babbitt, the government schoolteacher. The reformers toured the school and bathed in the hot springs. On Sunday Weinland delivered a sermon in the schoolhouse at Agua Caliente.[61] At Cahuilla they visited with N. J. Salsberry and met Anna Ritter, Dr. Anna Johnson's replacement. Then, on Easter Sunday, April 14, Weinland gave a sermon in the little Potrero church.[62]

The following day Weinland and Quinton set out to investigate a potential new site for a station among the Desert Cahuilla at Martínez (today's Torres-Martínez Indian Reservation). As head of the association's Missionary Committee, Quinton most often decided the location of a new station, but for the very first time a local Indian community had requested one. The Desert Cahuillas were familiar with Weinland's missionary efforts at Potrero, and although he visited their village monthly, they wanted their children to grow up in a society influenced by a permanent missionary family. Weinland and Quinton descended from their Southern Pacific Railroad coach at Walters and were met by John Morongo and a local government schoolteacher, then were driven by wagon another five miles to meet with more than fifty Indians, dressed in their best clothing, gathered at the council house. When Quinton inquired what kind of church they wanted, they responded: one like Potrero. Always short of money, Quinton agreed to build a cottage and chapel if the Moravian Board would provide the missionary and salary. Before the council ended, Weinland suggested the Indians also petition the government for artesian wells. Quinton agreed to hand-deliver their petition to the Indian commissioner.[63]

The Desert Cahuilla were not the only ones with confidence in Weinland. In her 1895 WNIA missionary report, Quinton wrote that compared to the "listlessness, poverty and want of enterprise" present five years before at Potrero and neighboring villages, there now was an "air of industry, thrift and prosperity." Comfortable homes were multiplying, more land was under production, and ambition and patriotism were increasing. The Indians held great "affection for their devoted pastor," which spoke "eloquently of the greater interior revolution which has taken place," she had written.[64] However, such an achievement had required a grueling schedule. Weinland reserved the Potrero Mission for Sunday school and Sunday morning and evening services; Cahuilla and Agua Caliente were visited during the week, a journey made more difficult because of mountainous terrain, especially during the rainy season. Between November 19 and 23, 1895, he had visited Cahuilla and Agua Caliente, and joined Morongo on a visit to Martínez, where he had preached two services, one for adults and another for the young. Weinland described the villagers in Martínez as "simple-minded, honest folks, who, in spite of their having been neglected so long, want to know the way to the better life," finding an "earnest spirit manifested." Between December 17 and 21, he retraced the 200 miles between Agua Caliente and Cahuilla, and home; from January 14 to 18, 1896, he returned to the two villages, finding "happy memories of a bright Christmas" fresh in the Indians' minds. He revisited them again, adding in Soboba between January 28 and February 1, and returned to Martínez in mid-February.[65]

A disturbing situation surfaced that put the proposed mission station at Martínez in jeopardy. Years earlier, in February 1891, Bishop H. T. Bachman had requested from the Board of Indian Commissioners a deed, "gratuitously if possible, or for such a reasonable price as you may deem just and fair," for the five acres initially granted the WNIA at Potrero and later transferred to the Moravians.[66] It is unknown if the deed was transferred, but five years later, in August 1896, Weinland informed Edmund A. Oerter, secretary of the Provincial Elders' Conference of the Northern Province of the church, of a concern with the Moravian Church's claim to land and water at Potrero. Whatever the issue, the matter was solved and Potrero remained a Moravian mission. Oerter, fearful that a similar situation might arise at Martínez, wrote that it had been a pity that greater care had not been taken at Potrero "to have the Catholic Indians consent, or were they simply out voted in the Council meeting of Tribe?" To avoid a similar problem, he urged Weinland to do everything possible at Martínez "to have the consent of the Indians so clear & positive that no question can ever be raised." And, to ensure adequate water, Oerter recommended a well be dug and a windmill constructed.[67]

Three weeks later, Oerter wrote to Weinland, concerned about a delay "in selecting land at Martínez, but as you & the chief had agreed upon a site, I suppose the Agent will not oppose your plans." He also informed Weinland that David J. Woosley, their choice for missionary, was leaving that evening for Banning, thanking the former for agreeing to put Woosley up at Potrero for a month.[68] Oerter was relieved when the Indians finally signed the paperwork on September 9, turning over the requested five acres. At year's end, he wrote Weinland that "the information given in regard to the situation at Potrero, & affair at Martínez is all very acceptable & we thank you for it."[69]

The decision to establish a station at Martínez had been easy; building the cottage proved more difficult, requiring numerous letters between Weinland

and Quinton. Aware of the extreme heat of the desert, she had recommended a double roof, with an air space of twenty inches between to keep the house cool. She also suggested large windows, adobe walls, and an open passage with no walls between the little kitchen and the bedroom and the large living room—the house should not "be roasting by being all small rooms," she concluded. Reviewing a copy of the plans she had requested, Quinton suggested another window for the sitting room and windows on each side of the fireplace. She assured Weinland she would find money for the upgrades. "We *don't want* a 'poor little tucked up' cottage on that *hot reservation*," she wrote in early September.[70]

Weinland's next obligation was to introduce the new missionary to his congregation. Joined by John Morongo and Reverend David Woosley, he met Agent Estudillo at the Martínez schoolhouse, where, during a council, the agent assured the Indians that he and the Indian Office approved of this new WNIA station. Following Woosley's introduction, the Indians spoke, and then each "touched the tip of the penholder" to his name on the agreement. In the meantime, Weinland and Woosley selected the site for the cottage and chapel.[71] After a subsequent visit to the Woosleys, Weinland described "the prospect for a successful work" as seemingly bright and promising. The older Indians had heartily welcomed the new mission, while the younger ones were "eager to know and learn the truth." Although "difficulties will arise from time to time," Weinland concluded that the "faith that can remove mountains is the faith that can live down and overcome difficulties." Financial worries were eased when the Brooklyn Indian Association and its Bay Ridge branch pledged Woosley's salary.[72] Then on December 12, 1896, providing an interesting ceremonial role of two generations, the Weinlands and their son Jamie, accompanied by Morongo and his daughter Annie, revisited the new station and, with the Woosleys, dedicated the new church.[73] On November 19, 1897, the station was formally handed over to the Moravian Church.[74]

Months earlier, the WNIA had held a meeting at New York City's Waldorf Hotel to raise money for proposed artesian wells. Angered by the tone of a *New York Times* article on the practicability of supplying the Desert Indians with water, Weinland wrote the editor on June 7 charging that his newspaper's article had "no more bearing upon the subject of supplying the Indians with needed water than an essay on green cheese would have." He feared that the false statements made by their correspondent, whom he portrayed as "riding his private hobby for the public benefit," would prejudice the readers' minds against this worthy enterprise. Weinland, who described himself as living and laboring among the Indians for years and interested in both their welfare and future progress, concluded that the mere fact that the Indians "succeed in keeping soul and body together under such hard conditions proves beyond a question that they are worthy of better facilities for making a living."[75]

During February 1898, Reverend Morris W. Leibert, on behalf of the Moravian Church, paid an official visit to Weinland. Invited by Sarah Morris to visit the government school on the Morongo Reservation, Leibert found twenty-five students, ranging from toddlers up, busy at age-appropriate assignments in a new building containing the school room, Morris's living quarters, and quarters for a matron. Weinland then took his visitor on a four-a-half-day buggy ride of some 150 miles to Soboba, Cahuilla, and Agua Caliente. Leibert reported that at Soboba the villagers paid respectful heed to Weinland's message, while the children appeared to be both "happy and attentive at school," and described Agua Caliente as primitive, with houses of thatched covered adobes. Leibert was surprised to see in the little village both a Catholic chapel at the foot of the village street and the special WNIA cottage in which French and Hallowell lived serving "all Indians who desire medical treatment." He then recounted that Weinland went house to house, inviting the Indians to the schoolhouse for a service which Leibert described as attended by "a respectable and attentive audience." A "short, practical sermon," with all joining "heartily in singing favourite familiar hymns," followed. After spending the night in the home of an Indian family, the two clerics returned to Potrero. Leibert was impressed by Weinland's achievements but disappointed by the sorry spectacle at Potrero, Soboba, and Cahuilla "of two hostile religious organizations engag[ing] in rival efforts in behalf of remnants of a race, on scraps of the national domain on which nobody else cares to live."[76]

That July, Weinland and his family moved to Banning as the Moravian Board had found a successor for him at Potrero.[77] As Superintendent of Southern California for the Moravian Church, Weinland was responsible for a large district, including all thirty Mission villages. A move from the isolated Potrero village to a more central location such as Banning enabled him to observe activities at Potrero and Martínez, to make more regular Sunday visits to the out-stations of Soboba, Cahuilla, and Agua Caliente, and to go "wherever else he could find an opening." It also would free up time for him to organize congregations at the three out-stations. On October 23, 1898, Reverend A. C. Delbo and his wife took charge at Potrero, and the Weinlands headed for Banning. Writing from Agua Caliente, Rebecca Hallowell congratulated him in a letter filled with events and news of Indians there and in nearby villages and activities of Indians known to him. One of her Indian informants had described his new home as "mucho grande"—very different from "the pretty home that rose out of the sage brush" at Potrero.[78]

Although the WNIA had one by one turned over its stations among the Mission Indians to the Moravian Church, their Southern California Auxiliary, or the NYCIA, the national association continued to retain close ties to Weinland, with Quinton negotiating with her auxiliaries to raise money for his ongoing work.[79] In return, she informed him that she expected his reports for publication in *The Indian's Friend*. Her complaints to Reverend Paul de Schweinitz, secretary and treasurer of the Provincial Elders' Conference, about his reports no longer including "points to catch or waken interest," prompted a letter to Weinland urging him to find incidents to "fire the zeal" of Quinton's members, using his "fertile imagination to play about [his] experiences" and "dress them up in an appropriate garb."[80] Weinland took his advice to heart. An article about the Mission Indians in an illustrated issue of the *Los Angeles Times* was described by *The Indian's Friend* as so excellent that "we cannot forbear reproducing it" for their readers' benefit.[81]

The new century brought renewed interest in Weinland's work. He wrote in his August 8, 1901, report to the Moravian Church that the previous autumn he had been invited to begin work among the Yuma Indians. Unfortunately, a lack of funding had made it impossible for his board to sanction the work. Instead, the Young Men's Missionary Society of Bethlehem, Pennsylvania, pledged money, enabling Reverend Woosley to begin monthly visits.[82] In reporting his own work at Soboba, Cahuilla, Rincon, La Jolla, and Agua Caliente, Weinland revealed he was especially well received at La Jolla and Rincon, where the Moravian Church had purchased land adjoining the reservation and was currently repairing a house on the property for a missionary couple, hopefully soon to be appointed. *The Indian's Friend* reported Weinland's continued travels from one reservation to another, "preaching and caring for his large and scattered flock," using "his influence against the gambling and liquor-selling," while his wife had started a lacemaking class at Potrero.[83]

Weinland concluded his report with mention that "during the past year [he had] worked very hard to prevent the reappointment of the present Indian Agent," Lucius A. Wright, "because of his undesirable character generally and because he was personally engaged in the sale of liquor." Weinland described his "kicking against the pricks of machine politics," and would "despair of accomplishing any good, were it not for the fact that God still rules."[84] Quinton supported his efforts, traveling to Washington the first week of February 1901 to confer with Commissioner William A. Jones and California Senator Thomas R. Bard. She had also forwarded Weinland's January 17 letter criticizing Wright to Merrill E. Gates, secretary of the Board of Indian Commissioners. Gates responded on February 11 that both Bishop Joseph H. Johnson of the Los Angeles Diocese of the Episcopal Church and Albert K. Smiley had endorsed Wright.[85] To her dismay, politicians had pelted Bard with letters in favor of Wright, and he had yielded, reappointing the "wicked agent." Quinton described his reappointment to Weinland as "*one* of the darkest transactions we have had to complain of, *if* so, in all these late years."[86] Other than a veiled reference to his drinking, neither Weinland nor Quinton provided any evidence of any wrongdoing on the agent's part.

During 1902, Weinland worked with Quinton to expand the existing missionary work among the Yuma, this time at the Fort Yuma Indian Boarding School in Imperial County, California, across the Colorado River from Yuma, Arizona. At an undisclosed date, Weinland had taken over Woosley's monthly visits. Short of funds, Quinton struggled to pull together finances. Waiting for several stations to be transferred, she conferred with two members of the Moravian Board and members of the NIA's Bethlehem, Pennsylvania, auxiliary. The latter branch with its Allentown auxiliary, joined by the Louisiana auxiliary at New Orleans and the Redlands Indian Association and other nearby auxiliaries, agreed to support this new work, with the Moravian Board and the Young Men's Missionary Society of Bethlehem rounding out the financing. Quinton hoped to eventually find funding for a permanent worker and a cottage.[87] In the meantime, Weinland promised to send a report after each visit to "keep up the interest . . . by this *living link*."[88]

In early February, Quinton had learned from the Moravian Board that because the Fort Yuma School had a Catholic superintendent, they would support only once-a-month preaching sessions. Personally displeased with sharing a mission with the Catholics, Quinton, nevertheless, planning a trip to California, decided to stop at Yuma en route and requested that Weinland meet her so they could look over the field together. A week later, she asked him to alert School Superintendent John S. Spear of her upcoming visit.[89] On March 17, 1902, Quinton met with Spear, who drove her across the Colorado River to the California side to visit the school, where she dined with the teachers. Weinland arrived the following day and toured her around the facility. Late the following month he returned, remaining until May 3 visiting Indian homes, giving illustrated sermons, and, as promised, sending his report to Quinton.⁹⁰

A day after their Yuma meeting, Weinland and Quinton traveled to Martínez to meet with Reverend Robert Staveley, the new missionary. They found positive changes implemented since their 1895 visit. During a five-hour-long Indian council, the two old friends listened to complaints about local whites who encroached upon Indian lands, stealing horses and cattle. Quinton agreed to take their requests for wire fencing to protect their livestock, eight more wells, and a land survey back to Commissioner Jones.⁹¹ Two months later, on May 5, 1902, Caroline Weinland joined her husband in a trip from Banning to Hemet to meet up with Quinton, who had remained in the state longer than usual. They drove the sixty miles to Agua Caliente, at the request of Josephine Babbitt, government schoolteacher. Both Weinland and Quinton identified marked changes. She described many Indian homes with new lights gleaming "from the windows on the hillside, in the vale, and the new schoolhouse with its comfortable living rooms alight" as a welcome sign from Babbitt. However, a profound sadness hung over the village as residents, dreading their upcoming removal, explained they did not want to leave their homes. They proposed sending a delegation to President Theodore Roosevelt to explain what was in their hearts and to convince Congress to buy their land. Initially advising against such a plan, Quinton, upon seeing their aggrieved faces, changed her mind, aware that the Cupeños would at least have the satisfaction of knowing they had done everything possible to save their village. The council over, the Weinlands and Quinton left for Banning, spending Sunday attending a church service at Potrero.⁹²

This visit to Agua Caliente unexpectedly involved both Weinland and Quinton in a conflict with Southern California Indian reformer Charles Fletcher Lummis, member of the Warner Ranch Indian Commission, who viewed Quinton as interfering with his authority. Lummis accused her of telling untruths that would only cause "greater distress and suffering," begging her to "be judicious and friendly to the Indians" and not give them any ideas. He had written: "If there were any possibility that by going to Washington the Indians could aid their cause, I would not only favor their going but would go with them and take them to the President, but everyone of common sense knows that neither the President nor Congress nor anyone else can reverse a decision of the Supreme Court."⁹³ The *Los Angeles Times* made matters worse, portraying Quinton as a female false pretender and a wild-brained person who had started a crusade to upset the plans of Lummis

Figure 20. Reverend William H. Weinland and his wife Caroline pose for the camera in this undated photograph taken during one of their many visits to Mission Indian villages to missionize and educate them. Note the small gathering of Indigenous people to the left. (The Huntington Library, San Marino, California, William H. Weinland Collection, [PhotCL 39 (366)].)

and his commission.[94] Weinland came to her defense, declaring forcefully that "she did not create, but found already existing, the dissatisfaction in the minds of the natives concerning their removal." In response, the *Times* attacked him, describing the cleric as "not conversant with the facts of the case."[95] In the end, Lummis was forced to admit that Quinton's motives "which appeared so insurrectionary at the time, were misunderstood." He apologized, "sorry to have the head of a national organization, as she is, discredited without cause."[96]

The removal of the Warner Ranch Indians from Agua Caliente reduced Weinland's visits by one village, giving him more time to visit other sites, especially Martínez, where in the summer of 1903 he learned that a Catholic priest had visited, asking permission to build a church. During their council meeting, the villagers had rejected the proposal, but the priest made the same request at neighboring Torres, offering one Indian a new home and a second some money, winning "several to favor his project." Subsequently, Martínez residents put together a petition, signed by "*the majority of the Indians of the entire desert*," protesting the building of the Catholic church, forwarding it to Commissioner Jones through Samuel Brosius of the IRA. Although the petition was "now on file in the Indian Office at Washington," Weinland informed Quinton that he had just received a letter from Pancho Torres, the village captain at Martínez, informing him that it had been ignored and land was being cleared at the eastern end of their village. Following an assurance by the Indians that they did not want a Catholic church, Weinland asked Quinton to "please bring this to the attention of Commissioner Jones at once."[97] Some weeks later, following one of his morning services, Weinland joined a group of Indians, who were sitting under a shade tree in the sand. One by one, they reassured him that should a Catholic church be built, they would remain faithful to him. Even though the temperature that day had been 110° in the shade, he rejoiced at his "whole experience during this trip." Sometime later, after ordering several Catholic Indians to cease their adobe brick making, Captain Torres reported the matter to Agent Wright, who contacted the Indian Office, asking "what action should be taken in the matter." Subsequently, Brosius filed a formal petition against the location, prompting Weinland to write to Quinton that he hoped "the result will be that the new church will be located *elsewhere*, and not at Martinez."[98]

The new few years witnessed changes in Weinland's routine. In June 30, 1905, he reported teaching monthly Bible classes at Sherman Institute, a government off-reservation boarding school in Riverside, at the invitation of School Superintendent Harwood Hall.[99] In late November 1906, Weinland received a letter from Quinton reminding him that these classes were underwritten by the Bethlehem auxiliary, and he had not sent her a report for an entire year. Then a month later she informed him that the NIA had elected a new president and her "heart [was] easy about the future of the Ass'n as never before." Longing to hear from him, she wrote in a postscript: "We have been friends for *many years* & I *care, really care*, to know how all goes with you all."[100] Weinland's letter, which included news that he and his family had moved back to their former cottage in Potrero, and his report, appeared in the February issue of *The Indian's Friend*.[101] He later explained that his classes at Sherman had been to "gather together the children of Moravian parents, not only from the Morongo Reservation, but from other Reservations" to keep them loyal to the Church. The children looked forward to these meetings with "pleasant anticipation, and we have reason to know that they have been used of God for good," he concluded.[102]

CHAPTER 7

Following Quinton's retirement, Weinland's reports become spotty; fewer letters passed between the two old friends. In an early January 1907 letter that included news of his children, he also reported that his Potrero church was prospering now that he was back at the helm. Quinton described his letter as refreshing, almost as good as a personal visit.[103] In a report to the Moravian Board two years later, Weinland wrote of hard times—four deaths to one birth among his parishioners, tuberculosis being the most common cause. Expanding his work, he had received several invitations to address "white people on the subject of Moravian Missions."[104] In January 1922, the Woman's Club of Oceanside announced he would be lecturing on Indian welfare. Two months later he participated in a conference on the same subject, recounting that he had encouraged the raising of fruit trees at Potrero to make "the Indians help themselves."[105] After a brief mention of two Easter celebrations at Potrero, news of Weinland disappeared altogether.[106]

Cornelia Taber, corresponding secretary of the Northern California Indian Association, described the Moravian cleric as clearing his five-acre mission plot, planting fruit trees, and giving "the Indians in whose midst he and his family lived, an object lesson on what can be done." He opened his mission home to them "with the view of planting in the minds both of the men and women the germ thought or desire for the making of Christian homes." Weinland, she explained, had created for them an idyllic "real family home-life," with a sewing machine in every home.[107]

Taber's praise may have been perceived as through rose-colored glasses, but there was truth to her words. For more than four decades, William Henry Weinland had ridden or driven hundreds of miles weekly to preach to the Mission Indians, believing he was providing them with a better life. His reports to the WNIA and the Moravian Church revealed a man thoroughly dedicated to his ministry. Weinland was well respected by the local white community and praised by visiting Moravian authorities. He had won the loyalty of such important Indian leaders as John Morongo. And most important, he had won the respect of Amelia Stone Quinton, who continually and creatively found support for his expanding missionary work. The lack of a formal representative Indian voice requires more effort on our part to divine what these Mission Indians thought of his efforts on their behalf. They obviously respected him or they would not have signed the petition supporting his appointment as agent, attended his Sunday school, listened to his sermons from the pulpit of his Potrero chapel, or promised to attend the Moravian Church even if there was a Catholic church in their village. His success at Potrero led the villagers at Martínez to ask Quinton to provide them with a full-time missionary to live in their midst, duplicating what Weinland had created at Potrero.

Weinland's role in the missionary work of Southern California was unusually influential. Although no single individual in Northern California played a similar role, there was an auxiliary that was equally influential. Members of the Northern California Indian Association in San Jose, California, conducted a successful petition drive on behalf of the Indians in their part of the state, which resulted in a large congressional appropriation to purchase land; sponsored an annual conference in which local Indian leaders played a leading role; established an Indian industrial boarding school; and supported more government field matrons than any other auxiliary. Three members of this association played a pivotal role in directing these activities: a lawyer and a mother-daughter team. They are the subjects of the next chapter.

CHAPTER 8

Cornelia and Anna Taber and C. E. Kelsey of the NCIA

On October 13, 1909, at San Francisco's St. Francis Hotel, Cornelia Taber, corresponding secretary of the Northern California Indian Association (NCIA), was one of several reformers who addressed the annual dinner of the Commonwealth Club during "ladies' night." The theme was "Indian Rights and Wrongs." She began by declaring that Robert Louis Stevenson had once described the redwood trees and the Indians as "the two noblest living indigenous things in the State and both were condemned." The trees had been saved, the legislature had even passed laws to protect California's songbirds and game birds, and now thoughts were turning to "wild flowers, to keep them from being entirely swept away." It was finally time to save the few remaining Indians and provide them with homes. "Will you not help us to save this race, these native Sons and Daughters of the Golden West," Taber had asked the audience. Her question drew loud applause.[1]

The *San Francisco Chronicle* described a group of beautifully gowned women circulating through the Red Room of the hotel during the reception and exhibition preceding the dinner, enthusiastically examining the large collection of rare and beautiful Indian baskets offered by the NCIA, and asking questions of NCIA president Mrs. S. W. Gilchrist (née Josephine Russell), Taber, and two other members on how to order the baskets they had selected. Blankets, rugs, and other Indian handicrafts were also visible. The *Chronicle* described artfully displayed compositions and drawings by Indian children, accompanied by "explanatory compositions not infrequently in verse." During her address, Taber directed the audience's attention to the Indian baskets that were displayed, explaining their sale was "one of the special works we are trying to do" to help the Indians become self-supporting and to fund NCIA missionary efforts.[2] One of Taber's many duties was the promotion of Indian arts and, by so doing, to carry out a commitment made two decades previously by the WNIA to encourage industries among Indians when it had established its Committee on Indian Libraries and Industries in 1891.

Addresses that evening included one by Alfred Louis Kroeber, a University of California professor of anthropology, and another by C. E. Kelsey, general secretary of the NCIA. During his talk, Kelsey estimated that the state's Indian population had declined by over 90 percent when faced by "a frontier population, many of whom had just fought their way across the plains against the warlike Indians there," although the majority of the state's Indians were not hostile. Kelsey also sadly related that Indian children were not tolerated in public schools, and the same racial prejudice could be found within churches. He described these evils suffered by the Indians as "a reflection of public sentiment among white people," concluding the cure was to create a "better and more reasonable public sentiment." The following week he presented this same message to an entirely different audience at the Lake Mohonk Conference.[3] During her address at the Commonwealth Club, Taber shifted the emphasis to the NCIA's efforts to improve Indian housing and their support of the government field matron program, asking attendees to aid their program by helping to purchase sewing materials and medical supplies, horses and wagons, a phonograph for Sunday meetings, school supplies and hymn books, candles, candies, and assorted little gifts for Christmas boxes.[4]

Almost two decades earlier, Amelia Stone Quinton, president of the Women's National Indian Association, had come to California on her first visit and organized auxiliaries of local women. Although it is unclear when Cornelia Taber,[5] and her mother, Anna Haviland Ferris Taber, first joined the WNIA, they both played a major role in supporting the association's station among the Natinook-wa (or Hupa) Indians on the Hoopa Indian Reservation in Humboldt County. Initially isolated from the worst of an invasion of white settlers, the Hupas had tolerated the intruders, traded with, worked for, and married them. However, suspicions that the Indians were aiding neighboring tribes prompted the government in 1858 to establish Fort Gaston in the Hoopa Valley. Six years later, on August 12, 1864, in an effort to bring about a peaceful end to decades of hostilities among Indians, miners, and settlers, the federal government set aside the entire Hoopa Valley, called "Natinook" by the Hupa, as a treaty reservation. In the early years there was little consistency in administration. Eight different agents, many of whom were uncaring and inexperienced, served at the Hoopa Agency between 1864 and 1877, and a self-sufficient agricultural economy continually eluded the Indians. J. L. Broaddus, the last of the eight agents, made the situation worse, reducing rations and planting fewer acres in the hopes of forcing the residents to relocate to the Round Valley Reservation. Although the Hupas ultimately remained in their beloved valley, between 1877 and 1890 they were under military supervision when the secretary of war finally took over jurisdiction of the valley.[6]

Quinton had initially been alerted to the worsening conditions on the reservation by Mrs. Dorcas J. Spencer, corresponding secretary of the California Woman's Christian Temperance Union. While giving a temperance lecture in Hydesville in the summer of 1889, Spencer had been approached by William Beckwith, a Hupa Indian, who pleaded with her to come with him to his reservation to see the negative influence that the personnel of Fort Gaston had upon his people.[7] Mounted on a mule, Spencer accompanied Beckwith to the almost inaccessible reservation in the heart of the Trinity Mountains in the northwestern part of Humboldt County. She described her visit in a letter to Herbert Welsh, executive secretary of the Indian Rights Association, sending a copy to Quinton, who after making a few changes published it in *The Indian's Friend*.[8]

Among the WNIA members who read Spencer's letter was Mrs. Stephen H. Bullard (née Elizabeth Lyman Eliot), president of the Massachusetts Indian Association (MIA) and sister to Harvard's president, Charles W. Eliot. The worsening situation on the Hoopa Reservation appealed to her compassion and that of the reform-minded members of her MIA. In September 1890, Bullard wrote Commissioner Thomas Jefferson Morgan requesting 160 acres on the Hoopa Reservation for educational and missionary purposes. The project never got off the ground because Agent Isaac A. Beers expressed grave concerns about such a large grant of Indian land, and the MIA soon realized they would not be able to fund the project on their own.[9]

A year later, Quinton, on her lengthy coast-to-coast organizing tour, visited the Hoopa Reservation. Two days after founding the Northern California Women's Indian Association (NCWIA) on August 10, 1891, at the Occidental Hotel in San Francisco,[10] she sailed for Eureka and, like Spencer, accompanied Beckwith over the same dangerous route. Several days after her return, Quinton addressed the first formal meeting of the NCWIA, chaired by Mrs. Nellie Blessing Eyster, a prominent author, member of the WCTU, and founder of the Women's Press Club of San Francisco.[11] Quinton described the Hupas' condition as the most hopeless degradation she had ever seen, suggesting to the fifty women in attendance that they should immediately adopt the reservation "as their field of work." They agreed by the next meeting to have plans formulated and to invite Spencer to give her illustrated lecture on the Indians at a future date.[12] However, little was accomplished on behalf of the Hupa Indians until reformers in San Jose, California, reorganized.

Immediately upon her return from the Hoopa Reservation, Quinton had formed an Indian Committee in San Jose, some fifty miles south of San Francisco. A committee was the simplest of all WNIA associations, with no regular monthly meetings and little if any press coverage. With the support of former San Jose residents Edward N. Ament and his wife Floy, the few members of the committee reorganized on July 23, 1894, initially calling themselves the San Jose Indian Association. The Aments had been living in Plumas County since 1891, supervising the WNIA's Greenville Indian Industrial School, a boarding facility. During their 1894 summer vacation, they returned to San Jose to participate in the reorganization, delivering addresses and holding meetings. Their efforts may well have been partially self-serving because the newly reconfigured Indian association pledged funding for the construction of a new school dormitory wing at Greenville. By year's end, San Jose reformers were supporting Harriet Newell, Greenville's new school assistant, who, joined by her mother, boarded at the school. By October, with help from the Aments, the San Jose Indian Association had grown from thirty-three to fifty members.[13] When the Aments returned to

Greenville, the Taber women took charge of the association. In the fall of 1895, Cornelia was reelected as corresponding secretary while her mother became one of the two vice presidents. Three years later Anna Taber was elected president.[14]

One of Cornelia Taber's regular duties was to send branch reports to the national headquarters. She included interesting and sometimes amusing anecdotes and personal achievements from Harriet Newell's letters and those of other association workers, with requests for food, clothing, school supplies, and other items.[15] One "happy feature of San José helpfulness" towards the Indians was the sale of Indian baskets, Taber noted, quoting from Floy Ament, who had recommended that basketmaking be encouraged, with weekly lessons given.[16] In her spring 1895 column, she reported that since its reorganization the previous July, San Jose women had already raised $245.13 ($9,111 in 2025 dollars) for the Greenville School and sent boxes and barrels of clothing worth $270 to them. Auxiliary interest shifted to the Hoopa Valley when San Jose resident Emma Hapgood Denton was appointed as the government kindergarten teacher to the Hupa Indians. Taber's reports soon included cheerful extracts from Denton's letter, encouraging San Jose women to transfer all their energies to the new field at Hoopa Valley.[17]

On November 10, 1895, Nellie Eyster, branch president of the NCWIA in San Francisco, wrote to Commissioner Daniel M. Browning requesting a gift of eighty to a hundred acres at Hoopa to build an industrial school where a resident missionary would be employed to teach elements of farming. She explained that her association had chosen San Jose resident Reverend Lyman Paul Armstrong, "a man of unusual capabilities in his chosen field of labor," as their missionary. She reminded the commissioner that the NCWIA was already supporting Miss Denton, a kindergarten teacher.[18] Browning denied Eyster's request upon learning from Hoopa Indian Agent William E. Dougherty that, because every foot of land except for the school tract had been allotted under the Dawes Act, there was no land available for such missionary work. Furthermore, the agent explained, the Indians were already good farmers and their current conditions were satisfactory. Dougherty described Eyster's plan as benevolent but "inopportune and wholly impracticable."[19]

Quinton apologized to Browning, explaining that Eyster's "request for a farm, like her statement that the kindergarten teacher was supported by the Ind. Ass'n, was only a blunder." She assured him that Eyster had little to do with the actual work among the Hupas; her only obligation was to help gather Armstrong's salary. It would be the "San Jose ladies [who were] the responsible ones, & *they* are practical women," and would no doubt "see the need of great care on the part of this missionary & will request it." Quinton assured Browning "that no friction will arise, & that Mr. Armstrong's work may be wholly wise & greatly helpful to the Indians."[20]

With Quinton siding with the more practical San Jose reformers, work at Hoopa moved forward primarily because of Cornelia Taber's diplomatic skills. Learning from Denton that the agent was most interested in reservation missionary work, she wrote to Quinton, enclosing Denton's letter, asking her to "lay the matter before the Commissioner." Taber also explained that the Indian associations of San Francisco and San Jose had already pledged three-quarters of the missionary's first year salary, and Agent Dougherty seemed inclined to the idea; therefore, all that was lacking was the commissioner's permission. Knowing Quinton's powers of persuasion, Taber concluded, "I trust that this will be speedily granted." On January 30, Quinton asked Browning for his approval, explaining the agent was in favor, and "a capital man has been found for the field." She inquired if there might be "a vacant cottage of the old barracks," or possibly any other government room available to house the missionary. If not, she sensibly requested, a small grant of an acre or so might be provided for the building of a missionary cottage.[21]

When Browning did not respond immediately, Quinton wrote again in March, stressing that "*the Work* needs to begin *at once*,"[22] an urgency highlighted by an article decrying that despite a government school in their midst and forty years of white control, the Hupas still preserved many of their "old beliefs and superstitions. Witchcraft still retains a hold upon them and the custom of heathenish and immoral dances is kept up." In addition, the schoolchildren "are surrounded by and return to the corrupting influences of their uncivilized and unchristianized parents." Missionary work was now more crucial than ever before. Browning approved the request, and the Tabers and their fellow San Jose reformers provided $300 toward Armstrong's salary.[23]

If there had been any rift between San Francisco and San Jose, it was not apparent in the August 1896 *San Francisco Chronicle* article describing an afternoon mass meeting of the NCWIA in the Maple Room of the Palace Hotel with members of both associations attending. After calling the meeting to order, Eyster reported that since the government had recently donated land, all that remained was to raise money for a cottage and chapel.[24] Armstrong served as the NCIA missionary only a short time. He was replaced by Pliny E. Goddard and his wife.²⁵ By the spring of 1897 the San Jose association was supporting the Goddards, and Taber began forwarding extracts of their letters to *The Indian's Friend*.²⁶

San Jose reformers' links with the government were further strengthened when in August 1898 Emma Denton was appointed as a field matron, a program reflective of society's attitude that domesticity was woman's "sphere."²⁷ The previous year Commissioner Browning had explained that although the position required much "toil, hardship, wisdom, courage, and patience," a field matron "touches the mainsprings of life and character, and slowly develops a finer womanhood, childhood and manhood."²⁸ Cornelia Taber developed especially close ties to her association's field matrons, supporting them when possible, sharing their letters, including those written by Denton, and describing their work in her short book on California Indians.²⁹

Initially, the San Jose group had been a branch of the San Francisco NCWIA, which because of its more central location was recognized in Philadelphia as headquarters for Northern California work. When the San Francisco group disbanded, San Jose became the headquarters, in large part because of the leadership of the Taber women. Initially known as the Northern California State Branch of the WNIA, members soon came to identify themselves as the Northern California Indian Association (NCIA). Taber, as association chronicler, during the October 1898 annual meeting described the first aim of her association as awakening "public sentiment to aid our Government in its present policy of granting citizenship to Indians, and the same protection of law enjoyed by other races among us." Their second goal was to support suitable missionaries and teachers working on the Indians' behalf.³⁰

To spread the NCIA's message to wider audiences, Taber spoke before various philanthropic groups. In an address during a Chautauquan Program in Pacific Grove, she revealed her position on the 1887 Dawes Act. Like many reformers, she viewed the legislation as positive, explaining that it lifted "the Indians morally, intellectually and industrially." They were no longer "the pauperized eater of rations." Already, she explained, some 66,000 Indians had taken their allotments, with 22,000 full citizens, and another 35,000 paying taxes. She was also concerned with California's failure to recognize Indians' right to occupancy of their land. They had never been compensated for the lands taken from them; therefore, she believed the state's debt to them remained unpaid.³¹ During the next three years, Taber and the NCIA would devote most of their efforts toward fulfilling this unpaid debt, initiating a campaign to raise money to purchase land for the landless Indians of Northern California.

During the summer of 1899, Taber stepped out from behind her desk and traveled to the Hoopa Valley. Like Spencer and Quinton before her, she endured a lengthy and uncomfortable journey. Her party boarded a steamer in San Francisco, disembarking at Eureka, and climbed aboard a railroad car, finally mounting mules for the last forty miles. At times she and her party were forced to dismount because the narrow path was often blocked by fallen trees. Two exhausting days later, tired and thankful, the reformers stood before the door of the association's mission chapel. They investigated the little three-acre farm, surrounded by a post and wire fence, and visited the chapel, the barn, and the new four-room Huntington Cottage, named after Collis P. Huntington, a financier of the Central Pacific Railroad, who had contributed $500 towards its construction.[32]

Standing on the front porch of the Goddards' new home, Taber had a clear view of the fine vegetable garden, grape vines, strawberry patches, and irrigated fields of corn and alfalfa. The missionary couple had literally cultivated every available spot on what a mere eighteen months before had been unfenced wild land. Taber listened carefully as Pliny Goddard educated her about the Indians' customs and religion, their fear of witchcraft, and their weekly gambling, which he described as "a great curse of the reservation." He stated that there were two hundred children attending the government school, and job prospects were improving now that the Indians were employed hauling supplies in and out of the valley. Some Hupas had begun to fence portions of the valley, and Taber could personally see their fields of newly planted grain. The Hoopa Mission Church had been organized, and already thirty-three schoolchildren had asked to become members and were currently undergoing religious instruction. Nine adults were also interested in joining, including a married couple whom Emma Denton had been instructing.[33]

Taber had anticipated a happy reunion with her friend during this visit, but Denton had drowned on January 19, 1899, probably having suffered a heart attack—a decision thus reported to the editor of *The Indian's Friend* by Anna Taber because there had been no signs of a struggle. During the memorial service in San Jose's First Congregational Church, Cornelia Taber described her friend as a soldier "storming a height," planting her banner. "She was our color bearer, leading us on to victory, she herself following her Captain as seeing Him who is invisible."³⁴ Months later, in homage, Cornelia read a compelling paper on Denton's life before a Young Men's Christian Association meeting.³⁵ The following year, when Alice Goddard fell ill, missionary work on the Hoopa Reservation suffered yet another setback. The Goddards left their post in June 1900. The following month, the WNIA Missionary Committee turned control of the work over to the Presbyterian Board in New York City. In December, Mary E. Chase of Los Angeles and her assistant, Miss Dayton, began their missionary work among the 435 Indians in the Hoopa Valley.³⁶

Although continuing to support their former mission, San Jose reformers turned much of their attention to the purchase of land for Northern California's homeless Indians. They first decided to buy land for sixty Indians recently evicted from their forty-acre home adjoining a large ranch in Manchester, where the men had worked for years clearing land and harvesting crops. When the story of this eviction appeared in a June 1901 article in *The Indian's Friend*, NCIA member Hannah Elliott Shipley Bean sent a copy to IRA president Philip C. Garrett, a fellow Quaker. The Taber women were also Quakers. Bean explained that her association had located forty acres near the Indians' former Manchester home that could be purchased for $250. However, having recently spent $400 for twenty acres near Ukiah, currently held in Anna Taber's name for the Indians' benefit, the San Jose reformers could only raise $50. Bean, who described the Tabers as "devoted in a variety of ways to the cause of the Indians of California," asked Garrett for assistance, assuring him that lands purchased for the Manchester group would be held "the same way, made legally safe to the Indians that we may protect it." IRA members quickly raised $312.³⁷

To more easily facilitate future land purchases, the NCIA organized as a corporation. Ten of their members, including the Taber women, signed the papers of incorporation on January 23, 1902. Article II declared the corporation was formed "for benevolent, charitable and Missionary purposes for the benefit of the Indians of California," to aid the government "in preventing all oppression of Indians," to engage in educational and missionary work, and to purchase and hold in trust lands to be sold or leased to Indians.³⁸ By the following June, the NCIA reported that new homes had been built near Manchester and vegetable gardens and fruit trees planted.³⁹

Taber wrote of three more endangered groups, one nine miles south of Colusa, another on Grande Island, ten miles south of Colusa where forty-six people, including a dozen children, refused attendance at the public school, were confined to a four-acre plot of land. Three of the acres were "the old *grave yard* of their people." Another two hundred or more Indians lived some forty miles from Colusa. She also reported during their regular quarterly meeting in July that an NCIA committee was scheduled to confer with Commissioner Jones during his upcoming visit to San Jose.[40] Quinton, already impressed with the NCIA, described the auxiliary as "freshly and from consciences vital and energetic" in their study of the situation of the Indians of their state. She concluded: "How clear in such circumstances is the duty of Christian women, not being in politics to plead for those who have no voice."[41]

To raise more money, in the summer of 1903 the NCIA adopted a new plan of action—to write a memorial letter to President Theodore Roosevelt to get his attention and then initiate a petition drive to secure federal funding. Roosevelt's scheduled visit to San Francisco and San Jose in the summer of 1903 provided an opportunity for C. E. Kelsey, a San Jose lawyer and the association's general secretary, to welcome the president and present him with the NCIA's lengthy memorial letter, signed by Cornelia Taber, corresponding secretary; Mrs. Thomas C. Edwards (née Mary Haven), president; and Mrs. Mary L. Bacon, financial secretary.[42] Kelsey sent a typed copy of the letter to Charles Fletcher Lummis, describing the "condition of the Indians here [as] very disheartening," requesting his "moral support and backing."[43] This ambitious plan had been made possible because membership had grown from eleven to ninety with a treasury of $4,770, described by Taber as having "been expended in careful seed sowing."[44]

In their memorial letter, Taber and her fellow reformers called Roosevelt's attention to the present condition of Northern California Indians "whose title and ownership to this beautiful land have never been extinguished, either in law or morals." While nearly all Indians in Southern California had been provided with land, only the Hupas and the small tribes at Round Valley had designated reservations in the north, leaving the remainder, an estimated 10,000 to 12,000, homeless. Representing a little over 10 percent of their original population, Northern California's Indigenous population had witnessed the seizing of their land, the killing of their game, and the muddying of their rivers by runoff from mining operations, "all apparently done wantonly." The memorialists continued that as land values rose, Indian evictions became more common, forcing some to take refuge on an ocean beach, squat upon a levee, or occupy an old cemetery of three or four acres, where "every turn of the spade brings up the bones of their ancestors." One old woman had recently asked an NCIA member: "Do the people think we are birds and can live in the trees?" The San Jose reformers concluded that it was "doubtful if there [were] any people in America, even on the East Side of New York City, whose present is so miserable or whose future is so appalling as some of the Indian bands in Northern California."[45]

Taber and her fellow members assured Roosevelt that their intention was not to deprive the Indians of their independence but to provide them with a home "in the neighborhood where they now live," enabling them the opportunity to "develop into intelligent, self-respecting citizens." The NCIA had conferred with Commissioner Jones during his recent visit to the state, and he had assured them of his cooperation. At his suggestion, the NCIA had begun gathering information on the location and size of each landless band of Indians in the northern part of the state.[46] Meanwhile, Roosevelt forwarded their memorial to the commissioner for his recommendation. Although he appeared to be sympathetic, Jones informed the president that he doubted "if any action of the National Government in the direction suggested by the memorialists would be of any permanent benefit to the Indians." Five days later, Roosevelt sent Jones's response to Kelsey, who addressed all the commissioner's concerns, providing additional details.[47]

The Taber women had little good to say about Commissioner Jones. In a January 30, 1904, letter to Mathew K. Sniffen, assistant to Herbert Welsh, Cornelia Taber expressed her gratitude for his association's support, noting that Samuel M. Brosius had characterized Jones as careless. "We hardly know how to forgive" Jones, she wrote, "his attitude toward us has been most vacillating and hypocritical," even though he had promised to do everything he could for them during his recent visit to California.[48] In a mid-March letter to Sniffen, Anna Taber echoed her daughter's opinion, describing Jones as being, in their minds, "poorly qualified for the office he fills—no doubt he means well, but he makes serious mistakes." She was still complaining about him to Sniffen in September, wishing "that a somewhat different man could occupy the position."[49]

To reach a larger audience, the NCIA also prepared a "memorial" petition addressed to Congress requesting the allotment of lands to Northern California's landless Indians. Signed by Edwards and Kelsey, it was presented by California Senator Thomas R. Bard on January 21, 1904.[50] The petitioners explained that in other areas the government paid the Indians for land cessions, but because the treaties negotiated with the eighty to ninety bands in Northern California had never been ratified by the Senate, no payment had been made for "more than 100,000 square miles of the most beautiful and valuable country in the world."⁵¹ As a result, these Indians had become squatters and tenants on their former lands, "victims of a constantly increasing series of evictions" as white populations encroached. And, furthermore, "race prejudice [had] for the most part debarred their children from the public schools." Describing the rejection of the California treaties as "*a great wrong*," Kelsey later wrote that it was only just "that the General Government should take some steps to repair the wrong inflicted upon a helpless people."⁵²

Because landholding Indians tended to be in a better situation, the petitioners determined that the government "may in some measure repair the wrong it has done these people by giving them individually small tracts of land and increasing the school privileges for their children." Instead of creating costly reservations, the NCIA recommended land allotments "in the neighborhoods where they now live." Along with the petition, the NCIA included a detailed list of non-reservation bands of Indians north of Tehachapi at 418 settlements with a population of 13,733—all landless.⁵³

Kelsey turned to the IRA for support, sending a copy of their petition to Sniffen on December 4, 1903, urging him to "take charge of the matter at Washington." He stated that individual petitions, gathered by various auxiliaries, would soon follow. Receiving a positive response, Kelsey suggested that Bard, a member of the Senate Indian Committee and the Sequoya League, present it.⁵⁴ Eight days later, Brosius informed Sniffen that Bard had confided that the Senate Indian Committee, with his urging, had agreed to have the petition printed the day before, giving "it further standing, as of more than usual interest." Because Congress could not be expected to appropriate funds without a formal report from an official of their choice, Bard intended to ask for a responsible inspector to investigate the condition of the Indians. However, Brosius correctly assumed that the NCIA would not want to depend solely upon an outside investigation.⁵⁵ Kelsey later confided to California Senator George C. Perkins that a "tenderfoot's" report would be valueless because such an investigation would require some 15,000 miles of very rough travel to visit the many isolated *rancherias* (small California Indian settlements). The NCIA was only asking for modest plots of land, "so small that after cabins, corrals, etc., are put up there will be room for nothing but small gardens." The association had no intention of starting these Indians out on a career of farming, for "they are now laborers (after a fashion) and our purpose is that they shall remain laborers." Kelsey assured Perkins that government officials should not be alarmed about the NCIA petition.⁵⁶

In late January 1904, days after Bard presented the petition, NCIA president Mrs. Thomas Edwards summarized the good work of her association to the *San Francisco Chronicle*, explaining their reform work generally went unrecognized because absolutely no politics was involved. They were philanthropists who had raised $5,000, with $3,000 already spent on the Hoopa Reservation. Swayed by her words, several months later the *Chronicle* published an editorial supporting their petition, concluding that "for justice and honest and fair dealing" the government should "make what reparation it can to the remnant of these Indians."⁵⁷ Not all reformers agreed. Richard Henry Pratt, founder of the Carlisle Indian School, adamantly opposed the petition, but then he also clashed often with the IRA. Where Herbert Welsh saw value in reservation schools, Pratt "could see no good in the reservation experience in any form."⁵⁸ Kelsey dismissed Pratt's criticism, believing his opposition was based on a hasty misreading of the petition and an assumption that the NCIA intended to create reservations. Furthermore, Kelsey believed Pratt was objecting "to things not in our proposition at all."⁵⁹

Anna Taber expressed great concern about Pratt's criticism, explaining to Sniffen on February 19 that it had created considerable anxiety among the membership. Pratt's success at Carlisle had made him powerful in the community, which she noted was not good in this case for he showed "much ignorance of California conditions and of our purpose." She had shown Pratt's written criticisms to a certain gentleman who for years had lived in personal contact with Indians in Northern California. The man had called Pratt a fool. Anna Taber was presumably referring to Judge J. R. Lewis,⁶⁰ who during frequent meetings with Pratt at Lake Mohonk had soon learned that it was impossible to convince him on any issue. Lewis had confided to Taber that Pratt might possibly be right for Carlisle, "but he does not know as much outside as he thinks." Therefore, concerned about Pratt's influence, Anna Taber was in hopes that the IRA would take up the NCIA's cause, showing the public how ignorant he was, nullifying his influence. She firmly believed that if Indians owned land and could vote, "whites would treat them as men, and not as animals as they so frequently do now." Taber concluded that "perhaps the subject is foolish or impracticable, but I knew the whites will rob the Indians if they can, and make them drunk in order to do it."⁶¹

Annie Ellicott Kennedy Bidwell, western vice president of the WNIA, wrote to Pratt in support of the NCIA petition. Anna Taber, upon receiving a letter

Figure 21. Born in Westchester, New York, and raised in the Quaker faith, Anna Haviland Ferris Taber, pictured in this undated photograph, was, along with her daughter Cornelia, a powerful presence in the Northern California Indian Association, serving as vice president and president. (California Historical Society, San Francisco, California, [(FN-27750/CHS2010.441].)

from Bidwell, informed Sniffen of the wonderful success that Bidwell and her husband John had accomplished at Chico, explaining that "by an appropriation of their own land & by intelligent kind treatment they changed a band of almost naked savages into a respectable Christian community." Taber continued that Bidwell also had recently written a letter to the *San Francisco Chronicle* in support of the NCIA work and their petition, believing she had the right to do so because of her extensive work on behalf of the Indians.[62]

Initially, Kelsey and Edwards had been unconcerned about Pratt's criticism, but Taber's correspondence with Sniffen may have prompted them to finally rebut Pratt's "effusion." In mid-February under their signature, they sent Pratt an open letter recognizing that because his "well known zeal in the Indian service" had given weight to anything he said, the NCIA realized it was essential to set the record straight. The situation with the California Indians was unlike that of other tribes and, therefore, his "arguments [had] absolutely no bearing upon the problem" and especially upon the NCIA's attempt to solve it. The association had no intention of restricting the individual liberty of Northern California Indians, or placing them under the control of any bureau. Instead, their goal was to "give the Northern California Indians as a whole, their only chance to attain independent citizenship." Because they held no title to their lands and were continually subjected to evictions, using the Indian Homestead Law,[63] which Pratt had suggested, was not the answer. The petition had clearly stated that the NCIA had no intention of establishing reservations as they were expensive and, furthermore, the Indians did not want them. Instead, the NCIA proposed to grant land in severalty in the areas where they now lived, unless "unfit for human habitation." It was essential to protect what little land they held because the smallest improvements became an incentive for eviction. Pratt was totally ignoring the Indians' right to occupancy, a right acknowledged by other civilized nations and by every state but California. Furthermore, California Indians would not end up in the "opulent ease of those in Oklahoma," as Pratt had suggested. The NCIA was not looking for any kind of charity, only for justice. Kelsey respectfully requested that Pratt re-read the petition to see more clearly what the NCIA was asking and their reasons for doing so.[64]

On February 19, Judge J. R. Lewis, prominent western attorney, director of the NCIA, husband of one of the association's five vice presidents, and a signer of the NCIA petition, wrote to Congress in defense of the petition. He could only assume that Pratt had attacked it because he either failed to read it properly or misunderstood its purpose. Lewis explained to Congress that "in all Northern California there cannot be found a tract of public land for entry under the homestead law, fit for a white man to live upon and no Indian can make a living where a white man cannot." Therefore, Pratt's reliance on the Indian Homestead Act was unsound—the idea of "filing homestead claims upon the *mountain peaks of our State is absurd* ." Lewis concluded that Pratt must have seen in their petition "the 'Shadow' of the 'Ghosts of the Indian Reservation' and has 'tackled' it." Lewis's letter was widely circulated within the reforming community.[65]

Cornelia Taber, serving temporarily as Kelsey's assistant, enclosed a copy of Lewis's letter to Commissioner Jones, describing the writer as a wealthy man with social standing. He was moreover president of the San Jose Board of Education and respected by both the rich and the poor. By now she trusted that Washington officials fully understood the reasoning behind the NCIA's appeal on behalf of California's landless Indians. Their sole intent was to ask for "enough land to keep them above ground not under it." Reinforcing their case, Taber enumerated nine previous arguments, including the lack of title to Indian-occupied lands, subjecting them to dispossession at any moment, and because they had no legal standing, she concluded, they were neither citizens nor wards. She also alerted Jones to three more bands, numbering one hundred fifty-five individuals, who were now facing eviction.[66]

Anna Taber forwarded Senator Bard's response to Lewis's letter on to Sniffen in mid-March, describing it as very friendly and showing a gratifying interest in the Indians. Addressing Bard's recommendation of a formal investigation of the Indians' condition, she criticized such investigations as generally careless, often imperfectly done, and requiring "a peculiarly careful consideration by whoever is sent out here." She warned that only honest, conscientious, intelligent men be appointed as investigators. The NCIA had already suggested Kelsey and now had added Judge Lewis. In an earlier letter, Anna Taber had cautioned that it would be best to send a California man. "To approach an Indian one must understand them & know how to earn their confidence," otherwise "there would be no possibility of getting at the truth."[67]

While Cornelia Taber was assisting Kelsey, her mother, now a director of the NCIA, continued her flurry of letters to IRA officials. She informed Sniffen that the NCIA were sending appeals out all over the state and elsewhere, but that getting endorsements from "white people in *Indian* neighborhoods" was proving particularly difficult because of indifference in these areas. "If the Indians were wild animals they [local whites] could not care less for their welfare, and they are driven from any spot a white man desires without the least sympathy," she confided. "I don't wish to jest on a serious subject," she concluded, "but we are really respectable people and have among our members some very intelligent men & women."⁶⁸ In the meantime, a committee of Kelsey and two ministers, a Congregational and a Quaker, were addressing various ministers' Union meetings and getting endorsements for their petition.⁶⁹

The April issue of *The Indian's Friend* included Cornelia Taber's report describing the circulation of their petition as arousing interest for Indians as never before. It had even been espoused by the 28,000 members of the California Federation of Women's Clubs.⁷⁰ Despite herculean efforts, the petition failed, partially because Senator Orville H. Platt of Connecticut sponsored one in opposition, prompting the *Los Angeles Herald* to write that Congress "is in doubt as to what to do."⁷¹ In mid-June, Anna Taber informed Sniffen of the defeat of their petition, and although the NCIA membership was greatly disappointed, they were not deterred. They planned to gather signatures during the summer and submit a new petition that fall at the Lake Mohonk Conference. Explaining to Sniffen that her husband, Augustus, had been an active member of the conference before they moved to California, she asked him if he would present their petition, concluding, "As far as I know, missions are a blessing to the Indians who are grateful and responsive when approached with tact and good sense." On the first of September she sent Sniffen a copy of the new petition, along with an old one marked to indicate changes made to address all objections. She also asked if he could bring it before the IRA and encourage them to take it up as part of their work.⁷²

As fall approached, Anna Taber increased her letter writing to Sniffen, explaining that the reformers were sending out petitions to a great many Californians as well as people living out of state. Kelsey would send Sniffen all they had collected before October 1. She again expressed displeasure with many Californians who were "utterly indifferent and in many cases have regarded the Indians about as they do the wild animals that are being gradually exterminated." A week later, noting that although she had been sick for the last month, she had continued to write personal letters to friends. She sent Sniffen names of a few visitors expected to attend Lake Mohonk, all of whom she thought would do what they could to influence the conference. Among the names included were Anna Laurens Dawes, daughter of Senator Dawes; Taber's cousin, James Wood, clerk of the

Yearly Meeting of Friends in New York;[73] and Benjamin Cappock, former superintendent of Chilocco Indian Agricultural School. Anna Taber explained that although she and her husband had visited a number of Indian schools, Chilocco was distinct. She described the students much like members of the family, taking their meals with them and behaving like ladies and gentlemen. She concluded that she was sending some papers prepared by her daughter, Cornelia, "to meet honest objections to our plans. You may encounter people who can be made to change adverse opinions."[74]

In an early October letter to Sniffen, Anna Taber wrote that Stanford President David Starr Jordan,[75] whose wife was an NCIA vice president, had written the previous year to government officials on behalf of the NCIA. Although their earlier effort had failed, in one way it had been successful, because more people were now writing for information and offering to help than ever before.[76] A week later, Cornelia Taber sent additional information to Sniffen before his presentation of their petition, noting that her mother was ill. She explained that Quakers in Baltimore had "taken a special interest in our Indians," and that if he needed more witnesses to evictions, Reverend H. C. Meredith of Lakeport, California, could easily provide them.[77] On October 11, Kelsey forwarded Sniffen some 500 petitions, writing at month's end that in addition to California's two senators, a majority of congressmen had responded favorably.[78]

During the fifth session of the twenty-second Lake Mohonk Conference on October 21, Samuel Brosius addressed the attendees, declaring in good conscience that California Indians should be "entitled to have at least a few acres for each family," five-acre parcels that "secured wherever possible will, in a measure meet the present need." Quinton followed with a shorter but no less passionate address, describing one band of some one hundred Indians living on four acres, most of which included the "burial place of their fathers." At conference's end, the members resolved that the government was "duty bound to provide homes" for these landless Indians and recommended that Congress appoint a three-man commission, one being a California resident, to investigate their conditions and to purchase small plots of five to ten acres for each to enable "these Indians [to live] among white settlers, where employment may be found for them."[79]

In early November, Anna Taber thanked Sniffen for his account of events at Mohonk and updated him on the petition drive. "Certainly the interest in the landless Indians has developed wonderfully in this State," she remarked, and the NCIA hoped for good results on their petition that winter. Then, on

November 13, she acknowledged that Commissioner Jones had expressed a willingness to include an application for $10,000 ($359,325 in 2025 dollars) on behalf of the NCIA's work, although she had learned from Quinton that Jones had no intention of including the NCIA petition "or any part of it in his paper for appropriations."[80]

Copies of this new petition flooded in as the national association encouraged support from their state branches and auxiliaries through *The Indian's Friend*. Pastors' associations, California clergymen, the IRA, the California WCTU, the General Federation of Women's Clubs, Stanford University president David Starr Jordan, and many faculty members joined the effort.[81] A news account of the October 29, 1904, annual meeting of the NCIA reported that 2,000 petitions representing some 12,000 members of religious and charitable organizations had already been received.[82] During their annual conference in December, the NIA had adopted five resolutions addressed to Congress and President Roosevelt in support of their Northern California auxiliary. One in particular required Congress "to provide individual land holdings sufficient for self-support" for Indians whose land had been taken from them without compensation and who were now homeless.[83]

The following month between sixty and seventy people gathered at the Trinity Parish House to hear Kelsey report on the petition and its endorsement by the Lake Mohonk Conference. They also listened to addresses by Dorcas J. Spencer, secretary for the Indian Department of the Woman's Christian Temperance Union, and to Cornelia Taber, who read extracts from letters written by teachers and workers at several NCIA mission stations. At her request, they took up donations to purchase a horse and buggy for one worker, enabling her to more easily visit additional Indian homes.[84] Then, on April 12, 1905, one hundred seventy-five NCIA members packed the Baptist Church schoolroom in San Jose for their regular meeting to learn from Kelsey that Congress had appropriated $10,000 to investigate the condition of Northern California Indians. Six days later, Kelsey informed Sniffen that the NCIA had unanimously passed a resolution thanking him for his kindness and for his assistance in their efforts on behalf of Northern California Indians.[85] Unjustly, the IRA took credit for getting this appropriation, although Lummis in his Sequoya League reports and in *Out West* had recognized Kelsey's work, praising him and his associates, and offering League assistance if needed. Lummis's praise may also have been the result of the NCIA's earlier thanks "for his virile championship of the rights of the Northern California Indians."[86]

CHAPTER 8

In June 1905, Commissioner Francis Ellington Leupp[87] briefly visited San Francisco, and according to Anna Taber, in his interview with Kelsey, the commissioner showed that he had a "clear understanding of even local conditions in California and hearty accord with our views."[88] Following his California visit, in June 1905 Leupp selected Kelsey as the special agent to conduct the investigation, prompting NCIA members to describe the appointment as "the best work done for our Indians in all the years of our association's life." Anna Taber had known for months that Kelsey was being considered. She informed Sniffen in January 1905 that Kelsey had lived on the Oneida Reservation when his father was their agent and was thus familiar with the Indian character. Therefore, he "would be a very suitable person for appointment either to make inquiries or to distribute the appropriation." The Sequoya League was also pleased that a Californian, a lawyer, and someone with experience in the Indian service had been appointed.[89]

Kelsey's father, Charles Sheffield Kelsey, had been appointed in 1890 as the Green Bay Indian Agent for the Menominee, Stockbridge, and Oneida Reservations in northeastern Wisconsin. The younger Kelsey had not only lived on the reservation with his father but had served as an agency clerk from 1891 to 1893. According to Larisa K. Miller, during his stay Kelsey acquired firsthand experience of the Indian Office bureaucracy and "with tribes and individuals in different circumstances who were dealing with great pressures to acculturate." He witnessed Indians living communally and individually on allotted and unallotted lands, experiences that served as the incubator for his "later advocacy for individually owned, small home sites for the landless Indians of Northern California." Kelsey had also met his future wife, Abigail, whose father, Solomon Stevens Burleson, was the Episcopal missionary to the Oneidas. Kelsey left his reservation position to attend the University of Wisconsin, graduating with a law degree in 1896, opening up his own law practice in Eau Claire with a friend. He and Abigail had married in 1897 and four years later moved to San Jose. It is unknown when he first joined the NCIA.[90]

Between August 8, 1905, and March 8, 1906, Kelsey traveled some twelve thousand miles, conducting his census of the state's non-reservation Indians. The area's size limited him to spending less than three days per county, when he would have much preferred a "hut to hut canvass." With most settlements located away from existing railroad lines, he found it "impossible to hurry the inquiry beyond the speed of a horse." His final count revealed a total population of slightly more than 17,000 Native people, 3,500 living in the south. With 5,200 living on reservations, there were some 11,800 homeless. He also learned that the Northern California Indian population had declined by 1,100 in the previous three years.[91] Kelsey began his report with a history of the Mission Period, concluding with the eighteen rejected treaties. "Had the Government given these Indians the same treatment as it did other Indians in the United States," he wrote, "their conditions today would be very different." Non-California Indians at least had been assigned reservations, giving them at a minimum a land base. He recommended protecting the land and water rights of all Indian allotees, additional field matrons and industrial teachers, more day schools, stronger legislation to stop the liquor traffic, and the proper surveying and marking of all reservation boundaries. The latter issue had become very apparent to Kate Foote when she was engaged in participating in the eleventh federal census among the Mission Indians.[92]

On March 19, 1906, Anna Taber informed Sniffen that Kelsey had been summoned by Commissioner Leupp to Washington to place his report before the Senate Committee. She stated that he had devoted several months to his investigation, forced to ride or walk to visit the isolated areas to which many of the Indians had been forced. He had, she noted, found conditions worse than expected. Hoping "his account should meet with some justice from Congress," Taber explained that the NCIA was continuing to send postal cards, papers, and appeals everywhere. "When we consider that the government has received millions from the sale of California lands and have dishonestly broken every treaty and never paid a cent to the rightful owners, it seems a disgrace that should attract the attention of all respectable honest citizens," she concluded.[93] The following month, Cornelia Taber reported that Kelsey's investigation had revealed greater destitution than originally claimed, with some Indians "literally dying of starvation." She determined that an appropriation "for the purchase of land for small allotments is imperatively needed to save the remnants of our landless Indians."[94] During her travels through Mission villages, Constance Goddard DuBois had also discovered the same grim circumstances.

With Kelsey busy in the field, Cornelia Taber, aided by her mother, remained a consistent voice, publicizing the NCIA work, writing reports, and giving talks. Invited by the Federated Women's Club to talk, she instead entertained them with Indian music. "We are glad of this chance to call attention of the representative women of the state to our Indians," she wrote in *The Indian's Friend*, hoping in time that other clubs would sponsor an Indian Day, and that the NCIA might become a reference bureau for all California clubs. In support, *The Indian's Friend* carried a notice to all association members to send their papers to Taber to be read before other groups.⁹⁵

Cornelia Taber's message quoted in the 1906 NIA annual report alerted the widely scattered membership that Kelsey's report had been approved, and Congress had appropriated $100,000 ($3,553,322 in 2025 dollars) for the purchase of land for non-reservation Indians in the north. That July, Indian Commissioner Leupp appointed Kelsey as the special disbursing agent. Taber explained that Kelsey was "now at work negotiating for the purchase of land . . . and we hope soon to report some bands settled in homes from which they cannot be evicted."⁹⁶ During the NCIA quarterly meeting the following June, unusually well attended because Commissioner Leupp was present, Kelsey reported that he had examined one hundred fifty tracts of land, negotiating the purchase of $60,000 worth of land. Cornelia Taber also reported on field matron work, reading extracts from several letters, urging that "the Indians' Christmas should be remembered during the leisure of the summer, and articles suitable for holiday gifts be prepared and collected."⁹⁷

In the summer of 1906, the NCIA added an innovative approach to their reform efforts, the only NIA auxiliary to do so: an annual local conference to "start a new era of true interest and helpfulness among the Indians' white neighbors in his behalf." It was even more unique in that Indian leaders were invited to air their grievances. The NCIA's first Zayante Indian Conference was held July 29–31 in Santa Cruz, California, at Mount Hermon, a 400-acre summer camp equipped with a hotel and cottages. A circular letter invitation, addressed "To the Friends of the Indians of California," was sent under the signatures of NCIA members Cornelia Taber, Kelsey, Spencer, and Mary Edwards, and thirteen other clergymen, missionaries, and university professors.⁹⁸ The facility, which hosted Christian conferences, was owned by the Mount Hermon Association and managed by Reverend Hugh W. Gilchrist, whose cousin, Mrs. S. W. Gilchrist, had recently been reelected as NCIA president.⁹⁹ Taber expressed hope in a report in the September issue of *The Indian's Friend* that this first conference would reach "a new and thoughtful audience." She was most pleased with the presence of William R. Benson,¹⁰⁰ an educated Pomo Indian, who after relating the history of his band and its many evictions, appealed for an end to the liquor traffic. "You brought it and you ought to take it away," he had exclaimed. Quinton, in her report, also noted his speech, as well as one by Dorcas J. Spencer, concluding that this expanded movement by the NCIA would, no doubt, bring "great progress for Indian uplift throughout that state" in the near future.[101]

The following year, additional invitations were mailed. Twenty Indians from nine different tribes attended, including one Indian woman, Maggie Sowilleno Lafonso, a Mechoopa Indian from Chico, who had accompanied her benefactress, Annie E. K. Bidwell. *The Indian's Friend* reported that the conference had awakened fresh hope in Indian attendees, and after holding a council, they came up with their five most important needs. These were: land for homes, protection from the liquor traffic, a common school education for their children, field physicians, and legal protection. All Indian attendees signed the final document. The Prudential Committee, the governing body of the conference, endorsed all five pleas as "essential to the welfare of the Indians of California" and recommended that the document be sent to various governmental entities and organizations, beginning with the president of the US and the Indian commissioner.[102] In a small way, the NCIA's Zayante conferences played a role not unlike that of Thomas A. Bland's earlier National Indian Defense Association, where Indians were invited to speak. Indian attendance at Zayante prompted historian Cathleen D. Cahill to describe these conferences as creating Indian middlemen trained to do outreach work among their own people.[103] The third conference focused on an educational plan no longer aimed at Indian assimilation. To carry out this goal, in 1913 the NCIA opened an industrial school at Guinda.[104]

Because Indian participants had cited land as their first priority, the NCIA remained focused on purchasing such. On February 28, 1908, California Senator Frank P. Flint informed Lummis that he had secured an additional $50,000 to not only buy land for the Mission Indians in the southern part of the state but to build a wagon road through the Hoopa Valley Indian Reservation.[105] This latest infusion of money prompted Lake Mohonk founder Albert K. Smiley to declare that "great credit is due to a little band of women at San Jose the leading spirit of which is Miss Cornelia Taber, formerly of New York City." Through extraordinary persistence and a successful petition drive, the NCIA had succeeded in getting a total of $150,000 from Congress for land purchases.[106]

To reach other interested parties, between April 27 and 29 Cornelia Taber and NCIA members joined the Sequoya League and other reformers at a California "Mohonk-style" conference in Riverside, hosted at the Glenwood Mission Inn by Frank Augustus Miller, who had acquired his interest in Indian reform from his Quaker mother and a childhood among the Winnebago Indians in his hometown of Tomah, Wisconsin.[107] Some 150 delegates and between fifty and sixty Indians attended the three-day conference. Cornelia Taber and Quinton, in California on a visit, spoke. Lummis was most impressed with the common sense reflected in the discussions, describing Kelsey's plainspoken talk as "without a flower of rhetoric, the most encouraging" one he had ever heard "on any phase of the Indian question."[108] Then, in mid-October, Taber addressed the Missionary Society of the Presbyterian Church of Gilroy, "setting forth the condition of and what is being done for the Indians of this Coast in the way of education and other matters pertaining to their moral and spiritual welfare."[109]

In a 1909 annual report, the national association praised the NCIA for reaching a wider audience than ever before in their efforts on behalf of their state's Indians.[110] The branch had added twenty-four new members; opened their long-awaited nondenominational mission in Bishop, Inyo County, named in honor of Hannah Elliott Bean, who had died in January;[111] and addressed such diverse groups as the Young Women's Christian Association, the Century Club of San Francisco, and the prestigious Annual Dinner and Ladies' Night at the Commonwealth Club. A week later, Kelsey gave his address before the Lake Mohonk Conference.[112] In early June, the San Jose Woman's Club hosted an Indian day, decorating their clubhouse with Indian blankets and baskets and playing Indian music. NCIA president, Mrs. S. W. Gilchrist, in charge of the festivities, spoke before the gathering, as did Cornelia Taber, who after retelling the shameful story of the mistreatment of the Indians read from some field matron letters.[113] At the Fourth Zayante Conference in mid-August, attended by seventeen Indians, including two women, attendees learned that Kelsey had purchased some 1,800 acres for thirty-two bands, with fifteen already settled in new homes, prompting one Indian to exclaim: "We got land! When I heard that I could not sleep four nights"; he said he felt he had "wings and could fly."[114] After learning this news, Cornelia Taber wrote that NCIA members returned home "singing our Doxology, and with a thousand new plans in our heads."[115] However, according to Larisa K. Miller, as early as 1910 some of Kelsey's purchases in Lake and Mendocino Counties proved to be unsuitable "for homesites, with value only for pasture and wood for fuel and fence posts." Years later, Edgar B. Meritt, assistant Indian commissioner, conceded that land purchased was not of "the highest grade," a shortcoming he "attributed to the paucity of funds appropriated."[116]

The NCIA had an especially successful year in 1910. The high point was the Fifth Zayante Indian Conference held in early August. In her report, Cornelia

Figure 22. This photograph was most likely taken during the Fourth Zayante Indian Conference at Mount Hermon, California, in August 1909. Sitting in the front row are two Indigenous women, a Mrs. Lockhart and Alma Yee. (Cal Poly Humboldt University Library [Genzoli Collection (1999.07.3058)].)

Taber described that Kelsey's land purchases had provided homes for nine hundred formerly landless Indians, with another 1,300 soon to receive homes. She described by name each Indian at the conference and praised the work of the four field matrons in attendance, concluding with a discussion of the building of their industrial school in eastern Yolo County—a school similar to Tuskegee, the Alabama normal school for African American teachers. Reverend Hugh W. Gilchrist had proposed such a school two years earlier, viewing it as a "center of moral and industrial instruction and influence" where students would be trained to be Christian leaders among their people. Taber later wrote to Mathew Sniffen on behalf of Reverend L. L. Legters, a missionary among the Comanche of Oklahoma, who was under consideration as school superintendent.[117] It was hoped that the Indian part of the next Zayante Conference could meet there. Great progress was also made by the Presbyterians, who had adopted the NCIA missionary field at Bishop, Inyo County, and the Baptists, who had continued their work at Auberry, Fresno County.[118]

Taber's report reflected progress made in the sixteen years "since a few people met one hot day in July and organized an association with eleven members." Now only about 2,000 Indians were homeless, and nine cheerful and faithful NCIA-sponsored field matrons were busy providing clothing, medicine,

Christmas gifts, and other items to the Indians. Finally, land had been purchased for an industrial school in Yolo County. Taber concluded that the goal of the NCIA was to "exert a strong Christian influence" in the young to ensure that "our Indians, long shut out from Christian churches as well as other means of culture, may come to realize their claim in common with all mankind upon the love and care of the One Father."[119]

The following year the industrial school at Guinda opened. The Indian contingent of the Sixth Zayante conference held their part of the meeting on school grounds in August while white educators, clergy, and reformers met the previous month at Mount Hermon. The September issue of *The Indian's Friend* described the year's meeting at Guinda as "probably the first of its kind—namely, that the Indians did most of the talking, while the white contingent made excellent and attentive listeners."[120] The October issue included a lengthy article on the Guinda meeting, describing it as unique in that attendees had been invited to meet with members of the NCIA "and suggest the kind of education they, the Indians, desired should be given to their children in the new Industrial school." During the first session, Legters asked specifically what kind of education they wanted. Captain Tom Odock, head of a small band of Indians from Colusa, for example, urged that all students be taught to read and write, with the young men learning carpentering, engineering, and blacksmithing. Another maintained that although it was good for the young to be taught how to make a living, "our people need to be uplifted," and, thus, he believed, it was also important they "be taught to be honest, truthful, reliable and good in character." He was not so concerned about what his children chose to do for a living, but "in this matter of character they all need to be taught. It should be set before them every day." During the afternoon session, attendees discussed issues within the Indian home. Since marital relationships were without binding ceremony, several participants made a plea for "marriage in white man's fashion," viewing it as the "basis of the home." Others recommended a stable home with "the marriage bond indissoluble (except for serious cause)." They also advocated "for the complete suppression of" the liquor traffic. On Sunday all participants, white and Indian, joined in a simple service, which *The Indian's Friend* described as "a remarkable exhibition of the real brotherhood of true Christianity which showed red and white worshipping side by side . . . all looking up to the same God for His divine blessing."[121]

Also in 1911, Taber's monograph, *California and Her Indian Children*, was published by the NCIA. The *San Jose Mercury-News* described it as not only lovingly and carefully written but of value to anyone studying Indian problems. Selling for 25 cents, it was advertised as written for Mission study classes and "brimful of facts you ought to know about California Indians."[122] Taber had dedicated her book to her mother, "who through many shut-in years worked unceasingly with pen and with needle for the Indians of California, and whose sympathetic encouragement made possible the preparation of this book."[123]

Taber had begun with a history of the state's Indians followed by the arrival of white settlers and Indian evictions, writing that "hardly a band in Northern California ... does not have its tale of repeated evictions." As late as the winter of 1910, Indians near Healdsburg had been turned out, leaving them without shelter in the midst of an unusually wet season. She wrote of current conditions and the opportunities to support the Indigenous people, emphasizing that "every dweller in California lives where once an Indian lived. Our hearth fires burn where their camp fires burned; their whispering voices still haunt the oaks of our valleys, the pines of our mountains."[124] The second half of the book was devoted to depicting missionary work, with heart-warming extracts from field matrons' letters.

In mid-October, Taber attended the Lake Mohonk Conference, describing the splendid work done by the NIA and the NCIA among the Indians of her state.[125] Then, in early December, she attended the thirty-second annual conference of the NIA in New York City, where she addressed the need for more religious work among the Indians. Other races, she noted, came to religion on their own volition because they were free to enter schools and churches, but the eleven thousand Indians in California, who had never heard the Gospel, were isolated either by geography or by neglect. They were often "unwelcomed in the churches they try to attend, ignored by the better elements of society." Given this situation, "What can such Indian girls do but drift into companionship with the lower?" She also praised field matrons, who regularly wrote to her about how well the Indians responded to their efforts, explaining that, for example, gambling and drinking at Auberry had declined. Taber concluded that the solution to the disadvantaged condition of the state's Indian population was to establish better Christian missions and appoint more field matrons.[126] Like most reformers, she believed that the curative light of Christianity would transform the Indians, rid them of their ignorance and superstition, and turn them into "civilized" Indian citizens.

Taber's 1913 report to the national association reflected "one of the most fruitful years in its history." The NCIA was now responsible for seventeen sites staffed by twenty missionaries representing six different denominations and serving eighty-five hundred Indians. Some six thousand Indians still remained without missions, however. Kelsey reported that some nine thousand Indians had homes and that education was improving. Three new government day schools had opened, more students were attending public schools, and that fall their Industrial and Christian Training School at Guinda had begun teaching classes in agriculture, carpentry, blacksmithing, painting, and plumbing, just some of the subjects suggested by Indian attendees at the 1911 Zayante Conference held on school grounds. Only three boys attended that first year. More traditional domestic science classes such as sewing, embroidering, crocheting, and butter-making were taught to the eight girls who attended. Starting small, the campus grew to include a superintendent's home, dormitories, and a two-story structure housing the dining room, kitchen, and storeroom. Four wells provided water needed for domestic use and irrigation of the hay crop. During the annual meeting in San Jose in November 1913, Mrs. E. A. Ripley, chairman of the Guinda School committee, reported the school's purpose was not to "turn out concert singers or public speakers" but "to give [the Indian students] a Christian training corresponding to what white children get in their homes."[127]

The following year, Taber reported fifteen pupils attending, and readers of the *San Jose Mercury-News* learned from a Miss E. T. Gray, a recent visitor, that the Guinda School demonstrated "the clear, sound note of morality, [and] the gentle spirit of love which distinguishes it from other schools."[128] In a February 12, 1917, letter, school superintendent Charles A. Olsen informed NIA members that the student population had grown to thirty-two, with an average attendance of eighteen. The facility had expanded, with additional classroom offerings, including engineering, machine work, and shoe and harness repairing. An almond orchard had been planted, and a hay crop sowed.[129] On July 17, a fire of unknown origin destroyed the largest building, which included the Olsens' residence, and the girls' dorm and bathroom. Although insurance money was paid promptly, the loss was more than double the reimbursement. Fortunately, classes were not cancelled, for local residents supplied the school with beds and bedding.[130] However, the destructive fire and subsequent developments meant that this WNIA missionary station was never turned over to a reliable missionary society or to the government as had been the case with the Greenville School in Plumas County and other association missions. Sniffen, now the IRA executive secretary, described Guinda as "conducted in a practical manner and [meeting] an urgent need." He hoped it would continue. However, a nervous breakdown suffered by Mrs. Olsen prompted her husband to resign. With the demands of World War I, a replacement could not be found; furthermore, many young Indian men had joined the service. The NCIA closed the school, found homes for the children, and rented out the property. The ultimate goal was to sell and use the money for the education of worthy young Indian students.[131]

By 1914, the NCIA had made great strides, purchasing forty-five tracts of land with congressional funding—homes for 19,839 California Indians. Nine thousand California Indians were now living on non-reservation lands, with the remainder living on reservations, allotments, in national forests,[132] or on church-owned land. The NCIA, estimating that $20,000 would be needed to provide for the remaining 1,841 Indians without secure homes, described prejudice against the Indians declining, with more children attending schools and "a four-fold increase in the number of white people working for the uplift of the Indians."[133] The NCIA may have overestimated their success. During a three-month-long tour of California in 1920, Sniffen discovered there were still sixty-five hundred landless Indians, many times the number reported by the NCIA. He did find more Indian children in public schools but little religious work—a troubling fact considering that was a main association goal. He described his rare pleasure in finding the constructive efforts of the Baptist Church in Fresno and Madera Counties.[134]

Times had grown difficult for the NCIA. The fire at Guinda was followed on March 9, 1918, by the death of Annie E. K. Bidwell, one of the NCIA's strongest advocates. Cornelia Taber, now living in Berkeley, assumed her role.[135] By 1921, the NCIA was only supporting Episcopal missionaries at Orleans, in Humboldt County. The following year there was no mention of this work; the 1924 report did note it was supporting NIA missionary work in Montana and at Manchester and Orleans in California.[136] Taber's death on March 1, 1929, was a crucial blow. An unnamed coworker described the success of the NCIA as due largely to her having given "freely of strength, time and means for [its] furtherance." Taber's "sound judgment and optimistic outlook in conducting" their work would be sorely missed, concluding she had "left a large place which no one else can fill."[137]

As the twentieth century moved into its second decade, the NCIA became generally viewed as too slow and conservative. Newer organizations had emerged, such as the Indian Board of Co-Operation (IBC), which used confrontational methods to achieve its ends.[138] The IBC was founded by Reverend Frederick George

Figure 23. Possibly taken at a Zayante Indian Conference at Mount Hermon, California, this photograph includes Indian and white attendees. Annie E. K. Bidwell, of Chico, with her white hair and dark dress, sits prominently in the middle of the second row from the front. Among the other white women are likely some of the field matrons sponsored by the Northern California Indian Association. (Cal Poly Humboldt University Library [Genzoli Collection (1999.07.3059)].)

Collett, a Methodist minister, who, along with his wife, Beryl Bishop-Collett, became acquainted with the NCIA after attending the Fifth Zayante Indian Conference in 1910. They had volunteered as teachers and missionaries to a small group of Indians living on a *rancheria* four miles north of Colusa.[139] Eventually they parted ways with the NCIA, and on August 26, 1914, Collett filed the IBC's articles of incorporation, declaring his purpose as aiding "the development of Indians in Christian citizenship in California and adjoining states, by securing for them the advantages of the public schools." If unable to get Indian children registered in schools, the IBC simply established an all-Indian school district, sued, or resorted to court orders.[140] The IBC was joined by the General Federation of Women's Clubs, which filled the void left by NCIA inactivity. Founded in 1890, the organization described itself as one of the oldest "nonpartisan, nondenominational women's volunteer service organizations." At their annual convention in Salt Lake City in May 1921, they established a committee on Indian welfare with Stella Atwood, a resident of Riverside, California, as the first chair.[141]

There were many reasons for the decline of the NCIA. American society was changing: the concept of "separate spheres" was diminishing, especially in the post–World War I era; founding leaders died; and the government was moving away from assimilation toward a more inclusive approach to a government Indian policy. For more than two decades, San Jose reformers, efficiently led by the Tabers and Kelsey, had served as one of the NIA's more effective auxiliaries, with land purchases as their most enduring legacy. Cornelia Taber tactfully described the California land situation in the following way: "Commissioner Leupp says that the red and white races in America stand in the relation of host and guest. As sometimes happens, the guest has dwelt so long in his adopted home, that he has quite forgotten the courtesies of the relation, and has well nigh turned his host out of doors."[142]

To appreciate the breadth of the work of San Jose reformers since their reorganization on July 23, 1894, one need only consult their fifteenth annual report. That first year they donated only one Christmas box and paid half of the $400 salary for Harriet Newell at the Greenville School. Before long they had funded missionary work on the Hoopa Reservation; bought land in Manchester; conducted a census of Northern California Indians; participated in a successful petition drive; organized an annual Indian conference; and founded an Indian industrial school, while at the same time furnishing almost a dozen field matrons with medical supplies, sewing items, horses and buggies, and school equipment. On a smaller scale they had founded a second mission in Bishop; supported an Indian student at the Bible Training School in Los Angeles; sent speakers to missionary meetings and various club meetings; and published numerous pamphlets. To support their growing work, they had also organized two auxiliaries, one at Auberry, in Fresno County, working with the Missionary Society of the Baptist Church among the local Mono Indians, and a second at Middletown, in southern Lake County.[143] Initially formed to missionize, Christianize, and promote the US government's policy of assimilation, the NCIA had gone well beyond its initial purposes, improving the lives of thousands of California Indians along the way.

One thorny issue that plagued all reservations and was often the topic of field matron letters to Taber was the constant and disturbing presence of alcohol in Indian communities. NCIA missionary work on the Hoopa Reservation had been the direct result of a temperance lecture delivered by Dorcas J. Spencer. The next chapter expands on her role and provides a more detailed history of the work of the Woman's Christian Temperance Union within the Women's National Indian Association.

CHAPTER 9

Dorcas J. Spencer

The Hupa Indians and the WCTU

During her November 1885 address, Women's National Indian Association president Mary Caroline Lowe Dickinson described "the frightful demoralization of Indian character under the curse of drink." She declared that "the crowning shame of our nation" was that after robbing the Indians of all rights, "we thrust upon him this most debasing wrong." In conclusion, she noted that although there should be no effort spared on the part of the WNIA to secure protection and rights for the Indians, the same should be said of using the association's relationship with the Woman's Christian Temperance Union on their behalf.[1]

From the very beginning, these two female-driven associations formed an amicable working relationship. The year before Dickinson's address, the WNIA had created a short-lived Committee on Friendly Relations with the WCTU. Then, eight years later, it established a Committee on Temperance Appeals, which continued until 1905.[2] A possible reason for this close association may have been Amelia Stone Quinton's previous role as an organizer for the Brooklyn branch of the WCTU. WNIA literature, however, never mentioned Quinton's prior WCTU work. Temperance was a logical path for her. She had been born in Upstate New York, known for its involvement in reform movements, and her father had been a member of a temperance society in Homer, New York, where the Stone family lived. Furthermore, the Baptist Church, in which she had been raised, although more conservative in their view of women's rights, actually encouraged an expanded role for women in certain benevolent causes, especially the temperance crusade, "as long as these efforts remain dissociated with the feminist agitation and politics."[3]

The earliest evidence of Quinton's WCTU membership can be found in 1876.[4] Although it is unknown when she moved to Brooklyn, she could have been part of the founding membership, which met in rooms provided by the YMCA on March 16, 1874. Brooklyn women immediately began making hundreds of saloons visits, distributing temperance literature and Bibles, and holding daily prayer meetings. Mrs. Annie Wittenmyer, the first WCTU president, described these meetings as "filled nightly with the same changing class, from the jails and saloons, the gutter and the homes of wealth, all bitten by this serpent of sin, intemperance." Members also held meetings in local jails, inebriate asylums, private homes, and churches across the city. When a local saloonkeeper invited them to speak before his patrons and lead a Sabbath evening prayer meeting, hundreds attended. Brooklyn members soon organized a flourishing juvenile society, and in the first saloon they closed, they founded a restaurant and an inn that provided free meals and lodgings. Other saloons were closed, and in others, no liquor was sold on Sundays.[5]

Subsequent references to Quinton's temperance activities are scant. In an 1877 temperance publication, she was described as a faithful worker, presenting the association's message in "every town and village in [New York] state." That same year in the *Third Annual Report of the Brooklyn Temperance Union*, she was listed as a member of the executive committee. The previous June, she had been a delegate to the International Temperance Conference in Philadelphia.[6] She likely engaged in traditional organizing work, preparing propaganda, giving addresses, encouraging others to join, and leading an occasional prayer meeting. Identified as Mrs. A. C. Swanson, she gave an evening Bible reading in January 1877 at the Tabernacle Baptist Church where Dr. Thomas Rambaut, who later married Mary Lucinda Bonney, was pastor.[7] Once Quinton turned her full attention to Indian reform, she may well not have had time to continue her temperance work; possibly there was no need to do so because Dorcas J. Spencer, an officer in the Northern California Indian Association and supervisor of the California branch of the WCTU's Department of Work Among Indians, had filled the void.[8]

Spencer was born in Rhode Island on January 7, 1841, to Joseph T. Barber and his wife Nancy James Barber. A decade later, the senior Barber headed off to California's gold country with his sons, leaving his wife and young daughter behind. They settled in Grass Valley, Nevada County, and worked in construction. Several years later Joseph returned East to bring his wife Nancy and their daughter back with him. On January 17, 1858, Dorcas married William Kenyon Spencer, who had come to California in 1852. They, too, settled in Grass Valley, where beginning in late 1852 he became the first telegraph operator for the Alta Telegraph Company, later running a bookstore and a stationery business.[9]

The presence of some forty saloons in Grass Valley presented a concern for the Spencer family, which had grown to include six children. Dorcas Spencer and her neighbor, Mrs. A. B. (Emma) Dibble, had begun to take an interest in the growing temperance movement then sweeping the east. Unable to find a male willing to speak before such a gathering, Spencer gave her first public address. She was later quoted as rehearsing her talk "at home with her babies as auditors." On March 24, 1874, she and her fellow workers founded a Woman's Temperance Union in Grass Valley. During her long and distinguished career within the California branch of WCTU, Spencer held various positions, serving as secretary of the San Francisco union and chairman of the department for Indian relief. She was soon recognized as an authority on Indian matters.[10] National WCTU president Frances Willard confirmed her contributions decades later, identifying Grass Valley as the site of the first local WCTU.[11] To highlight the town's unique role, in April 1926, the WCTU organized an automobile caravan to commemorate the event, at the end of which, on the 25th, Spencer unveiled a bronze marker placed on Grass Valley's First Congregational Church.[12]

Almost four decades earlier, Spencer, then a 48-year-old wife and mother, described by an unidentified observer as a "little woman with a knot of white ribbons," had been guided by a Hupa man to the isolated Hoopa Indian Reservation in Northern California in late 1889 to personally view reservation conditions—a visit that led to a long association with reservation residents, continued return visits, membership in the Northern California Indian Association, and the founding of a missionary station.[13] Returning home, Spencer wrote to Herbert Welsh of the Indian Rights Association, explaining that while in the small Humboldt County community of Hydesville to give a WCTU temperance lecture, she had noticed a Hupa Indian sitting in the front row with his daughter. He was listening intently.

The following day, he approached her, and, in terms she described as "positively pathetic," pleaded for her to accompany him to his reservation to see the wrongs endured by his people. This was her first meeting with William Beckworth, who declared he had tried unsuccessfully to "get a hearing on the subject," but trade and politics had proven to be a barrier. He was confident that because she represented Christian women with "neither political [nor] commercial interests" and with no axe to grind, others would believe her when they would not listen to him. Long familiar with the issue of Indians and alcohol and curious to see whether the rumors about reservation conditions were true, Spencer could not resist his plea. Climbing aboard a mule, she accompanied this Hupa activist through rugged county to the isolated reservation where she saw enough to corroborate what she had heard over the years.[14]

Beckwith had been raised by whites, could read and write, and had served in the Army. For decades he had been dealing with government officials on his people's behalf. When Agent J. L. Broaddus tried to force his people to move to the Round Valley Reservation, even cutting rations and planting fewer acres to force them to leave, Beckwith convinced tribal members to remain, asserting that "their social and ceremonial world was inextricably linked" to the Hoopa Valley. Even after Broaddus sold off the agency's movable property and removed the rest to the Round Valley Agency, the Hupas continued to heed Beckwith. Food became so scarce that the new agent was forced to distribute rations. Following repeated complaints of profiteering and abuse at the hands of Fort Gaston's soldiers, the Hoopa Agency was finally returned to civilian control under Agent Isaac A. Beers. Beckwith's continued efforts on behalf of the Hupas eventually led Beers to banish him from the reservation. In his defense, Beckwith wrote a letter to the local *Western Watchman*, a copy of which was reprinted in the April 1891 issue of *The Indian's Friend*. He had explained that for three decades he and his people had "been kept in wicked hands." His simple question was: "When will the white man give us our land and send good men to teach us, instead of bad men such as we have now?"[15]

Spencer's visit to the reservation was delayed until Beckwith could get time off from his work, and, according to M. E. Chase, pastor of the reservation's Presbyterian Mission Church, to also find the appropriate moment when the soldiers were absent on an inspection tour. Even then, he followed a thoroughly obscure route.[16] When they reached the reservation, Spencer initially met with a group of Indians gathered at the government school. In a later account, she claimed she had never seen "a picture more impressive than Billy speaking in the soft, plaintive tones of the Hoopa language to 'his people,' as he always calls them, in the school room at Hoopa" that quiet Sunday.[17] She also visited a number of Indian homes and listened as they explained that in the past they had met with officials who promised to improve their situation. Nothing ever happened; they had grown accustomed to being disappointed. Moved by their predicament, Spencer professed to Welsh that she was now "taxed to show what a woman could do." She felt "the force of all & saw so deeply, that [she] gladly promised to do the only thing a woman can do, to *talk*—for them, and not to stop until a hearing shall be had."[18] Both seemed to recognize the commonality of powerlessness faced by Indians and women; however, Beckwith realized that although white women reformers were at times powerless, they still had privileges that could be used on the Indians' behalf.

The letter was read by many. Welsh had forwarded a copy to Indian Commissioner Thomas Jefferson Morgan, who responded that he fully sympathized with her view of the situation,[19] while Spencer, herself, had sent another to Quinton, who printed a slightly abridged version in the January 1890 issue of *The Indian's Friend* to be read by the entire WNIA membership.[20] Spencer had graphically emphasized the Hupas' main grievance as the presence of Fort Gaston, where four times a year "a new lot of petty officials, too often wholly unprincipled men, [were] turned loose to range through the Reservation, to find and debauch the girls, and in every way aid to the degradation of these people." The result was the birth of numerous illegitimate children without a thought towards any responsibility to be borne by the fathers. Describing the soldiers as "unprincipled vagabonds who would be arrested for vagrancy in the cities," Spencer was heartsick "to see what these lawless, worthless men do, and the effect of these things on the people." Government patronage had led local politicians and businessmen to favor the presence of the fort, while the Indians wanted it, the soldier residents, and their accompanying liquor removed and replaced with a church and school. Spencer could easily envision the abandoned buildings serving admirably as an Indian industrial school. The Indians' desire for their church and a school prompted her to write: "I hereby give my testimony that it is what they *need*."[21]

During her visit, Spencer declared, she had found that the Hupas were intelligent, with some speaking fairly good English and apparently self-supporting. She was also especially touched by the appeals of the young men, who not only wanted something better for themselves but wanted to protect their women and educate their children. She personally understood "by what enormity of wrong they have in the first place been driven from their homes to this mountain fastness, where no eye but the All-Seeing, can witness their present oppressions." She concluded her letter, exclaiming that "our voices must be raised in behalf of outraged womanhood, and of bestialized maternity, for these degraded women are the mothers of a race for whose very being the nation is responsible."[22]

Her letter to Welsh, written in the spirit of "maternalism" specific to women's political activism at the time, propelled Spencer headlong into the late nineteenth-century Indian reform arena. She never lost interest in the well-being of the Hupa, continually returning to the subject in addresses and articles. Months after her initial visit, she lectured before the San Francisco Women's Educational and Industrial Union, describing them as "bright, intelligent-looking people."[23] She realized that Beckwith had recognized her as his peer and that they shared a common status: each had "no votes and no rights." In one interview, she recounted that she had dined in the home of a local white farmer who was married to a Hupa woman. Their children spoke English, and their home had carpets on the floors, pictures on the walls, and a piano in the drawing room, refinements reformers equated with civilization.[24] The adoption by Indians of such accoutrements found in white households was a sign to WNIA members that the government's assimilationist Indian policy was working.

During her organizational tour in the summer of 1891, Quinton, after founding the NCWIA auxiliary in San Francisco in mid-August,[25] accompanied Beckwith to the Hoopa Valley. Her mode of transportation was only slightly more comfortable than Spencer's. Instead of riding a mule for the entire journey, Quinton spent a day and a half in a horse-drawn wagon before walking a mile on an unfinished road along the mountain edge, completing the last rugged nine miles to the Hoopa Valley in a two-wheeled cart, hand-carried to the site.[26] Returning to San Francisco, Quinton convinced the membership of her newly founded auxiliary to undertake missionary work among the Hupas.[27] When Beckwith died on December 11, 1891, only months after having escorted her to the Hoopa Valley, Quinton wrote a lengthy eulogy in *The Indian's Friend*. "There is not one who knew Billy's true character but will keenly mourn his too early death, and feel that a great prop of the true interests of his tribe has fallen." Beckwith had lived long enough, wrote Quinton, that he had planted "in many hearts an earnest, loving and persistent purpose to take no rest until that which is sorely needed for the relief and elevation of the Hoopas shall be secured." She described his life as a success, concluding that "he triumphs in death." She informed WNIA members to "let our tribute to his memory be pauseless work for his people's redemption."[28]

Spencer had argued, however, that Fort Gaston had to be removed before any missionary work could begin. She presided over a February 9, 1892, NCWIA meeting during which a petition, addressed to Interior Secretary John M. Noble and requesting the post be abolished and its buildings repurposed as an Indian industrial school, was presented and read.[29] When it arrived at WNIA headquarters, Quinton quickly forwarded it to Commissioner Noble. There was intense local opposition to the petition. One unidentified observer who complained to the *Humboldt Times* described "a certain set of sentimental enthusiastics" who wanted to assume guardianship over the Indians without considering "the demands of either reason or common sense." He described the replacement of "the firm, practical and wise government of the army officers" with "a triumvirate consisting of the female reformer, the tramp preacher, and the hungry office seeker." Claiming that "the people of Humboldt county cannot afford to have the mining and grazing interests of the northern part of the country be jeopardized" by any potential Indian outbreak, the individual demanded that the Board of Trade and the Chamber of Commerce protest the withdrawal of the fort's military.[30] Regardless, with eastern WNIA auxiliaries joining in the petition drive, the fort was abandoned in late June 1892. There is some evidence, however, that this move was already in the works.[31]

A year later, *The Indian's Friend* reported that forty students were now attending the new Hoopa Valley government boarding school.[32] Several years later, an August 2, 1896, issue of the *San Francisco Call* described the removal of the soldiers, with the barracks having been "turned into an industrial school, manned and womaned by efficient, wise and sympathetic teachers."[33] Although Spencer's vision of a school became a reality quickly, missionary work took longer. An article in the March 1896 issue of *The Indian's Friend* alerted WNIA membership to a crying need for a missionary to lead the residents of the Hoopa Reservation "out of the darkness of heathenism into the light of Christianity." The Indians were described as continuing to practice their old beliefs and superstitions, engaging in witchcraft and "heathenish and immoral dances."[34] By this time, the Philadelphia headquarters of the national association had a well-honed process of acquiring land from the government, appointing missionaries, and setting up missionary stations. Guidelines, initially set during a February 13, 1883, board meeting, had, by the founding of the Hoopa station, been scaled down to "pioneer missionary work in tribes unprovided with religious teaching and domestic instruction."[35]

During an August 1896 NCIA mass meeting in the Maple Room of the Palace Hotel, attendees learned their association was about to underwrite the support of a missionary at Hoopa Valley. The following day, the *San Francisco Chronicle* reported that Mrs. Nellie Blessing Eyster, NCWIA president, announced that the government had donated land for a WNIA missionary station, and her association would raise money to sponsor a missionary and build a chapel.[36] A three-acre plot had been secured with an old schoolhouse, later repaired and enlarged for use as a chapel. The NCIA proposed to build a small cottage and a stable and to hire Reverend Lyman Paul Armstrong, a San Jose resident, as their missionary. He was soon visiting homes and conducting Sunday Bible classes and evening reading classes, and traveling down the Klamath River to visit other Native groups.[37] He served only one year before he was replaced in 1897 by Pliny E. Goddard, who held religious services while his wife, Alice, organized a women's Bible class and a sewing society; several Hupa women owned sewing machines.[38] Mrs. Goddard's illness in 1900 ended the ministry, and in July of that year the NCIA mission station was transferred to the Presbyterian Board of New York. The board selected Miss M. E. Chase of Los Angeles as their missionary.[39]

Spencer soon befriended Chase. In the summer of 1904, Spencer spent a month on the reservation, describing to *The Indian's Friend* the marvelous changes she had witnessed.[40] Chase later wrote that during her visit Spencer gave a Sunday address before some forty to fifty adult Hupa Indians, asserting that fifteen years before "not a soul could read except Billy Beckwith." Now they were not only using three or four dozen hymnals but singing beautifully.[41] On January 11, 1905, Spencer gave a talk before some sixty to seventy NCIA members, gathered in the classrooms of the Trinity Parish House. The *San Jose Mercury News* reporter called her "instrumental in securing the removal of the military post from the Indian camp at Hoopa Valley." He noted her attendance at the Hoopa boarding school's closing exercises, where she witnessed "the drill and band play of the boys, and the basketball of the girls." During Spencer's first visit to the reservation, she had found the Indians living under "unspeakable degradation," but now they were living in comfortable, well-furnished homes, with "floors scrupulously washed and bedding aired," a strong argument "for the work of the association [NCIA] in endeavoring to secure settled homes for the landless Indians on lands of their own."⁴² The NCIA's allotment process called for small plots, often ten acres or less, awarded from public lands or lands purchased by congressional funding. In contrast, under the provisions of the Dawes Act, large communally held reservations were allotted into parcels of 40 to 160 acres, with remaining lands open to white homesteading. Under this latter legislation, untold millions of acreage passed out of Indian hands.

An editorial in the same issue of the *Mercury News* described how clearly it could be seen that when "Indians have been given security of tenure that they can under proper conditions develop into the same measure of civilization as marks white people in similar circumstances." They could live in neat, clean, well ornamented homes, and have "a general appreciation of civilized conditions just as great as are found among their white neighbors." The editor praised Spencer and the NCIA for working toward enabling these Indians to "possess their own lands and homes."⁴³

Spencer had set two goals during her 1904 visit: to learn about the Hupa Indians' present conditions and to use their successes to promote the government's policy of assimilation. She continued to pursue this latter goal in a 1907 article describing Hupa lifestyle as resembling that "of any county hamlet or town." Frame houses of several rooms, some even two stories, had replaced "the old pit with a roof over it," and the residents were sending off for seeds from catalogs to plant around their homes. Their church service, which included an Indian elder, was as well attended "as could be expected of a people utterly unaccustomed to the observance of time, system, or worship."⁴⁴ The following year, as superintendent of Indian work for the national WCTU, Spencer reported that the former WNIA Missionary Station at Hoopa had developed into an organized church of twenty-three members, with Reverend James Hayes, a Nez Perce evangelist, now visiting them. She also noted that Chase had introduced the Medal Contest there several years earlier. These medals were part of an elocution contest, a feature of the WCTU, encouraging women and children to develop speaking skills and to bring attention to their temperance agenda, with the students selecting subjects related to temperance principles. Six young Hupa Indians had already received silver medals, and that summer one had achieved a gold medal, Spencer proudly noted.⁴⁵

Spencer made one more extended visit to Hoopa in July 1917, staying over through two Sundays—a visit she described in a letter presented before the annual NIA meeting in December. By this time, Chase, who had served the

CHAPTER 9

Figure 24. Three prominent members of the Northern California Indian Association are photographed attending a missionary function. (L–R): Mrs. S. W. Gilchrist, clapping; Annie E. K. Bidwell; and Dorcas J. Spencer. Note the Indian men standing behind the three seated women. (Cal Poly Humboldt University Library [Genzoli Collection (1999.07.3032)].)

Presbyterian Board of Missions for twelve years, had been replaced as head of the Hoopa church by Reverend William Baesler and his wife. Spencer described him as an excellent pastor, and the Hupas as "a civilized community, with the interests of civilized life." She had felt great joy standing "before the worshipping congregation, looking into their eager, intelligent and kindly faces, and [speaking] to them as a Christian people." Describing them as living in comfortable homes with fruitful fields and gardens, she only wished that Quinton could personally see this change. Spencer was pleased to convey in her letter "a sense of the changes that have come to this scene of their early labors."[46]

Active in the local auxiliary of the WNIA, Spencer traveled east twice to attend two national meetings. In December 1902 she was in Washington, DC, for the twenty-third annual meeting, presenting a touching reminiscence of the work at Hoopa, explaining that since her original appeal she had aided the association's work by making numerous church appeals for cooperation. She rejoiced in the strong missionary presence the association had initially established among the Hupas and was pleased that their station was now under the care of the Presbyterian Board. She concluded "that the white man's law, the white man's school, and the white man's church if provided for the tribes would solve the entire [Indian] question."⁴⁷ Four years later she attended the annual meeting in New York City. Instead of reminiscing about the Hupas, she discussed the dire situation facing all of California's landless Indians, relating the case of a Lake County Indian family who were forced to move at least seven different times in four decades. Each time after the Indian man had improved his plot of land, making it more desirable, a local white resident had filed a claim on it.⁴⁸

Although Spencer never attended another national association meeting, for the next several years, beginning in 1914, her temperance reports were printed in the annual reports. In her first one she explained she was serving as the temperance secretary of the NCIA auxiliary and had taken on the job of director of the Indian Board of Co-Operation largely because her Indian temperance work was sporadic. The goal of the Board, she explained, was to bring "our scattered Indians under the public school system of the state."⁴⁹ Her next temperance report was more hopeful, because Indian Commissioner Cato Sells had required Indians and employees, all six thousand in the Indian service, to take the following pledge: "I hereby promise that I will not use intoxicating liquors as a beverage, and that I will do everything that I can to protect my people from this great evil." To further the work, during the last political campaign, Spencer had sent out a circular letter to the nearly seven hundred Indians eligible to vote, reminding them that this was "their first opportunity of patriotic service." She reported "that nearly all voted dry," concluding that "some few who depended on vineyards and hopfields for employment proved themselves, by voting wet, to be amenable to the same influences that control many white men." She concluded with the news that the case of the seven saloon keepers arrested the previous year had been transferred to a federal court.⁵⁰ In 1916 she reported that, with support by the IBC, some one hundred Indians from California joined by a few from Arizona, Nevada, and Oregon had spent a week the previous year at the San Francisco Panama-Pacific International Exposition. They all had paid their own travel and living expenses "and not one was dressed up as an Indian, or attracted undue attention"—another example, in her opinion, of the success of the government's assimilation program. She concluded that more Indians were voting and that an amendment to a California school law finally enabled Indian children to attend public schools.⁵¹

America's entrance into World War I impacted all reservations. Spencer informed John W. Clark, NIA executive secretary, that the "promise of their upcoming citizenship" encouraged many to enlist and that reservation members at Hoopa had established a Red Cross Society and from their meager earnings were purchasing, along with the rest of the country, Liberty Bonds and War Savings Stamps.[52] The Hupas, who served honorably, returned "with ideas broadened, and a new appreciation of themselves." Now was the perfect time to end the reservation system, she had concluded. She queried, "Why should a system be continued that prolongs the childhood of a race and retards their general development?" She also questioned the continuation of educating Indian children in reservation schools while the country was educating immigrants in "common schools, the best of all means of Americanization."[53]

Although Spencer was an active member of the NCIA, her primary role was to serve the California branch of the WCTU.[54] During almost sixty years of temperance work, she held various positions. Initially she was a state organizer, joining twenty other women from six California counties in 1879 to meet in the Northern California town of Petaluma to establish a union, a role recognized almost fifty years later when the May 1927 issue of the *Mill Valley Record* reported an upcoming WCTU jubilee convention in Petaluma with hundreds of delegates from Northern California counties expected to attend. In 1887 she was sent by the state president to organize in Stockton; the town paper describing her as a good soldier, engaging in a "long, wearisome house-to-house canvass."[55] She also served as a WCTU grand lecturer, giving twenty-seven different addresses from one end of Sonoma County to the other between April 20 and May 13, 1888.[56] In the 1890s, she recounted that she and her husband and their six children had joined in the procession in Grass Valley that had opened the proceedings of a crusade begun twenty-three years before.[57] In August of the following year, she participated in a series of temperance addresses at Pacific Grove during a sort of "summer school" to discuss methods used by the WCTU. Her topic was, "Is Temperance Work Church Work?"[58]

Spencer also served as the first female lobbyist to the California state legislature in Sacramento in 1887, working for the passage of the first bill for temperance education in the state's public schools. And early on she introduced the model for giving medals and prizes for temperance essays.[59] Other positions she held included recording secretary and corresponding secretary.[60] While in the latter position, she coordinated the activities of one hundred thirty-five local unions in the northern part of California, covering eighteen county organizations representing thirty-eight counties. She kept track of thirty-five hundred active members and five hundred honorary members.⁶¹ After 1905 she served as the superintendent of the WCTU's Department of Work Among Indians.⁶² Five years later, in a report, she wrote that for the past three years only eighteen state or territorial unions, mostly in the West, were even reporting Indian work. During that same time period, her department had sent out 120,000 pages of literature as well as numerous letters and had attended several missionary and other meetings presenting the Indians' cause, explaining that strong drink was their "special temptation and bane," leading to "slaughter and destruction of the race by warfare, and decimation by disease and death." She was convinced that only total abstinence and "civilization" would save the Indians, whom she described as "capable of all the achievements of superior people."⁶³ Three years later she reported that the WCTU was "peculiarly adaptable to their [Indians'] needs" and that on older reservations in the east there were several WCTU branches "consisting entirely of Indians."⁶⁴

Spencer's varied roles within the WCTU required attendance at annual temperance conventions throughout the state. A brief look at her activities at only one conference held in San Jose from October 18 to 21, 1892, reveals a diligent, efficient, dedicated temperance worker. During the meeting, she gave a formal address; presented a financial statement on the condition of the *Pacific Ensign*, a temperance magazine published in San Francisco, for which she served as business manager; and read her corresponding secretary report, representing over one hundred eighty state unions. To maintain contact during the year with these various unions, she wrote 2,247 letters and postal cards.⁶⁵ The following year, during the 1893 Stockton convention, she reported on one hundred ninety-three unions, covering 4,329 members.⁶⁶

Spencer also wrote numerous WCTU leaflets and pamphlets and *A History of the Woman's Christian Temperance Union of Northern and Central California*, published in 1911 in Oakland. A cursory glance at several of her articles reveals the passion she brought to her writing. In one 1893 article, she wrote that "perhaps no organization has ever been at once so well known and so imperfectly comprehended by the general public as the Woman's Christian Temperance Union." She described the national association as "a living entity, sentient and potent, in all its multiplying branches." Its organizational machinery approached "perfection in the systematic arrangement of local, county, State and National Unions, but the grand culmination [was] reached in the world's Union—a federation of the national unions of many countries."⁶⁷

Figure 25. This photograph, identified as a local Woman's Christian Temperance Union meeting, includes at least eight Indigenous women with four small children. Dorcas J. Spencer is probably the woman in the exact middle of the back row. (Cal Poly Humboldt University Library [Genzoli Collection (1999.07.3043)].)

In *The Californian Illustrated Magazine*, Spencer discussed their "Great Petition," which had been circulated in 1893 and already had a million signatures in forty-two different languages. It was to go on a grand tour the following year, presented to the principal countries that had signed. "Whatever may be thought of its direct effectiveness, there is something inspiring in this extensive cooperation of women," she wrote. If temperance reform is a "desire of woman's heart," it required "patient toil, persistent struggle and unlimited sacrifice." The varied work of the WCTU qualified "women for the exercise of all the duties of citizenship, as nothing else can." More important, because temperance was a cause of humanity and right, it "cannot be satisfied with a little reform here and there, but holds that the whole body-politic needs regeneration; the masses must be uplifted and the work must begin at the foundations."[68] Not only did the temperance cause demand "the ballot for woman," she declared, but it stood for "the defense of *home* from all the powers that can assail its purity or threaten its security." It recognized only one standard of "morality for all, requiring the record of man's life to be as stainless as woman's." She concluded that temperance "heralds the day when swords shall be beaten to plough-shares; wine-vats turned into kneading troughs, and the still shall have no deadlier use than to please the senses with soft odors distilled from sweetest flowers."[69]

In a 1916 article titled "Indians and Prohibition," Spencer wrote a short history of the temperance movement among Native peoples, explaining that the very first meeting, suggested by French Jesuits, had been somewhere in the St. Lawrence Valley at an Indian council where Indian representatives had complained about the availability of "white man's firewater." The chiefs in council had recommended that anyone who got drunk was to be turned over, along with the alcohol dealer, to the French for punishment, with the penalty of sale being death. And it had been the Cherokee of the southeast who had sent the first petition addressing prohibition to President Andrew Jackson. Based on this extensive early history, Spencer concluded that the current WCTU had merely joined an already well-established crusade movement.[70]

Spencer lived another decade and a half after writing this article. She died on May 1, 1933, in Berkeley, age 92. The *Oakland Tribune* portrayed her at age seventeen as a bride "crossing the plains with her husband," and later as the "founder of the temperance movement in California, Arizona, and Oregon, organizing for the W.C.T.U. long before the railways came to the West, and traveling vast distances on horse-back or by wagon."[71]

Spencer had been a tireless worker on behalf of the Hupa Indians and other California Natives, serving in an official capacity in both the WCTU and the WNIA for decades, struggling to protect Indians from the ravages of alcohol. Her visit to the Hoopa Reservation in 1889 had only been the beginning. She helped in a petition drive to remove Fort Gaston and worked to ensure that the NCIA mission station among the Hupas was a success. She extolled their improved living condition in public addresses and articles, returning to the reservation and working closely with their Presbyterian minister. Her work on behalf of the NCIA and the WNIA complemented her work as the national superintendent of the WCTU Department of Work Among Indians. Spencer was not the only WNIA member who worked on behalf of the temperance movement, but she was one of the most visible.

Conclusion

On December 7, 1929, the fiftieth anniversary luncheon of the National Indian Association was held at the Hotel McAlpin in New York City. The IRA's Mathew K. Sniffen was one of almost one hundred fifty guests in attendance. His presence was a testimony not only to the acceptance of women in the Indian reform movement but the decades-long harmonious working relationship between his association and the NIA. He had visited every mission station operated by the NIA, declaring that he "had everywhere found excellent work done by efficient and devoted missionaries."[1]

Amelia Stone Quinton, who died three years earlier on June 23, 1926, would have been most pleased with the written comments of Dr. Henry Roe Cloud, which were read before the gathering. "I recall vividly now [Quinton's] inspiring personality, [and] her untiring devotion to the welfare of the Indian people," he wrote. The two had met numerous times, beginning when he was a student at Yale. And because of his "intimate friendship" with John W. Clark, association secretary and editor of *The Indian's Friend*, Cloud knew well the "great trials and difficulties confronting" the work of the NIA. He asserted that these obstacles had easily been overcome through prayers by the membership and by the "inspiring leadership of Mrs. Quinton" until the "work of the association itself long ago became one of the outstanding pieces of constructive and redeeming work for the Red Man in America." He credited her with laying "the foundations that meant the future freedom and security of the Indian race in the nation."[2] One must wonder how many other Indians shared a similar sentiment but had found no way of expressing it.

Cloud, who had been born into the Bird Clan in 1884 in a Ho-Chunk bark home on the Winnebago Reservation in Nebraska, would go on to become the first Indian to graduate from Yale University, receiving a bachelor's degree in 1910 and a master's degree in anthropology in 1914. He had earned a divinity degree in theology in 1913 from Auburn Theological Seminary. He was also a founding member of the Society of American Indians and the founder of the Roe Indian Institute in Wichita, Kansas, the first college preparatory school for Native Americans. Cloud represented the educated assimilated Indian citizen that Quinton and her association had labored for more than half a century to create.[3]

The NIA continued their work for another quarter of a century after this celebratory luncheon. At one time there were members in every state and territory, but it is impossible to know exactly how many joined during its more than seventy years of operation. The average member was a foot soldier, who paid dues, attended meetings, signed petitions, and left behind little if any historical footprint. Their stories will forever remain in the shadows. The women presented in these pages were prominent community members, who at times engaged in heroic activities, leaving behind an easily identified and documented imprint. They, however, represented only a tiny fraction of the total membership. Many unanswered questions remain, as does the inability to access the long-term legacy of the association. We will never know how many sisters, daughters, or granddaughters followed in the footsteps of their relatives, either becoming Indian reformers or, for that matter, members of any reform movements.

Indian reformers were largely driven by their evangelical Protestant beliefs, assured that they had the answer to the so-called "Indian problem." Unlike the earliest settlers who warred with the Indians or simply pushed them aside, these reformers believed they were saving them from extinction by converting and Americanizing them. To achieve the ideal "civilized" Indian, reformers promoted policies that were harmful, the most destructive being the Dawes Act which divested Indigenous peoples of some ninety million acres of land. Another equally destructive policy was shipping Indian children off to distant boarding schools, where they were stripped of their culture while undergoing the so-called "civilization process."

The work of male and female Indian reformers differed. There were some men of sufficient wealth, such as Herbert Welsh, who approached reform as an avocation, but most were otherwise regularly employed. They may only have had time to attend an occasional IRA meeting, confer with a fellow member of the Boston Committee, or attend a Lake Mohonk Conference. A tour of an Indian reservation or a personal meeting with Indigenous people was not essential to their reform efforts. There were, of course, exceptions, including the IRA's Washington, DC, agents, Charles C. Painter and Samuel Brosius, and Welsh's assistant, Mathew K. Sniffen, and members of the Board of Indian Commissioners, who were required to make regular tours of reservations as part of their responsibilities.

The same hands-off approach might have been true of WNIA members had their association not turned over much of their political work to the IRA and returned to their missionary roots, born within the Home Missionary Society of Philadelphia's First Baptist Church. Financially secure on their own, or supported by families and husbands, many WNIA officers and members engaged in Indian reform as a full-time occupation. Once the national association began to establish mission stations, their work resembled that of various Protestant home missionary societies of the day. As early as 1883, the WNIA executive board already represented ten different denominations. Amelia Stone Quinton said it best in an 1895 article when she portrayed her association as a Christian organization with a history largely of missionary activity. By participating in this work, WNIA members gained not only a voice but power that had not been afforded them previously.

Any WNIA-sponsored worker in one of the more than sixty mission stations by necessity engaged in a daily face-to-face contact with Indian people as they converted, educated, or cared for them in a maternalistic relationship. These field-workers were joined by officers including Amelia Stone Quinton, Constance Goddard DuBois, Myra E. Frye, Dorcas J. Spencer, Laura Tileston, Kate Foote, Annie Beecher Scoville, and others who at times engaged in their own fieldwork, often enduring primitive traveling and accommodation conditions. Although the numbers of these hands-on workers and officials were not necessarily large, for each one there were many more members at home supporting them, encouraging them, holding fundraisers, and helping in any way possible to aid their missionary efforts.

At times it is difficult to find mention of women in the historical record because their contributions were often not recorded or valued. Fortunately for scholars working on the WNIA, there is a wealth of primary source material, making it possible to highlight the work of many of these extraordinary women, contributing not only to the understanding of Indigenous history but to the role that white women played in the Indian reform arena as well as in other reform movements. For seven decades, members of the WNIA labored among more than fifty different tribal groups to, from their point of view, improve their lives and welcome them into the broader American society as citizens. The histories of the auxiliaries and the women presented in this volume represent the positive contributions of decades of missionary work under the aegis of the Women's National Indian Association, the first of the "friends of the Indian" associations.

Appendix

Missionary stations founded by the WNIA and/or its state associations

1884

Ponca, Indian Territory
A Miss Howard first arrived on May 12, 1884. This station was transferred on February 3, 1886, to the Brooklyn Congregational Women's Indian Committee and in June 1887 to the Women's Methodist Episcopal Home Missionary Society.

Otoe, Indian Territory
A Mrs. H. O. McGlashan of New York began this work. The station was transferred on February 3, 1886, to the Brooklyn Congregational Women's Indian Committee and in June 1887 to the Women's Methodist Episcopal Home Missionary Society.

1886

Sioux, Rosebud Agency, South Dakota
Cora Fellows, who taught English at the Santee Training School, received traveling and incidental expenses from the WNIA to study the Dakota language at this agency. She began temporary work at a camp on the Cut Meat Creek some fifteen miles from Rosebud Agency, living with the government teacher in the government-provided school cottage. In March/April 1886 she resigned for health reasons, and in 1887 the WNIA combined her work with that begun at Corn Creek, Rosebud Agency.

Lower Brulé (Sioux), South Dakota
Indirect WNIA aid was given to the ladies of St. John's Episcopal Church, Yonkers, New York.

Round Valley, California (comprised of six linguistically diverse tribes: the Yuki, Concow, Little Lake Pomo, Nomlacki, Pit River, and Wailaki)
Claudia White of Rockville, Maryland, and Anna Boorman of Jersey City, a graduate of the Chicago Missionary Training School, served as WNIA missionaries until this station was transferred on April 5, 1887, to the Women's Baptist Home Missionary Society of Chicago.

Piegan, Blackfeet Agency, Montana
In June 1886, Sarah J. Williams, MD, a graduate of Holyoke Seminary, was appointed medical missionary by the WNIA Missionary Committee. With the approval of the Indian Office, the New Haven Women's Indian Association assumed her support. The mission never became a reality.

1887
Sitka, Alaska
The WNIA's Home Building Department built a number of model homes.

Sioux, Rosebud Agency, South Dakota
Temporary work, from November 1885 to April 1886, was begun at the agency. In 1887, Reverend Joseph E. Taylor, a Sioux Indian and Episcopal cleric, spent a year and two months at Corn Creek Mission at the agency. His work was partially funded by the Eastern New York Indian Association, which constructed a missionary cottage, chapel, and outbuildings. The station was transferred to the care of Bishop William Hobart Hare of the Episcopal Church, who at WNIA's request had selected the original site.

Bannock and Shoshoni, Fort Hall, Idaho
Funded by the New Haven Women's Indian Association and the Connecticut Indian Association, Amelia J. Frost of Albion, New York, and Miss Ella Stiles arrived in July 1887 to begin work at the Ross Fork Mission School. When Stiles resigned, she was replaced by Miss Agnes Decker, who also resigned for health reasons. In September 1888, the WNIA Missionary Committee transferred sole

care to the Connecticut auxiliary, which funded the Connecticut Mission Home on 160 acres obtained from the government. Completed in the spring of 1892, it housed the family of the Connecticut-sponsored farmer on one side and Frost on the other, with a school room and dormitory for the children under Frost's care in between. On January 10, 1900, it was transferred to the Board of Management of the Episcopal Board of Missions.

Omaha, Nebraska
Funded by the Massachusetts Indian Association (MIA) and the Kentucky auxiliary, Dr. and Mrs. L. M. Hensel of Oregon served as medical missionaries among the Omaha Indians at two different sites, one at the agency, with a night school, sewing school, and one room for a hospital, and a second location at Omaha Creek, initially with a day school. On May 1890, the missionary station—with five acres, a five-room cottage, barn and outbuildings, and an additional twelve acres at Omaha Creek with a new missionary cottage and chapel—was transferred to the Presbyterian Board of Home Missions. The WNIA continued to fund the medical missionary work of Dr. Susan La Flesche Picotte, an Omaha Indian woman whose medical education had been underwritten by the Connecticut Indian Association.

Navajo, Chinle, New Mexico Territory
The WNIA temporarily gave indirect aid.

1888

Chiricahua Apache, Mount Vernon Barracks, Alabama
In 1888, a member of the MIA's executive committee, with help from the Boston Indian Citizenship Committee, spearheaded a subscription to raise money to support education among the children of imprisoned Chiricahua Apache prisoners of war. The first teachers were a Miss Booth from Carlisle Indian School and a Miss Stevens from Hampton Institute. Within two years, the MIA was funding the educational and Christianization work of Sophie Shepard and her sister Margaret. The work ended in 1894 when the War Department relocated the Apaches to Fort Sill, Oklahoma.

1889

Nooksack, Stickney Memorial Home, Washington Territory
This facility, among the Nooksack (a Salish tribe), was funded by the WNIA

Home Building Department with a $400 contribution from Mrs. Leander Stickley of Albany. It was recommended by John Tennant, a Methodist missionary who had lived among these Indians for a quarter century.

Ramona Mission, California missionary and preaching stations among the Mission Indians at La Jolla, Temecula, Pechanga, Potrero, Soboba, Rincon, Cahuilla
Initially to have begun among the Cahuilla, in 1889, Reverend William H. Weinland and his wife Caroline began missionary work at Soboba and at Potrero (on the Morongo Reservation near Banning in San Gorgonio Pass). He held a regular Sunday school, while his wife opened up a sewing school. Missionary work eventually expanded into neighboring Mission villages.

Kiowa, Indian Territory
Reverend Joshua Given, a Kiowa Indian and a graduate of Carlisle Indian School and Lincoln University and its Theological Seminary, served as a missionary funded by the Brooklyn Auxiliary, which built a missionary cottage. From its inception, the Presbyterian Board of Home Missions agreed to take over this station.

1890

Potrero, California (Ramona Mission)
The Allegheny Cottage, gift of the Western Pennsylvania Indian Association, was completed in March 1890. The missionary station with the new cottage, chapel, and five acres of land granted to the WNIA in December 1889 by the government was turned over to the Missionary Board of the Moravian Church in May 1890.

Soboba, California (Ramona Mission)
Reverend Weinland turned over his duties to Mary Elizabeth Sheriff, who was supported by the NYCIA, which provided $500 for the building of a chapel. She ran a Sunday school, held sewing sessions, and engaged in house-to-house visits until 1891 when the work was suspended because of the construction of a Catholic church in the village.

Greenville Indian Industrial School, Plumas County, California
The facility was initially constructed by Charles W. Hall with $200 from the WNIA. He left in 1891, replaced by Edward N. and Florence Ament, who turned

it into a boarding school, with the WNIA funding a dormitory in November 1893. In April 1897 the government purchased the facility.

Sunday school, Plumas County, California
Amelia Martin, who had opened a Sunday school in February 1889, became a WNIA missionary in November 1890.

Sioux, Crow Creek, South Dakota
Laura Tileston, chair of the WNIA Hospital Department, with WNIA funding, transformed a small cottage at Crow Creek Reserve into a temporary working hospital in the fall of 1890. In 1891, Ada J. Porter, former head nurse at Hampton Institute, was appointed as a field matron. The federal government adopted the work and built the Crow Creek Hospital.

1891

Absentee Shawnee, Indian Territory
The Maine Indian Association built a missionary cottage for William Shawnee, a returning Indian student, who began pioneering work among a band of some three hundred Shawnees. After he left, missionary work continued among the Shawnees and some Kickapoos. Eight years later it was transferred to the Society of Friends (Quakers).

Seminole Mission, Florida
Dr. Jacob E. Brecht and his wife Clara opened this station at the Allen Place, some forty miles east of Fort Myers, with the government's cooperation. In March 1891, the WNIA purchased 320 acres for missionary use and an Indian industrial school. Although the intended school was never built, the Brechts opened a school temporarily in a tent. In December 1893 this site was transferred to the care of Bishop William Crane Gray of the Protestant Episcopal Church of Southern Florida. The Kentucky and Eastern Pennsylvania auxiliaries continued to fund Mrs. Brecht's work.

Cahuilla, California
C. M. Fleming, supported by the Ladies' Missionary Society of Riverside, began missionary work on her own until, at Quinton's recommendation, she was appointed a government field matron, and the Southern California Indian

Association built her a missionary cottage. She resigned in the fall of 1892 and was replaced by Dr. Anna Hayward Johnson, a Vassar College graduate, who began her medical missionary work in January 1893. In early 1896 the WNIA Missionary Committee transferred this work to its Southern California auxiliary.

1892

Hopi, at Oraibi, Arizona
The New Jersey auxiliary and its branches, the Philadelphia auxiliary and its branches, and the Delaware Women's Indian Association supported the work of Henry R. Voth and his wife Martha. This short-lived mission station at Oraibi, some forty miles from Keams Canyon, was transferred to the Mennonite Board in July 1893.

Home for Aged Women, Porcupine Creek, South Dakota
[Little is known about this station.]

1893

Agua Caliente (Cupeño) on Warner Ranch, California
In January 1893, WNIA medical missionary Dr. Rebecca C. Hallowell and government field matron Julia M. French moved into WNIA-financed housing at Agua Caliente. This work, funded largely by the NYCIA, was closed in January 1899.

Piegan, Montana
The Brooklyn Indian Association founded this mission station among the Piegans with the arrival on April 1, 1893, of Reverend and Mrs. E. S. Dutcher. Brooklyn women funded a missionary cottage and chapel on the 160 acres provided by the government. On August 1, 1894, the completely equipped station was turned over to the Methodist Episcopal Board of New York City.

Navajo, San Juan Valley, New Mexico
In the interests of supporting Mary E. Raymond, a Methodist Episcopal missionary and field matron, the CIA began an irrigation project known as the Cambridge Ditch. Following her death, the association continued to support her replacement, Mary Louise Eldridge, who had come with Raymond in 1891. Together they founded the Navajo Methodist Mission at Jewett, New Mexico.

1894

Hualapai (Walapai), Arizona

Frances S. Calfee, a government field matron, lived in MIA-sponsored housing and ran a day school among the Hualapai Indians. In the summer of 1896, the MIA purchased the Hope Ranch in Truxton Cañon to convert to a boarding school and model farm. In March 1903, the federal government assumed this missionary work with congressional appropriation of $60,000 for the building of the Truxton Canyon Training School on site.

1895

Middle Spokane, Washington

Helen W. Clark, a Canadian, sponsored by the Rhode Island Woman's Indian Association at Providence, began work in January 1895 among Chief Lot's band, a branch of the Flatheads. On the five acres granted by the government, she supervised the building of a two-room hewed log house as a school and living quarters. Funds were the gift of Mrs. W. C. (Mary Amanda) Greene, recently deceased president of the auxiliary. Opened on January 3, 1895, the school grew from twenty-four students to fifty-six within months. The site was transferred to the Presbyterian Board in 1899.

Hopi, First Mesa, Arizona

In September 1895, the New Jersey auxiliary sent Louise A. Young, a graduate of the Philadelphia Missionary Training School, as their missionary to live temporarily with Miss E. O. Stilwell, the new government field matron nominated by the WNIA. Young established a Sunday school and sewing classes.

Apache, Hampton, Virginia

The MIA spent $1,218.61 to educate eight Chiricahua Apache students at Hampton, Virginia—a several-year-long project.

1896

Hupa, Hoopa Reservation

Although WNIA interest here dated to 1891, missionary work was not undertaken until Emma Hapgood Denton, a member of the San Jose Indian Association and a reservation kindergarten teacher, convinced her association to sponsor a missionary. Reverend Lyman Paul Armstrong arrived in April 1896. He was soon replaced by Pliny Earle Goodard and his wife Alice and his sister Nellie. In July 1900 this three-acre station with its $500 missionary house, chapel, and barn was transferred to the Presbyterian Board of New York.

Desert Cahuilla, Desert Mission station at Martínez, California
Although Reverend Weinland preached monthly at their village, the Desert Cahuilla requested their own permanent missionary. The WNIA complied. With funding from the Brooklyn Association and its Bay Ridge branches, this mission opened in September 1896, building a missionary cottage for Reverend and Mrs. David J. Woosley. Mrs. Woosley soon organized the young girls into singing and sewing classes. In November 1897, the site was transferred to the Moravian Church of the United States.

Big Jim's Band of Absentee Shawnee, Indian Territory
The Maine Indian Association in 1896, with oversight from Dr. Charles Kirk's wife Rachel, an experienced missionary and with Big Jim's consent, bought forty acres and built a three-room cottage with a stable and wagon shed. In July 1897, Philander Blackledge and his wife were employed as missionaries. This work was transferred to the Associated Executive Committee of the Society of Friends in 1899.

1897

Hopi, Second Mesa, Arizona
This New Jersey Association–supported mission station twelve miles west of Keams Canyon opened with the arrival of Miss Mabel Collins as missionary and Flora M. Watkins as missionary and industrial teacher. Watkins was sponsored by auxiliaries in Western Pennsylvania and Washington, DC. In September their WNIA-funded missionary cottage was completed. The station was transferred to the Women's Baptist Home Mission Society in 1901.

Uncompahgre Ute, Colorado
The Wilmington, Delaware Association supported a field matron among these Indians in this little-known mission station. It was eventually turned over to the care of the Episcopal Church.

1898

Navajo, Two Grey Hills, New Mexico

Overseen by Mary Louise Eldridge, a government field matron and superintendent for the WNIA, this work began in March 1898 with the building of a $500 missionary cottage, a legacy of Mrs. J. Lewis (Mary S.) Crozer. Support staff included Henrietta G. Cole, who had been in charge of the infirmary at Williams College, and Sarah H. Munger, kindergarten teacher. The MIA and its branches in Cambridge and Jamaica Plain provided Munger's salary. In 1901 this work was taken over by the New Mexico Baptist Convention.

1899

Navajo, Rebecca Collins Hospital, Jewett, New Mexico

The NYCIA opened this eight-bed hospital (at a cost of $1,278) with living quarters for Eldridge and her assistant Edith M. Dabb. Eldridge supervised its construction on thirty-five acres she had donated from her own homestead. Eldridge had also donated five acres for the Indian room constructed by the Indian Industries League. Other auxiliaries that supported the station included the CIA, the Jamaica Plain auxiliary, the Connecticut Indian Association, and the Brooklyn branch. On December 1, 1902, it was turned over to the Presbyterian Board of Missions.

Helen R. Foote School and Mission, Shasta County, California

This station at Fall River Mills begun in 1894 by Isabella M. Cadwallader was initially only a Sunday school, underwritten by the Eastern Philadelphia auxiliary. Following the death of Helen R. Foote, the WNIA's longtime treasurer, the site was renamed in her honor, an additional forty acres was purchased, and a new schoolhouse constructed with $450 donated by Mrs. J. Lewis Crozer of Philadelphia, a member of the WNIA Executive Board. In July 1900 the facility was turned over to the Presbyterian Board.

1900

Tlingit, Sitka, Alaska

Anna Dean Wilbur, wife of Dr. Bertrand K. Wilbur, served as WNIA missionary, beginning among needy women and children on January 1, 1900. To provide housing, the WNIA built eight three-room cottages adjacent to the hospital, forming a model cottage settlement.

1902

Navajo, Closiah, New Mexico
With the closing of the Rebecca Collins Hospital, Eldridge moved down the San Juan River to engage in missionary work among the Navajos. In 1903, members of the Cambridge Indian Association funded the construction of an industrial building at the Closiah mission station, located near the Shiprock Agency. During 1904, Cambridge and Connecticut branches continued to fund Eldridge's work.

1903

Navajo, Tuba, Arizona
Opening in January 1903 on the site of a new government boarding school, this was the third WNIA mission station among the Navajo. The NYCIA pledged $600 for the work, while the Brooklyn auxiliary pledged $300 toward building a cottage to serve as home and headquarters for Ethel Sawyer and Jennie J. Johnson. The mission was transferred to the Presbyterian Board on August 4, 1905.

Navajo at Chinle, Arizona
Henrietta G. Cole was appointed by the WNIA Missionary Committee to work as a missionary among the Navajos. Her work was transferred to the government when she became their field matron on November 1. The Cambridge branch funded a housekeeper for her in 1904.

Yuma Indians, California
Initially beginning in 1902 with occasional visits by Weinland, the MIA with the support of its Jamaica Plain branch built a four-room missionary cottage and funded the work of Reverend and Mrs. Frank T. Lea, who reached Yuma on September 19, 1903. In November 1904, the Missionary Committee transferred this station to the Springfield, Massachusetts, auxiliary. In April 1907 it was transferred to the Women's Home Mission Society of the Methodist Episcopal Conference of Southern California.

Hopi, at Moencopi, Third Mesa, Arizona
Located two miles from Tuba, this station opened on December 3, 1903, with the arrival of Emma M. Houpt, a graduate of the missionary training school in Philadelphia. She was partially supported by the Bryn Mawr branch of the

Philadelphia auxiliary. In November 1904 this station was transferred to the Mennonite Board.

Greenville Chapel, Plumas County, California
Constructed with $500 of WNIA money, the chapel was used by Reverend G. J. Wentzell, who held meetings every other Sunday afternoon. WNIA involvement was minimal.

1904
Mojave-Apaches (Yavapai), Arizona
On January 14, 1904, the Philadelphia auxiliary opened a mission among the 1,000 Mojave-Apache (Yavapai) at Old Fort McDowell with the wife of Reverend W. H. Gill as field matron. The Indians had previously petitioned President Theodore Roosevelt to set aside land for them, and the Camp McDowell Indian Reservation was created. Old military buildings were granted to the WNIA for missionary and educational purposes. The station and its chapel were transferred in April 1907 to the Presbyterian Board of Home Missions.

1905
Navajo, Mary G. Fisk Home, near Farmington, New Mexico
The CIA, aided by the Connecticut auxiliary, established this new Navajo mission under Eldridge's care two miles from Farmington, New Mexico. The association built a $700 home for her in which she cared for the sick and engaged in industrial training. She took temporary leave in October 1906 to work among off-reservation Navajos in the checkerboard.

1906
Greenville, California
Rev. John M. Johnson and his wife Cora began missionary work from the WNIA-built chapel at the Greenville School. He established a nondenominational Indian Gospel Church in December 1906. In September 1908, the property was transferred to the Woman's Home Missionary Society of the Methodist Episcopal Church.

Navajo, Waro's Camp, east of Farmington, New Mexico
In October 1906, Eldridge moved temporarily from the Mary G. Fisk Home to

Waro's camp on public lands off the reservation, some fifty miles southeast of Farmington, to continue her work among the Navajos. She was partially funded by a member of the Executive Committee of the Cambridge branch and by government funding secured by Samuel Brosius of the IRA.

1907
Paiute, Walker River Reservation, Nevada
With the transfer of their Mojave-Apache (Yavapai) mission, Mr. and Mrs. W. H. Gill took over as missionaries among the 600 Paiute in October 1907 on five acres granted by the government. The NYCIA adopted this site in November 1907, building a chapel. In November 1909, this station was transferred to the permanent care of the Board of Home Missions and Church Extension of the Methodist Episcopal Church.

1908
Navajo, Saahtoye, Blanco Canyon, New Mexico
Supported by the MIA, Eldridge moved to Blanco Canyon to continue her work of allotment and missionary work for off-reservation Navajos living on public lands. The association built the Topliff Mission Home for her. Because of ill health, in 1910 she returned to the Fisk Home and the mission home was closed in 1914. The following year the MIA closed the Mary G. Fisk Home.

Klamath, Oregon
Missionary work was begun in October at Yainax, Oregon, a sub-agency forty miles east of the Klamath agency, by Mr. and Mrs. H. W. Peffley, who for nine years had engaged in missionary work in St. Louis. They worked not only among the Klamath but also the Modocs and Paiutes who shared the Klamath Reservation. Mrs. Peffley served half time as a WNIA missionary and a government field matron. The missionary station with a new church, missionary cottage, and barns were transferred to the Board of Home Missions and Church Extension of the Methodist Episcopal Church in July 1912.

1909
Hannah Elliott Bean Mission, Bishop, California
This nondenominational mission in Bishop, Inyo County was sponsored by the Northern California Indian Association and named in honor of one of its members. In 1910 it was turned over to the Presbyterian Board.

1910

Navajo, Indian Wells, Arizona

The fifth mission among the Navajo was opened at Castle Butte, thirty-five miles northeast of Winslow, Arizona, with missionary housing for E. A. Schwab and his wife provided by the government. A lack of water forced a permanent move in June 1911 to Indian Wells, with the NYCIA providing the salary and the construction of a $1,100 missionary cottage. In April 1912, the facility was transferred to the Presbyterian Board of Home Missions.

1912

Navajo, Good Samaritan Hospital, Indian Wells, Arizona

The NYCIA supported the medical missionary work of Mrs. W. R. Johnston, wife of a missionary among the Navajos. Other WNIA auxiliaries helped fund almost $10,000 for hospital construction costs. On December 1, 1919, the hospital was transferred to the care of the Woman's Board of Home Missions of the Presbyterian Church.

1913

Industrial and Christian Training School at Guinda, Yolo County, California

Opened by the NCIA, this school offered classes in agriculture, carpentry, blacksmithing, painting, and plumbing for boys and sewing, embroidering, crocheting, and butter-making for girls. A fire of unknown origin destroyed the largest building in July 1917 and the following year the school was closed.

1920

Rocky Boy Band of Chippewas and Crees, Montana

The government granted eighty acres to the NIA for missionary purposes, and Elmer D. and Mary M. Burroughs, graduates of the Moody Bible Training Institute, were chosen as the directing missionaries. The association constructed a mission house and chapel. On October 1, 1928, this site was transferred to the Board of American Missions of the United Lutheran Church in America.

1928

Turtle Mountain Band of Chippewa, Turtle Mountain Mission, North Dakota

Reverend and Mrs. Wilbur Doudna were the initial missionaries, followed by Mr. and Mrs. L. P. Wegenast. This site was transferred on September 1, 1933, to the Episcopal Diocese of North Dakota, becoming known as St. Sylvan Mission, serving as the center of all missions in the state.

1933
Paiute, Yerington Indian Mission, Nevada
Mr. and Mrs. Elmer D. Burroughs served as missionaries until the site was transferred on January 15, 1941, to the Methodist Episcopal Board. The Burroughs conducted sewing classes, held church services, at times offered a vacation church school, and provided headboards as grave markers.

1941
Sequoyah Indian Mission, Vian, Oklahoma
This station was founded among several small Cherokee Indian villages of Red Bird Smith, Pin Hook (West View), and Evening Shade, in the vicinity of Vian. Marion Lewis, who first came to work for the NIA in 1921, served as missionary. Unlike other NIA mission stations, this one was not turned over to a missionary society to run. When the national association disbanded in 1951, they gave the current missionary a jeep and a year's salary. Remaining missionary funds were donated to the Charles H. Cook Christian Training School in Phoenix, Arizona.

Notes

Introduction

1. Francis Paul Prucha, "Indian Policy Reform and American Protestantism, 1880–1900," *Indian Policy in the United States: Historical Essays* (Lincoln: University of Nebraska Press, 1981), 230–31. See also Margaret D. Jacobs, "Friends of the Indian," *After One Hundred Winters: In Search of Reconciliation of America's Stolen Lands* (Princeton: Princeton University Press, 2021), 126–47.
2. Francis Paul Prucha, "The Dawning of a New Era: The Spirit of Reform and American Indian Policy," in *Indian Policy in the United States*, 36–48, quotes on 37.
3. Russel Blaine Nye, *Social and Culture in America, 1830–1860* (New York: Harper & Row, 1974), quotes on 36, 39.
4. Prucha, "The Dawning of a New Era," 37–38.
5. Robert A. Trennert, *Alternative to Extinction: Federal Indian Policy and the Beginnings of the Reservation System, 1846–51* (Philadelphia: Temple University Press, 1975), 31.
6. Francis Paul Prucha, *The Great Father: The United States Government and the American Indians*, vol. 1 (Lincoln: University of Nebraska Press, 1984), 33. On paternalism, see Helen Marie Bannan, "Reformers and the 'Indian Problem,' 1878–1887 and 1912–1934" (PhD diss., Syracuse University, 1976), 215–23.
7. "Abolition of Treaty Making, March 3, 1971," and *"United States v. Kagama*, May 10, 1886," in *Documents of United States Indian Policy*, ed. Francis Paul Prucha, 2nd ed. (Lincoln: University of Nebraska Press, 1975), 136, 168–69.
8. Prucha, *The Great Father*, vol. 1, 177.
9. A. S. Quinton, *Indians and Their Helpers* (Publications of the WNIA, 1886), 1.
10. Margaret D. Jacobs, *White Mother to a Dark Race: Settler Colonialism, Maternalism, and the Removal of Indigenous Children in the American West and Australia, 1880–1940* (Lincoln: University of Nebraska Press, 2009), especially 88–103. Jacobs viewed Quinton's approach as equally harmful.
11. For policy, see Prucha, *The Great Father*, vol. 1, 479–606. On p. 481 he calls it "a state of mind," employing "a new emphasis on kindness and justice" which "cannot be precisely dated or rigidly defined." See also Prucha, *Documents of United States Indian Policy*, 141–43; for a current view, see Samantha M. Williams, "Establishing a Permanent Peace': Civilizing and Subjugating Native Americans During the Peace Policy Era (1869–1877)" (MA thesis, California State University, Stanislaus, 2013). The Catholic Church, with a long history of working among Indians, was assigned only seven reservations.
12. Prucha, "Federal Indian Policy in United States History," in *Indian Policy in the United States*, 21.

NOTES

13. See Prucha, *The Great Father*, vol. 1, 501–12; and "Authorization of the Board of Indian Commissioners," 126, and "Instructions to the Board of Indian Commissioners," 127–29, in *Documents of United States Indian Policy*.
14. Prucha, *The Great Father*, vol. 1, 512.
15. Prucha, *The Great Father*, first quote, 480; second quote, 39, in Prucha, "The Dawning of a New Era," see also 36–48.
16. Prucha, "Indian Policy Reform and American Protestantism, 1880–1900," 230–31. See also Jacobs, *After One Hundred Winters*, 126–47.
17. William G. McLoughlin, ed., *The American Evangelicals, 1800–1900: An Anthology* (New York: Harper & Row, 1968), 1, explains that evangelicalism molded Americans into "a unified, pietistic-perfectionist nation," which spurred them on to "heights of social reform, missionary endeavor, and imperialistic expansionism which constitute the moving forces of our history in that [the nineteenth] century."
18. Prucha, "Indian Policy Reform and American Protestantism," all quotes, 250.
19. Prucha, "General Allotment Act (Dawes Act)," *Documents of United States Indian Policy*, 171–74. Reservation lands were allotted in parcels of 40, 80, or 160 acres to individuals or families. For a different approach, see Siobhan Senier, *Voices of American Indian Assimilation and Resistance: Helen Hunt Jackson, Sarah Winnemucca, and Victoria Howard* (Norman: University of Oklahoma Press, 2001), 5–7, 41–49, 63–64.
20. C. Joseph Genetin-Pilawa, *Crooked Paths to Allotment: The Fight over Federal Indian Policy after the Civil War* (Chapel Hill: University of North Carolina Press, 2012): for Bland's beliefs see 112–33; quotes on 113, 114, 131. Bland edited the *Council Fire*, an Indian reform newspaper founded by Alfred B. Meacham, former superintendent of Indian affairs in Oregon. Although the membership of the NIDA was supposedly large, they were unable to hinder the "friends of the Indians."
21. For Tibbles's 1905 memoir and role, see *Buckskin and Blanket Days: Memoirs of a Friend of the Indians* (Lincoln: University of Nebraska Press, 1969). For reviews, see "Books and Authors," July 18, 1957, 22; "A Major Literary Find!," August 20, 1957, 18; Charles Poore, "Books of the *Times*, August 27, 1957, 25; and "Redman's Champion," December 29, 1957, 129, *New York Times*.
22. Valerie Sherer Mathes and Richard Lowitt, *The Standing Bear Controversy: Prelude to Indian Reform* (Urbana: University of Illinois Press, 2003); and Valerie Sherer Mathes, "Boston, the Boston Indian Citizenship Committee, and the Poncas," *The Massachusetts Historical Review* 14 (2012): 119–48. See also Jacobs, *After One Hundred Winters*, 67–86, 88–106, 109–31.
23. Valerie Sherer Mathes, "Helen Hunt Jackson and the Ponca Controversy," *Montana: The Magazine of Western History* 39, no. 1 (Winter 1989): 42–53; Valerie Sherer Mathes, *Helen Hunt Jackson and Her Indian Reform Legacy* (Austin: University of Texas Press, 1990), 21–37; and "Part One: The Ponca Cause and the Writing of *A Century of Dishonor*," in *The Indian Reform Letters of Helen Hunt Jackson, 1879–1885*, ed. Valerie Sherer Mathes (Norman: University of Oklahoma Press, 1998), 1–199.
24. Joshua W. Davis to Smiley, September 14, 1907; and Smiley to Davis, September 18, 1907, A. K. Smiley Family Papers, Quaker Collection, Haverford College, Haverford, Pennsylvania.
25. As late as the 1890 Lake Mohonk Conference, several women still identified as members of the Boston Committee. See "List of Members," *Twenty-Second Annual Report of the Board of Indian Commissioners* (BIC), *1890* (Washington, DC: GPO, 1891), 151–54. For names of early female members, see Mathes, "Boston, the Boston Indian Citizenship Committee," 138.
26. Henry S. Pancoast, *Impressions of the Sioux Tribes in 1882, with Some First Principles in the Indian Question* (Philadelphia: Franklin Printing House, 1883), and Herbert Welsh, *Four Weeks Among Some of the Sioux Tribes of Dakota and Nebraska, Together with a Brief Consideration of the Indian Problem* (Germantown, PA: Horace F. McCann, Steam-Power Printer, 1882).

27. Genetin-Pilawa, *Crooked Paths to Allotment*, writes that Welsh tried to mold "Native Americans to fit into his elite, Christian vision of 'civilized' people by eliminating tribal autonomy and destroying Indian communities": 95 for quote; see also 96–99. For investigative tour, see Herbert Welsh, *Report of a Visit to the Sioux and Ponka [sic] Indians on the Missouri River, Made by Wm. Welsh. July, 1872* (Philadelphia: M'Calla & Stavey, Printers, 1872).

28. Martha L. Edwards, "A Problem of Church and State in the 1870's," *The Mississippi Valley Historical Review* 11, no. 1 (June 1924): 37–53, especially 46–47, quote on 47.

29. For their work, see *The Spirit of Missions, 1873* (New York: Published for the Board of Missions of the Protestant Episcopal Church in the U.S. of America, 1873), 656–58; and *Constitution and By-laws of the Indians' Hope Association, 1892*, copies courtesy of the Archives of the Episcopal Church, Austin, Texas.

30. IRA, "The Object of the Association," *The Fourth Annual Report of the Executive Committee of the IRA* (Philadelphia: Office of the IRA, 1887), 3–4, quote on 3; William T. Hagan, *The Indian Rights Association: The Herbert Welsh Years, 1882–1904* (Tucson: University of Arizona Press, 1985), 11–19, (hereafter, Hagan, *The IRA*); and Genetin-Pilawa, *Crooked Paths to Allotment*, 135–45. For an interesting discussion of the founding of the IRA from his perspective see Herbert Welsh, "The Indian Question of 1882 and 1925," *The General Magazine and Historical Chronicle*, January 1926, 106–11.

31. Hagan, *The IRA*, 25 and 48; and Amelia Stone Quinton, "Care of the Indian," *Woman's Work in America*, ed. Annie Nathan Meyer (New York: Henry Holt, 1891), 385.

32. IRA, Cambridge Branch, *Secretary's Records, March 1885*, Cambridge Public Library, Cambridge, Massachusetts, 2; and "Cambridge and the Indians," *The Cambridge Tribune*, December 24, 1887, 2. The youngest child of Congressman Stephen Longfellow and Zilpah Wadsworth Longfellow, Samuel attended Harvard Divinity School. He was a clergyman, abolitionist, pacifist, and supporter of women's rights.

33. Sniffen served as assistant and clerk to Welsh from 1884 to 1909; as IRA executive secretary from 1909 to 1939; and recording secretary from 1939 to 1942. He joined the Board of Directors in 1903, serving until his death in 1942; see *Indian Rights Association Papers: A Guide to the Microfilm Edition, 1864–1973* (Glen Rock: Microfilming Corporation of America, 1975), 5.

34. Hagan, *The IRA*, 23, 256–57; and Valerie Sherer Mathes, *Charles C. Painter: The Life of an Indian Reform Advocate* (Norman: University of Oklahoma Press, 2020).

35. Larry Burgess, in an e-mail dated June 6, 2024, wrote that in 1889 Rev. Sherman Coolidge, an Episcopal cleric and an Arapaho, was the first Indian invited to Lake Mohonk. In 1890, Chester Cornelius, an Oneida, and Dr. Charles Eastman, a Sioux and physician at the Pine Ridge Indian agency, were invited.

36. Larry E. Burgess, "The Lake Mohonk Conferences on the Indian, 1883–1916" (PhD diss., Claremont, 1972), 19–20 for inner circle, 71, 73, for unity and approach to women reformers. Invitees were members of various Protestant denominations; the first Roman Catholic representative did not attend until 1902 (142, 189–90). See also Larry E. Burgess, "What Is a Woman Worth?" 1–22, and Cathleen D. Cahill, "'Noble Women Not a Few': The Lake Mohonk Conferences," 213–39, both in *The Women's National Indian Association: A History*, ed. Valerie Sherer Mathes (Albuquerque: University of New Mexico Press, 2015); and Bannan, "Reformers and the 'Indian Problem,'" 90–105, 136–43, 240–52.

37. The first four were ethnologist Alice Cunningham Fletcher, Peabody Museum; Sara T. Kinney, vice president of the Connecticut Indian Association; and Sarah F. Smiley and Eliza Smiley, the sister and wife of Albert K. Smiley.

38. BIC, "Woman's Work for the Indian," *Seventeenth Annual Report of the BIC for the Year 1885* (Washington, DC: GPO, 1886), 92. For cooperation between the WNIA and Lake Mohonk, see Valerie Sherer Mathes, "A Place at the Table: The Women's National Indian Association in the Indian Reform Arena," in *Gender, Race, and Power in the Indian Reform Movement: Revisiting the History of the*

NOTES

WNIA, ed. Valerie Sherer Mathes (Albuquerque: University of New Mexico Press, 2020), 85–104, especially 92–93.

39. BIC, "List of Members," *Twenty-Second Annual Report of the BIC, 1890* (Washington, DC: GPO, 1891), 151–54.
40. Anne Firor Scott, *Making the Invisible Woman Visible* (Urbana: University of Illinois Press, 1984), 281 for quote, 282 for categories.
41. Helen M. Wanken, "'Woman's Sphere' and Indian Reform: The Women's National Indian Association, 1879–1901" (PhD diss., Marquette University, 1981); Gregory Coyne Thompson, "The Origins and Implementation of the American Indian Reform Movement: 1867–1912" (PhD diss., University of Utah, 1981); and Bannan, "Reformers and the 'Indian Problem.'"

Chapter 1

1. "Mary L. Bonney Rambaut," *The National Cyclopaedia of American Biography Being the History of the United States*, vol. VI (New York: James T. White & Company, 1896), 100–101; "Mrs. Mary L. Bonney Rambaut," *A Woman of the Century: Fourteen Hundred-Seventy Biographical Sketches Accompanied by Portraits of Leading American Women in All Walks of Life*, ed. Francis E. Willard and Mary A. Livermore (Buffalo: Charles Wells Moulton, 1893), 595; WNIA, "Mrs. Mary L. Bonney Rambaut," *The Indian's Friend*, September 1896, 2; and Valerie Sherer Mathes, "Mary Lucinda Bonney and Amelia Stone Quinton, Founders of the Women's National Indian Association," *American Baptist Quarterly* 28, no. 4 (Winter 2009): 421–40.
2. No formal school history exists, only pamphlets, such as Chestnut Street Female Seminary, *Boarding and Day School, Philadelphia, No. 525 Chestnut Street* (Philadelphia: Henry B. Ashmead, 1855). See Valerie Sherer Mathes, "Mary Lucinda Bonney Rambaut: Educator and Indian Reformer," *Gender, Race, and Power*, 143–61, brief school history, 146–49.
3. *Records of the [ITKPA] from Dec. 1880* [handwritten by Quinton (ASQ)], Box 1, Folder 1, *Women's National Indian Association Papers*, Division of Rare and Manuscript Collections, Carl A. Kroch Library, Cornell University, Ithaca, NY (hereafter cited as *ITKPA Records*), quote on 1.
4. "Catharine Beecher: Circular Addressed to Benevolent Ladies of the U. States," in *The Cherokee Removal: A Brief History with Documents*, ed. Theda Perdue and Michael D. Green (Boston: Bedford/St. Martin's 2005), 113–14. For non-Beecher petitions, see Sara Northrop Romeyn, "A Sentimental Empire: White Women's Responses to Native American Policy, 1824–1894" (PhD diss., George Washington University, 2003), 56–90; Mary Hershberger, "Mobilizing Women, Anticipating Abolition: The Struggle Against Indian Removal in the 1830s," *Journal of American History* 86, no. 1 (June 1999), 15–40; and Alisse Theodore, "A Right to Speak on the Subject': The U.S. Women's Antiremoval Petition Campaign, 1829–1831," *Rhetoric & Public Affairs* 5, no. 4 (2002), 601–24.
5. Valerie Sherer Mathes, *Amelia Stone Quinton and the Women's National Indian Association: A Legacy of Indian Reform* (Norman: University of Oklahoma Press, 2022), 14–15 as WCTU organizer.
6. For her work in the field of microscopic crystallography, see *Proceedings of the American Association for the Advancement of Science* (Salem: Published by the Permanent Secretary, 1883), xxxvi; and "The Naturalists' Directory," *The International Scientist's Directory* (Boston: S. E. Cassino and Company, 1883), 22.
7. For founding, see William Williams Keen, ed., *The Bi-Centennial Celebration of the Founding of the First Baptist Church of the City of Philadelphia, 1898* (Philadelphia: American Baptist Publication Society, 1899), 391–92. Boardman died on September 12, 1915: see WNIA, "Mrs. George Dana Boardman," *The Indian's Friend*, November 1915, 6.

NOTES

8. *ITKPA Records*, 2 in preface.
9. For marriage announcement, see *Cortland County Democrat*, March 8, 1878.
10. WNIA, "A Historical Sketch," *The Indian's Friend*, October 1896, 2. This sketch was written in April 1881 by Bonney.
11. While living in Madison, Georgia, ASQ married James Franklin Swanson in 1854; he later became a Baptist minister; and Bonney married Rev. Thomas Rambaut in 1888.
12. See Mathes, "Mary Lucinda Bonney Rambaut," 143–46; and Mathes, *Amelia Stone Quinton*, 14–17.
13. For Bonney's attendance, see Mrs. John A. Logan, *The Part Taken by Women in American History* (Wilmington: The Perry-Nalle Publishing Co., 1912), 711–12; and Mathes, "Mary Lucinda Bonney Rambaut," 146–49.
14. Scott, *Making the Invisible Woman Visible*, 72.
15. Keen, ed., *The Bi-Centennial Celebration*, 123–24, quote on 124.
16. Francis Paul Prucha, *American Indian Policy in the Formative Years: The Indian Trade and Intercourse Acts, 1790–1834* (Lincoln: University of Nebraska Press, 1970), for background to legislation, 219–22; and "Civilization Fund Act," *Documents of United States Indian Policy*, 33.
17. John B. Boles, "Henry Holcombe, A Southern Baptist Reformer in the Age of Jefferson," *The Georgia Historical Quarterly* 54, no. 3 (Fall 1970): 381–407; for Philadelphia work, see 395–403.
18. For founding and quote, see Keen, ed., *The Bi-Centennial Celebration*, 391; for his tenure, 107–19. See also "George Dana Boardman," *Prominent and Progressive Pennsylvanians of the Nineteenth Century*, vol. I, Leland M. Williamson, et. al, eds. (Philadelphia: The Record Publishing Company, 1898), 114–16. They established "The Boardman Lectureship in Christian Ethics" at the University of Pennsylvania in 1899.
19. For founding, see *The Women's Baptist Home Mission Society, 1877 to 1882* (Chicago: R. R. Donnelley & Sons, Printers, 1883), 1. For Ingalls, see John M. Rhea, *A Field of Their Own: Women and American Indian History, 1830–1941* (Norman: University of Oklahoma Press, 2016), 39–40; and "Women's Baptist Home Mission Society," *The National Baptist*, May 17, 1877, 1. *The Baptist* was founded in 1865; Heman Wayland was editor from 1872 to 1894; see "The Rev. Dr. H. L. Wayland Dead," *New York Times*, November 8, 1898, 3.
20. John M. Rhea, "From Indian Territory to Philadelphia: A Critical Reexamination of the Origins and Early History of the Women's National Indian Association, 1877–1881," in *Gender, Race, and Power in the Indian Reform Movement: The Women's National Indian Association*, ed. Valerie Sherer Mathes, 27–54 (Albuquerque: University of New Mexico Press, 2020), quotes 31, 49. For Blackall's founding, and for Choctaw and Chickasaw, see *The Women's Baptist Home Mission Society*, 26–27; and also "Blackall, Mrs. Emily Lucas," Willard and Livermore, eds., *A Woman of the Century*, 89–90.
21. For founding and quote, see *The Women's Baptist Home Mission Society*, 1; and Mathes, *Amelia Stone Quinton*, 17–20.
22. "Missions," *The National Baptist*, May 30, 1878, 4. Boardman reported a meeting of young adults and children, supported by church women, which raised $1,000 "for the education of heathen children."
23. Rhea, *A Field of Their Own*, 40, 43; and Mathes, *Amelia Stone Quinton*, 18–20.
24. Rhea, "From Indian Territory to Philadelphia," 27.
25. WNIA [Bonney], "A Historical Sketch," 1896, 2, 10–11, quotes on 2.
26. Mary Bonney Rambaut, "A Sketch of the life of Mrs. Mary L. Bonney Rambaut given by herself to her friend Mrs. Amelia S. Quinton, September, 1894," American Baptist Historical Society Archives Center, Mercer University, Atlanta, Georgia. Bonney provided funds, and ASQ worked "as God opened the way"; see "A Brief Historical Sketch," in *ITKPA Records*, 21.
27. Rhea, "From Indian Territory to Philadelphia," 27–28.

NOTES

28. Ingalls was accused of mishandling monies while an Indian Agent. Absolved, he was still dismissed as ABHMS missionary; see "A Disgrace to the Nation," *New York Times*, January 8, 1878, 1.

29. Rhea, "From Indian Territory to Philadelphia," quotes on 27–28, 49; for Ingalls, see 30, for conflict within the Baptist Church, see 31–35, 39–40. Rhea writes (50) that "'Maternal patriotism' or Christian patriotism was a construct that Quinton developed, independently and long before historians developed the 'maternalism' concept to describe this ideology." Jacobs, in *White Mother to a Dark Race*, describes maternalism as "a type of feminism, concerned as it was with mobilizing women to address the disadvantages of other women and to gain greater political authority," quote 89, see also 88–95.

30. Mary P. Ryan, *Womanhood in America: From Colonial Times to the Present* (New York: New Viewpoints / Franklin Watts, 1979), 88.

31. For presentation, see Quinton, "Care of the Indian," 378; and "Women's Home Mission Union," *The National Baptist*, February 26, 1880, 5. For Bonney's quote, see "A Historical Sketch," 2. See also U.S. Congress, House, vol. 10, part 2, 46th Cong., 2nd sess., *Congressional Record*, February 20, 1880, 1044.

    ASQ wrote a three-page leaflet, *An Earnest Petition Needed: A Few Historical Facts*, describing the government's mistreatment of the Five Civilized Tribes, to accompany the petition. On the top of a copy in the Historical Society of Pennsylvania, ASQ had written: "The first leaflet of the Woman's Ind. Assc'n circulated in the summer of 1879 with the first petition of the assoc'n & before any organization was effected indeed."

32. For text, see "To the Editor of the National Baptist," *National Baptist*, February 19, 1880, 5, written by "Justice"; and Quinton, "Care of the Indian," 378–79. Petitions were clipped, signed, mailed to one central location, pasted together, and hand-delivered in Washington, DC, by association officials. Early ones were accompanied by pamphlets and memorials, often written by ASQ. To organize such work, the WNIA founded the Memorials to Government Committee; see WNIA, *Fourth Annual Report of the WNIA* (Philadelphia: Press of Grant & Faires, 1884), 5.

33. For friendship with Whipple and quote, see WNIA [Bonney], "A Historical Sketch," 2. See also undated letters signed by Chase, Bonney, Boardman, and Mrs. H. L. Wayland (née Elizabeth Arms) to Hayes, in Rutherford B. Hayes Papers, Rutherford B. Hayes Presidential Center, Spiegel Grove, Fremont, Ohio. Wayland's husband authored the petition.

34. Mrs. T. L. Tomkinson, *Twenty Years' History of the Woman's Home Missionary Society of the Methodist Episcopal Church, 1880–1900* (Cincinnati: The Woman's Home Missionary Society, 1903), 38; and Emily Apt Geer, "Lucy W. Hayes and the Woman's Home Missionary Society," *The Hayes Historical Journal: A Journal of the Gilded Age* 4, no. 4 (Fall 1984), 5–14.

35. English Congregational minister Robert Whitaker McAll founded his McAll Mission in Paris in 1872; see "Robert Whitaker McAll—A Character Sketch," *The Altruistic Review*, ed. Hazlitt Alva Cuppy, vol. 1 (July–December) (Chicago: The Altruistic Review Company, 1893), 243–48. According to *The American McAll Record* 1, no. 1 (October 1883), 4, the association "diffuses information, invokes prayer, and collects funds ... transmitted, with no slightest deduction for personal service ... to the Mission in France." See also Robert Whitaker McAll and Horatius Bonar, "American McAll Association," *A Cry from the Land of Calvin and Voltaire: Records of the McAll Mission* (London: Hodder and Stoughton, 1887), 77–79.

    Auxiliaries were in at least fourteen states and the District of Columbia. WNIA members included Anna L. Dawes, daughter of Senator Dawes; Elizabeth Arms Wayland; and Mrs. J. Lewis (née Mary A. Stotesbury) Crozer, a major supporter of WNIA work among the Navajo. Mrs. James A. Garfield was also a member.

36. "The American McAll Association," *Handbook of French and Belgian Protestantism* (New York: Federal Council of the Churches of Christ in America, 1919) 180–81, lists Hayes, Chase, and Lea as officers.

NOTES

Lea was the daughter of Isaac Lea, LL.D., a publisher, scientist, author, member of the American Philosophical Society, and president of the American Association for the Advancement of Science. She hosted activities from the family home on Locust Street, Philadelphia; see "American Home of the McAll Mission," in McAll and Bonar, *A Cry from the Land*, 77.

37. New members were Lea, Episcopal; Mrs. Margaretta C. Sheppard, Presbyterian; Mrs. Joshua R. (Mary) Jones, Methodist Episcopal; and Mrs. Edward Cope, Quaker; see WNIA [Bonney], "A Historical Sketch," 10.

38. *ITKPA Records*, 5–6. During the January 20, 1881, meeting Bonney moved to change their name to the Indian Treaty-Keeping Committee, 9.

39. During the November 21, 1882, meeting, Boardman submitted her resignation. She was a member from the beginning; the *ITKPA Records*, 62, described her as devoted, faithful, and efficient.

40. See *ITKPA Records*, 10, for Chase's resignation and quote; 11 for Bonney; and 15–22 for the June meeting, constitution, and a printed history.

41. *ITKPA Records*, 28–29.

42. "Headquarters Changed," *Rochester Democrat and Chronicle*, December 10, 1903, 17. The room, open daily, was manned by May Field McKean, correspondence secretary, who handed out NIA publications; see NIA, "Our New Headquarters," *The Indian's Friend*, March 1904, 7.

43. WNIA, "A Historical Sketch," quote on 11.

44. For text of petition and ASQ's memorial letter, see Quinton, "In Care of the Indian," 379–81.

45. For text of 1882 petition and memorial letter, see Quinton, "In Care of the Indian," 382–84; for quote see 383–84; see also *ITKPA Records*, 8, 10, 18–20 for constitution, and 55–57 for NIA constitution.

46. *The Women's Baptist Home Mission Society*, 22.

47. *ITKPA Records*, 47 for quote, 54–57 for constitution, quotes on 54 and 55; and "Our Association's Chronology. Number Five," *The Indian's Friend*, May 1897, 2.

48. Terri Christian Theisen, in "'With a View Toward Their Civilization': Women and the Work of Indian Reform" (MA thesis, Portland State University, 1996), 20, writes: "Changes in American Protestantism, Victorian tenets of domesticity and moral superiority, and the effects of expanding economic and commercial opportunities on the roles of men and women, all contributed to women's entrance into missionary work."

49. WNIA, "New Work," *Annual Meeting and Report of the WNIA, October 27, 1883* (Philadelphia: 1883), 10.

50. Prucha, "Indian Policy Reform and American Protestantism, 1880–1900," 232.

51. WNIA, *Missionary Work of the WNIA and Letters of Missionaries* (Philadelphia: Grant & Faires, Printers, 1885); remarks also on the cover of WNIA, *The WNIA Report of Missionary Work, November, 1885 to November 1886* (Philadelphia: Royal Printing Company), 2. In 1874, Cook, a graduate of the Andover Theological Seminary, led the Monday noon prayer meetings in Boston's Tremont Temple. A Ponca supporter, his 131st Monday lecture was on the "Wrongs of the Ponca Indians"; see "The Monday Lectures: by the Rev. Joseph Cook—with Preludes," *Boston Daily Advertiser*, November 4, 1879, 4. See also "Joseph Cook," *The Congregationalist and Christian World*, July 6, 1901, 10.

52. WNIA, "The Mass Meeting," *Fourth Annual Report of the WNIA*, 53.

53. Jacobs, *White Mother to a Dark Race*, 93–95, quotes on 94, 91; see also, 96–103; and Margaret D. Jacobs, "The Great White Mother: Maternalism and American Indian Child Removal in the American West, 1880–1940," *Faculty Publications, Department of History* 106 (University of Nebraska, 2008): 191–213. On 192 she writes that "through a politics of maternalism, many white women reformers claimed for themselves the role of a 'Great White Mother,' who would save her benighted Indian 'daughters.'"

NOTES

54. Quinton, *Indians and Their Helpers*, 8.
55. Dana L. Robert, "The Influence of American Missionary Women on the World Back Home," *Religion and American Culture: A Journal of Interpretation* 12, no. 1 (Winter 2002): 59–89, quote 69. The *Indian's Friend*, WNIA's monthly, resembled publications of women's missionary societies as "first person articles by women missionaries, testimonies from new converts, and news from mission circles" (75).
56. WNIA, "Our Association's Chronology. Number Six," *The Indian's Friend*, June 1897, 12.
57. Mrs. J. B. Dickinson, *Address of the President of the Women's National Indian Association, November 17, 1885* (Philadelphia: Grant & Faires Printers, 1885), 9.
58. Edward E. Hale, "The Indian Rights Association: What It Is," *Lend a Hand: A Record of Progress and Journal of Organized Charity* 1, no. 1 (January 1886): 57. Hale founded his private nonsectarian Boston charitable organization, the Lend a Hand Society, in 1891. It still exists. The monthly reported on the work of Lend a Hand Clubs and social issues of the day, including Indian rights. For more, see the abstract of the Lend a Hand Society Records, Massachusetts Historical Society, Boston, Massachusetts.
59. Hannah E. Bean to Philip Garrett, June 19, 1901, *The Indian Rights Association Papers, 1864–1973*, Series 1-A, Incoming correspondence, 1864–1968, microfilm edition (hereafter *IRA Papers*), Reel 15. Originals are with the Historical Society of Pennsylvania, Philadelphia. See also Constance Goddard DuBois (CGD) and her correspondence with Herbert Welsh, in Valerie Sherer Mathes, "Constance Goddard DuBois, Indian Reformer," *The Journal of San Diego History* 68, nos. 3–4 (Winter 2022): 184–219, specifically 188, 193.
60. According to "Cambridge and the Indians," *The Cambridge Tribune*, December 24, 1887, 2, this IRA branch admitted men and women. For more see Mathes, "The Banner Association: Twenty-Five Years in Massachusetts," in *Gender, Race, and Power*, 153–72.
61. See Cambridge branch and Boston Committee joint public meeting in "Indian Association," *Cambridge Chronicle*, March 3, 1888, 1; or a joint public meeting of the MIA and the Boston Committee, in "Absorbing Indians," *Boston Daily Globe*, March 28, 1890, 7; and for an address by a Boston Committee member to the Cambridge branch, see "The Indian Association," *Boston Daily Advertiser*, January 21, 1887, 1.
62. "President's Report," *Constitution of the Cambridge Branch of the Massachusetts Indian Association* (Cambridge: John Ford & Son, Printers, 1893), 13.
63. IRA, Cambridge Branch, *Secretary's Records*, March 1885, 22; see also 1, 18, 20–22, 51–52 for more examples of cooperation.
64. "Cambridge," *Annual Report of the MIA, January 1887* (Boston: Frank Wood, Printer, 1887), 13; see also Valerie Sherer Mathes, "James Bradley Thayer in Defense of Indian Legal Rights," *The Massachusetts Historical Review* 21 (2020): 41–74, for sponsorship of his address, 47.
65. Born in Fitchburg, Massachusetts, in 1839 to Timothy and Ruth Underwood, Dickinson taught at Hartford Female Seminary, later served as principal at Vassar College, and was chair of the literature department at the University of Denver. A published poet, author of a dozen books, numerous short stories, editor of her magazine, *The Silver Cross*, and of the WCTU's *National Reformer*, she contributed regularly to the *New York Tribune* and other journals. After her first husband, George Preston Lowe, died, she married John B. Dickinson, a prominent New York banker, who died five years later. See Logan, *The Part Taken by Women in American History*, 713–15; William A. Emerson, "Mary Caroline Dickinson," *Fitchburg, Massachusetts, Past and Present* (Fitchburg: Press of Blanchard & Brown, 1887), 101–4; and "Mary Lowe Dickinson," *Famous American Men and Women*, ed. Stanley Waterloo and John Wesley Hanson (Chicago: Wabash Publishing Company, 1896), 190.
66. For her appointment, see "Women to Guide Women. Officers of the National Council Elected Yesterday.

Mary Lowe Dickinson President," *New York Times*, February 27, 1895, 5.

67. For secretary role, see "The Years of Useful Love. International Order of King's Daughters and Sons Celebrates," *New York Times*, April 10, 1896, 2.

68. "League for Social Service," *New York Times*, January 24, 1899, 12. See also Ms. Mary Lowe Dickinson, "The Next Thing in Education," *The Congress of Women Held in the Woman's Building, World's Columbian Exposition, Chicago, U.S.A. 1893*, ed. Mary Kavanaugh Oldham Eagle (Denver: Charles Westley, 1894), 637.

69. Mary Lowe Dickinson, "Women and Religious Delusions," *Public Opinion*, October 10, 1901, 465.

70. May Wright Sewall, "Organization Among Women as an Instrument in Promoting Religion—Address by Mary Lowe Dickinson of New York," *The World's Congress of Representative Women*, vol. 2 (Chicago: Rand, McNally & Company, 1894), 296–97.

71. Dickinson, *Address of the President of the Women's National Indian Association, November 17, 1885*, quotes 2, 3, 11.

72. Bannan, "Reformers and the 'Indian Problem,'" 90–105, 136–43, 240–52; pp. 342–50 for her tables; see also "Journal of the Fourteenth Annual Conference with Representatives of Missionary Boards and Indian Rights Associations," *Sixteenth Annual Report of Indian Commissioners, 1884* (Washington, DC: GPO, 1885), 50.

73. Susan M. Cruea, "Changing Ideals of Womanhood During the Nineteenth-Century Woman Movement," *University Writing Program Faculty Publications* (2005), 187–204, quote on 190. See also Barbara Welter's chapter, "The Cult of True Womanhood, 1820–1860," in her *Dimity Convictions: The American Woman in the Nineteenth Century* (Athens: Ohio University Press, 1976), 21–41, notes 204–11. Linda K. Kerber in "Separate Spheres, Female Worlds, Woman's Place: The Rhetoric of Women's History," *Journal of American History* 75 (June 1988), explains that "sphere" is a trope used by historians to describe "women's part in American culture" (9–39, quote on 10). See also Mary P. Ryan, "American Society and the Cult of Domesticity, 1830–1860" (PhD diss., University of California at Santa Barbara, 1971); Nancy F. Cott, *The Bonds of Womanhood: "Woman's Sphere" in New England, 1780–1835* (New Haven: Yale University Press, 1977); Louise Michele Newman, "The 'Indian Problem' as a Woman Question," in her *White Women's Rights: The Racial Origins of Feminism in the United States* (New York: Oxford University Press, 1999), 116–31; and Jacobs, "Maternalist Politics," in *White Mother to a Dark Race*, 88–93.

74. J. F. Stearns, *A Discourse Delivered in the First Presbyterian Church in Newburyport, July 30, 1837* (Newburyport: John G. Tilton, 1837), 10–11.

75. Helen M. Bannan, "'True Womanhood' and Indian Assimilation," *Selected Proceedings of the Third Annual Conference on Minority Studies*, vol. II, ed. George E. Carter and James R. Parker (La Crosse, WI: Institute for Minority Studies, 1987), 187.

76. Theda Perdue, "Domesticating the Natives: Southern Indians and the Cult of True Womanhood," *Women, Families and Communities: Readings in American History*, vol. 1 to 1877, ed. Nancy A. Hewitt (Glenview: Scott Foreman, 1990), 159–70, quotes, 169, 161.

77. For a list, see Sarah R. Ames, "A History of the Cambridge Branch of the Massachusetts Indian Association from 1886 to 1923," *Proceedings of the Cambridge Historical Society* 17 (February 1901), 84–91. Sarah was married to James Barr Ames, who was associated with Harvard Law School for forty years, first as professor and finally in 1895 as dean. See James Barr Ames, "Memoir of James Barr Ames," *Lectures on Legal History and Miscellaneous Legal Essays* (Cambridge: Harvard University Press, 1913), "Preface," v, and 4, 6, 8.

78. WNIA, "The Report of the Committee on Amendments," *Annual Report of the WNIA, December, 1901* (Philadelphia: George Dukes, 1901), 36.

NOTES

79. Wanken, "'Woman's Sphere' and Indian Reform," 340–41.
80. A mimeograph machine printed copy from a stencil.
81. Wanken, "'Woman's Sphere' and Indian Reform," quotes, 346, 348, 350, 356, 359. See 366 for merger and 362 for remaining auxiliaries. For *The Indian's Friend*, see 358–60.
82. Born in Germany, Cook left his position as a minister at the Halsted Street Methodist Episcopal Church in Chicago in 1870 to establish a mission among the Akimel O'odham (Pima) in Sacaton on the Gila River Indian Reservation in Arizona Territory. A decade later he was ordained in the Presbyterian Church, establishing a Pima congregation in 1889. In 1911 he founded the Cook Bible School to train Native pastors to serve on reservations. See Charles A. Anderson, "Day Book of Rev. Charles H. Cook (of a Journey from Chicago, Illinois to the Pima Indian Agency in Arizona Territory Between September 1, 1870, and February 24, 1871)," *Journal of the Presbyterian Historical Society* 37, no. 2 (June 1959): 104–21; and Edward Drewry Jervey, "Methodism in Arizona: The First Seventy Years," *Arizona and the West* 3, no. 4 (Winter 1961): 341–50.
83. They included the MIA, Madeline G. Haynes Indian Association, NCIA, Washington, DC, and Brooklyn and Bryn Mawr Indian Associations.
84. Taber is the subject of chapter 8.
85. NIA, "Annual Meeting," and "Receipts," *The Indian's Friend*, June 1951, 3, 7. The Connecticut Indian Association had voted to dissolve during an April 9, 1924, meeting. See formal letter dated March 13, 1924, in "Miscellaneous," *Litchfield Branch Connecticut Indian Association Records*, Litchfield Historical Society, Helga J. Ingraham Memorial Library, Litchfield, Connecticut.
86. Wanken, "'Woman's Sphere' and Indian Reform," 375–76.
87. Wanken, "'Woman's Sphere' and Indian Reform," ii.
88. For travel, see WNIA, "Meetings Addressed," *Annual Report of the WNIA, November 1891*, 17–19.

Chapter 2

1. "The Chronology of Our Organization," *The Indian's Friend*, February 1897, 2.
2. The March issue of *The Council Fire and Arbitrator*, 42, described the Philadelphia Indian Association as actively distributing petitions calling for justice, citizenship, and permanent homes for the Indians. Bland, the editor, described its officers, including Quinton, as "ladies of well-known benevolence, and of the highest standing in the community, and of nine denominations."
3. *ITKPA Records*, 28–29; see also WNIA, *Annual Meeting and Report of the WNIA, October 27, 1883*, 4, 7, 9.
4. WNIA, *Fourth Annual Report*, 16, 20, for new branches.
5. "Our Association's Chronology," *The Indian's Friend*, September 1897, 2. For Dakota tour see Mathes, *Amelia Stone Quinton*, 34–37.
6. Amelia Stone Quinton, *The Mohonk Indian Conference* (Leaflet of the WNIA, 1885), 1 for quotes. For a pictorial history see Larry E. Burgess, *Mohonk: Its People and Spirit: A History of One Hundred Years of Growth and Service* (Fleischmanns, NY: Purple Mountain Press, 1996). In 1986 the resort became a U.S. National Historic Landmark and in 1999 became one of the Historic Hotels of America. It is still owned by the Smiley family.
7. "Miss M. C. Collins," in "Proceedings of the Lake Mohonk Conference," *Twentieth Annual Report of the BIC, 1888* (Washington, DC: GPO, 1889), 82 for quote, and 55–56 for her other comments; see "Mrs. A. S. Quinton," 56 for her comment. In 1899, Collins was ordained in the Congregational Church; see NIA, "Rev. Mary C. Collins," *The Indian's Friend*, July 1930, 7.
8. WNIA, "Our Association's Chronology. Number Nine," *The Indian's Friend*, September 1897, 2;

NOTES

WNIA, *Fourth Annual Report*, 21 for quote.

9. For ASQ's organizing skills, see Wanken's chapter on auxiliaries, in "'Woman's Sphere' and Indian Reform," 39–58; for quote, see 43.
10. WNIA, *Annual Report of the WNIA, November 17th, 1885* (Philadelphia: Grant & Faires, 1885), 16.
11. WNIA, *Official Pamphlet of the National Indian Association, with Suggestions and Facts for Its Helpers* (Philadelphia, November 1882), quotes 12, 9.
12. WNIA members were exclusively Protestant, and some, like Quinton, were anti-Catholic, but "it [the prejudice] was subtle and surfaced overtly only a few times in its publications," writes Wanken, "'Woman's Sphere' and Indian Reform," 50.
13. For committee definition, see Amelia Stone Quinton, "The Indian," *The Literature of Philanthropy*, ed. Francis Goodale (New York: Harper & Brothers Publishers, 1893), 119. For her pamphlet, see Mrs. A. S. Quinton, *Suggestions to Friends of the WNIA* (Philadelphia: Publication of the WNIA, 1886), 1 for quotes. See also WNIA, *How to Organize an Indian Association* (Philadelphia: Publications of the WNIA, 1889), and for dues see Wanken, "'Woman's Sphere' and Indian Reform," 49–50.
14. WNIA, *Annual Report of the WNIA, November 1886* (Philadelphia: Royal Printing Company, 1886), 10–11, quotes on 16, 13, 8.
15. Lori Jacobson, "Shall We Have a Periodical?" in *The Women's National Indian Association: A History*, ed. Valerie Sherer Mathes, 46–61 (Albuquerque: University of New Mexico Press, 2015).
16. WNIA, *Annual Report of the WNIA, November 30, 1887* (Philadelphia: Royal Printing Company, 1887), 11; for itinerary, see "Meetings Addressed," 13–14; and WNIA "Our Association's Chronology. Number Fourteen," *The Indian's Friend*, April 1898, 2. See Wanken, "'Woman's Sphere' and Indian Reform," 54, for number of branches.
17. Rose Stremlau, "WNIA Chapters in the South," in *The Women's National Indian Association: A History*, ed. Valerie Sherer Mathes (Albuquerque: University of New Mexico Press, 2015), quotes 175, 176, 184.
18. WNIA, *Annual Report of the WNIA, November 1891* (Philadelphia: Press of J. A. Wilbour Printing House, 1891), 15–16, quote on 15, see also 18.
19. Wanken, "'Woman's Sphere' and Indian Reform," 55.
20. Wanken, "'Woman's Sphere' and Indian Reform," quotes on 56–57, and 59.
21. "Massachusetts Indian Association," *Boston Journal*, January 23, 1883, 3; WNIA, "The Auxiliaries," *Fourth Annual Report of the WNIA*, 17; and *Annual Report of the MIA, January 1888* (Boston: Frank Wood, Printer, 1888), 7–10.
22. Mathes, "The Banner Association," 155, 165, photo of, 156.
23. Residents of Round Valley were the Yuki, Concow, Pomo, Nomlaiki, Pit River, and Wailaki. The station was turned over to the Women's Baptist Home Mission Society of Chicago the following spring. See Valerie Sherer Mathes, "Baptist Missionary Work at Round Valley, California," *American Baptist Quarterly* 29, no. 3 (Fall 2010): 172–86; Valerie Sherer Mathes, "The Women's National Indian Association Comes to Round Valley," in *Divinely Guided: The California Work of the Women's National Indian Association* (Lubbock: Texas Tech University Press, 2012), 51–77; and Mathes, "The Banner Association," 153–72.
24. See Wanken, "Massachusetts Indian Association," in "'Woman's Sphere' and Indian Reform," 106–40; for Mount Vernon, the Hualapai, Navajo work, and Hensel, see Mathes, "The Banner Association," 151–72.
25. Wanken, "'Woman's Sphere' and Indian Reform," quotes on 109, 115, 116, 117.
26. MIA, *Eighth Annual Report of the MIA, November 1890* (Boston: J. Stilman Smith & Co., 1890), 6; and Wanken, "'Woman's Sphere' and Indian Reform," 140.

27. See Massachusetts Indian Association, Stockbridge Auxiliary Records, 1886–1909, Special Collections and University Archives, University of Massachusetts, Amherst, Massachusetts. Dues were $.50 for women, $5.00 for men with no voting rights.
28. Born in Hawaii to missionary parents, Armstrong commanded African American troops during the Civil War and served as superintendent in Virginia of the Freedmen's Bureau. See the Samuel Chapman Armstrong Papers, Hampton University Archives, Hampton, Virginia, and Special Collections, Williams College, Williamstown, Massachusetts, the latter for a biographical chronology. Armstrong was an 1862 graduate of the college,
29. "Stockbridge," *Annual Report of the MIA, January 1887* (Boston: Frank Wood, Printer, 1887), 14.
30. "Stockbridge," *Annual Report of the MIA, January 1888* (Boston: Frank Wood, 1888), 8.
31. "Stockbridge," *Twelfth Annual Report of the MIA, November 1894* (Boston: J. Stilman Smith & Co., 1894), 9; "Stockbridge," *Twenty-First Annual Report of the MIA, November 1903* (Cambridge: The Powell Press, 1903), 10; and "Stockbridge," *Twenty-Third Annual Report of the MIA, November 1905* (Canton: Office of the Journal Press, 1905), 10.
32. *Twenty-Sixth Annual Report of the MIA, November 1908* (Boston: Frank Wood, 1909), 8–9; branches were in Amherst, Cambridge, Jamaica Plain, and Springfield.
33. WNIA, "Association News and Notes," *The Indian's Friend*, April 1893, 3.
34. Wanken, "'Woman's Sphere' and Indian Reform," 57 for quote.
35. Sarah Whitmer Foster and John T. Foster Jr., "Historic Notes and Documents: Harriet Ward Foote Hawley: Civil War Journalist," *The Florida Historical Quarterly* 83, no. 4 (Spring 2005): 448–67, quote 450. See also Maria Huntington, *Harriet Ward Foote Hawley* (Bibliolife: n.d.), 5–7, a historical reproduction of a work published prior to 1923, written by Maria Huntington and Kate Foote for Hawley's nieces and nephews.
36. Henry S. Cohn, "Mark Twain and Joseph Roswell Hawley," *Mark Twain Journal* 53, no. 2 (Fall 2015): 67–84. Hawley later purchased the *Hartford Courant*, merging the two newspapers.
37. Foster and Foster, "Historic Notes and Documents," 448, quotes on 467.
38. A Unitarian minister, Higginson was an abolitionist, colonel of a regiment of African American troops, advocate for women's rights, author of numerous books and essays, co-editor of a collection of Emily Dickinson's poems, a longtime friend of Helen Hunt Jackson, and a longtime associate with the *Atlantic Monthly*. His papers are in the Boston Public Library; the Houghton Library at Harvard University; and at the University of Nebraska–Lincoln.
39. Foster and Foster, "Historic Notes and Documents," 454–55; see also Huntington, *Harriet Ward Foote Hawley*, 30–35.
40. *The Nation: A Weekly Journal*, vol. 62, March 11, 1886, 205; for descriptions of her nursing career, see Huntington, *Harriet Ward Foote Hawley*, 53–77.
41. Hawley's death moved the WNIA to put together a memorial record of letters by Electa Dawes, Ann Whittlesey, Annie W. Halstead, Anna L. Dawes, and Alice C. Fletcher, for her husband and sister. For quote, see "In Memoriam: Copy of Resolution passed by the WNIA at a meeting held at Mrs. Dawes' residence, March 11, 1886," Harriet Foote Hawley Correspondence, Papers of Joseph Roswell Hawley, Library of Congress, Manuscript Division, Washington, DC, container 27, Reel 15, 9–10 (hereafter cited as "In Memoriam: Copy of Resolution," Hawley Papers). See also Huntington, *Harriet Ward Foote Hawley*, 55–59.
42. For hospital and House of Refuge, see Huntington, *Harriet Ward Foote Hawley*, 96–97, quote on 97.
43. "In Memoriam: Copy of Resolution," Hawley Papers, 5 for quote. For Dawes as vice president, see Mary R. C. Wilbur, *Sketch of the Washington Auxiliary of the National Indian Association, 1882–1903* (Women's National Indian Association, 1903), 3.

44. Quinton, "Care of the Indian," 383. Eliza's husband was Joseph Warren Keifer, an Ohio senator and Speaker of the House.
45. WNIA, "Our Association's Chronology. Number Three," *The Indian's Friend*, March 1897, 2; Wanken, "'Woman's Sphere' and Indian Reform," 42; and Mathes, *Amelia Stone Quinton*, 18.
46. Ellen Terry Johnson, *Historical Sketch of the Connecticut Indian Association from 1881 to 1888* (Hartford: Press of the Fowler & Miller Company, 1888), 9.
47. WNIA, "The Auxiliaries," *Fourth Annual Report*, 19.
48. There is little on Mrs. Whittlesey. Her husband was born in New Britain, Connecticut, attended Yale, taught school, studied theology at Yale and Andover Seminary, and served as pastor of the Central Congregational Church at Bath, Maine. A professor of rhetoric and oratory at Bowdoin College, he served in the Civil War; served as an adjutant general of the Freedmen's Bureau; and aided in the establishment of Howard University, where he also taught. He served on the BIC from 1874 to 1900. For more, see Whittlesey Family Papers, Special Collections and Archives, Bowdoin College Library, Brunswick, Maine.
49. Unitarian minister, abolitionist, coronel of a regiment of African American troops, women's rights advocate, Union general, and member of the Tennessee Freedmen's Bureau, Fisk supported the American Missionary Association in the founding of Fisk University, Nashville. He was a member of WNIA's advisory board.
50. For comments, see BIC, "Journal of the Thirteenth Annual Conference with Representatives of Missionary Boards," in *Fifteenth Annual Report of the BIC for the Year 1883* (Washington, DC: GPO, 1884), 62. For observer's quote, see Huntington, *Harriet Ward Foote Hawley*, 97. She was on crutches because she had injured her knee the previous summer, 96–97.
51. WNIA, "Auxiliaries," *Annual Report of the WNIA, November 17th, 1885*, 22. For other speakers, see Wilbur, *Sketch of the Washington Auxiliary*, 8–9.
52. For background, see Wanken, "Chapter VI: Home Building and Loan," in "'Woman's Sphere' and Indian Reform," 153–81.
53. Wilbur, *Sketch of the Washington Auxiliary*, 4 for quote; and WNIA, "The Auxiliaries," *Annual Report of the WNIA, November 1886*, 23. For last comment, see WNIA, "Auxiliaries," *Annual Report of the WNIA, November 1889* (Philadelphia: J. A. Wilbour Printing House, 1889), 18.
54. LMC, "Education," *Second Annual Address to the Public of the LMC* (Philadelphia: Printed by Order of the Executive Committee of the IRA, 1884), 28. See also W. Roger Buffalohead and Paulette Fairbanks Molin, "'A Nucleus of Civilization': American Indian Families at Hampton Institute in the Late Nineteenth Century," *Journal of American Indian Education* 35, no. 3 (Spring): 59–94.
55. Johnson, *Historical Sketch of the Connecticut Indian Association*, 11–12 for quotes.
56. WNIA, "The Report of the General Secretary," *Annual Report of the WNIA, November 17th, 1885* (Philadelphia: Grant & Faires, 1885), 11.
57. "Outside Testimony: A Letter from Miss Alice C. Fletcher, February 8, 1888," *Ten Years' Work for Indians at Hampton Institute, Virginia* (Hampton, VA: The Hampton Institute, 1888), 62.
58. WNIA, "The Annual Address of the President, Mrs. A. S. Quinton," *The Indian's Friend*, January 1889, 3; this November 7, 1888, address was reprinted as a pamphlet.
59. Lori Jacobson, "'Environed by Civilization': WNIA Home-Building and Loan Department," in *The Women's National Indian Association: A History*, ed. Valerie Sherer Mathes, 65–83 (Albuquerque: University of New Mexico Press, 2015), quote on 71. See also Jane E. Simonsen, "Object Lessons: Domesticity on Display in Native American Assimilation," in her *Making Home Work: Domesticity and Native American Assimilation in the American West, 1860–1919* (Chapel Hill: University of North Carolina Press, 2006), 71–109.

NOTES

60. "The National Capital. Death of Senator Hawley's Wife," March 4, 1886, 3; and "Obituary. Mrs. General Hawley," March 4, 1886, 2, both in the *Hartford Daily Courant*; see also *The Hamilton Literary Monthly. Conducted by the Senior Class of Hamilton College* 20, no. 9 (May 1886), 337. Hawley attended the college. For quote, see WNIA, *Annual Report of the WNIA, November, 1886* (Philadelphia: Royal Printing Company, 1886), 34.

61. For resolution, see 4; for Sunderland, see 6; for Anna, see "Memorial Address by Miss Anna L. Dawes," quotes 11, 16, 17, all in "In Memoriam: Copy of Resolution," Hawley Papers. For tablet, see Huntington, *Harriet Ward Foote Hawley*, 104.

62. For Fletcher, see "The closing tribute was given with tearful emotion by Miss Alice C. Fletcher," quotes 21, 22, 23; and for Ann, see "Mrs. Gen'l Whittlesey said," 7, in "In Memoriam: Copy of Resolution," Hawley Papers.

63. WNIA, "Auxiliaries," *Annual Report of the WNIA, November, 1890* (Philadelphia: Press of J. A. Wilbour, 1890), 15; and WNIA, "Auxiliaries," *Annual Report of the WNIA, November 1891*, 14.

64. "Kate Foote Coe," *An Historic Record and Pictorial Description of the Town of Meriden, Connecticut*, compiled by C. Bancroft Gillespie (Meriden: Journal Publishing Co., 1906), 320–22, quote on 321; and *Society in Washington. Its Noted Men, Accomplished Women, Established Customs, and Notable Events* (Washington, DC: Harrisburg Publishing Company, 1887), 98.

65. Beecher was the eldest of the nine children of Roxana Foote and Lyman Beecher. In "dame schools," girls learned manners, languages, and fine arts while at Beecher's, they learned world history, philosophy, natural sciences, and Latin, and took physical education classes; see "May 20: Catharine Beecher Opens Hartford Female Seminary," https://todayincthistory.com/2019/05/20/may-20-hartford-female-seminary-opens/.

66. The society, founded in Boston in 1862, disbanded in 1874, published a monthly, *The Freedmen's Record*. For description, see New England Freedmen's Aid Society Records, Massachusetts Historical Society, Boston, Massachusetts.

67. "Letters from the People. Mrs. Coe," *Hartford Courant*, December 26, 1923, 14, an obituary written by an anonymous contributor.

68. For a short story, see "A Pistol Shot," in *Century*; see "Literature: Late Publications and Gossip About Authors," *San Jose Mercury*, September 19, 1886, 6; and for an article in *The Independent*, see "A Hint to the Evolutionist," *Truckee* (California) *Republican*, May 10, 1884, 4.

69. "Kate Foote Coe," *An Historic Record and Pictorial Description*, 320–21. See also "D.A.R. Memorial," *Centennial of Meriden, June 10–16, 1906* (Meriden: The Journal Publishing Co., 1906), 146; and *The Spirit of '76*, no. 15 (November 1895), 70.

70. Founded in 1868 by journalists Jane Cunningham Croly and Sara Willis Parton, chapters were established in other cities. In 1873, 400 club members organized the Association for the Advancement of Women, with Fletcher elected as association secretary. See Sorosis Records, Sophia Smith Collection of Women's History, Smith College, Northampton, Massachusetts. For Fletcher's membership, see Joan Mark, *A Stranger in Her Native Land: Alice Fletcher and the American Indians* (Lincoln: University of Nebraska Press, 1988), 17–19; for Foote in Alaska, see 138. For more on Fletcher, see Jacobs, *White Mother to a Dark Race*, numerous pages, 98 for membership in Sorosis.

71. During her visit, Fletcher formed a friendship with Francis La Flesche, Susette's brother. Francis, a clerk in the Indian Office, was a respected ethnologist, an expert on the Omaha and Osage, and co-author of *The Omaha Tribe* with Fletcher. See Mark, *A Stranger in Her Native Land*, 45–53; Sherry L. Smith, "Francis La Flesche and the World of Letters," *American Indian Quarterly* 25, no. 4 (Autumn 2001): 570–603; and Jacobs, *After One Hundred Winters*, 131–46, 152, 155–57, 160–61. In 1887, Fletcher allotted Winnebago land, and in 1889 the Nez Perce reservation.

NOTES

72. Fletcher to Dawes, February 4, 1882, Henry L. Dawes Papers, Library of Congress, Washington, DC, reprinted with an introduction and editorial comments as "'I Plead for Them': An 1882 Letter from Alice Cunningham Fletcher to Senator Henry Dawes," ed. Valerie Sherer Mathes and Richard Lowitt, *Nebraska History* 84, no. 1 (Spring 2003): 36–41, quote on 38.
73. Mark, *A Stranger in Her Native Land*, quotes on 265, 267; and Senier, *Voices of American Indian Assimilation*, 63.
74. Jackson went to Alaska in 1877, the first of twenty-six trips, opening missions in Sitka and Point Barrow and founding an industrial school in Sitka, later known as the Sheldon Jackson Junior College. It continued until 2007. See Sheldon Jackson Papers, the Presbyterian Historical Society, Philadelphia, Pennsylvania.
75. For trip, see Mark, *A Stranger in Her Native Land*, 138–46. For blankets, see *Science*, New Series, vol. 17, February 20, 1903 (New York: The MacMillan Company, 1903), 289. Chilkat blankets, woven by Tlingit and Haida women out of mountain goat hair and cedar bark, were worn over the shoulder during ceremonial dances.
76. BIC, "Journal of the Seventeenth Annual Conference with Representatives of Missionary Boards and Indian Rights Association," *Nineteenth Annual Report of the BIC, 1887* (Washington, DC: GPO, 1887), 136; and WNIA, "Our Association's Chronology. Number Fourteen," *The Indian's Friend*, April 1898, 2. Electa Dawes, an officer of the Washington auxiliary and president of the Pittsfield, Massachusetts, auxiliary, came up with the idea of sponsoring farmers.
77. For first quote, see WNIA, *Our Work: What? How? Why?* (Philadelphia: January 1893), 25. Wanken, "'Woman's Sphere' and Indian Reform," 144–46, second quote on 145.
78. *The Indian Bulletin*, June 1892, 1.
79. Kate Foote, *Indian Bills in Congress* (Philadelphia; November 1889), quote 7. See also Kate Foote, *The Indian Legislation of 1888* (Philadelphia: Press of the J. F. Dickson Printing Company, 1888), and Kate Foote, *Indian Legislation—As Far As It Goes* (Philadelphia: November 1891).
80. "Annual Session of the Women's National Indian Association at Newark," *Sacramento Daily Union*, November 22, 1889, 1.
81. WNIA, June 1894, 1; and WNIA, "Needed Indian Legislation: Read at the Annual Convention," January 1894, 8, both in *The Indian's Friend*.
82. LMC, *Proceedings of the Eighth Annual Meeting of the LMC, 1890* (LMC: 1890), 98.
83. "A Prominent Indian Worker," *Pittsburg Dispatch*, November 18, 1891, 5.
84. For his tenure, see Gregory C. Thompson, "John D. C. Atkins, 1885–88," *The Commissioners of Indian Affairs, 1824–1977*, ed. Robert M. Kvasnicka and Herman J. Viola (Lincoln: University of Nebraska Press, 1979), 181–88; and David H. DeJong, "Commissioner John D. Atkins," *The Commissioners of Indian Affairs: The United States Indian Service and the Making of Federal Indian Policy, 1824–2017* (Salt Lake City: University of Utah Press, 2020), 76–80.
85. Foote to Atkins, November 15, 1887, Letter Received (LR) #30655-1887, Record Group 75, Office of Indian Affairs, National Archives and Records Administration (hereafter LR, RG 75, OIA, NARA). It is unknown if Atkins complied. Chippewa lands were opened in October 1882 by the interior secretary; see *The History and Culture of the Turtle Mountain Band of Chippewa*, a 1997 publication of the North Dakota Department of Public Instruction, 15–16.
86. In a letter to the editor, Father Jean Baptiste Marie Genin described Chippewa deaths; see www.chippewaheritage.com/heritage-blog2/archives/03-2012/2#:~:text.
87. Foote to Atkins, May 17, 1888, LR #13024-1888, RG 75, OIA, NARA.
88. WNIA, "Latest Indian Legislation," *The Indian's Friend*, February 1889, 1.
89. WNIA, "Legislation at Headquarters," *The Indian's Friend*, March 1889, 1.

NOTES

90. The "Act for the Relief of the Mission Indians in the State of California," see U.S. Congress, Senate, "Message from the President of the U.S.; S. Ex. Doc. 49, 48th Cong. 1st Sess., 1884, 1–7 (text of Jackson/Kinney Report followed), 7–37. The text is reprinted as "Report on the Condition and Needs of the Mission Indians of California, Made by Special Agents Helen Jackson and Abbot Kinney, to the Commissioner of Indian Affairs," in Helen Hunt Jackson, *A Century of Dishonor: A Sketch of the United States Government's Dealings with Some of the Indian Tribes* (Norman: University of Oklahoma Press, 1995 [Boston: Roberts Brothers, 1888]), 458–514; for her recommendations, see 464–74; 467 for quotes. See also Senier, *Voices of American Indian Assimilation*, 5–7, 41–49, 63–64.

91. Foote, *The Indian Legislation of 1888*, 5, for first quote, and WNIA, "Indian Legislation," *The Indian's Friend*, September 1890, 1, for the second.

92. For clipping, see Mrs. John Hiles to Cleveland, August 12, 1885, LR #19236-1885, RG 75, OIA, NARA. See also Francis Paul Prucha, "A 'Friend of the Indian' in Milwaukee: Mrs. O. J. Hiles and the Wisconsin Indian Association," *Indian Policy in the United States*, 214–28; Mathes, *Helen Hunt Jackson and Her Indian Reform Legacy*, 92, 95, 100–106, 108, 119–21, 153, 155; and Mathes, *Divinely Guided*, 183–89, 191–92, 194, 262.

93. For appointment, see "Short Locals," *The Daily Courier* (San Bernardino), November 21, 1890, 3 noting that Foote, a "special agent of the eleventh census, left yesterday for New York."

94. For Rust's tenure, see Valerie Sherer Mathes and Phil Brigandi, "A Controversial Collector: Horatio Nelson Rust, 1889–1893," *Reservations, Removal, and Reform: The Mission Indian Agents of Southern California, 1878–1903* (Norman: University of Oklahoma Press, 2018), 98–132. For edited versions of some articles, see *A Call for Reform: The Southern California Indian Writings of Helen Hunt Jackson*, ed. Valerie Sherer Mathes and Phil Brigandi (Norman: University of Oklahoma Press, 2015).

95. WNIA, "Association News and Notes," *The Indian's Friend*, November 1890, 1. For census taken "as fully as possible," see "Rust, Report of Mission Agency, August 8, 1890," *Fifty-Ninth Annual Report of the Commissioner of Indian Affairs to the Secretary of the Interior, 1890 [ARCIA]* (Washington, DC: GPO, 1890), 17.

96. For the Cupeño, see A. L. Kroeber, *Handbook of the Indians of California* (New York: Dover Publications, Inc., 1976), 689–92.

97. Caroline H. Dall, "Concerning Women," *The Cambridge Tribune*, December 27, 1890, 4. Dall—a reformer, feminist, essayist, and author of numerous books, articles, and newspaper columns, and an abolitionist—also founded the American Social Science Association. See the Caroline Wells Healey Dall Papers, Massachusetts Historical Society, Boston, Massachusetts.

98. Funding from the IRA and a court case in 1888 saved Soboba; see Mathes, *Helen Hunt Jackson*, 38–94; Mathes and Brigandi, eds, *A Call for Reform*, 23, 35, 42, 44–48, 75, 76, 98–101, 158–60, 173–83; Mathes, *Divinely Guided*, 177–203; and Van H. Garner, "Soboba," *The Broken Ring: The Destruction of the California Indians* (Tucson: Westernlore Press, 1982), 75–95.

99. LMC, "Fifth Session," *Proceedings of the Eighth Annual Meeting of the LMC*, 96. For letter mention, see "Mission Indian Conference. A Bit of Sensation," *Sacramento Daily Union*, October 11, 1890, 1. Foote was reported as "making an official visit to the Mission Indians of California," whom she described as "still the victims of the greed of their white neighbors." The letter was also reported in *The San Francisco Morning Call*, October 11, 1890, 1.

100. LMC, "Fifth Session," *Proceedings of the Eighth Annual Meeting of the LMC*, 96–97.

101. Lawrence C. Kelly, *The Navajo Indians and Federal Indian Policy, 1900–1935* (Tucson: University of Arizona Press, 1970), writes, an "executive-order reservation was a unilateral creation of the President which the Congress had neither the power to approve nor reject" (20).

102. There were in fact eighteen treaties negotiated between 1851 and 1852 but never ratified by the Senate;

see Larisa K. Miller, "The Secret Treaties with California's Indians," *Prologue* 45, no. 3 (Fall–Winter 2013): 38–45. This lack of ratification meant no annuities or goods were ever issued; thus the NCIA went to great lengths to provide the Indians with small parcels of land after they had been dispossessed by white settlers.

103. "Mission Indians: Report of Special Agent Miss Kate Foote," *Report of the Indians Taxed and Indians not Taxed in the United States. Eleventh Census: 1890* (Washington, DC: GPO, 1894), report 207–16, quotes on 212, 214, 215.

104. WNIA, "Indian Legislation," January 1891, 1; and "Indian Legislation," February 1891, 1, both in *The Indian's Friend*. "An Act for the Relief of the Mission Indians in the State of California" was listed in "Indian Legislation Passed During the Second Session of the Fifty-First Congress," *Sixtieth ARCIA, 1891* (Washington, DC: GPO, 1891), 612–14; see also 47–48.

105. For Dawes's comment, see 24 and for Smiley and Foote, 24–25, in LMC, *Proceedings of the Ninth Annual Meeting of the LMC, 1891* (LMC: 1891). For Foote, see "The Indian Conference. Encouraging Reports of Work Among the Red Men," *New York Times*, October 8, 1891, 3.

106. See Prucha, "Thomas Jefferson Morgan, 1889–93," *The Commissioners of Indian Affairs*, 193–203; and DeJong, "Commissioner Thomas Jefferson Morgan," *The Commissioners of Indian Affairs*, 83–87. Morgan promoted assimilation and education.

107. Mathes, "A Hospital at Warner Ranch," in *Divinely Guided*, 231–61.

108. The third member was a Michigan attorney, Joseph B. Moore. Only Painter remained in California for eleven months to complete the task. See WNIA, "Association News and Notes," *The Indian's Friend*, May 1892, 1; Valerie Sherer Mathes, "The California Mission Indian Commission of 1891: The Legacy of Helen Hunt Jackson," *California History* 72, no. 4 (Winter 1993/94): 339–58, notes 390–95; Larry E. Burgess, "Commission to the Mission Indians, 1891," *San Bernardino County Museum Quarterly* (Spring 1988): 1–47; and Mathes, *Charles C. Painter*, 162–82.

109. For $100, see WNIA, "Washington," *The Indian's Friend*, June 1892, 41.

110. For Bidwell's reform work, see Valerie Sherer Mathes, "Indian Philanthropy in California: Annie Bidwell and the Mechoopda Indians," *Arizona and the West* 25, no. 2 (Summer 1983): 153–66; Valerie Sherer Mathes, "Annie E. K. Bidwell: Chico's Benefactress," *California History* 68, nos. 1–2 (Winter 1993/94): 339–58, notes 390–95; and Valerie Sherer Mathes, "The Indian Reform Work of Annie Ellicott Kenney Bidwell," in *Divinely Guided*, 153–76. Bidwell died on March 9, 1918; see NIA, "In Memoriam: Mrs. Annie E. K. Bidwell," *The Indian's Friend*, May 1918, 2, 5, 6.

111. "Thomson H. Alexander," *Eminent and Representative Men of Virginia and the District of Columbia of the Nineteenth Century* (Madison: Brant & Fuller, 1893), 36–37; and WNIA, "Washington," *The Indian's Friend*, March 1893, 3.

112. For May meeting, see WNIA, "Washington," *The Indian's Friend*, June 1892, 41. See also Valerie Sherer Mathes, "Dr. Susan La Flesche Picotte: The Reformed and the Reformer," in *Indian Lives: Essays on Nineteenth- and-Twentieth-Century Native American Leaders*, ed. L. G. Moses and Raymond Wilson (Albuquerque. University of New Mexico Press, 1985), 61–90; for her alcohol crusade, see 74–77, 80; and also, Peggy Pascoe, *Relations of Rescue: The Search for Female Moral Authority in the American West, 1874–1939* (Oxford: Oxford University Press, 1990), 123–27, 134–35, 139–43, 152–53, 202–3.

113. WNIA, "Washington," *The Indian's Friend*, March 1893, 3, for ASQ.

114. For Foote, see WNIA, "Washington," *The Indian's Friend*, March 1893, 3.

115. "Miss Kate Foote Appointed," *Evening Journal*, July 28, 1892, 5. This Wilmington, Delaware, newspaper used the same wording as her commission; see "Commission for Appointment of Miss Kate Foote," July 27, 1892, LS #27160-1892, RG 75, OIA, NARA.

116. Foote to Morgan, July 29, 1892, LR #27419-1892, SC 147, RG 75, OIA, NARA.

NOTES

117. Morgan to Foote, August 5, 1892 [Letters Sent: Accounts Division], LS Div. A, #27160 & 27767-1892, Vol. 133, Letter Book 265, p. 177, RG 75, OIA, NARA.
118. Morgan to Foote, August 20, 1892, LS, Div. A, #29753-1892, Vol. 133, LB 266, p. 136, RG 75, OIA, NARA.
119. Painter to Welsh, September 19, 1892, *IRA Papers*, Reel 9.
120. Foote to Morgan, October 22, 1892, LR #39009-1892, SC 31, RG 75, OIA, NARA.
121. Morgan to Bussey, November 3, 1892, LS, Land Division, #89009-1892, Vol. 124, LB 247, pp. 257–58, RG 75, OIA, NARA.
122. Bussey to Morgan, November 5, 1892, LR #40040-1892, RG 75, OIA, NARA.
123. Belt to Foote, November 18, 1892, LS, Land Division, Vol. 124, LB 248, p. 81, RG 75, OIA, NARA.
124. Foote to Morgan, November 24, 1892, LR #41997-1892, SC 31, RG 75, OIA, NARA.
125. Noble to Foote, December 23, 1892, LR #45613-1892, RG 75, OIA, NARA.
126. Painter to Morgan, January 9, 1893, LR #1223-1893, SC 31, RG 75, OIA, NARA.
127. Agua Caliente Indian Reservation was home of the Agua Caliente band of Cahuillas.
128. Painter to Morgan, January 9, 1893. For his work with Dorn, see Mathes, *Charles C. Painter*, 171, 174, and 212–13.
129. To avoid confusion with the village of Agua Caliente on Warner Ranch, the Agua Caliente band at Palm Springs was designated as No. 2.
130. Foote to Bradford, February 17, 1893, LR #6264-1893, RG 75, OIA, NARA.
131. Foote to Bradford, February 17, 1893.
132. WNIA, "Association News and Notes," *The Indian's Friend*, November 1892, 2.
133. WNIA, "Association News and Notes," *The Indian's Friend*, February 1893, 1.
134. "To Meet Today. The New Haven Indian Association," *Morning Journal and Courier* (New Haven), May 6, 1893, 2.
135. WNIA, "Association News and Notes," *The Indian's Friend*, May 1893, 3.
136. "Estudillo, Report of Mission Tule River Agency, August 31, 1893," *Sixty-Second ARCIA, 1893* (Washington, DC: GPO, 1893), 128.
137. For tenure, see William T. Hagan, "Daniel M. Browning, 1893–97," *The Commissioners of Indian Affairs*, eds. Kvasnicka and Viola, 205–9, and DeJong, "Commissioner Daniel Browning," *The Commissioners of Indian Affairs*, eds. Kvasnicka and Viola, 87–91. In 1876, by executive order, President Grant created the Los Torres and Martínez reservations; they were combined in 1891.
138. Foote to Browning, September 4, 1893, LR #33323-1893, RG 75, OIA, NARA.
139. Salmons had a 37-year teaching career in government schools, beginning circa 1885 at Rincon, and from 1904 to 1922 at Pala. See Joel R. Hyer, *"We Are Not Savages": Native Americans in Southern California and the Pala Reservation, 1840–1920* (East Lansing: Michigan State University Press, 2001), 151, 154–67, 169–70. For comments about allotment, see WNIA, "News and Notes," *The Indian's Friend*, February 1894, 2.
140. "In and About the City. Miss Howard's Mission," *New York Times*, June 21, 1887, 8, for quotes; for her address, see WNIA, "Auxiliaries," *Annual Report of the WNIA, December, 1893* (Lancaster: Examiner Printing House, 1893), 19. For her father, see "Joseph Howard's Funeral," *New York Times*, April 4, 1908, 9.
141. "Report of W. W. Anderson, Agent Crow Creek and Lower Brulé Agency, Dakota," *The Executive Documents of the House of Representatives for the First Session of the Fiftieth Congress, 1887–'88* (Washington, DC: GPO, 1889), 878.
142. WNIA, "Grace Mission," *The Indian's Friend*, February 1890, 3.
143. "Alice Robertson Dies. Aided Indians, Second Woman Elected to Congress, Representing Oklahoma

District," *New York Times*, July 2, 1931, 27.

144. For addresses, see WNIA, "Association News and Notes," *The Indian's Friend*, April 1893, 3; and WNIA, "Auxiliaries," *Annual Report of the WNIA, December, 1893* (Lancaster: Examiner Printing House, 1893), 19.

145. WNIA, "Auxiliaries," *Annual Report of the WNIA, December, 1893*, 9–10 for annual meeting, and 35–36 for delegates.

146. LMC, "Miss Kate Foote," *Proceedings of the Twelfth Annual Meeting of the LMC, 1894* (LMC, 1894), 152.

147. "Miss Kate Foote Is to Wed," *The Inter Ocean* (Chicago), December 18, 1894, 6.

148. WNIA, "News and Notes," *The Indian's Friend*, February 1895, 4.

149. Swiss born, Hailmann founded the first kindergarten in the US and served as Superintendent of Indian Education from 1894 to 1898. He died in Pasadena, California, in 1920. For more, see Dorothy W. Hewes, "Those First Good Years of Indian Education: 1894–1898," *American Indian Culture and Research Journal* 5, no. 2 (1981): 63–82.

150. Foote to Hailmann, February 6, 1895, LR #5848-1895, RG 75, OIA, NARA.

151. For talk, see WNIA, "News and Notes," *The Indian's Friend*, May 1895, 2; and WNIA, "Auxiliaries," *Annual Report of the WNIA, December 1895* (Lancaster: Examiner Publishing House, 1895), 17, for presidency. Foote died December 23, 1923.

152. For a detailed report on her work, see WNIA, "Agua Caliente," *Sunshine Work* (WNIA: December 1894), 14–24, and chapter 5 in this book.

153. See Nicole Tonkovich, "'Lost in the General Wreckage of the Far West': The Photographs and Writings of Jane Gay," in *Trading Gazes: Euro-American Women Photographers and Native North Americans, 1880–1940*, Susan Bernardin, Melody Graulich, Lisa MacFarlane, and Nicole Tonkovich (New Brunswick: Rutgers University Press, 2003), 32–70.

154. WNIA, "News and Notes," *The Indian's Friend*, April 1895, 2; see also WNIA, "Auxiliaries," *Annual Report of the WNIA, December, 1895* (Lancaster: Examiner Publishing House, 1895), 21–22. See also Frank B. Williams, "John Eaton, Jr.: Editor, Politician, and School Administrator, 1865–1870," *Tennessee Historical Quarterly* 10, no. 4 (December 1951), 291–319. For Pratt, see Richard Henry Pratt Papers, Beinecke Rare Book & Manuscript Library, Yale University, New Haven, Connecticut.

155. WNIA, "Our Washington Auxiliary," *The Indian's Friend*, May 1895, 3, 6, quotes on 6; and *The Indian's Friend*, July 1895, 5.

156. WNIA, "News and Notes," *The Indian's Friend*, April 1896, 4. For Leupp's tenure, see Donald L. Parman, "Francis Ellington Leupp, 1905–1909," *The Commissioners of Indian Affairs*, 221–32; and DeJong, "Commissioner Francis E. Leupp, *The Commissioners of Indian Affairs*, 99–107.

157. WNIA, "News and Notes," *The Indian's Friend*, April 1896, 4. For background, see Mathes, *Amelia Stone Quinton*, 242–44.

158. WNIA, "News and Notes," June 1900, 4; and "News and Notes," October 1900, 4, in *The Indian's Friend*. See also WNIA, "The Mission of New Jersey," *The Report of Missions for 1900* (WNIA: 1900), 27.

159. NIA, *Annual Report of the NIA, December 1902* (Philadelphia, 1902), quote 9, and NIA, "News and Notes," *The Indian's Friend*, June 1903, 4.

160. Hastings, with a Cherokee grandmother, graduated with a law degree from Vanderbilt University, opening a law practice in Tahlequah, Indian Territory in 1889. He was principal of the Cherokee Orphan Asylum, superintendent of tribal education, attorney general, and national attorney for the Cherokee Nation. Elected to the House of Representatives in 1914, he lost in 1920 to Alice Robertson, but was elected again in 1922, serving until 1935. See https://www.okhistory.org/publications/enc/

entry?entry=HA051.
161. Owen taught at the Cherokee Orphan Asylum in Tahlequah, studied law on his own, practiced in the Cherokee National courts, and was appointed in 1885 as the agent for the Union Agency, becoming the "principal federal official overseeing an area of approximately 19.5 million acres in the eastern half of present-day Oklahoma." Advocating for separate statehood for Indian Territory, one month after Oklahoma was granted statehood, he took his seat in the Senate. See Kenny Lee Brown, "Robert Latham Owen, Jr.: His Careers as Indian Attorney and Progressive Senator" (PhD diss., Oklahoma State University, 1975), 49.
162. A reference used by historians and genealogists during pre-statehood. As a viable territory, Indian Territory was not formally organized until the May 1890 Organic Act.
163. NIA, "Auxiliaries and Branches," *Annual Report of the NIA, December 1906* (New York, 1906), 19–20. For background, see Prucha, *The Great Father*, vol. 2, 737–57.
164. NIA, "The Washington, D.C. Association," *The Indian's Friend*, February 1908, 4; for more on Woodruff, see "Assistant Attorney General," *Yale Alumni Weekly* 16, no. 30 (April 17, 1907): 687.
165. NIA, "Auxiliaries and Branches," *Annual Report of the NIA, December 1907* (New York: 1907), 17.
166. NIA, "The Washington, D.C. Auxiliary," *Annual Report of the NIA, 1908* (New York: 1908), 18; for another meeting, see NIA, "The Washington, D.C., Indian Association," *The Indian's Friend*, June 1908, 4.
167. "Jane Douglas Butler Chany," *Woman's Who's Who of America*, ed. John William Leonard (New York: The American Commonwealth Company, 1915), 171. She died in November 1914; see NIA, "News and Notes," "Mrs. William H. Chany," *The Indian's Friend*, December 1914, 4. For memorial service, see NIA, "Washington, D.C. Indian Association. Memorial Service," *The Indian's Friend*, January 1915, 4.
168. NIA, "Washington, D.C. Indian Association," December 1910, 5, and "Washington, D.C., Indian Association," December 1911, 4–5, 5, in *The Indian's Friend*. For a history of the Society, see Lucy Maddox, *Citizen Indians: Native American Intellectuals, Race & Reform* (Ithaca, NY: Cornell University Press, 2005).
169. NIA, "Washington D.C. Indian Association," *The Indian's Friend*, December 1913, 5. See also NIA, "Our Navajo Mission and Hospital," *The Report of Missions, 1913* (WNIA: 1913), 5–14.
170. NIA, "Washington, D.C. Indian Association," *The Indian's Friend*, January 1914, 5. Sculpting the full-size statue of Lincoln in the basement of the Capitol, using an earlier clay mask she made while observing him sitting at his desk and clothing he had worn the night of his assassination, she also crafted the bronze monument to Admiral David Farragut. Cutting back after her 1878 marriage to Hoxie, in 1906 she created the bronze statue of Samuel Kirkwood for the National Statuary Hall, and had completed the plaster model of Sequoyah, the creator of the Cherokee syllabary, before her death on November 20, 1914. Her friend and fellow sculptor George Zolnay completed the monument. https://www.womenhistoryblog.com/1007/01/vinnie-ream.html; and "Hoxie, Vinnie Ream," *Woman's Who's Who of America, 1914–1915* (New York: The American Commonwealth Company, 1914), 410.
171. NIA, "The Year's Work," Forty-First Annual Report of the NIA (New York: 1920), 16, 19.
172. NIA, "Reports of Our Auxiliaries and Branches," *Fifty-Fourth Annual Report of the NIA* (New York: 1933), 11.

Chapter 3

1. Hawley was listed as a committee member in "Twenty Years of Work by the Association," *The Indian Bulletin*, November 1901, 3.
2. Nick Streifel, "Crisis Management during the American Civil War: The Hartford Soldiers' Aid Society,"

NOTES

ConnecticutHistory.org, and letter from Sarah S. Cowan [*sic*] on Hartford Soldiers Aid Association stationery to Sarah Low, August 13, 1864, Call Number: 1965.010, New Hampshire Historical Society, Concord, New Hampshire. Cowen was born on June 29, 1820, in Brooklyn, Connecticut, and died in Hartford on June 24, 1887; see Willard I. Tyler Brigham, "3379: Sarah Sophia Tyler, *The Tyler Genealogy: The Descendants of Job Tyler, of Andover Massachusetts, 1619–1700*, vol. II (Plainfield: Published by Cornelius B. Tyler, 1912), 577. Her husband, a lawyer, authored a treatise on civil jurisdiction.

3. Wanken, "'Woman's Sphere' and Indian Reform," 61.
4. Kinney was born on April 21, 1842, to Dr. Charles Steele Thomson, a Fair Haven, Connecticut, physician, and Susan Coit Belcher Thomson. She married J. C. Kinney, editor of the *Hartford Courant*. Interested in genealogy, she served on various commissions at governors' discretion, the last to save the flagship *Hartford*, rotting in Charleston Harbor. She died on December 14, 1922. For more, see the introduction to the Sara A. Thomson-Kinney Papers, Connecticut State Library, Hartford, Connecticut.
5. Johnson, *Historical Sketch of the Connecticut Indian Association*, 5 for Hawley, 9–10 for dates, 54 for charter and quote. See also WNIA, "Honorary Vice-Presidents," *Annual Report of the WNIA, November 30, 1887*, 5, for Stowe; and WNIA, *Annual Report of the WNIA, December 1898*, 7, for Scoville.
6. Johnson, *Historical Sketch of the Connecticut Indian Association*, 33.
7. For election, see "Waterbury," *The Indian Bulletin*, April 1901, 1. For her work, see Mathes, "Constance Goddard DuBois: Indian Reformer," 184–219; Don Laylander, "Early Ethnographic Notes from Constance Goddard DuBois on the Indians of San Diego County," *Journal of California and Great Basin Anthropology* 26, no. 2 (2006): 205–14; and Erik Krenzen Trump, "The Indian Industries League and Its Support of American Indian Arts, 1893–1922: A Study of Changing Attitudes Toward Indian Women and Assimilationist Policy" (PhD diss., Boston University, 1996), 303–33.
8. Don Laylander, ed., "Constance Goddard DuBois," in *Listening to the Raven: The Southern California Ethnography of Constance Goddard DuBois* (Salinas, CA: Coyote Press, 2004), 14. The 1900 federal census listed her as Conkey's partner, in 1910 as a boarder; see also "Caroline Root Conkey, MD, Waterbury," *Proceedings of the Connecticut State Medical Society, 1918* (Published by the Society, 1918), 209–10. For Conkey's membership, see *The Indian Bulletin*, December 1892, 1, and for attendance at October meeting, see *Waterbury Evening Democrat*, October 16, 1889, 4.
9. Laylander, ed., *Listening to the Raven*, 14, claims CGD was visiting her sister, Mary Delafield DuBois, and her husband (John J. Mathers).
10. For a list of her 239 photographs, see the finding aid for the CGD Collection, San Diego Museum of Us (formerly the Museum of Man), San Diego, California. On page 4 under Lipay Nation of Santa Ysabel, she had written: "My first trip among the Mission Indians-1897."
11. Erik Trump, "'The Idea of Help': White Women Reformers and the Commercialization of Native American Women's Arts," in *Selling the Indian: Commercializing & Appropriating American Indian Cultures*, ed. Carter Jones Meyer and Diana Royer (Tucson: University of Arizona Press, 2001), 173, 175 for quotes; see also 177. He described three Indian art markets: the curio, the art market, and "the philanthropist, the white women who bought Indian arts from the conviction that doing so gave economic support to individual Indians" (159). He put CGD in this third category.
12. For Kinney's support to open a market for Indian-made products, see "Report for the Nineteenth Year of the Connecticut Indian Association," *The Indian Bulletin*, April 1901, 2.
13. According to "Founding a National Movement," *Out West*, January 1902, 66, the League's slogan was "To Make Better Indians," and its mandate was "to forward and assist a more tolerable policy toward the Indians of California." See also "To Make Better Indians," *Out West*, February 1902, 177–79. Lummis (CFL) informed President William Howard Taft that he had founded it to "focus public

sentiment locally to aid the Indian service"; see CFL to Taft, March 7, 1909, Sequoya League Series (folder-Correspondence, 1909), Charles F. Lummis Manuscript Collection, Braun Research Library, Southwest Museum, Autry Museum of the American West, Los Angeles, California (hereafter CFL Collection, Braun Research Library). See also Frances E. Watkins, "Charles F. Lummis and the Sequoya League," *The Quarterly: Historical Society of Southern California* 26, nos. 2–3 (June–September 1944), 99–114. Board members included George Bird Grinnell, editor-in-chief of *Forest and Stream*; Phoebe A. Hearst, founder of the University of California's anthropology department; Major John Wesley Powell, head of the Bureau of American Ethnology; Thomas R. Bard, California U.S. Senator; F. W. Hodge, of the Smithsonian Institution; David Starr Jordan, president of Stanford University; Estelle Reel, Superintendent of Indian education; and Hamlin Garland, novelist, poet, and essayist; see Mark Thompson, *American Character: The Curious Life of Charles Fletcher Lummis and the Rediscovery of the Southwest* (New York: Arcade Publishing, 2001), 216, for names.

14. Valerie Sherer Mathes, "C. E. Kelsey and California's Landless Indians," *Gender, Race, and Power*, 163–81.
15. For ethnological contributions, see Laylander, ed., *Listening to the Raven*.
16. See the finding aid in the CGD Collection.
17. *Bulletin of the Gray Memorial Botanical Chapter of the Agassiz*, no. 1 (Second Quarter, 1893): 10 for her listing as general secretary; *The Asa Gray Bulletin*, no. 2 (Third Quarter, 1893): 1 as general secretary; *The Asa Gray Bulletin* 3, no. 8 (January 1895): 2, 6, for a short article, 6 for associate editor; and *The Asa Gray Bulletin* 4, no. 1 (January 1896): as publisher, 9. The January 1897 issue of the *Bulletin*, 15, announced a change of management, with the publisher's office moving to the Agricultural College in Michigan. Asa Gray, a graduate of the Fairfield Medical School of New York, was a self-educated botanist, accepting a professorship of natural history at Harvard in 1842. He published and edited the *American Journal of Science*.
18. For a list, see Laylander, ed., *Listening to the Raven*, 171–72.
19. Constance Goddard DuBois, *A Soul in Bronze: A Novel of Southern California* (Chicago: Herbert S. Stone and Company, 1900), dedication in the front, 220 for quote.
20. Lummis, "In the Lion's Den," *The Land of Sunshine*, July 1898, 80, first quote and in "In Western Letters," *The Land of Sunshine*, January 1901, 27, for second quote.
21. Lummis, "In the Lion's Den," *The Land of Sunshine*, May 1899, 351. Phil Brigandi, in "Her Soul Is Marching On': Helen Hunt Jackson's Followers in the Indian Reform Movement," in *Gender, Race, and Power*, longtime historian for the Ramona Pageant Association in Hemet, describes *A Soul in Bronze* as tracing "the often sad history of Antonio Lachusa, who suffers stoically and philosophically through it all." This novel, as in *Ramona*, has Anglo characters "who must learn to change their views about Indians, and she even borrows Father Gaspara from Jackson as a character." He concludes, however, that the novel "lacks the geography of *Ramona* and is built on a smaller scale, lacking the broad events drawn from the actual history of the region" (115–16).
22. "Literary Notes," *City and State*, December 6, 1900, 364.
23. Constance Goddard DuBois, "Our American 'Reconcentrados,'" *City and State*, November 8, 1900, 297–99.
24. Hagan, *The IRA*, quotes, 4, 150. Donald W. Disbrow, "Herbert Welsh, Editor of City and State, 1895–1904," *Pennsylvania Magazine of History and Biography* 94, no. 1 (January 1970), 62–74; on 62 he describes Welsh as "a humanitarian, who subscribed to the credo of the times—idealism, progress, and Anglo-Saxon Culture," immersing himself "in various reform causes as a young man."
25. DuBois, "Our American 'Reconcentrados,'" quotes on 297, 298, 299. For Cuban conditions, see Mark David Ledbetter, *America's Forgotten History: Part Three: A Progressive Empire* (published by the author,

2015), 398–99.
26. DuBois, "Our American 'Reconcentrados,'" 298.
27. First quote, see Dubois, "Some Unknown Missions of California," *The Land of Sunshine*, November 1899, 318; final quote, see DuBois, "Our American 'Reconcentrados,'" 297–98.
28. DuBois, "The Song of Death," *The Southern Workman*, April 1909, 229.
29. DuBois, "A Fiesta at Mesa Grande," *The Land of Sunshine*, January 1900, 89.
30. "Employees in School Service," *ARCIA, 1898* (Washington, DC: GPO, 1898), 651 for Watkins. DuBois, in "Report of the Industrial Art Committee, *The Indian Bulletin*, November 1901, 2, wrote she had known Watkins for four years, describing her as "thoroughly reliable, and capable of administering" a perpetual fund to enable the purchasing of Indian basketry. Trump, "The Indian Industries League," 143–56 described her relationship to CGD, noting that her living conditions were as primitive as those of the Indians she served.
31. "Some Aid Offered Starving Indians. Response to Appeal Made in Their Behalf by Rev. Restarick," *San Diego Union and Daily Bee*, November 22, 1900, 8; see also "Indian Relief: How the Money Is being Spent," *San Diego Union and Daily Bee*, December 1, 1900, 5. For other articles on baskets, see "Manzanita Basketry: A Revival" (1903) and "The Indian Woman as a Craftsman" (1904), in Laylander, ed., *Listening to the Raven*, 59–63.
32. "Will Visit the Indians. Rev. H. B. Restarick Starts Today, "*San Diego Union and Daily Bee*, December 5, 1900, 4. See also "Starving Indians at La Posta. Bishop Johnson and Rev. H. B. Restarick Home from Long Trip," *San Diego Union and Daily Bee*, December 16, 1900, 6.
33. WNIA, *Annual Report of the WNIA, December 1900* (Philadelphia: George Dukes, 1900), 28, for letter; and 29, for CGD as the Waterbury delegate to the annual WNIA meeting.
34. "Starving Indians of Mesa Grande. Their Condition Even Worse Than Was at First Reported," *Los Angeles Herald*, December 14, 1900, 10. See also "Reconcentrados Right Here in Your Own State! Forced Exodus, Mission Indians, Great Privation, Many Deaths," *San Francisco Examiner* (Sunday edition), December 9, 1900, 27; and "Homeless Indians Starving in a Land of Plenty: Tragic Story of the White Man's Cruelty in California," *The Standard Gauge* (Brewton, AL), January 3, 1901, 1.
35. "Indians in Bad Plight: Suffering at Mesa Grande Reservation," *Los Angeles Herald*, November 22, 1900, 8.
36. For tenure, see W. David Baird, "William A. Jones, 1897–1904, *The Commissioners of Indian Affairs*, 211–20; and DeJong, "Commissioner William A. Jones, *The Commissioners of Indian Affairs*, 91–97.
37. For trip, see "Congress to Aid Needy Mission Indians. Bishop Johnson and Senator Bard Do Good Work at Washington," *San Diego Union and Daily Bee*, January 15, 1901, 5.
38. "New Indian Policy," *The Land of Sunshine*, December 1901, quote on 460. The League's goal was to work with the government on commonsense policies with Indian consent.
39. Constance Goddard DuBois, *The Condition of the Mission Indians of Southern California* (Philadelphia: Office of the IRA, 1901), 9.
40. WNIA, "The Mission Indians," January 1901, quote on 6, and "The Mission Indians Again," February 1901, quote on 7, in *The Indian's Friend*.
41. For appointment, see "Los Angeles," *The Churchman*, August 24, 1901, vii. *The Churchman* was an American Episcopalian Church periodical.
42. DuBois, "Report of the Industrial Art Committee," 2.
43. "Starving to Death. Indians in Pitiable Condition," *San Diego Union and Daily Bee*, October 18, 1901, 4.
44. For more, see BIC, "Work for Indian Women" (Address of Miss Sybil Carter), "Proceedings of the BIC at the Twelfth LMC," in *Twenty-Sixth Annual Report of the BIC, 1894* (Washington, DC: GPO, 1895), 84. The WNIA praised her work, invited her to speak, and included articles on her; see NIA, "Miss Sybil

NOTES

Carter," October 1908, 7–8 and "An Enduring Memorial of a Noble Life: Indian Lace Designed by Miss Sybil Carter on Cathedral Altar," May 1911, 7–8 in *The Indian's Friend*. See also Trump, "The Indian Industries League," 50–52.

45. Sybil Carter Indian Mission and Lace Industry Association, *Annual Report, 1905–1906* (New York: 1906), 7. "Lace-Making at Santa Fe," *The Native American* (Phoenix Indian School), September 16, 1916, 248, also listed a school at Santa Ysabel.

46. Simonsen, *Making Home Work*, quotes on 105, 103. See also Jane Simonsen, "Your Indian Friend,' Indigenous Women and Strategic Alliances with the WNIA," in *Gender, Race, and Power*, 195–97.

47. See chapters 5 and 6 for background on field matrons.

48. WNIA, "Historical Sketch of Missions," *Annual Report of the WNIA, December 1901* (Philadelphia: George Dukes), 1901, 24.

49. DuBois, "Paths of Hope for the Mission Indians," *The Southern Workman*, April 1903, 216–17. For Johnson's work at La Posta and Manzanita, see "Indian Relief: How the Money Is Being Spent," *San Diego Union and Daily Bee*, December 1, 1900, 5.

50. DuBois, "Report of the Industrial Art Committee," 2.

51. Trump, "'The Idea of Help,'" 180.

52. "Sequoyah League," *Out West*, August 1905, 184 for quote. In 1907 the Indian Industries League opened a second-floor salesroom in Boston across from the Park Street Church, selling $1,201 worth of Indian goods. At year's end, it moved to the first floor of a bookstore for better visibility; see Trump, "The Indian Industries League," 248–49.

53. David Wallace Adams writes that the initial purpose had been to introduce "wholesome reading materials to Indians schools," the latter aimed to "open individual opportunities of work to individual Indians and to build up self-supporting industries in Indian communities"; see Adams, "'In the Shadow of Ramona': Frances Campbell Sparhawk and the Fiction of Reform," in *Gender, Race, and Power*, 123. For Sparhawk's literary work, see 123–38.

54. "Sparhawk, Miss Frances Campbell," *A Woman of the Century*, 672; and "Frances Campbell Sparhawk," *Book News [A Monthly Survey of General Literature]*, October 1903, 152–53.

55. See Wanken, "Department of Indian Industries and the Indian Industries League," in "'Woman's Sphere' and Indian Reform," 222–52, quotes on 237, 238; Trump, "The Indian Industries League," 16–17, for founding, also 28–30; and Cathleen D. Cahill, "Making and Marketing Baskets in California," in *The WNIA: A History*, 126–49.

56. Wanken, "'Woman's Sphere' and Indian Reform," 239–40.

57. Wanken, "'Woman's Sphere' and Indian Reform," 251–52 for quote.

58. Trump, "The Indian Industries League," 6 for quote, see 9 also.

59. Wanken, "'Woman's Sphere' and Indian Reform," 249–50; see WNIA, "A New Industrial Department," *The Indian's Friend*, June 1901, 6–7; Trump, "The Indian Industries League," 196–209, 217–19, 228–30, 234; and Trump, "The Idea of Help," 170–73.

60. Trump, "The Idea of Help," quotes on 170–71. For her reasoning, see 171–73.

61. Trump, "The Indian Industries League," 196. For his chapter on CGD, see 303–33. CGD also challenged compulsory Indian education. In "A New Phase of Indian Education," in the June 7, 1900, issue of *City and State*, 363, she wrote, "no white child can be forcibly carried from his home without the consent of his parents, taken to a school inaccessible and remote, and kept a prisoner under close restraint during the term of his education." Her conclusion was to "let native industries be fostered, and all that is good in the old customs be preserved."

62. For background, see "Samuel M. Brosius," *Indian Truth* (Published by the IRA), December 1936, 1.

63. CGD to Welsh, July 15, 1900, *IRA Papers*, Reel 15.

64. DuBois, "Paths of Hope for the Mission Indians," 215.
65. "The Warner's Ranch Indians," "The Jackson/Kinney Report," 486–87.
66. CGD to Welsh, July 15, 1900, *IRA Papers*, Reel 15. For Jackson's recommendation to purchase, see "The Jackson/Kinney Report," 472–73.
67. C. Hart Merriam, in "The Acorn, a Possibly Neglected Source of Food," *Food in California Indian Culture*, ed. Ira Jacknis (Phoebe Hearst Museum of Anthropology, University of California, Berkeley, 2004), 144, writes, "the acorn is, and always has been, the staff of life" for California natives.
68. CGD to Sniffen, August 3 and August 21, 1900, *IRA Papers*, Reel 15. These reservations were closest to Mexico.
69. Sniffen to CGD, December 4, 1900, and Welsh to CGD, December 27, 1900, Box 1, Folder 6, Constance Goddard DuBois Papers, Division of Rare and Manuscript Collections, Carl A. Krock Library, Cornell University, Ithaca, New York (hereafter, CGD Papers).
70. CGD to CFL, February 18, 1901, in CGD, MS 1.1.1218 B, Braun Research Library. Apparently, he never published it; but see Laylander, in "Early Ethnographic Notes from Constance Goddard DuBois," 205–12.
71. March 8, 1901, 8, and March 2, 1901, 8, issue of the *Waterbury Democrat* for quotes.
72. Constance Goddard DuBois, "Our Work for the Mission Indians," *The Indian Bulletin*, April 1901, 3–4.
73. DuBois, *The Condition of the Mission Indians*, quotes on 10, 15. For list, see 12–13.
74. Brosius to William Henry Weinland (WHW), April 11, 1901 (copy), Box 5, Papers of William Henry Weinland, Huntington Library, San Marino, California (hereafter, WHW Papers). However, Colonel John S. Lockwood, who later served as president of the Indian Industries League, was most impressed, writing in Lockwood to CGD, June 28, 1906, CGD Papers, Box 1, Folder 11, that "no one person has done so much in my opinion, as the lady whose name is at the head of this sheet, and I consider it an honor to have worked with her in this matter." He was founder of Lockwood, Brooks and Company; see Edwin M. Bacon, *The Book of Boston: Fifty Years' Recollections of the New England Metropolis* (Boston: The Book of Boston Company, 1916), 129.
75. Brosius to Welsh, July 25, 1901, *IRA Papers*, Reel 15.
76. Brosius to John S. Lockwood, April 6, 1906, CGD Papers, Box 1, Folder 11.
77. Relevantly, Helen Hunt Jackson's writings were viewed by some as sentimental; see Theodore Roosevelt, *The Winning of the West*, vol. 1 (New York: G. P. Putnam's Sons, 1889), 288–90; and Allan Nevins, "Helen Hunt Jackson, Sentimentalist vs. Realist," *The American Scholar* 10, no. 3 (Summer 1941): 269–85. For Agent S. S. Lawson's criticism of Jackson, see Mathes, *Helen Hunt Jackson*, 64–68; and for similar criticisms against Quinton, see Mathes, *Amelia Stone Quinton*, 90–93, 100–103, 106, 108–13.
78. WNIA, "The Report of Charles L. Partridge, Esq.," *The Indian's Friend*, September 1901, 9–10, quotes on 10; and WNIA, CGD, "The Mission Indians Again," *The Indian's Friend*, September 1901, 8. For more on Redlands, see Valerie Sherer Mathes, "The Redlands Indian Association: The WNIA in Southern California," *The WNIA: A History*, 192–210.
79. WNIA, "News and Notes," June 1901, 11; see also WNIA, "Editorial," August 1901, 8 for ASQ, both in *The Indian's Friend*.
80. ASQ to WHW, August 5, 1901, WHW Papers, Box 1.
81. DuBois, "Paths of Hope for the Mission Indians," 214.
82. A reservation established by a presidential proclamation which can be modified and does not need Senate approval.
83. Jones to CGD, March 26, 1901, CGD Papers, Box 1, Folder 7.
84. CGD to Welsh, June 8, 1901, *IRA Papers*, Reel 15. It is not known if Welsh complied.
85. CGD to Welsh, May 28, 1901, *IRA Papers*, Reel 15. In a June 2, 1901, letter to Welsh, Reel 15, CGD

NOTES

expressed hope that he would join their "corporation for work in Calif."

86. ASQ to WHW, August 20, 1901, WHW Papers, Box 1.
87. Brosius to Welsh, July 25, 1901, *IRA Papers*, Reel 15.
88. Brosius to WHW, September 16, 1901, WHW Papers, Box 6. C. E. Kelsey would accomplish this goal.
89. Collier to CGD, July 29, 1901, CGD Papers, Box 1, Folder 7. The July 13, 1901, 8, issue of the *Daily Morning Journal and Courier* (New Haven) reported that CGD had left for a three-month tour among the Mission Indians. The *Los Angeles Herald*, in "Getting Homes for the Indians," September 8, 1901, 5, reported Collier's return from Warner Ranch, and at the suggestion of Senator Bard, he was examining potential properties with Mission Agent Wright. Wright and Collier later returned with Bard; see "Visiting Indians. Senator Bard at Warners," *San Diego Union and Daily Bee*, October 27, 1901, 5.
90. "I do not believe there is a single one where it will be safe to allot with a hope of avoiding complications, but I do believe that [it] is far better and more economical for the Government to allow the matter to stand and the title to remain in trust for the band or village," he wrote in "Collier to Attorney General P. C. Knox, October 23, 1901," *Annual Report of the Attorney-General of the United States for the Year 1901* (Washington, DC: GPO, 1901), 311; see also his comments in "The Warner Ranch Indians," 377–78, ibid.
91. WNIA, CGD, "The Mission Indians—a Crisis," *The Indian's Friend*, October 1891, 2.
92. Constance Goddard DuBois, "The Mission Indian Exiles," *The Land of Sunshine*, October 1901, 248–52, quotes 250, 251.
93. This is not intended to be a complete history of the Warner Ranch removal. See Mathes and Brigandi, *Reservations, Removal, and Reform*, 144–48, 168–69; and Mathes, *Divinely Guided*, 237, 243–45, 250–51; 231–61 for WNIA missionary work at Agua Caliente. For League's support, see Thompson, *American Character*, 213–43, also 180–243 for CFL's work as editor and efforts on behalf of the Mission Indians.
94. In an 1888 appeal to save Soboba (*Byrne v. the San Jacinto Indians*), Welsh and the IRA supported Shirley C. Ward, a Special Assistant U.S. District Attorney for the California Mission Indians. See Mathes and Brigandi, *Reservations, Removal, and Reform*, 44, 58, 75–79, 93–94; and Garner, "Soboba," *The Broken Ring*, 75–95.
95. In Partridge to CGD, August 12, 1902, CGD Papers, Box 1, Folder 8, he wrote that the J. Downey Harvey Estate, owner of the ranch, had offered to sell 28,000 acres for $245,000—"impossible with our appropriation," which was only $70,000.
96. "Collier to Knox, October 27, 1902," *Annual Report of the Attorney-General of the U.S. for the Year 1902* (Washington, DC: GPO, 1902), 275. See also "Final Report of the Warner's Ranch Indian Advisory Commission," CFL Collection, Braun Research Library; "New Home for Mission Indians," *San Francisco Call*, May 30, 1902, 2; and NIA, Amelia Stone Quinton, "The Agua Calientes," *The Indian's Friend*, October 1902, 2.
97. "Wagons Start for Reservation: Warner Ranch Indians Will Begin Moving Saturday," *San Francisco Call*, May 8, 1903, 2. See Steven M. Karr, "The Warner's Ranch Indian Removal: Cultural Adaptation, Accommodation, and Continuity," *California History* 86, no. 4 (2009): 24–43, notes 82–84; Phil Brigandi, "In the Name of the Law: The Cupeño Removal of 1903," *Journal of San Diego History* 64, no. 1 (2018); and Damon B. Akins and William J. Bauer Jr., *We Are the Land: A History of Native California* (Oakland: University of California Press, 2021), 184–87.
98. Constance Goddard DuBois, "The Exiles of San Felipe," *The Southern Workman*, December 1903, 607–10, quote on 609. See also "Removal of San Felipe Indians. Have Joined Contingent at Pala Reservation," *Los Angeles Herald*, September 8, 1903, 5; and "San Felipe Indians Object to Removal," *San Francisco Call*, September 6, 1903, 27.

NOTES

99. "Miss DuBois," *Proceedings of the Nineteenth Annual Meeting of the LMC of Friends of the Indian, 1901* (LMC, 1902), 112–13. In "The Lake Mohonk Indian Conference," *The Indian's Friend*, November 1901, 11, it was reported that CGD "made an appeal, full of heart, for land for the Mission Indians" and that she had seen for herself during her many visits "their great destitution." For talks, see *Waterbury Democrat*, October 26, 1901, 8, and November 7, 1901, 3; and "Indian Association: Twentieth Annual Meeting of State Organization," *Hartford Courant*, November 23, 1901, 11.
100. WNIA, "Historical Sketch of Missions," *Annual Report of the WNIA, December 1901* (Philadelphia: George Dukes, 1901), 24; see 38 for her as delegate. See also NIA, "The Annual Meeting," *The Indian's Friend*, January 1901, 7, for mention of her report on Connecticut's Indian work.
101. NIA, *Annual Report of the NIA, December, 1903* (Philadelphia: Times Printing House, 1903), 16, 19, 23, 35.
102. Constance Goddard DuBois, "How to Help the Mission Indians," *The Southern Workman*, December 1901, 673–76 quote, 676.
103. CGD to CFL, February 17, 1902, CGD MS, CFL Collection, Braun Research Library.
104. According to C. W. Goodman, superintendent of the Indian School at Phoenix, Campo had a population of fewer than twenty inhabitants, as did La Posta, with perhaps only fifty-five at Manzanita; see WNIA, "A Visit to Campo," *The Indian's Friend*, December 1906, 2.
105. DuBois, *The Condition of the Mission Indians*, 12–13. These reservations were created in 1893 under the authority of the January 21, 1891, Mission Indian bill. For details, see Robert V. Belt to John Noble, December 19, 1891, LR #9299-1891 [#44477-1891], SC 31, RG 75, OIA, NARA.
106. For CFL quote, see "Two Noble Girls," *Out West*, March–April 1905, 203–4. Lachappa attended the Mesa Grande day school and the Perris Boarding School, later serving as a matron of her local day school before going to the Phoenix Indian School and an Episcopal Mission near Reno among the Paiutes. Nejo, who attended San Diego Mission School, was also a matron at Mesa Grande School. See "Mission Indians, California," *ARCIA, 1905* (Washington, DC, 1905), 105, for wagon. See also Trump, "The Indian Industries League," 235–39.
107. Davis's fascination with local Indian culture led to his appointment as their ceremonial chief. See Daisy Edith Kessler in "El Capitan Blanco—The White Chief of the Mesa Grandes," *The Southern Workman*, December 1909, 665–71, 671, who described him as "a white man pledged to blood brotherhood, to hold the sacred traditions and faiths." See also Dana Ruth Hicks Dunn, "Strategies and Survival: Indian Transitions in the Mountains of San Diego County, 1846–1907" (PhD diss., University of California, Riverside, 2013), 213–16, 226–30. In 1916, Davis became the field collector for the Museum of the American Indian in New York City.
108. Davis to CGD, March 27 and May 18, 1905, CGD Papers, Box 1, Folder 10. For a dispute that threatened their position, see Lisa E. Emmerich, "'Right in the Midst of My Own People': Native American Women and the Field Matron Program," *American Indian Quarterly* 15, no. 1 (Spring 1991): 201–16, esp. 209–10.
109. "City News," *Waterbury Evening Democrat*, October 17, 1903, 1.
110. Shell to CGD, December 27, 1903, CGD Papers, Box 1, Folder 8. In C. E. Kelsey, *Report of the Special Agent for California Indians to the Commissioner of Indian Affairs, March 21, 1906* (San Jose: Cleveland Printing Company, 1906), 30–31, he described these portable houses as "far from satisfactory"; made of three-quarter-inch board, they were "hot in summer and cold in winter," and "neither dust-proof, wind-proof, nor water-proof, and are far inferior to the despised adobes."
111. CGD to CFL, October 21 [1904], CGD MS, CFL Collection, Braun Research Library.
112. CGD to CFL, November 10, 1904, CGD MS, CFL Collection, Braun Research Library.
113. CFL to CGD, November 15, 1904, CGD MS, CFL Collection, Braun Research Library.

NOTES

114. "Sequoya League," *Out West*, March–April 1905, 230; see also "Aid Coming in for the Campo Indians," *San Diego Union and Daily Bee*, November 18, 1904, 3.
115. Watkins to CGD, May 12, 1903, CGD Papers, Box 1, Folder 8.
116. CFL to CGD, November 24, 1904, CGD MS, CFL Collection, Braun Research Library.
117. Davis to CGD, March 27 and May 18, 1905, CGD Papers, Box 1, Folder 10.
118. Wissler to CGD, June 23, 1905, CGD Papers, Box 1, Folder 10; and Trump, "The Indian Industries League," 211 for quote.
119. Kroeber to CGD, August 18, 1905, CGD Papers, Box 1, Folder 10.
120. "Anthropologists Discuss Dying Civilizations," *Riverside Enterprise*, September 2, 1905, 3; see also "Anthropologists Discuss Dying Civilizations: Merriam Blames State for Treatment of Indians," *San Francisco Chronicle*, August 30, 1905, 7; and "American Anthropological Society Convenes at Affiliated Colleges to Exchange Views," *San Francisco Examiner*, August 30, 1905, 5.
121. Kroeber to CGD, September 8, 1905, CGD Papers, Box 1, Folder 10. Her paper, "Religious Ceremonies and Myths of the Mission Indians," appeared in the 1905 issue of the *American Anthropologist*, 620–29; reprinted in Laylander, ed., *Listening to the Raven*, 87–92.
122. Shell to CGD, enclosed with Shell to Leupp, August 7, 1905, CGD Papers, Box 1, Folder 10.
123. Leupp to CGD, August 21, and October 4, 1905, CGD Papers, Box 1, Folder 10. In his October 4 letter, Shell enclosed copies of letters from the Indian Office showing there was only $600 for doctor's services and relief of destitute Indians, to be divided between his agency and San Jacinto. In 1904 the government divided the Mission Tule River (Consolidated) Agency, placing equal parts under a bonded superintendent at the training school of San Jacinto and at Pala; see "Abolishment of Agencies," *Annual Reports of the Department of the Interior* (1903), (Indian Affairs, Part 1) (Washington, DC: GPO, 1904), 28.
124. Leupp to CGD, November 8, 1905, CGD Papers, Box 1, Folder 10.
125. CGD to Leupp, October 26, 1905, and Leupp to CGD, November 2, 1905, in CGD Papers, Box 1, Folder 10.
126. Brosius to John S. Lockwood [League of Indian Industries], April 6, 1906, CGD Papers, Box 1, Folder 11.
127. For background, see Mathes, "C. E. Kelsey and California's Landless Indians," *Gender, Race, and Power*, 163–81; Larisa K. Miller, "Primary Sources on C. E. Kelsey and the Northern California Indian Association, *Journal of Western Archives* 4, no. 1 (2013): 1–20.
128. CGD to Kelsey, October 27, 1905, and Kelsey to CGD, November 13, 1905, CGD Papers, Box 1, Folder 10.
129. Kroeber to CGD, December 22, 1905, CGD Papers, Box 1, Folder 10.
130. Kroeber to CGD, April 26, May 11, 17 and 19, 1906, CGD Papers, Box 1, Folder 11. On May 11, he wrote that although the April earthquake had not damaged the Berkeley campus, he had been personally "burned out, but lost none of [his] manuscripts and saved enough to live on."
131. Kroeber to CGD, May 29, June 20, 1906, CGD Papers, Box 1, Folder 11.
132. Kroeber to CGD, August 18, 1906, CGD Papers, Box 1, Folder 11. Based on this fieldwork, CGD wrote "The Religion of the Luiseño Indians of Southern California," published in the June 27, 1908, issue of *American Archaeology and Ethnology* and reprinted in Laylander, ed., *Listening to the Raven*, 120–65. In his "Editor's Note" (121–22), Kroeber wrote that in 1906 DuBois had spent "some weeks in San Diego county, in field studies with the Luiseño Indians," work carried on under the Ethnological and Archaeological Survey of California for the Department of Anthropology at the University of California.
133. *Pittsburg Press*, September 11, 1906, 6; see the same announcement in "The Hall of Fame," *Barre* (VT) *Daily Times*, November 13, 1906, 3.

134. Kelsey to CGD, September 17, 1906, CGD Papers, Box 1, Folder 11. See *Out West*, March 1906, 240, for CFL report on Kelsey's investigations of Southern California reservations.
135. Kelsey to CGD, November 2, 1906, CGD Papers, Box 1, Folder 11. A notice in the *Waterbury Evening Democrat*, October 27, 1906, 16, reported that CGD was one of several representing the Waterbury Indian Association at the state conference in Hartford in November.
136. Leupp to CGD, November 22, 1906, CGD Paper, Box 1, Folder 12.
137. "Twenty-Five Years' Work for Indians: Mrs. Kinney's Review of Association," *Hartford Courant*, December 19, 1906, 15. The $200 was worth $7,107 in 2025 dollars.
138. Trump, "The Indian Industries League," 330.
139. See Lawrence C. Kelly, *The Assault on Assimilation: John Collier and the Origins of Indian Policy Reform* (Albuquerque: University of New Mexico Press, 1983), and Lois Palken Rudnick, *Mabel Dodge Luhan: New Woman, New Worlds* (Albuquerque: University of New Mexico Press, 1984).
140. Watkins to CGD, February 7, 1907, CGD Papers, Box 1, Folder 12.
141. CFL to CGD, February 20, 1907, CGD Papers, Box 1, Folder 12. From 1905 to 1910 Lummis served as director of the library.
142. Larrabee to CGD, May 7, 1907, CGD Papers, Box 1, Folder 12. For the 1908 purchase of 1,200 acres at Campo, see Charles E. Kelsey, "Indian Reservations in Southern California, and What Has Been Accomplished in the Last Three Years," in Wayland H. Smith, "In Re California Indians to Date," *Out West*, February–March 1909, 141–44. See also "County's Indians Well Provided with Land," *San Diego Union and Daily Bee*, May 10, 1908, 5; "From the Seventy-Sixth Annual Report of the Commissioner of Indian Affairs," *The Native American* [Phoenix Indian School], February 22, 1908; and "The Sequoya League," *Out West*, November 1908, 393.
143. For reelection, see "Fraternal and Social," *Waterbury Evening Democrat*, January 28, 1908, 12; "What Private Philanthropy Can Do for Red Man," *Hartford Courant*, December 9, 1908, 7; and "To the Members and Friends of the Waterbury Indian Association," undated, CGD Papers, Box 1, Folder 41.
144. "Indians in Poverty Going Fast Now," *Bridgeport Times*, November 16, 1910, 1. Watkins in Mesa Grande and CGD in Chula Vista established a branch of the International Sunshine Society. Founded in 1896 by philanthropist and author Cynthia M. Westover Alden, the society had no initiation fees, dues, or salaried officers, requiring the performance of one kind act each year—work done "by all for the good of the cause and the love of mankind." See "Cynthia Westover Alden: President General and Founder of the International Sunshine Society," *Los Angeles Herald*, January 26, 1902, 8; and "Alden, Cynthia M. Westover," *The National Cyclopaedia of American Biography*, Supplement I (New York: James T. White & Company, 1910), 288–89, quote on 289. At the time of this publication, the membership was 100,000 strong. For the year's work and a brief history, see Frederic J. Haskin, "The International Sunshine Society," *Los Angeles Herald*, May 21, 1909, 4.
145. Laylander, ed., *Listening to the Raven*, 14, for death certificate and final years. CGD left $14,831 ($353,951 in 2025 dollars) in her estate, "in railroad company bonds, stocks and cash." See "$14,000 Estate Left by Woman Research Aide," *Waterbury Democrat*, December 15, 1934, 1.

Chapter 4

1. Valerie Sherer Mathes, "New York Women and Indian Reform," *New York History* 94, nos. 1/2 (Winter/Spring 2013): 84–109.
2. WNIA, "The Chronology of Our Organization," *The Indian's Friend*, February 1897, 2.
3. The sanitarium, incorporating the sulphur springs once used by local Indians, was developed by Dr. Henry Foster in the 1850s as a water cure. ASQ visited several times. See Jim Connors, Village Historian,

NOTES

"Bath Treatments at the Clifton Springs Sanitarium, Company," https://www.fostercottage.org/content/museum/Bath-Treatments; and Mathes, *Amelia Stone Quinton*, 170.

4. WNIA, "Our Association's Chronology, Number Three," *The Indian's Friend*, March 1897, 2.

5. "13th Meeting. Dec. 19th 1882," *ITKPA Records*, 66; WNIA, "Our Association's Chronology. Number Five," *The Indian's Friend*, May 1897, 2; and "Women to Aid the Indians," *New York Times*, December 6, 1882), 2.

6. "Mrs. Melissa Phelps Dodge," *The National Advocate*, April 1903, 55. William Earl Dodge, a one-term congressmen, had, with his father in-law, founded Phelps, Dodge & Company, a prominent mining concern. Prucha, in *The Great Father*, vol. 1, 506, described Dodge as "an active Presbyterian, with antislavery, temperance, Sunday school, foreign mission, Bible Society, and YMCA interests and engagements."

7. Newman, who married Angeline in 1855, served in two of the largest New York City churches between 1859 and 1864. He was later appointed to the Metropolitan ME Church in Washington, DC, and served as pastor to the Grant family. In 1888 he was appointed bishop. See John Philip Newman Collection, Archives & History, United Methodist Church, Drew University, Madison, New Jersey.

8. For D. P. Kidder, see the short history in the Archives of the Drew University, Madison, New Jersey.

9. Cynthia Rogers, "Composing a Useful Life: The Diary (1844–1902) of Harriette Smith Kidder (1816–1915)," *Methodist History* 50, no. 3 (2012): 161–70; Victoria G. Harrison, "Little Matters and a Great Mission: The Life and Diary of Harriette Smith Kidder," *Journal of the Rutgers University Library* 46, no. 2 (1984): 58–66; and "Mrs. Harriette Smith Kidder," *The Christian Advocate*, April 22, 1915, 557.

10. WNIA, "The New York City Indian Association," *The Indian's Friend*, June 1895, 2, for Kidder quote; and for Sitka, see "Efforts in Behalf of the Indians," *New York Herald-Tribune*, March 20, 1888, 3.

11. For more on the Ramona Mission and the aged women's home, see "Annual Report," *Eighteenth Annual Report of the NYCIA, November 1900* (New York: 1900), 8.

12. Both the NYCIA and Eastern New York Indian Association had an auxiliary in Poughkeepsie.

13. WNIA, "The New York City Indian Association," *The Indian's Friend*, June 1895, 2, 9.

14. WNIA, "Our Association's Chronology. Number Seven," *The Indian's Friend*, July 1897, 2.

15. "Summary of the Year's Work," *Annual Report of the Women's Eastern New York Indian Association, Albany, January 1886* (Albany: Weed, Parsons and Company, 1886), 5; 14 for Troy founding, 16 for Poughkeepsie founding; and WNIA, "Auxiliaries," *Annual Report of the WNIA, November 17th, 1885*, 19.

16. *Annual Report of the Women's Eastern New York Indian Association, Albany, January 1887* (Albany: Weed, Parsons and Company, 1887), 5–9, quote on 7–8; WNIA, "The Auxiliaries," *Annual Report of the WNIA, November, 1886*, 20.

17. WNIA, "The Auxiliaries," *Fourth Annual Report*, 17. See also WNIA, "Our Association's Chronology. Number Eleven," *The Indian's Friend*, November 1897, 2.

18. WNIA, "Meetings Addressed," *Annual Report of the WNIA, November 17th, 1885*, 15, 19 for Brewster.

19. WNIA, "Meetings Addressed," *Annual Report of the WNIA, November 1889* (Philadelphia: Press of J. A. Wilbour Printing House, 1889), 16, 21, 22. For quote, see WNIA, *The Indian's Friend*, July 1889, 2.

20. WNIA, "Meeting Addressed," *Annual Report of the WNIA, December, 1896* (Lancaster: Examiner Publishing House, 1896), 23; and WNIA, "Meetings Addressed," *Annual Report of the WNIA, December, 1897* (Philadelphia: Hudson Wagenseller, Printer, 1897), 14.

21. Mathes, *Amelia Stone Quinton*, 21–22.

22. Amelia Stone Quinton, "The Woman's National Indian Association," in *The Congress of Women Held in the Woman's Building, World's Columbia Exposition*, ed. Mary Kavanaugh Oldham Eagle (Chicago: W. B. Conkey Company, Publishers, 1894), 71.

23. Amelia Stone Quinton, "Woman's Work in Solving the Indian Problem," *Christian Educators in Council: Sixty Addresses by American Educators* (New York: Phillips & Hunt, 1884), 103.
24. WNIA, *Missionary Work of the WNIA* (Philadelphia: WNIA Leaflet, 1884), 1. Their ethnocentrism is apparent.
25. For resolution, see WNIA, "Our Association's Chronology: Number Seven," *The Indian's Friend*, July 1897, 2; and Wanken, "'Woman's Sphere' and Indian Reform," 255, also 256–68.
26. WNIA, "What Our Missionary Work Will Be," *Annual Meeting and Report of the WNIA, October 27, 1883*, 12; and Simonsen, *Making Home Work*, 75; see also 71–109.
27. A copy of "Sixty-Six Indian Tribes Still Without Missionaries" can be found in WHW Papers, Box 7. Although the WNIA Board decided to send only evangelical Protestants as teachers and missionaries, many members of the MIA were Unitarians, who because of their "liberal theology" were not considered "mainstream, evangelical Protestant." Implying they might withdraw, the MIA executive committee recommended wording be modified to read that "all Christian women can still solicit sympathy and aid." On January 12 the national board agreed. See MIA, "Report of the Secretary," *Annual Report of the MIA, January 1884* (Boston: Frank Wood Printer, 1884), 11; and Wanken, "'Woman's Sphere' and Indian Reform," 262–63.
28. Amelia Stone Quinton, "The Original Indian Association," *Christian Union*, October 6, 1887, 346.
29. Amelia S. Quinton, "Women's Work for Indians," in *The National Exposition Souvenir*, ed. Lydia Hoyt Farmer (Buffalo: Charles Wells Moulton, 1893), 301 for quote.
30. NIA, *Report of Missions, 1907* (New York: The Volunteer Press Print, 1907), quotes, 3–4, 6.
31. See the appendix for a complete list; see also NIA, "The Work of the National Indian Association," *The Indian's Friend*, June 1907, 12.
32. Robert F. Berkhofer Jr., *Salvation and the Savage: An Analysis of Protestant Missions and American Indian Response, 1787–1862* (New York: Atheneum, 1972), 15. Francis Paul Prucha, *The Churches and the Indian Schools, 1888–1912* (Lincoln: University of Nebraska Press, 1979), 5, writes that "the missionary influence over the Indians came from their [reservation] boarding schools." Harvey Markowitz, *Converting the Rosebud: Catholic Mission and the Lakotas, 1886–1916* (Norman: University of Oklahoma Press, 2018), 24, in his study of the Saint Francis Boarding School in South Dakota, confirms the role of education, quoting Superintendent William Ketcham, longtime director of the Bureau of Catholic Indian Missions: "the schools did not comprise all that there was of mission work, but it is safe to say that they were the major part of it, and that they afforded much of the inspiration that made the Catholic Indian Missions successful in a remarkable degree."
33. Berkhofer, *Salvation and the Savage*, 13,
34. Lori Jacobson, "Foreword," to Mathes, *Amelia Stone Quinton*, vii.
35. To Berkhofer, *Salvation and the Savage*, 76–77, child-rearing and keeping house were important "in developing a civilized society," therefore missionaries "elevated the transformed female role," viewing it as "the chief dividing points between barbarism and civilization."
36. WNIA, "Report of the Missionary Committee," *Fourth Annual Report*, 33; and "Report of Agent Scott, Ponca, Pawnee, Otoe Agency, Indian Territory, August 15, 1884," *ARCIA, 1884* (Washington, DC: GPO, 1884), 86.
37. WNIA, "Auxiliaries," *Annual Report of the WNIA, November 17th, 1885*, 20; see also WNIA, "The Auxiliaries," *Annual Report of the WNIA, November, 1886*, 22.
38. This letter, written in 1887, was not published until 1936; see NIA, "Henry Ward Beecher and the National Indian Association," *The Indian's Friend*, July 1936, 2, 4. For February transfer, see WNIA, "Missions of the Year," *Report of Missionary Work, November 1885, to November 1886* (Philadelphia: Royal Printing Company, 1886), 10.

39. WNIA, "The Auxiliaries," *Annual Report of the WNIA, November 30, 1887*, 18. See also WNIA, "Fruits of the Work," *Christian Civilization and Missionary Work of the WNIA, November 30, 1887* (Philadelphia: Royal Printing Company, 1887), 3, 5, for transfer.
40. "Civilizing Poor Lo," *San Francisco Bulletin*, January 30, 1884, 2.
41. WNIA, "Auxiliaries," *Annual Report of the WNIA, November 1889* (Philadelphia: J. A. Wilbour Printing House, 1889), 16; and WNIA, "The Kiowa Mission," *Report of Missionary Work, November 1889* (Philadelphia: Wilbour Printing House, 1889), 19.
42. "Indians Speak at the Meeting of the National Association," *Brooklyn Eagle*, January 24, 1889, 1.
43. "Indians Speak at the Meeting of the National Association." For Lone Wolf as a Baptist, see WNIA, "Work Among the Kiowas," *The Indian's Friend*, October 1889, 3. For his becoming a minister, see "Lone Wolf Obit," *Phillipsburg* (Kansas) *News and Phillips County Post*, October 18, 1923, 5.
44. For letter, see WNIA, "Work Among the Kiowas," *The Indian's Friend*, October 1889, 3.
45. "Report of John Charlton," in "Report of the Board of Indian Commissioners, February 7, 1891," *The Executive Documents of the House of Representatives for the Second Session of the Fifty-First Congress, 1890–91* (Washington, DC: GPO, 1891), 897.
46. WNIA, "A New Field," *Report of Missionary Work, November 1889*, 19–20. For background, see WNIA, "The Brooklyn Mission for the Piegans of Montana," *Sketches of Delightful Work* (WNIA: January 1893), 56–60.
47. WNIA, "New Work," *Annual Meeting and Report of the WNIA, October 27, 1883*, 10. See also *ARCIA, 1882* (Washington, DC: GPO, 1882), 514, for lack of missionary work among the Piegans. Commissioner Price, p. vi, described the influence of Christian men and women teachers and missionaries as serving an "important auxiliary in transforming men from savage to civilized life."
48. John Taliaferro, in *Grinnell: America's Environmental Pioneer and His Restless Drive to Save the West* (New York: Liveright Publishing Company, 2019), xv, lists four bands: Blackfoot, Blood, Northern Piegan, and Southern Piegan. The first three are in Canada; the Southern Piegan are on the Montana Blackfeet Indian Reservation and simply referred to as Piegans.
49. See "Biographical Note," John Young Papers, Brown University Library, Providence, Rhode Island. For the school, see "John Young, Blackfeet Agency, Montana, August 1, 1877," *ARCIA, 1877* (Washington, DC: GPO, 1877), 131.
50. "Young, Blackfeet Agency, Montana, July 25, 1878," *ARCIA, 1878* (Washington, DC: GPO, 1878), 83.
51. "Young, Blackfeet Agency, Montana, July 31, 1881," *ARCIA, 1881* (Washington, DC: GPO, 1881), 112.
52. WNIA, "More Great Wrongs," *The Indian's Friend*, April 1889, 3. For Baldwin, see Taliaferro, *Grinnell*, 173, 174–77. On 175 he describes Baldwin as shortchanging the Piegans, lining his own pockets and looking away "while whisky traders poisoned his wards." Grinnell's complaints took up twenty-eight pages.
53. "Wood, Blackfeet Agency, Montana, September 25, 1875," *ARCIA, 1875* (Washington, DC: GPO, 1875), 300.
54. "Young, Blackfeet Agency, Montana, August 6, 1883," *ARCIA, 1883* (Washington, DC: GPO, 1883), 98.
55. "Allen, Blackfeet Agency, Montana, August 14, 1884," *ARCIA, 1884* (Washington, DC: GPO, 1884), 106.
56. "Indians Dying from Starvation," June 25, 1884, 5, and "Starving Indians in Montana," June 30, 1884, 1, both in the *New York Times*.
57. See Jackson to Henry C. Bowen, October 15, 1884, *The Indian Reform Letters of Helen Hunt Jackson*, 331–32; poem on 332–33.
58. Valerie Sherer Mathes, "Investigating Negligence in Indian Affairs: Charles C. Painter, the Indian Rights

NOTES

Association, and the Blackfeet Famine of 1883–1885," *Montana: The Magazine of Western History* 70, no. 3 (Autumn 2020): 3–20; and Mathes, *Charles C. Painter*, 35, 42–54.

59. "H. Price, Report of the CIA, October 15, 1884," *ARCIA, 1884* (Washington, DC: GPO, 1884), v.

60. WNIA, *Fourth Annual Report*, 11, for Bonney quote; 44–45, and "Appendix: The Starving Piegans," 70 for final quote. For Quinton's comments, see 48; and for Welsh, see 55.

61. WNIA, "Work of the Committee," *The WNIA Report of Missionary Work, November, 1885 to November 1886*, 7–9. See also Wanken, "'Woman's Sphere' and Indian Reform," 79–81. The Connecticut association claimed Williams left in June 1866; letters from the Indian Office reflect that as late as October 4 she had not arrived; see Wanken, 81.

62. Terry served as treasurer of the Western Reserve branch of the U.S. Sanitary Commission during the Civil War. Her war service and that of eight other women, including Mrs. Rutherford B. Hayes, was recognized by the placement of a relief statue on the Soldiers and Sailors Monument in Cleveland, Ohio. The relief statue, created by Heidi Kathleen Elise, represents the Sanitary Commission, Soldiers' Aid Society, and hospital service. Ellen, a descendant of Rev. Thomas Hooker, a founder of the colony of Connecticut, was a member of the Connecticut Society of Colonial Dames of America; see "Mrs. Charles Frederick Johnson (Ellen Terry)," *Register of the Connecticut Society of the Colonial Dames of America, 1893–1907* (Published by the Connecticut Society, 1907), 46. She served as secretary of the New York State Charities Aid Association before marrying Johnson and moving to Hartford. See WNIA, "Mrs. Ellen Terry Johnson," *The Indian's Friend*, February 1897, 8; and "Mrs. Ellen Terry Johnson," *The Indian Bulletin*, February 1897, 1.

63. Johnson, *Historical Sketch of the Connecticut Indian Association*, 21; and WNIA, "The Brooklyn Mission for the Piegans of Montana," *Sunshine Work*, 26–29, 27 for quote.

64. "Baldwin, Blackfeet Agency, August 20, 1887," *ARCIA, 1887* (Washington, DC: GPO, 1887), 132.

65. "Indians. An Eloquent Plea for the Rights of the Red Men," *Brooklyn Eagle*, March 1, 1883, 2, was a lengthy article, noting an address by Welsh. For a speech by Reverend Beecher, see "The Indians. A Fine Demonstration Promised for Monday Evening," *Brooklyn Eagle*, April 28, 1883, 1. Entertainment included a band from the Carlisle Indian School; see also "From the Indian Training School," *New York Times*, January 22, 1884, 2.

66. "Some Benevolent Ladies," *Brooklyn Eagle*, February 26, 1888, 12.

67. "The Good Work Goes on. News of Brooklyn Women Who Are Ever Usefully Active," *Brooklyn Eagle*, December 17, 1893, 7.

68. WNIA, "The Brooklyn Mission for the Piegans of Montana," *Sunshine Work*, 27 for quote, also 26–28.

69. WNIA, "More Great Wrongs," *The Indian's Friend*, April 1889, 3. Taliaferro, in *Grinnell*, 130, 133, details his visits to the Blackfeet reservation.

70. WNIA, "The Home of the Piegans," *The Indian's Friend*, August 1889, 3. For portion quoted, see "M. D. Baldwin, Blackfeet Agency, Montana Territory, August 20, 1886," 171.

71. For excerpts, see WNIA, "The Brooklyn Mission for the Piegans of Montana," *Sketches of Delightful Work*, 57–59.

72. WNIA, "The Piegans of Montana," *The Indian's Friend*, August 1892, 49.

73. WNIA, "The Piegans of Montana," 49. See Jacobson, "Environed by Civilization," 65–83, and Lisa E. Emmerich, "Promoting Homemaking on the Reservations: WNIA Field Matrons," 84–101, both in *The WNIA: A History*.

74. ASQ to Dutcher, September 28, 1892, Eugene S. Dutcher Photographs, Box 2, Correspondence 1892–1899, National Anthropological Archives, Smithsonian Institution, Suitland, Maryland.

75. Amelia Stone Quinton, "A Visit to the Piegans," *The Indian's Friend*, August 1893, 1.

76. WNIA, "Editorial," *The Indians Friend*, February 1889, 2. Quinton served four times as editor: see

Daniel F. Littlefield Jr. and James W. Parins, *American Indian and Alaska Native Newspapers and Periodicals, 1826-1924* (Westport, CT: Greenwood Press, 1984), 242-45.

77. "Steell, Blackfeet Agency, Piegan, Montana, August 15, 1893," *Sixty-Second ARCIA, 1893* (Washington, DC: GPO, 1893), 174 for quote. He noted their arrival as April 2; in Rev. E. S. Dutcher, Superintendent, "Epworth Piegan Indian Mission," *The Gospel in All Lands*, November 1894, 527, the date is April 30.

78. George Bird Grinnell, "The Indian on the Reservation," *The Atlantic Monthly* (February 1899), 255-67, quote on 258.

79. Quinton, "A Visit to the Piegans," August 1893, 1.

80. Quinton, "A Visit to the Piegans," 1.

81. "Matson, Report of Superintendent of Blackfeet School, Kipp, Montana, July 18, 1893," in *Sixty-Second ARCIA*, 174-77. Another major issue was abuse in boarding schools; see Margaret Jacobs's "Indian Boarding Schools," in *After One Hundred Winters*, 148-64; for general histories, see *The Indian School on Magnolia Avenue: Voices and Images from Sherman Institute*, ed. Clifford E. Trafzer, Matthew Sakiestewa Gilbert, and Lorene Sisquoc (Corvallis: Oregon State University, 2012); *Boarding School Blues: Revisiting American Indian Educational Experiences*, ed. and intro by Clifford E. Trafzer, Jean A. Keller, and Lorene Sisquoc (Lincoln: University of Nebraska Press, 2006); and Amelia V. Katanski, *Learning to Write "Indian": The Boarding-School Experience and American Indian Literature* (Norman: University of Oklahoma Press, 2005).

82. Quinton, "A Visit to the Piegans," 1, a reference to individual landholdings under the Dawes Act; and Taliaferro, *Grinnell*, 239; see also 212-13, 220-22.

83. See "Army Officers as Indian Agents, July 13, 1892," *Documents of United States Indian Policy*, 186.

84. Quinton, "A Visit to the Piegans," 1. ASQ's praise is unique; she generally criticized agents, especially the agents at the Mission Agency in Southern California. For example, see Mathes, *Amelia Stone Quinton*, 81, 83, 88-93, 96-98, 100-103, 105-6, 108-9, 177, 199 for her complaints about Horatio Nelson Rust; and 107-14, 124-25, 147-48, 165-66 for Francisco Estudillo.

85. Quinton, "A Visit to the Piegans," 2.

86. Quinton, "A Visit to the Piegans (Continued)," *The Indian's Friend*, September 1893, 1-3.

87. Quinton, "A Visit to the Piegans (Concluded)," *The Indian's Friend*, October 1893, 1.

88. Quinton, "A Visit to the Piegans (Concluded)," 1, 3, quote on 3.

89. WNIA, "Association News and Notes," May 1893, 1, and June 1893, 1, in *The Indian's Friend*. See "Discussion of Same Subject by Mrs. Amelia S. Quinton of Pennsylvania," *The World's Congress of Representative Women*, ed. May Wright Sewall, vol. I (Chicago: Rand, McNally & Company, 1894), 240-41, quote on 241. See also Quinton, "The Woman's National Indian Association," 71-73.

90. "The Coming Congress of Women," *New York Times*, May 7, 1893, 12; Quinton, "Women's Work for Indians," 293-304; and "Growing Influence of Women in Literature and Business," *Brooklyn Eagle*, October 15, 1893, 4.

91. For booth work see WNIA, "82nd Meeting," *Minutes of the Executive Board, November 20, 1890, to October 29, 1913* (p. 112), WNIA Papers, Box 1, Folder 4, Cornell. See also Lori Jacobson, "Indians Can be Educated: The WNIA at the 1893 World's Columbian Exposition," *Gender, Race, and Power*, 209-25.

92. "Mrs. A. S. Quinton was asked to speak of the Piegans," *Proceedings of the Eleventh Annual Meeting of the LMC, 1893* (LMC, 1893), 19-22, quotes on 20.

93. Quinton, "A Visit to the Piegans," *The Indian's Friend*, August 1893, 1. Cooke took over on July 22, 1893; see "L. W. Cooke, Report of Blackfeet Agency, August 15, 1894," *ARCIA, 1894* (Washington, DC: GPO, 1895), 156.

94. Prucha, *The Great Father*, vol. 2, quote, 724; for background, see 723-26, 733-36.

NOTES

95. Hagan, *The IRA*, 81, writes that civil service reform had "become almost an obsession with Welsh"; see also 82, 113–14, 124–25, 161–62. Prucha, *The Great Father*, vol. 2, 721, described Welsh "as the driving force behind the growing demand that civil service rules be applied to the Indian service."
96. Prucha, *Indian Policy in the United States*, 15–16.
97. "Remarks of Mrs. A. T. [*sic*] Quinton," found in "Journal of the Sixteenth Annual Conference with Representatives of Missionary Boards and Indian Rights Associations," *Eighteenth Annual Report of the BIC, 1886* (Washington, DC: GPO, 1887), 115.
98. *The Annual Address of the President, Mrs. A. S. Quinton, November 7th, 1888* (Philadelphia: Publications of the WNIA, 1888), 2.
99. "Work for Christian Women. The Moral and Physical Improvement of the Indian," *New York Times*, November 28, 1888, 6.
100. LMC, *Proceedings of the Ninth Annual Meeting of the LMC, 1891* (LMC, 1891), for Welsh's address, 74–76, and 78 for ASQ quote.
101. During the December 1893 meeting, one session was devoted to "How to Get the Indian out of Politics." They concluded that "when the people recognize a great wrong they move to remedy it. Let us see that the constituencies of public men are rightly informed, for congressmen vote as their constituencies require," see WNIA, *Annual Report of the WNIA, December 1893* (Lancaster: Examiner Printing House, 1893), 27.
102. LMC, "Mr. Herbert Welsh," *Proceedings of the Eleventh Annual Meeting of the LMC, 1893* (LMC, 1893), 22. Grinnell's changed opinion is unexplained. See also "Mr. Welsh's Address at Mohonk" on civil service reform in the November 1893 issue of *The Indian's Friend*, 1, 3, reporting that Harrison had already extended the rules to cover 700 positions in the Indian Service but not yet that of agent.
103. ASQ to Welsh, October 31, 1893, *IRA Papers*, Reel 10.
104. BIC, "Journal of the Twenty-Third Annual Conference of the United States Board of Indian Commissioners, with Representatives of Missionary Boards and Indian Rights Associations," *Twenty-Fifth Annual Report of the BIC, 1893* (Washington, DC: GPO, 1894), 126; and WNIA, "Meeting of the BIC," *The Indian's Friend*, January 1894, 3.
105. Hagan writes that Roosevelt's "real education in Indian affairs began" with his appointment to the Civil Service Commission; he was comfortable dealing with Welsh, who enlisted his help often; see William T. Hagan, *Theodore Roosevelt and Six Friends of the Indian* (Norman: University of Oklahoma Press, 1997), quote 11, 12, and for civil service and work with Welsh, see also 13–25, 30–32, 49, 53.
106. "Journal of the Twenty-Third Annual Conference," 125–27, 131–32. On April 13, 1891, Harrison extended civil service rules to include Indian service physicians, school superintendents and assistants, teachers, and matrons, in Prucha, *The Great Father*, vol. 2, 731. For agent coverage, see IRA, "The Extension of the Civil Service Reform Rules to the Indian Service," *The Ninth Annual Report of the Executive Committee of the IRA* (Philadelphia: Office of the IRA, 1892), 4–9, 8 for the law.
107. "Journal of the Twenty-Third Annual Conference," 149–50. For a summary, see WNIA, "Platform of the Indian Conference," *The Indian's Friend*, January 1894, 6. For November 1888 address, see WNIA, "The Annual Address," *The Indian's Friend*, January 1889, 3.
108. ASQ to WHW, December 23, 1893, WHW Papers, Box 7.
109. ASQ to Welsh, January 13, 1894, *IRA Papers*, Reel 11.
110. "Resolutions of the Indian Commissioners," in "Journal of the Twenty-Fourth Annual Conference of the United States BIC with Representatives of Missionary Boards and Indian Rights Associations," *Twenty-Sixth Annual Report of the BIC, 1894* (Washington, DC: GPO, 1895), 68–69; for committee work, see "The Meeting of the Commissioners," *The Indian's Friend*, February 1895, 9; and for Cleveland meeting, see "Meetings Addressed, by Mrs. Quinton," *Annual Report of the WNIA*,

December, 1894 (Lancaster: Examiner Publishing House, 1894), 13.

111. For Garrett, see "Journal of the Twenty-Fifth Annual Conference of the United States BIC with Representatives of Missionary Boards and Indian Associations," *Report of the Secretary of the Interior; Being Part of the Message and Documents Communicated to the Two Houses of Congress*, vol. II (Washington, DC: GPO, 1896), 1082.

112. "The Indian Association: Special Meeting of the Cambridge Branch to Hear Mrs. Quinton's Account of Her Experiences," *Cambridge Chronicle*, January 28, 1899, 11.

113. WNIA, "A Piegan Letter," *The Indian's Friend*, December 1893, 2. The new site, some six miles from the Great Northern Railroad tracks, made it easier to supply the agency.

114. WNIA, "News and Notes," *The Indian's Friend*, January 1894, 2–3.

115. WNIA, "News and Notes," *The Indian's Friend*, February 1894, 7. See also "The Indian Mission in Montana," *The Gospel in All Lands, Illustrated*, May 1895, 273.

116. WNIA, "News and Notes," in March 1894, 3; May 1894, 6; and September 1894, 2, all in *The Indian's Friend*.

117. WNIA, "A Piegan Letter," *The Indian's Friend*, September 1894, 5.

118. Rev. E. S. Dutcher, Superintendent, "Epworth Piegan Indian Mission," *The Gospel in All Lands*, November 1894, 527.

119. Dutcher, "Epworth Piegan Indian Mission," 527.

120. "Reservation Lands Occupied by Religious Societies," *Annual Reports of the Department of the Interior for 1897* (Washington, DC: GPO, 1897), 458 lists the transfer to the Missionary Society of the M. E. Church; see also "For the Benefit of the Indians," *The Brooklyn Eagle*, October 18, 1894, 4.

121. For a resolution of thanks from the M. E. Church, see WNIA, "Our Piegan Mission," *The Indian's Friend*, October 1894, 6; WNIA, "The Brooklyn Mission for the Piegans of Montana," *Sunshine Work*, 28; WNIA, "The Transferred Piegan Mission," *Our Missions for the Year . . . 1985* (WNIA: December 1895), 41–42; and WNIA, "The Brooklyn Association," *Annual Report of the WNIA, December 1894* (Lancaster: Examiner Publishing House, 1894), 19–20. For monies spent, see WNIA, "What It Cost," *The Indian's Friend*, October 1894, 4, and "American Indian Missions. Montana," *The Gospel in All Lands, Illustrated* (March 1895), 183. The Dutchers moved to Nebraska in 1889. His mission photographs and a collection of family letters are in the National Anthropological Archives, in Suitland, Maryland. The January 1902 issue of *The Indian's Friend*, 1, reported that he had been elected superintendent of schools for Red Willow County.

122. WNIA, "An Indian Letter," *The Indian's Friend*, July 1894, 6–7. It is unknown if ASQ sent Wolf Tail peacock feathers.

123. WNIA, "News and Notes," *The Indian's Friend*, February 1895, 6.

124. WNIA, "News and Notes," *The Indian's Friend*, November 1897, 4.

125. WNIA, *The Indian's Friend*, March 1895, 4–5.

126. "Steell, Report of the Blackfeet Agency, Montana, August 28, 1895," *ARCIA, 1895* (Washington, DC: GPO, 1896), 181.

127. "Steell, Report of Blackfeet Agency, Browning, Montana, August 15, 1896," *ARCIA, 1896* (Washington, DC: GPO, 1897), quotes, 176.

128. Taliaferro, *Grinnell*, 239.

129. For specific duties and quote, see "Field Matrons," *Sixty-First ARCIA* (Washington, DC: GPO, 1892), 100; U.S. Department of the Interior, Office of Indian Affairs, "Field Matrons," *ARCIA, 1892* (Washington, DC: GPO, 1892), 101; see also, WNIA, "Field Matrons," *The Indian's Friend*, December 1892, 2.

130. Lisa E. Emmerich, "To Respect and Love and Seek the Ways of White Women: Field Matrons, the Office

of Indian Affairs, and Civilization Policy, 1890–1938" (PhD diss., University of Maryland, College Park), 1987, quotes, 7–8. For comparison of missionary and field matron work, see 70–71.
131. Lisa E. Emmerich, "'Civilization' and Transculturation: The Field Matron Program and Cross-Cultural Contact," *American Indian Culture and Research Journal* 15, no. 4 (1991): 39.
132. In numerous tribes, Indigenous women practiced medicine after menopause, their power considered so dangerous that they were required to spend their menses in specially constructed huts. For a general study, see Virgil J. Vogel, *American Indian Medicine* (Norman: University of Oklahoma Press, 1977), and Ruth M. Underhill, *Red Man's Religion: Beliefs and Practices of the Indians North of Mexico* (Chicago: University of Chicago Press, 1965).

Chapter 5

1. "Eighth Annual Conference of the Connecticut Indian Association," *The Bulletin*, December 1889, 2 for quotes; Mathes, "Dr. Susan LaFlesche Picotte," 67, for Fletcher; and Wanken, "'Woman's Sphere' and Indian Reform," 66–71, for Kinney.
2. "A New Role," *The Indian Bulletin*, February 1896, 1
3. "Eighth Annual Conference of the Connecticut Indian Association," 2. See also Benson Tong, *Susan LaFlesche Picotte, M.D.: Omaha Indian Leader and Reformer* (Norman: University of Oklahoma Press, 1999).
4. WNIA, "From Dr. Susan La Flesche," *The Indian's Friend*, December 1889, 2.
5. WNIA, "Association News and Notes," *The Indian's Friend*, October 1890, 1. For report referenced, see WNIA, "Association News and Notes, 'Our Medical Mission,'" *The Indian's Friend*, May 1892, 3; for an expanded version, see "Good Work by Connecticut's 'Daughter,'" *The Indian Bulletin*, June 1892. See also "Letter from Dr. LaFlesche," February 1891, 3 and Susan LaFlesche, "The Home Life of the Indian," June 1892, 1, in *The Indian's Friend*; and WNIA, "Present Medical and Hospital Work," *Sketches of Delightful Work, January, 1893*, 46–52.
6. "A Letter from Dr. LaFlesche," *The Indian Bulletin*, December 1891, 4.
7. "News from Dr. Picotte," *The Indian Bulletin*, February 1897, 2.
8. In 2020, the California Nursing Students' Association chose Cornelius as their July representative; see https://www.cnsa.org/year-of-the-nurse. See "Nancy Cornelius Student Information Card," Archives & Special Collections, Waidner-Spahr Library, Dickinson College, Carlisle, Pennsylvania; and "Indian Trained Nurses," *Detroit Free Press*, June 15, 1898, 4. Four years earlier she had married Daniel Skenandore. See also Wanken, "'Woman's Sphere' and Indian Reform," 74–78; and "Indian Women as Nurses," *The Indian Bulletin*, June 1895, 3.
9. For work at Cahuilla and Agua Caliente, see Mathes, *Divinely Guided*, 204–61.
10. "Anna Hayward Johnson," *History of Essex and Hudson Counties, New Jersey*, vol. 1, compiled by William H. Shaw (Philadelphia: Everts & Peck, 1884), 345; and WNIA, "Association News and Notes," *The Indian's Friend*, December 1892, 3.
11. Impressed by Fleming, who, although supported by local reformers from Riverside, had begun missionary work on her own, ASQ asked Morgan to appoint her as a field matron; the WNIA would build her a cottage and garden. In ASQ to Morgan, June 28, 1891, LR #24191-1891, she wrote that with Fleming's hiring, "the best good of the Indians will at once be started"; see also ASQ to Morgan, August 4, 1891, LR #29440-1891, both in RG 75, OIA, NARA. Fleming had resigned for health issues; see "Arrow-Heads," *The Indian's Friend*, October 1891, 1.
12. ASQ to Morgan, November 1, 1892, LR #39462-1892, RG 75, OIA, NARA.
13. WNIA, "Coahuilla [sic]," *Sunshine Work*, 11.

NOTES

14. WNIA, "Progress at Coahuilla," *The Indian's Friend*, April 1893, 1–3, quote on 3.
15. WNIA, "Coahuilla Again," *The Indian's Friend*, May 1893, 2. This is another example of an Indian voice in appreciation of WNIA work on their behalf.
16. WNIA, "Coahuilla," *Sunshine Work*, 10–14, quotes on 12–13.
17. "The Convention. A Session of More than Ordinary Interest," October 19, 1894; see also "In Defense of Poor Lo," December 22, 1897, 2, from a lecture she delivered before a WCTU County Convention, both in the *Riverside Enterprise*. For more details and her death, see "Johnson, Anna Hayward," *Woman's Who's Who of America, 1914–1915* (New York: The American Commonwealth Company, 1914), 433.
18. ASQ to Browning, February 27, 1894, LR #9206-1894, RG 75, OIA, NARA wrote that Johnson would be retiring in early autumn. For death notice, see *Los Angeles Times*, March 17, 1929, 12.
19. For position, see Rachel L. Bodley, *The College Story; Woman's Medical College of Pennsylvania, Commencement Day, March 17, 1881*, in *Valedictory Address to the Twenty-Ninth Graduating Class of the Woman's Medical College of Pennsylvania* (Philadelphia: Jas. B. Rodgers Co., Printers, 1881), 1. For WNIA membership, see "To Educate Indians," *San Francisco Call*, August 13, 1891, 2.
20. ASQ to Morgan, September 1, 1891, LR #40821-1891, RG 75, OIA, NARA.
21. "Rust, October 28, 1889," *Fifty-Eighth ARCIA, 1889* (Washington, DC: GPO, 1889), 125.
22. Rust to Morgan, July 20, 1891, LR #27101-1891, RG 75, OIA, NARA.
23. "Mischief Record of 'La Gobernadora.' Former Indian Agent Tells of Devil She Raised," *Los Angeles Times*, May 26, 1902, 9. For troubles with Rust, see Mathes, "A Hospital at Warner Ranch," *Divinely Guided*, 233–45.
24. ASQ to WHW, April 4, and April 11, 1892, WHW Papers, Box 7.
25. "Mischief Record of 'La Gobernadora.' Former Indian Agent Tells of Devil She Raised," *Los Angeles Times*, May 26, 1902, 9.
26. WNIA, "From a Missionary Report," *The Indian's Friend*, July 1892, 3, for Weinland's trips.
27. ASQ to WHW, December 19, 1892, for request; see also January 4, 1893, WHW Papers, Box 7; and WNIA, "Letter from the New Mission," *The Indian's Friend*, March 1893, 2.
28. WHW, "The Indian Mission," *The Moravian*, February 1, 1893, 72, first quote; and WNIA, "Association News and Notes," *The Indian's Friend*, February 1893, 5.
29. WHW, "The Indian Mission," 72. For lawsuits, see Mathes, *Divinely Guided*, 237, 244–45; Mathes and Brigandi, *Reservations, Removal, and Reform*, 144–48, 168–70; and for a discussion of the case, see WNIA, "A Most Unjust Decision," *The Indian's Friend*, February 1897, 1.
30. For sponsorship, see *Eighteenth Annual Report of the NYCIA, November, 1900* (New York City: 1900), 8; WNIA, *Annual Report of the WNIA, 1894* (Lancaster: Examiner Publishing House, 1894), 19; WNIA "The New York City Indian Mission," *The Indian's Friend*, May 1895, 7; and WNIA, "Agua Caliente," *Sketches of Delightful Work, January, 1893*, 43–46.
31. WNIA, "Letter from the New Mission," *The Indian's Friend*, March 1893, 2.
32. ASQ to WHW, January 30, 1893, WHW Papers, Box 7.
33. WNIA, "From Agua Caliente," *The Indian's Friend*, April 1893, 2.
34. WNIA, "The Institute Paper of Miss French," *The Indian's Friend*, October 1896, 7. Her talk was continued in the November issue, 10. For an early letter from her, see WNIA, "From a New Correspondent," *The Indian's Friend*, May 1893, 3. Emmerich, in "'Civilization' and Transculturation," 37, writes that French discovered that the Indian women at Agua Caliente would not meet with her without a formal introduction by the Indian agent; therefore she "defused tension" by initially visiting them at the village springs and grinding stones, a place where they felt comfortable.

In WNIA, "The Agua Caliente, California, Mission," *Our Missions, for the Year … 1895* (WNIA: 1895), 12, it was noted that "glass windows and plank floors have increased in number, and the desire for these is also extending and deepening."

35. WNIA, "Agua Caliente," *Sunshine Work*, quotes on 24, 18; WNIA, "The New York City Indian Mission," *The Indian's Friend*, May 1895, 7 last quote.

    WNIA official Sarah Newlin wrote to Welsh of differences in medical missionary salaries. Hallowell was paid $800, while those under Episcopalian Bishop Hare, among the Sioux, received only $500, "a pittance, as they pay board I believe, but none are physicians"; see Newlin to Welsh, April 16, 1894, *IRA Papers*, Reel 11.

36. WNIA, "The Annual Meeting," *The Indian's Friend*, January 1897, 7.
37. WNIA, "The Mission of the New York City Indian Association," *Our Missionary Report for 1897* (WNIA: 1897), 29–34, for date of court decision, see p. 29.
38. NYCIA, *Sixteenth Annual Report of the NYCIA, November, 1898*, 9, for her visit, 10–11 for ASQ's visit; 8 for sum pledged.
39. WNIA, "The Annual Meeting," *The Indian's Friend*, January 1899, 9.
40. NYCIA, "Annual Report," *Seventeenth Annual Report of the NYCIA, November, 1899* (New York: 1899), 7–8.
41. See *Southern California Practitioner*, vol. 18 (Los Angeles: 1903), 503. See also "Obituary Notes," *Medical Record. A Weekly Journal of Medicine and Surgery*, October 23, 1909, 698.
42. WNIA, "The Omaha Creek Mission, Nebraska," *Christian Civilization and Missionary Work of the WNIA* (Philadelphia: Royal Printing Company, 1887) 9–10, quote on 9.
43. Alice Fletcher "allotted 75,931 acres in 954 separate allotments to 1,194 persons (wives were counted in the census but not given their own allotments)"; see Mark, *A Stranger in Her Native Land*, 93.
44. WNIA, "3d, The Omaha Mission," *The WNIA Report on Missionary Work* (Philadelphia: November 1888), 5–8; and for arrival and quotes from letters, see WNIA, "Our New Omaha Mission," and "Later Letters from Omaha Mission," 3, in *The Indian's Friend*, March 1888.
45. For gift, see WNIA, "Mission Notes," *The Indian's Friend*, April 1889, 2.
46. WNIA, "3d, The Omaha Mission," *The WNIA Report on Missionary Work*, 5–8, 7 specific to Omaha Creek; for cost, see WNIA, "The Omaha Mission," *Report of Missionary Work, November 1889*, 3.
47. "Chap. 255—An act for the relief of the Omaha tribe . . ." *The Statutes at Large of the United States of America from December 1887 to March 1889* (Washington, DC: GPO, 1889), 150–51, quote on 151; and ASQ to Oberly, February 18, 1889, LR #4927-1889, RG 75, OIA, NARA. In WNIA, "3d. The Omaha Mission," 6, it was explained that Quinton had received assurance from Dawes that such a provision was to be included. In ASQ, "The Late Omaha Council," *The Indian's Friend*, September 1889, 1, she confirmed that this legislation was "procured by Senator Dawes."
48. In Morgan to ASQ, July 27, 1889, Letters Sent: Land Division, vol. 94, LB 187, pp. 363–64, RG 75, OIA, NARA, he included a copy of his instructions to Gordon.
49. WNIA, "The Omaha Mission," *Report of Missionary Work, November, 1889* (Philadelphia: Wilbour Printing House, 1889), 3–7, quotes on 3, 5, 4. See also "Statistics of English Among the Omahas," *The Presbyterian Monthly Record*, October 1886, 378, explaining the need for missionaries to learn the native language, describing the use of interpreters as "a very imperfect way of reaching their mind," and on 379 recommending that day-school teachers use both English and the native tongue.
50. For departure, see "Editorial Note," August 1889, 2, and ASQ, "The Late Omaha Council," *The Indian's Friend*, September 1889, 1. Reports of the departure dates differed: either the 13th or 14th.
51. Chase, whose father was a government inspector and mother was the granddaughter of an Omaha chief, was born on the Omaha reservation. Receiving formal legal training in Cincinnati, he returned to Nebraska, was admitted to the bar, and, with Thomas L. Sloan, founded the law firm of Chase & Sloan in Pender, Nebraska. Chase was elected a county attorney in 1893, was reelected, and was the

first Indian lawyer to argue before the US Supreme Court. For a short biography, see Hiram Chase, 1861–1928, History Nebraska Manuscript Finding Aid. (History Nebraska was formerly the Nebraska State Historical Society.)

52. Quinton, "The Late Omaha Council," 1.
53. Quinton, "The Late Omaha Council," 1.
54. Quinton, "The Late Omaha Council," 1.
55. Wanken, "'Woman's Sphere' and Indian Reform," 166.
56. WNIA, "The Omaha Mission," WNIA, *Report of Missionary Work, November 1889*, 7 for homes, 3 for chapel dedication; see also "A Visit to the Omahas," *The Indian's Friend*, October 1889, 3.
57. Leicester Knickerbacker Davis, "Thomas L. Sloan—American Indian," *The American Indian Magazine* (published by the Society of American Indians), August 1920, 39–40. In 1919 Sloan was elected president of the Society of American Indians, the first pan-Indian association.
58. BIC, "The Women's National Indian Association," in "Proceedings of the LMC," *Twenty-First Annual Report of the BIC, 1889* (Washington, DC: GPO, 1890), 115–16.
59. WNIA, "The Omaha Mission," *The Report of the Missionary Department of the WNIA, November, 1890* (Philadelphia: 1890), 8–9.
60. WNIA, "Our Omaha Medical Mission," *The Report of the Missionary Department, November, 1891*, 9–13, 12 for quotes.
61. For hospital, see Valerie Sherer Mathes, "Susan La Flesche Picotte: Nebraska's Indian Physician, 1865–1915," *Nebraska History* 63, no. 4 (Winter 1982): 524. The structure, once used as a community center, is currently undergoing restoration.
62. For a brief sketch, see "Laura Elise Bates Tileston" and "Ruth Etta Gregg Tileston," in Gregg-Tileston Family Papers, Massachusetts Historical Society, Boston, Massachusetts.
63. Goodale later married Sioux physician Charles Eastman.
64. Elaine Goodale Eastman, *Sister to the Sioux: The Memoirs of Elaine Goodale Eastman, 1885–91*, ed. Kay Graber (Lincoln: University of Nebraska Press, 1978), 31, 44, 43 for quotes; for details of their stay, see 31–86; and Ruth Ann Alexander, "Finding Oneself through a Cause: Elaine Goodale Eastman and Indian Reform in the 1880s," *South Dakota History* 22, no. 1 (Spring 1992), 1–37, 23–27 for Tileston, quote on 27.

    Hare was on the WNIA advisory board, as were Dawes, Armstrong, and Smiley; see WNIA, "Advisory Board," *Annual Report of the WNIA, November 30, 1887*, 6.
65. WNIA, Laura E. Tileston, "A Letter on Hospitals," *The Indian's Friend*, January 1891, 3–4.
66. WNIA, Miss Laura E. Tileston, *Report of the Hospital Department* (Philadelphia: November 1891), 1–3. See WNIA, "Our Crow Creek Medical Mission," *The Report of the Missionary Department, November 1891* (Philadelphia: Wilbour Printing House, 1891), 13–15, for almost the same report.
67. WNIA, "The Year's Hospital Work," *Sketches of Delightful Work, January, 1893*, 52–53.
68. WNIA, Tileston, *Report of the Hospital Department*, 3. See also WNIA, "Our Hospital Work," *Report of Missions for 1900–1901* (WNIA: 1901), 42–43.
69. "Tileston Hall," *Where to Educate, 1898–1899* (Boston: Brown and Company, 1898), 364; and Gregg-Tileston Family Papers.
70. Robert A. Trennert, "Mary L. Eldridge: Serving God and Country on the San Juan," *New Mexico Historical Review* 77, no. 2 (2002): 145–72. On p. 159, he mistakenly attributes the hospital to the Ladies Missionary Society of New York instead of to the NYCIA. See also Scott Ashley Bruton, "The American Dream in Indian Country: Housing, Property, and Assimilation on the Navajo Reservation and Beyond" (PhD diss., Rutgers, October 2016), 210–12, 226, 228–29, 249–59, 262–83, 286–87; Trump, "The Indian Industries League," 132–39, 181–84, 189, 219, 258–68, 286, 288; and Will

NOTES

Steinsick, "Mary Louise Eldridge," *United Methodist Historical Journal* 2 (November 2015): 3–15.

MLE was born on September 1, 1849, in Williamstown, Berkshire County, Massachusetts, to Eli R. Deming and Harty Jane Johnson Deming; see *Genealogy of the Descendants of John Deming of Wethersfield, Connecticut*, compiled and ed. Judson Keith Deming (Dubuque, IA: Press of Mathis-Mets Co., 1904), 375.

71. The *San Juan Times*, January 20, 1899, 4, reported that she hired W. R. Shawver to build a hospital and industrial building at Jewett. For the 35 acres "for the purpose of a Hospital Mission for the Navajos," see *San Juan County Deed Books*, vol. 4: 158 [Warranty Deed], "Eldridge to WNIA," recorded November 9, 1898, witnessed by Mary A. Tripp; see also *San Juan County Deed Book*, vol. 4: 193 [Warranty Deed], "Eldridge to the Trustees of the WNIA," recorded January 28, 1899; both in Office of San Juan County Clerk.

72. "Bureau for New Mexico and Arizona (Indians)," *Tenth Annual Report of the Board of Managers of the Woman's Home Missionary Society of the Methodist Episcopal Church, 1890–91* (n.p.: WHMS, 1891), 70.

73. See Pauline G. Malehorn, "The Tender Plant: The History of the Navajo Methodist Mission Farmington, New Mexico, 1891–1948," in *Navajo Methodist Mission School History: Mission Magnets* (n.p., 1948), 14–15 for their arrival.

74. For her letter, see Emmerich, "To Respect and Love," 62. On p. 96, Emmerich describes the first two dozen appointees as exemplifying "the best of American womanhood": single Protestant women, reasonably well educated, familiar with domestic science, and able to teach.

75. Collins, a Quaker, who died in 1892, "was known in almost all the prominent societies for Christian charity and philanthropy in New York City"; see "Rebecca Collins," *The American Friend* 7, no. 12 (Philadelphia: 1900): 269.

76. WNIA, "News and Notes," *The Indian's Friend*, April 1899, 4. See also WNIA, "The New York Missionary Work," *The Report of Missions for 1900* (WNIA: 1900), 16–19.

77. The Cambridge branch also funded an industrial room; see Ellen S. Bulfinch, "Historical Sketch, 1886–1911," in *Historical Sketch Prepared for the Twenty-Fifth Anniversary with Officers... and Constitution, 1911* (Cambridge: Caustic-Claflin Co., Printers, 1911), 10. For contributions, see WNIA, "The New York Missionary Work," *The Report of Missions for 1900*, 16–19; NIA, "The New York Missionary Work," *Report of Missions for 1900–1901*, 14–17; according to "Our Hospital Work," 44–45, the "whole plant" cost about $2,500 ($94,549 in 2025 dollars); see also MIA, "Cambridge," *Seventeenth Annual Report of the MIA, November 1899* (Boston: Geo. H. Ellis Printer, 1899), 16; WNIA, "The Association's Chronology. Number 26," *The Indian's Friend*, November 1899, 2.

78. A large, sharply tilted sandstone monocline, the Hogback forms the northwest boundary of the San Juan Basin. Beginning north of Waterflow, it rises to almost 6,000 feet at the San Juan River, which carved a 1.5-mile gap into it. The Hogback then continues southward for some thirty miles, ending near Newcomb. See Stephen Lane Wood, *Place Names of San Juan County, NM: The Settlements* (Aztec: San Juan County Historical Society, 2016), 35; and Stephen Lane Wood, *Landscape Place Names: San Juan County, New Mexico* (Farmington: Stephen Lane Wood, 2019), 90.

79. "Indian Invasion," *San Juan County Index* (Aztec, NM), January 19, 1900, 1.

80. For land, see *San Juan County Deed Book*, vol. 4: 157 [Warranty Deed], "Eldridge to Indian Industries League," signed November 5, 1898; and *San Juan County Deed Book*, vol. 4: 297 [Warranty Deed], "Eldridge to Indian Industries League," recorded February 22, 1899, both in Office of San Juan County Clerk.

81. For letter, see WNIA, "News and Notes," *The Indian's Friend*, September 1899, quotes on 5, 11.

82. Born in Elizabeth, New Jersey, in 1873, Dabb attended Colorado College; in 1898 was employed by the

Methodist Episcopal Board; and in 1904 attended the YWCA training school in Chicago, eventually organizing and becoming director of the Indian Department of the national association and serving as secretary for Indian Schools for the YWCA. See "Edith M. Dabb, 96, Indians' Teacher: Retired Worker for Y.W.C.A. on Reservation Dies," *New York Times*, November 26, 1969, 45; see also "Beyond the Camp-Fire," *The Association Monthly* (Y.W.C.A.), November 1916, 454. Dabb wrote several articles, including "A New Era of Indian Life and Service," *Home Mission Monthly*, February 1921, 73–75.

83. "The Navajo Hospital," *The Cambridge Tribune*, September 30, 1899, 3 for quotes. For breadmaking, see WNIA, "News and Notes," *The Indian's Friend*, September 1899, 6. Trump, "The Indian Industries League," 183, noted the League had raised $152 toward a room to start "on a very small scale the woolen industry among the Navajo Indians now in the charge of Mary L. Eldridge."

   In a November 21, 1900, report, Sparhawk wrote that "blankets have been woven and work has been done upon the sewing machines," and "the fine cooking stove in the room has helped the Indian women to like and to make good bread"; see MIA, "The Indian Industries League," *Eighteenth Annual Report of the MIA, November 1900* (Boston: A. F. Grant, Printer, 1900), 11.

84. For quote, see WNIA, "News and Notes," *The Indian's Friend*, December 1898, 5. For Dabb, see WNIA, "The Indian Industries League," *Annual Report of the WNIA, December 1899* (Philadelphia: George Dukes), 15–16; see also Frances C. Sparhawk, in "An Important Work," *The Outlook*, vol. 61, January 1899, 75–76.

85. For letter, see "Indian Association: Reports of the Cambridge Branch of the Massachusetts Indian Association—Report of the Recording Secretary," *The Cambridge Tribune*, November 25, 1899, quote, 9. ASQ had commented on MLE's revolver when she had been toured around Two Grey Hills by MLE in September 1898; see WNIA, "Among the Bears," *The Indian's Friend*, October 1898, 2, 10.

86. Mary and her husband Edwin D. Harper were graduates of Starling Medical College (now Ohio State University College of Medicine). Encouraged by her brother, they moved to New Mexico, where Edwin served as a physician and surgeon for the Santa Fe Pacific Railroad. They divorced, and she returned to Mazomanie, Wisconsin. Specializing in the treatment of women and children, she accepted a position at the Hospital of the Good Shepherd at Fort Defiance in 1898 before coming to the Rebecca Collins Hospital. She died on December 16, 1908, in Madison, Wisconsin; for more, see Mazomanie Historical Society records.

87. WNIA, "News and Notes," *The Indian's Friend*, June 1900, 5 for two short notices. In WNIA, "Taking an Indian Census," *The Indian's Friend*, August 1900, 2, 11, she had written that she stayed in the home of prominent Navajo leader Henry Dodge, who had helped her take the census in his vicinity.

88. For stroke, see WNIA, "News and Notes," *The Indian's Friend*, October 1900, 4.

89. WNIA, "A Visit to Our Missions," *The Indian's Friend*, November 1901, 2, 8–10, quotes on 8, 9. Her letter was reprinted in "Our Correspondents: Editor," *The Cambridge Tribune*, December 14, 1901, 9. See also NIA, "News from an Old Mission," *The Indian's Friend*, July 1905, 8–9.

90. WNIA, "News and Notes," *The Indian's Friend*, November 1901, 10. See also E. E. Chivers, "In the Navajo Desert," *The Baptist Home Mission Monthly*, February 1905, 52–59; on 55 he noted the transfer and that the original name came from "two large masses of gray rock, which stand conspicuously out upon the plain" (56).

91. WNIA, "News and Notes," *The Indian's Friend*, September 1901, 5; letter partially reprinted in "The Navajo Mission," *The Cambridge Tribune*, September 21, 1901, 7; and in "Report of the Twentieth Annual Meeting of the Connecticut Indian Association," *The Indian Bulletin*, November 1901, 1. For visit, see "The Rebecca Collins Memorial Hospital," *Nineteenth Annual Report of the NYCIA* (New York: November 1901), 13–14 for MLE's description of the building as "fine, not beautiful but strongly built, substantial and should be a great benefit and comfort to the people."

92. "The Navajo Mission," *The Cambridge Tribune*, September 21, 1901, 7.
93. "Mr. Chase Tells of His Trip," *Durango Semi-Weekly Herald*, March 25, 1901, 4.
94. NIA, "Work Among the Navajos," *The Indian's Friend*, March 1902, 10. It was reported in "Cambridge," *Twentieth Annual Report of the MIA, November 1902* (Cambridge; The Powell Press, 1902), 11, that the branch spent $1,994 ($74,149 in 2025 dollars) for MLE's salary and other Navajo work.
95. MLE to Rogers, April 10, 1911, Board of National Missions, Presbyterian Historical Society, Box 8, Folder 27.
96. "The Rebecca Collins Memorial Hospital," *Twentieth Annual Report of the NYCIA*, 12–13. In "From Minutes of Board Meeting, November 6th, 1902," the Presbyterian Board accepted the gift of the hospital and thirty-five acres at Jewett; see Board of National Missions, RG. 301.7, Box 8, Folder 27, Presbyterian Historical Society. See also *San Juan County Deed Books*, vol. 5: 544 [Deed], "NIA to the Board of Home Missions of the Presbyterian Church," signed December 1, 1902, Office the San Juan County Clerk.
97. For Samuel Brosius's visit to the Tolchaco (Tolchico) mission, see LMC, S. M. Brosius, "Impressions from a Summer's tour Among the Indians," *Proceedings of the Eighteenth Annual Meeting of the LMC, 1900* (LMC, 1901), 126–27. He described Johnston as "thoroughly practical" and "in a position to be a great power for good among this people" (126). According to the biographical note to the Philip Johnston Papers, 1896–1982, Special Collections and Archives, Northern Arizona University, Flagstaff, Arizona, Johnston and Brosius together resolved major Navajo land use issues near Leupp, Arizona.
98. NIA, "The Tuba Mission," *Missionary Report for 1903* (NIA, 1903), 17–27; see 18 for his Philadelphia address. For the transfer, see *Twenty-Third Annual Report of the NYCIA* (New York: November 1905), 8. See also NIA, "The Navajo Mission at Tuba," *The Missions of 1905*, 17–18; NIA, "Tuba News," *The Indian's Friend*, April 1904, 8–9. For NYCIA's role, see *Twenty-Second Annual Report of the NYCIA* (New York: November 1904), 11, 13–15. See also IRA, "Missionary Johnston and the Navajos," *Twenty-Second Annual Report of the Executive Committee of the IRA, 1904* (Philadelphia: Office of the IRA, 1905), 66–68; and Michael J. Warner, "Protestant Mission Activity Among the Navajos," *New Mexico Historical Review* 45, no. 3 (1970), 217–18, 221–22.
99. NIA, "The Arizona Mission," *The Report of Missions, 1910* (NIA, 1910), 14–23, quote on 22–23.
100. NIA, "The Good Samaritan Hospital," *The Indian's Friend*, January 1913, 7.
101. Their son Philip, who grew up on the reservation, was the inspiration for the creation of the Navajo Code and the Navajo Code Talkers; see Biographical Note, Johnston Papers, Northern Arizona University.
102. NIA, "The Arizona Mission," *Report of Missions, 1911* (New York: The NIA: 1911), 13–23; NIA, "The Arizona Mission," *The Report of Missions, 1912* (NIA: 1912), 13–28, 14 for quote on her qualifications; NIA, "The Good Samaritan Hospital," *The Report of Missions* (New York: 1913), 16–24; NIA, "Our Navajo Mission and Hospital," *The Indian's Friend*, November 1913, 6–8; NIA, "Our Navajo Mission," and "The Good Samaritan Hospital," *The Indian's Friend*, January 1914, 6–7, and 7. For a drawing of the hospital and an article, see NIA, "Our Navajo Hospital," March 1912, 9; for a detailed first-floor plan, see NIA, "Our Navajo Hospital," May 12, 1912, 7, in *The Indian's Friend*. For her work, see "Work Among the Red Men: Annual Report of the Cambridge Branch of the Massachusetts Indian Association," *The Cambridge Tribune*, February 1, 1919, 8; and "Work of the National Indian Association," *The Red Man* 7, no. 3 (November 1914): 107–8.
103. NIA, "News from Our Navajo Mission," *The Indian's Friend*, December 1912, 7. See, for example, NIA, "The Good Samaritan Hospital, Indian Wells, Ariz.," *The Indian's Friend*, December 1914, 6, for one such visit.
104. NIA, "News from Our Navajo Mission," November 1912, 7 for quote. For December cases, see NIA, "Good Samaritan Hospital," February 1913, 8; for later cases, see "Our Navajo Mission and Hospital,"

November 1913, 7, in *The Indian's Friend*.
105. NIA, "The Report of Missions, 1913," 16–24, quote, 23–24; second quote in NIA, "Our Navajo Mission," *The Indian's Friend*, July 1913, 7.
106. For appointment, see NIA, "Our Navajo Hospital," *The Indian's Friend*, October 1914, 6.
107. NIA, "The Good Samaritan Hospital, Indian Wells, Ariz.," *The Indian's Friend*, December 1914, 6 and 7 for quotes. See also NIA, *Annual Report of the NIA, December 1915* (New York: 1915), 27. For a lengthy report, see NIA, "Good Samaritan Hospital," *The Indian's Friend*, January 1915, 6–7.
108. For her reports, see NIA, "News and Notes," September 1916, 4; NIA, "The Good Samaritan Hospital," January 1916, 6–7, 6 for Binghamton branch, in *The Indian's Friend*.
109. NIA, "The Good Samaritan Hospital," *The Indian's Friend*, July 1917, 4. David M. Brugge, in "A Comparative Study of Navajo Mortuary Practices," *American Indian Quarterly* 4, no. 4 (November 1978): 309–28, writes on 311–12 that Navajos' view of death, other than that of infants and the elderly, as due to "interference in the normal or expectable course of events," regardless of direct cause, could "be attributed at least indirectly to witchcraft." At death the *chindi* separates from the corpse and, if trapped in the hogan, causes ghost-sickness. Thus, the body of the deceased was removed through a hole "other than the entry" and the entrance, facing the "sunrise," was blocked, and the hogan abandoned. To save the hogan, the sick were removed before death. R. W. Shufeldt, MD, in "Mortuary Customs of the Navajo Indians," *The American Naturalist* 25, no. 292 (April 1891): 303–6, describes four ways of disposing of a body: cliff burial, brush burial, grave digging, and tree burial.
110. NIA, "The Good Samaritan Hospital," *The Indian's Friend*, July 1917, 4. In "Our Medical Work," same issue, 6, a call was put out to fund Thomas's work, estimated at $100 a week—"It is our duty, as well as privilege to sustain her in the work not alone by our prayers but as well by our gifts." This same letter was reprinted in NIA, "The Good Samaritan Hospital, Indian Wells, Arizona," *Annual Report of the NIA* (New York: 1917), 21–22.
111. NIA, "The Good Samaritan Hospital," *The Indian's Friend*, November 1917, 4–5. Kennedy, a medical missionary, served under the Board of Home Missions of the Presbyterian Church for eleven years; see "From Other Schools and Agencies," *The Native American*, September 6, 1919, 207. He worked at the Ganado hospital from 1910 to 1919, also treating patients at the mission and boarding school; see "Biographical Note," Hickok family/Ganado Mission, PC 168, Library and Archives, Arizona Historical Society, Tucson, Arizona. According to Edgar W. Moore, "The Bierkempers, Navajos, and the Ganado Presbyterian Mission, 1901–1912," *American Presbyterians* 64, no. 2 (Summer 1986): 125–35, Kennedy was known to the Navajos as the "Walking Doctor," visiting distant camps where no white doctor had ever been seen.
112. NIA, "The Good Samaritan Hospital," *The Indian's Friend*, January 1918, 5.
113. NIA, "The Good Samaritan Hospital," March 1918, 6–7; May 1918, 7–8; and July 1918, 4–5, all in *The Indian's Friend*.
114. NIA, "Our Medical Work," *The Indian's Friend*, November 1918, 6.
115. NIA, "The Good Samaritan Hospital," November 1919, 4, for transfer; and "The Good Samaritan Hospital," January 1820, 4, for treatments and quote, both in *The Indian's Friend*.
116. For more details on field matrons and medical care, see Emmerich, "To Respect and Love," 184–281.
117. Emmerich, "To Respect and Love," quotes, 14, 184.
118. Lisa E. Emmerich, "Marguerite Laflesche Diddock: Office of Indian Affairs Field Matron," *Great Plains Quarterly* 13, no. 3 (Summer 1903): 162–71.
119. For Quakers, see Emmerich, "To Respect and Love," 16–18, 27–41 and for Morgan, 48. For more Quaker efforts, see Clyde A. Milner II, *With Good Intentions: Quaker Work among the Pawneees, Otos, and Omahas in the 1870s* (Lincoln: University of Nebraska Press, 1982).

NOTES

120. ASQ to Morgan, September 1, 1891, LR #40821-1891, RG 75, OIA, NARA. For more on Morgan, see Emmerich, "To Respect and Love," 29, 31–33, 45–50, especially.
121. Emmerich, "To Respect and Love," 66 for Dorchester, 29–30 for Morgan.
122. WNIA, "Indian Mothers and Indian Girls," *The Indian's Friend*, June 1890, 1. She described them as "embryo angels"; for an interesting discussion, see Carol Anne Chase Lastowka, "At Home and Industriously Employed: The Women's National Indian Association" (MA thesis, University of Arizona, 1994), 15–16.
123. "Field Matrons," *Sixty-First ARCIA*, 101, and Emmerich, "To Respect and Love," 47–48, 47 for quote. Emmerich describes Morgan's program as combining "Victorian and modern values and beliefs" (49).
124. "Miss Annie Scoville, Held U.S. Indian Post," *New York Times*, March 15, 1953, 92; and "A Friend of the Indian," *College News* (Wellesley), January 17, 1906, 5. In 1905 she made a study of the Winnebagos and Omahas; for conditions at the Winnebago Agency, see "Friends of the Indians. Lake Mohonk Conference Listens to Reports," *Santa Barbara Weekly Press*, October 19, 1905. Her papers are in the Beecher Family Papers, Manuscripts and Archives, Yale University, New Haven, Connecticut.
125. See Annie Beecher Scoville, "Indians at Home," *The Evangelist*, June 29, 1899, 1–14; and Annie Beecher Scoville, "Today Among the Dakotahs," *The Southern Workman and Hampton School Record*, January 1899, 461–64.
126. Annie Beecher Scoville, "The Field Matron's Mission," *The Outlook*, August 24, 1901, quotes on 976, 977, 978; see also WNIA, Anna [*sic*] Beecher Scoville, "The Field Matron," *The Indian's Friend*, February 1899, 2; and Cathleen D. Cahill, *Federal Fathers & Mothers: A Social History of the United States Indian Service, 1869–1933* (Chapel Hill: University of North Carolina Press, 2011), 45–48.
127. WNIA, "Field Matrons for Indians," *The Indian's Friend*, May 1894, 6.
128. California Indian Association, C. E. Kelsey, *Field Matrons* (n.d.), *IRA Papers*, Reel 129, No. 314, 4.
129. Cornelia Taber, "California Indians Past and Present," Cornelia Taber Collection, California Historical Society (hereafter, Taber Collection, CHS).
130. Reprinted as Mary Ellicott Arnold and Mabel Reed, *In the Land of the Grasshopper Song: Two Women in the Klamath River Indian Country in 1908-09* (Lincoln: University of Nebraska Press, 1980). The 2011 University of Nebraska Press reprint included a foreword by André Cramblit and an afterword by Terry Supahan, both members of the Karuk Tribe. In her introduction, Susan Bernardin described the complexity of Arnold and Reed's narrative as "part travelogue, part ethnography ... and part feminist western." This memoir "gleefully subverts the era's expectations for white women," with Bernardin describing it as a "reverse acculturation narrative," holding "up Karuk values as vastly superior to the ones the two women were paid to disseminate" (xii). For letters, see Arnold to Taber, April 11, 1908, Taber Collection, CHS, folder 2; The California Indian Association, *Field Matron Work in Siskiyou County* (n.d., probably 1908), in *IRA Papers*, Reel 129, No. 314. See also Theisen, "With a View Toward Their Civilization," 86–99.
131. NIA, Cornelia Taber, "Cornell on the Klamath River," *The Indian's Friend*, April 1908, quote on 10. For other extracts in *The Indian's Friend*, see "'Mail-Bag' Missionaries," May 1908, 6; "With the Indians on the Klamath River," January 1909, 7; and "Progress in Northwest California," August 1908, 4–5. See also Mary Ellicott Arnold and Mabel Reed, "Report: Somesbar Matrons," in Arnold to Taber, April 9, 1908, Taber Collection, CHS, folder 2; and Anna R. Davis, "The Indians of California Today," *Out West*, April 1911, 340–43.
132. Emmerich, "To Respect and Love," 199.
133. Arnold and Reed, *In the Land of the Grasshopper Song* (1980 edition), 313. They gave no explanation as to why they decided to leave. In her introduction, Bernardin writes that after leaving the lower Klamath River region, Arnold and Reed "brought their humor and considerable managerial and accounting

134. Emmerich, "'Civilization' and Transculturation," 34–35, 43 specifically for Arnold and Reed.
135. Cornelia Taber, "Government Field Matron Stations: Requa," *California and Her Indian Children* (San Jose: NCIA, 1911), 31–33, quote 32. For a letter on alcohol use, see Johnston to Taber, October 2, 1907, Taber Collection, CHS, Folder 1. See also NIA, "The Excellent Work of California Field Matrons," *The Indian's Friend*, July 1910, 11. For an extract of other Johnson letters, see California Indian Association, *Field Matrons* (n.d.), *IRA Papers*, Reel 129, No. 314.
136. NIA, "From Mrs. H. M. Gilchrist, Coarse Gold," *The Indian's Friend*, July 1910, 11.
137. NIA, "From a California Field Matron," February 1911, 8; see also "Office Notes and Comment," May 1910, 9; "Letters from Mrs. Gilchrist," March 1911, 8, 11; and "New York City Indian Association," December 1910, 5; all in *The Indian's Friend*. For Canadian citizenship, see NIA, "The Fifth Zayante Indian Conference," 2; see also Taber, "Coarse Gold, Madera County," *California and Her Indian Children*, 39–42.
138. NIA, "News and Notes," *The Indian's Friend*, February 1914, 4. Most Indian land had already been allotted by this time.
139. Randolph to Taber, February 18, 1907, Taber Collection, CHS, Folder 1. For Faucette, see NCIA, *Wanted—A Missionary*, copy in *IRA Papers*, Reel 129, #314; and Taber, "Bishop, Inyo County—500 Indians," *California and Her Indian Children*, 65.
140. NIA, "From Mrs. C. A. Johnson, Middletown, Cal.," July 1910, 12 and "From a Field Matron to Miss Taber," November 1910, 10, in *The Indian's Friend*. See also NIA, "The Excellent Work of California Field Matrons," 12.

Chapter 6

1. "Mrs. T. M. F. Whyte," *The San Juan Times*, August 24, 1894, 2, a eulogy written by MLE. Mary was born about 1862 in Cedar Rapids, Iowa, to Alfred W. Raymond and Mary A. Raymond. See also Trennert, "Mary L. Eldridge," 147, and Bruton, "The American Dream in Indian Country," 211.
2. A government boarding school founded in 1884 in Lawrence. MLE was born on September 1, 1849, in Williamstown, Berkshire County, Massachusetts, to Eli R. Deming and Harty Jane Johnson Deming; see Deming, ed., *Genealogy of the Descendants of John Deming of Wethersfield, Connecticut*, 375. On February 15, 1869, she married William T. Eldridge. He died in 1887. Their children were Silas, George D., and Ruth.
3. "Bureau for New Mexico and Arizona (Indians)," *Tenth Annual Report of the Board of Managers of the WHMS of the Methodist Episcopal Church, 1890–91* (n.p.: WHMS, 1891), 70. For location, see Trennert, "Mary L. Eldridge," 145; for arrival date, see "Field Matrons," *The Cambridge Tribune*, February 25, 1893, 4. Eleanor Davenport MacDonald and John Brown Arrington, *The San Juan Basin: My Kingdom Was a Country* (Denver: Green Mountain Press, 1970), 64, describe Jewett as "the most remote settlement in the lower valley." Wood, *Place Names of San Juan County, NM*, 14, describes it as a "homestead settlement at Hogback Mountain."
4. "Bureau for New Mexico and Arizona (Indians)" *Eleventh Annual Report of the Board of Managers of the WHMS of the M. E. Church, 1891–92* (n.p.: WHMS, 1892), 72–71, quote on 72.
5. "Bureau for New Mexico and Arizona," *Eleventh Annual Report*, 71–72; and "Early History of the Navajo Mission," *Navajo Mission Collection*, WC116, Manuscripts Division, Princeton University Library, Princeton, New Jersey, 1. (This undated, unsigned handwritten document of twenty-six pages

was written by an unidentified teacher at the M. E. Mission.) See also Robert S. McPherson, *Traders, Agents, and Weavers: Developing the Northern Navajo Region* (Norman: University of Oklahoma Press, 2020), especially 67–73; also 75, 82–83, 97, 107, 109, 135, 266; and Malehorn, "The Tender Plant," 14–15 for arrival.

6. A notice in the *San Juan Index*, reprinted in *Santa Fe Daily New Mexican*, April 13, 1892, 1; see also Malehorn, "The Tender Plant," 15.

7. Tomkinson, *Twenty Years' History of the WHMS of the M. E. Church*, 172–73. For quote, see Sally J. Southwick, "Educating the Mind, Enlightening the Soul: Mission Schools as a Means of Transforming the Navajos, 1898–1928," *The Journal of Arizona History* 37, no. 1 (Spring 1996): 48.

8. For letter, see "Field Matrons: An Interesting Letter Received by the Cambridge Indian Association Detailing the Work of the Field Matrons Among the Navajo Indians," *The Cambridge Tribune*, February 25, 1893, 4; quoted in "Work for Indians: Cambridge Branch of the Massachusetts Association Observes Its Twenty-fifth Anniversary," *The Cambridge Tribune*, December 2, 1911, 6. See also "President's Report," *Constitution of the Cambridge Branch of the MIA* (Cambridge: John Ford & Sons, Printers, 1893), 17. In "Report of Field Matron, August 4, 1893," *Sixty-Second ARCIA, 1893* (Washington, DC: GPO, 1893), 113, Raymond wrote that she bought two small plows, shovels, axes, picks, regular and grubbing hoes, a hammer, and a grindstone. See also "The Navajo Indians," *The Indian Bulletin*, March 1894, 3.

9. "The Indian Association," *Cambridge Chronicle*, April 21, 1894, 9. See also Bulfinch, "Historical Sketch, 1886–1911," 9. In "Early History of the Navajo Mission," *Navajo Mission Collection*, 7–8, it was noted that the ditch was built "along the river, the other side of the Hog Back."

10. MLE's letter was reprinted in "Indian Association: Annual Report of the Massachusetts Indian Association," *The Cambridge Tribune*, November 23, 1895, 3. For completion, see CIA, *Annual Reports: Cambridge Branch of the MIA*, November 5, 1895 (n.p., 1895), 3. Samuel E. Shoemaker, Supervisor of Constructed Ditches, in his June 30, 1905, "Report of Supervisor of Ditches, San Juan River," mentioned "the Cambridge ditch, built and maintained by Mrs. M. L. Eldridge, field matron," in *House Documents* (59th Congress, 1st session), vol. 19 (Washington, DC: GPO, 1906), 269.

11. "Plummer, Report of Navajo Agency, August 22, 1893," 110–11, and "MLE, Report of Missionary, August 6, 1893," 113, both in *Sixty-Second ARCIA, 1893*; see also Bruton, "The American Dream in Indian Country," 249–50.

12. "Report of Missionary, Navajo Reservation," August 27, 1894, *ARCIA, 1894* (Washington, DC: GPO, 1895), 103.

13. "Death of Mrs. T. M. F. Whyte," August 17, 1894, 1; "Mrs. T. M. F. Whyte," August 24, 1894, 2, both in *San Juan Times*; see also "Death of a Field-Matron," *The Cambridge Tribune*, September 22, 1894, 2.

14. *San Juan Times*, July 27, 1894, 1. Short of funds, the WHMS had advised her to accept the position; see "Navajo M. E. Mission," *Farmington Times Hustler*, September 19, 1912, 1.

15. For addition and Tripp's employment, see Malehorn, "The Tender Plant," 19. In caring for Whyte, MLE had given up her Sunday school work, which Tripp assumed; see Rev. Thomas Harwood, *History of New Mexico Spanish and English Missions of the Methodist Episcopal Church from 1850 to 1910*, vol. II (Albuquerque: El Abogado Press, 1910), 279.

16. Robert A. Trennert, "Superwomen in Indian Country: U.S.I.S. Field Nurses in Arizona and New Mexico, 1928–1940," *The Journal of Arizona History* 41, no. 1 (Spring 2000): 33.

17. "Plummer, Report of Navajo (and Moqui) Agency, August 17, 1894," *ARCIA, 1894* (Washington, DC: GPO, 1895), 100; and Bulfinch, "Historical Sketch, 1886–1911," 9–10. MLE learned to farm from her father; see *Genealogy of . . . John Deming*, 375. Her husband managed a farm in South Williamstown for years; see "Among the Navajo Indians," *Pittsfield Berkshire County Eagle*, November 11, 1896, 10.

NOTES

18. "Williams, Report of Navajo Agency, August 29, 1895," *ARCIA, 1895*, vol. II (Washington, DC: GPO, 1896), 118.
19. "MLE, "Report of Field Matron, Jewett, New Mexico, August 15, 1895," *ARCIA, 1895*, vol. II, 120.
20. May 3, 1895, 3, *San Juan Times*, reprint, *The Santa Fe Daily New Mexican*, May 9, 1895, 1.
21. "MLE, "Report of Field Matron, Jewett, New Mexico, August 15, 1895," 120.
22. MLE to Welsh, June 22, 1895, *IRA Papers*, Reel 12. For Antes, see Robert S. McPherson, "Howard R. Antes and the Navajo Faith Mission: Evangelist of Southeastern Utah," *Utah Historical Quarterly* 65, no. 1 (1997): 4–24.
23. CIA, "Report of Recording Secretary," *Annual Reports: Cambridge Branch of the MIA*, 3. See also "Indian Association: Annual Report of the Massachusetts Indian Association," *The Cambridge Tribune*, November 23, 1895, 3. For Welsh's support, see Trennert, "Mary L. Eldridge," 154–55; and for the ferry, see Hagan, *The IRA*, 176.
24. See WNIA, "News and Notes," March 1894, 4–5, and "The Navajos Again," January 1895, 4 in *The Indian's Friend*. See also "Indian Association," *The Cambridge Tribune*, December 29, 1894, 6.
25. Herbert Welsh, *Report of a Visit to the Navajo, Pueblo, and Hualapais Indians of New Mexico and Arizona* (Philadelphia: Published by the IRA, 1885).
26. IRA, "The Navajos," *The Thirteenth Annual Report of the Executive Committee of the IRA, 1895* (Philadelphia: Office of the IRA, 1896), 63; and "The Hungry Navajos," 32–37. Hardy taught at Fort Defiance boarding school, June 1892 to April 1893; see BIC, "Address of Mr. Alfred Hardy, Farmington, Conn.," *Twenty-Seventh Annual Report of the BIC, 1895* (Washington, DC: GPO, 1896), 26. For tour, see Alban W. Hoopes, "The Indian Rights Association and the Navajo, 1890–1895," *New Mexico Historical Review* 21, no. 1 (1946): 22–46. See also Bruton, "The American Dream in Indian Country," 261–63, 262 for his time with Eldridge.
27. LMC, "Address of Mr. Alfred Hardy, Farmington, Connecticut," *Proceedings of the Thirteenth Annual Meeting of the LMC, 1895* (LMC, 1896), 23–24 for report, 24 for quote.
28. WNIA, "The Navajos," *The Indian's Friend*, May 1895, 5, and "Williams, "Report of Navajo Agency, August 28, 1896," *Annual Report of the SI, 1896*, vol. II (Washington, DC: GPO, 1897), 112, 113. Smiley was related to Albert K. Smiley (his great-grandfather, Hugh, was her great-great grandfather); the 1900 census placed her as a field matron in Utah on the Uintah Valley Indian Reservation.
29. Trennert, "Mary L. Eldridge," 155–56, and Bruton, "The American Dream in Indian Country," 267.
30. For expenses, see Trennert, "Mary L. Eldridge," 156–57.
31. Shipley did not mention his displeasure but did note the women's presence, in "Shipley, Report of Navajo Agency, August 31, 1891," *Sixtieth ARCIA, 1891*, 310. See LMC, "Mrs. Eldridge," *Proceedings of the Fourteenth Annual Meeting of the LMC*, 1896 (LMC, 1897), 30–31.
32. "Mrs. Eldridge," *Proceedings of the Fourteenth Annual Meeting of the LMC*, 31–33.
33. WNIA, "The Report of Our Indian Industries League," *Annual Report of the WNIA, December 1896* (Philadelphia: Examiner Publishing House, 1896), 13.
34. "Mrs. Eldridge," *Proceedings of the Fourteenth Annual Meeting of the LMC*, 103–5, and WNIA, "The Lake Mohonk Indian Conference," *The Indian's Friend*, November 1896, 7. For other burials, see WNIA, "An Indian Burial," 9–10, and "Death of Hausteen Teel-be-ga," 10, *The Indian's Friend*, February 1900.
35. "Annual Report of the Indian Industries League," *The Native American*, June 10, 1905, 234; WNIA, "The Report of the Indian Industries League," *Annual Report of the WNIA, December 1897*, 25; and Trump, "The Indian Industries League," 258–68. For letter, see MLE to Welsh, May 27, 1898, *IRA Papers*, Reel 13. Lamb, founded in 1867, still makes knitting machines.
36. The $500 cottage was donated by Mary S. Crozer, a Philadelphia executive board member, to honor

NOTES

     her husband, philanthropist and director of the Delaware County National Bank. He had died in 1897. She also founded the J. Lewis Crozer Home for Incurables in his honor. See "J. Lewis Crozer," *History of the Delaware County National Bank* (Chester: Press of the Chester Times, 1914), 129.
37. WNIA, "News and Notes," April 1898, 11; see also "Our New Mission," May 1898, 7, *The Indian's Friend*.
38. "Williams, Report of Navajo Agency, August 27, 1898," *Annual Reports of the Department of the Interior, 1898* (Washington: GPO, 1898), 123.
39. WNIA, "Our Association's Chronology. Number 26," *The Indian's Friend*, 2. Henrietta Grinnell, who married Truman E. Cole in 1864, was head of the college infirmary, located in her own home from 1893 to 1896; see Subject Files Collection, Archives & Special Collections, Williams College, Williamstown, Massachusetts. My thanks to Laura Zepka, Archives Assistant, for help on this topic.
40. WNIA, "News and Notes," *The Indian's Friend*, August 1898, 4. For more on Cole, see McPherson, *Traders, Agents, and Weavers*, 71–73, 266.
41. For her visit, see WNIA, ASQ, "Among the Bears," *The Indian's Friend*, October 1898, 2, 10. For additions, see "Our Association's Chronology. Number 26," *The Indian's Friend*, November 1899, 2.
42. LMC, "Mrs. Quinton," *Proceedings of the Sixteenth Annual Meeting of the LMC, 1898* (LMC, 1898), 30–32, 31 for MLE.
43. WNIA, "News and Notes," *The Indian's Friend*, March 1899, 4, for her arrival; and WNIA, "Our Two Gray Hills Mission," *The Report of Missions for 1900*, 20–24; and NIA, "Our Two Gray Hills Mission," *Report of Missions for 1900–1901* (NIA, 1901), 18–22, for teaching. WNIA literature referred to their mission as Two Gray Hills instead of the more traditional Two Grey Hills.
44. WNIA, "A Letter from Mrs. Eldridge," *The Indian's Friend*, July 1899, 8–9. Navajo agent G. W. Hayzlett complimented Eldridge and Tripp, in "Hayzlett, Report of Navajo Agent, August 18, 1899," *Annual Reports of the Department of the Interior, 1899 [Part I]* (Washington, DC: GPO, 1899), 158.
45. WNIA, "A Letter from Mrs. Eldridge," July 1899, 9, for quotes; for Cole's rest, see WNIA, "News and Notes," January 1900, 4, *The Indian's Friend*; for Dabb's replacement, see *San Juan Times*, April 6, 1900, 4. For one of her articles, see WNIA, Mrs. H. G. Cole, "Some Navajo Beliefs," October 1900, 7–8; and for return, see "Two Grey Hills Again," December 1900, 5, 11, in *The Indian's Friend*.
46. For sale and quote, see "Navajo Mission," *Twenty-First Annual Report of the General Board of Managers of the WHMS of the M. E. Church, 1901–1902* (Cincinnati: Western Methodist Book Concern Press, 1902), 115. The Board mistakenly called the WNIA the Woman's Navajo Indian Association. The Presbyterian Board paid $1,000 for the M. E. school property; see "From Minutes of Board Meeting, September 4th, 1902," Board of National Missions, RG 301.7, [Jewett Property Records (1899–1922)], Presbyterian Historical Society, Box 8, Folder 27. In "Excerpt from Minutes of Woman's Board," September 2, 1912, ibid.; the Presbyterian Board, unaware that the hospital was "so close to a Methodist school and home," in conference decided to purchase the school and land for $1,000.
47. For location, see "Methodists' Navajo Mission: Tribute to Human Fortitude: Founded in 1891, School Now Has 16 Buildings, Own Crops," *Durango Herald-Democrat*, May 13, 1951, 7; and "Navajo Mission 75 Years Old," *Farmington Daily Times*, May 22, 1966, 26. See also "Navajo Mission, Farmington, N.M.," *Twenty-Second Annual Report of the General Board of Managers of the WHMS of the M. E. Church, 1902–1903* (Cincinnati: Western Methodist Book Concern Press, 1903), 109; for Tripp, see Malehorn, "The Tender Plant," 27–28.
48. For flood, see "Methodists' Navajo Mission: Tribute to Human Fortitude," 7.
49. "Cambridge," *Twentieth Annual Report of the MIA*, 11.
50. "Among the Indians: Work of the Cambridge Branch of the Massachusetts Indian Association Described," *The Cambridge Tribune*, November 22, 1902, 2.

NOTES

51. With no supporting evidence, Malehorn, "The Tender Plant," 28, writes that MLE left Jewett in August 1902 and with Gaines established a mission at Shiprock, intending to add a school until Shelton was commissioned by the government to build the Navajo Northern Agency, later the Shiprock Agency, with a boarding school. In a February 27, 1903, letter reprinted in NIA, "Mrs. Eldridge's Work Among Navahoes," *The Indian's Friend*, May 1903, 9, MLE mentions a new school being proposed near her but does not identify her location. It only becomes clear that Closiah was at Shiprock in Frank Mead's Gen. Supr. Ind. Res., "Report, General Inspection of San Juan Training School, Shiprock, New Mexico," LR #28333-1905, RG 75, OIA, NARA. He had been sent to Shiprock to investigate Shelton's complaints against Eldridge and had recommended her resignation.
52. MIA, "Cambridge," *Twenty-First Annual Report of the MIA, November 1903* (Cambridge: Powell Press, 1903), 8–9; NIA, *Missionary Report for 1903* (NIA, 1903), 4; and NIA, "The Connecticut Missionary Report," *Missionary Report for 1903*, 7.
53. NIA, "Mrs. Eldridge's Work Among the Navahoes," *The Indian's Friend*, May 1903, 8–9; quotes on 9.
54. MLE to IRA, July 3, 1904, *IRA Papers*, Reel 17.
55. NIA, "News and Notes," *The Indian's Friend*, June 1904, 11.
56. Mead, "Report, General Inspection of San Juan Training School, Shiprock, New Mexico," LR #28333-1905, RG 75, OIA, NARA.
57. For Shelton and trouble with MLE, see McPherson, *Traders, Agents, and Weavers*, 58–59, 82–84, 97–125.
58. David M. Brugge, *A History of the Chaco Navajos* (Albuquerque: Division of Chaco Research, National Park Service, 1980), 193; McPherson, *Traders, Agents, and Weavers*, 67 for quote; for the agency and Shelton's twelve-year tenure, see 76–93, 97–104.
59. NIA, "News from Mrs. Eldridge," *The Indian's Friend*, January 1905, 11; and for position abolished, see MIA, *Twenty-Fourth Annual Report of the MIA, November 1906* (Boston: Frank Wood Printer, 1906), 8. See also Lockwood to CGD, August 1, 1905, Box 1, Folder 8, CGD Papers. Apparently, Eldridge provided no evidence in her letter to Lockwood, just stating that her resignation was "involuntary."
60. MIA, "Cambridge," *Twenty-Third Annual Report of the MIA, November 1905* (Canton, MA: Printed at the Office of the Journal Press, 1905), 9. For ASQ, see "Supplemental Work," *The Missions of 1905* (New York: Volunteer Press Print, 1905), 21; for appeal, see "Cambridge Indian Association," *The Cambridge Tribune*, October 21, 1905, 6; and for visitors, see *Twenty-Fourth Annual Report of the MIA*, 8. See also "Mrs. Mary G. Fisk," *The Cambridge Tribune*, October 3, 1903, 5; Fisk died on September 25.
61. Brugge, in *A History of the Chaco Navajos*, 219, describes his camp as extending for 60 to 75 miles south from Farmington and 50 to 60 miles east from the reservation boundary.
62. For a general history of the Navajo, see Peter Iverson, *Diné: A History of the Navajos* (Albuquerque: University of New Mexico, Press, 2002).
63. "Treaty with the Navaho, 1868," *Indian Treaties, 1778–1883* (Interland Publishing Inc., 1972), 1019; for background on the Navajos' wars and internment, see Iverson, *Diné*, 4, 35, 51–58, 62–64, 66–67.
64. Kelly, *The Navajo Indians and Federal Indian Policy*, 16–22, for maps of executive-order additions, 17–18. He describes an executive-order reservation as a unilateral creation of a president, an administrative expediency that fit "into no well-defined public policy," and that created an "insecure status [which] brought great anxiety to those for whom it was originally fashioned" (20). Bruton, in "The American Dream in Indian Country," 70, wrote that the 1868 treaty had given the Navajos "broad rights to use lands outside the reservation" and was written "in language that allowed liberal interpretation based on their social organization and modes of subsistence."
65. Kelly, *The Navajo Indians and Federal Indian Policy*, 16, see also 17.
66. MIA, *Twenty-Fourth Annual Report of the MIA*, quotes on 9.

NOTES

67. MLE to Sniffen, May 16, 1906, *IRA Papers*, Reel 20. This letter, with only May 16 on the bottom and no year, was mistakenly identified as written in 1908; based on content, it was written in 1906.
68. For letter, see NIA, "Mrs. Eldridge's Work for Navajos," *The Indian's Friend*, December 1906, 9. Damon, of Navajo and Scotch-Irish descent, served for sixteen years as interpreter. He also made adobes, hauled water, and assisted in the care and discipline of the children. Blinded by trachoma in one eye, he lost sight in the other due to an infection; see "Beginnings—50 Years Ago," *Mission Echoes*, (Navajo Methodist Mission School, Farmington, New Mexico), June 1949, 130.
69. NIA, "Mrs. Eldridge's Work for Navajos," 9–10.
70. Typed and undated with only "1908, May" penciled in at the top, in *IRA Papers*, Reel 20; this letter, containing the exact same information as her May 21, 1906, letter, printed in the December 1906 issue of *The Indian's Friend*, was clearly written in 1906.
71. For his report, see, IRA, "The Navajos—Allotment upon Public Lands," *Twenty-Fourth Annual Report of the Executive Committee of the IRA, 1906* (Philadelphia: Office of the IRA, 1907), 70–74 for quotes. See also Bruton, "The American Dream in Indian Country," 282–85, for IRA involvement.
72. NIA, "Mrs. Eldridge's Work for Navajos," *The Indian's Friend*, December 1906, 8; for Ebbs and Gaines at the Fisk Home, see "Indians' Friends: Annual Reports Show a Good Year's Work Done by the Cambridge Indian Association: Recording Secretary's Report," *The Cambridge Tribune*, January 11, 1908, 3.
73. For time off and first part of quote, see MIA, *Twenty-Fifth Annual Report of the MIA, November 1907* (Boston: Frank Wood, Printer, 1907), 8; for Brosius and quote about pioneer work, see "Work for Indians: A Letter Showing What the Agent of the Cambridge Indian Association Is Doing," *The Cambridge Tribune*, August 24, 1907, 3.
74. IRA, "Navajos on Public Lands–Day Schools Proposed," *Twenty-Fifth Annual Report of the Executive Committee of the IRA, 1907* (Philadelphia: Office of the IRA, 1908), 35. This report located her work "on public lands about sixty miles southeast of Farmington, New Mexico, near El Huerfano (Lonely Mountain)."
75. "Work for Indians: A Letter Showing What the Agent of the Cambridge Indian Association Is Doing," *The Cambridge Tribune*, August 24, 1907, 3.
76. Letter, with return address of a Largo P.O. Box, reprinted in "Indians' Friends: Annual Reports Show a Good Year's Work Done by the Cambridge Indian Association," *The Cambridge Tribune*, January 11, 1908, 3.
77. "Work for Indians. A Letter Showing What the Agent of the Cambridge Indian Association Is Doing," *The Cambridge Tribune*, August 24, 1907, 3. *The Cambridge Tribune* in "Indian Association Fair," November 16, 1907, 8, reported Eldridge was teaching the Indians "scientific cultivation of the soil and has been instrumental in having irrigation ditches built in their territory."
78. MIA literature uses Saahtoye instead of Saahtohe, as Eldridge does.
79. MIA, *Twenty-Sixth Annual Report of the MIA*, 6 and 8 for quotes; see also "Cambridge Indian Association," *The Cambridge Tribune*, May 22, 1909, 3. In "Massachusetts Indian Association Holds 26th Annual Meeting," *Boston Daily Globe*, November 13, 1908, 9, it was reported that Eldridge was to take charge of the Saahtoye mission "in the center of a population of about 500 Indians."
80. MIA, *Twenty-Seventh Annual Report of the MIA, November 1909* (Boston: Frank Wood, Printer, 1910), 6–7, 6 for Topliff. That year the Cambridge branch sent $912.55 ($32,237 in 2025 dollars) to support the Fisk Home. For land, see MIA, *Twenty-Eighth Annual Report of the MIA, November 1910* (Boston: Frank Wood, Printer, 1911), 8.
81. MIA, *Twenty-Eighth Annual Report of the MIA, November 1910*, 10.
82. "Indians Seek Medicines. Massachusetts Association Hears Report from Miss Gaines, Among the

NOTES

Navajos in New Mexico," *Boston Daily Globe*, November 29, 1911, 11.

83. *Durango Wage Earner*, October 12, 1911. For an eyewitness account, see "Letter from Mattie to her folks, October 11, 1911," copy in the San Juan County Historical Society. The cornerstone for the replacement of the Navajo Methodist Mission was laid in Farmington on what was to become Apache Street. "History of M. E. Mission. Cornerstone Laying Last Sunday Attended with Impressive Ceremonies. Good Crowd Present," *Farmington Enterprise*, September 13, 1912, 1; same quote in "Methodists' Navajo Mission: Tribute to Human Fortitude," *Durango Herald-Democrat*, May 13, 1951.

84. For Damon's role, see "Forty Years Ago—1901," *Mission Echoes* (Navajo Methodist Mission School), June 1949, 130; see also Marilu Waybourn, *Water: Lifeline of the Valley: Rivers, Ditches & Floods of San Juan County, NM* (n.p., 2004), 11–13. Malehorn, in "The Tender Plant," 34, writes that by the time of Damon's arrival, water was as high as his wagon wheel hub; he took the children to the Fisk Home a mile distant. For Eldridge letter, see "Work for Indians," *Cambridge Tribune*, December 2, 1911, 6.

85. "Teaching the Indian to Live Properly: Report of Progress to Be Made in Cambridge," *Boston Daily Globe*, November 26, 1911, 41; for *The Cambridge Tribune*, see "Work for Indians: Cambridge Branch of the Massachusetts Association Observes Its Twenty-Fifth Anniversary," 6. For money, see "Mrs. Gray's Will," *Cambridge Chronicle*, August 7, 1909, 2. Jane's husband, Professor Asa Gray, was a preeminent nineteenth-century botanist. CGD had been general secretary of the Gray Memorial Botanical Association.

For a photograph of Annie in traditional clothing, see Ellen Bulfinch, "Historical Sketch, 1886-1911," *Cambridge Branch of the Massachusetts Indian Association: Historical Sketch Prepared for the Twenty-Fifth Anniversary with Officers and Members, The Annual Report of the Treasurer and the Constitution, 1911* (Cambridge: Caustic-Clafin Co., Printers, 1911), 7.

86. "From the Navajos: Recent Letter Written by Mrs. Eldridge Gives Interesting Facts," *The Cambridge Tribune*, April 19, 1913, 11. See also MIA, "Cambridge," *Thirtieth Annual Report of the MIA, 1912–1913* (Boston: Frank Wood, Printer, 1913), 10.

87. MIA, "Cambridge," *Thirty-First Annual Report of the MIA, 1913–1914* (Boston: David Clapp & Son, Printers, 1914), 9–10. The shade cover is a ramada.

88. MIA, "Cambridge," *Thirty-First Annual Report of the MIA, 1913–1914* (Boston: David Clapp & Son, Printers, 1914), 9–10; for closure, see MIA, "Cambridge," *Thirty-Second Annual Report of the MIA* (Boston: David Clapp & Son, Printers, 1914), 7, 9.

89. For resignation, see MIA, "Cambridge," *Thirty-Fourth Annual Report of the MIA, 1916* (Boston: David Clapp & Son, Printers), 9. The CIA continued to support the Good Samaritan Hospital; for end of project, see MIA, "Cambridge," *Thirty-Third Annual Report of the MIA, 1915–1916* (Boston: David Clapp & Son, 1915), 9.

90. "Mrs. Eldridge—Pioneer Missionary, Has Passed On," *The Farmington Times Hustler*, April 7, 1933, 8.

91. Trennert, "Mary L. Eldridge," 168.

92. Martha C. Knack, "Philene T. Hall, Bureau of Indian Affairs Field Matron: Planned Culture Change of Washakie Shoshone Women," *Prologue: Quarterly of the National Archives* 22, no. 2 (Summer 1990): 151–67, quote, 165.

93. "Navajoes in Fruit Business," *Albuquerque Citizen*, May 1, 1902, 3; "Early History of the Navajo Mission," *Navajo Mission Collection*, 7–8.

94. Bruton, "The American Dream in Indian Country," 287. In a February 27, 1903, letter to the CIA, MLE related that a father had given his son, John Cambridge, to her to raise; see "Mrs. Eldridge's Work Among Navahoes," *The Indian's Friend*, May 1903, 9.

Chapter 7

1. The Moravians, a Protestant denomination originating in what is now the Czech Republic, arrived in North America 1735, working initially among the Indians in Georgia. The most famous among them were David Zeisberger and John Heckewelder; the latter influenced the writings of James Fenimore Cooper.
2. Mathes, *Amelia Stone Quinton*, 81, 94–95, 121–22, 130, 133, 142, 192.
3. "Rev. William H. Weinland," *New York Times*, March 11, 1930, 22; "Rev. W. H. Weinland," *Indian Truth*, April 1930, 4; and "Death of Pioneer Minister Mourned by Pass Communities; Started Work Among Tribesmen," *San Bernardino Sun*, March 9, 1930, 16.
4. Mary C. B. Watkins, Mesa Grande government teacher, described him to CGD as "hating [Catholics] with a bitterness that poisons his own better judgment." See Watkins to CGD, March 7, 1900, CGD Papers, Box 1, Folder 6.
5. "The Moravian Mission in Alaska," *New York Times*, November 29, 1884, 5. "The Alaska Number of the 'Moravian,'" *Periodical Accounts Relating to the Foreign Missions of the Church of the United Brethren* (hereafter cited as *Periodical Accounts*), September 1895, 552–53; see 553–54 for WHW's account. See also Wendell H. Oswalt, *Historic Settlements along the Kuskokwim River, Alaska* (Juneau: Alaska Division of State Libraries and Museums, 1980), 12, 27–28.
6. Rev. Paul de Schweinitz, "The Moravian Mission on the Kuskokwim," *Periodical Accounts*, March 1890, 19–20; "Alaska, The Alaska Number of the 'Moravian,'" *Periodical Accounts*, September 1895, 554; "The Drowning of Hans Torgersen in Alaska, 1885," *This Month in Moravian History*, issue 58 (October/November 2010); and "First Moravian Mission," AHRS Site No. BTH-013, (OMB No. 1024-0018), United States Department of the Interior National Park Service, National Register of Historic Places Registration Form, September 7, 1990, 3–4, 7, 8–9. At Bethel the Moravians developed a Yup'ik alphabet and grammar, conducting services and printing literature in Yup'ik.
7. Sheldon Jackson, "Education in Alaska," February 1, 1886, *Report of Education in Alaska with Maps and Illustration by Sheldon Jackson, 1886* (Washington, DC: GPO, 1886), 29 [580] found in *The Executive Documents of the Senate of the United States for the First Session of the Forty-Ninth Congress*, vol. 6 (Washington, DC: GPO, 1886). For appointment to operate the signal station, see "F. M. M. Beall, Second Lieut. Signal Corps. to Lieut. Robert Craig, San Francisco," *Report of the Secretary of War Being Part of the Message and Documents Communicated to the Two Houses of Congress at the Beginning of the First Session of the Forty-Ninth Congress*, vol. IV, Part 1 (Washington, DC: GPO, 1885), found in *Index to the Executive Documents of the House of Representatives for the First Session of the Forty-Ninth Congress, 1885–86* (Washington, DC: GPO, 1886), 63.
8. Edmund de Schweinitz Brunner, "History of the Moravian Mission to the Indians of Southern California," reprinted from the *Proceedings of the Society for Propagating the Gospel* (1909) (Bethlehem: Times Publishing Company, 1923), 9 (copy in WHW Papers, Box 17). For WNIA providing all monies, see Rev. Paul de Schweinitz, "The Ramona Mission," *The Missionary Review of the World*, May 1890, 358.
9. For quote, see Brunner, "History of the Moravian Mission to the Indians of Southern California," 10. For arrival, see WHW, "Ramona Mission [Diary], 1889," 1, and WHW, "Report of Ramona Mission for Decade 1889–1899," 1, both in WHW Papers, Box 15 and Box 18. See also "Our New Remona [sic] Mission," *The Indian's Friend*, June 1889, 2; and Mathes, *Divinely Guided*, 177–203.
10. In Jackson to ASQ, April 2, 1884, MA 4571, Pierpont Morgan Library, New York, she wrote: "I do not dare to think I have written a second Uncle Tom's Cabin," but "I do think I have written a story which will be a good stroke for the Indian cause." Reprinted in *The Indian Reform Letters of Helen Hunt*

Jackson, 1879–1885, 319, and Valerie Sherer Mathes, "Helen Hunt Jackson and Southern California's Mission Indians," *California History* 78, no. 4 (Winter 1999/2000): 271.

11. WNIA, "The Cohuilla [Cahuilla] Indians," *The Indian's Friend*, October 1888, 4. In March 1889 and for the next three months, an article on the Mission Indians, written by an unidentified contributor, appeared in the monthly periodical to acquaint the membership of the new missionary work. The Cahuillas were included with a number of Southern California tribes as Mission Indians; see George Harwood Phillips, *Chiefs and Challengers: Indian Resistance and Cooperation in Southern California, 1769–1906* (Norman: University of Oklahoma Press, 2014), 17–20.

12. ASQ to Oberly, February 18, 1889, LR #4927-1889; Oberly to ASQ, February 28, 1889, Letters Sent: Education Division, Volume 6, LB, pg. 32, 33; ASQ to Oberly, March 1, 1889, LR #5839-1889 enclosed in LR #19602-1889 [Special Case 143]; and ASQ to Oberly, April 12, 1889, LR #9615-1889, all in RG 75, OIA, NARA.

13. ASQ to WHW, June 4 and June 26, 1889, WHW Papers, Box 7. Few of his letters survived; hers are in the Huntington Library.

14. WHW, "Ramona Mission, 1889," 1, and WHW, "Report of Ramona Mission for Decade 1889–1899," 1, WHW Papers, Box 15, Box 18. Nancy Jane Ticknor came to Cahuilla in October 1881 as their first government schoolteacher; see Mrs. O. J. Hiles, "Another Worker Fallen," *The Indian's Friend*, October 1888, 1, for quote. Ticknor's being much loved, Preston reported that her death on May 8, 1888, had "so affected the whole tribe" that "it was not deemed advisable to re-open the school during the term." See "Preston to Oberly, August 20, 1888," *Fifty-Seventh ARCIA, 1888* (Washington, DC: GPO, 1888), 17.

15. ASQ to WHW, July [?] 1889, WHW Papers, Box 7.

16. WHW, "Ramona Mission, 1889," 1, WHW Papers, Box 15.

17. ASQ to WHW, July [?] 1889, WHW Papers, Box 7. Soboba was not a government reservation, thus Morgan had no authority to authorize a grant of land. In Morgan to ASQ, July 27, 1889 (copy), WHW Papers, Box 8, he suggested: "I can see no reason why your Association could merely with the consent of the Indians of said village, use the quantity of land desired for the purpose indicated." On July 23 (Box 7), ASQ wrote WHW that if the Soboba Indians "cordially consent you *might* perhaps built a cottage there & take the rest of our getting the government permission later."

18. In 1899, Morris married M. French Gilman, a rancher and fruit grower, who worked closely with the U.S. Department of Agriculture, experimenting on various crops. Born in Banning in 1871, he had been a teacher, postmaster, horticultural inspector, member of the Riverside County forestry board, councilman, and later mayor of Banning. Sarah died in 1941, and he died in 1944; see Philip A. Munz, "M. French Gilman," *Madroño: A West American Journal of Botany* 8 no. 1 (1945): 27–29.

19. She also taught crocheting, quilt making, and, at Potrero, how to care for the sick; see WNIA, "News and Notes," *The Indian's Friend*, October 1893, 1.

20. WHW, "Ramona Mission, 1889," 1–2, 13, Box 15, and WHW, "Report of Ramona Mission for Decade 1889–1899," 1–2, WHW Papers, Box 18.

21. "A Letter from Our New Ramona Mission," *The Indian's Friend*, July 1889, 1. At the time, ASQ was editor of the monthly.

22. Brunner, "History of the Moravian Mission to the Indians of Southern California," 11–15, 26 for quote.

23. "Rust to Morgan, October 28, 1889," *Fifty-Eighth ARCIA, 1889* (Washington, DC: GPO, 1889), 125. For his attendance, see WNIA, "The Ramona Mission," *Report of Missionary Work, November 1889*, 10, 7–19 for entire report on this station.

24. "The Ramona Mission," *Report of Missionary Work, November 1889*, 9, 13 and 14 for quotes.

25. Morgan to Belt, November 17, 1890, LR #35960-1890, RG 75, OIA, NARA.

26. ASQ to WHW, July 29, 1889; see also December 20, 1889, WHW, Box 7. For Soboba work, see Mathes,

Divinely Guided, 191, 193–94, 196, 198–202, 210, 224, 230, 239, 246, and Mathes, *Helen Hunt Jackson*, 19–39.

27. "The Ramona Mission, California," *Periodical Accounts*, September 1890, 130 for quote.
28. Rust to WHW, December 11, 1889, copy in WHW Papers, Box 6; and WHW, "From the Ramona Mission," *The Indian's Friend*, January 1890, 2. See also WHW, "Ramona Mission, 1889," 13; and WHW, "Report of Ramona Mission for Decade 1889–1899," 2, for continuation of Soboba work, WHW Papers, Box 15 and Box 18; see also Brunner, "History of the Moravian Mission," 12–14, 18–19.
29. WNIA, *The Ramona Mission and the Mission Indians* (WNIA: May 1889), quotes 1, 18. Hiles had made two extensive tours through Mission villages prior to 1889.
30. ASQ to WHW, January 17, and February 5, 1890, WHW Papers, Box 7. Quote from an undated letter.
31. WNIA, "From the Ramona Mission," March 1890, 1, and "Mrs. Weinland's Letter," March 1890, 3; for cottage, see "Association News," "Pittsburg and Allegheny Honors," January 1890, 1; and "Our New California Chapel," May 1890, 3, for dedication and baptism, all in *The Indian's Friend*. See also WHW, "The Ramona Mission, California," *Periodical Accounts*, September 1890, 130.
32. WNIA, "Missions Transferred," *The Indian's Friend*, May 1890, 2.
33. ASQ to WHW, May 3, 1890, WHW Papers, Box 7.
34. WNIA, "Our Ramona Missions," *The Report of the Missionary Department*, November 1891, 8; and WNIA "Association News and Notes," *The Indian's Friend*, September 1891, 1.
35. ASQ to WHW, August 7, 1891, WHW Papers, Box 7.
36. For more on Morongo, see Mathes and Brigandi, *Reservations, Removal and Reform*, numerous pages; and Phillips, *Chiefs and Challengers*, 231, 235, 294–95, 297–98, 301–2, 305, 312–13, 317.
37. Ida Goepp, "A Visit to the Ramona Mission at Potraro [sic]," *Periodical Accounts*, December 1890, 170–75.
38. WNIA, "The Ramona Missions," *Report of the Missionary Department of the WNIA* (WNIA: November 1890), 11–12. For more on Sheriff, see Mathes, *Helen Hunt Jackson*, 48–50, 58–60, 68–69, 71–72, 78, 90, 100, 123,126; Mathes, *Divinely Guided*, 178, 189, 200–203; and Mathes and Brigandi, eds., *A Call for Reform*, 23, 29, 37, 44, 46, 126–27, 149, 154–55, 157–60, 177.
39. Mary Sheriff Fowler wrote "The San Jacinto Valley," in Elmer W. Holmes, *History of Riverside County, California with Biographical Sketches* (Los Angeles: Historic Record Company, 1912) describing this meeting, quote on 242, see 218–52. She died on September 29, 1921; see "Mrs. Mary Fowler Is Called Home," *The Hemet News*, September 30, 1921, 1; and "Noted Life Comes to Close," *San Jacinto Register*, September 29, 1921.
40. Stockman to Morgan, August 2, 1890, LR #24390-1890, SC 143, RG 75, OIA, NARA; and ASQ to WHW, September 5, 16, and December 9, 1890, WHW Papers, Box 7.
41. WNIA, "The New York City Mission," *The Report of the Missionary Department*, November 1891, 7–8.
42. WNIA, "From a Missionary Report," *The Indian's Friend*, July 1892, 3.
43. "North American Indians. Notes from Afar," *Periodical Accounts*, March 1892, 450–51, quotes on 451.
44. WHW, "The Indian Mission," *The Moravian*, February 1, 1893, 72; and WNIA, "Association News and Notes," *The Indian's Friend*, February 1893, 5.
45. ASQ to Morgan, February 4, 1893, LR #4665-1893, RG 75, OIA, NARA. For other issues, see Mathes, *Divinely Guided*, 213–16.
46. WHW to Smith, March 15, 1893, WHW Papers, Box 10.
47. Hallowell and French to Smith, March 16, 1893, WHW Papers, Box 1.
48. Salsbery and Salmons to Smith, March 18, 1893; and Fowler to Smith, March 16, 1893, WHW Papers, Box 6 and Box 1.
49. Johnson to Smith, March 18, 1893; and Cadwallader to Cleveland, March 4, 1893, in WHW Papers,

Box 4 and Box 1.
50. Gibson to WHW, March 21, 1893, WHW Papers, Box 6.
51. ASQ to Smith (copy), March 29, 1893, WHW Papers, Box 7 with March 16 enclosures by French, Hallowell, and Fowler.
52. His father served as a public official under both Mexican and American rule. For his term of service, see Mathes and Brigandi, "A Troubled Tenure: Francisco Estudillo, 1893–1897," *Reservations, Removal, and Reform*, 133–59, 135 on positions and fiesta.
53. For appointment, see *Journal of the Executive Proceedings of the Senate of the United States of America*, vol. 28 (Washington, DC: GPO, 1909), 461.
54. ASQ to WHW, April 13, and 15, see also April 26, and May 7, 1893, WHW Papers, Box 7, the latter for Jones and quote. Quinton provided no proof that Estudillo was a poor candidate.
55. ASQ to WHW, May 2 and May 19, 1893, WHW Papers, Box 7; ASQ to Browning, May 8, 1893, LR #17196-1893, RG 75, OIA, NARA.
56. WNIA, *The Indian's Friend*, July 1893, 2; and ASQ to WHW, April 16 and April 26, 1893, WHW Papers, Box 7.
57. ASQ to WHW, September 4 and October 31, 1893, WHW Papers, Box 7.
58. ASQ to WHW, July 30, 1894, WHW Papers, Box 7.
59. February 1894, 5, March 1894, 7, and December 1894, 7, *The Indian's Friend*. For Palm Springs, see Eliza W. Jones [WNIA corresponding Secretary] to WHW, February 17, 1894, WHW Papers, Box 6.
60. For friendship between Jackson and Quinton, see Valerie Sherer Mathes, "Helen Hunt Jackson, Amelia Stone Quinton, and the Mission Indians of California," *Southern California Quarterly* 96, no. 2 (Summer 2014): 172–205.
61. WNIA, ASQ, "From California," *The Indian's Friend*, May 1895, inside cover page, and page 6.
62. WNIA, ASQ, "From California. No. 2," *The Indian's Friend*, June 1895, 7–8.
63. WNIA, ASQ, "From California. No. 3. Into the Desert," *The Indian's Friend*, July 1895, 6–7. When WHW drew up a second petition, the Indians requested he get ASQ's support. See WHW to ASQ, November 30, 1901, Amelia Stone Quinton Papers, Division of Rare and Manuscript Collections, Cornell University Library, Ithaca, New York (hereafter ASQ Papers, Cornell). Because this collection had not yet been transferred from the Phillips Free Library in Homer, New York, to Cornell when I used it, it had not been catalogued—hence no folder or box numbers.
64. WNIA, "At the Potrero," *Our Missions, for the Year . . . 1895* (WNIA: Executive Board, December 1895), 17.
65. WNIA, "From a Late Report," *The Indian's Friend*, June 1896, 9.
66. Bachman to BIC on Appropriations of Indian Lands, February 12, 1891, LR #46165-1891, SC 31, RG 75, OIA, NARA.
67. Oerter to WHW, August 11, 1896 (copy), WHW Papers, Box 4.
68. Oerter to WHW, August 31, 1896, WHW Papers, Box 4. WHW had agreed in a June 4 letter to accommodate the Woosleys; see Oerter to WHW, June 12, 1896, ibid.
69. Oerter to WHW, December 8, 1896, WHW Papers, Box 4. For signing, see "Progress in the Ramona Mission, South California," December 1896, *Periodical Accounts*, December 1896, 160.
70. ASQ to WHW, March 15, 1896; see also June 8, September 10, 21, and 28, 1896, WHW Papers, Box 7. In "Progress in the Ramona Mission, South California," *Periodical Accounts*, December 1896, 182, Weinland noted the highest heat that summer had been 126°.
71. "Progress in the Ramona Mission, South California," *Periodical Accounts*, December 1896, 181–82; see WHW, "The Desert Mission," *The Indian's Friend*, November 1896, 2. For a letter by WHW describing this meeting, see "Progress in the Ramona Mission, South California," *Periodical Accounts*, December

1896, 180–82.
72. WNIA, "Our Superintendent's Report," *Our Missionary Report for 1896* (WNIA: December 1896), 40–41; for pledge, see 25, and WNIA, *Annual Report of the WNIA, December, 1896* (Lancaster: Examiner Publishing House, 1896), 17.
73. WNIA, "Dedication of the New Mission Church," *The Indian's Friend*, February 1897, 7. Unable to endure the heat, the Woosleys were reassigned to Rincon, La Jolla, and Pechanga; the Robert Staveleys served instead: see Brunner, *History of the Moravian Mission to the Indians of Southern California*, 30.
74. WNIA, "The Reports of Mission," *Annual Report of the WNIA, December 1897* (Philadelphia: Hudson Wagenseller, Printer, 1897), 20.
75. "California's Arid Lands. Practicality of Supplying the Desert Indians with Water," *New York Times*, June 16, 1897, 2.
76. Rev. Morris W. Leibert, "Narratives from the Report of an Official Visitation," *Periodical Accounts*, June 1899, 96–108, quotes on 103, 106, 107; for Morris, see 101–2.
77. According to Oerter, in the minutes of the April 16, 1895, Provincial Elders' Conference, WHW had proposed that if a married brother was stationed at Potrero, Weinland would move "to Banning & take charge of the out-stations."
78. For Delbo, see WHW, "Ramona Mission, 1889," 17, WHW Papers, Box 15. In ASQ to WHW, August 1, 1898, Quinton wrote she was glad he had "a successor at Potraro [sic]," WHW Papers, Box 7. For move to Banning, see WNIA, "News and Notes," *The Indian's Friend*, September 1898, 4; and for his district, see "The District Br. Weinland Works," *Periodical Accounts*, March 1901, 482. See also Hallowell to WHW, October 6, 1898, WHW Papers, Box 1.
79. In ASQ to WHW, August 1, 1898, WHW Papers, Box 7, she noted that she had raised $200 from Redland and Pasadena branches, hoping to raise an additional $300.
80. Paul de Schweinitz to WHW, July 28, 1899, WHW Papers, Box 2.
81. WHW, "Mission Indians of California. Present Condition of a Race That Is Rapidly Growing Extinct," *Los Angeles Times*, April 16, 1899, 8; reprinted in the December 1899 and the February and April 1900 issues of *The Indian's Friend*.
82. "The Mission in Southern California," *Proceedings of the Society of the United Brethren for Propagating the Gospel Among the Heathen* (Bethlehem: Published by the Society, 1901), 44–48, quote on 47. For Yuma work, see WNIA, "News and Notes," *The Indian's Friend*, April 1901, 4; and ASQ to WHW, March 19, 1901, WHW Papers, Box 7, in which she expressed pleasure with Woosley's work.
83. WNIA, "News and Notes," *The Indian's Friend*, June 1901, 11.
84. "The Mission in Southern California," *Proceedings of the Society of the United Brethren*, quote on 48.
85. ASQ to WHW, January 22 and February 13, 1901, and Gates to ASQ, February 11, 1901 (with her February 13 letter to WHW), in WHW Papers, Box 7.
86. ASQ to WHW, March 19, and May 13, 1901 (for quote), WHW Papers, Box 7.
87. In 1904, Rev. Frank T. Lea and his wife were appointed; see NIA, "The Yuma Mission," *Missions of 1904* (Publications of the NIA: 1904), 22–25.
88. ASQ to WHW, January 25, 1902, WHW Papers, Box 7. For New Orleans, see NIA, ASQ, "Westward Ho," *The Indian's Friend*, April 1902, 2.
89. ASQ to WHW, February 3, 12, 1902, WHW Papers, Box 7. The school had been founded by the Sisters of St. Joseph of Carondelet in 1886.
90. NIA, ASQ, "A Visit to the Yumas," May 1902, 2 and NIA, "Work Among the Yumas," July 1902, 10, both in *The Indian's Friend*.
91. NIA, ASQ, "A Visit to the Desert Indians," *The Indian's Friend*, June 1902, 2, 7.
92. NIA, ASQ, "At Agua Caliente," 2, and NIA, "News and Notes," 5, *The Indian's Friend*, July 1902.

NOTES

93. CFL to ASQ, May 23, 1902, ASQ MS, CFL Collection, Braun Research Library.
94. "Poor Indians Victimized. Female False Pretender Among Them," *Los Angeles Times*, May 23, 1902, A1. See also Valerie Sherer Mathes and Phil Brigandi, "The Mischief Record of 'La Gobernadora': Amelia Stone Quinton, Charles Fletcher Lummis, and the Warner Ranch Indian Removal," *The Journal of San Diego History* 57, nos. 1–2 (Winter/Spring 2011), 69–96.
95. "Says She Is Blameless," *Los Angeles Times*, May 30, 1902, 5.
96. "Fight Till Last Ditch. Trouble Is Brewing at Warner's Ranch," *Los Angeles Times*, July 26, 1902, A1.
97. WHW to ASQ, August 21, 1903, ASQ Papers, Cornell. The text of the petition is unknown.
98. WHW to ASQ, September 6, 1903, ASQ Papers, Cornell. For report, see NIA, "News and Notes," *The Indian's Friend*, June 1903, 5. The outcome of his filing is unknown. But in 1904 the Chapel of the Sacred Hearts of Mary and Jesus was built on the Torres-Martínez Reservation.
99. WHW, "The Potrero," "Proceedings of the Society for Propagating the Gospel Among the Heathen," *Annual Report of the Foreign Mission Board of the Moravian Church* (1905), 42; see ASQ to WHW November 1, 1905, ASQ Papers, Cornell.
100. ASQ to WHW, November 28, and December 21, 1906, WHW Papers, Box 7.
101. NIA, Rev. William Henry Weinland, "Indian Student Work," *The Indian's Friend*, February 1907, 8; see "Fruitage," ibid.
102. NIA, "The Bible at Sherman," *The Indian's Friend*, September 1908, 5.
103. ASQ to WHW, January 9, 1907, WHW Papers, Box 7.
104. WHW, "Report of the Potrero Indian Mission for the Year 1909," *The Moravian*, February 2, 1910, 66–67, quote on 66.
105. "Observe Fourth Anniversary," *Oceanside Blade*, January 14, 1922, 2; and "Conference on Indian Welfare," *Riverside Daily Press*, March 21, 1922, 2.
106. NIA, "Eastern Day at the Potrero," May 1922, 4–5; and NIA, "Easter at the Moravian Mission in Southern California," May 1926, 6, *The Indian's Friend*.
107. Taber, *California and Her Indian Children*, 50.

Chapter 8

1. "Remarks by Miss Cornelia Taber," *Transactions of the Commonwealth Club of California* 47 (December 1909), 438, 441; and "Indian Night at the St. Francis," *San Francisco Chronicle*, October 14, 1909, 3. For this meeting, see Frances J. Fischer, "The Third Force: The Involvement of Voluntary Organizations in the Education of the American Indian with Special Reference to California, 1880–1933" (PhD diss., University of California, Berkeley, 1980), 70–72.
2. "Remarks by Miss Cornelia Taber," 440, and "Indian Night at the St. Francis," 3. She wrote a regular column for the California Federation of Women's Clubs' bulletin, *Club Life*, and spoke regularly on the lecture circuit.
3. Kelsey explained that reformers were fighting "against [a] most powerful adverse Indian sentiment" which had denied the California Indians all rights "absolutely," especially access to a public education; see LMC, "Providing for the California Indians, Address of Mr. Charles E. Kelsey," *Report of the Twenty-Seventh Annual Meeting of the LMC* (LMC, 1909), 44–47.
4. C. E. Kelsey, "The Rights and Wrongs of the California Indians," *Transactions of the Commonwealth Club of California*, quotes on 419, 422, 424. For Taber's remarks, see 438–41. For comments on Kelsey's talk and his attitude toward Indian education, see Fischer, *The Third Force*, 70–73.
5. For biographical information, see "The Damon and Taber Family Connections," http://www.richard.damon.name/genealogy/p990.htm; Jane Thompson-Stahr, *The Burling Book: Ancestors and Descendants*

of *Edward and Grace Burling, Quakers (1600–2000)*, vol. II (Baltimore: Gateway Press, Inc., 2001), 719.

    Cornelia was born on April 11, 1858, in New York City to New Bedford, Massachusetts–born Augustus Taber, a marble merchant, and his wife, Anna Haviland Ferris, who had been born in Westchester, New York. The Tabers were Quakers. In the 1880 census, the household, including Cornelia, her sister Mary Ferris and Mary's husband Edward W. Parsons and one-year-old daughter Edith, were living in Westchester. It is not known when they moved to California. Per the 1900 federal census, Cornelia was living with her mother and widowed brother-in-law and two children, Edith and Augustus T., in San Jose. Mary Ferris Parsons died in 1896, followed by her father Augustus Taber in 1898. Anna died in 1911 and Cornelia on March 1, 1929, at age 70.

6. Byron Nelson Jr., *Our Home Forever: The Hupa Indians of Northern California* (Salt Lake City: Howe Brothers, 1988), 3 explains that the term "Hupa" refers to the people, and "Hoopa" to the valley and agency. For treaty provisions, see 187–92. See also chapters 4 and 5 in David Rich Lewis, *Neither Wolf nor Dog: American Indians, Environment, & Agrarian Change* (Oxford: Oxford University Press, 1994), 71–117. On p. 91 he describes the Hoopa Valley as so isolated it took pack mules two days to travel from Eureka, 54 miles away, or five days from Crescent City, 83 miles' distance over difficult mountain trails.

7. For Spencer's meeting with Beckwith, see Belle M. Brain, *The Redemption of the Red Man* (New York: The Board of Home Missions of the Presbyterian Church in the U.S.A., 1904), 64–70; and Nelson, *Our Home Forever*, 124–26; for more on Beckwith, see 128–30.

8. Spencer to Welsh, November 10, 1889, *IRA Papers*, Reel 5; and WNIA, "Another Dark Region," *The Indian's Friend*, January 1890, 1. See also Mathes, "Northern California Members and Their Work at the Hoopa Reservation," in *Divinely Guided*, 78–100.

9. Bullard to Morgan, September 12, 1890, LR #28298-1890 included with George Chandler to Morgan, November 19, 1890, LR #24930-1890, SC 143, RG 75, OIA, NARA. See also Bullard to Morgan, December 6, 1890, LR #37960-1890; and Beers to Morgan, December 13, 1890, LR #40010-1890, ibid. Elizabeth's husband was Stephen H. Bullard, president of the Mercantile Marine Insurance Company. See "The Harleian Society," *The New England Historical & Genealogical Register and Antiquarian Journal, for 1869* (Boston: Published by The Society, 1869), 340; and "Mercantile Marine Insurance Company," *The Massachusetts Register, 1872* (Boston: Rand, Avery, & Co., 1872), 594.

10. "Women's Indian Association," *Daily Evening Bulletin* (San Francisco), August 12, 1891, 1; "For the Indians: An Address by Mrs. Amelia S. Quinton: The Northern California Women's Indian Association Organized," *San Francisco Chronicle*, August 12, 1891, 10.

11. Eyster came to California in the 1870s from her native Maryland. She was a member of the Pen Women's Club and lived in San Jose before moving to Berkeley in 1906, where she became president of the local WCTU. See "Mrs. N. B. Eyster, Author, Dies, Aged 92 Years," *San Francisco Chronicle*, February 23, 1922.

12. WNIA, "In Northern California: Letter Number Eight," *The Indian's Friend*, November 1891, 1, 3; for ASQ's visit to Hoopa, see Mathes, *Amelia Stone Quinton*, 75–77, 144–46.

13. For committee, see "The Northern California Women's Indian Association," *San Francisco Call*, August 28, 1891, 8; for Amenta, see WNIA, "Taking Vacation," August 1894, 8; and "Good News for Greenville," October 1894, 6–7; and "News and Notes," December 1894, 2, all in *The Indian's Friend*. For the school, see Mathes, "Greenville Indian Industrial School," *Divinely Guided*, 101–26.

14. WNIA, "News and Notes," November 1895, 6; and "News and Notes," July 1898, 4, for Taber's presidency, both in *The Indian's Friend*.

15. The exact date of Taber's appointment is unknown. For an early report, see WNIA, "From a New Teacher," *The Indian's Friend*, December 1894, 8–9.

16. WNIA, *Annual Report, December 1896*, 21.

17. WNIA, "News and Notes," and "Meeting of San Jose Workers," in *The Indian's Friend*, October 1895, 3, 7.
18. Eyster to Browning, November 10, 1895, LR #46735-1895 [in LR #49516-1895], SC 143, RG 75, OIA, NARA.
19. Dougherty to Browning, November 30, 1895, LR #49516-1895, SC 143, RG 75, OIA, NARA.
20. ASQ to Browning, May 10, 1896, LR #18070-1896, SC 143, RG 75, OIA, NARA.
21. Denton to Taber, January 12, 1896, Taber to ASQ, January 14, 1896, and ASQ to Browning, January 30, 1896, all in LR #4632-1896, RG 75, OIA, NARA.
22. ASQ to Browning, March 4, 1896, LR #8859-1896, RG 75, OIA, NARA.
23. WNIA, "In the Hoopa Valley," *The Indian's Friend*, March 1896, 9.
24. "Women Who Take Care of Indians: A Meeting at the Palace," *San Francisco Chronicle*, August 4, 1896, 8.
25. Born in Maine, a graduate of Earlham College, Goddard left his mission duties to pursue a PhD in linguistics at the University of California, Berkeley. Doctorate completed in 1904, he was hired to teach in the new Department of Anthropology. In 1909 the family moved to New York, where he became the assistant curator at the American Museum of Natural History. For a letter from Mrs. Goddard to Taber, see WNIA, "News and Notes," *The Indian's Friend*, June 1897, 9.
26. WNIA, "News and Notes," May 1896, 5, and "Mission of the San Jose Indian Association, California," March 1897, 10, both in *The Indian's Friend*.
27. WNIA, "News and Notes," *The Indian's Friend*, August 1898, 4; and WNIA, *Annual Report* (Philadelphia, December 1898), 25.
28. Connecticut Indian Association, "Field Matron Work. The Views of Com. Browning and Dr. Hailmann on an Important Subject," *The Indian Bulletin*, April 1897, 2, 3.
29. Taber, "Government Field Matron Stations," *California and Her Indian Children*, 31–42.
30. "For the Indians. Good Word for the Redmen by Their San Jose Friends," *San Jose Mercury News*, October 8, 1898, 7; and WNIA, "News and Notes," *The Indian's Friend*, May 1899, 4.
31. "Miss Taber's Talk on the Indians," *San Jose Mercury-News*, July 21, 1898, 7.
32. WNIA, "A Trip to Hoopa," *The Indian's Friend*, May 1899, 10–11.
33. WNIA, "A Trip to Hoopa," May 1899, 10; "News and Notes," June 1899, 6–7, 9, and "The Children of the Lord's Supper," August 1899, 2, 11, all in *The Indian's Friend*.
34. "Memorial Service. Tribute to Life and Work of Miss Emma H. Denton," *San Jose Mercury-News*, January 30, 1899, 5; and WNIA, "News and Notes," April 1899, 9, for quote; see also "News and Notes," March 1899, 4, in *The Indian's Friend*. For an obituary, see WNIA, *Annual Report* (Philadelphia, December 1899), 24.
35. "State Normal School," *San Jose Mercury-News*, June 18, 1899, 10.
36. WNIA, "News and Notes," *The Indian's Friend*, December 1900, 4. For a brief undated history of "The Hoopa [sic] Indians" by M. E. Chase, see Taber Collection, CHS.
37. WNIA, "Another Sad Story," June 1901, 7; "News and Notes," October 1901, 5, in *The Indian's Friend*; Bean to Garrett, June 19, 1901, *IRA Papers*, Reel 15; and IRA, *Nineteenth Annual Report* (Philadelphia: Office of the IRA, 1902), 32–34; see 34 for Bean's acknowledgment.
38. *Articles of Incorporation of the Northern California Indian Association, 34724*, filed January 24, 1902, Office of the Secretary of State Records, California State Archives, Sacramento, California.
39. WNIA, "News and Notes," December 1901, 4; and "News and Notes," June 1902, 4, in *The Indian's Friend*.
40. NIA, "Colusa Indians," August 1902, 9; "News and Notes," September 1902, 4; and for her letter about landless Indians at Upper Lake, see "News and Notes," March 1902, 4, in *The Indian's Friend*.

41. NIA, ASQ, "Dear Friends of *The Indian's Friend*," *The Indian's Friend*, September 1902, 2.
42. For printed version, see U.S. Congress, Senate, *Memorial of the Northern California Indian Association* (hereafter cited as *Memorial of the NCIA*), S. Doc. 131, 58th Cong., 2d sess., 1904, 10–12. See also NIA, "News and Notes," *The Indian's Friend*, July 1903, 4; and IRA, "Other Needy California Indians," *Twenty-First Annual Report* (Philadelphia: Office of the IRA, 1904), 31–32.
43. A May 18, 1903, letter from Kelsey to CFL, along with a typed "draft of the memorial," can be found in C. E. Kelsey MS, CFL Collection, Braun Research Library.
44. WNIA, "News and Notes," *The Indian's Friend*, March 1903, 4.
45. "Draft of the Memorial," 1, 2, CFL Collection, Braun Research Library.
46. "Draft of the Memorial," 3–4, CFL Collection, Braun Research Library.
47. Jones to Roosevelt, July 22, 1903, in *Memorial of the NCIA*, 13. For response, see Kelsey to Roosevelt, August 10, 1903, ibid., 14–16.
48. C. Taber to Sniffen, January 30, 1904, *IRA Papers*, Reel 16.
49. A. Taber to Sniffen, March 17 and September 1, 1904, 1904, *IRA Papers*, Reel 17,
50. For presentation, see "Many Indians Are Homeless: Northern California Association Asks Aid for Some Ten Thousand, Said to Be in Need," January 22, 1904, 1; and "editorial," January 23, 1904, 6, both in *San Francisco Chronicle*. See also "The California Indians," *The Southern Workman*, October 1904, 516–17.
51. In NIA, "Mrs. Dorcas J. Spencer," *Annual Report of the NIA* (New York, December 1906), 35, it was written these treaties were unknown until "at the request of Mr. Kelsey of the NCIA they were unearthed from the archives of Congress."
52. Ordered printed on January 28, 1904, the petition appeared in the Senate document, *Memorial of the NCIA*, 1–4, with quotes on 1, 2. It was also reprinted as an NCIA pamphlet, dated December 24, 1903, a copy in *IRA Papers*, Reel, 132, No. 344; in NIA, "Petition to Congress," *The Indian's Friend*, February 1904, 2, 10; and as "Memorial of the NCIA, Praying That Lands Be Allotted to the Landless Indians of the Northern Part of the State of California," in *Federal Concern About Conditions of California Indians 1853 to 1913: Eight Documents*, ed. Robert F. Heizer (Socorro, NM: Ballena Press, 1979), 95–109. For Kelsey's last quote, see NIA, "A California Letter," *The Indian's Friend*, December 1905, 10, an article by ASQ that included the text of his letter.
53. *Memorial of the NCIA*, 2–3, list on 4–9; reprinted as "Statistics of the Northern California Indians," *The Indian's Friend*, March 1904, 10–11. See also a *San Francisco Chronicle* article with these statistics reprinted in the April 1904 issue, 2 of *The Indian's Friend*; and "The Sequoya League," *Out West*, April 1904, 382. On December 15, 1910, Kelsey informed Commissioner Robert Grosvenor Valentine that only 1,720 out of 14,000 Indians in Northern California had reservation lands; see Administrative Files, 1895–1923, Greenville, Box 79, RC 75, OIA, NARA [San Bruno, California].
54. Kelsey to Sniffen, December 4 and 26, 1903, *IRA Papers*, Reel 16.
55. Brosius to Sniffen, January 29, 1904, *IRA Papers*, Reel 16.
56. Kelsey to Perkins, March 30, 1904; for a similar sentiment, see Kelsey to Sniffen, April 1, 1904, both in *IRA Papers*, Reel 17.
57. "Good Work for Indians: How Northern California Association Has Provided Homes for Many Scattered Bands," January 27, 1904, 5; and "Our California Indians," March 7, 1904, 6, in *San Francisco Chronicle*.
58. Hagan, *The IRA*, 84 for quote; see also 87, 107, and 160–61 for other examples.
59. Kelsey to Sniffen, February 10, 1904, Reel 16; see also Kelsey to Sniffen, April 1, 1904, *IRA Papers*, Reel 17. David Wallace Adams, *Education for Extinction: American Indians and the Boarding School Experience, 1875–1928* (Lawrence: University Press of Kansas, 1995), 53, writes that Pratt favored "rapid

and absolute assimilation of the Indians," even opposing the Dawes Act because he believed education should precede land allotment. Even though allotment broke up reservations, Pratt viewed it as still continuing "to perpetuate Indian communities."

60. From 1869 to 1897, Lewis served as an Associate Justice of the Supreme Courts of Idaho and Washington Territories, meeting Indians as witnesses.
61. A. Taber to Sniffen, February 19, 1904, *IRA Papers*, Reel 16.
62. In A. Taber to Sniffen, November 13, 1904, *IRA Papers*, Reel 17, she noted that Pratt had responded to Bidwell "of the inevitable result of the carrying out of our plan as involving the appointment of agents and the putting the Indians under the Indian Bureau—This is all a mistake," Taber concluded.
63. The Indian Homestead Act of March 3, 1875, extended to any Indian born in the country, head of a household or twenty-one, the right to select land from the public domain under provision of the May 20, 1862, Homestead Act. To comply, the applicant had to abandon their tribal affiliation. Many were unwilling to do so.
64. Kelsey to Sniffen, April 1, 1904; and open letter from Edwards and Kelsey to Col. R. H. Pratt, February 15, 1904, pamphlet published by the NCIA (n.d.), *IRA Papers*, Reel 16. See also "Memorial of the NCIA," *Federal Concern*. Pratt's response is unknown.
65. Lewis to the Honorable Members of the Senate and House of Representatives, February 19, 1904, LR #16531-1904, RG 75, OIA, NARA; a copy is in *IRA Papers*, Reel 16.
66. C. Taber to Jones, February 25, 1904, *IRA Papers*, Reel 16. Bard forwarded Lewis's letter to Jones on March 2, 1905; see Bard to Jones, March 2, 1904, included in LR #16531-1904, RG 75, OIA, NARA.
67. A. Taber to Sniffen, February 11, 1904, *IRA Papers*, Reel 16.
68. A. Taber to Sniffen, February 11, 1904, *IRA Papers*, Reel 16.
69. "Ask Justice for Indians, Ministers' Unions Take up the Fight to Secure Land for Those North of Tehachapi," *San Francisco Chronicle*, February 16, 1904.
70. NIA, "News and Notes," *The Indian's Friend*, April 1904, 4.
71. "Bard's Petition Is Contradicted. California Indians' Welfare at Stake," *Los Angeles Herald*, February 17, 1904, 5.
72. A. Taber to Sniffen, June 16 and September 1, 1904, *IRA Papers*, Reel 17. See "Good Success in Rousing Interest. Northern California Indian Association in Annual Meeting—Encouraged over the Year's Work," *San Jose Mercury-News*, October 30, 1904, 5, for the reasoning behind the rewriting. A. Taber included this article in a January 20, 1905, letter to Sniffen, *IRA Papers*, Reel 18.
73. In C. Taber to Sniffen, October 11, 1904, *IRA Papers*, Reel 17, Cornelia wrote that Wood was "a member of the Com. on Restitutions at the Mohonk Conference."
74. A. Taber to Sniffen, September 18 and 26, 1904, *IRA Papers*, Reel 17. The school was opened in 1884 and lasted almost a century. See K. Tsianina Lomawaima, *They Called It Prairie Light: The Story of Chilocco Indian School* (Lincoln: University of Nebraska Press, 1994). For a brief history of Coppock, see a description of his papers at DeGolyer Library, Southern Methodist University, Dallas, Texas.
75. Jordan received a PhD at Northwestern Christian University (later Butler University) in Indianapolis and taught at Indiana University, becoming president in 1885. In 1891 he became the first president of Stanford University and its chancellor in 1913. See Kevin Starr, *Americans and the California Dream, 1850–1915* (New York: Oxford University Press, 1973), 307–44.
76. A. Taber to Sniffen, October 3 and 11, 1904, *IRA Papers*, Reel 17.
77. C. Taber to Sniffen, October 11, 1904, *IRA Papers*, Reel 17.
78. Kelsey to Sniffen, October 11, 31, 1904, *IRA Papers*, Reel 17.
79. LMC, S. M. Brosius, "A Plea for the Northern California Indians," *Proceedings of the Twenty-Second Annual Meeting of the LMC of Friends of the Indian and Other Dependent Peoples* (LMC, 1904),

150–52; 152–53 for ASQ, 163 for resolutions. See also NIA, "Resolutions," *The Indian's Friend*, December 1904, 7.

80. A. Taber to Sniffen, November [8] 1904, and November 13, 1904; see also C. Taber to Sniffen, October 11, 1904, all in *IRA Papers*, Reel 17.
81. NIA, "News and Notes," December 1904, 6; see also "News and Notes," April 1904, 5, in *The Indian's Friend*.
82. "Good Success in Rousing Interest," *San Jose Mercury-News*, October 30, 1904, 5.
83. NIA, *Annual Report* (New York: December 1904), 33. For NCIA work that year, see 19.
84. "Improvement in Hoopa Indians' Home Life: Northern California Indian Association Has Big Meeting," *San Jose Mercury-News*, January 12, 1905, 3.
85. For meeting, see NIA, "News and Notes," *The Indian's Friend*, May 1905, 4; for quotes, see Kelsey to Sniffen, April 18, 1905, *IRA Papers*, Reel 18. See also "The Northern California Indians" and "The Treatment of the Northern California Indians," in *Twenty-Second Annual Report* (Philadelphia: Office of the IRA, 1905), 33–34, 57–60, and especially 42–43 for resolution supporting the establishment of homes and the creation of a committee to investigate their condition. See also IRA, "A Beginning for the Northern California Indians," *Twenty-Third Annual Report* (Philadelphia: Office of the IRA, 1906), 29.
86. IRA, "The Landless Indians in California," *Twenty-Fourth Annual Report* (Philadelphia: Office of the IRA, 1907), 16; for CFL, see Kelsey to Lummis, May 23, 1904, and CFL to Kelsey, May 26, 1904, C. E. Kelsey MS, CFL Collection, Braun Research Library.
87. NIA, "Our New Commissioner," *The Indian's Friend*, February 1905, 5, quotes Leupp as saying: "Let us not make the mistake in the process of absorbing them, of washing out of them whatever is distinctly Indian"—a statement reflective of the gradual waning of the government's assimilation policy. Leupp wrote *The Indian and His Problem*, published by Charles Scribner's Sons in 1910.
88. Phoenix Indian School, *The Native American*, September 9, 1905, 304.
89. NIA, *Annual Report* (New York City, 1905), 22–23, quote on 23; A. Taber to Sniffen, January 20, 1905, *IRA Papers*, Reel 18; and "The Sequoya League," *Out West*, March 1906, 240. In a June 16, 1904, letter to Sniffen, she wrote that Kelsey "lived for six years among the Oneidas his father being the agent," and in her November [8?], 1904, letter to Sniffen, she wrote that he was the son of an agent and that his wife was the daughter of "a devoted Indian missionary," Reel 17.
90. Larisa K. Miller, "Made in Wisconsin: The Shaping of a Federal Indian Agent," *Voyageur* 33, no. 1 (Summer/Fall 2016): 10–18, quote on 16. For law firm in Eau Claire, see *The American Lawyer: A Monthly Journal Serving the Interests of the Legal Profession in America*, New York, July 1899, 299; and for a short obituary, see *Wisconsin Alumnus* 38, no 4 (March 1937): 247.
91. Kelsey, *Report of the Special Agent*, 4; see 24 for decline. See also Charles E. Kelsey, *Census of Non-reservation California Indians, 1905–1906*, ed. Robert F. Heizer (Berkeley: University of California, Archaeological Research Facility, Department of Anthropology, 1971). Heizer wrote that Kelsey physically visited 36 counties, providing figures for the nine he did not, using the 1900 census figures (i). He was called back to Washington before he could finish the task. See also M. E. Crane, "Red Men Are Unable to Cultivate Holdings," *San Francisco Call*, November 26, 1906, 9.
92. Kelsey, *Report of the Special Agent*, 24 and 37 for quotes. For a history of these lost treaties, see Akins and Bauer, *We Are the Land*, 187–89.
93. A. Taber to Sniffen, March 19, 1906, *The IRA Papers*, Reel 18. Kelsey also wrote *Indian Rights and Wrongs* (1907). For comments on his tour at the NCIA's annual meeting in November, see NIA, "News and Notes," *The Indian's Friend*, January 1906, 4.
94. NIA, "California Indians," *The Indian's Friend*, April 1906, 7.

95. NIA, "News and Notes," *The Indian's Friend*, March 1906, 5.
96. NIA, *Annual Report* (New York, December 1906), 22, and NIA, "News and Notes," *The Indian's Friend*, July 1906, 6. See also Taber, *California and Her Indian Children*, 13.
97. NIA, "News and Notes," *The Indian's Friend*, August 1907, 4; quote from "Leupp in Strong Plea to Assist 'Poor Lo,'" *San Jose Mercury-News*, June 12, 1907, 3.
98. For a list and quote, see NIA, *The Indian's Friend*, August 1906, 4. Signers included Annie E. K. Bidwell; Frank P. Flint, California US Senator; Mrs. David Starr Jordan, wife of Stanford's president; Dr. C. Hart Merriam, zoologist, ethnographer, and naturalist in Washington, DC; and Pliny E. Goddard, former NCIA missionary.
99. Her husband, Samuel W. Gilchrist, was active in the First Presbyterian Church, a director of the Farmers Union, and in the Oak Hill Cemetery association. See "S. W. Gilchrist, Well Known San Jose Man Dead at Home Here," *San Jose Mercury-News*, July 21, 1916, 7.
100. For more on Benson, see Mathes, *Divinely Guided*, 141–42, 145, 320n51. As a friend of Grace Nicholson, a Pasadena collector of Indian art, see William R. Benson, *"My Dear Miss Nicholson": Letters and Myths*, ed. Maria del Carmen Gasser (Carmel: published by author, 1995). Benson, who had a career as a basket maker, ethnographer, and political activist, also wrote an account from the Pomo perspective of the murder of two white men, Charles Stone and Andrew Kelsey, and the subsequent Bloody Island Massacre; see William Ralganal Benson, "The Stone and Kelsey 'Massacre' on the Shores of Clear Lake in 1849: The Indian Viewpoint," *California Historical Society Quarterly* 11, no. 3 (September 1932): 266–73; and Jeremiah J. Garsha, "'Reclamation Road': A Microhistory of Massacre Memory in Clear Lake, California," *Genocide Studies and Prevention: An International Journal* 9, no. 2 (2015): 61–75.
101. For Taber, see NIA, "News and Notes," September 1906, 9; and ASQ, "The California Indian Conference," 5, same issue, *The Indian's Friend*.
102. NIA, "An Indian Conference in California," *The Indian's Friend*, September 1907, 2, 11; see NCIA, *Assembled in the Zayante Indian Conference* (NCIA, 1907), copy in *IRA Papers*, Reel 132, No. 344; for demands and Indian signatures, see 2–3, recipients, 4. For Maggie Lafonso, see Mathes, *Divinely Guided*, 160, 162–64, 166, 168, 170, 331n49; photo on 137.
103. Cathleen D. Cahill, "Reassessing the Role of the 'Native Helper': Christian Indians and the Woman's National Indian Association (WNIA), 1905–1926," paper presented at the "Women and American Religion: Reimagining the Past" Conference, University of Chicago, October 9, 2003, 5. She compares these conferences and the Guinda school with Dwight L. Moody's academies in Northfield, Massachusetts, as "a training ground for future evangelists," 4.
104. NIA, "The Third Annual Zayante Indian Conference," *The Indian's Friend*, September 1908, 2, 7–8, and California Indian Association and Mount Hermon Association, *The Third Annual Zayante Indian Conference* (Mount Hermon, August 4–6, 1908), in Sequoya League Series (folder-correspondence, 1908), CFL Collection, Braun Research Library. The focus was to educate Indians to work on behalf of their people, replacing white reservation workers. Not until the 1928 publication of *The Problem of Indian Administration* (Meriam Report) did the government move away from education aimed at assimilation. According to Fischer, "The Third Force," 61, the WNIA was the "most directly concerned and most effective in terms of Indian education"; see also 16–17, 22–25, 32, 52–55, 61–67, 70–81, 83–87.
105. Flint to CFL, February 28, 1908, Sequoya League Series (folder-correspondence, 1908), CFL Collection, Braun Research Library; see also "The Sequoya League," *Out West*, April 1908, 335. The legislation did not stipulate the money be used exclusively for Mission Indians but for non-reservation Indians and those living on reservations without suitable cultivatable lands in California; see "Indian Appropriation Act of April 30, 1908," http://www.standupca.org/gaming-law/unique-federal-indian-law-california-specific, accessed October 5, 2013. For both the 1906 and 1908 appropriations, see Kelsey to Flint, January 5,

NOTES

1909, in Wayland H. Smith, "In Re California Indians to Date," *Out West*, February–March 1909, 131, see also 130, reprinted as the *Fifth Bulletin of the Los Angeles Council of the Sequoya League*.

106. LMC, *Report of the Twenty-Sixth Annual Meeting of the LMC* (LMC, 1908), 76.

107. Holmes, *History of Riverside County, California*, 289–91, for Miller. In 1880 he bought the Glenwood Cottage from his father, enlarged it once, and again in 1902 into the popular Mission Revival style. Reopened in January, it was renamed the Glenwood Mission Inn. After Miller's death, family members ran it for decades. It was closed in 1985 for renovations and reopened in 1992 as the Mission Inn Hotel and Spa.

108. CFL to [an unknown recipient], c. early May 1908, Sequoya League Series (folder-Indian Affairs, 1910), CFL Collection, Braun Research Library. The same sentiment appeared in his article, "Getting Together," *Out West*, June 1908, 504–6; see also 507–8 for a list of delegates. See NIA, "The California Conference," *The Indian's Friend*, June 1908, 6–7, an article written by ASQ; and "Indian Conference Closes with Great Church Meeting," *Enterprise* [Riverside], April 30, 1908, 2.

109. "Chinese Members of Gilroy M. E. Church," *San Jose Mercury-News*, October 15, 1908, 5.

110. NIA, *Annual Report* (New York, December 1909), quote, 19.

111. The Bishop site, supported by the American Sunday School Union, was turned over to the Presbyterian Board the following year. See also NIA, "Good News from Bishop, California," *The Indian's Friend*, August 1909, 8–10.

112. LMC, "Providing for the California Indians," Address of Mr. Charles E. Kelsey," *Report of the Twenty-Seventh Annual Meeting of the LMC* (LMC, 1909), 44–47.

113. "Indian-Day a Success at the Woman's Club," *San Jose Mercury-News*, June 6, 1909, 9.

114. NIA, *Annual Report* (New York, December 1909), 19–20, 20 for quote; and NCIA, *Fifteenth Annual Report of the NCIA* (January 1, 1910), 13–16, for the Zayante Conference. The cover photograph shows the Indian men in suits and ties and the women, Mrs. Lockhart and Alma Yee, in dresses, each holding a fancy hat.

115. NIA, "Zayante Conference Notes: by Miss Cornelia Taber, Saratoga, Cal.," *The Indian's Friend*, September 1909, 4–5, quote 5; an article condensed from the *San Jose Mercury-News* appeared as "The Fourth Zayante Indian Conference," 2, same issue.

116. Larisa K. Miller, "The Decline of the Northern California Indian Association," *California History* 99, no. 3 (Fall 2022): 32.

117. C. Taber to Sniffen, October 14, 1910, *IRA Papers*, Reel 22. For more on Legters, see "New York City Indian Association," *The Indian's Friend*, December 1910, 5.

118. NIA, *Annual Report* (New York, December 1910), 18; and NCIA, *The Fifth Zayante Indian Conference* (NCIA, 1910), 2, 11.

119. NIA, *Annual Report* (New York, December 1910), quotes, 19, 20. For land purchase, see "Buying Land for Indian School," *Sacramento Union*, October 17, 1910, 7, and "Will Purchase Land for Indian Reservation," *Los Angeles Herald*, October 18, 1910, 6. For the transfer of two parcels to the federal government and the setting aside of $20,000 for the initial school building, see "Deed Indian School Site to Government," *San Francisco Chronicle*, December 28, 1910, 3.

120. NIA, "News and Notes," 4, and for the Mount Hermon portion, see "Sixth Zayante Indian Conference," 10–11, both in the September 1911 issue of *The Indian's Friend*.

121. NIA, "The First Indian Conference at Guinda, Cal.," *The Indian's Friend*, October 1911, 2, 12. See also Miller, "The Decline of the Northern California Indian Association," 34–37.

122. "With New Books and Magazines. California and Her Indian Children," *San Jose Mercury-News*, December 10, 1911, 32; and NIA, "California and Her Indian Children," *The Indian's Friend*, December 1911, 4.

NOTES

123. Dedication page, Taber, *California and Her Indian Children*. For Anna's death on September 13, see "In Memoriam: Anna Ferris Taber," *The Indian's Friend*, January 1912, 5. On October 3, 1911, Dorcas Spencer, startled to learn of Taber's mother's death, wrote to her: "We become too acquainted to continued illness to apprehend the end," in Spencer to Taber, Taber Collection, CHS.
124. Taber, *California and Her Indian Children*, for quotes, see 9, 17–18; see also NIA, *Annual Report* (December 1911), 19, and Cahill, "Reassessing the Role of the 'Native Helper,'" 8–10 for an interesting analysis of Taber's book.
125. NIA, "The Lake Mohonk Conference," *The Indian's Friend*, November 1911, 12. Her address was not printed in the annual report.
126. NIA, *Annual Report* (December 1911), 23–25, quotes on 24; for the NCIA's work in 1911, see 19–21; also see NIA, "The Annual Meeting of the National Indian Association," *The Indian's Friend*, December 1911, 10–11.
127. NIA, *Annual Report* (New York, December 1913), 21–23, 21 for quote. For subjects, see NIA, "California Indian Industrial School," March 1917, 4–5, and "Guinda School," January 1918, 4, *The Indian's Friend*. See also Fischer, "The Third Force," 77–81. For Ripley's comment, see NIA, "Northern California Indian Association," *The Indian's Friend*, December 1913, 5. In a letter to a Quaker cousin, C. Taber wrote that the NCIA had a "plant worth $25,000" but lacked money for daily expenses, in Taber to "my dear Cousin," April 2, 1913, the Quaker Collection, Haverford College, Haverford, Pennsylvania.
128. NIA, *Annual Report* (New York, December 1914), 16; NCIA, *The Guinda Indian Industrial School* (n.d.), and NCIA, "Indian Industrial School" (n.d.), in *IRA Papers*, Reel 132, No. 344. For Gray's comment, see NIA, *Annual Report* (New York, December 1915), 18.
129. NIA, "California Indian Industrial School," *The Indian's Friend*, March 1917, 4–5, quote, 4.
130. NIA, "Guinda School," January 1918, 4, and "Guinda Indian Industrial School," March 1918, 4–5, in *The Indian's Friend*; and NIA, *Annual Report* (New York, December 1917), 16.
131. For Sniffen's quote, see IRA, *Thirty-Seventh Annual Report* (Philadelphia, 1919), 20, *IRA Papers*, Reel 104, D37. For closure, see NIA, *Annual Report* (New York, December 1918), 17; (New York, December 1919), 19; and (New York, December 1920), 17. It is not known when this sale occurred.
132. For an article on land allotment for Indians in national forests, see Larisa K. Miller, "Native American Land Ownership in California's National Forests," *Forest History Today* (Fall 2017): 3–13. By 1913, Kelsey estimated that 3,600 Indians lived in forests, and because allotments were made only to heads of families, he estimated 500 allotments would be sufficient. By 1916, only 145 allotments had been processed by the Forest Service, and the Indian Office had approved only 137 of them (11).
133. NIA, "Office Notes and Comment," *The Indian's Friend*, May 1914, 9.
134. IRA, "Non-Reservation Indians in California," *The Thirty-Eighth Annual Report* (Philadelphia, 1920), 10–14, *IRA Papers*, Reel 104, D 38.
135. "Bidwell Is Dead," *Chico Record*, March 10, 1918, 1, 8.
136. NIA, *Forty-Second Annual Report* (New York, December 1921), 13; and *Forty-Fifth Annual Report* (December 1924), 14.
137. NIA, *Fiftieth Annual Report* (New York, December 1929), 18. For second quote, see NIA, "Office Notes," *The Indian's Friend*, May 1929, 7. Kelsey, who had returned to his law practice in 1914, died on July 3, 1936.
138. Miller, "The Decline of the Northern California Indian Association," 37–47.
139. Fischer, "The Third Force," 80–81, 236. See also NIA, *Annual Report* (December 1911), 20; NIA, "Sixth Zayante Indian Conference," September 1911, 10; and "California Indians," March 1912, 12, both in *The Indian's Friend*.

NOTES

140. Fischer, "The Third Force," 99 for quote. She devotes an entire chapter to the IBC; see 82–130, and also 238–39, 242, 248, 252–55.
141. Quote from *"Capsule History: The General Federation of Women's Clubs,"* cover page, courtesy of the Women's History and Resource Center, General Federation of Women's Clubs, Washington, DC. See also *Twenty-Five Years, 1921-1946, Indian Welfare* (Washington, DC: General Federation of Women's Clubs, n.d.). For a history, see Mary Jean Houde, *A Story of the General Federation of Women's Clubs* (Chicago: The Mobium Press, 1989). The GFWC was an umbrella organization serving more than 500 women's clubs. They were very active in supporting John Collier in the next big reform wave that started shortly after they established the Indian Welfare Committee.
142. "California Indians Past & Present," Cornelia Taber Collection, CHS. Most likely the manuscript was written to be a speech.
143. NCIA, *Fifteenth Annual Report*, 4 and 9. Field matrons were located in Requa, Del Norte County; Weitchpec, Humboldt County; Happy Camp, Siskiyou County; Eureka, Humboldt County; Middletown, Lake County; Lookout, Modoc County; Colusa, Colusa County; Bishop, Inyo County; Coarse Gold, Madera County; and Auberry, Fresno County. For auxiliary work, see Taber, *California and Her Indian Children*, 72–73 and 36–38; and NIA, *Annual Report* (New York City, December 1910), 19–20.

Chapter 9

1. Dickinson, *Address of the President of the Women's National Indian Association*, 6.
2. WNIA, *Fourth Annual Report of the WNIA*, 5, and *Annual Report of the WNIA* (Lancaster: Examiner Publishing House, 1892), 7.
3. *Temperance Society of the Town of Homer, Minutes, 1841-1842*, 10, copy in Cortland County Historical Society. According to Curtis D. Johnson, *Islands of Holiness: Rural Religion in Upstate New York, 1790-1860* (Ithaca, NY: Cornell University Press, 1989), 115–19, by 1825 Cortland County had twenty-two distilleries, and as consumption increased, members of evangelical churches "were at the heart of the county's early temperance movement" (117). See Scott, "Women, Religion, and Social Change in the South, 1830–1930," in *Making the Invisible Woman Visible*, 199, for final quote.
4. "Women's State Temperance Union," *Buffalo Evening Courier & Republic*, May 26, 1876, 1, notes a Mrs. A. C. Swanson (she had married James Franklin Swanson in 1854 in Madison, Georgia) from Brooklyn in attendance.
5. Mrs. Annie Wittenmyer, *History of the Woman's Temperance Crusade* (Philadelphia: Published at the Office of the Christian Woman, 1878), 544–56 for "Crusade at Brooklyn," quote on 548. Mrs. Swanson is listed on p. 552 under "officers and earnest workers."
6. In *Third Annual Report of the Brooklyn Temperance Union* (New York: N. Tibbals & Son, 1877) 7–11, she is listed as a member of the Executive Committee (2); see also *Centennial Temperance Volume, A Memorial of the International Temperance Conference Held in Philadelphia, June, 1876* (New York: National Temperance Society and Publication House, 1877), 693–94. Her poem, "A Centennial Tea-Bell," 394–95, was read aloud at the International Temperance Breakfast.
7. Church notices, *Brooklyn Eagle*, January 20, 1877, 3.
8. For the WCTU and Indians, see Thomas J. Lappas, *In League Against King Alcohol: Native American Women and the Woman's Christian Temperance Union, 1874–1933* (Norman: University of Oklahoma Press, 2020).
9. On December 31, 1890, the Spencers moved to San Francisco; see "Leman and Spencer: Death of Two

NOTES

Well-Known Residents of This State," *Daily Alta California*, January 1, 1891, 8. Dorcas died on May 2, 1933, in Grass Valley. For background, see Prof. J. M. Guinn, "Gardner C. Barber," *History of the State of California and Biographical Record of Coast Counties, California* (Chicago: The Chapman Publishing Co., 1904), 1117; and "Joseph T. Barber," *Representative Men and Old Families of Rhode Island*, vol. II (Chicago: J. H. Beers & Company, 1908), 1137.

10. "Veteran in Prohibition Fight Tells of First Temperance Lecture," *Stockton Independent*, August 9, 1921, 4. See also "Original Organizer to Attend Convention," *Madera Mercury*, August 9, 1921, 3.

11. "W.C.T.U. Started in Grass Valley," *Sacramento Daily Union*, September 3, 1918, 5. In "A Notable Citizen: Pioneer Woman of Eighty Still Active in Welfare Work," the *Mill Valley Record*, August 27, 1921, 1, reported that Willard "publicly acknowledged that to Mrs. Spencer was due the honor of priority in supplying a name" to the organization. When the national society was organized in Cleveland, Ohio, the word "Christian" was added. The *Record* also described the 81-year-old Spencer as "an authority on Indian history in California." The *San Francisco Chronicle*, in "Pioneer in Work for Dry California Attends Sessions," on August 21, 1921, 4, reported she had written "The California W.C.T.U.," largely from memory, her notes having been destroyed in the 1906 San Francisco earthquake and fire.

12. *The Madera Tribune*, "Will Celebrate First W.C.T.U," April 20, 1926, 4: cars were driven from as far south as Tulare and Kings Counties, with two pennants, one naming its starting point and the second identifying Grass Valley as destination. See also "W.C.T.U. Caravan," *Mill Valley Record*, April 24, 1926, 2.

13. For quote, see Belle M. Brain, *The Redemption of the Red Man*, 68, article, 64–70. For Spencer, see Mathes, *Divinely Guided*, 81–85, 98–99, 147, 151–52, 169–70, 259; and Mathes, *Amelia Stone Quinton*, 76, 144, 194.

14. Spencer to Welsh, November 10, 1889, *The IRA Papers*, Reel 5. At the bottom of the letter, Mrs. R. R. Johnson, president of the California WCTU, had written: "This statement of Mrs. Spencer's is not the immature impression of a stranger. She has been long aware of the facts she states and made this journey to verify her previous knowledge by actual sight and hearing. The Cal. W.C.T.U. endorses her plea and writes in this appeal in behalf of these Native Americans."

15. Lewis, *Neither Wolf nor Dog*, 93 for removal of equipment; WNIA, "Who Is Billy Beckwith?" *The Indian's Friend*, April 1891, 3 for quote. The situation became worse in 1889 when the government temporarily combined the Hoopa and Mission agencies.

16. "Miss M. E. Chase Tells of Work Among Hupa Indians: Presbyterian Pastor Has Faith in Her Wards," [Santa Rosa] *Press Democrat*, August 23, 1907, 5; see also "Tells of Work Among Hupas," *The Humboldt Times*, August 28, 1907, 2. See also Dorcas J. Spencer, "The Woman Pastor and Her Parish," *The Pacific*, July 14, 1904, 12. *The Pacific* was a weekly published in San Francisco by the Congregational Churches.

17. Dorcas J. Spencer, "An Indian's Work. What William Beckwith Has Done for the Hoopas," *San Francisco Chronicle*, February 7, 1891, 8.

18. Spencer to Welsh, November 10, 1889.

19. Morgan to Spencer, November 23, 1889, *IRA Papers*, Reel 5.

20. WNIA, "Another Dark Region," *The Indian's Friend*, January 1890, 1.

21. Spencer to Welsh, November 10, 1889.

22. Spencer to Welsh, November 10, 1889.

23. "Advancement of Women: Organization of an Education and Industrial Union," *Daily Alta California*, October 14, 1888, 1. The San Francisco Union was organized in October 1888 to lighten "the burden of working women" and see that employers provide "comfortable working rooms for their female employees." The first union, founded in Boston, Massachusetts, in 1877 by Harriet Clisby, supported that city's women and children.

NOTES

24. "Hoopa Indians: A Visit to Their Home in Humboldt," *San Francisco Chronicle*, February 21, 1890, 5.
25. "Women's Indian Association," *San Francisco Daily Evening Bulletin*, August 12, 1891, 1.
26. ASQ, "In Northern California. Letter Number Eight," *The Indian's Friend*, November 1891, 1, 3.
27. "The Hoopa [sic] Indians. A Ladies' Society Discusses their Condition," *San Francisco Chronicle*, August 29, 1891, 8.
28. WNIA, "William Beckwith," *The Indian's Friend*, January 1892, 2.
29. "Plumas Red Men. A Petition for the Removal of Fort Gaston in Hoopa Valley," *San Francisco Chronicle*, February 10, 1892, 12.
30. "The Abandonment of Fort Gaston," *Humboldt Times*, March 17, 1892, 2.
31. For date, see "Aiding the Indians. The Woman's Association and Its Work," *San Francisco Chronicle*, August 10, 1892, 5. According to WNIA, "Our New Hoopa Valley Mission," *The Report of the Missionary Department, November 1891* (Philadelphia: Wilbour Printing House, 1891), 19, and WNIA, *Annual Report of the WNIA, December 1893* (Lancaster: Examiner Printing House, 1893), 20, the petition drive was largely responsible for the removal. Nelson, *Our Home Forever*, 131–32, provides evidence that the War Department was planning on closing the fort and turning it over for a school. "Abandonment of Forts," *San Francisco Call*, August 9, 1890, 1, substantiates that conclusion. By January 1893, students were studying in buildings where soldiers had once lived. See "The Last of Fort Gaston," *San Francisco Call*, May 13, 1892, 3; and "Fort Gaston Abandoned," *Blue Lake Advocate*, July 2, 1892, 3.
32. WNIA, "Association News and Notes," *The Indian's Friend*, May 1893, 3. "Dougherty, Report of Hoopa Valley Agency, August 31, 1893," *Sixty-Second ARCIA* (Washington, DC: GPO, 1893), 124 reported the school had about forty-five students.
33. "The Hoopa Valley Indians," *San Francisco Call*, August 2, 1896, 24. Cahill, in "The Hoopa Valley Reservation," *Federal Fathers & Mothers*, 170–206, writes, 182, that the opening of the school in 1893 created new employment opportunities for women in the federal Indian Service.
34. WNIA, "In the Hoopa Valley," *The Indian's Friend*, March 1896, 9.
35. Quinton, "Women's Work for Indians," 301 for quote.
36. "Women Who Take Care of Indians: The Work in Hoopa Valley Presented," *San Francisco Chronicle*, August 4, 1896, 8.
37. For Armstrong and extracts of his letters, see WNIA, "The Mission of the Northern California Auxiliary," *Our Missionary Work for 1896* (WNIA: 1896), 33–38.
38. For appointment, see WNIA, *The Indian's Friend*, April 1897, 5, and WNIA, *Our Missionary Report for 1897* (Philadelphia: 1897), 51–56. Goddard was joined by his wife and their 17-month-old daughter, Myra.
39. WNIA, *The Report of Missions for 1900* (Philadelphia: 1900), 3.
40. NIA, "News and Notes," *The Indian's Friend*, October 1904, 5. For Spencer's article on Chase, see Dorcas J. Spencer, "Woman's Board of Home Missions. A Woman Pastor and Her Parish," *Herald and Presbyter*, June 21, 1905, 13.
41. NIA, "News and Notes," *The Indian's Friend*, January 1905, 5.
42. "Improvement in Hoopa Indians' Home Life: Interesting Account of Their Progress by Mrs. Dorcas Spencer," *San Jose Mercury-News*, January 12, 1905, 3.
43. "The Indians of California," *San Jose Mercury-News* (editorial), January 12, 1905, 6.
44. Dorcas J. Spencer, "Some California Aborigines: A Historical Sketch of Hoopa," *The Home Mission Monthly*, February 1907, 79–81, quotes on 81. The monthly was published by the Woman's Board of Home Missions of the Presbyterian Church.
45. NIA, "Work at the Hoopa Mission," *The Indian's Friend*, September 1908, 4. For her explanation of

NOTES

medals, see "The Prevention of the Sale of Intoxicants to Native Races," *Report of the Ninth Convention of the World's WCTU* (New York: October 23–28, 1913), 142.

46. "Visiting the Indians," *Blue Lake Advocate*, June 30, 1917, 2; and NIA, *Annual Report of the NIA* (New York: Published by Order of the Executive Board, 1917), 18–19.
47. NIA, "Mrs. D. J. Spencer's Address," *Annual Report of the NIA, December 1902* (New York: 1902), 25.
48. NIA, "Mrs. Dorcas J. Spencer," *Annual Report of the NIA, December 1906* (New York: 1906), 35–36.
49. NIA, "Temperance Work for Indians," *Annual Report of the NIA* (New York: Published by Order of the Executive Board, 1914), 30–33, quotes on 32–33.
50. NIA, "Temperance and Indians," *Annual Report of the NIA* (New York: 1915), 31–33, pledge quote on 31, and voting on 32.
51. NIA, "Temperance and Indians This Year," *Annual Report of the NIA* (New York: 1916), 26–27.
52. NIA, *Annual Report of the NIA* (New York: 1918), 17–18, quotes 18.
53. NIA, "California Indians," *Fortieth Annual Report of the NIA* (New York: 1919), 20–21.
54. See Lappas, "The Dorcas Spencer Difference," *In League Against King Alcohol*, 145–49.
55. "W.C.T.U. Jubilee. A Celebration Coming to Petaluma in October," *Mill Valley Record*, May 21, 1927, 6; and "The Woman's Christian Temperance Union," *Stockton Record*, April 10, 1900, 7. For another reference as an organizer of the Stockton WCTU, see "Grand Diamond Medal Contest," *Stockton Independent*, October 13, 1911, 8. See also "W.C.T.U. Meeting," *Morning Union [Grass Valley Daily Union]*, April 6, 1889, 3.
56. "Temperance Lectures," *Healdsburg Enterprise*, April 20, 1888, 4. For a mid-May reception on her behalf, see "A Reception," 3, ibid.
57. "Celebrated the Ohio Crusades: Exercises by the Women's Christian Temperance Union," *San Francisco Call*, December 24, 1896, 9.
58. "Women Talk on Temperance Topics," *San Francisco Chronicle*, August 3, 1897, 4.
59. "W.C.T.U. Started in Grass Valley," *Sacramento Daily Union*, September 3, 1918, 5. For more on this legislation, see "Western States," *History of the First Decade of the Department of Scientific Temperance Instruction in Schools and Colleges, of the Woman's Christian Temperance Union, Part II* (Boston: Geo. E. Crosby & Co., Printers, 1892), 72 with mention of Spencer's 1889 report that "work [was] growing, and much enthusiasm manifested, with a movement on foot to secure a chair in the State Normal School for this study." For more on medal contests, see Lappas, *In League Against King Alcohol*, 41, 43, 44, 142, 200, 225–26.
60. For recording secretary, see "Women in Convention. Seventeenth Annual Gathering in California Meet in Petaluma," *Sonoma Democrat*, October 17, 1896, 2; and for corresponding secretary, see "Christian Temperance Union Names Officers," *San Francisco Call*, October 25, 1900, 11. For an early appointment as corresponding secretary of the Napa WCTU, see "Officers Elected," *San Jose Herald*, October 12, 1889, 2.
61. For her report as secretary, see "State Convention of W.C.T.U. at Stockton," *Humboldt Times*, November 6, 1901, 3. See also "Temperance Workers to Meet: Mrs. Dorcas Spencer, the Corresponding Secretary, Will Make an Address," *Morning Tribune* [San Luis Obispo], February 13, 1903, 1; and "For Cause of Temperance: Mrs. Dorcas J. Spencer Addresses Local W.C.T.U.," *Humboldt Times*, June 17, 1904, 5.
62. WNIA, *The Indian's Friend*, July 1905, 5, reported on her appointment as superintendent of work among the Indians, describing her as "exceptionally well prepared for her new department." *A Brief History of the Woman's Christian Temperance Union*, 3rd ed. (Evanston: The Union Signal, 1907), 36, claims she assumed the position of superintendent in 1904. For a detailed state-by-state report in 1909, see Dorcas J. Spencer, "Work Among Indians," *Report of the Thirty-Sixth Annual Convention of the National WCTU* (1909). As the national superintendent, she gave an address on the "Relations

of Temperance to Mission"; see "To Talk Before W.C.T.U.," *Sacramento Union*, July 11, 1910, 2. For more as superintendent of Indian work, see *A Brief History of the WCTU*, 36.

63. Her report is printed in "The Protection of Native Races," *Report of the Eighth Convention of the World's WCTU* (Glasgow, Scotland, June 4–11, 1910), quotes on 206–7.
64. Spencer's report is in "The Prevention of the Sale of Intoxicants to Native Races," 142.
65. *Minutes of the Thirteenth Annual Convention of the WCTU of California* (Woodland: Lee & Warren Printers, 1892), 11, has her residence in Grass Valley; for talk, see 49; for business report, see 55; and for corresponding secretary, see 79–80.
66. *Minutes of the Fourteenth Annual Convention of the WCTU of California* (San Francisco: Brunt & Co., Printers, 1893), 52, 54, see also 81–85 for her corresponding secretary's report.
67. Dorcas J. Spencer, "Woman's Christian Temperance Union," *The Californian Illustrated Magazine* 3, no. 2 (January 1893): 161–71, quotes on 161, 162, 163.
68. Spencer, "Woman's Christian Temperance Union," quotes on 165, 166, 169.
69. Spencer, "Woman's Christian Temperance Union," quotes 170–71.
70. Dorcas J. Spencer, "Indians and Prohibition," *The American Indian Magazine*, October–December 1916, 311–14. This is the quarterly journal of the Society of American Indians. The article was reprinted in *The Indian's Friend*, September 1916, 1, 7–8. Unlike the WCTU, the WNIA did not promote women's suffrage.
71. "Woman Author, Pioneer, Dies," *Oakland Tribune*, May 2, 1933, 3. See also "Pioneer Citizen of State Passes Away: Mrs. Dorcas Spencer, Noted for Work Among California Indians," *Mill Valley Record*, May 5, 1933, 4.

Conclusion

1. NIA, "The Fiftieth Anniversary Luncheon," *The Indian's Friend*, January 1930, 5. For his visit to the Good Samaritan hospital, see NIA, "With the Navajos," *The Indian's Friend*, October 1913, 7.
2. NIA, "An Indian Tribute to Mrs. Quinton," *The Indian's Friend*, January 1930, 7.
3. His granddaughter, Renya K. Ramirez, noted that the death of his grandmother and parents during a flu epidemic when he was in his early teens was central to his "decision to informally adopt the Roes [Dr. and Mrs. Walter C. Roe], a white missionary couple, as his 'mother' and 'father' when he was in his early twenties." This "informal adoption was consistent with the Ho-Chunk cultural custom to adopt others to take the place of those who had passed away." See Renya K. Ramirez, "Ho-Chunk Warrior, Intellectual, and Activist: Henry Roe Cloud Fights for the Apache," *Studies in American Indian Literatures* 25, no. 2, The Society of American Indians and Its Legacies: A Special Combined Issue of *SAIL*, and *American Indian Quarterly* (Summer 2013): 291–309, quote, 292. See also Steven J. Crum, "Henry Roe Cloud, A Winnebago Indian Reformer: His Quest for American Indian Higher Education," *Kansas History* 11 (1988): 171–84; and Joel Pfister, *The Yale Indian: The Education of Henry Roe Cloud* (Durham, NC: Duke University Press, 2009).

Bibliography

Manuscript Collections

American Baptist Historical Society Archives Center, Mercer University. Atlanta, Georgia.
Archives of the Episcopal Church. Austin, Texas.
Board of National Missions, Presbyterian Historical Society. Philadelphia, Pennsylvania.
Cambridge Branch of the Massachusetts Indian Association. Records. Brinkler Library, Cambridge Historical Society (now History Cambridge). Cambridge, Massachusetts.
Dawes, Henry Laurens. Papers. Library of Congress, Washington, DC.
DuBois, Constance Goddard. Papers. Division of Rare and Manuscript Collections, Carl A. Krock Library, Cornell University. Ithaca, New York.
Dutcher, Eugene S. Correspondence and Photographs. National Anthropological Archives, Smithsonian Institution. Suitland, Maryland.
Hawley, Joseph R. Papers. Library of Congress. Washington, DC.
Hayes, Rutherford B. Papers. Rutherford B. Hayes Presidential Center, Spiegel Grove. Fremont, Ohio.
Indian Industries League. Papers. Massachusetts Historical Society. Boston, Massachusetts.
Indian Rights Association. Papers, 1864–1973. Historical Society of Pennsylvania. Philadelphia, Pennsylvania.
———. Cambridge Branch. Secretary's Records. Cambridge Public Library. Cambridge, Massachusetts.
Jackson, Helen Hunt. Collection. Bancroft Library, University of California, Berkeley.
Johnston, Philip. Papers. Special Collections and Archives, Northern Arizona University. Flagstaff, Arizona.
Lend a Hand Society. Records. Massachusetts Historical Society. Boston, Massachusetts.
Litchfield Branch Connecticut Indian Association. Records. Helga J. Ingraham Memorial Library, Litchfield Historical Society. Litchfield, Connecticut.
Lummis, Charles Fletcher. Manuscript Collection. Braun Research Library, Southwest Museum, Autry Museum of the American West. Los Angeles, California.
National Archives and Records Administration. Letters Received and Letters Sent, Record Group 75, Office of Indian Affairs. Washington, DC.
Navajo Mission Collection. Manuscripts Division, Princeton University Library. Princeton, New Jersey.
Perry, America E. Hamilton. Papers. Atkins Library, University of North Carolina. Charlotte, North Carolina.
Quinton, Amelia Stone. Papers. Division of Rare and Manuscript Collections, Carl A. Krock Library, Cornell University. Ithaca, New York.
———. MS1.1.3648, Charles F. Lummis Manuscript Collection, Braun Research Library, Southwest Museum,

Autry Museum of the American West. Los Angeles, California.
Rust, Horatio Nelson. Papers. Henry E. Huntington Library, Art Museum, and Botanical Gardens. San Marino, California.
Smiley Family Papers. Quaker Collection, Haverford College. Haverford, Pennsylvania.
Taber, Cornelia. Collection. California Historical Society. (CHS collections now housed at Stanford University.)
Thomson-Kinney, Sara A. Papers. Connecticut State Library. Hartford, Connecticut.
Young, John. Papers. Brown University Library. Providence, Rhode Island.
Weinland, William Henry. Papers. Henry E. Huntington Library, Art Museum, and Botanical Gardens. San Marino, California.
Women's National Indian Association. *Minutes of Executive Board Meetings from November 17, 1883 to October 21, 1890.* Rare and Manuscript Collections, Carl A. Krock Library, Cornell University. Ithaca, New York.
———. Papers. *Records of the Indian Treaty-Keeping and Protective Association from Dec., 1880.* Rare and Manuscript Collections, Carl A. Krock Library, Cornell University. Ithaca, New York.
Woosley, David. Diaries and Correspondence. Henry E. Huntington Library, Art Museum, and Botanical Gardens. San Marino, California.

Government Documents

"Act for the Relief of the Mission Indians in the State of Congress," U.S. Congress, Senate, "Message from the President of the U.S.; S. Ex. Doc 49, 48th Cong. 1st Sess., 1884, 1–7.
"An Act for the Relief of the Omaha Tribe . . ." *The Statutes at Large of the United States of America from December 1887 to March 1889.* Washington, DC: GPO, 1889, 150–51.
Annual Report of the Attorney-General of the United States for the Year 1901. Washington, DC: GPO, 1901.
Annual Report of the Commissioner of Indian Affairs to the Secretary of the Interior. Washington, DC: GPO. Various years.
Board of Indian Commissioners. *Annual Reports of Conference with Representatives of Missionary Boards and Indian Rights Associations.* Various years.
The Executive Documents of the Senate of the United States. Washington, DC: GPO, 1889.
The Executive Documents of the Senate of the United States for the First Session of the Forty-Ninth Congress, vol. 6. Washington, DC: GPO, 1886.
Index to the Executive Documents of the House of Representatives for the First Session of the Forty-Ninth Congress, 1885–86. Washington, DC: GPO, 1886.
Journal of the Executive Proceedings of the Senate of the United States of America, vol. 28. Washington, DC: GPO, 1909.
Proceedings on the Occasion of the Presentation of the Petition of the Women's National Indian Association, by Hon. H. L. Dawes, February 21, 1882. Washington, DC, 1882.
Report of Education in Alaska with Maps and Illustration by Sheldon Jackson, 1886. Washington, DC: GPO, 1886.
Report of the Secretary of the Interior; Being Part of the Message and Documents Communicated to the Two Houses of Congress. Vol II. Washington, DC: GPO, 1896.
"Testimony Taken Before the Committee of Indian Affairs." House of Representatives, 44th Congress, 1st sess., Misc. Doc. #167. *Index of the Miscellaneous Documents of the House of Representatives for the First Session of the Forty-Fourth Congress.* Washington, DC: GPO, 1876.
U.S. Congress. House. Vol. 10, Part 2, 46th Cong., 2nd sess. February 20, 1880. *Congressional Record,* 1044.
U.S. Congress. Senate. *Memorial of the Northern California Indian Association,* S. Doc. 131, 58th Cong., 2d sess., 1904.

U.S. Congress. Senate. "Senator Dawes Presents Petition," 46th Cong., 3rd sess., January 27, 1881. *Congressional Record*, 953–54.

U.S. Congress. Senate. Vol. XIII, Part II, 47th Cong., 1st sess., February 21, 1882. *Congressional Record*, 1326–30.

Contemporary Sources

The American McAll Record. Various issues.

Ames, James Barr. *Lectures on Legal History and Miscellaneous Legal Essays*. Cambridge: Harvard University Press, 1913.

Annual Reports of the Board of Indian Commissioners. Various issues

Annual Reports of the Indian Commissioner to the Secretary of the Interior. Various years.

The Asa Gray Bulletin. Various issues.

Bodley, Rachel L. *The College Story: Woman's Medical College of Pennsylvania, Commencement Day, March 17, 1881*. In *Valedictory Address to the Twenty-Ninth Graduating Class of the Woman's Medical College of Pennsylvania*. Philadelphia: Jas. B. Rodgers, Co., Printers, 1881.

Brain, Belle M. *The Redemption of the Red Man*. New York: The Board of Home Missions of the Presbyterian Church in the U.S.A., 1904.

A Brief History of the Woman's Christian Temperance Union, 3rd ed. Evanston: The Union Signal, 1907.

Brunner, Edmund de Schweinitz. "The First Protestant Mission in Southern California. Its Establishment." *History of the Moravian Mission to the Indians of Southern California*. Bethlehem: Times Publishing Company, 1923.

———. "History of the Moravian Mission to the Indians of Southern California." *Proceedings of the Society for Propagating the Gospel Among the Heathen, for the Year Ending August 19, 1914*.

———. "The Ramona Mission." *The Missionary Review of the World*, May 1890.

Bulfinch, Ellen S. "Historical Sketch, 1886–1911." In *Historical Sketch Prepared for the Twenty-Fifth Anniversary with Officers . . . and Constitution, 1911*. Cambridge: Caustic-Clafin Co., Printers, 1911.

"Catharine Beecher: Circular addressed to Benevolent Ladies of the U. States." In *The Cherokee Removal: A Brief History with Documents*, ed. Theda Perdue and Michael D. Green, 113–14. Boston: Bedford/St. Martin's, 2005.

Centennial Temperance Volume, A Memorial of the International Temperance Conference Held in Philadelphia, June, 1876. New York: National Temperance Society and Publication House, 1877.

Chestnut Street Female Seminary. Boarding and Day School, Philadelphia, No. 525 Chestnut Street. Philadelphia: Printed by Henry B. Ashmead, 1855.

Chestnut Street Female Seminary. Boarding and Day School, Philadelphia, No. 1615 Chestnut Street. Philadelphia: Henry B. Ashmead, Books and Job Printer, 1860.

Connecticut Indian Association. *Historical Sketch of the Connecticut Indian Association from 1881 to 1888*. Hartford: Press of the Fowler & Miller Company, 1888.

Constitution and By-laws of the Indians' Hope Association, 1892.

Constitution of the Cambridge Branch of the Massachusetts Indian Association, Cambridge: John Ford & Son, Printers, 1893.

Davis, Leicester Knickerbacker. "Thomas L. Sloan—American Indian." *The American Indian Magazine* (published by the Society of American Indians), August 1920, 39–4.

Deming, Judson Keith, comp. and ed. *Genealogy of the Descendants of John Deming of Wethersfield, Connecticut*. Dubuque, IA: Press of Mathis-Mets Co., 1904.

Dewey, Mary E. *Historical Sketch of the Formation and Achievements of the Women's National Indian Association*. National Indian Association, 1900.

Dickinson, Mrs. J. B. *Address of the President of the Women's National Indian Association, November 17, 1885*. Philadelphia: Grant & Faires Printers, 1885.

DuBois, Constance Goddard. *The Condition of the Mission Indians of Southern California*. Philadelphia: Office of the Indian Rights Association, 1901.

———. "Our American 'Reconcentrados.'" *City and State*, November 8, 1900, 297–99.

———. *A Soul in Bronze: A Novel of Southern California*. Chicago: Herbert S. Stone and Company, 1900.

Dutcher, Rev. E. S., "Epworth Piegan Indian Mission." *The Gospel in All Lands*, November 1894.

Eagle, Mary Kavanaugh Oldham, ed. *The Congress of Women Held in the Woman's Building, World's Columbia Exposition, Chicago, U.S.A., 1893*, vol. 1. Chicago: W. W. Conkey Company, Publishers, 1894.

Emerson, William A. *Fitchburg, Massachusetts, Past and Present*. Fitchburg: Press of Blanchard & Brown, 1887.

Executive Committee of the Indian Rights Association. *Annual Reports*. Various years.

Foote, Kate. *Indian Legislation—As Far as It Goes*. Philadelphia: November 1891.

———. *The Indian Legislation of 1888*. Philadelphia: Press of the J. F. Dickson Printing Company, 1888.

———. *Report of the Indians Taxed and Indians not Taxed in the United States. Eleventh Census: 1890*. Washington, DC: GPO, 1894, 207–16.

Eminent and Representative Men of Virginia and the District of Columbia of the Nineteenth Century. Madison: Brant & Fuller, 1893.

Forty-Seventh Annual Report of the American Baptist Home Mission Society. New York: American Baptist Home Mission Rooms, 1879.

Frye, Myra E. "Among the Omahas." *Annual Report of the Maine Branch of the Women's National Indian Association, October 24th, 1889*. Portland, ME, 1889.

Grinnell, George Bird. "The Indian on the Reservation." *The Atlantic Monthly*, February 1899, 255–67.

Handbook of French and Belgian Protestantism. New York: Federal Council of the Churches of Christ in America, 1919.

Harwood, Rev. Thomas. *History of New Mexico Spanish and English Missions of the Methodist Episcopal Church from 1850 to 1910*, vol. II. Albuquerque: El Abogado Press, 1910.

An Historic Record and Pictorial Description of the Town of Meriden, Connecticut. Compiled by C. Bancroft Gillespie. Meriden, CT: Journal Publishing Company, 1906.

History of the State of California and Biographical Record of Coast Counties, California. Chicago: The Chapman Publishing Co., 1904.

Holmes, Elmer W. *History of Riverside County, California with Biographical Sketches*. Los Angeles: Historic Record Company, 1912.

The Home Mission Monthly. Various issues.

Index of the Miscellaneous Documents of the House of Representatives for the First Session of the Forty-Fourth Congress. Washington, DC: GPO, 1876.

The Indian Bulletin. [Connecticut Indian Association newsletter]. Various years.

Indian Rights Association. *Annual Report of the Executive Committee*. Various issues.

The Indian's Friend. Various issues

Jackson, Helen Hunt Jackson. *A Century of Dishonor: A Sketch of the United States Government's Dealing with Some of the Indian Tribes*. Norman: University of Oklahoma Press, 1995 [Boston: Roberts Brothers, 1888].

Johnson, Ellen Terry. *Historical Sketch of the Connecticut Indian Association from 1881 to 1888*. Hartford: Press of the Fowler & Miller Company, 1888.

Journal of the Thirtieth Annual Convention of the Protestant Episcopal Church in the Diocese of Central New York, 1898. Utica: Herald Job Department, 1898.

Kelsey, C. E. *Census of Non-Reservation California Indians, 1905–1906*. Edited by Robert F. Heizer. Berkeley: University of California, Archaeological Research Facility, Department of Anthropology, 1971.

―――. *Report of the Special Agent for California Indians to the Commissioner of Indian Affairs, March 21, 1906*. San Jose: Cleveland Printing Company, 1906.
Kessler, Daisy Edith. "El Capitan Blanco—The White Chief of the Mesa Grandes." *The Southern Workman*, December 1909, 665-71.
Kingsbury, George Washington. *History of Dakota Territory: South Dakota. Its History and Its People*, vol. 3. Chicago: S. J. Clarke Publishing Company, 1915.
Lake Mohonk. *Proceedings of.* Various years.
The Land of Sunshine. Various issues.
Lend a Hand: A Record of Progress and Journal of Organized Charity. Various issues.
Leonard, John William, ed. *Woman's Who's Who of America*. New York: The American Commonwealth Company, 1915.
Logan, Mrs. John A. *The Part Taken by Women in American History*. Wilmington: The Perry Nalle Publishing Co., 1912.
Marshall, Clara. *The Woman's Medical College of Pennsylvania*. Philadelphia: R. Blakiston, Son & Company, 1897
Massachusetts Indian Association. *Annual Reports*. Various years.
McAll, Robert Whitaker, and Horatius Bonar. "American McAll Association." *A Cry from the Land of Calvin and Voltaire: Records of the McAll Mission*. London: Hodder and Stoughton, 1887.
Minutes of the Yearly Meeting of Friends for New England, 1905. Portland: Press of the Southworth Bros., 1905.
The Missionary Review of the World, January to December 1889. New York: Funk & Wagnalls, 1889.
National Indian Association. *Annual Reports*. Various years
―――. *Missions of 1904*. Publication of the NIA, 1904.
―――. *Report of Missions, 1906*. New York: The Volunteer Press Print, 1906.
―――. *Report of Missions, 1907*. New York: The Volunteer Press Print, 1907.
The Native American. [Phoenix Indians school newspaper.] Various issues
New York City Indian Association. Annual Reports (various).
Painter, Charles C. *A Visit to the Mission Indians of California*. Philadelphia: Indian Rights Association, 1887.
Pancoast, Henry S. *Impressions of the Sioux Tribes in 1882, with Some First Principles in the Indian Question*. Philadelphia: Franklin Printing House, 1883.
Periodical Accounts Relating to the Foreign Missions of the Church of the United Brethren. Various issues.
Proceedings of the Cambridge Historical Society. Various issues.
Proceedings of the Connecticut State Medical Society, 1918. Published by the Society, 1918.
Quinton, Amelia Stone. *Address of the President on Current Indian Legislation, Work Needed, Etc.* Philadelphia: Royal Printing Company, 1887.
―――. "The Annual Address of the President, Mrs. A. S. Quinton, November 7, 1888." Philadelphia: Publications of the WNIA, 1888.
―――. "Care of the Indian." In *Woman's Work in America*, edited by Annie Nathan Meyer, 373-91. New York: Henry Holt and Company, 1891.
―――. "The Indian." In *The Literature of Philanthropy*, edited by Francis Goodale. New York: Harper & Brothers Publishers, 1893.
―――. *Indians and Their Helpers*. Publications of the WNIA, 1886.
―――. *The Mohonk Indian Conference*. Women's National Indian Association Leaflet, 1885.
―――. "The Original Indian Association." *Christian Union*, October 6, 1887.
―――. *A Retrospect and its Lessons*. WNIA: Annual Address, December 6, 1894.
―――. *Suggestions to Friends of the Women's National Indian Association*. Publications of the WNIA [1886].
―――. *What It Has Done: What It Ought to Do*. Philadelphia: WNIA, November 1889.

———. "The Woman's National Indian Association." In *The Congress of Women Held in the Woman's Building, World's Columbia Exposition*, edited by Mary Kavanaugh Oldham Eagle, 71–73. Chicago: W. B. Conkey Company, Publishers, 1894.

———. "Woman's Work in Solving the Indian Problem." *Christian Educators in Council: Sixty Addresses by American Educators*. New York: Phillips & Hunt, 1884.

———. "Women's Work for Indians." In *The National Exposition Souvenir: What America Owes to Women*, edited by Lydia Hoyt Farmer, 293–304. Buffalo: Charles Wells Moulton, 1893.

———. "The Work and Objects of the Woman's National Indian Association." *Report of the International Council of Women, Assembled by the National Woman Suffrage Association, March 25 to April 1, 1888*. Washington, DC: Rufus H. Darby, Printer, 1888.

Representative Men and Old Families of Rhode Island, vol. II. Chicago: J. H. Beers & Company, 1908.

The Sailors' Magazine and Seamen's Friend for the Year Ending December, 1873, vol. XLV. New York: American Seamen's Friend Society, 1873.

Scoville, Annie Beecher. "Today Among the Dakotahs." *The Southern Workman and Hampton School Record*, January 1899, 461–64.

Sewall, May Wright, ed. *The World's Congress of Representative Women*, vol. 2. Chicago: Rand McNally, 1894.

Smith, Wayland H. "In Re California Indians to Date." *Out West*, February–March 1909, 141–44.

Society in Washington: Its Noted Men, Accomplished Women, Established Customs, and Notable Events. Washington, DC: Harrisburg Publishing Company, 1887.

Southern Workman. Various issues.

Spencer, Dorcas J. "Indians and Prohibition." *The American Indian Magazine*, October–December 1916, 311–14.

———. "Woman's Christian Temperance Union." *The Californian Illustrated Magazine* 3, no. 2 (January 1893): 161–71.

Taber, Cornelia. *California and Her Indian Children*. San Jose: Northern California Indian Association, 1911.

Ten Years Work for Indians at Hampton Institute, Virginia. Hampton, VA: The Hampton Institute, 1888.

Tibbles, Susette. "Perils and Promises of Indian Citizenship." *Our Day: A Record and Review of Current Reform* 5, no. 30 (June 1890): 460–71.

Tileston, Laura E. *Report of the Hospital Department*. Philadelphia: November 1891. Tomkinson, Mrs. T. L. *Twenty Years' History of the Woman's Home Missionary Society of the Methodist Episcopal Church, 1880–1900*. Cincinnati: The Woman's Home Missionary Society, 1903.

Transactions of the Commonwealth Club of California, 4–7 (December 1909).

Waterloo, Stanley, and John Wesley Hanson, eds. *Famous American Men and Women*. Chicago: Wabash Publishing Company, 1896.

Weinland, William Henry. "The Indian Mission." *The Moravian*, February 1, 1893.

Welsh, Herbert. *Four Weeks Among Some of the Sioux Tribes of Dakota and Nebraska, Together with a Brief Consideration of the Indian Problem*. Germantown, PA: Horace F. McCann, Steam-Power Printer, 1882.

———. "The Indian Question of 1882 and 1925." *The General Magazine and Historical Chronicle*, January 1926, 106–11.

———. *Report of a Visit to the Navajo, Pueblo, and Hualapais Indians of New Mexico and Arizona*. Philadelphia: Published by the IRA, 1885.

Welsh, William. *Report of a Visit to the Sioux and Ponka Indians on the Missouri River, Made by Wm. Welsh, July, 1872*. Philadelphia: M'Calla & Stavey, Printers, 1872.

"Western States." *History of the First Decade of the Department of Scientific Temperance Instruction in Schools and Colleges, of the Woman's Christian Temperance Union, Part II*. Boston: Geo. E. Crosby & Co., Printers, 1892.

Wilbur, Mary C. *Sketch of the Washington Auxiliary of the National Indian Association, 1882–1903.* Women's National Indian Association, 1903.

Willard, Frances E., and Mary A. Livermore, eds. *A Woman of the Century: Fourteen Hundred-seventy Biographical Sketches Accompanied by Portraits of Leading American Women in All Walks of Life.* Buffalo: Charles Wells Moulton, 1893.

Wittenmyer, Mrs. Annie. *History of the Woman's Temperance Crusade.* Philadelphia: Published at the Office of the Christian Woman, 1878.

Woman's Home Mission Society of the Methodist Episcopal Church. Annual Reports. Various years.

The Women's Baptist Home Mission Society, 1877 to 1882. Chicago: R. R. Donnelley & Sons, Printers, 1883.

Women's Eastern New York Indian Association. Annual Reports (various).

Women's National Indian Association. *Annual Reports.* Various years.

——. *How to Organize an Indian Association.* Publications of the WNIA, 1888.

——. *The Indian's Friend.* Various issues.

——. *Minutes of the Trustees.* Various years.

——. *Missionary Reports.* Various years and different titles.

——. *Official Pamphlet of the National Indian Association, with Suggestions and Facts for its Helpers.* Philadelphia: Women's National Indian Association, 1882.

——. *The Ramona Mission and the Mission Indians.* Philadelphia: May 1889.

Zayante Indian Conferences. Annual Reports.

Secondary Sources
Books

Adams, David Wallace. *Education for Extinction: American Indians and the Boarding School Experience, 1875–1928.* Lawrence: University Press of Kansas, 1995.

Akins, Damon B., and William J. Bauer Jr. *We Are the Land: A History of Native California.* Oakland: University of California Press, 2021.

Arnold, Mary Ellicott, and Mabel Reed. *In the Land of the Grasshopper Song: Two Women in the Klamath River Indian Country in 1908–09.* Lincoln: University of Nebraska Press, 1980.

Benson, William R. *"My Dear Miss Nicholson": Letters and Myths,* edited by Maria del Carmen Gasser. Carmel: published by author, 1995.

Berkhofer, Robert F. *Salvation and the Savage: An Analysis of Protestant Missions and American Indian Response, 1787–1862.* New York: Atheneum, 1972.

Bordin, Ruth. *Woman and Temperance: The Quest for Power and Liberty, 1873–1900.* Philadelphia: Temple University Press, 1981.

Brugge, David M. *A History of the Chaco Navajos.* Albuquerque: Division of Chaco Research, National Park Service, 1980.

Burgess, Larry E. *Mohonk: Its People and Spirit: A History of One Hundred Years of Growth and Service.* Fleischmanns, NY: Purple Mountain Press, 1996.

Cahill, Cathleen D. *Federal Fathers & Mothers: A Social History of the United States Indian Service, 1869–1933.* Chapell Hill: University of North Carolina Press, 2011.

Cott, Nancy F. *The Bonds of Womanhood: "Woman's Sphere" in New England, 1780–1835.* New Haven: Yale University Press, 1977.

Douglas, Ann. *The Feminization of American Culture.* New York: Alfred A. Knopf, 1977.

Eastman, Elaine Goodale. *Sister to the Sioux: The Memoirs of Elaine Goodale Eastman, 1885–91,* edited by Kay Graber. Lincoln: University of Nebraska Press, 1978.

Federal Concern About Conditions of California Indians 1853 to 1913: Eight Documents, edited by Robert F. Heizer. Socorro, New Mexico: Ballena Press, 1979.

Garner, Van H. *The Broken Ring: The Destruction of the California Indians*. Tucson: Westernlore Press, 1982.

Genetin-Pilawa, C. Joseph. *Crooked Paths to Allotment: The Fight over Federal Indian Policy after the Civil War*. Chapel Hill: University of North Carolina Press, 2012.

Hagan, William T. *The Indian Rights Association: The Herbert Welsh Years, 1882–1904*. Tucson: University of Arizona Press, 1985.

———. *Theodore Roosevelt and Six Friends of the Indian*. Norman: University of Oklahoma Press, 1997.

Houde, Mary Jean. *A Story of the General Federation of Women's Clubs*. Chicago: The Mobium Press, 1989.

Huntington, Maria. *Harriet Ward Foote Hawley*. BiolioLife, L.L.C., 1923.

Hyer, Joel R. *"We are Not Savages": Native Americans in Southern California and the Pala Reservation, 1840–1920*. East Lansing: Michigan State University Press, 2001.

Iverson, Peter. *Diné: A History of the Navajos*. Albuquerque: University of New Mexico, Press, 2002.

Jacobs, Margaret D. *After One Hundred Winters: In Search of Reconciliation on America's Stolen Lands*. Princeton: Princeton University Press, 2021.

———. *White Mother to a Dark Race: Settler Colonialism, Maternalism, and the Removal of Indigenous Children in the American West and Australia, 1880–1940*. Lincoln: University of Nebraska Press, 2009.

Johnson, Curtis D. *Islands of Holiness: Rural Religion in Upstate New York, 1790–1860*. Ithaca, NY: Cornell University Press, 1989.

Katanski, Amelia V. *Learning to Write "Indian": The Boarding-School Experience and American Indian Literature*. Norman: University of Oklahoma Press, 2005.

Keen, William Williams, ed. *The Bi-Centennial Celebration of the Founding of the First Baptist Church of the City of Philadelphia, 1698–1898*. Philadelphia: American Baptist Publication Society, 1899.

Kelly, Lawrence C. *The Assault on Assimilation: John Collier and the Origins of Indian Policy Reform*. Albuquerque: University of New Mexico Press, 1983.

———. *The Navajo Indians and Federal Indian Policy, 1900–1935*. Tucson: University of Arizona Press, 1970.

Kroeber, A. L. *Handbook of the Indians of California*. New York: Dover Publications, Inc., 1976.

Kvasnicka, Robert M., and Herman J. Viola, eds. *The Commissioners of Indian Affairs, 1824–1977*. Lincoln: University of Nebraska Press, 1979.

Lappas, Thomas J. *In League Against King Alcohol: Native American Women and the Woman's Christian Temperance Union, 1874–1933*. Norman: University of Oklahoma Press, 2020.

Laylander, Don, ed. *Listening to the Raven: The Southern California Ethnography of Constance Goddard DuBois*. Salinas, CA: Coyote Press, 2004.

Ledbetter, Mark David. *America's Forgotten History: Part Three; A Progressive Empire*. Published by the author, 2015.

Lewis, David Rich. *Neither Wolf nor Dog: American Indians, Environment, & Agrarian Change*. Oxford: Oxford University Press, 1994.

Littlefield, Daniel, Jr., and James W. Parins. *American Indian and Alaska Native Newspapers and Periodicals, 1826–1924*. Westport, CT: Greenwood Press, 1984.

Lomawaima, K. Tsianina. *They Called It Prairie Light: The Story of Chilocco Indian School*. Lincoln: University of Nebraska Press, 1994.

MacDonald, Eleanor Davenport, and John Brown Arrington. *The San Juan Basin: My Kingdom Was a Country*. Denver: Green Mountain Press, 1970.

Maddox, Lucy. *Citizen Indians: Native American Intellectuals, Race & Reform*. Ithaca, NY: Cornell University Press, 2005.

Malehorn, Pauline G. "The Tender Plant: The History of the Navajo Methodist Mission Farmington, New

Mexico, 1891–1948." In *Navajo Methodist Mission School History: Mission Magnets*. N.p., 1948.

Mark, Joan. *A Stranger in Her Native Land: Alice Fletcher and the American Indians*. Lincoln: University of Nebraska Press, 1988.

Markowitz, Harvey. *Converting the Rosebud: Catholic Missions and the Lakotas, 1886–1916*. Norman: University of Oklahoma Press, 2018.

Mathes, Valerie Sherer. *Amelia Stone Quinton and the Women's National Indian Association: A Legacy of Indian Reform*. Norman: University of Oklahoma Press, 2022.

———. *Charles C. Painter: The Life of an Indian Reform Advocate*. Norman: University of Oklahoma Press, 2020.

———. *Divinely Guided: The California Work of the Women's National Indian Association*. Lubbock: Texas Tech University Press, 2012.

———, ed. *Gender, Race, and Power in the Indian Reform Movement: The Women's National Indian Association*. Albuquerque: University of New Mexico Press, 2020.

———. *Helen Hunt Jackson and her Indian Reform Legacy*. Austin: University of Texas Press, 1990.

———, ed. *The Indian Reform Letters of Helen Hunt Jackson, 1879–1885*. Norman: University of Oklahoma Press, 1998.

———, ed. *The Women's National Indian Association: A History*. Albuquerque: University of New Mexico Press, 2015.

Mathes, Valerie Sherer, and Phil Brigandi, eds. *A Call for Reform: The Southern California Indian Writings of Helen Hunt Jackson*. Norman: University of Oklahoma Press, 2015.

Mathes, Valerie Sherer, and Phil Brigandi. *Reservations, Removal, and Reform: The Mission Indian Agents of Southern California, 1878–1903*. Norman: University of Oklahoma Press, 2018.

Mathes, Valerie Sherer, and Richard Lowitt. *The Standing Bear Controversy: Prelude to Indian Reform*. Urbana: University of Illinois Press, 2003.

Mattingly, Carol. *Well-Tempered Women: Nineteenth-Century Temperance Rhetoric*. Carbondale: Southern Illinois University Press, 1998.

McLoughlin, William G., ed. *The American Evangelicals, 1800–1900: An Anthology*. New York: Harper & Row, 1968.

McPherson, Robert S. *Traders, Agents, and Weavers: Developing the Northern Navajo Region*. Norman: University of Oklahoma Press, 2020.

Milner, Clyde A., II. *With Good Intentions: Quaker Work among the Pawneees, Otos, and Omahas in the 1870s*. Lincoln: University of Nebraska Press, 1982.

Nelson, Byron, Jr. *Our Home Forever: The Hupa Indians of North California*. Salt Lake City: Howe Brothers, 1988.

Newman, Louise Michele. *White Women's Rights: The Racial Origins of Feminism in the United States*. New York: Oxford University Press, 1999.

Nye, Russel Blaine. *Society and Culture in America, 1830–1860*. New York: Harper & Row, 1974.

Oswalt, Wendell H. *Historic Settlements along the Kuskokwim River, Alaska*. Juneau: Alaska Division of State Libraries and Museums, 1980.

Pascoe, Peggy. *Relations of Rescue: The Search for Female Moral Authority in the American West, 1874–1939*. Oxford: Oxford University Press, 1900.

Pfister, Joel. *The Yale Indian: The Education of Henry Roe Cloud*. Durham, NC: Duke University Press, 2009.

Phillips, George Harwood. *Chiefs and Challengers: Indian Resistance and Cooperation in Southern California, 1769–1906*. Norman: University of Oklahoma Press, 2014.

Prucha, Francis Paul. *American Indian Policy in Crisis: Christian Reformers and the Indian, 1865–1900*. Norman: University of Oklahoma Press, 1976.

———. *American Indian Policy in the Formative Years: The Indian Trade and Intercourse Acts 1790–1834*. Lincoln: University of Nebraska Press, 1970.

———. *The Churches and the Indian Schools, 1888–1912*. Lincoln: University of Nebraska Press, 1979.

———. *Documents of United States Indian Policy*, 2nd ed. Lincoln: University of Nebraska Press, 1990.

———. *The Great Father: The United States Government and the American Indian*, 2 vols. Lincoln: University of Nebraska Press, 1984.

———. *Indian Policy in the United States: Historical Essays*. Lincoln: University of Nebraska Press, 1981.

Rhea, John M. *A Field of Their Own: Women and American Indian History, 1830–1941*. Norman: University of Oklahoma Press, 2016.

Rudnick, Lois Palken. *Mabel Dodge Luhan: New Woman, New Worlds*. Albuquerque: University of New Mexico Press, 1984.

Ryan, Mary P. *Womanhood in America: From Colonial Times to the Present*. New York: New Viewpoints / Franklin Watts, 1979.

San Juan, County, New Mexico: A Photographic History, vol. II. Farmington: The Farmington Daily Times, 2009.

Scott, Anne Firor. *Making the Invisible Woman Visible*. Urbana: University of Illinois Press, 1984.

Senier, Siobhan. *Voices of American Indian Assimilation and Resistance: Helen Hunt Jackson, Sarah Winnemucca, and Victoria Howard*. Norman: University of Oklahoma Press, 2001.

Simonsen, Jane E. *Making Home Work: Domesticity and Native American Assimilation in the American West, 1860–1919*. Chapel Hill: University of North Carolina Press, 2006.

Starr, Kevin. *Americans and the California Dream, 1850–1915*. New York: Oxford University Press, 1973.

Taliaferro, John. *Grinnell: America's Environmental Pioneer and His Restless Drive to Save the West*. New York: Liveright Publishing Company, 2019.

Thompson, Mark. *American Character: The Curious Life of Charles Fletcher Lummis and the Rediscovery of the Southwest*. New York: Arcade Publishing, 2001.

Thompson-Stahr, Jane. *The Burling Book: Ancestors and Descendants of Edward and Grace Burling, Quakers (1600–2000)*, vol. II. Baltimore: Gateway Press, Inc., 2001.

Tibbles, Thomas Henry. *Buckskin and Blanket Days: Memoirs of a Friend of the Indians*. Lincoln: University of Nebraska Press, 1969.

Tong, Benson. *Susan La Flesche Picotte, M.D. Omaha Leader and Reformer*. Norman: University of Oklahoma Press, 1999.

Trafzer, Clifford E., Matthew Sakiestewa Gilbert, and Lorene Sisquoc, eds. *The Indian School on Magnolia Avenue: Voices and Images from Sherman Institute*. Corvallis: Oregon State University, 2012.

Trafzer, Clifford E., Jean A. Keller, and Lorene Sisquoc, intro and eds. *Boarding School Blues: Revisiting American Indian Educational Experiences*. Lincoln: University of Nebraska Press, 2006.

Trennert, Robert A. *Alternative to Extinction: Federal Indian Policy and the Beginnings of the Reservation System, 1846–51*. Philadelphia: Temple University Press, 1975.

Underhill, Ruth M. *Red Man's Religion: Beliefs and Practices of the Indians North of Mexico*. Chicago: University of Chicago Press, 1965.

Vogel, Virgil J. *American Indian Medicine*. Norman: University of Oklahoma Press, 1977.

Waybourn, Marilu. *Water: Lifeline of the Valley: Rivers, Ditches & Floods of San Juan County, NM*. 2004.

Wood, Stephen Lane. *Landscape Place Names: San Juan County, New Mexico*. Farmington: Stephen Lane Wood, 2019.

———. *Place Names of San Juan County, NM: The Settlements*. Aztec: San Juan County Historical Society, 2016.

Woman's Who's Who of America, 1914–1915. New York: The American Commonwealth Company, 1914.

Wood, Stephen Lane. *Places of San Juan County, N.M: The Settlements*. Aztec: San Juan County Historical

Society, 2016.

Zaeske, Susan. *Signatures of Citizenship: Petitioning, Antislavery, & Women's Political Identity*. Chapel Hill: University of North Carolina Press, 2003.

Articles, Anthologies, and Book Chapters

Adams, David Wallace. "'In the Shadow of Ramona': Frances Campbell Sparhawk and the Fiction of Reform." In *Gender, Race, and Power in the Indian Reform Movement: Revisiting the History of the WNIA*, edited by Valerie Sherer Mathes, 123–38. Albuquerque: University of New Mexico Press, 2020.

Alexander, Ruth Ann. "Finding Oneself Through a Cause: Elaine Goodale Eastman and Indian Reform in the 1880s." *South Dakota History* 22, no. 1 (Spring 1992): 1–37.

Anderson, Charles A. "Day Book of Rev. Charles H. Cook." *Journal of the Presbyterian Historical Society* 37, no. 2 (June 1959): 104–21.

Bannan, Helen M. "'True Womanhood' and Indian Assimilation." In *Selected Proceedings of the Third Annual Conference on Minority Studies*, vol. II, edited by George E. Carter and James R. Parker, 187–94. La Crosse, WI: Institute for Minority Studies, 1987.

———. "True Womanhood on the Reservation: Field Matrons in the United States Indian Service." *Southwest Institute for Research on Women*, Working Paper No. 18. Women's Studies, University of Arizona, Tucson (1984): 1–25.

Benson, William Ralganal. "The Stone and Kelsey 'Massacre' on the Shores of Clear Lake in 1849: The Indian Viewpoint." *California Historical Society Quarterly* 11, no. 3 (September 1932): 266–73.

Boles, John B. "Henry Holcombe, A Southern Baptist Reformer in the Age of Jefferson." *The Georgia Historical Quarterly* 54, no. 3 (Fall 1970): 381–407.

Brigandi, Phil. "Debating the Existence of a 'Real' Ramona." *The Valley Chronicle* (Hemet, California), February 9, 2002.

———. "'Her Soul Is Marching On': Helen Hunt Jackson's Followers in the Indian Reform Movement." In *Gender, Race, and Power in the Indian Reform Movement: Revisiting the History of the WNIA*, edited by Valerie Sherer Mathes, 109–20. Albuquerque: University of New Mexico Press, 2020.

———. "In the Name of the Law: The Cupeño Removal of 1903." *Journal of San Diego History* 64, no. 1 (2018).

Brigandi, Phil, and John W. Robinson. "The Killing of Juan Diego: From Murder to Mythology." *Journal of San Diego History* 40, nos. 1 & 2 (Winter/Spring 1994): 1–22.

Brugge, David M. "A Comparative Study of Navajo Mortuary Practices." *American Indian Quarterly* 4, no. 4 (November 1978): 309–28.

Buffalohead, W. Roger, and Paulette Fairbanks Molin. "'A Nucleus of Civilization': American Indian Families at Hampton Institute in the Late Nineteenth Century." *Journal of American Indian Education* 35, no. 3 (Spring 1996): 59–94.

Burgess, Larry E. "Commission to the Mission Indians, 1891." *San Bernardino County Museum Quarterly* (Spring 1989): 1–47.

———. "What Is a Woman Worth?" In *The Women's National Indian Association: A History*, edited by Valerie Sherer Mathes, 1–22. Albuquerque: University of New Mexico Press, 2015.

Cahill, Cathleen D. "Making and Marketing Baskets in California." In *The Women's National Indian Association: A History*, edited by Valerie Sherer Mathes, 126–49. Albuquerque: University of New Mexico Press, 2015.

———. "'Noble Women Not a Few': The Lake Mohonk Conferences." In *The Women's National Indian Association: A History*, edited by Valerie Sherer Mathes, 213–39. Albuquerque: University of New Mexico

Press, 2015,

———. "Reassessing the Role of the 'Native Helper': Christian Indians and the Woman's National Indian Association (WNIA), 1905–1926." Paper presented at the "Women and American Religion: Reimagining the Past" Conference, University of Chicago, October 9, 2003.

Cruea, Susan M. "Changing Ideals of Womanhood During the Nineteenth-Century Woman Movement." *University Writing Program Faculty Publication* (2005), 187–204.

Crum, Steven J. "Henry Roe Cloud, A Winnebago Indian Reformer: His Quest for American Indian Higher Education. *Kansas History* 11 (1988): 171–84.

DeJong, David H. "Commissioner John D. Atkins." *The Commissioners of Indian Affairs: The United States Indian Service and the Making of Federal Indian Policy, 1824–2017*. Salt Lake City: University of Utah Press, 2020, 76–80.

Disbrow, Donald W. "Herbert Welsh, Editor of City and State, 1895–1904." *Pennsylvania Magazine of History and Biography* 94, no. 1 (January 1970): 62–74.

Edwards, Martha L. "A Problem of Church and State in the 1870's." *The Mississippi Valley Historical Review* 11, no. 1 (June 1924): 37–53.

Emmerich, Lisa E. "'Civilization' and Transculturation: The Field Matron Program and Cross-Cultural Contact." *American Indian Culture and Research Journal* 15, no. 4 (1991): 33–47.

———. "Marguerite Lafleshe Diddock: Office of Indian Affairs Field Matron." *Great Plains Quarterly* 13, no. 3 (Summer 1903): 162–71.

———. "Promoting Homemaking on the Reservation. WNIA Field Matrons." In *The Women's National Indian Association: A History*, edited by Valerie Sherer Mathes, 84–101. Albuquerque: University of New Mexico Press.

———. "'Right in the Midst of My Own People': Native American Women and the Field Matron Program." *American Indian Quarterly* 15, no. 1 (Spring 1991): 201–16.

Foster, Sarah Whitmer, and John T. Foster Jr. "Historic Notes and Documents: Harriet Ward Foote Hawley: Civil War Journalist." *The Florida Historical Quarterly* 83, no. 4 (Spring 2005): 448–67.

Garsha, Jeremiah J. "'Reclamation Road': A Microhistory of Massacre Memory in Clear Lake, California." *Genocide Studies and Prevention: An International Journal* 9, no. 2 (2015): 61–75.

Geer, Emily Apt. "Lucy W. Hayes and the Woman's Home Missionary Society." *The Hayes Historical Journal: A Journal of the Gilded Age* 4, no. 4 (Fall 1984): 5–14.

Hershberger, Mary. "Mobilizing Women, Anticipating Abolition: The Struggle Against Indian Removal in the 1830s." *The Journal of American History* (June 1999): 15–40.

Hewes, Dorothy W. "Those First Good Years of Indian Education: 1894–1898." *American Indian Culture and Research Journal* 5, no. 2 (1981): 63–82.

Hoopes, Alban W. "The Indian Rights Association and the Navajo, 1890–1895." *New Mexico Historical Review* 21, no. 1 (1946): 22–46.

Jacobs, Margaret D. "The Great White Mother: Maternalism and American Indian Child Removal in the American West, 1880–1940." *Faculty Publications, Department of History* 106 (University of Nebraska, 2008): 191–213.

Jacobson, Lori. "'Environed by Civilization': WNIA Home-Building and Loan Department." In *The Women's National Indian Association: A History*, edited by Valerie Sherer Mathes, 65–83. Albuquerque: University of New Mexico Press, 2015.

———. "Indians Can be Educated: The WNIA at the 1893 World's Columbian Exposition." In *Gender, Race, and Power in the Indian Reform Movement: Revisiting the History of the WNIA*, edited by Valerie Sherer Mathes, 209–25. Albuquerque: University of New Mexico Press, 2020.

———. "Shall We Have a Periodical?" In *The Women's National Indian Association: A History*, edited by

Valerie Sherer Mathes, 46–61. Albuquerque: University of New Mexico Press, 2015.

Jervey, Edward Drewry. "Methodism in Arizona: The First Seventy Years." *Arizona and the West* 3, no. 4 (Winter 1961): 341–50.

Karr, Steven M. "The Warner's Ranch Indian Removal: Cultural Adaptation, Accommodation, and Continuity." *California History* 86, no. 4 (2009): 24–43.

Kerber, Linda K. "Separate Spheres, Female Worlds, Woman's Place: The Rhetoric of Women's History." *Journal of American History* 75 (June 1988): 9–39.

Knack, Martha C. "Philene T. Hall, Bureau of Indian Affairs Field Matron: Planned Culture Change of Washakie Shoshone Women." *Prologue: Quarterly of the National Archives* 22, no. 2 (Summer 1990): 151–67.

Laylander, Don. "Early Ethnographic Notes from Constance Goddard DuBois on the Indians of San Diego County." *Journal of California and Great Basin Anthropology* 26, no. 2 (2006): 205–14.

Mathes, Valerie Sherer. "Annie E. K. Bidwell: Chico's Benefactress." *California History* (Spring/Summer 1989): 14–25, notes 60–64.

———. "The Banner Association: Twenty-Five Years in Massachusetts." In *The Women's National Indian Association: A History*, edited by Valerie Sherer Mathes, 153–72. Albuquerque: University of New Mexico Press, 2015.

———. "Baptist Missionary Work at Round Valley, California." *American Baptist Quarterly* 29, no. 3 (Fall 2010): 172–86.

———. "Boston, the Boston Indian Citizenship Committee, and the Poncas." *The Massachusetts Historical Review* 14 (2012): 119–48.

———. "C. E. Kelsey and California's Landless Indians." In *Gender, Race, and Power in the Indian Reform Movement: Revisiting the History of the WNIA*, edited by Valerie Sherer Mathes, 163–81. Albuquerque: University of New Mexico Press, 2020.

———. "The California Mission Indian Commission of 1891: The Legacy of Helen Hunt Jackson." *California History* 73, no. 4 (Winter 1993/94): 339–59, notes 390–95.

———. "Constance Goddard DuBois, Indian Reformer." *The Journal of San Diego History* 68, nos. 3–4 (Winter 2022): 184–219.

———. "Dr. Susan LaFlesche Picotte: The Reformed and the Reformer." In *Indian Lives: Essays on Nineteenth- and Twentieth-Century Native American Leaders*, edited by L. G. Moses and Raymond Wilson, 61–90. Albuquerque: University of New Mexico Press, 1985.

———. "Helen Hunt Jackson, Amelia Stone Quinton, and the Mission Indians of California." *Southern California Quarterly* 96, no. 2 (Summer 2014): 172–205.

———. "Helen Hunt Jackson and Southern California's Mission Indians." *California History* 78, no. 4 (Winter 1999/2000): 262–73, notes 303–4.

———. "Helen Hunt Jackson and the Ponca Controversy." *Montana: The Magazine of Western History* 39, no. 1 (Winter 1989): 42–53.

———. "Indian Philanthropy in California: Annie Bidwell and the Mechoopda Indians." *Arizona and the West* (Summer 1893): 153–66.

———. "Investigating Negligence in Indian Affairs: Charles C. Painter, the Indian Rights Association, and the Blackfeet Famine of 1883–1885. *Montana: The Magazine of Western History* 70, no. 3 (Autumn 2020): 3–20.

———. "James Bradley Thayer in Defense of Indian Legal Rights." *The Massachusetts Historical Review* 21 (2020): 41–74.

———. "Mary Lucinda Bonney and Amelia Stone Quinton, Founders of the Women's National Indian Association." *American Baptist Quarterly* (Winter 2009): 421–40.

———. "Mary Lucinda Bonney Rambaut: Educator and Indian Reformer." In *Gender, Race, and Power in the*

Indian Reform Movement: Revisiting the History of the WNIA, edited by Valerie Sherer Mathes, 143–61. Albuquerque: University of New Mexico Press, 2020.

———. "New York Women and Indian Reform." *New York History* 94, nos. 1/2 (Winter/Spring 2013): 84–109.

———. "A Place at the Table: The Women's National Indian Association in the Indian Reform Arena." In *Gender, Race, and Power in the Indian Reform Movement: Revisiting the History of the WNIA*, edited by Valerie Sherer Mathes, 85–104. Albuquerque: University of New Mexico Press, 2020.

———. "The Redlands Indian Association: The WNIA in Southern California." In *The Women's National Indian Association: A History*, edited by Valerie Sherer Mathes, 192–210. Albuquerque: University of New Mexico Press, 2015.

———. "Susan La Flesche Picotte: Nebraska's Indian Physician, 1865–1915." *Nebraska History* 63, no. 4 (Winter 1982): 502–30.

Mathes, Valerie Sherer, and Phil Brigandi. "Charles C. Painter, Helen Hunt Jackson and the Mission Indians of Southern California." *The Journal of San Diego History* 55, no. 3 (Summer 2009): 89–118.

Mathes, Valerie Sherer, and Phil Brigandi. "The Mischief Record of 'La Gogernadora' Amelia Stone Quinton, Charles Fletcher Lummis, and the Warner Ranch Indian Removal." *Journal of San Diego History* 57, nos. 1–2 (Winter/Spring 2011): 69–96.

Mathes, Valerie Sherer, and Richard Lowitt, eds. "'I Plead for Them': An 1882 Letter from Alice Cunningham Fletcher to Senator Henry Dawes." *Nebraska History* 84, no. 1 (Spring 2003): 36–41.

McPherson, Robert S. "Howard R. Antes and the Navajo Faith Mission: Evangelist of Southeastern Utah." *Utah Historical Quarterly* 65, no. 1 (1997): 4–24.

Miller, Larisa K. "The Decline of the Northern California Indian Association." *California History* 99, no. 3 (Fall 2022): 25–52.

———. "Made in Wisconsin: The Shaping of a Federal Indian Agent." *Voyageur* 33, no. 1 (Summer/Fall 2016): 10–18.

———. "Native American Land Ownership in California's National Forests." *Forest History Today* (Fall 2017): 3–13.

———. "Primary Sources on C. E. Kelsey and the Northern California Indian Association." *Journal of Western Archives* 4, no. 1, article 8 (2013): 1–20.

———. "The Secret Treaties with California's Indians." *Prologue* (Fall–Winter 2013): 38–45.

Moore, Edgar W. "The Bierkempers, Navajos, and the Ganado Presbyterian Mission, 1901–1912." *American Presbyterians* 64, no. 2 (Summer 1986): 125–35.

Munz, Philip A. "M. French Gilman." *Madroño: A West American Journal of Botany* 8 no. 1 (1945): 27–29.

Newman, Louise Michele. "The 'Indian Problem' as a 'Woman Question.'" In *White Women's Rights: The Racial Origins of Feminism in the United States*. New York: Oxford University Press, 1999.

Perdue, Theda. "Domesticating the Natives: Southern Indians and the Cult of True Womanhood." *Women, Families and Communities: Readings in American History*, vol. 1 to 1877, edited by Nancy A. Hewitt, 159–70. Glenview: Scott Foreman, 1990.

Prucha, Francis Paul. "A 'Friend of the Indian' in Milwaukee: Mrs. O. J. Hiles and the Wisconsin Indian Association." *Historical Messenger of the Milwaukee County Historical Society* (Autumn 1893): 78–95.

———. "Indian Policy Reform and American Protestantism, 1880–1900." In *Indian Policy in the United States: Historical Essays*. Lincoln: University of Nebraska Press, 1981.

Ramirez, Renya K. "Ho-Chunk Warrior, Intellectual, and Activist: Henry Roe Cloud Fights for the Apache." *Studies in American Indian Literatures* 25, no. 2. The Society of American Indians and Its Legacies: A Special Combined Issue of SAIL, and *American Indian Quarterly* (Summer 2013): 291–309.

Rhea, John M. "From Indian Territory to Philadelphia: A Critical Reexamination of the Origins and Early History of the Women's National Indian Association, 1877–1881." In *Gender, Race, and Power in the*

Indian Reform Movement: The Women's National Indian Association, edited by Valerie Sherer Mathes, 27–54. Albuquerque: University of New Mexico Press, 2020.

Robert, Dana L. "The Influence of American Missionary Women on the World Back Home." *Religion and American Culture: A Journal of Interpretation* 12, no. 1 (Winter 2002): 59–89.

Roddis, Louis H. "The Last Indian Uprising in the United States." *Minnesota History Bulletin* 3, no. 5 (February 1920): 273–90.

Shufeldt, R. W. "Mortuary Customs of the Navajo Indians." *The American Naturalist* 25, no. 292 (April 1891): 303–6.

Simonsen, Jane. "'Your Indian Friend': Indigenous Women and Strategic Alliances with the WNIA." In *Gender, Race, and Power in the Indian Reform Movement: The Women's National Indian Association*, edited by Valerie Sherer Mathes, 185–208. Albuquerque: University of New Mexico Press, 2020.

Smith, Sherry. "Francis LaFlesche and the World of Letters." *American Indian Quarterly* 25, no. 4 (Autumn 2001): 570–603.

Southwick, Sally J. "Educating the Mind, Enlightening the Soul: Mission Schools as a Means of Transforming the Navajos, 1989–1928." *The Journal of Arizona History* 37, no. 1 (Spring 1996): 47–66.

Steinsick, Will. "Mary Louise Eldridge." *United Methodist Historical Journal* 2 (November 2015): 3–15.

Stremlau, Rose. "WNIA Missions in the South." In *The Women's National Indian Association: A History*, edited by Valerie Sherer Mathes, 102–25. Albuquerque: University of New Mexico Press, 2015.

Theodore, Alisse. "'A Right to Speak on the Subject': The U.S. Women's Antiremoval Petition Campaign, 1829–1831." *Rhetoric & Public Affairs* 5, no. 4 (2002): 601–24.

Tonkovich, Nicole. "'Lost in the General Wreckage of the Far West': The Photographs and Writings of Jane Gay." In *Trading Gazes: Euro-American Women Photographers and Native North Americans, 1880–1940*, Susan Bernardin, Melody Graulich, Lisa MacFarlane, and Nicole Tonkovich, 32–70. New Brunswick: Rutgers University Press, 2003.

Trennert, Robert A. "Mary L. Eldridge: Serving God and Country on the San Juan." *New Mexico Historical Review* 77, no. 2 (2002): 145–72.

———. "Superwomen in Indian Country: U.S.I.S. Field Nurses in Arizona and New Mexico, 1928–1940." *The Journal of Arizona History* 41, no. 1 (Spring 2000): 31–56.

Trump, Erik. "'The Idea of Help': White Women Reformers and the Commercialization of Native American Women's Arts." In *Selling the Indian: Commercializing & Appropriating American Indian Cultures*, edited by Carter Jones Meyer and Diana Royer, 159–89. Tucson: University of Arizona Press, 2001.

Warner, Michael J. "Protestant Mission Activity Among the Navajos." *New Mexico Historical Review* 45, no. 3 (1970): 209–32.

Watkins, Frances E. "Charles F. Lummis and the Sequoya League." *The Quarterly: Historical Society of Southern California* 26, nos. 2–3 (June–September 1944): 99–114.

Welter, Barbara. "The Cult of True Womanhood, 1820–1860." In *Dimity Convictions: The American Woman in the Nineteenth Century*, edited by Barbara Welter. Athens: Ohio University Press, 1976.

Williams, Frank B. "John Eaton, Jr.: Editor, Politician, and School Administrator, 1865–1870." *Tennessee Historical Quarterly* 10, no. 4 (December 1951): 291–319.

Dissertations and Theses

Bannan, Helen Marie. "Reformers and the 'Indian Problem,' 1878–1887 and 1922–1934." PhD diss., Syracuse University, 1976.

Brown, Kenny Lee. "Robert Latham Owen, Jr: His Careers as Indian Attorney and Progressive Senator." PhD diss., Oklahoma State University, 1975.

Bruton, Scott Ashley. "The American Dream in Indian Country: Housing, Property, and Assimilation on the Navajo Reservation and Beyond." PhD diss., Rutgers, October 2016.
Burgess, Larry E. "The Lake Mohonk Conferences on the Indian, 1883–1916." PhD diss., Claremont, 1972.
Dunn, Dana Ruth Hicks. "Strategies and Survival: Indian Transitions in the Mountains of San Diego County, 1846–1907." PhD diss. University of California, Riverside, 2013.
Emmerich, Lisa E. "To Respect and Love and Seek the Ways of White Women: Field Matrons, the Office of Indian Affairs, and Civilization Policy, 1890–1938." PhD diss., University of Maryland, College Park, 1987.
Fischer, Frances J. "The Third Force: The Involvements of Voluntary Organizations in the Education of the American Indian with Special Reference to California, 1880–1933." PhD diss., University of California, Berkeley, 1980.
Lastowka, Carol Anne Chase. "At Home and Industriously Employed: The Women's National Indian Association." MA thesis, University of Arizona, 1994.
Romeyn, Sara Northrop. "A Sentimental Empire: White Women's Responses to Native American Policy, 1824–1894." PhD diss., George Washington University, 2003.
Ryan, Mary P. "American Society and the Cult of Domesticity, 1830–1860." PhD diss., University of California at Santa Barbara, 1971.
Theisen, Terri Christian, "'With a View Toward their Civilization': Women and the Work of Indian Reform." MA thesis, Portland State University, 1996.
Thompson, Gregory Coyne. "The Origins and Implementation of the American Indian Reform Movement: 1867–1912." PhD diss., University of Utah, 1981.
Trump, Erik Krenzen. "The Indian Industries League and Its Support of American Indian Arts, 1893–1922: A Study of Changing Attitudes Toward Indian Women and Assimilationist Policy." PhD diss., Boston University, 1966.
Wanken, Helen M. "'Woman's Sphere' and Indian Reform: The Women's National Indian Association, 1879–1901." PhD diss., Marquette University, 1981.
Williams, Samantha M. "'Establishing a Permanent Peace': Civilizing and Subjugating Native Americans During the Peace Policy Era (1869–1877)." MA thesis, California State University, Stanislaus, 2013.

Newspapers

Albuquerque Citizen
Blue Lake Advocate
Boston Daily Advertiser
Boston Evening Journal
Bridgeport Times
Brooklyn Eagle
Buffalo Evening Courier & Republic
Cambridge Chronicle
Cambridge Tribune
Chicago Chronicle
Cortland County Democrat
Daily Alta California
Daily Courier (San Bernardino)
Daily Evening Bulletin (San Francisco)
Detroit Free Press

Durango Herald-Democrat
Durango Wage Earner
Evening Journal (Wilmington, Delaware)
Farmington Daily Times
Farmington Times Hustler
Hartford Courant
Healdsburg Enterprise
Humboldt Times
Inter Ocean (Chicago)
La Jolla Light and La Jolla Journal
Los Angeles Herald
Madera Mercury
Madera Tribune
Mill Valley Record
Morning Journal and Courier (New Haven)
Morning Tribune (San Luis Obispo)
The National Baptist
New Haven Daily Morning Journal and Courier
New York Herald-Tribune
New York Times
Newark Advertiser
Newark Evening Star
Oceanside Blade
Pittsburg Dispatch
Pittsburg Press
Pittsfield Berkshire County Eagle
Riverside Daily Press
Riverside Enterprise
Rochester Democrat and Chronicle
Sacramento Daily Union
San Bernardino Sun
San Diego Union and Daily Bee
San Francisco Bulletin
San Francisco Call
San Francisco Chronicle
San Francisco Daily Evening Bulletin
San Jose Mercury-News
San Juan County Index (Aztec, NM)
San Juan Times
Santa Barbara Weekly Press
Santa Fe Daily New Mexican
Santa Rosa Press Democrat
Sonoma Democrat
Standard Gauge (Brewton, AL)
Stockton Independent
St. Louis Post-Dispatch

Truckee (California) *Republican*
Waterbury (Connecticut) *Evening Democrat* (later *Waterbury Democrat*)

Index

Note: Page numbers in italics refer to images.

Agua Caliente (Cupeño village on Warner's Ranch), 49, 55, 76–77, 83, 90, 133–34, 185, 192–94, 196–97; Hallowell's medical work at, 130, 132, 190, 262; NYCIA station at, 60, 64; proposed WNIA hospital at, 49, 51–52, 133–34, 143, 189; removal of Warner Ranch Indians, 85, 88, 133, 199–200; station transferred, 136; Warner Ranch legal case, 77, 82–84, 136
Alaska, Moravian Mission at, 179–80, 189
Alexander, Sarah Jane, 52, 62
Allen, R. A. (Indian agent), 107, 109
allotment, 3, 6–8, 171–73, 211, 216, 225, 233; of Mission Indians, 52–57, 81; of Omaha, 44–45, 138
Ament, Edward N., 208–9, 260
Ament, Floy, 208, 260
American Baptist Home Mission Society (ABHMS), 14–16
Armstrong, Gen. Samuel C., 35, 40, 100, 127, 282n28; death of, 58
Armstrong, Rev. Lyman Paul, 209–10, 244, 263
Arnold, Mary Ellicott, 153, 154
Arthur, President Chester A., 38, 107
assimilation, xiii, 4, 6–7, 20, 26, 33, 52, 60, 75–76, 96, 102, 112, 151, 227, 235, 242, 245, 247, 254, 332n59, 334n104
Atkins, John D. C. (Indian Commissioner), 47, 109

Babbitt, Josephine, 193, 199
Bachman, Bishop H. T., 181, 186, 188, 194
Baldwin, Marcus (Indian agent), 106, 108–9
Bannan, Helen M., xiii, 23–24
Baptist Home Missionary Society (Women's Home Missionary Society of Philadelphia's First Baptist Church), xi, 11–15, 255
Bard, Thomas R., 72, 92, 198, 215–17, 220
Bay Ridge Branch of the Brooklyn Indian Association, 96, 110, 120, 195, 264
Bean, Hannah Elliott, 228; mission station in honor of, 268
Beckwith, William, 207–8, 239–42; death of, 242–44
Beecher, Catharine, 11, 44, 103, 284n65
Beecher, Rev. Henry Ward, 36–37, 57, 66, 103–4, 109
Beers, Isaac A. (Indian agent), 208, 240
Belt, Robert V. (acting commissioner), 54, 18
Berkhofer, Robert E., 102, 124
Bethel, Alaska, 180–81
Bidwell, Annie E. K., 52, 60, 153, 217, 219, 227, 234; death of, 233, 246

Blackfeet Agency, 105–6, 108–9, 111, 115
Bland, Thomas A., 6, 227, 272n20, 280n2
Board of Home Missions of the Presbyterian Church, 147, 167
Board of Indian Commissioners (BIC), 5, 8–9, 38, 45, 48, 61, 75, 98, 105, 116–19, 180, 194, 198, 255
Boardman, Ella Covell (Mrs. George Dana Boardman), 12–16
Boardman, Rev. George Dana, 8, 12–13
Bonney, Mary Lucinda, 8, 11–12, 15–17, 30, 100, 103, 107; married Rev. Thomas Rambaut, 238
Boston Indian Citizenship Society, 3, 7–9, 22, 25, 75, 255, 259
Broaddus, J. L. (Indian agent), 207, 240
Brooklyn Eagle, 104, 108–9, 121
Brooklyn Indian Association, 96, 98, 103–5, 108–10, 144, 148, 167, 195, 260, 264–66; establishes Piegan Mission Station, 108–12, 120–21, 151, 262
Brosius, M. Samuel, 76–77, 79–83, 92, 171–73, 201, 215–16, 222, 255, 268
Browning, Daniel M. (Indian commissioner), 56–57, 117, 162, 163, 191, 209–11
Bulfinch, Ellen Susan, 158–59, 161, 174
Bullard, Elizabeth Lyman (Mrs. Stephen H. Bullard), 207–8, 329n9

Cahuilla, 50, 130–31, 133–34, 182, 186, 189–90, 192–94, 196–97, 260–61; WNIA among, 181, 185, 189
Cambridge Ditch, 145, 159, 161, 168, 174, 178, 262
Cambridge Indian Association (MIA branch and WNIA auxiliary), 8, 22, 25, 35, 143, 158–59, 262, 265–68; funds Eldridge's work, 144–45, 147, 159, 161–63, 167–68, 170–71, 173–74, 176–77; sponsors Rebecca Collins Hospital, 143–45, 147
Campo Reservation, 73, 87–80, 90, 92–94, 96; land purchased by Kelsey, 299n142
Carlisle Indian Industrial School, 60, 74, 104, 130, 140, 217, 259–60
Carrere, John F., 54–55
Carter, Sybil, 72–73, 75
Chase, Hiram, 139–40, 309n51
Chase, M. E., 240, 244–45
Chase, Mariné, 12, 16–17, 19
Cherokee, 11, 24–25, 62; petition on behalf of, 11; WNIA Mission on behalf of, 270
Chestnut Street Female Seminary, 11–12
City and State, 69, 71, 76–78
Clark, John W., 147–48, 150, 247, 253
Cleveland, President Grover, 48, 117–19, 189–90
Closiah Mission Station, 168, 174, 266, 320n51
Cloud, Dr. Henry Roe, 253–54, 341n3
Coe, Mrs. A. J. *See also* Kate Foote
Cole, Henrietta G., 146, 165, *166*, 167, 170, 265–66, 319n39
Collette, Rev. Frederick George, 233–34
Collier, William, 83, 85, 89, 91–92
Collins, Rebecca, 142–43
Conkey, Dr. Caroline Root, 66, 291n8
Connecticut Indian Association, xii, 25, 32, 36, 38–40, 42, 63–64, 78, 86, 93, 95, 103, 108, 144, 152, 259, 266–67; beginnings of, 65–66; funds La Flesche's medical education, 52, 127–30; funds Rebecca Collins Hospital, 147, 265; supports Eldridge's work, 168, 170
Cooke, Captain L. W. (Indian agent), 116, 119
Costa, Gabriel, 131–32
Cowan, Sarah Sophia Tyler (Mrs. Sidney Joseph Cowan), 38, 65–66, 291n2
Crannell, Elizabeth Keller Shaule (Mrs. William Winslow Crannell), 99–100
Crozer, J. Lewis, 164, 167, 265, 319n36
Crozer, Mary S. (Mrs. J. Lewis Crozer), 265, 276n35, 318–19n36
Crow Creek Reservation and Agency, 57,

141–42, 261

Dabb, Edith M., 144–46, 167, 265, 311–12n82
Dall, Caroline H., 49, 52, 286n97
Damon, Frank, 171–72, 176, 321n68, 322n84
Daughters of the American Revolution (DAR), 39, 44, 63, 66
Dawes, Anna Laurens, 41, 221
Dawes, Electa Allen Sanderson, 38, 41, 285n76
Dawes, Henry Laurens, 19, 38, 40, 45, 47–48, 51, 138
Dawes Act, 6, 171, 209, 211, 245, 254, 304n82, 332n59
Davis, Edward H., 88, 90, 95
Denton, Emma Hapgood, 209–10, 212, 263; as field matron, 211; death of, 212–13
Dewey, Mary, 34, 152
Dickinson, Mary Caroline Lowe (Mrs. J. B. Dickinson), 21–23, 97, 237, 278n65
Dorchester, Rev. Dr. Daniel, 109, 151
Dorn, Edward L., 53–55
Doubleday, Nellie Blanchan De Graff, 75–76, 82, 96, 110
Dougherty, William E. (Indian agent), 209–10
Downey, John G., 77, 134–35; death of, 84
DuBois, Constance Goddard, 22, 64, 67, *68*, 75–78, 80–83, 85–95, 170, 173, 225, 255; at Lake Mohonk, 85, 89; challenges Indian education, 294n61; death of, 95; promotes basket making, 67, 71, 75, 76, 86–87, 90, 93–94; supported by Welsh, 64, 67, 69–70, 76; tours Mission Indian villages, 64, 66–72, 77–78, 82–83, 85–86, 89, 91–93; writes on Kumeyaay and Luiseño religion, 67–68; writes *A Soul in Bronze*, 69, 71
Dutcher, Mary Bishop, 110, 112, 119, 122–25

Dutcher, Rev. Eugene S., 110–12, 114, 119–22, 124–25, 262

Eastern New York Indian Association, 99, 258
Edwards, Mary Haven (Mrs. Thomas C. Edwards), 214–15, 217, 219, 226
Eldridge, Mary Louise, xii, 22, 124, 142, 151, 157–59, 162–63, *169*, 170, *175*, 262, 265, 311n70, 320n51; addresses Lake Mohonk, 163–65; as a field matron, 142–43, 155, 161, 167, 169, 177–78, 316n2; at Closiah Station, 168, 170; at Fisk House, 170, 172–74, 176–77, 267–68; at Rebecca Collins Hospital and Two Grey Hills, 145, 146–47, 165, 167; death of, 177; promotes Navajo weaving, 75, 158, 164; Waro's camp, 171–73
Emmerich, Lisa, 125, 151, 154
Epworth Piegan Indian Mission, Montana, xii, 96–97, 102, 105, 108–15, 119–22, 124
Estudillo, Francisco (Mission Indian agent), 56, 191, 195, 326n52
executive order reservations, 81, 171, 286n101, 295n82, 320n64
Eyster, Nellie Blessing, 208–10, 244, 329n11

First Baptist Church of Philadelphia, xi, 8, 11–12, 38; petition efforts of, 12–13
Fisk, Clinton B., 39, 283n49
Five Campo Reservations (Campo, La Posta, Manzanita, Laguna, Cuyapipa), 88–90, 93
Fleming, C. M., 131, 134, 189, 261, 307n11
Fletcher, Alice Cunningham, 40–42, 48, 51, *61*, 127; Nez Perce allotment, 60–61; Omaha allotment, 45, 61, 138; to Alaska with Kate Foote, 44
Foote, Katherine Elisabeth (Kate Foote Coe), 27, *43*, 44, 46, 58–59, 64–65,

363

255; at Lake Mohonk, 45, 49–50; head WNIA Committee on Indian Legislation, 46, 48; interest in Indian schools, 47, 56–57, 59–60; marries, 59; Mission Indian census and allotment at Rincon, 48–57, 60, 81, 225; president of the Washington, DC, auxiliary, 43–45, 46, 57; president of Meriden Indian Association, 60; travels with Fletcher to Alaska, 44–45

Fort Gaston (Hoopa Valley, Northern California), 207, 240–41, 251; petition to remove, 243

French, Julia M., 132–33, 135–36, 151, 189–91, 193, 196, 262

"Friends of the Indian," 3, 6, 87, 256

Frissell, Rev. Hollis Burk, 58, 100, 130

Gaines, Mary E., 147, 168, 172, 175, 320n31

Garrett, Philip C., 119, 213

General Allotment (Dawes) Act, 6, 56, 171, 209, 211, 245, 254

Gilchrist, Josephine Russell (Mrs. S. W. Gilchrist), 206, 226, 228, *246*, 334n99

Gilchrist, Rev. Hugh W., 26, 229

Given, Rev. Joshua H., 104–5, 260

Goddard, Pliny E., 211–12, 244, 264, 330n25

Good Samaritan Hospital (Navajo, Indian Wells), 63–64, 148, 150, 269

Gordon, George W. (special agent), 138–39

government field matrons, 21, 73, 75, 87, 100, 125, 130, 132–33, 142, 150–51, 153, 155, 158, 163, 165, 169, 173, 178, 180, 189, 206, 225, 229, 234, 263–64, 266

government Indian boarding schools, 47, 52, 74–75

Grace Mission (on Crow Creek Reservation), 57–58

Grant, Ulysses S., 5, 98, 105

Greenville Indian Industrial School (WNIA boarding school), 34, 102, 208–9, 232, 235, 260

Grinnell, George Bird, 106, 109–10, 112–13, 117, 124

Guinda Indian Industrial School, 203, 227, 229–31, 233, 269

Hailmann, William N., 59, 289n149

Hallowell, Dr. Rebecca Cooper, 60, 77, 130, 133–37, 189, 190–91, 193, 196; death of, 137

Hampton Normal and Agricultural Institute (Hampton, VA), 35, 40, 47, 57–58, 60, 100, 127, 130, 140–42, 152, 250, 261

Hardy, Alfred, 162–63, 318n26

Harper, Dr. Mary Pradt, 145, 312n86; enaged in Navajo census taking, 312n87

Harrison, President Benjamin, 48, 53, 117–18

Hartford Evening Press, 36–37, 42

Hastings, William Wirt, 62, 289n160

Hawley, Harriet Ward Foote, 27, 36–38, 42, 43, 64–65; death of, 41, 282n41

Hawley, Joseph Roswell, 36, 40, 42, 44, 53, 65

Hayes, Lucy Ware Webb, 16–17

Hensel, Dr. L. M., 34, 137, 139–40, 259

Hiles, Osia Jane Joslyn, 48–49, 69, 185

Holcombe, Henry, 13–14

Hoopa Indian Reservation, 207–9, 212–13, 227, 235, 239–40, 242–45, 248, 251; NCIA supports, 208–13, 217, 239–40

Hoppock, Louise, 80–81, 192

hospitals, 20, 49, 51–52, 102, 124–25, 140–43, 154, 186

Howard, Grace, 57–58

Hupa Indians, 207–10, 212, 214, 239, 241–44, 246–47, 251, 263

Indian Board of Co-Operation (IBC), 233–34, 247

Indian Bulletin, The (Connecticut Indian Association), 46, 78, 129

Indian Home-Building and Loan Department (WNIA), 40–41, 45, 66, 99, 103, 139–40, 258, 260
Indian Industries League, 73–74, 170, 206, 265, 294n52; funds Eldridge's work, 144, 147, 164
Indian Office, 4, 9, 32, 45, 47–48, 53–54, 58, 67, 100, 107–8, 116, 141, 152–53, 172, 178, 180, 195, 201, 224, 258
"Indian problem," 3–5, 26, 101, 254
Indian Rights Association (IRA), 3, 8, 19–22, 41, 46, 61, 69, 76–77, 92, 107–8, 116, 119, 162, 169, 172, 179, 201, 207, 213, 216, 239, 254; assumes part of WNIA's political duties, 10, 20, 255; Cambridge branch, 9, 22; funds the Warner Ranch defense, 84, 183; publishes DuBois's writings, 69, 71, 76, 78–79, 81; saves Soboba Reservation, 50, 188; supports NCIA, 213, 215–17, 220
Indian Territory (modern-day Oklahoma), 14–15, 62, 100, 103–4, 260, 289n162
Indian Treaty Keeping and Protective Association, 19, 65
Indian's Friend, The, 21, 26, 32, 46, 49, 56–60, 63, 67, 72, 80, 99–100, 105–6, 109–11, 115, 119–20, 122–23, 129, 133, 136, 148–50, 152–53, 162–64, 170, 182, 185, 192, 197, 201, 211–13, 221, 223, 225–27, 230, 240, 242–44, 253, 338n11; DuBois's articles in, 83, 85; Spencer's letter in, 207, 241–42
Ingalls, George Washington, 14–16

Jackson, Helen Hunt, 7, 48–51, 67, 69, 107, 188, 192; government report, 67, 77; *Ramona*, 48, 56, 69, 182, 185, 323n10
Jackson, Shelton, 45, 180, 285n7
Jamaica Plain Indian Association, 115, 142, 144, 148, 265–66
Johnson, Dr. Anna Hayward, 130, 134, 137, 161, 193, 262; as field matron, 130–31, 190; medical work at Cahuilla, 130, 132, 189, 190
Johnson, Ellen Terry, 108, 303n62
Johnson, H. M., 73, 90
Johnson, Right Rev. Joseph Horsfall, 71–73, 76, 80, 198
Johnston, Margaret Wray, 147–50, 269
Johnston, Rev. William Riley, 147–50
Jones, William A. (Indian commissioner), 72, 81, 89, 198–99, 201, 214–15, 220, 223
Jordan, David Starr, 222–23, 332n75

Karok Indians, 153–54
Kelsey, C. E., 67, 93–94, 153, 203, 205, 206, 214, 216, 219, 221, 228, 235, 333n89, 333n91, 336n132; memorial letter and petition, 215, 217, 221–23; special census agent, 92, 220, 223–25, 235; special land disbursing agent, 226, 229, 232
Kidder, Harriette Smith (Mrs. D. P. Kidder), 98–99
Kinney, Abbot, 48–50
Kinney, Sara Thomson (Mrs. John Coddington Kinney), 38, *39*, 40, 65–66, 127, 291n4
Kiowa Reservation, 104–5
Kroeber, L. Alfred, 67, 91–93, 206

La Flesche, Susan (Susan La Flesche Picotte), xii, 52, 125, 127, *128*, 129, 140–41, 151, 259; death of husband, 52
La Jolla, 53, 73, 184–85, 197, 260
Lachappa, Frances, 99, 297n106
Lake Mohonk Conference of the Friends of the Indian, 3, 7, 9–10, 30, 40, 45–46, 48–49, 51, 59, *86*, 92, 117, 165, 206, 217, 221–22, 227–28, 231, 255; DuBois attends, 85, 89; Eldridge attends, 163–64; Quinton attends, 9, 10, 30, 46, 115, 117, 140, 165
Land of Sunshine, 67, 60; DuBois' articles in, 83–85; renamed *Out West*, 87
Lea, Frances, 17, 277n36

Leupp, Francis E., 62, 90–91, 93, 172, 224–26, 235
Lewis, Judge J. R., 217, 219–22, 332n600
Lockwood, John S., 170, 295n74
Lone Wolf, 104–5
Longfellow, Henry Wadsworth, 9, 34
Los Angeles Times, 133, 197, 199
Lummis, Charles Fletcher, 67, 73, 78, 87–92, 94, 214, 223, 227–28; criticizes Quinton, 199–200; serves on Warner Ranch Indian Commission, 84–85, 199

Maine Indian Association, 137, 261, 264
Manzanita Reservation, 70, 73, 78–79, 82–83, 87
Martínez, California, 89, 199–201, 203, 264; new WNIA station, 192–96
Mary G. Fisk Home, 170, 172–77, 267–68
Massachusetts Indian Association (WNIA auxiliary), 22, 25–26, 35, 63, 115, 152, 177, 207–8, 259, 263, 265–66, 268; organized, 34; sponsors Eldridge's work, 143–44, 168, 173, 175
maternalism, 5, 16, 21, 101, 242, 255, 276n29, 277n53
Mesa Grande Reservation, 70–73, 76–78, 82–83, 86–88, 90, 93, 96
Miller, Larisa K., xiii, 224, 228
Miller, Sophie R., 72–73, 86
Mission Indian Bill, 48–52
Mission Indians (California), 25, 65–73, 77–78, 80–82, 84–85, 89, 91, 95, 118, 185, 237; allotment of land, 50–56; DuBois writes about and visits, 64, 66–71, 77–78, 82–83, 89, 91–93; subject of Jackson's writings, 48–50, 56, 67, 69, 182, 185, 188, 192; Weinland's work among, 179, 187, 200, 202
Moravian, The, 134, 189
Moravian Church and Board, 66, 82, 136, 180–81, 186, 192–98, 202–3, 260, 264, 323n1
Morgan, Thomas Jefferson (Indian commissioner), 51–54, 56–57, 130–33, 138, 142–43, 151–52, 183–84, 188–89, 208, 241
Morongo, John, 186–88, 193, 195, 202
Morris, Sarah Elizabeth, 183–84, *185*, 187–88, 196; marries M. French Gilman, 324n18
Mount Vernon Barracks missionary work, 25, 34
Munger, Sara, 166–67, 265

National Baptist, 38
National Indian Association, 147–50, 201, 231, 235, 245, 253–54. *See also* Women's National Indian Association
National Indian Defense Association (NIDA), 6–7, 22
Native lace industry, 67, 71–73, 79, 86
Navajo Methodist Mission, at Jewett, 143, 158, 160, 152, 262; at Farmington, 167, 176
Navajo Reservation, xii, 34, 63, 102, 136, 142, 149, 162, 167
Navajo Tribe, 25, 64, 75, 86, 143–50, 157–59, 161–62, 165–67, 169–72, 175–76, 267–69; weaving, 145, 158, 163–64, 168, 262, 165
Nejo, Rosalia, 88, 297n106
New England Freedmen's Aid Society, 43–44
New Haven Women's Indian Association, 32, 56, 108, 258
New York City Indian Association (WNIA auxiliary), 22, 26, 56, 63, 80, 99, 148, 154, 197, 266, 268; funds Good Samaritan Hospital, 147; funds Rebecca Collins Hospital, 143–44, 146–47, 265; funds work at Soboba, 187; mission station at Agua Caliente, 60, 64, 77, 135–36, 143, 262; organized, 98
New York Independent, 44, 49, 56, 107
New York Times, 106–7, 109, 115, 117, 195
Newell, Harriet, 208–9, 235
Noble, John W. (Interior Secretary), 48,

53–54, 243
Noble, Mary L., 183, 188
Northern California Indian Association (NCIA), xi, 22, 26, 63, 67, 202–3, 208, 211, 214–15, 218, 222, 224, 227, 231, 246, 268; at Hoopa, 207–10, 243–44, 263; decline of, 235; field matrons, 153–55, 203, 235, 337n143; Indian census, 223, 235; Guinda Indian Industrial School, 203, 227, 229, 232, 235, 269; memorial letter and petition, 92, 203, 214, 216–17, 219–20, 222–23, 225; promotes Indian basket making, 206, 209, 228; purchases land for homeless Indians, 212–13, 229, 233, 245; Zayante Indian Conferences, 226–30, *229*, 232, *234*
Northern California Women's Indian Association (NCWIA), 132, 208–10, 242
Nye, Russel Blaine, 3, 4

Oberly, John H. (Indian commissioner), 138, 182
Omaha Creek Station, 137–38, 259; transferred, 140
Omaha Indians, 34, 52, 125, 127–30, 137, 139–140; allotment of reservation, 44–45; Hensel as their physician, 137, 259
Owen, Robert Latham, 62, 290n161

Painter, Charles C., 19, 35, 48, 52, 54–55, 255; death of, 59; displeased with Foote's appointment, 53–54; investigates Piegan condition, 107
Pala Reservation, 85, 88, 93; portable houses at, 297n110
Partridge, Charles L., 80–81, 85, 91
paternalism in Indian policy, 4, 6, 272n6
Peace Policy, 5, 98, 105
Perkins, George C., 216–17
Piegan Indians, 105, 111–13, 115–16, 119, 120–21, 124, 151, 258
Piegan Indians, The (Doubleday), 96, 110

Plummer, E. H. (Indian agent), 159, 161
Ponca Indians, 7, 44, 103–4, 257
Porter, Ada J., 141–42, 151, 261
Potrero, 178, 183, 185–86, 188, 191–94, 196–97, 199, 201–3, 260, 327n77
Pratt, Richard Henry, 60, 74, 179, 217, 219
Presbyterian Board of Home Missions, 104, 147, 259–60, 267, 269
Prucha, Francis Paul, 3–6, 20, 116

Quaker reformers, 9, 151, 213, 221–22, 261, 311n75
Quinton, Amelia Stone, x, 4–5, 8–12, 15–17, *18*, 19, 21–22, 26–27, 29, 31, 38, 40, 45, 48, 52, 56, 66, 69, 75, 80–82, 97–98, 102, 109, 122, 129, 138, 141, 148, 181, 183, 186, 190, 214, 223, 228, 241, 254–55, 261; and Beckwith, 242–43; and the Omahas, 138–39; addresses of, 17, 32–33, 52, 61, 101, 103, 115, 238; as a field matron, 151; at Agua Caliente, 49, 130, 132–33, 135, 189, 200; at Hoopa, 208, 210, 212; first visit to Mission Indians, 189; at Cahuilla, 133, 182, 189, 193; at Martínez, 193, 195, attends Lake Mohonk Conference, 9, 10, 30, 46, 115, 117, 140, 165, 222; death of, 25, 253; defends Agent Steell, 113–16; editor of *The Indian's Friend*, 80, 109, 112, 123; friendship with Weinland, 179, 197–99, 201–2; head of Missionary Committee, 18, 100–101, 110, 131, 135, 147, 165, 193; promotes Civil Service reform for Indian Service, 117–19; visits Piegan Station, 110–16; WCTU organizer, 11, 237–38

Rambaut, Mary. *See* Bonney, Mary Lucinda
Ramona (Jackson), 48–49, 56, 69, 78, 182
Ramona Mission, 66, 99, 130, 182, 185, 260; under Weinland's supervision,

79–80, 118, 125, 134
Raymond, Mary E., 142–43, 157–59; death of, 159–60, 163–64, 262, 316n1, 317n8
Rebecca Collins Memorial Hospital (Navajo Reservation), 136, 142–43, 147, 155, 159, 164–65, 167–68, 173–74; closure, 266; sale of, 167–68
Redlands Indian Association, 80, 192, 198
Reed, Mable, 153–54
Restarick, Rev. H. B., 71–72, 76, 80
Rhea, John M., 14–16
Rincon Indian Reservation, 53–57, 81, 184, 190, 192, 197
Riverside Conference, 227–28
Robinson, Mamie, 73, 88–89, 92–94
Roman Catholic, 180–82, 184, 188, 191, 194, 196, 198, 200–201, 203, 260, 272 1n11, 273n36; anti-Catholic, 180, 281n12, 323n4
Roosevelt, Theodore, 85, 92, 118, 199, 214–15, 223, 267
Round Valley Reservation (California), 25, 34, 207, 214, 240, 258, 282n23
Rust, Horatio Nelson (Indian agent), 49–50, 72, 133, 184, 189, 192

Saahtoye (Blanco Canyon), 174–75, 268, 321n79
Salmons, Ora M., 57, 190, 192, 288n139; at La Jolla, 184
Salsberry, N. J., 189–90, 193
Santa Ysabel village and ranch, 70, 76–77, 82, 87
Scott, Anne Firor, 10, 12
Scoville, Annie Beecher, 66, 103, 152, 255
Sequoya League, 67, 72–73, 76, 84, 87–88, 90, 92, 216, 223–24, 227
Shell, Charles E., 87–89, 90–91
Sheriff, Mary, 187, 188, 190, 260; married William P. Fowler, 188, 191
Simonsen, Jane, 73, 101
Sloan, Thomas L., 47, 140, 309–10n51
Smiley, Albert K., 7, 9, 30, 49, 51–52, 59, 75, 131, 192, 198, 227, 318n28

Smith, Hoke (Interior Secretary), 117–18, 123, 189, 191
Sniffen, Mathew K., 9, 77–78, 171, 219, 253, 255, 273n33; supports NCIA, 215–16, 220–23, 225, 229, 232–33
Soboba Reservation (California), 99, 132, 135, 182–88, 192, 194, 196–97, 260, 296n94, 324n17; IRA defends, 50, 84, 183
Society of American Indians, 63, 254
Soul in Bronze, A (DuBois), 69, 71
Southern Workman (Hampton Institute), 67; DuBois articles in, 85, 87
Sparhawk, Frances Campbell, 25, *74*, 74–75
Spencer, Dorcas J., xii, 238, *246*; attends WNIA annual meetings, 246–47, 255; death of, 251; letter to Welsh, 207, 239–42; NCIA member, 226, 245–48; with Beckwith, 207, 239, 242; work at Hoopa, 212, 244–46; WCTU member, 223, 235, 245, 248–51, 340n62
Steell, George (Indian agent), 112–19, 121, 123–24
Stowe, Harriet Beecher, 11, 36–37, 66, 103
Swanson, Mrs. A. C., 238; for marriage, 275n11, 337n4. *See* Amelia Stone Quinton

Taber, Anna Haviland Ferris, 203, 205, 207, 209–10, 212–13, 215, *218*, 224, 235; works with IRA, 217, 219–22, 225, 329n5
Taber, Cornelia, 152, 202–3, 205–7, 213–15, 218–20, 223, 225, 227–28, 232–33, 235, 329n5; attends Lake Mohonk, 231; death of, 233; efforts on Hupas' behalf, 209–12; Fund, 26; petition work, 221–22, 226; supports field matrons, 153–55, 211, 226, 228–29, 231; writes book, 230–31
Teller, Henry M., 61, 103
Tileston, Laura Elise Bates, 141, 255, 262

Tolchaco Mission, 147–48
Topliff, M. M., 175–77; Mission Home, 268
Trennert, Robert A., 161, 177
Tripp, Mary, 143, 160–63, 167
"true womanhood," 24–25, 27
Trump, Erik Krenzen, 67, 73, 75–76, 90, 94
Two Grey Hills Stations, 145, 164–67, 263

Vest, George, 15, 39
Volcan (reservation), 78, 82

Wainwright, Dr. C. C., 131, 135
Wanken, Helen W., 25–26, 31, 34–36, 46, 75
Waro's camp (Huerfano), 171, 173–74, 178, 267–68, 320n61
Washington Women's Indian Association, Washington, DC (WNIA auxiliary), xi, 27, 29–30, 33, 35, 37–38, 40–41, 43–46, 51–52, 61, 63, 65, 264; hosts annual WNIA meetings, 58–59, 62
Waterbury Indian Association, 64, 66, 68, 85, 87, 95–96; DuBois elected president of, 88, 94, 170
Watkins, Mary, 71, 76–77, 83, 85, 90, 93–95, 293n30
Weinland, Caroline Yost, 180–81, 183, 186, 199–200, *200*, 260
Weinland, William Henry, xii, 18, 66, 79–82, 134–36, 178, 182–83, 192–94, 196–98, *200*, 202, 260; among Yuma Indians, 197–99, 266; applies for Mission agent position, 180, 189–91, 202; at Martínez, 193–95, 203; death of, 179; defends Quinton, 200; in Alaska, 180–81, 190, 323n7; supervises Ramona station, 79–80, 118, 125, 133–34, 179–80, 185–89; survey of mission reservations, 183–84
Welsh, Herbert, 8–9, 22, 46, 48, 53, 75, 77–79, 81–83, 107–8, 116, 124, 162–64, 215, 217, 254–55, 292n24;

letter from Spencer, 207, 239, 241–42; supports civil service reform, 116–18, 305n95; supports DuBois, 64, 67, 69–70, 76
Welsh, William, 8
Whipple, Bishop Henry B., 16–17, 73
Whittlesey, Anna Augusta Patten (Mrs. Eliphalet Whittlesey), 38, 42
Whittlesey, Eliphalet, 48, 118, 283n48
Wilkinson, Mrs. A. G., 59–60; death of, 64
Williams, Capt. Constant (Indian agent), 161, 163, 165
Willow Creek Indian Boarding School, 113–15, 119, 121
Wissler, Clark, 67, 90, 92
Wolf Tail, 122, 124
Woman's Board of Home Missions of the Presbyterian Church, 150, 269
Woman's Christian Temperance Union (WCTU), xii, 10–12, 23, 33, 52, 157, 207–8, 223, 235, 237–39, 250–25
Woman's Home Missionary Society of the Methodist Episcopal Church, 16, 103–4, 143, 157–60, 163, 167
Woman's Medical College of Pennsylvania, 52, 129–30, 132
Women's Baptist Home Mission Society (WBHMS), 14–16, 19, 145, 258
Women's Methodist Episcopal Home Missionary Society, 257, 266–67
Women's [Home] Missionary Societies, 3, 10, 15–16, 20–21, 102, 255
Women's National Indian Association (WNIA), xi, 3–4, 7–8, 10–11, 13, 15, 20–22, 25–26, 29–31, 33, 38, 40–41, 46, 49, 56, 59, 73–76, 82, 92, 96–97, 101, 103, 110, 112, 115, 151, 153, 182, 184, 190–91, 197, 237, 242, 251, 256; allows men to join, 25, 74–75, 147; annual meetings, 19, 23, 29, 32, 40, 46, 71, 73, 86, 116, 136, 246; Central Indian Committee, 12, 17; Committee of Ways & Means, 11, 15; funds Cahuilla station, 130–31;

granted Omaha land, 138–39; hospital at Agua Caliente, 49, 51–52, 84, 108, 124, 129–30, 132–35, 137, 140, 186–87, 213, 258, 262, 266; Hospital Department, 141–42; Indian Home-Building and Loan Department, 40–41, 66, 99, 103, 139–40; Missionary Committee of, xii, 18, 34, 100, 105, 108, 124, 129, 131, 135, 137, 140, 165, 186–87, 213, 245, 258; missionary reports, 20, 61, 86, 108, 136, 140, 193; name change to National Indian Association, 147; Navajo Missionary work of, 142, 145; petitions of, 12, 16–17, 19–20, 31–32, 38, 66; Piegan Mission, 110–15, 119–23; Ramona Mission, 66, 79–80, 99, 118, 125, 130, 134, 185, 188; supports missions among the Navajos, 159, 164; various mission stations, 257–70

Wood, John S. (Indian agent), 106

Woosley, Rev. David J., 194–95, 197–98, 264

Wright, Lucius A. (Indian agent), 79, 84, 197–98

Young, John (Indian agent), 105–7

Yuma, 64, 104, 197–99, 257, 266

Zayante conferences, 226–30, 232, 234

About the Author

Valerie Sherer Mathes, professor emerita of City College of San Francisco, is the author of numerous books on the Indian reform movement, including *Amelia Stone Quinton and the Women's National Indian Reform Association: A Legacy of Indian Reform* (2022) and *Charles C. Painter: The Life of an Indian Reform Advocate* (2020), and coauthor with Phil Brigandi of *Reservations, Removal, and Reform: The Mission Indian Agents of Southern California, 1878–1909* (2018). She is also the author and editor of books on Helen Hunt Jackson's Indian reform legacy and more than sixty articles.

AUTHOR PHOTO BY LYNN DOWNEY

www.ingramcontent.com/pod-product-compliance
Lightning Source LLC
Chambersburg PA
CBHW032012300426
44117CB00008B/994